40 Best Fields for Your Career

Part of JIST's Best Jobs™ Series

Michael Farr and Laurence Shatkin, Ph.D.

Also in JIST's *Best Jobs* Series

- *Best Jobs for the 21st Century*
- *300 Best Jobs Without a Four-Year Degree*
- *200 Best Jobs for College Graduates*
- *250 Best Jobs Through Apprenticeships*
- *50 Best Jobs for Your Personality*
- *225 Best Jobs for Baby Boomers*
- *250 Best-Paying Jobs*

JIST
Works
America's Career Publisher

40 Best Fields for Your Career

© 2006 by JIST Publishing, Inc.

Published by JIST Works, an imprint of JIST Publishing, Inc.
8902 Otis Avenue
Indianapolis, IN 46216-1033

Phone: 1-800-648-JIST   Fax: 1-800-JIST-FAX
E-mail: info@jist.com   Web site: www.jist.com

Some Other Books by the Authors

Michael Farr

Seven-Step Job Search
The Quick Resume & Cover Letter Book
Getting the Job You Really Want
The Very Quick Job Search

Laurence Shatkin

90-Minute College Major Matcher

Quantity discounts are available for JIST products. Please call 1-800-648-JIST or visit www.jist.com for a free catalog and more information. Have future editions of JIST books automatically delivered to you on publication through our convenient standing order program.

Visit www.jist.com for information on JIST, free job search information, book excerpts, and ordering information on our many products. For free information on 14,000 job titles, visit www.careeroink.com.

Acquisitions Editor: Susan Pines
Development Editor: Stephanie Koutek
Cover and Interior Designer: Aleata Howard
Illustrator: Katherine Knutson

Interior Layout: Carolyn J. Newland
Proofreader: Linda Seifert
Indexer: Kelly D. Henthorne

Printed in the United States of America

11 10 09 08 07 06   9 8 7 6 5 4 3 2 1

Library of Congress Cataloging-in-Publication Data

Farr, J. Michael.
    40 best fields for your career / Michael Farr and Laurence Shatkin.
        p. cm. —   (JIST's best jobs series)
    Includes index.
    ISBN-13: 978-1-59357-315-7 (alk. paper)
    ISBN-10: 1-59357-315-4 (alk. paper)
    1. Vocational guidance—United States. 2. Occupations—United
    States. I. Shatkin, Laurence. II. Title. III. Title: Forty best fields for your career. IV. Series.
    HF5382.5.U5F363 2006
    331.702—dc22

                                                    2006011525

ISBN-13: 978-1-59357-315-7
ISBN-10: 1-59357-315-4

This Book Is Filled with Facts, But It Is Very Easy to Use

This book is designed to start you thinking in terms of career *fields*. During your childhood, probably nobody ever asked you, "What *field* do you want to work in when you grow up?" But how you answer that question can have a big influence on your future success. It's a fact of life that some fields are growing rapidly whereas others are stagnating or even shrinking. So it's helpful to aim for a field that will offer you lots of opportunity.

What exactly do we mean by a "field"? We use this term to refer to industries, only we prefer to call them fields so you won't think only in terms of smokestacks and assembly lines. Education, health care, Internet services, and investing are some fields that don't readily come to mind when the word "industries" is used, but they are some of the hottest fields in today's economy.

Probably you're used to thinking in terms of hot jobs—that is, occupations. Perhaps you're thinking, "If I choose a promising occupation as my goal, I won't need to think about fields." In some cases that's true; for example, the vast majority of nurses are working in the health care field. But for many occupations, there are openings in several different fields. For example, consider how many fields employ salesworkers. Doesn't it make sense to be selling in a hot field rather than in a sluggish one?

Also consider that you're not likely to stay in the same occupation throughout your working life-time—but, as you change occupations in the future, you're likely to stay in the field that you know well and where you're well known. So why not establish yourself in a field with a lot of potential?

In this book, we identify the fields that have the best combination of earnings, growth rate through 2014, and expected expansion of the workforce. You'll find useful lists comparing these fields, plus detailed descriptions of each field, including the kinds of employers and jobs that make up the fields.

We are not suggesting that the 40 best fields in this book are all good ones for you to consider—some will not be. But the 40 fields that met our criteria present such a wide range of jobs that you are likely to find one or more that will interest you.

(continued)

(continued)

Some Things You Can Do with This Book

- ◎ Identify high-potential fields where you are most likely to find a career that pays well and has lots of job openings.
- ◎ Decide how to tailor your college major or other educational or training program to prepare for a promising field.
- ◎ Decide which fields you should target for part-time work experience, a summer job, or an internship.
- ◎ Prepare for interviews and the job search.
- ◎ Find reliable earnings information to negotiate pay.

These are a few of the many ways you can use this book. We hope you find it as interesting to browse as we did to put together. We have tried to make it easy to use and as interesting as occupational information can be.

When you are done with this book, pass it along or tell someone else about it. We wish you well in your career and in your life.

Credits and Acknowledgments: While the authors created this book, it is based on the work of many others. The selection and descriptions of fields are based on the *Career Guide to Industries,* 2006–2007 edition, a publication of the U.S. Department of Labor. The occupational information is based on data obtained from the U.S. Department of Labor and the U.S. Census Bureau. These sources provide the most authoritative occupational information available. The job titles and the facts about their characteristics are from the O*NET database, which was developed by researchers and developers under the direction of the U.S. Department of Labor. They, in turn, were assisted by thousands of employers who provided details on the nature of work in the many thousands of job samplings used in the database's development. We used the most recent version of the O*NET database, release 9.0. We appreciate and thank the staff of the U.S. Department of Labor for their efforts and expertise in providing such a rich source of data.

Table of Contents

Summary of Major Sections

Introduction. A short overview to help you better understand and use the book. *Starts on Page 1.*

Part I—The Best Fields Lists. Very useful for exploring career options! Lists are arranged into easy-to-use groups. The first group of lists presents the best fields overall–fields with the highest earnings, projected growth, and increase in workforce size. More-specialized lists follow, presenting the best fields for workers age 16–24, workers 55 and over, part-time workers, self-employed workers, women, and men. The column starting at right presents all the list titles within the groups. *Starts on Page 13.*

Part II—Descriptions of the Fields. Provides complete descriptions of 45 fields identified by the U.S. Department of Labor. Each description contains information on earnings, projected growth, nature of the work, working conditions, skills and abilities required, work-related values that are satisfied, types of employers, related occupations, education and training required, advancement routes, earnings, and factors affecting the outlook. *Starts on page 71.*

Detailed Table of Contents

Introduction

We kept this introduction short to encourage you to actually read it. For this reason, we don't provide many details on the technical issues involved in creating the lists or descriptions of fields. Instead, we give you short explanations to help you understand and use the information the book provides for career exploration or planning. We think this brief and user-oriented approach makes sense for most people who will use this book.

Why Focus on Fields?

Most people, when planning their careers, think mainly about the job they want and the education or training need to get it. Unfortunately, they often overlook the enormous importance of the *field* (or industry) where they will work. This book is designed to help open your eyes to the importance of choosing the right field for your career.

For example, let's say you are thinking of becoming a chemist. Have you given any thought to what *field* you'd like to work in as a chemist? Here are two bits of information that might shape your thinking:

- Chemists working in the field of Pharmaceutical and Medicine Manufacturing earn an average of $56,910, whereas those in Scientific Research and Development Services average $65,380.
- Employment of chemists in the field of Scientific Research and Development Services is expected to grow by 6.9% between 2004 and 2014, whereas in the field of Chemical Manufacturing (Except Drugs), employment is expected to *shrink* by 27.7%.

Maybe you're thinking, "Okay, it's nice to know about conditions in different fields, but can't I postpone the decision about what field I should aim for? When I'm ready to send out resumes, then I'll choose a field." Some people do this, but if you have a field in mind while you're still in school, you can better choose the courses, summer jobs, and internships that will help you prepare for that field, gain experience in it, and make contacts in it.

Of course, you may not yet have chosen a specific career goal, such as chemist. Here again, focusing on fields can be helpful by making you aware of where future earnings and job opportunities will be greatest. You can move toward a career choice by following a narrowing-down process at whatever pace seems right to you: first settling on a high-potential field, then—whenever you're ready—deciding on a promising occupation.

Finally, focusing on fields is useful because people tend to shift from one occupation to another during a career, although during these shifts they often stay within the same field. For example, within the same field they may move from being a technician to being a sales-person, from being a professional to being a manager, or from being the practitioner of a skilled trade to being a union representative. These workers' chances of moving from success to success are better if they are in industries that are prospering. And these workers' chances of satisfaction are better if the characteristics of the industry—for example, the physical demands and the skill requirements—are consistent with their abilities and preferences.

Of course, people sometimes jump from one field to another, especially when making a career change late in life. For example, a pediatrician who has spent 25 years looking into children's ears may decide to take up teaching at a medical school, thus jumping from Health Care to Educational Services. If you are considering such a major change, you would be wise to investigate the prospects of the new field you are planning to enter.

Whether you are planning your career move early or later in life, the facts in this book can be very helpful. The lists in Part I show you which fields—and the jobs within them—hold the most promise. To create the lists, we started with 45 major fields identified by the U.S. Department of Labor and selected those with the best combination of earnings, projected job growth rate, and size of workforce. We created lists of the fields that pay the best, are expected to have the fastest job growth, and are expected to add the most workers. We also created lists of fields that attract certain kinds of workers, such as young, part-time, or female workers. Then we created lists of the best-paying and fastest-growing jobs associated with the 40 best fields. Part II contains descriptions for all 45 of the fields. Finally, the appendices will help you identify fields that are characterized by certain skills, abilities, and work-related values.

Where the Information Comes From

The information we used in creating this book comes from four major sources provided by the U.S. Department of Labor:

- The publication *Career Guide to Industries,* 2006–2007 edition, identified the 45 fields compared in Part I and provided most of the descriptive text that appears in Part II. These 45 fields cover about 75 percent of the wage and salary jobs in the U.S. economy.
- For information about the jobs linked to the 40 best fields, we used the O*NET data-base, which is now the primary source of detailed information on occupations. The Labor Department updates the O*NET on a regular basis, and we used the most recent update available, release 9.

- For information about earnings in the various fields and jobs, we relied on the Occupational Employment Statistics (OES) program. The OES uses a slightly different system of job titles than the O*NET does, but we were able to link the OES data to the fields and O*NET job titles that we used to develop this book.

- Information about projected employment in fields and jobs comes from the Office of Occupational Statistics and Employment Projections, which develops information about the labor market for the nation as a whole for 10 years in the future.

- Information about the proportion of workers who are part time, self-employed, female, and of various ages is derived from the Current Population Survey, which is conducted for the Department of Labor by the Census Bureau. This information is based on surveys conducted in 2005 and thus is a year more up to date than other economic figures that appear in this book.

Data Complexities

For those of you who like details, we present here some of the complexities inherent in our sources of information and what we did to make sense of them. You don't need to know this to use the book, so jump to the next section of the introduction if you are bored with details.

We include information on earnings, projected job growth, and size of workforce for each field and job throughout this book. We think this information is important to most people, but getting it for each field and job is not a simple task.

Earnings

The employment security agency of each state gathers information on earnings for various jobs and fields and forwards it to the U.S. Bureau of Labor Statistics. This information is organized in standardized ways by a BLS program called the Occupational Employment Statistics, or OES. To keep the earnings for the various jobs and regions comparable, the OES screens out certain types of earnings and includes others, so the OES earnings we use in this book represent straight-time gross pay, exclusive of premium pay. More specifically, the OES earnings include the job's base rate; cost-of-living allowances; guaranteed pay; hazardous-duty pay; incentive pay, including commissions and production bonuses; on-call pay; and tips, but they do not include back pay, jury duty pay, overtime pay, severance pay, shift differentials, non-production bonuses, or tuition reimbursements. Also, self-employed workers are not included in the earnings estimates, and they can be a significant segment in certain occupations and fields.

The OES earnings data are reported not only by occupation, but also by the *field* in which workers are employed. (The Department of Labor uses the term "industry," but because some people interpret this term to mean only manufacturing or production environments, we use the term "field" instead in this book.) When reporting earnings by fields, the OES uses a classification scheme called NAICS (North American Industry Classification System), which allowed us to link the earnings data to the 45 fields compared and described in this book.

Projected Job Growth

The most recent projections available from the Office of Occupational Statistics and Employment Projections cover the years from 2004 to 2014. The projections are based on information about people moving into and out of occupations and fields. The BLS uses data from various sources in projecting the job growth for each occupation and field—some data comes from the Census Bureau's Current Population Survey and some comes from an OES survey. The projections assume that there will be no major war, depression, or other economic upheaval. Like the earnings figures, the figures on projected job growth are also reported according to the NAICS classification, so again we were able to link it to the 45 fields analyzed in this book.

While salary figures are fairly straightforward, you may not know what to make of job growth figures for fields and occupations. For example, is projected job growth of 15.0% good or bad? You should keep in mind that the average (mean) job growth projected for wage-earners in all occupations and fields in the OES survey is 14.2%. For the 45 fields (which do not cover all occupations), the average job growth projected is 17.3%.

Size of Workforce

When you look at the lists in Part I, you may notice that one figure we use to determine the best 40 fields is the "workforce increase." You may be wondering, "Isn't that the same thing as the *rate of job growth?*" Also, in Part II, you'll observe that the description of every field begins with three statistics, one of which is "size of workforce." Perhaps you're wondering why it matters whether a field has a big workforce or a small one.

To understand our methods, consider two fields: Software Publishers and Health Care. Software Publishers is growing like a weed, with an expected expansion of 67.6%. Health Care, by contrast, is growing less than half as fast, at a rate of 27.3% (still well above average). It sounds as if the faster-growing field of Software Publishers will offer a lot more job opportunities, doesn't it? But Software Publishers is actually a tiny field, with a total workforce of 238,700 people. Even at its outstanding job-growth rate, it will not take on a large number of new workers. Now compare that field to Health Care, which has a workforce of over 13 *million* people—over *50 times as big* as Software Publishers. Even at its slower job-growth rate, the Health Care field will take on many more workers than Software Publishers.

To get a useful idea of the job opportunities in a field, we need to know how many workers the field will actually take on. Unfortunately, accurate figures of that kind are not available for fields. Nevertheless, we can compute a rough-and-ready approximation by computing how many more workers will be in the workforce in 2014 than were employed in 2004— not the *percent* of increase (that's the job-growth rate), but the absolute increase in numbers of people employed. This is the figure we call the "workforce increase."

The workforce increase is only a rough measure of the actual number of job openings because some occupations have a higher turnover rate than others. To understand this, consider your local fast-food restaurant and the often restless teenagers who work there. Job turnover there is really high, so even if there are 20 workers at the restaurant this year and 21 workers there next year (a workforce increase of one), the restaurant actually may have hired dozens of people over that time span. So the figure for workforce increase does not necessarily reflect the number of job openings that an employer can generate. Fortunately, a field consists of a large collection of employers and occupations with varying rates of job turnover—some fast, some slow—so the workforce increase figure can still be useful for comparing one field to another.

When we get to the level of individual occupations, however, we can't rely on the workforce increase figure as a meaningful measure. And, alas, we have no other useful measure of expected job openings at the occupational level *within a field*. That's why, in the lists of the best jobs in each field, you'll see a figure for "workforce size," but not the possibly misleading figure for workforce increase.

How the 40 Best Fields Were Selected

The "This Book Is Filled with Facts" section at the beginning of this book gives a brief description of how we determined the best fields for this book. Here are a few more details:

1. We began by gathering information about the 45 fields included in the Department of Labor's publication *Career Guide to Industries*. We matched the 45 fields to Labor Department data on their earnings, expected job growth, and increase in workforce size.

2. We also matched the 45 fields to the occupations in the O*NET database, taking care to assign only O*NET occupations that truly belong in the fields. For example, labor market data indicate that one of the important jobs in the field of Wholesale Trade is Laborers and Freight, Stock, and Material Movers, Hand. The problem is that this is an "umbrella" occupation that the O*NET does not have information about; instead the O*NET has information about three detailed occupations that fit under this umbrella, and some of them have nothing to do with the field of Wholesale Trade. (One of them is Grips and Set-Up Workers, Motion Picture Sets, Studios, and Stages.) So when we assembled O*NET-derived information about the characteristics of the Wholesale Trade field, we used only data about the one occupation that belongs in this field.

3. We created three lists that ranked the 45 fields based on three major criteria: median annual earnings, projected job growth through 2014, and increase in the size of the workforce between 2004 and 2014.

4. We then added the numerical ranks for each field from all three lists to calculate its overall score.

5. To emphasize fields that tend to pay more, are likely to experience more rapid job growth, and are expected to have more job openings, we set the 40 fields with the best numerical scores in our list of the best fields in boldface type. These fields are the focus of the remaining 89 lists.

How the Best Jobs in Each Field Were Selected

We realized that once you get interested in a field, you're probably going to want to plan for a *job within* that field. So we assembled the available information about jobs within the fields and created 40 pairs of lists: the best-paying jobs in each field and the fastest-growing jobs in each field.

1. First we identified the most important jobs within each field—those that employ more than 2 percent of the workforce for that field. This produced a list of about 20 jobs for each field, but we removed a few jobs for which little or no information is available.

2. We then ranked the jobs by their earnings and by their projected growth from 2004 to 2014. Note that in every case these figures are true *only for the jobs in that specific field*, not for the whole occupation. For example, when we report the earnings for Financial Managers in the Banking field as $66,727, this figure may be more or less than what Financial Managers earn in other fields. In fact, in the field of Securities, Commodities, and Other Investments, they average $129,500. So you can understand that a job may be high-ranked in one field but less distinguished in another field. That's what makes these lists so useful—they help you plan for a winning combination of a job and a field.

3. Because these lists are fairly short, we decided not to set a cutoff for the "best-paying 10" or the "fastest-growing 15." Each list includes *all* the important jobs linked to the field, so look to the top of each list to find the best jobs. When you look at the lists of fastest-growing jobs, don't forget to consider the figure for workforce size that is listed for each job; as we explained earlier, it is another factor that affects the number of job openings.

4. There are some ties in these lists, just as there are in the lists of the best fields, so don't assume that a small difference in ranking represents a big advantage of one job over another.

Why This Book Has More Than 40 Fields

We didn't think you would mind that this book actually provides information on more than 40 fields. We decided that a really good job can be rewarding even if it is in a lackluster field. That's why in Part II you'll find descriptions of all 45 fields described in the Department of Labor's *Career Guide to Industries*.

The Data in This Book Can Be Misleading

We use the most reliable data we can obtain for the earnings, projected growth, workforce increase, and other information to create this book, but keep in mind that this information may or may not be accurate for your situation. This is because the information is true on the average. But just as there is no precisely average person, there is no such thing as a statistically average example of a particular field. We say this because data, while helpful, can also be misleading.

Take, for example, the yearly earnings information in this book. This is highly reliable data obtained from a very large U.S. working population sample by the Bureau of Labor Statistics. It tells us the median annual pay received by people in various fields. This sounds very useful until you consider that a field is a large collection of diverse jobs at widely varying levels of pay. The median merely means that half of all people in that field earned less than that amount and half earn more. (We often use "average" instead of "median" elsewhere in this book for ease of explanation.)

For example, people who work in a clerical or manual-labor job will typically earn less than people in the same field who work as technicians or professionals. They will also earn less than the average for the exact same occupation if they have few years of work experience, live in rural areas, or work for smaller employers.

Finally, don't forget that the job market consists of both job openings and job-seekers. The figures on job growth and workforce increase don't tell you how many people will be competing with you to be hired. The Department of Labor does not publish figures on the supply of job candidates, so we are unable to tell you about the level of competition you can expect. Competition is an important issue that you should research for any tentative career goal. In some cases the outlook statements in Part II and for related occupations in the *Occupational Outlook Handbook* can provide some useful information. You should speak to people who educate or train tomorrow's workers; they probably have a good idea of how many graduates find rewarding employment and how quickly. People in the workforce also can provide insights into this issue. Use your critical thinking skills to evaluate what people tell you. For example, educators or trainers may be trying to recruit you, whereas people in the workforce may be trying to discourage you from competing. Get a variety of opinions to balance out possible biases.

So, in reviewing the information in this book, please understand the limitations of the data it presents. You need to use common sense in career decision-making as in most other things in life. Even so, we hope that you find the information helpful and interesting.

Part I: The Best Fields Lists

There are 90 separate lists in Part I of this book—look in the table of contents for a complete list of them. The lists are not difficult to understand because they have clear titles and are organized into groupings of related lists.

Depending on your situation, some of the lists of fields in Part I will interest you more than others. For example, if you are young, you may be interested to learn the fields that employ above-average percentages of workers age 16–24. Other lists show fields with above-average percentages of older workers, part-time workers, self-employed workers, women, or men.

Whatever your situation, we suggest that you use the lists that make sense for you to help explore career options. Following are the names of each group of lists along with short comments on each group. You will find additional information in a brief introduction provided at the beginning of each group of lists in Part I.

Here is an overview of each major group of lists you will find in Part I.

40 Best Fields: Lists of Fields with the Highest Pay, Fastest Growth, and Biggest Increase in Workforce Size

Four lists are in this group, and they are the ones that most people want to see first. The first list presents all 45 fields in order of their combined scores for earnings, growth, and increase in workforce size, with the 40 best fields in boldface type. Three more lists in this group present the 20 fields with the highest earnings, the 20 fields projected to grow most rapidly, and the 20 fields with the biggest workforce increases.

Best Fields Lists with Above-Average Percentages of Workers Age 16–24, Workers Age 55 and Over, Part-Time Workers, Self-Employed Workers, Women, and Men

This group of lists presents interesting information for a variety of types of people based on data from the U.S. Census Bureau. We created one list each for fields that employ an above-average percentage of workers age 16–24, workers age 55 and older, part-time workers, self-employed workers, women, and men.

Lists of Best Jobs in Each of the 40 Best Fields

We created a pair of lists for each of the 40 best fields based on the jobs that employ more than 2 percent of the workforce of that field. The first list in each pair orders these jobs by their average earnings, so you can see the best-paying jobs in that field. Note that this ordering and the earnings figures represent the average earnings for that job *in that field*, not the overall average for that job throughout the economy. The second list orders the jobs by percentage of growth for that occupation *in that field* so you can find the fastest-growing jobs in that field. (For each job we also list the size of the workforce in that field to give you additional insight into the potential for job openings.)

Part II: Descriptions of the Fields

This part of the book provides an information-packed description for each of the 45 fields. Because most of the text is taken from the Department of Labor's *Career Guide to Industries*, 2006–2007 edition, the descriptions are ordered as they are in that publication.

For example, the fields related to Information are grouped together. You can also use the table of contents to locate any field you identify in a list from Part I that you want to learn more about, and you can use the appendices to identify fields with certain characteristics.

Here are the topics that are covered in the descriptions:

- **Title and Data Elements:** Immediately following the title are bulleted facts about the field, including average annual earnings, projected job growth 2004–2014, size of workforce in 2004, percentage of self-employed workers (based on 2005 data), and percentage of part-time workers (also based on 2005 data).

- **Significant Points:** The bullet points under Significant Points highlight key characteristics for the field.

- **Nature of the Field:** This section discusses the kinds of business establishments that employ workers, the parts of the country where these establishments are located, major work activities, and the impact of changes in technology and business practices. For most fields, a bar chart provides information about the sizes of the establishments that employ the bulk of the workers.

- **Working Conditions:** This section identifies the typical hours worked, the workplace environment, physical activities and susceptibility to injury, special equipment, and the extent of travel required. In many fields, people work regular business hours—40 hours a week, Monday through Friday—but many do not. For example, waiters and waitresses often work evenings and weekends.

- **Important Characteristics of the Field:** This section identifies the important skills, abilities, and work-related values that characterize the field. We derived this information from the O*NET database by focusing on the major jobs in the field.

- **Employment:** This section reports the number of people who were employed in the field in 2004 and the number or proportion of self-employed workers in the field, if significant. For most fields, a table identifies how employment in the field is divided up by detailed fields—that is, specializations within the field. For example, the field of Agriculture, Forestry, and Fishing covers the detailed fields of Crop Production; Animal Production; Logging; Fishing, Hunting, and Trapping; Forestry; and Support Activities for Agriculture and Forestry.

- **Occupations in the Field:** This part of the field description identifies the occupations that employ significant numbers of workers in this field. It provides brief explanations of the tasks the various occupations perform. You may want to look up interesting occupations elsewhere; for suggestions, see the next section, "Additional Information About Jobs."

- **Training, Other Qualifications, and Advancement:** After knowing what workers do in a field, you need to understand how to train for it. This section describes the most significant sources of education and training, including the pathways preferred by employers, the typical length of training, and advancement possibilities. It also mentions desirable skills, aptitudes, and personal characteristics, plus any certification or licensing that may be necessary.

◉ **Outlook:** When planning for the future, you probably are thinking about potential job opportunities. This section describes the factors that will result in employment growth or decline in the field. For example, demographic changes, which affect what services the public requires, can influence the growth or decline of a field. So can technological change; changes in business practices, such as the outsourcing of work or the restructuring of businesses; the substitution of one product or service for another; and competition from foreign trade. Variation in job opportunities by educational attainment, size of firm, or geographic location also may be discussed here.

◉ **Earnings:** This section discusses typical earnings and how workers are compensated—by means of annual salaries, hourly wages, commissions, piece rates, tips, or bonuses. Within every field and occupation, earnings vary by experience, responsibility, performance, tenure, and geographic area.

◉ **Sources of Additional Information:** This section lists mailing addresses for associations, government agencies, unions, and other organizations that can provide information on the field and the important jobs in it. In some cases, toll-free phone numbers and Internet addresses are also listed. Free or relatively inexpensive publications offering more information may be mentioned.

Additional Information About Jobs

Because this book focuses on fields, there was no room to provide detailed descriptions of the major jobs associated with the fields. Fortunately, hundreds of sources of career information exist that do provide detailed information at the job level, so here are a few we consider most helpful for your further exploration.

Print References

◉ *O*NET Dictionary of Occupational Titles:* Revised on a regular basis, this book provides good descriptions for nearly one thousand jobs at all levels of education and training. It also includes lists of related job titles in other major career information sources, educational programs, and other information. Published by JIST.

◉ *Enhanced Occupational Outlook Handbook:* Updated regularly, this book provides thorough descriptions for nearly 270 major jobs in the current *Occupational Outlook Handbook,* brief descriptions for the O*NET jobs that are related to each, brief descriptions of thousands of more-specialized jobs from the *Dictionary of Occupational Titles,* and other information. Published by JIST.

Internet Resources

◉ **The U.S. Department of Labor Bureau of Labor Statistics Web site:** The Department of Labor Bureau of Labor Statistics Web site (http://www.bls.gov) provides a lot of career information, including links to other Web pages that provide information on the jobs referred to in this book. This Web site is a bit formal and, well, confusing, but it will take you to the major sources of government career information if you explore its options.

- ☉ **O*NET site:** Go to http://www.onetcenter.org for a variety of information on the O*NET database, including links to sites that provide detailed information on the O*NET job titles listed in Part I of this book.
- ☉ **CareerOINK.com:** This site (http://www.careeroink.com) is operated by JIST and includes free information on thousands of jobs (including all O*NET jobs included in *40 Best Fields for Your Career*), easy-to-use crosswalks between major career information systems, links from military to civilian jobs, sample resumes, and many other features. A link at http://www.jist.com will also take you to the CareerOINK Web site.

Thanks

Thanks for reading this introduction. You are surely a more thorough person than those who jumped into the book without reading it, and you will probably get more out of the book as a result.

We wish you a satisfying career and, more importantly, a good life.

PART I

The Best Fields Lists

Tips on Using These Lists

We've tried to make the best fields and jobs lists in this section both fun to use and informative. You can use the table of contents at the front of the book to find a complete listing of all the list titles in this section. You can then review the lists that most interest you or simply browse the lists in this section. Most, such as the list of highest-paying fields, are easy to understand and require little explanation. We provide comments on each group of related lists to inform you of the selection criteria or other details we think you may want to know.

As you review the lists, mark the titles of fields and jobs that appeal to you (or, if someone else will be using this book, write them on a separate sheet of paper). You can look up the descriptions of the fields in Part II, and you can find descriptions of the jobs in books such as JIST's *O*NET Dictionary of Occupational Titles* and the *Occupational Outlook Handbook* or online at sites such as JIST's CareerOINK (http://www.careeroink.com).

Understand the Limitations of the Information

The lists emphasize fields with high pay or high growth because most people consider these factors important in selecting a desirable job and because they are also easily quantifiable. While these measures are important, we believe that you should also think about other factors in considering your career options. For example, location, liking the people you work with, having an opportunity to serve others, and enjoying your work are just a few of the many factors that may define the ideal field and job for you.

Some of these "soft" measures are reflected in the *work-related values* that are linked to each of the fields and are included in the descriptions of the fields in Part II under the heading "Important Characteristics of the Field." For example, if it is important to you for your work to offer opportunities to serve others, you might look for fields that are characterized by the value Social Service. Other "soft" factors listed under "Important Characteristics of the Field" are the *skills* and *abilities* that are required by the work. (In appendices A, B, and C, you can look up fields by their associated skills, abilities, and work-related values.)

Nevertheless, many of the factors that make work pleasant or unpleasant are difficult or impossible to quantify, measure objectively, or infer readily from observation and are not, therefore, presented in this book. For this reason, we suggest that you consider the importance of these issues yourself and that you thoroughly research any field or job before making a firm decision.

For example, the field ranked last among the best 40 is Chemical Manufacturing, Except Drugs, and of the nine major jobs linked to it, Chemical Equipment Tenders ranks seventh in pay ($41,407) and eighth in rate of growth (the workforce actually will *shrink* by 19.8% and numbers only 25,255 people). Is this a "bad" combination of field and job, one you should avoid? No, of course not. It all depends on what you like or want to do. Another example is in the field that had the very best overall score for earnings, growth, and increase in workforce: Computer Systems Design and Related Services. Of the 13 major jobs linked to this dynamic field, Computer Software Engineers, Applications, is ranked fourth in pay ($76,130) and second in rate of growth (62.7%, with a workforce of 133,095). Is this job a great job to consider? Many people (the authors included) would not want to work in this job or may not have the skills or interests needed to do it well. It would be a great job for someone who was good at it and who would enjoy doing it, but it would simply not be right for someone else. On the other hand, the perfect job for some people would be Chemical Equipment Tenders in the Chemical Manufacturing field because they enjoy it and are good at it. It may be hard to find work at this job in this field because it has a small and shrinking workforce, but a person with the right skills and motivation may be able to land a job regardless.

So, as you look at the lists that follow, keep in mind that earnings, growth, and workforce size are just three things to consider. Also consider that half of all people in a given field or job earn more than the earnings you will see in this book—and half earn less. If a field or job really appeals to you, you should consider it even if it is not among the highest paying. And you should also consider fields and jobs not among the fastest growing for similar reasons, because openings are always available, even in fields and jobs with slow or negative growth projections.

Some Details on the Lists

The sources of the information we used in constructing these lists are presented in this book's introduction. Here are some additional details on how we created the lists and how to interpret them:

- Some fields or jobs have the same scores for one or more data elements. For example, in the category of best fields overall, the fields Automobile Dealers and Federal Government, Excluding the Postal Service, have the same combined score for the three features we use to rank fields in this list. Therefore we ordered these two fields alphabetically, and their order has no other significance. There was no way to avoid these ties, so simply understand that the difference of several positions on a list may not mean as much as it seems.

🌀 Some of these ties in the lists of jobs occur because two or more jobs are similar and "share" economic information. For example, in the list of fastest-growing jobs in the field Child Day Care Services, you'll find Child Care Workers and Nannies listed one atop the other, and you'll see that they share the same statistics: a projected growth rate of 37.4% and a workforce size of 222,010. This happens because the Department of Labor does not report separate economic figures for these two jobs; it reports one figure for a job called Child Care Workers. If you want to find noneconomic information about that job by looking in other books, you'll find different information under *each* title, Child Care Workers and Nannies. So we thought it would be helpful for your further exploration if we listed both titles here. But remember that the workforce size represents the *total* for both of these jobs, and the growth rate is the *average* for both. One may be growing faster than the other, but we do not have information on that.

40 Best Fields: Lists of Fields with the Highest Pay, Fastest Growth, and Biggest Increase in Workforce Size

The three lists that follow show the fields with the best "payoffs" in terms of earnings, rate of employment growth, and increase in number of workers.

To create these lists, we started with the 45 fields that are described in a publication of the U.S. Department of Labor called the *Career Guide to Industries*. We ranked these 45 fields according to a combination of the *earnings* of people working in the fields, the projected percent of employment *growth* of the fields, and the projected increase in the *total number* of workers. We then selected the 40 fields with the best combined scores for use in this book. (The process for ranking the fields is explained in more detail in the introduction.)

The first list presents all 45 fields according to these combined rankings for pay, growth, and workforce increase, with the best 40 fields bolded. Three additional lists present the 20 fields with the best annual earnings, the 20 with the highest projected percentage growth through 2014, and the 20 with the biggest projected gain in number of workers. Descriptions for all 45 fields are included in Part II.

The 40 Best Fields Overall

This list arranges all 45 fields from the *Career Guide to Industries* in order of their overall scores for pay, growth, and workforce increase. Computer Systems Design and Related Services was the field with the best combined total score, and it is on the top of the list. The other fields follow in descending order based on their total combined scores. Some fields had tied scores and were simply listed one after another, so there are often only very small or even no differences between the scores of fields that are near each other on a list. All the lists that follow use these 40 fields as their source list. You can find descriptions for each of these fields in Part II, beginning on page 71.

The 40 Best Fields Overall

Field	Annual Earnings	Percent Growth	Workforce Increase
1. Computer Systems Design and Related Services	$63,320	39.5%	452,900
2. Software Publishers	$71,170	67.6%	161,300
3. Management, Scientific, and Technical Consulting Services	$46,570	60.5%	471,200
4. Educational Services	$36,370	16.6%	2,121,165
5. Internet Service Providers, Web Search Portals, and Data Processing Services	$48,370	27.8%	107,900
6. Health Care	$32,149	27.3%	3,563,998
7. Securities, Commodities, and Other Investments	$53,140	15.8%	121,198
8. Employment Services	$21,320	45.5%	1,579,900
9. Pharmaceutical and Medicine Manufacturing	$44,420	26.1%	76,000
10. Scientific Research and Development Services	$58,310	11.9%	65,300
11. State and Local Government, Excluding Education and Hospitals	$35,598	11.4%	894,800
12. Advertising and Public Relations Services	$38,370	22.4%	95,200
13. Construction	$35,060	11.4%	792,400
14. Social Assistance, Except Child Day Care	$22,979	32.6%	444,700
15. Insurance	$38,590	9.5%	215,400
16. Arts, Entertainment, and Recreation	$20,190	25.1%	459,700
17. Child Day Care Services	$18,400	38.4%	294,800
18. Truck Transportation and Warehousing	$32,152	14.0%	267,300
19. Wholesale Trade	$33,170	8.4%	475,900
20. Food Services and Drinking Places	$15,720	16.4%	1,450,801
21. Aerospace Product and Parts Manufacturing	$53,270	8.2%	36,400
22. Automobile Dealers	$33,270	12.2%	152,800
23. Federal Government, Excluding the Postal Service	$54,980	2.5%	49,500
24. Advocacy, Grantmaking, and Civic Organizations	$28,007	14.5%	178,800
25. Hotels and Other Accommodations	$18,840	16.9%	304,200
26. Air Transportation	$42,810	8.8%	45,200
27. Motion Picture and Video Fields	$26,210	17.1%	62,700
28. Utilities	$51,760	−1.3%	−7,500
29. Motor Vehicle and Parts Manufacturing	$38,011	5.6%	61,600
30. Broadcasting	$36,238	10.7%	34,900
31. Clothing, Accessory, and General Merchandise Stores	$18,360	10.1%	422,800
32. Oil and Gas Extraction	$39,973	−6.1%	−19,200
33. Telecommunications	$48,180	−6.5%	−67,700
34. Publishing, Except Software	$33,630	6.5%	43,700

The 40 Best Fields Overall

Field	Annual Earnings	Percent Growth	Workforce Increase
35. Computer and Electronic Product Manufacturing	$47,070	−7.1%	−94,200
36. Grocery Stores	$18,270	6.6%	160,300
37. Food Manufacturing	$24,180	3.8%	57,100
38. Steel Manufacturing	$36,599	−13.4%	−20,900
39. Mining	$36,380	−12.9%	−26,600
40. Chemical Manufacturing, Except Drugs	$38,869	−14.4%	−86,000
41. Banking	$28,784	−1.8%	−31,405
42. Machinery Manufacturing	$35,000	−12.8%	−146,500
43. Printing	$30,210	−9.8%	−64,900
44. Agriculture, Forestry, and Fishing	$19,090	−10.7%	−230,000
45. Textile, Textile Product, and Apparel Manufacturing	$23,912	−44.6%	−331,600

The 20 Best-Paying Fields

We sorted the 40 best fields based on their annual median earnings from highest to lowest. *Median earnings* means that half of all workers in these fields earn more than that amount and half earn less. We then selected the 20 fields with the highest earnings to create the list that follows.

A quick review of the list will tell you that most of the best-paying fields are associated with high technology or energy. But there are also many high-paying jobs in the fields of federal government and finance. Keep in mind that the earnings reflect the national average for all workers in the field. This is an important consideration, because some of the jobs in a particular field pay much better than others. For example, in the highest-paying field, Software Publishers, people working as Computer and Information Systems Managers earn on average almost three times as much as people working as Adjustment Clerks. You can get more detailed information about the earnings of jobs within these fields by looking at the lists of best jobs in each of the 40 best fields later in Part I.

The 20 Best-Paying Fields

Field	Annual Earnings
1. Software Publishers	$71,170
2. Computer Systems Design and Related Services	$63,320
3. Scientific Research and Development Services	$58,310
4. Federal Government, Excluding the Postal Service	$54,980

(continued)

(continued)

The 20 Best-Paying Fields

Field	Annual Earnings
5. Aerospace Product and Parts Manufacturing	$53,270
6. Securities, Commodities, and Other Investments	$53,140
7. Utilities	$51,760
8. Internet Service Providers, Web Search Portals, and Data Processing Services	$48,370
9. Telecommunications	$48,180
10. Computer and Electronic Product Manufacturing	$47,070
11. Management, Scientific, and Technical Consulting Services	$46,570
12. Pharmaceutical and Medicine Manufacturing	$44,420
13. Air Transportation	$42,810
14. Oil and Gas Extraction	$39,973
15. Chemical Manufacturing, Except Drugs	$38,869
16. Insurance	$38,590
17. Advertising and Public Relations Services	$38,370
18. Motor Vehicle and Parts Manufacturing	$38,011
19. Steel Manufacturing	$36,599
20. Mining	$36,380

The 20 Fastest-Growing Fields

We created this list by sorting the 40 best fields by their projected growth over the ten-year period from 2004 to 2014. Growth rates are one measure to consider in exploring career options, as fields with higher growth rates tend to provide more job opportunities. But note that you need to consider more than just growth rate when you think about job opportunities. That's why we include the list following this one.

Also remember that even in a high-growth field, some jobs are growing much faster than others. For example, in the fastest-growing field, Software Publishers, the job Computer Software Engineers, Applications, is growing almost three times as fast as the job Computer Programmers. The lists of best jobs in each of the 40 best fields, later in this part, provide more detailed information about comparative growth rates of jobs within these fields.

The 20 Fastest-Growing Fields

Field	Percent Growth
1. Software Publishers	67.6%
2. Management, Scientific, and Technical Consulting Services	60.5%
3. Employment Services	45.5%
4. Computer Systems Design and Related Services	39.5%
5. Child Day Care Services	38.4%
6. Social Assistance, Except Child Day Care	32.6%
7. Internet Service Providers, Web Search Portals, and Data Processing Services	27.8%
8. Health Care	27.3%
9. Pharmaceutical and Medicine Manufacturing	26.1%
10. Arts, Entertainment, and Recreation	25.1%
11. Advertising and Public Relations Services	22.4%
12. Motion Picture and Video Fields	17.1%
13. Hotels and Other Accommodations	16.9%
14. Educational Services	16.6%
15. Food Services and Drinking Places	16.4%
16. Securities, Commodities, and Other Investments	15.8%
17. Advocacy, Grantmaking, and Civic Organizations	14.5%
18. Truck Transportation and Warehousing	14.0%
19. Automobile Dealers	12.2%
20. Scientific Research and Development Services	11.9%

The 20 Fields with the Biggest Workforce Increases

As we explained in the introduction, the gain in *total number* of people in the workforce tells you something that *percentage* of growth doesn't. It gives you a clearer idea of how many jobs are actually going to open (or disappear). So we sorted the 40 best fields by their projected absolute increase in workers over the ten-year period from 2004 to 2014. A field that is high on both this list and the one before it will provide lots of employment in the years ahead. Do keep in mind, however, that even small, shrinking fields have some job openings for highly qualified and determined job candidates.

The 20 Fields with the Biggest Workforce Increases

Field	Increase in Workforce
1. Health Care	3,563,998
2. Educational Services	2,121,165
3. Employment Services	1,579,900
4. Food Services and Drinking Places	1,450,801
5. State and Local Government, Excluding Education and Hospitals	894,800
6. Construction	792,400
7. Wholesale Trade	475,900
8. Management, Scientific, and Technical Consulting Services	471,200
9. Arts, Entertainment, and Recreation	459,700
10. Computer Systems Design and Related Services	452,900
11. Social Assistance, Except Child Day Care	444,700
12. Clothing, Accessory, and General Merchandise Stores	422,800
13. Hotels and Other Accommodations	304,200
14. Child Day Care Services	294,800
15. Truck Transportation and Warehousing	267,300
16. Insurance	215,400
17. Advocacy, Grantmaking, and Civic Organizations	178,800
18. Software Publishers	161,300
19. Grocery Stores	160,300
20. Automobile Dealers	152,800

Best Fields Lists with Above-Average Percentages of Workers Age 16–24, Workers Age 55 and Over, Part-Time Workers, Self-Employed Workers, Women, and Men

We decided that it would be interesting to include lists in this section that show what sorts of fields are likely to have high representations of different types of people. For example, what fields have the above-average percentages of men or younger workers? We're not saying that men or younger workers should consider these fields over others, but it is interesting information to know.

In some cases, the lists can give you ideas for fields to consider that you might otherwise overlook. For example, perhaps women should consider some fields that traditionally have high percentages of men in them. Older workers might consider some fields with a high percentage of younger ones. Although these are not obvious ways of using these lists, the lists may give you some good ideas on fields to consider. The lists may also help you identify fields that work well for others in your situation—for example, fields with plentiful opportunities for self-employment, if that is a work arrangement you prefer.

All of the lists in this section were created by using a similar process. We began with all 40 best fields and sorted those fields in order of the primary criterion for each set of lists. Then, we selected the fields with an above-average percentage of workers fitting the primary criterion. (For example, to create the first list for this group, we sorted all 40 fields based on the percentage of workers age 16 to 24 and then selected the 10 fields with a greater-than-average percentage.) Finally, we sorted each list again by the fields' combined scores for earnings, growth, and workforce increase, and these economic figures are presented below for each field. One limitation to some of the lists is that we were unable to obtain separate data for federal and state government; you'll find these two fields together wherever they appear on the lists that follow.

Best Fields with an Above-Average Percentage of Workers Age 16–24

From our list of the 40 best fields used in this book, this list contains the 10 fields with an above-average percentage of workers age 16 to 24, presented in order of their overall score for earnings, growth, and workforce increase. Younger workers are found in all fields (the average representation is about 14 percent), but fields with higher percentages of younger workers may present more opportunities for initial entry or upward mobility. Many fields with an above-average percentage of younger workers are dominated by jobs that don't require extensive training, education, or experience.

If you are a young person thinking about what field to enter, think about whether you are going to want to *stay* in that field as you get older. Many of the fields with high percentages of young workers have limited opportunities for income; in fact, none of the 10 fields on this list can be found on the list of the 20 best-paying fields. So if you want to work in a field with a lot of young people, you may want to plan on eventually gaining experience or (better yet) education that will help you move into a better-paying field, or at least into one of the higher-paying jobs in that youthful field.

Best Fields with an Above-Average Percentage of Workers Age 16–24

Field	Percent Age 16–24	Annual Earnings	Percent Growth	Workforce Increase
1. Employment Services	14.4%	$21,320	45.5%	1,579,900
2. Arts, Entertainment, and Recreation	24.5%	$20,190	25.1%	459,700
3. Child Day Care Services	18.3%	$18,400	38.4%	294,800
4. Hotels and Other Accommodations	17.2%	$18,840	16.9%	304,200
5. Motion Picture and Video Fields	30.0%	$26,210	17.1%	62,700
6. Automobile Dealers	15.4%	$33,270	12.2%	152,800
7. Food Services and Drinking Places	44.2%	$15,720	16.4%	1,450,801
8. Broadcasting	14.1%	$36,238	10.7%	34,900
9. Clothing, Accessory, and General Merchandise Stores	31.8%	$18,360	10.1%	422,800
10. Grocery Stores	32.1%	$18,270	6.6%	160,300

Best Fields with an Above-Average Percentage of Workers Age 55 and Over

For all fields, the average representation of workers age 55 or older is about 16 percent. Of the 40 best fields, 18 have a percentage of older workers that exceeds this average. They are listed here, ordered by their overall score for earnings, growth, and workforce increase.

Older workers don't change careers as often as younger ones do, and on the average, they tend to have been in their fields for quite some time. Many of the fields with an above-average percentage of workers age 55 and over—and those fields with the highest earnings—include jobs that require considerable preparation, either through experience or through education and training. Young people are less likely to be able to get these jobs, and people who have a lot of education or experience are likely to try to squeeze additional earning years out of the time and money they have invested in career-building—so they may retire later than average.

In addition, some fields on this list are characterized by a lot of job security, which has allowed a high percentage of workers to stay in their field. The two government fields, for example, offer the job security that comes with civil service positions. Steel Manufacturing and Mining are shrinking rapidly and therefore are not attracting young workers, and their older workers are more likely to be unionized and thus have better-than-average job security. The field of Educational Services is characterized by jobs that require advanced degrees, often lead to job tenure, and impose few physical demands, so workers who started in this field tend to stay in it well into late middle age and beyond.

However, some people with track records in *other* fields enter Educational Services late in life by taking up teaching jobs, especially at the postsecondary level. Similarly, some workers with expertise in other fields become management analysts, thus swelling the ranks of Management, Scientific, and Technical Consulting Services, or go to work for nonprofit organizations (perhaps in a "retirement" job) and thus enter the field of Advocacy, Grantmaking, and Civic Organizations. Therefore, if you are in the baby-boom generation, this list may give you some ideas about fields you may be able to move into at this stage of your life.

Best Fields with an Above-Average Percentage of Workers Age 55 and Over

Field	Percent Age 55 and Over	Annual Earnings	Percent Growth	Workforce Increase
1. Management, Scientific, and Technical Consulting Services	27.1%	$46,570	60.5%	471,200
2. Educational Services	21.0%	$36,370	16.6%	2,121,165
3. Health Care	17.3%	$32,149	27.3%	3,563,998
4. Securities, Commodities, and Other Investments	17.0%	$53,140	15.8%	121,198
5. Advertising and Public Relations Services	18.0%	$38,370	22.4%	95,200
6. State and Local Government, Excluding Education and Hospitals	19.0%	$35,598	11.4%	894,800
7. Insurance	18.2%	$38,590	9.5%	215,400
8. Social Assistance, Except Child Day Care	21.8%	$22,979	32.6%	444,700
9. Federal Government, Excluding the Postal Service	19.0%	$54,980	2.5%	49,500
10. Aerospace Product and Parts Manufacturing	19.1%	$53,270	8.2%	36,400
11. Truck Transportation and Warehousing	17.1%	$32,152	14.0%	267,300
12. Wholesale Trade	17.2%	$33,170	8.4%	475,900
13. Automobile Dealers	18.5%	$33,270	12.2%	152,800
14. Advocacy, Grantmaking, and Civic Organizations	22.2%	$28,007	14.5%	178,800
15. Utilities	16.1%	$51,760	–1.3%	–7,500
16. Publishing, Except Software	17.6%	$33,630	6.5%	43,700
17. Steel Manufacturing	19.3%	$36,599	–13.4%	–20,900
18. Mining	16.5%	$36,380	–12.9%	–26,600

Best Fields with an Above-Average Percentage of Part-Time Workers

Look over the list of the fields with above-average percentages (more than 17 percent) of part-time workers and you will find some interesting things. For example, several are dominated by retail and service jobs. In some cases, people work part time in these fields because they want the freedom of time this arrangement can provide, but others may do so because they can't find full-time employment in these areas. These folks may also work in another full- or part-time job to make ends meet.

If you want to work part time now or in the future, this list will help you identify fields that are more likely to provide that opportunity. However, you probably should consider whether you want to stay in part-time work throughout your career. If not, you should either plan on getting the experience or education you'll need to move into a field with more full-time opportunities or focus on the fields on this list that have both high growth and large workforce size, such as Employment Services, Health Care, and Educational Services—fields that, even with a comparatively low percentage of full-time jobs, still will have a large number of full-time openings.

The 14 fields listed here are ordered by their overall score on earnings, growth, and workforce increase.

Best Fields with an Above-Average Percentage of Part-Time Workers

Field	Percent Part-Time Workers	Annual Earnings	Percent Growth	Workforce Increase
1. Management, Scientific, and Technical Consulting Services	19.1%	$46,570	60.5%	471,200
2. Health Care	20.0%	$32,149	27.3%	3,563,998
3. Educational Services	21.9%	$36,370	16.6%	2,121,165
4. Employment Services	18.4%	$21,320	45.5%	1,579,900
5. Social Assistance, Except Child Day Care	24.6%	$22,979	32.6%	444,700
6. Arts, Entertainment, and Recreation	32.0%	$20,190	25.1%	459,700
7. Child Day Care Services	28.7%	$18,400	38.4%	294,800
8. Motion Picture and Video Fields	27.1%	$26,210	17.1%	62,700
9. Advocacy, Grantmaking, and Civic Organizations	24.6%	$28,007	14.5%	178,800
10. Hotels and Other Accommodations	18.7%	$18,840	16.9%	304,200
11. Food Services and Drinking Places	41.1%	$15,720	16.4%	1,450,801
12. Publishing, Except Software	23.8%	$33,630	6.5%	43,700
13. Clothing, Accessory, and General Merchandise Stores	31.8%	$18,360	10.1%	422,800
14. Grocery Stores	35.3%	$18,270	6.6%	160,300

Best Fields with an Above-Average Percentage of Self-Employed Workers

Across all fields, about 7 percent of workers are self-employed. Although you may think of the self-employed as having similar jobs, they actually work in an enormous range of fields, situations, and work environments that you may not have considered. Of the 40 best fields, 10 have an above-average representation of self-employed workers, and they are listed here, ordered by their overall score for earnings, growth, and workforce increase.

Among the self-employed are people who own small or large businesses; professionals such as lawyers, psychologists, and medical doctors; part-time workers; people working on a contract basis for one or more employers; people running home consulting or other businesses; and people in many other situations. They may go to the same office every day, as an attorney might; visit multiple employers during the course of a week; or do most of their work from home. Some work part time, others full time, some as a way to have fun, some so they can spend time with their kids or go to school.

The point is that there is an enormous range of situations, and one of them could make sense for you now or in the future. You may plan on entering one of these fields as a wage-earning or salaried worker and acquiring experience and capital with the long-term goal of starting your own business.

Best Fields with an Above-Average Percentage of Self-Employed Workers

Field	Percent Self-Employed Workers	Annual Earnings	Percent Growth	Workforce Increase
1. Computer Systems Design and Related Services	8.8%	$63,320	39.5%	452,900
2. Management, Scientific, and Technical Consulting Services	24.2%	$46,570	60.5%	471,200
3. Internet Service Providers, Web Search Portals, and Data Processing Services	8.2%	$48,370	27.8%	107,900
4. Arts, Entertainment, and Recreation	14.6%	$20,190	25.1%	459,700
5. Construction	15.9%	$35,060	11.4%	792,400
6. Securities, Commodities, and Other Investments	9.6%	$53,140	15.8%	121,198
7. Child Day Care Services	28.0%	$18,400	38.4%	294,800
8. Advertising and Public Relations Services	11.2%	$38,370	22.4%	95,200
9. Truck Transportation and Warehousing	12.1%	$32,152	14.0%	267,300
10. Motion Picture and Video Fields	10.8%	$26,210	17.1%	62,700

Best Fields with an Above-Average Percentage of Women and Men

To create the two lists that follow, we sorted the 40 best fields according to the percentages of women and men in the workforce and kept those fields that have an above-average percentage of women (more than 46 percent) for one list and of men (more than 54 percent) for the other list. We then ordered each list by the fields' overall scores on earnings, growth, and workforce increase.

These are our most controversial lists, and we knew we would create some controversy when we first included lists of *jobs* with above-average percentages of men and women in other books in the *Best Jobs* series. But these lists are not meant to restrict women or men from considering options in fields and jobs—our reason for including these lists is exactly the opposite. We hope the lists help people see possibilities that they might not otherwise have considered.

The fact is that fields with above-average percentages of women or men offer good opportunities for both men and women if they want to work in one of these fields. So we suggest that women browse the list of fields that employ above-average percentages of men and that men browse the list of fields with above-average percentages of women. The fields on both lists include jobs that pay well, and women or men who are interested in these fields and who have or can obtain the necessary education and training for the jobs should consider them.

An interesting and unfortunate tidbit to bring up at your next party is that the average earnings for the fields with an above-average percentage of women are $27,278, compared to average earnings of $37,962 for the fields with an above-average percentage of men. But earnings don't tell the whole story. We computed the average growth and total workforce increase of the fields with an above-average percentage of women and found statistics of 20.8% growth and a workforce increase of 10,953,495, compared to 11.3% growth and a workforce increase of 4,447,998 for the fields with an above-average percentage of men. This discrepancy reinforces the idea that men have had more problems than women in adapting to an economy dominated by service and information-based fields. Many women may simply be better prepared for these fields, possessing more appropriate skills for the fields that are now growing rapidly and have more job openings.

Best Fields with an Above-Average Percentage of Women

Field	Percent Women	Annual Earnings	Percent Growth	Workforce Increase
1. Health Care	78.0%	$32,149	27.3%	3,563,998
2. Employment Services	57.4%	$21,320	45.5%	1,579,900
3. Educational Services	69.0%	$36,370	16.6%	2,121,165
4. Social Assistance, Except Child Day Care	73.8%	$22,979	32.6%	444,700
5. Pharmaceutical and Medicine Manufacturing	46.3%	$44,420	26.1%	76,000
6. Advertising and Public Relations Services	52.3%	$38,370	22.4%	95,200
7. Child Day Care Services	95.8%	$18,400	38.4%	294,800
8. Insurance	60.9%	$38,590	9.5%	215,400
9. Hotels and Other Accommodations	57.0%	$18,840	16.9%	304,200
10. Advocacy, Grantmaking, and Civic Organizations	66.9%	$28,007	14.5%	178,800
11. Food Services and Drinking Places	52.5%	$15,720	16.4%	1,450,801
12. Clothing, Accessory, and General Merchandise Stores	62.7%	$18,360	10.1%	422,800
13. Publishing, Except Software	49.7%	$33,630	6.5%	43,700
14. Grocery Stores	50.8%	$18,270	6.6%	160,300

Best Fields with an Above-Average Percentage of Men

Field	Percent Men	Annual Earnings	Percent Growth	Workforce Increase
1. Software Publishers	74.3%	$71,170	67.6%	161,300
2. Computer Systems Design and Related Services	73.3%	$63,320	39.5%	452,900
3. Management, Scientific, and Technical Consulting Services	57.4%	$46,570	60.5%	471,200
4. Internet Service Providers, Web Search Portals, and Data Processing Services	59.6%	$48,370	27.8%	107,900
5. Securities, Commodities, and Other Investments	61.9%	$53,140	15.8%	121,198
6. Scientific Research and Development Services	54.7%	$58,310	11.9%	65,300
7. State and Local Government, Excluding Education and Hospitals	54.5%	$35,598	11.4%	894,800
8. Construction	90.4%	$35,060	11.4%	792,400
9. Arts, Entertainment, and Recreation	54.8%	$20,190	25.1%	459,700
10. Truck Transportation and Warehousing	86.1%	$32,152	14.0%	267,300

(continued)

(continued)

Best Fields with an Above-Average Percentage of Men

Field	Percent Men	Annual Earnings	Percent Growth	Workforce Increase
11. Aerospace Product and Parts Manufacturing	75.2%	$53,270	8.2%	36,400
12. Automobile Dealers	80.2%	$33,270	12.2%	152,800
13. Federal Government, Excluding the Postal Service	54.5%	$54,980	2.5%	49,500
14. Wholesale Trade	71.3%	$33,170	8.4%	475,900
15. Air Transportation	63.8%	$42,810	8.8%	45,200
16. Motion Picture and Video Fields	61.3%	$26,210	17.1%	62,700
17. Motor Vehicle and Parts Manufacturing	75.6%	$38,011	5.6%	61,600
18. Utilities	78.7%	$51,760	−1.3%	−7,500
19. Broadcasting	61.0%	$36,238	10.7%	34,900
20. Oil and Gas Extraction	79.8%	$39,973	−6.1%	−19,200
21. Telecommunications	61.3%	$48,180	−6.5%	−67,700
22. Food Manufacturing	61.3%	$24,180	3.8%	57,100
23. Computer and Electronic Product Manufacturing	66.4%	$47,070	−7.1%	−94,200
24. Steel Manufacturing	85.0%	$36,599	−13.4%	−20,900
25. Mining	87.8%	$36,380	−12.9%	−26,600
26. Chemical Manufacturing, Except Drugs	69.3%	$38,869	−14.4%	−86,000

Lists of Best Jobs in Each of the 40 Best Fields

Once you have identified a field that interests you, you probably want to consider which jobs within that field are most promising. That's why we assembled the 40 pairs of lists that follow: the best-paying and fastest-growing jobs within each field.

As the introduction explains, these lists actually include *all* the most important jobs (for which information is available) that are linked to each field. So to find the best jobs, concentrate on the high performers on each list. On the lists of fastest-growing jobs, look for combinations of high percent growth *and* large workforce size. For example, in the list of Fastest-Growing Jobs in Hotels and Other Accommodations, the top-ranked job, Maintenance and Repair Workers, General, has the impressive growth rate of 27.2%, but the workforce is only 64,269. By comparison, the third-ranked job, Hotel, Motel, and Resort Desk Clerks, has the smaller (but still outstanding) growth rate of 17.4% and a workforce almost three times as big as that of the top-ranked job. It will probably produce more job openings.

One especially valuable aspect of these lists is that they are based on *field-specific* information about the job. In almost any other book you'll find an *overall average* figure for the earnings or the growth of a job. But here you can see the economic rewards of holding the job in a particular field.

When you peruse the salary figures, remember that starting pay in any occupation is usually a lot less than the pay that workers can earn with several years of experience. Earnings also vary significantly by region of the country, so actual pay in your area could be substantially different.

Also remember that these lists do not include every job in each field—only those that employ more than two percent of the workforce. This is why occasionally a familiar job is missing from a list. For example, Dentists is missing from the best-paying jobs in the Health Care field. This job does, in fact, pay much better than most of the jobs on that list, but it has only a small workforce (about 95,000 workers), representing less than one percent of the Health Care field.

The lists are ordered by the scheme used in the *Career Guide to Industries,* which is the same ordering used in Part II. For example, the six Information-related fields are listed together.

Best-Paying Jobs in Mining

Job	Median Earnings
1. First-Line Supervisors and Manager/Supervisors—Extractive Workers	$58,340
2. Electricians	$42,960
3. Mobile Heavy Equipment Mechanics, Except Engines	$39,890
4. Roof Bolters, Mining	$38,770
5. Continuous Mining Machine Operators	$38,440
6. Maintenance and Repair Workers, General	$37,970
7. Grader, Bulldozer, and Scraper Operators	$34,740
8. Operating Engineers	$34,740
9. Helpers—Extraction Workers	$32,420
10. Dragline Operators	$32,080
11. Excavating and Loading Machine Operators	$32,080
12. Crushing, Grinding, and Polishing Machine Setters, Operators, and Tenders	$31,870
13. Tractor-Trailer Truck Drivers	$31,580
14. Truck Drivers, Heavy	$31,580
15. Freight, Stock, and Material Movers, Hand	$24,920

Fastest-Growing Jobs in Mining

Job	Percent Growth	Size of Workforce
1. Tractor-Trailer Truck Drivers	–5.5%	14,719
2. Truck Drivers, Heavy	–5.5%	14,719
3. Crushing, Grinding, and Polishing Machine Setters, Operators, and Tenders	–7.0%	6,733
4. Dragline Operators	–9.0%	10,679
5. Excavating and Loading Machine Operators	–9.0%	10,679
6. Grader, Bulldozer, and Scraper Operators	–9.9%	21,178
7. Operating Engineers	–9.9%	21,178
8. Maintenance and Repair Workers, General	–12.4%	7,315
9. First-Line Supervisors and Manager/Supervisors—Extractive Workers	–14.0%	8,038
10. Continuous Mining Machine Operators	–14.2%	7,443
11. Mobile Heavy Equipment Mechanics, Except Engines	–15.3%	6,758
12. Helpers—Extraction Workers	–16.1%	6,188
13. Freight, Stock, and Material Movers, Hand	–19.1%	5,333
14. Electricians	–19.8%	5,016
15. Roof Bolters, Mining	–29.9%	4,415

Best-Paying Jobs in Oil and Gas Extraction

Job	Median Earnings
1. Geologists	$98,783
2. Petroleum Engineers	$95,470
3. General and Operations Managers	$90,448
4. Accountants	$54,095
5. Auditors	$54,095
6. Gaugers	$49,384
7. Petroleum Pump System Operators	$49,384
8. Petroleum Refinery and Control Panel Operators	$49,384
9. Executive Secretaries and Administrative Assistants	$38,090
10. Wellhead Pumpers	$35,086
11. Service Unit Operators, Oil, Gas, and Mining	$30,900
12. Bookkeeping, Accounting, and Auditing Clerks	$30,799
13. Secretaries, Except Legal, Medical, and Executive	$25,199
14. Roustabouts, Oil and Gas	$24,205
15. Office Clerks, General	$22,710

Fastest-Growing Jobs in Oil and Gas Extraction

Job	Percent Growth	Size of Workforce
1. Service Unit Operators, Oil, Gas, and Mining	−1.8%	15,374
2. Roustabouts, Oil and Gas	−1.9%	27,956
3. Petroleum Engineers	−3.6%	9,198
4. General and Operations Managers	−5.8%	9,924
5. Gaugers	−8.2%	13,929
6. Petroleum Pump System Operators	−8.2%	13,929
7. Petroleum Refinery and Control Panel Operators	−8.2%	13,929
8. Accountants	−9.0%	6,805
9. Auditors	−9.0%	6,805
10. Geologists	−11.1%	6,481
11. Executive Secretaries and Administrative Assistants	−12.4%	5,015
12. Office Clerks, General	−16.5%	6,615
13. Bookkeeping, Accounting, and Auditing Clerks	−16.6%	6,748
14. Secretaries, Except Legal, Medical, and Executive	−20.5%	6,180
15. Wellhead Pumpers	−26.1%	9,520

Best-Paying Jobs in Aerospace Product and Parts Manufacturing

Job	Median Earnings
1. Aerospace Engineers	$79,360
2. Mechanical Engineers	$71,770
3. Industrial Engineers	$67,440
4. Management Analysts	$65,750
5. First-Line Supervisors/Managers of Production and Operating Workers	$57,690
6. Aircraft Body and Bonded Structure Repairers	$43,900
7. Aircraft Engine Specialists	$43,900
8. Aircraft Rigging Assemblers	$43,900
9. Aircraft Structure Assemblers, Precision	$43,900
10. Aircraft Systems Assemblers, Precision	$43,900
11. Airframe-and-Power-Plant Mechanics	$43,900
12. Electrical and Electronic Inspectors and Testers	$40,860
13. Materials Inspectors	$40,860
14. Mechanical Inspectors	$40,860
15. Precision Devices Inspectors and Testers	$40,860
16. Production Inspectors, Testers, Graders, Sorters, Samplers, Weighers	$40,860
17. Machinists	$37,830

Fastest-Growing Jobs in Aerospace Product and Parts Manufacturing

Job	Percent Growth	Size of Workforce
1. Aircraft Body and Bonded Structure Repairers	30.9%	15,306
2. Aircraft Engine Specialists	30.9%	15,306
3. Airframe-and-Power-Plant Mechanics	30.9%	15,306
4. Industrial Engineers	19.9%	11,832
5. Mechanical Engineers	9.0%	13,426
6. Management Analysts	7.8%	10,388
7. Machinists	7.8%	15,844
8. Aircraft Rigging Assemblers	7.8%	15,896
9. Aircraft Structure Assemblers, Precision	7.8%	15,896
10. Aircraft Systems Assemblers, Precision	7.8%	15,896
11. First-Line Supervisors/Managers of Production and Operating Workers	7.8%	8,905
12. Aerospace Engineers	5.6%	45,060
13. Electrical and Electronic Inspectors and Testers	−1.9%	13,970
14. Materials Inspectors	−1.9%	13,970
15. Mechanical Inspectors	−1.9%	13,970
16. Precision Devices Inspectors and Testers	−1.9%	13,970
17. Production Inspectors, Testers, Graders, Sorters, Samplers, Weighers	−1.9%	13,970

Best-Paying Jobs in Chemical Manufacturing, Except Drugs

Job	Median Earnings
1. Chemists	$60,548
2. First-Line Supervisors/Managers of Production and Operating Workers	$53,240
3. Chemical Plant and System Operators	$45,537
4. Industrial Machinery Mechanics	$44,082
5. Chemical Technicians	$41,759
6. Chemical Equipment Controllers and Operators	$41,407
7. Chemical Equipment Tenders	$41,407
8. Maintenance and Repair Workers, General	$40,656
9. Mixing and Blending Machine Setters, Operators, and Tenders	$30,122

Fastest-Growing Jobs in Chemical Manufacturing, Except Drugs

Job	Percent Growth	Size of Workforce
1. Mixing and Blending Machine Setters, Operators, and Tenders	–6.6%	36,034
2. First-Line Supervisors/Managers of Production and Operating Workers	–13.7%	24,202
3. Maintenance and Repair Workers, General	–14.5%	20,004
4. Chemists	–15.7%	13,369
5. Industrial Machinery Mechanics	–16.0%	11,333
6. Chemical Technicians	–16.7%	17,406
7. Chemical Equipment Controllers and Operators	–19.8%	25,255
8. Chemical Equipment Tenders	–19.8%	25,255
9. Chemical Plant and System Operators	–22.0%	50,640

Best-Paying Jobs in Computer and Electronic Product Manufacturing

Job	Median Earnings
1. Engineering Managers	$114,280
2. Computer Software Engineers, Systems Software	$86,650
3. Computer Hardware Engineers	$86,490
4. Computer Software Engineers, Applications	$86,080
5. Electronics Engineers, Except Computer	$77,800
6. Electrical Engineers	$76,850
7. Industrial Engineers	$71,120
8. First-Line Supervisors/Managers of Production and Operating Workers	$50,500
9. Calibration and Instrumentation Technicians	$42,870
10. Electrical Engineering Technicians	$42,870
11. Electronics Engineering Technicians	$42,870
12. Semiconductor Processors	$29,950
13. Electrical and Electronic Inspectors and Testers	$29,190
14. Materials Inspectors	$29,190
15. Mechanical Inspectors	$29,190
16. Precision Devices Inspectors and Testers	$29,190
17. Production Inspectors, Testers, Graders, Sorters, Samplers, Weighers	$29,190
18. Electrical and Electronic Equipment Assemblers	$24,800
19. Team Assemblers	$23,670

Fastest-Growing Jobs in Computer and Electronic Product Manufacturing

Job	Percent Growth	Size of Workforce
1. Computer Software Engineers, Systems Software	14.1%	43,060
2. Industrial Engineers	11.1%	26,656
3. Computer Software Engineers, Applications	6.6%	40,250
4. Electrical Engineers	2.2%	36,647
5. Electronics Engineers, Except Computer	1.3%	35,130
6. Calibration and Instrumentation Technicians	0.3%	44,560
7. Electrical Engineering Technicians	0.3%	44,560
8. Electronics Engineering Technicians	0.3%	44,560
9. Engineering Managers	0.1%	28,086
10. Team Assemblers	−2.6%	64,423
11. Computer Hardware Engineers	−3.6%	33,030
12. First-Line Supervisors/Managers of Production and Operating Workers	−9.8%	30,116
13. Semiconductor Processors	−10.2%	42,190
14. Electrical and Electronic Equipment Assemblers	−12.3%	119,803
15. Electrical and Electronic Inspectors and Testers	−14.0%	34,725
16. Materials Inspectors	−14.0%	34,725
17. Mechanical Inspectors	−14.0%	34,725
18. Precision Devices Inspectors and Testers	−14.0%	34,725
19. Production Inspectors, Testers, Graders, Sorters, Samplers, Weighers	−14.0%	34,725

Best-Paying Jobs in Construction

Job	Median Earnings
1. Construction Managers	$70,510
2. First-Line Supervisors and Manager/Supervisors—Construction Trades Workers	$51,200
3. Pipe Fitters	$41,870
4. Pipelaying Fitters	$41,870
5. Plumbers	$41,870
6. Electricians	$41,840
7. Grader, Bulldozer, and Scraper Operators	$38,090
8. Operating Engineers	$38,090
9. Boat Builders and Shipwrights	$35,670
10. Brattice Builders	$35,670
11. Carpenter Assemblers and Repairers	$35,670

Best-Paying Jobs in Construction

Job	Median Earnings
12. Construction Carpenters	$35,670
13. Rough Carpenters	$35,670
14. Ship Carpenters and Joiners	$35,670
15. Heating and Air Conditioning Mechanics	$35,260
16. Refrigeration Mechanics	$35,260
17. Cement Masons and Concrete Finishers	$31,630
18. Bookkeeping, Accounting, and Auditing Clerks	$31,030
19. Painters, Construction and Maintenance	$30,150
20. Construction Laborers	$25,890
21. Office Clerks, General	$22,450

Fastest-Growing Jobs in Construction

Job	Percent Growth	Size of Workforce
1. Heating and Air Conditioning Mechanics	27.4%	142,924
2. Refrigeration Mechanics	27.4%	142,924
3. Pipe Fitters	16.7%	341,248
4. Pipelaying Fitters	16.7%	341,248
5. Plumbers	16.7%	341,248
6. Cement Masons and Concrete Finishers	15.9%	179,220
7. Electricians	14.2%	429,729
8. Construction Managers	14.0%	152,352
9. First-Line Supervisors and Manager/Supervisors—Construction Trades Workers	13.8%	425,105
10. Boat Builders and Shipwrights	13.1%	736,818
11. Brattice Builders	13.1%	736,818
12. Carpenter Assemblers and Repairers	13.1%	736,818
13. Construction Carpenters	13.1%	736,818
14. Rough Carpenters	13.1%	736,818
15. Ship Carpenters and Joiners	13.1%	736,818
16. Grader, Bulldozer, and Scraper Operators	13.1%	225,518
17. Operating Engineers	13.1%	225,518
18. Painters, Construction and Maintenance	12.7%	195,358
19. Bookkeeping, Accounting, and Auditing Clerks	2.4%	139,811
20. Construction Laborers	2.0%	699,596
21. Office Clerks, General	1.2%	168,933

Best-Paying Jobs in Food Manufacturing

Job	Median Earnings
1. First-Line Supervisors/Managers of Production and Operating Workers	$41,720
2. Maintenance and Repair Workers, General	$33,930
3. Industrial Truck and Tractor Operators	$26,770
4. Packaging and Filling Machine Operators and Tenders	$24,250
5. Food Batchmakers	$23,070
6. Bakers, Bread and Pastry	$21,860
7. Bakers, Manufacturing	$21,860
8. Freight, Stock, and Material Movers, Hand	$21,680
9. Slaughterers and Meat Packers	$20,890
10. Production Helpers	$20,800
11. Production Laborers	$20,800
12. Packers and Packagers, Hand	$19,260
13. Meat, Poultry, and Fish Cutters and Trimmers	$19,250

Fastest-Growing Jobs in Food Manufacturing

Job	Percent Growth	Size of Workforce
1. Meat, Poultry, and Fish Cutters and Trimmers	14.8%	104,093
2. Slaughterers and Meat Packers	14.2%	130,273
3. Production Helpers	8.7%	68,342
4. Production Laborers	8.7%	68,342
5. First-Line Supervisors/Managers of Production and Operating Workers	7.1%	50,403
6. Bakers, Bread and Pastry	6.8%	47,541
7. Bakers, Manufacturing	6.8%	47,541
8. Maintenance and Repair Workers, General	6.7%	40,564
9. Packers and Packagers, Hand	5.8%	73,290
10. Food Batchmakers	4.4%	68,288
11. Industrial Truck and Tractor Operators	0.4%	39,937
12. Freight, Stock, and Material Movers, Hand	–4.1%	60,404
13. Packaging and Filling Machine Operators and Tenders	–10.2%	106,902

Best-Paying Jobs in Motor Vehicle and Parts Manufacturing

Job	Median Earnings
1. First-Line Supervisors/Managers of Production and Operating Workers	$49,188
2. Electrical and Electronic Inspectors and Testers	$37,692
3. Materials Inspectors	$37,692
4. Mechanical Inspectors	$37,692
5. Precision Devices Inspectors and Testers	$37,692
6. Production Inspectors, Testers, Graders, Sorters, Samplers, Weighers	$37,692
7. Machinists	$36,814
8. Industrial Truck and Tractor Operators	$33,790
9. Brazers	$31,964
10. Solderers	$31,964
11. Welder-Fitters	$31,964
12. Welders and Cutters	$31,964
13. Welders, Production	$31,964
14. Team Assemblers	$31,431
15. Press and Press Brake Machine Setters and Set-Up Operators, Metal and Plastic	$28,341
16. Punching Machine Setters and Set-Up Operators, Metal and Plastic	$28,341
17. Sawing Machine Tool Setters and Set-Up Operators, Metal and Plastic	$28,341
18. Shear and Slitter Machine Setters and Set-Up Operators, Metal and Plastic	$28,341

Fastest-Growing Jobs in Motor Vehicle and Parts Manufacturing

Job	Percent Growth	Size of Workforce
1. Machinists	10.2%	23,647
2. Team Assemblers	9.6%	203,670
3. Brazers	9.5%	35,478
4. Solderers	9.5%	35,478
5. Welder-Fitters	9.5%	35,478
6. Welders and Cutters	9.5%	35,478
7. Welders, Production	9.5%	35,478
8. First-Line Supervisors/Managers of Production and Operating Workers	9.3%	36,661
9. Industrial Truck and Tractor Operators	1.5%	24,270
10. Electrical and Electronic Inspectors and Testers	–0.7%	35,823
11. Materials Inspectors	–0.7%	35,823
12. Mechanical Inspectors	–0.7%	35,823

(continued)

(continued)

Fastest-Growing Jobs in Motor Vehicle and Parts Manufacturing

Job	Percent Growth	Size of Workforce
13. Precision Devices Inspectors and Testers	–0.7%	35,823
14. Production Inspectors, Testers, Graders, Sorters, Samplers, Weighers	–0.7%	35,823
15. Press and Press Brake Machine Setters and Set-Up Operators, Metal and Plastic	–11.9%	32,701
16. Punching Machine Setters and Set-Up Operators, Metal and Plastic	–11.9%	32,701
17. Sawing Machine Tool Setters and Set-Up Operators, Metal and Plastic	–11.9%	32,701
18. Shear and Slitter Machine Setters and Set-Up Operators, Metal and Plastic	–11.9%	32,701

Best-Paying Jobs in Pharmaceutical and Medicine Manufacturing

Job	Median Earnings
1. Medical Scientists, Except Epidemiologists	$76,410
2. Sales Representatives, Chemical and Pharmaceutical	$65,410
3. Sales Representatives, Medical	$65,410
4. Chemists	$56,910
5. First-Line Supervisors/Managers of Production and Operating Workers	$54,150
6. Maintenance and Repair Workers, General	$42,480
7. Biological Technicians	$39,340
8. Separating, Filtering, Clarifying, Precipitating, and Still Machine Setters, Operators, and Tenders	$37,230
9. Chemical Equipment Controllers and Operators	$33,270
10. Chemical Equipment Tenders	$33,270
11. Electrical and Electronic Inspectors and Testers	$31,770
12. Materials Inspectors	$31,770
13. Mechanical Inspectors	$31,770
14. Precision Devices Inspectors and Testers	$31,770
15. Production Inspectors, Testers, Graders, Sorters, Samplers, Weighers	$31,770
16. Mixing and Blending Machine Setters, Operators, and Tenders	$29,630
17. Packaging and Filling Machine Operators and Tenders	$26,480

Fastest-Growing Jobs in Pharmaceutical and Medicine Manufacturing

Job	Percent Growth	Size of Workforce
1. Medical Scientists, Except Epidemiologists	41.8%	10,222
2. Maintenance and Repair Workers, General	28.9%	5,845
3. Mixing and Blending Machine Setters, Operators, and Tenders	28.9%	7,783
4. First-Line Supervisors/Managers of Production and Operating Workers	28.9%	7,244
5. Chemical Equipment Controllers and Operators	28.9%	7,625
6. Chemical Equipment Tenders	28.9%	7,625
7. Separating, Filtering, Clarifying, Precipitating, and Still Machine Setters, Operators, and Tenders	28.9%	5,878
8. Sales Representatives, Chemical and Pharmaceutical	28.9%	5,900
9. Sales Representatives, Medical	28.9%	5,900
10. Biological Technicians	28.2%	8,076
11. Chemists	23.6%	14,454
12. Electrical and Electronic Inspectors and Testers	16.3%	7,801
13. Materials Inspectors	16.3%	7,801
14. Mechanical Inspectors	16.3%	7,801
15. Precision Devices Inspectors and Testers	16.3%	7,801
16. Production Inspectors, Testers, Graders, Sorters, Samplers, Weighers	16.3%	7,801
17. Packaging and Filling Machine Operators and Tenders	9.8%	22,131

Best-Paying Jobs in Steel Manufacturing

Job	Median Earnings
1. First-Line Supervisors/Managers of Production and Operating Workers	$50,173
2. Electricians	$46,851
3. Industrial Machinery Mechanics	$43,741
4. Metal-Refining Furnace Operators and Tenders	$39,038
5. Maintenance and Repair Workers, General	$37,963
6. Production, Planning, and Expediting Clerks	$37,930
7. Rolling Machine Setters, Operators, and Tenders, Metal and Plastic	$35,493
8. Materials Inspectors	$34,419
9. Mechanical Inspectors	$34,419
10. Precision Devices Inspectors and Testers	$34,419
11. Production Inspectors, Testers, Graders, Sorters, Samplers, Weighers	$34,419
12. Crane and Tower Operators	$34,172
13. Extruding and Drawing Machine Setters, Operators, and Tenders, Metal and Plastic	$31,687

(continued)

(continued)

Best-Paying Jobs in Steel Manufacturing

Job	Median Earnings
14. Brazers	$30,785
15. Solderers	$30,785
16. Welder-Fitters	$30,785
17. Welders and Cutters	$30,785
18. Welders, Production	$30,785
19. Industrial Truck and Tractor Operators	$30,514
20. Press and Press Brake Machine Setters and Set-Up Operators, Metal and Plastic	$28,552
21. Punching Machine Setters and Set-Up Operators, Metal and Plastic	$28,552
22. Sawing Machine Tool Setters and Set-Up Operators, Metal and Plastic	$28,552
23. Shear and Slitter Machine Setters and Set-Up Operators, Metal and Plastic	$28,552
24. Freight, Stock, and Material Movers, Hand	$28,391
25. Production Helpers	$24,033
26. Production Laborers	$24,033

Fastest-Growing Jobs in Steel Manufacturing

Job	Percent Growth	Size of Workforce
1. Industrial Truck and Tractor Operators	−9.4%	3,739
2. Brazers	−9.6%	3,176
3. Solderers	−9.6%	3,176
4. Welder-Fitters	−9.6%	3,176
5. Welders and Cutters	−9.6%	3,176
6. Welders, Production	−9.6%	3,176
7. First-Line Supervisors/Managers of Production and Operating Workers	−9.9%	6,749
8. Production Helpers	−10.1%	5,287
9. Production Laborers	−10.1%	5,287
10. Rolling Machine Setters, Operators, and Tenders, Metal and Plastic	−10.2%	6,887
11. Maintenance and Repair Workers, General	−11.0%	7,706
12. Industrial Machinery Mechanics	−11.6%	3,205
13. Electricians	−12.0%	4,161
14. Crane and Tower Operators	−12.2%	5,586
15. Production, Planning, and Expediting Clerks	−12.8%	3,596
16. Metal-Refining Furnace Operators and Tenders	−13.1%	3,761
17. Materials Inspectors	−15.2%	4,362
18. Mechanical Inspectors	−15.2%	4,362

Fastest-Growing Jobs in Steel Manufacturing

Job	Percent Growth	Size of Workforce
19. Precision Devices Inspectors and Testers	−15.2%	4,362
20. Production Inspectors, Testers, Graders, Sorters, Samplers, Weighers	−15.2%	4,362
21. Freight, Stock, and Material Movers, Hand	−18.9%	5,844
22. Extruding and Drawing Machine Setters, Operators, and Tenders, Metal and Plastic	−25.1%	5,485
23. Press and Press Brake Machine Setters and Set-Up Operators, Metal and Plastic	−26.6%	7,259
24. Punching Machine Setters and Set-Up Operators, Metal and Plastic	−26.6%	7,259
25. Sawing Machine Tool Setters and Set-Up Operators, Metal and Plastic	−26.6%	7,259
26. Shear and Slitter Machine Setters and Set-Up Operators, Metal and Plastic	−26.6%	7,259

Best-Paying Jobs in Utilities

Job	Median Earnings
1. First-Line Supervisors/Managers of Mechanics, Installers, and Repairers	$66,100
2. Electrical and Electronics Repairers, Powerhouse, Substation, and Relay	$55,440
3. Auxiliary Equipment Operators, Power	$54,390
4. Power Generating Plant Operators, Except Auxiliary Equipment Operators	$54,390
5. Electrical Power-Line Installers and Repairers	$52,760
6. Electric Meter Installers and Repairers	$50,260
7. Meter Mechanics	$50,260
8. Valve and Regulator Repairers	$50,260
9. Maintenance and Repair Workers, General	$46,560
10. Adjustment Clerks	$34,860
11. Customer Service Representatives, Utilities	$34,860
12. Meter Readers, Utilities	$33,310

Fastest-Growing Jobs in Utilities

Job	Percent Growth	Size of Workforce
1. Maintenance and Repair Workers, General	3.7%	11,609
2. Adjustment Clerks	3.1%	32,448
3. Customer Service Representatives, Utilities	3.1%	32,448
4. First-Line Supervisors/Managers of Mechanics, Installers, and Repairers	0.7%	15,481
5. Electric Meter Installers and Repairers	0.6%	17,973
6. Meter Mechanics	0.6%	17,973
7. Valve and Regulator Repairers	0.6%	17,973
8. Electrical Power-Line Installers and Repairers	–0.5%	54,118
9. Auxiliary Equipment Operators, Power	–1.6%	22,824
10. Power Generating Plant Operators, Except Auxiliary Equipment Operators	–1.6%	22,824
11. Electrical and Electronics Repairers, Powerhouse, Substation, and Relay	–4.2%	14,786
12. Meter Readers, Utilities	–49.8%	21,934

Best-Paying Jobs in Automobile Dealers

Job	Median Earnings
1. General and Operations Managers	$108,170
2. First-Line Supervisors/Managers of Retail Sales Workers	$66,440
3. First-Line Supervisors/Managers of Mechanics, Installers, and Repairers	$53,510
4. Automotive Master Mechanics	$38,160
5. Automotive Specialty Technicians	$38,160
6. Retail Salespersons	$38,100
7. Counter and Rental Clerks	$37,750
8. Automotive Body and Related Repairers	$37,060
9. Parts Salespersons	$32,230
10. Bookkeeping, Accounting, and Auditing Clerks	$27,420
11. Office Clerks, General	$22,020
12. Cleaners of Vehicles and Equipment	$18,910

Fastest-Growing Jobs in Automobile Dealers

Job	Percent Growth	Size of Workforce
1. Counter and Rental Clerks	23.6%	30,377
2. First-Line Supervisors/Managers of Mechanics, Installers, and Repairers	17.7%	35,420
3. Automotive Master Mechanics	17.7%	227,429
4. Automotive Specialty Technicians	17.7%	227,429
5. Retail Salespersons	17.7%	269,314
6. General and Operations Managers	16.5%	27,173
7. First-Line Supervisors/Managers of Retail Sales Workers	8.3%	51,858
8. Cleaners of Vehicles and Equipment	6.7%	80,769
9. Bookkeeping, Accounting, and Auditing Clerks	6.0%	35,335
10. Office Clerks, General	4.8%	36,491
11. Automotive Body and Related Repairers	3.2%	42,453
12. Parts Salespersons	–5.8%	66,178

Best-Paying Jobs in Clothing, Accessory, and General Merchandise Stores

Job	Median Earnings
1. First-Line Supervisors/Managers of Retail Sales Workers	$30,151
2. Marking Clerks	$18,211
3. Order Fillers, Wholesale and Retail Sales	$18,211
4. Stock Clerks, Sales Floor	$18,211
5. Stock Clerks—Stockroom, Warehouse, or Storage Yard	$18,211
6. Freight, Stock, and Material Movers, Hand	$17,479
7. Retail Salespersons	$17,306
8. Cashiers	$16,183

Fastest-Growing Jobs in Clothing, Accessory, and General Merchandise Stores

Job	Percent Growth	Size of Workforce
1. Retail Salespersons	14.3%	1,795,169
2. Freight, Stock, and Material Movers, Hand	6.4%	123,890
3. Cashiers	5.9%	600,948
4. First-Line Supervisors/Managers of Retail Sales Workers	5.8%	264,940
5. Marking Clerks	–3.8%	428,620
6. Order Fillers, Wholesale and Retail Sales	–3.8%	428,620
7. Stock Clerks, Sales Floor	–3.8%	428,620
8. Stock Clerks—Stockroom, Warehouse, or Storage Yard	–3.8%	428,620

Best-Paying Jobs in Grocery Stores

Job	Median Earnings
1. First-Line Supervisors/Managers of Retail Sales Workers	$31,410
2. Butchers and Meat Cutters	$27,520
3. Adjustment Clerks	$18,710
4. Food Preparation Workers	$18,460
5. Marking Clerks	$18,450
6. Order Fillers, Wholesale and Retail Sales	$18,450
7. Stock Clerks, Sales Floor	$18,450
8. Stock Clerks—Stockroom, Warehouse, or Storage Yard	$18,450
9. Combined Food Preparation and Serving Workers, Including Fast Food	$17,710
10. Cashiers	$16,340
11. Packers and Packagers, Hand	$14,910

Fastest-Growing Jobs in Grocery Stores

Job	Percent Growth	Size of Workforce
1. Adjustment Clerks	24.6%	57,891
2. Food Preparation Workers	21.8%	103,394
3. Combined Food Preparation and Serving Workers, Including Fast Food	15.1%	97,645
4. First-Line Supervisors/Managers of Retail Sales Workers	12.0%	129,307
5. Packers and Packagers, Hand	11.0%	194,789

Fastest-Growing Jobs in Grocery Stores

Job	Percent Growth	Size of Workforce
6. Butchers and Meat Cutters	9.6%	88,146
7. Cashiers	–2.6%	824,084
8. Marking Clerks	–6.7%	372,846
9. Order Fillers, Wholesale and Retail Sales	–6.7%	372,846
10. Stock Clerks, Sales Floor	–6.7%	372,846
11. Stock Clerks—Stockroom, Warehouse, or Storage Yard	–6.7%	372,846

Best-Paying Jobs in Wholesale Trade

Job	Median Earnings
1. General and Operations Managers	$90,630
2. Sales Representatives, Wholesale and Manufacturing, Except Technical and Scientific Products	$45,620
3. Tractor-Trailer Truck Drivers	$33,030
4. Truck Drivers, Heavy	$33,030
5. Adjustment Clerks	$29,940
6. Bookkeeping, Accounting, and Auditing Clerks	$29,280
7. Shipping, Receiving, and Traffic Clerks	$25,060
8. Truck Drivers, Light or Delivery Services	$24,210
9. Office Clerks, General	$23,100
10. Marking Clerks	$22,990
11. Order Fillers, Wholesale and Retail Sales	$22,990
12. Stock Clerks, Sales Floor	$22,990
13. Stock Clerks—Stockroom, Warehouse, or Storage Yard	$22,990
14. Freight, Stock, and Material Movers, Hand	$21,450

Fastest-Growing Jobs in Wholesale Trade

Job	Percent Growth	Size of Workforce
1. Adjustment Clerks	17.9%	149,833
2. Sales Representatives, Wholesale and Manufacturing, Except Technical and Scientific Products	13.9%	813,886
3. Truck Drivers, Light or Delivery Services	12.9%	184,747

(continued)

(continued)

Fastest-Growing Jobs in Wholesale Trade

Job	Percent Growth	Size of Workforce
4. General and Operations Managers	11.8%	136,212
5. Tractor-Trailer Truck Drivers	8.3%	201,963
6. Truck Drivers, Heavy	8.3%	201,963
7. Shipping, Receiving, and Traffic Clerks	3.4%	160,759
8. Freight, Stock, and Material Movers, Hand	1.3%	372,562
9. Bookkeeping, Accounting, and Auditing Clerks	1.1%	145,105
10. Office Clerks, General	0.6%	169,599
11. Marking Clerks	−12.6%	177,276
12. Order Fillers, Wholesale and Retail Sales	−12.6%	177,276
13. Stock Clerks, Sales Floor	−12.6%	177,276
14. Stock Clerks—Stockroom, Warehouse, or Storage Yard	−12.6%	177,276

Best-Paying Jobs in Air Transportation

Job	Median Earnings
1. Airline Pilots, Copilots, and Flight Engineers	$143,020
2. Aircraft Body and Bonded Structure Repairers	$54,240
3. Aircraft Engine Specialists	$54,240
4. Airframe-and-Power-Plant Mechanics	$54,240
5. Flight Attendants	$46,030
6. Cargo and Freight Agents	$37,570
7. Reservation and Transportation Ticket Agents	$32,620
8. Travel Clerks	$32,620
9. Baggage Porters and Bellhops	$31,780
10. Adjustment Clerks	$27,770

Fastest-Growing Jobs in Air Transportation

Job	Percent Growth	Size of Workforce
1. Airline Pilots, Copilots, and Flight Engineers	19.4%	70,234
2. Adjustment Clerks	16.8%	13,978
3. Flight Attendants	16.4%	100,586
4. Aircraft Body and Bonded Structure Repairers	4.1%	41,593
5. Aircraft Engine Specialists	4.1%	41,593
6. Airframe-and-Power-Plant Mechanics	4.1%	41,593
7. Baggage Porters and Bellhops	3.4%	10,419
8. Reservation and Transportation Ticket Agents	–6.3%	97,421
9. Travel Clerks	–6.3%	97,421
10. Cargo and Freight Agents	–9.9%	14,420

Best-Paying Jobs in Truck Transportation and Warehousing

Job	Median Earnings
1. Tractor-Trailer Truck Drivers	$35,807
2. Truck Drivers, Heavy	$35,807
3. Bus and Truck Mechanics and Diesel Engine Specialists	$34,250
4. Truck Drivers, Light or Delivery Services	$27,916
5. Industrial Truck and Tractor Operators	$27,396
6. Shipping, Receiving, and Traffic Clerks	$26,993
7. Marking Clerks	$26,120
8. Order Fillers, Wholesale and Retail Sales	$26,120
9. Stock Clerks, Sales Floor	$26,120
10. Stock Clerks—Stockroom, Warehouse, or Storage Yard	$26,120
11. Freight, Stock, and Material Movers, Hand	$24,125
12. Office Clerks, General	$23,157

Fastest-Growing Jobs in Truck Transportation and Warehousing

Job	Percent Growth	Size of Workforce
1. Shipping, Receiving, and Traffic Clerks	21.5%	39,307
2. Industrial Truck and Tractor Operators	18.2%	100,916
3. Truck Drivers, Light or Delivery Services	16.1%	81,878
4. Freight, Stock, and Material Movers, Hand	13.6%	211,558
5. Bus and Truck Mechanics and Diesel Engine Specialists	13.4%	45,511
6. Tractor-Trailer Truck Drivers	13.2%	765,490
7. Truck Drivers, Heavy	13.2%	765,490
8. Office Clerks, General	5.2%	43,676
9. Marking Clerks	4.6%	51,366
10. Order Fillers, Wholesale and Retail Sales	4.6%	51,366
11. Stock Clerks, Sales Floor	4.6%	51,366
12. Stock Clerks—Stockroom, Warehouse, or Storage Yard	4.6%	51,366

Best-Paying Jobs in Broadcasting

Job	Median Earnings
1. General and Operations Managers	$91,977
2. Directors—Stage, Motion Pictures, Television, and Radio	$46,314
3. Producers	$46,314
4. Program Directors	$46,314
5. Talent Directors	$46,314
6. Technical Directors/Managers	$46,314
7. Advertising Sales Agents	$40,245
8. Telecommunications Line Installers and Repairers	$37,230
9. Reporters and Correspondents	$35,394
10. Camera Operators, Television, Video, and Motion Picture	$31,774
11. Adjustment Clerks	$29,452
12. Broadcast Technicians	$26,488
13. Office Clerks, General	$25,262
14. Radio and Television Announcers	$22,628

Fastest-Growing Jobs in Broadcasting

Job	Percent Growth	Size of Workforce
1. Adjustment Clerks	48.4%	13,849
2. Telecommunications Line Installers and Repairers	46.9%	11,238
3. General and Operations Managers	10.2%	8,989
4. Directors—Stage, Motion Pictures, Television, and Radio	10.0%	21,374
5. Producers	10.0%	21,374
6. Program Directors	10.0%	21,374
7. Talent Directors	10.0%	21,374
8. Technical Directors/Managers	10.0%	21,374
9. Camera Operators, Television, Video, and Motion Picture	5.3%	9,348
10. Broadcast Technicians	5.2%	22,484
11. Office Clerks, General	3.7%	9,362
12. Advertising Sales Agents	2.7%	31,788
13. Reporters and Correspondents	2.2%	10,688
14. Radio and Television Announcers	–7.3%	38,919

Best-Paying Jobs in Internet Service Providers, Web Search Portals, and Data Processing Services

Job	Median Earnings
1. General and Operations Managers	$109,730
2. Computer and Information Systems Managers	$100,510
3. Computer Software Engineers, Systems Software	$76,360
4. Computer Software Engineers, Applications	$75,130
5. Computer Systems Analysts	$70,360
6. Computer Programmers	$65,980
7. Computer Security Specialists	$60,520
8. Network and Computer Systems Administrators	$60,520
9. Network Systems and Data Communications Analysts	$60,300
10. First-Line Supervisors, Administrative Support	$45,590
11. First-Line Supervisors, Customer Service	$45,590
12. Computer Support Specialists	$37,790
13. Bookkeeping, Accounting, and Auditing Clerks	$31,130
14. Computer Operators	$28,710
15. Adjustment Clerks	$28,370
16. Office Clerks, General	$23,110
17. Data Entry Keyers	$21,110

Fastest-Growing Jobs in Internet Service Providers, Web Search Portals, and Data Processing Services

Job	Percent Growth	Size of Workforce
1. Network Systems and Data Communications Analysts	69.2%	9,024
2. Computer Software Engineers, Systems Software	56.5%	18,320
3. Computer Software Engineers, Applications	56.3%	19,491
4. Computer Security Specialists	50.4%	12,602
5. Network and Computer Systems Administrators	50.4%	12,602
6. Computer Systems Analysts	47.6%	18,582
7. Computer and Information Systems Managers	36.8%	12,198
8. Adjustment Clerks	31.5%	26,753
9. General and Operations Managers	28.0%	8,399
10. Computer Support Specialists	27.9%	21,534
11. Office Clerks, General	20.3%	13,689
12. First-Line Supervisors, Administrative Support	20.0%	8,261
13. First-Line Supervisors, Customer Service	20.0%	8,261
14. Bookkeeping, Accounting, and Auditing Clerks	19.0%	7,886
15. Computer Programmers	8.4%	21,917
16. Data Entry Keyers	5.8%	19,335
17. Computer Operators	−23.9%	8,191

Best-Paying Jobs in Motion Picture and Video Fields

Job	Median Earnings
1. General and Operations Managers	$97,010
2. Directors—Stage, Motion Pictures, Television, and Radio	$67,940
3. Producers	$67,940
4. Program Directors	$67,940
5. Talent Directors	$67,940
6. Technical Directors/Managers	$67,940
7. Film and Video Editors	$47,590
8. Audio and Video Equipment Technicians	$34,980
9. Motion Picture Projectionists	$16,870
10. Cashiers	$14,760
11. Ushers, Lobby Attendants, and Ticket Takers	$14,070
12. Counter Attendants, Cafeteria, Food Concession, and Coffee Shop	$13,870

Fastest-Growing Jobs in Motion Picture and Video Fields

Job	Percent Growth	Size of Workforce
1. Audio and Video Equipment Technicians	27.7%	8,036
2. Film and Video Editors	27.3%	10,069
3. Directors—Stage, Motion Pictures, Television, and Radio	26.5%	13,317
4. Producers	26.5%	13,317
5. Program Directors	26.5%	13,317
6. Talent Directors	26.5%	13,317
7. Technical Directors/Managers	26.5%	13,317
8. Counter Attendants, Cafeteria, Food Concession, and Coffee Shop	23.0%	32,575
9. General and Operations Managers	17.6%	9,481
10. Ushers, Lobby Attendants, and Ticket Takers	4.2%	41,579
11. Cashiers	−5.7%	22,389
12. Motion Picture Projectionists	−16.4%	9,075

Best-Paying Jobs in Publishing, Except Software

Job	Median Earnings
1. Editors	$44,080
2. Advertising Sales Agents	$35,830
3. Design Printing Machine Setters and Set-Up Operators	$34,350
4. Embossing Machine Set-Up Operators	$34,350
5. Engraver Set-Up Operators	$34,350
6. Letterpress Setters and Set-Up Operators	$34,350
7. Marking and Identification Printing Machine Setters and Set-Up Operators	$34,350
8. Offset Lithographic Press Setters and Set-Up Operators	$34,350
9. Precision Printing Workers	$34,350
10. Printing Press Machine Operators and Tenders	$34,350
11. Screen Printing Machine Setters and Set-Up Operators	$34,350
12. Graphic Designers	$32,810
13. Camera Operators	$30,910
14. Dot Etchers	$30,910
15. Electronic Masking System Operators	$30,910
16. Electrotypers and Stereotypers	$30,910
17. Hand Compositors and Typesetters	$30,910
18. Paste-Up Workers	$30,910

(continued)

(continued)

Best-Paying Jobs in Publishing, Except Software

Job	Median Earnings
19. Photoengravers	$30,910
20. Photoengraving and Lithographing Machine Operators and Tenders	$30,910
21. Plate Finishers	$30,910
22. Platemakers	$30,910
23. Scanner Operators	$30,910
24. Strippers	$30,910
25. Typesetting and Composing Machine Operators and Tenders	$30,910
26. Reporters and Correspondents	$30,130
27. Adjustment Clerks	$27,050
28. Office Clerks, General	$23,020
29. Truck Drivers, Light or Delivery Services	$22,490
30. Telemarketers	$21,030
31. Freight, Stock, and Material Movers, Hand	$20,110

Fastest-Growing Jobs in Publishing, Except Software

Job	Percent Growth	Size of Workforce
1. Graphic Designers	16.0%	21,412
2. Advertising Sales Agents	15.7%	47,878
3. Adjustment Clerks	15.1%	20,160
4. Editors	12.1%	58,816
5. Design Printing Machine Setters and Set-Up Operators	8.0%	18,287
6. Embossing Machine Set-Up Operators	8.0%	18,287
7. Engraver Set-Up Operators	8.0%	18,287
8. Letterpress Setters and Set-Up Operators	8.0%	18,287
9. Marking and Identification Printing Machine Setters and Set-Up Operators	8.0%	18,287
10. Offset Lithographic Press Setters and Set-Up Operators	8.0%	18,287
11. Precision Printing Workers	8.0%	18,287
12. Printing Press Machine Operators and Tenders	8.0%	18,287
13. Screen Printing Machine Setters and Set-Up Operators	8.0%	18,287
14. Truck Drivers, Light or Delivery Services	5.0%	13,666
15. Reporters and Correspondents	4.2%	38,527
16. Freight, Stock, and Material Movers, Hand	–0.3%	15,090
17. Office Clerks, General	–1.8%	19,382
18. Camera Operators	–3.2%	17,783

Fastest-Growing Jobs in Publishing, Except Software

Job	Percent Growth	Size of Workforce
19. Dot Etchers	−3.2%	17,783
20. Electronic Masking System Operators	−3.2%	17,783
21. Electrotypers and Stereotypers	−3.2%	17,783
22. Hand Compositors and Typesetters	−3.2%	17,783
23. Paste-Up Workers	−3.2%	17,783
24. Photoengravers	−3.2%	17,783
25. Photoengraving and Lithographing Machine Operators and Tenders	−3.2%	17,783
26. Plate Finishers	−3.2%	17,783
27. Platemakers	−3.2%	17,783
28. Scanner Operators	−3.2%	17,783
29. Strippers	−3.2%	17,783
30. Typesetting and Composing Machine Operators and Tenders	−3.2%	17,783
31. Telemarketers	−13.7%	14,407

Best-Paying Jobs in Software Publishers

Job	Median Earnings
1. General and Operations Managers	$119,670
2. Computer and Information Systems Managers	$109,080
3. Computer Software Engineers, Systems Software	$85,550
4. Computer Software Engineers, Applications	$81,310
5. Computer Programmers	$74,360
6. Computer Systems Analysts	$72,160
7. Computer Support Specialists	$45,650
8. Adjustment Clerks	$34,830

Fastest-Growing Jobs in Software Publishers

Job	Percent Growth	Size of Workforce
1. Computer Software Engineers, Applications	93.0%	39,358
2. Computer Software Engineers, Systems Software	91.8%	21,296
3. Computer Systems Analysts	76.9%	9,803
4. Computer and Information Systems Managers	68.4%	8,750
5. Adjustment Clerks	64.7%	4,784
6. Computer Support Specialists	60.8%	18,663
7. General and Operations Managers	59.2%	4,831
8. Computer Programmers	31.2%	18,486

Best-Paying Jobs in Telecommunications

Job	Median Earnings
1. Computer Software Engineers, Systems Software	$76,640
2. Electronics Engineers, Except Computer	$70,050
3. First-Line Supervisors/Managers of Mechanics, Installers, and Repairers	$64,570
4. First-Line Supervisors, Administrative Support	$53,080
5. First-Line Supervisors, Customer Service	$53,080
6. Central Office and PBX Installers and Repairers	$51,940
7. Communication Equipment Mechanics, Installers, and Repairers	$51,940
8. Frame Wirers, Central Office	$51,940
9. Station Installers and Repairers, Telephone	$51,940
10. Telecommunications Facility Examiners	$51,940
11. Telecommunications Line Installers and Repairers	$49,830
12. Office Clerks, General	$35,290
13. Telemarketers	$34,780
14. Central Office Operators	$33,080
15. Directory Assistance Operators	$33,080
16. Adjustment Clerks	$32,130
17. Customer Service Representatives, Utilities	$32,130
18. Retail Salespersons	$24,350

Fastest-Growing Jobs in Telecommunications

Job	Percent Growth	Size of Workforce
1. Retail Salespersons	12.6%	24,388
2. Adjustment Clerks	11.3%	132,864
3. Customer Service Representatives, Utilities	11.3%	132,864
4. Telecommunications Line Installers and Repairers	2.5%	78,905
5. Electronics Engineers, Except Computer	–2.8%	25,024
6. Computer Software Engineers, Systems Software	–6.7%	24,829
7. First-Line Supervisors/Managers of Mechanics, Installers, and Repairers	–11.7%	22,075
8. First-Line Supervisors, Administrative Support	–12.3%	23,530
9. First-Line Supervisors, Customer Service	–12.3%	23,530
10. Central Office and PBX Installers and Repairers	–17.2%	140,295
11. Communication Equipment Mechanics, Installers, and Repairers	–17.2%	140,295
12. Frame Wirers, Central Office	–17.2%	140,295
13. Station Installers and Repairers, Telephone	–17.2%	140,295
14. Telecommunications Facility Examiners	–17.2%	140,295
15. Office Clerks, General	–18.8%	21,477
16. Telemarketers	–34.7%	24,855
17. Central Office Operators	–42.3%	26,810
18. Directory Assistance Operators	–42.3%	26,810

Best-Paying Jobs in Insurance

Job	Median Earnings
1. Insurance Underwriters	$49,630
2. First-Line Supervisors, Administrative Support	$48,510
3. First-Line Supervisors, Customer Service	$48,510
4. Claims Examiners, Property and Casualty Insurance	$46,500
5. Insurance Adjusters, Examiners, and Investigators	$46,500
6. Insurance Sales Agents	$42,240
7. Executive Secretaries and Administrative Assistants	$37,240
8. Bookkeeping, Accounting, and Auditing Clerks	$30,490
9. Insurance Claims Clerks	$29,850
10. Insurance Policy Processing Clerks	$29,850
11. Adjustment Clerks	$29,650
12. Secretaries, Except Legal, Medical, and Executive	$25,590
13. Office Clerks, General	$22,720

Fastest-Growing Jobs in Insurance

Job	Percent Growth	Size of Workforce
1. Adjustment Clerks	20.0%	253,127
2. Claims Examiners, Property and Casualty Insurance	14.6%	205,249
3. Insurance Adjusters, Examiners, and Investigators	14.6%	205,249
4. Executive Secretaries and Administrative Assistants	11.3%	57,545
5. Insurance Sales Agents	8.6%	283,489
6. Bookkeeping, Accounting, and Auditing Clerks	6.7%	47,744
7. Office Clerks, General	6.5%	106,246
8. Insurance Underwriters	6.0%	86,702
9. First-Line Supervisors, Administrative Support	4.4%	68,403
10. First-Line Supervisors, Customer Service	4.4%	68,403
11. Insurance Claims Clerks	3.6%	216,253
12. Insurance Policy Processing Clerks	3.6%	216,253
13. Secretaries, Except Legal, Medical, and Executive	–3.0%	64,192

Best-Paying Jobs in Securities, Commodities, and Other Investments

Job	Median Earnings
1. Financial Managers, Branch or Department	$129,500
2. Treasurers, Controllers, and Chief Financial Officers	$129,500
3. General and Operations Managers	$127,130
4. Sales Agents, Financial Services	$81,610
5. Sales Agents, Securities and Commodities	$81,610
6. Financial Analysts	$72,820
7. Personal Financial Advisors	$70,940
8. Accountants	$56,140
9. Auditors	$56,140
10. First-Line Supervisors, Administrative Support	$50,660
11. First-Line Supervisors, Customer Service	$50,660
12. Executive Secretaries and Administrative Assistants	$42,570
13. Brokerage Clerks	$36,180
14. Bookkeeping, Accounting, and Auditing Clerks	$33,760
15. Adjustment Clerks	$32,810
16. Secretaries, Except Legal, Medical, and Executive	$29,960
17. Office Clerks, General	$23,970

Fastest-Growing Jobs in Securities, Commodities, and Other Investments

Job	Percent Growth	Size of Workforce
1. Personal Financial Advisors	30.2%	55,665
2. Adjustment Clerks	24.0%	35,762
3. Accountants	23.4%	19,381
4. Auditors	23.4%	19,381
5. General and Operations Managers	21.5%	16,951
6. Financial Analysts	19.0%	38,757
7. Financial Managers, Branch or Department	17.4%	27,409
8. Treasurers, Controllers, and Chief Financial Officers	17.4%	27,409
9. Bookkeeping, Accounting, and Auditing Clerks	10.7%	19,094
10. First-Line Supervisors, Administrative Support	10.7%	19,326
11. First-Line Supervisors, Customer Service	10.7%	19,326
12. Executive Secretaries and Administrative Assistants	9.8%	42,644
13. Sales Agents, Financial Services	9.4%	160,532
14. Sales Agents, Securities and Commodities	9.4%	160,532
15. Brokerage Clerks	9.4%	58,355
16. Office Clerks, General	8.5%	39,476
17. Secretaries, Except Legal, Medical, and Executive	4.2%	18,136

Best-Paying Jobs in Advertising and Public Relations Services

Job	Median Earnings
1. General and Operations Managers	$115,120
2. Art Directors	$67,290
3. Sales Representatives, Wholesale and Manufacturing, Except Technical and Scientific Products	$49,730
4. Public Relations Specialists	$49,530
5. Advertising Sales Agents	$46,260
6. Graphic Designers	$39,080
7. Executive Secretaries and Administrative Assistants	$37,680
8. Bookkeeping, Accounting, and Auditing Clerks	$31,710
9. Adjustment Clerks	$30,240
10. Office Clerks, General	$23,380
11. Mail Clerks, Except Mail Machine Operators and Postal Service	$20,480
12. Mail Machine Operators, Preparation and Handling	$20,480
13. Demonstrators and Product Promoters	$17,570

Fastest-Growing Jobs in Advertising and Public Relations Services

Job	Percent Growth	Size of Workforce
1. Public Relations Specialists	39.8%	22,158
2. Graphic Designers	38.9%	22,171
3. Adjustment Clerks	30.1%	13,889
4. Advertising Sales Agents	27.2%	43,273
5. Art Directors	27.1%	9,886
6. Sales Representatives, Wholesale and Manufacturing, Except Technical and Scientific Products	27.1%	9,552
7. General and Operations Managers	25.8%	14,663
8. Demonstrators and Product Promoters	22.4%	18,549
9. Executive Secretaries and Administrative Assistants	20.5%	10,630
10. Bookkeeping, Accounting, and Auditing Clerks	14.4%	10,859
11. Office Clerks, General	13.1%	13,168
12. Mail Clerks, Except Mail Machine Operators and Postal Service	–34.9%	15,836
13. Mail Machine Operators, Preparation and Handling	–34.9%	15,836

Best-Paying Jobs in Computer Systems Design and Related Services

Job	Median Earnings
1. General and Operations Managers	$119,100
2. Computer and Information Systems Managers	$105,430
3. Computer Software Engineers, Systems Software	$81,340
4. Computer Software Engineers, Applications	$76,130
5. Management Analysts	$72,480
6. Computer Systems Analysts	$69,030
7. Computer Programmers	$66,540
8. Network Systems and Data Communications Analysts	$64,480
9. Computer Security Specialists	$64,210
10. Network and Computer Systems Administrators	$64,210
11. Computer Support Specialists	$42,360
12. Adjustment Clerks	$28,580
13. Office Clerks, General	$23,530

Fastest-Growing Jobs in Computer Systems Design and Related Services

Job	Percent Growth	Size of Workforce
1. Network Systems and Data Communications Analysts	81.5%	28,502
2. Computer Software Engineers, Applications	62.7%	133,095
3. Computer Software Engineers, Systems Software	62.2%	86,693
4. Computer Security Specialists	58.1%	39,726
5. Network and Computer Systems Administrators	58.1%	39,726
6. Computer Systems Analysts	49.2%	87,003
7. Computer and Information Systems Managers	42.0%	35,603
8. Adjustment Clerks	40.6%	35,525
9. Computer Support Specialists	35.6%	82,972
10. Management Analysts	35.6%	24,333
11. General and Operations Managers	34.2%	32,971
12. Office Clerks, General	20.7%	24,168
13. Computer Programmers	10.6%	112,146

Best-Paying Jobs in Employment Services

Job	Median Earnings
1. Registered Nurses	$64,160
2. Adjustment Clerks	$23,290
3. Office Clerks, General	$21,080
4. Team Assemblers	$18,130
5. Construction Laborers	$17,970
6. Packaging and Filling Machine Operators and Tenders	$17,600
7. Freight, Stock, and Material Movers, Hand	$17,160
8. Production Helpers	$16,850
9. Production Laborers	$16,850
10. Packers and Packagers, Hand	$16,290

Fastest-Growing Jobs in Employment Services

Job	Percent Growth	Size of Workforce
1. Adjustment Clerks	74.4%	79,115
2. Construction Laborers	66.7%	71,765
3. Registered Nurses	50.5%	76,711
4. Office Clerks, General	49.3%	181,508
5. Team Assemblers	42.9%	122,157
6. Packaging and Filling Machine Operators and Tenders	39.1%	72,008
7. Production Helpers	35.0%	84,203
8. Production Laborers	35.0%	84,203
9. Freight, Stock, and Material Movers, Hand	34.7%	545,495
10. Packers and Packagers, Hand	19.1%	150,674

Best-Paying Jobs in Management, Scientific, and Technical Consulting Services

Job	Median Earnings
1. General and Operations Managers	$117,480
2. Management Analysts	$73,810
3. Employment Interviewers, Private or Public Employment Service	$52,530
4. Personnel Recruiters	$52,530
5. Executive Secretaries and Administrative Assistants	$37,550
6. Bookkeeping, Accounting, and Auditing Clerks	$31,540
7. Adjustment Clerks	$28,480
8. Secretaries, Except Legal, Medical, and Executive	$27,470
9. Office Clerks, General	$23,440

Fastest-Growing Jobs in Management, Scientific, and Technical Consulting Services

Job	Percent Growth	Size of Workforce
1. Adjustment Clerks	69.6%	26,833
2. Management Analysts	66.2%	95,451
3. Employment Interviewers, Private or Public Employment Service	65.6%	16,951
4. Personnel Recruiters	65.6%	16,951
5. General and Operations Managers	64.5%	28,186
6. Bookkeeping, Accounting, and Auditing Clerks	49.6%	18,244
7. Executive Secretaries and Administrative Assistants	48.9%	29,539
8. Office Clerks, General	48.0%	36,244
9. Secretaries, Except Legal, Medical, and Executive	30.1%	21,826

Best-Paying Jobs in Scientific Research and Development Services

Job	Median Earnings
1. General and Operations Managers	$123,440
2. Computer Software Engineers, Systems Software	$92,280
3. Medical Scientists, Except Epidemiologists	$68,750
4. Chemists	$65,380
5. Executive Secretaries and Administrative Assistants	$40,910
6. Biological Technicians	$37,220
7. Office Clerks, General	$28,140

Fastest-Growing Jobs in Scientific Research and Development Services

Job	Percent Growth	Size of Workforce
1. Computer Software Engineers, Systems Software	33.4%	17,910
2. Medical Scientists, Except Epidemiologists	22.6%	17,710
3. Executive Secretaries and Administrative Assistants	11.4%	19,002
4. Biological Technicians	10.8%	14,776
5. General and Operations Managers	9.9%	12,899
6. Chemists	6.9%	11,482
7. Office Clerks, General	−1.4%	11,330

Best-Paying Jobs in Child Day Care Services

Job	Median Earnings
1. Education Administrators, Preschool and Child Care Center/Program	$33,770
2. Preschool Teachers, Except Special Education	$20,060
3. Teacher Assistants	$17,320
4. Cooks, Institution and Cafeteria	$16,880
5. Child Care Workers	$15,530
6. Nannies	$15,530

Fastest-Growing Jobs in Child Day Care Services

Job	Percent Growth	Size of Workforce
1. Preschool Teachers, Except Special Education	41.2%	261,522
2. Teacher Assistants	41.2%	95,045
3. Child Care Workers	37.4%	222,010
4. Nannies	37.4%	222,010
5. Education Administrators, Preschool and Child Care Center/Program	32.9%	34,202
6. Cooks, Institution and Cafeteria	12.9%	18,135

Best-Paying Jobs in Educational Services

Job	Median Earnings
1. Teachers, Postsecondary	$61,130
2. Secondary School Teachers, Except Special and Vocational Education	$46,160
3. Middle School Teachers, Except Special and Vocational Education	$44,200
4. Elementary School Teachers, Except Special Education	$43,720
5. Executive Secretaries and Administrative Assistants	$34,970
6. Secretaries, Except Legal, Medical, and Executive	$26,990
7. Office Clerks, General	$22,970
8. Janitors and Cleaners, Except Maids and Housekeeping Cleaners	$22,740
9. Teacher Assistants	$20,010

Fastest-Growing Jobs in Educational Services

Job	Percent Growth	Size of Workforce
1. Teachers, Postsecondary	42.3%	559,370
2. Elementary School Teachers, Except Special Education	17.9%	1,411,336
3. Executive Secretaries and Administrative Assistants	14.5%	196,604
4. Janitors and Cleaners, Except Maids and Housekeeping Cleaners	14.5%	482,574
5. Secondary School Teachers, Except Special and Vocational Education	14.3%	1,017,234
6. Middle School Teachers, Except Special and Vocational Education	13.6%	622,072
7. Teacher Assistants	10.9%	1,067,400
8. Office Clerks, General	8.1%	367,319
9. Secretaries, Except Legal, Medical, and Executive	–5.1%	394,919

Teachers, Postsecondary, represents a combination of the following separate job titles: Agricultural Sciences Teachers, Postsecondary; Anthropology and Archeology Teachers, Postsecondary; Architecture Teachers, Postsecondary; Area, Ethnic, and Cultural Studies Teachers, Postsecondary; Atmospheric, Earth, Marine, and Space Sciences Teachers, Postsecondary; Biological Science Teachers, Postsecondary; Chemistry Teachers, Postsecondary; Communications Teachers, Postsecondary; Computer Science Teachers, Postsecondary; Economics Teachers, Postsecondary; Education Teachers, Postsecondary; Engineering Teachers, Postsecondary; Environmental Science Teachers, Postsecondary; Forestry and Conservation Science Teachers, Postsecondary; Geography Teachers, Postsecondary; Health Specialties Teachers, Postsecondary; Home Economics Teachers, Postsecondary; Law Teachers, Postsecondary; Mathematical Science Teachers, Postsecondary; Nursing Instructors and Teachers, Postsecondary; Physics Teachers, Postsecondary; Political Science Teachers, Postsecondary; Psychology Teachers, Postsecondary; Recreation and Fitness Studies Teachers, Postsecondary; and Sociology Teachers, Postsecondary.

Best-Paying Jobs in Health Care

Job	Median Earnings
1. Physicians and Surgeons	more than $145,600
2. Registered Nurses	$53,489
3. Licensed Practical and Licensed Vocational Nurses	$34,332
4. Medical Secretaries	$27,093
5. Medical Assistants	$24,971
6. Office Clerks, General	$23,529
7. Receptionists and Information Clerks	$22,893
8. Nursing Aides, Orderlies, and Attendants	$21,033
9. Home Health Aides	$18,443
10. Personal and Home Care Aides	$16,175

Fastest-Growing Jobs in Health Care

Job	Percent Growth	Size of Workforce
1. Home Health Aides	66.4%	457,804
2. Personal and Home Care Aides	60.5%	312,238
3. Medical Assistants	53.7%	361,434
4. Receptionists and Information Clerks	31.3%	352,599
5. Registered Nurses	30.5%	1,988,352
6. Physicians and Surgeons	30.0%	289,660
7. Nursing Aides, Orderlies, and Attendants	22.2%	1,229,572
8. Medical Secretaries	17.3%	347,444
9. Office Clerks, General	16.8%	327,359
10. Licensed Practical and Licensed Vocational Nurses	14.2%	585,718

Physicians and Surgeons represents a combination of the following separate job titles: Anesthesiologists; Family and General Practitioners; Internists, General; Obstetricians and Gynecologists; Pediatricians, General; Psychiatrists; and Surgeons.

Best-Paying Jobs in Social Assistance, Except Child Day Care

Job	Median Earnings
1. Social and Community Service Managers	$46,413
2. Child, Family, and School Social Workers	$30,888
3. Rehabilitation Counselors	$26,650
4. Social and Human Service Assistants	$23,275
5. Office Clerks, General	$20,516
6. Home Health Aides	$17,973
7. Personal and Home Care Aides	$17,923
8. Janitors and Cleaners, Except Maids and Housekeeping Cleaners	$17,008

Fastest-Growing Jobs in Social Assistance, Except Child Day Care

Job	Percent Growth	Size of Workforce
1. Social and Human Service Assistants	45.6%	99,128
2. Personal and Home Care Aides	44.2%	183,896
3. Home Health Aides	33.5%	90,842
4. Child, Family, and School Social Workers	33.4%	52,484
5. Janitors and Cleaners, Except Maids and Housekeeping Cleaners	32.5%	29,598
6. Social and Community Service Managers	32.5%	41,680
7. Rehabilitation Counselors	23.6%	51,965
8. Office Clerks, General	18.1%	36,544

Best-Paying Jobs in Arts, Entertainment, and Recreation

Job	Median Earnings
1. Fitness Trainers and Aerobics Instructors	$29,020
2. Security Guards	$20,520
3. Landscaping and Groundskeeping Workers	$19,280
4. Janitors and Cleaners, Except Maids and Housekeeping Cleaners	$17,670
5. Receptionists and Information Clerks	$17,550
6. Cashiers	$16,580
7. Bartenders	$16,260
8. Ushers, Lobby Attendants, and Ticket Takers	$15,930
9. Waiters and Waitresses	$15,710
10. Amusement and Recreation Attendants	$15,150

Fastest-Growing Jobs in Arts, Entertainment, and Recreation

Job	Percent Growth	Size of Workforce
1. Amusement and Recreation Attendants	30.0%	155,385
2. Janitors and Cleaners, Except Maids and Housekeeping Cleaners	29.8%	40,428
3. Fitness Trainers and Aerobics Instructors	28.7%	115,891
4. Landscaping and Groundskeeping Workers	24.5%	115,089
5. Receptionists and Information Clerks	22.6%	39,011
6. Bartenders	19.0%	40,276
7. Ushers, Lobby Attendants, and Ticket Takers	18.1%	37,113
8. Waiters and Waitresses	16.4%	93,033
9. Cashiers	16.3%	55,237
10. Security Guards	4.3%	39,378

Best-Paying Jobs in Food Services and Drinking Places

Job	Median Earnings
1. First-Line Supervisors/Managers of Food Preparation and Serving Workers	$24,970
2. Cooks, Restaurant	$19,390
3. Food Preparation Workers	$16,140
4. Counter Attendants, Cafeteria, Food Concession, and Coffee Shop	$15,660
5. Hosts and Hostesses, Restaurant, Lounge, and Coffee Shop	$15,570
6. Bartenders	$15,450
7. Dishwashers	$15,170
8. Cashiers	$14,950
9. Cooks, Fast Food	$14,710
10. Dining Room and Cafeteria Attendants and Bartender Helpers	$14,590
11. Combined Food Preparation and Serving Workers, Including Fast Food	$14,300
12. Waiters and Waitresses	$14,000

Fastest-Growing Jobs in Food Services and Drinking Places

Job	Percent Growth	Size of Workforce
1. Food Preparation Workers	25.3%	424,938
2. First-Line Supervisors/Managers of Food Preparation and Serving Workers	17.9%	548,182
3. Counter Attendants, Cafeteria, Food Concession, and Coffee Shop	17.4%	277,443
4. Combined Food Preparation and Serving Workers, Including Fast Food	16.9%	1,710,635
5. Hosts and Hostesses, Restaurant, Lounge, and Coffee Shop	16.5%	282,247
6. Cooks, Fast Food	16.4%	620,136
7. Waiters and Waitresses	16.4%	1,893,099
8. Cooks, Restaurant	16.3%	668,179
9. Dining Room and Cafeteria Attendants and Bartender Helpers	15.9%	267,209
10. Dishwashers	15.5%	390,299
11. Bartenders	14.2%	337,236
12. Cashiers	6.5%	284,915

Best-Paying Jobs in Hotels and Other Accommodations

Job	Median Earnings
1. Maintenance and Repair Workers, General	$23,250
2. Cooks, Restaurant	$22,430
3. Janitors and Cleaners, Except Maids and Housekeeping Cleaners	$19,080
4. Hotel, Motel, and Resort Desk Clerks	$17,660
5. Bartenders	$17,010
6. Dishwashers	$16,960
7. Food Servers, Nonrestaurant	$16,450
8. Maids and Housekeeping Cleaners	$16,330
9. Dining Room and Cafeteria Attendants and Bartender Helpers	$16,190
10. Waiters and Waitresses	$14,830

Fastest-Growing Jobs in Hotels and Other Accommodations

Job	Percent Growth	Size of Workforce
1. Maintenance and Repair Workers, General	27.2%	64,269
2. Janitors and Cleaners, Except Maids and Housekeeping Cleaners	20.2%	49,255
3. Hotel, Motel, and Resort Desk Clerks	17.4%	183,377
4. Maids and Housekeeping Cleaners	17.0%	404,510
5. Cooks, Restaurant	16.7%	56,144
6. Bartenders	13.1%	38,768
7. Food Servers, Nonrestaurant	11.9%	39,458
8. Waiters and Waitresses	9.5%	133,398
9. Dining Room and Cafeteria Attendants and Bartender Helpers	9.1%	42,981
10. Dishwashers	8.3%	38,279

Best-Paying Jobs in Advocacy, Grantmaking, and Civic Organizations

Job	Median Earnings
1. General and Operations Managers	$76,783
2. Public Relations Specialists	$44,080
3. Executive Secretaries and Administrative Assistants	$35,085
4. Bookkeeping, Accounting, and Auditing Clerks	$28,796
5. Secretaries, Except Legal, Medical, and Executive	$26,449
6. Fitness Trainers and Aerobics Instructors	$21,411
7. Office Clerks, General	$21,405
8. Receptionists and Information Clerks	$20,116
9. Janitors and Cleaners, Except Maids and Housekeeping Cleaners	$17,965
10. Recreation Workers	$17,404
11. Child Care Workers	$15,988
12. Nannies	$15,988
13. Bartenders	$15,246

Fastest-Growing Jobs in Advocacy, Grantmaking, and Civic Organizations

Job	Percent Growth	Size of Workforce
1. Public Relations Specialists	22.0%	28,142
2. Janitors and Cleaners, Except Maids and Housekeeping Cleaners	18.0%	27,141
3. General and Operations Managers	17.6%	40,625
4. Receptionists and Information Clerks	13.7%	27,984
5. Recreation Workers	13.5%	40,317
6. Fitness Trainers and Aerobics Instructors	13.2%	36,803
7. Bartenders	12.9%	38,324
8. Child Care Workers	12.4%	31,670
9. Nannies	12.4%	31,670
10. Executive Secretaries and Administrative Assistants	10.2%	47,866
11. Office Clerks, General	5.6%	52,194
12. Bookkeeping, Accounting, and Auditing Clerks	4.9%	30,631
13. Secretaries, Except Legal, Medical, and Executive	–5.8%	48,688

Best-Paying Jobs in Federal Government, Excluding the Postal Service

Job	Median Earnings
1. Management Analysts	$72,580
2. Registered Nurses	$64,000
3. Coroners	$52,180
4. Environmental Compliance Inspectors	$52,180
5. Equal Opportunity Representatives and Officers	$52,180
6. Government Property Inspectors and Investigators	$52,180
7. Licensing Examiners and Inspectors	$52,180
8. Pressure Vessel Inspectors	$52,180

Fastest-Growing Jobs in Federal Government, Excluding the Postal Service

Job	Percent Growth	Size of Workforce
1. Registered Nurses	14.4%	52,430
2. Coroners	4.0%	46,658
3. Environmental Compliance Inspectors	4.0%	46,658
4. Equal Opportunity Representatives and Officers	4.0%	46,658
5. Government Property Inspectors and Investigators	4.0%	46,658
6. Licensing Examiners and Inspectors	4.0%	46,658
7. Pressure Vessel Inspectors	4.0%	46,658
8. Management Analysts	4.0%	45,925

Best-Paying Jobs in State and Local Government, Excluding Education and Hospitals

Job	Median Earnings
1. Highway Patrol Pilots	$45,752
2. Police Patrol Officers	$45,752
3. Sheriffs and Deputy Sheriffs	$45,752
4. Forest Fire Fighters	$39,175
5. Municipal Fire Fighters	$39,175
6. Executive Secretaries and Administrative Assistants	$35,399
7. Correctional Officers and Jailers	$33,550
8. Office Clerks, General	$26,192

Fastest-Growing Jobs in State and Local Government, Excluding Education and Hospitals

Job	Percent Growth	Size of Workforce
1. Forest Fire Fighters	25.4%	265,383
2. Municipal Fire Fighters	25.4%	265,383
3. Highway Patrol Pilots	15.0%	602,188
4. Police Patrol Officers	15.0%	602,188
5. Sheriffs and Deputy Sheriffs	15.0%	602,188
6. Correctional Officers and Jailers	4.8%	397,656
7. Executive Secretaries and Administrative Assistants	4.2%	163,048
8. Office Clerks, General	0.3%	337,842

PART II

Descriptions of the Fields

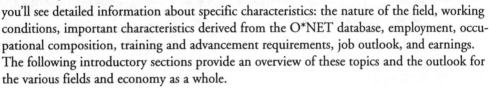

The U.S. economy can be broken down into numerous fields, each with its own set of characteristics. The Department of Labor has identified 45 fields that account for three-quarters of all workers, and these fields are described here. For each field, you'll see detailed information about specific characteristics: the nature of the field, working conditions, important characteristics derived from the O*NET database, employment, occupational composition, training and advancement requirements, job outlook, and earnings. The following introductory sections provide an overview of these topics and the outlook for the various fields and economy as a whole.

Nature of the Field

Fields are defined by the processes they use to produce goods and services. Workers in the United States produce and provide a wide variety of products and services and, as a result, the types of fields in the U.S. economy range widely—from agriculture, forestry, and fishing to aerospace manufacturing. Each field has a unique combination of occupations, production techniques, inputs and outputs, and business characteristics. Understanding the nature of the field is important because it is this unique combination that determines working conditions, educational requirements, and the job outlook for each of the fields described here in Part II.

Fields consist of many different places of work, called establishments. Establishments are physical locations in which people work, such as the branch office of a bank, a gasoline service station, a school, a department store, or a plant that manufactures machinery. Establishments range from large factories and corporate office complexes employing thousands of workers to small community stores, restaurants, professional offices, and service businesses employing only a few workers. Establishments should not be confused with companies or corporations, which are legal entities. Thus, a company or corporation may have a single establishment or more than one establishment. Establishments that use the same or similar processes to produce goods or services are organized together into fields (the Department of Labor uses the term "industries"). Fields are, in turn, organized together into field groups such as Information and Trade.

71

There were slightly more than 8 million private business establishments in the United States in March 2004. Business establishments in the United States are predominantly small; 59.9 percent of all establishments employed fewer than 5 workers in March 2004. However, the medium-sized to large establishments employ a greater proportion of all workers. For example, establishments that employed 50 or more workers accounted for only 4.6 percent of all establishments, yet employed 56.3 percent of all workers. The large establishments—those with more than 500 workers—accounted for only 0.2 percent of all establishments, but employed 17.3 percent of all workers. Table 1 presents the percent distribution of employment according to establishment size.

The average size of these establishments varies widely across fields. Most establishments in the construction; wholesale trade; retail trade; finance and insurance; real estate and rental and leasing; and professional, scientific, and technical services fields are small, averaging fewer than 20 employees per establishment. However, wide differences within fields can exist. Hospitals, for example, employ an average of 724.9 workers, while physicians' offices employ an average of 10.1. Similarly, although there is an average of 14.3 employees per establishment for all of retail trade, department stores employ an average of 124.1 people but jewelry stores employ an average of only 5.8.

Establishment size can play a role in the characteristics of each job. Large establishments generally offer workers greater occupational mobility and advancement potential, whereas small establishments may provide their employees with broader experience by requiring them to assume a wider range of responsibilities. Also, small establishments are distributed throughout the nation—every locality has a few small businesses. Large establishments, in contrast, employ more workers and are less common, but they play a much more prominent role in the economies of the areas in which they are located.

Table 1. Percent distribution of nongovernment establishments and employment by establishment size, March 2004

Establishment size (number of workers)	Establishments	Employment
Total	100.0	100.0
1 to 4	59.9	6.8
5 to 9	16.9	8.4
10 to 19	11.1	11.2
20 to 49	7.6	17.3
50 to 99	2.6	13.3
100 to 249	1.4	16.4
250 to 499	0.4	9.3
500 to 999	0.1	6.6
1,000 or more	0.1	10.7

Working Conditions

Just as the goods and services produced in each field are different, working conditions vary significantly among fields. In some fields, the work setting is quiet, temperature-controlled, and virtually hazard-free, while other fields are characterized by noisy, uncomfortable, and sometimes dangerous work environments. Some fields require long workweeks and shift work, but standard 40-hour workweeks are common in many other fields. In still other fields, a lot of the jobs can be seasonal, requiring long hours during busy periods and abbreviated schedules during slower months. Production processes, establishment size, and the physical location of work usually determine these varying conditions.

One of the most telling indicators of working conditions is a field's injury and illness rate. Overexertion, being struck by an object, and falls on the same level are among the most common incidents causing work-related injury or illness. In 2003, approximately 5.0 million nonfatal injuries and illnesses were reported across the various nongovernment fields. Among major field divisions, manufacturing and construction tied for the highest rate of injury and illness—6.8 cases for every 100 full-time workers—while financial activities had the lowest rate—1.7 cases. About 5,700 work-related fatalities were reported in 2004; the most common events resulting in fatal injuries were transportation incidents, contact with objects and equipment, assaults and violent acts, and falls.

Work schedules are another important reflection of working conditions, and the operational requirements of each field lead to large differences in hours worked and in part-time versus full-time status. In food services and drinking places, for example, fully 41.1 percent of employees worked part time in 2005 compared with only 1.7 percent in motor vehicles and motor vehicle equipment manufacturing. Table 2 presents fields having relatively high and low percentages of part-time workers.

Table 2. Part-time workers as a percent of total employment, selected fields, 2005

Field	Percent part-time
All fields	17.4
Many part-time workers	
Food services and drinking places	41.1
Grocery stores	35.3
Clothing, accessory, and general merchandise stores	33.8
Arts, entertainment, and recreation	32.0
Child day care services	28.7
Motion picture and video fields	27.1
Social assistance	24.6
Educational services	21.9

(continued)

(continued)

Table 2. Part-time workers as a percent of total employment, selected fields, 2005

Field	Percent part-time
Few part-time workers	
Pharmaceutical and medicine manufacturing	3.6
Utilities	3.2
Oil and Gas Extraction	3.2
Computer and electronic product manufacturing	2.8
Steel manufacturing	2.4
Mining	2.3
Aerospace product and parts manufacturing	1.9
Motor vehicles and parts manufacturing	1.7

The low proportion of part-time workers in some manufacturing fields often reflects the continuous nature of the production processes that makes it difficult to adapt the volume of production to short-term fluctuations in product demand. Once these processes are begun, it is costly to halt them; machinery must be tended and materials must be moved continuously. For example, the chemical manufacturing field produces many different chemical products through controlled chemical reactions. These processes require chemical operators to monitor and adjust the flow of materials into and out of the line of production. Because production may continue 24 hours a day, 7 days a week under the watchful eyes of chemical operators who work in shifts, full-time workers are more likely to be employed. Retail trade and service fields, on the other hand, have seasonal cycles marked by various events that affect the hours worked, such as school openings or important holidays. During busy times of the year, longer hours are common, whereas slack periods lead to cutbacks in work hours and shorter workweeks. Jobs in these fields are generally appealing to students and others who desire flexible, part-time schedules.

Important Characteristics of the Field

Although the working conditions of a field can be observed directly, such as loud noise or little part-time work, some other characteristics of the field can only be inferred. For example, to determine the *skills* required in a field, a job analyst needs to infer from work tasks what kinds and levels of skill are needed for successful performance of the major jobs in that field. The most important physical and mental *abilities* that are required in the field similarly can be inferred from the work tasks of major jobs.

Work also provides certain rewards, both intrinsic (for example, variety, social status, or creativity) and extrinsic (for example, compensation). These rewards are commonly called *work-related values,* and job analysts have been able to quantify the differing potentials of various occupations to provide these rewards.

Therefore it is possible to determine the most important skills, abilities, and work-related values for each field in the U.S. economy. To prepare this section of the field description, we identified the most important jobs in each field (those that represent more than 2 percent of the workforce) and assembled the ratings of these occupations on these inferred characteristics according to the Labor Department's O*NET database. We calculated the average rating of the characteristic for all occupations, and then for each occupation we computed how much the rating exceeds the average rating and used this difference as a measure of the level of the skill or ability or the importance of the work-related value. Finally, we combined the ratings of multiple occupations to create a field-wide average, computing a *weighted* average in order to give greater weight to the jobs that account for a greater fraction of the workforce. We listed the characteristics in declining order of their average scores, including the top six skills, abilities, and values. In some cases there were fewer than six with average ratings above the average for all occupations, so in those cases we list fewer. One field had no skills with an above-average rating, so we reported that "none met the criteria." A few fields had no values with an above-average rating, but since values say so much about the flavor of a field, we decided to include the one highest-rated value regardless.

Table 3 shows how fields differ in their skill requirements for mathematics. The fields requiring a lower level are dominated by jobs where mathematics is used mainly in calculations (for example, in sales or production roles), whereas the fields requiring a higher level are dominated by jobs in which people must also think about mathematical concepts (for example, in engineering or research roles).

Table 3. Level of mathematics skill required, selected fields

Field	Amount by which rating exceeds average
Higher level required	
Software Publishers	1.3
Scientific Research and Development Services	1.2
Computer Systems Design and Related Services	1.1
Computer and Electronic Product Manufacturing	1.0
Securities, Commodities, and Other Investments	0.9
Lower level required	
Arts, Entertainment, and Recreation	−0.9
Food Manufacturing	−1.0
Printing	−1.0
Mining	−1.2
Hotels and Other Accommodations	−1.3

Some of the names of the abilities, skills, or work-related values may not be familiar to you. For example, you may wonder what "Category Flexibility" or "Supervision, Technical" means. You can find definitions of all of these characteristics in appendices A, B, and C, where you can also see all fields that have a high level of each characteristic.

Employment

The total number of jobs in the United States in 2004 was 145.6 million. This included 12.1 million self-employed workers, 141,000 unpaid workers in family businesses, and 133.5 million wage and salary jobs—including primary and secondary job holders. The total number of jobs is projected to increase to 164.5 million by 2014, and wage and salary jobs are projected to account for more than 152.1 million of them.

As shown in table 4, wage and salary jobs are the vast majority of all jobs, but they are not evenly divided among the various fields. Education, health, and social services had the largest number of jobs in 2004 with almost 28 million. Manufacturing, construction, and utilities had almost 21.9 million jobs, including 14.3 million manufacturing and 7.0 million construction jobs. The trade supersector was nearly as large, with about 20.7 million jobs, followed by professional and business services with 16.4 million jobs in 2004. Among the fields covered in this book, wage and salary employment ranged from only 156,200 in steel manufacturing to over 13 million in health services. The three largest fields—education services, health services, and food services and drinking places—together accounted for 34.7 million jobs, over one-quarter of the nation's wage and salary employment.

Table 4. Wage and salary employment in fields covered in this book, 2004, 2014, and projected change, 2004–2014 (Employment in thousands)

	2004		2014		2004–2014	
Field	Employment	Percent distribution	Employment	Percent distribution	Percent change	Employment change
All fields	133,478	100.0	152,093	100.0	13.9	18,615
Agriculture and natural resources	1,672	1.3	1,567	1.0	–6.3	–105
Agriculture, forestry, and fishing	1,149	0.9	1,090	0.7	–5.2	–60
Mining	207	0.2	180	0.1	–12.9	–27
Oil and gas extraction	316	0.2	297	0.2	–6.1	–19
Manufacturing, construction, and utilities	21,864	16.4	21,872	14.4	0.0	8
Aerospace product and parts manufacturing	444	0.3	480	0.3	8.2	36

Table 4. Wage and salary employment in fields covered in this book, 2004, 2014, and projected change, 2004–2014 (Employment in thousands)

Field	2004		2014		2004–2014	
	Employment	Percent distribution	Employment	Percent distribution	Percent change	Employment change
Chemical manufacturing, except drugs	596	0.5	510	0.3	–14.4	–86
Computer and electronic product manufacturing	1,326	1.0	1,232	0.8	–7.1	–94
Construction	6,964	5.2	7,757	5.1	11.4	792
Food manufacturing	1,498	1.1	1,555	1.0	3.8	57
Machinery manufacturing	1,142	0.9	995	0.7	–12.8	–146
Motor vehicle and parts manufacturing	1,109	0.8	1,171	0.8	5.6	62
Pharmaceutical and medicine manufacturing	291	0.2	367	0.2	26.1	76
Printing	665	0.5	600	0.4	–9.8	–65
Steel manufacturing	156	0.1	135	0.1	–13.4	–21
Textile, textile product, and apparel manufacturing	701	0.5	380	0.2	–44.6	–321
Utilities	570	0.4	563	0.4	–1.3	–8
Trade	20,689	15.5	22,814	15.0	10.3	2,125
Automobile dealers	1,254	0.9	1,407	0.9	12.2	153
Clothing, accessory, and general merchandise stores	4,205	3.1	4,628	3.0	10.1	423
Grocery stores	2,447	1.8	2,607	1.7	6.6	160
Wholesale trade	5,655	4.2	6,131	4.0	8.4	476
Transportation	4,250	3.2	4,756	3.1	11.9	506
Air transportation	515	0.4	560	0.4	8.8	45
Truck transportation and warehousing	1,907	1.4	2,174	1.4	14.0	267
Information	3,138	2.4	3,502	2.3	11.6	364
Broadcasting	327	0.2	362	0.2	10.7	35
Motion picture and video fields	368	0.3	430	0.3	17.1	63
Publishing, except software	671	0.5	715	0.5	6.5	44
Software publishers	239	0.2	400	0.3	67.6	161
Telecommunications	1,043	0.8	975	0.6	–6.5	–68

(continued)

(continued)

Table 4. Wage and salary employment in fields covered in this book, 2004, 2014, and projected change, 2004–2014 (Employment in thousands)

Field	2004		2014		2004–2014	
	Employment	Percent distribution	Employment	Percent distribution	Percent change	Employment change
Internet service providers, Web search portals, and data processing services	388	0.3	496	0.3	27.8	108
Financial activities	8,052	6.0	8,901	5.9	10.5	849
Banking	1,783	1.3	1,751	1.2	–1.8	–31
Insurance	2,260	1.7	2,476	1.6	9.5	215
Securities, commodities, and other investments	767	0.6	888	0.6	15.8	121
Professional and business services	16,414	12.3	20,980	13.8	27.8	4,566
Advertising and public relations services	425	0.3	520	0.3	22.4	95
Computer systems design and related services	1,147	0.9	1,600	1.1	39.5	453
Employment services	3,470	2.6	5,050	3.3	45.5	1,580
Management, scientific, and technical consulting services	779	0.6	1,250	0.8	60.5	471
Scientific research and development services	548	0.4	613	0.4	11.9	65
Education, health, and social services	27,973	21.0	34,399	22.6	23.0	6,426
Child day care services	767	0.6	1,062	0.7	38.4	295
Educational services	12,778	9.6	14,901	9.8	16.6	2,123
Health services	13,062	9.8	16,626	10.9	27.3	3,564
Social assistance, except child day care	1,365	1.0	1,810	1.2	32.6	445
Leisure and hospitality	12,479	9.3	14,694	9.7	17.7	2,215
Arts, entertainment, and recreation	1,833	1.4	2,293	1.5	25.1	460
Food services and drinking places	8,850	6.6	10,301	6.8	16.4	1,451
Hotels and other accommodations	1,796	1.3	2,100	1.4	16.9	304

Table 4. Wage and salary employment in fields covered in this book, 2004, 2014, and projected change, 2004–2014 (Employment in thousands)

Field	2004 Employment	2004 Percent distribution	2014 Employment	2014 Percent distribution	2004–2014 Percent change	2004–2014 Employment change
Government and advocacy, grantmaking, and civic organizations	11,047	8.3	12,170	8.0	10.2	1,123
Advocacy, grantmaking, and civic organizations	1,231	0.9	1,410	0.9	14.5	179
Federal government	1,943	1.5	1,993	1.3	2.5	50
State and local government, except education and health	7,872	5.9	8,767	5.8	11.4	895

Note: May not add to totals due to omission of fields not covered.

Although workers of all ages are employed in each field, certain fields tend to possess workers of distinct age groups. For the previously mentioned reasons, retail trade employs a relatively high proportion of younger workers to fill part-time and temporary positions. The manufacturing sector, on the other hand, has a relatively high median age because many jobs in the sector require a number of years to learn and perfect specialized skills that do not easily transfer to other firms. Also, manufacturing employment has been declining, providing fewer opportunities for younger workers to get jobs. As a result, one-fourth of the workers in retail trade were 24 years of age or younger in 2004, compared with only 8.2 percent of workers in manufacturing. Table 5 contrasts the age distribution of workers in all fields with the distributions in five very different fields.

Table 5. Percent distribution of wage and salary workers by age group, selected fields, 2004

Field	Age group 16 to 24	Age group 25 to 44	Age group 45 to 64	Age group 65 and older
All fields	14	47	36	4
Computer systems design and related services	7	63	29	1
Educational services	9	42	45	3
Food services and drinking places	44	39	15	2
Telecommunications	8	56	34	2
Utilities	5	43	50	2

Employment in some fields is concentrated in one region of the country. Such fields often are located near a source of raw or unfinished materials upon which the field relies. For example, oil and gas extraction jobs are concentrated in Texas, Louisiana, and Oklahoma; many textile mills and products manufacturing jobs are found in North Carolina, South Carolina, and Georgia; and a significant proportion of motor vehicle manufacturing jobs are located in Michigan and Ohio. On the other hand, some fields—such as grocery stores and educational services—have jobs distributed throughout the nation, reflecting the general population density.

Occupations in the Field

The occupations found in each field depend on the types of services provided or goods produced. For example, because construction companies require skilled trades workers to build and renovate buildings, these companies employ large numbers of carpenters, electricians, plumbers, painters, and sheet metal workers. Other occupations common to construction include construction equipment operators and mechanics, installers, and repairers. Retail trade, on the other hand, displays and sells manufactured goods to consumers. As a result, retail trade employs numerous retail salespersons and other workers, including more than three-fourths of all cashiers. Table 6 shows the field sectors and the occupational groups that predominate in each.

Table 6. Field sectors and their largest occupational group, 2004

Field sector	Largest occupational group	Percent of field wage and salary jobs
Agriculture, forestry, fishing, and hunting	Farming, fishing, and forestry occupations	61.1
Mining	Construction and extraction occupations	33.3
Construction	Construction and extraction occupations	66.2
Manufacturing	Production occupations	52.1
Wholesale trade	Sales and related occupations	24.7
Retail trade	Sales and related occupations	52.5
Transportation and warehousing	Transportation and material moving occupations	56.0
Utilities	Installation, maintenance, and repair occupations	25.6
Information	Professional and related occupations	29.1
Finance and insurance	Office and administrative support occupations	51.4
Real estate and rental and leasing	Sales and related occupations	22.7
Professional, scientific, and technical services	Professional and related occupations	42.6
Management of companies and enterprises	Office and administrative support occupations	33.6

Table 6. Field sectors and their largest occupational group, 2004

Field sector	Largest occupational group	Percent of field wage and salary jobs
Administrative and support and waste management and remediation services	Office and administrative support occupations	23.2
Educational services, private	Professional and related occupations	59.6
Health care and social assistance	Professional and related occupations	42.6
Arts, entertainment, and recreation	Service occupations	57.2
Accommodation and food services	Service occupations	84.0
Government	Professional and related occupations	43.7

The nation's occupational distribution clearly is influenced by the structure of its fields, yet there are many occupations, such as general managers or secretaries, that are found in all fields. In fact, some of the largest occupations in the U.S. economy are dispersed across many fields. For example, the group of professional and related occupations is among the largest in the nation while also experiencing the fastest growth rate. (See table 7.) Other large occupational groups include service occupations; office and administrative support occupations; sales and related occupations; and management, business, and financial occupations.

Table 7. Total employment and projected change by broad occupational group, 2004–2014 (Employment in thousands)

Occupational group	Employment, 2004	Percent change, 2004–2014
Total, all occupations	145,612	13.0
Professional and related occupations	28,544	21.2
Service occupations	27,673	19.0
Office and administrative support occupations	23,907	5.8
Sales and related occupations	15,330	9.6
Management, business, and financial occupations	14,987	14.4
Production occupations	10,562	–0.1
Transportation and material moving occupations	10,098	11.1
Construction and extraction occupations	7,738	12.0
Installation, maintenance, and repair occupations	5,747	11.4
Farming, fishing, and forestry occupations	1,026	–1.3

Training and Advancement

Workers prepare for employment in many ways, but the most fundamental form of job training in the United States is a high school education. Better than 88 percent of the nation's workforce possessed a high school diploma or its equivalent in 2004. However, many occupations require more training, so growing numbers of workers pursue additional training or education after high school. In 2004, 28.7 percent of the nation's workforce reported having completed some college or an associate's degree as their highest level of education, while an additional 29.5 percent continued in their studies and attained a bachelor's or higher degree. In addition to these types of formal education, other sources of qualifying training include formal company-provided training, apprenticeships, informal on-the-job training, correspondence courses, Armed Forces vocational training, and non-work-related training.

The unique combination of training required to succeed in each field is determined largely by the field's production process and the mix of occupations it requires. For example, manufacturing employs many machine operators who generally need little formal education after high school, but sometimes complete considerable on-the-job training. In contrast, the educational services field employs many types of teachers, most of whom require a bachelor's or higher degree. Training requirements by field sector are shown in table 8.

Table 8. Percent distribution of workers by highest grade completed or degree received, by field sector, 2004

Field sector	High school diploma or less	Some college or associate degree	Bachelor's or higher degree
All fields	41.6	28.7	29.5
Agriculture, forestry, fishing, and hunting	64.3	21.4	14.2
Mining	60.4	21.8	17.8
Construction	64.7	24.5	10.8
Manufacturing	51.5	25.1	23.4
Wholesale trade	42.7	29.0	28.3
Retail trade	50.6	32.3	17.1
Transportation and warehousing	52.6	31.7	15.6
Utilities	38.7	34.1	27.0
Information	26.7	31.3	42.0
Finance and insurance	24.9	31.6	43.4
Real estate and rental and leasing	36.2	31.7	32.2
Professional, scientific, and technical services	14.4	25.1	60.6
Administrative and support and waste management services	55.3	28.4	16.3
Educational services	17.8	19.0	63.2
Health care and social assistance	30.6	34.8	34.7
Arts, entertainment, and recreation	39.5	31.8	28.6
Accommodation and food services	60.7	28.4	11.0

Persons with no more than a high school diploma accounted for about 64.7 percent of all workers in construction; 64.3 in agriculture, forestry, fishing, and hunting; 60.7 percent in accommodation and food services; 60.4 percent in mining; 51.5 percent in manufacturing; and 50.6 in retail trade. On the other hand, those who had acquired a bachelor's or higher degree accounted for 63.2 percent of all workers in private educational services; 60.6 percent in professional, scientific, and technical services; 43.4 percent in finance and insurance; and 42.0 percent in information.

Education and training also are important factors in the variety of advancement paths found in different fields. Each field has some unique advancement paths, but workers who complete additional on-the-job training or education generally help their chances of being promoted. In much of the manufacturing sector, for example, production workers who receive training in management and computer skills increase their likelihood of being promoted to supervisory positions. Other factors that impact advancement and that may figure prominently in the fields covered in this book include the size of the establishments, institutionalized career tracks, and the mix of occupations. As a result, persons who seek jobs in particular fields should be aware of how these advancement paths and other factors may later shape their careers.

Earnings

Like other characteristics, earnings differ by field, the result of a highly complicated process that reflects a number of factors. For example, earnings may vary due to the nature of occupations in the field, average hours worked, geographical location, workers' average age, educational requirements, profits, and the degree of union representation of the workforce. In general, wages are highest in metropolitan areas to compensate for the higher cost of living. Also, as would be expected, fields that employ a large proportion of unskilled minimum-wage or part-time workers tend to have lower earnings.

The difference in earnings between the fields of software publishers and of food services and drinking places illustrates how various characteristics of fields can result in great differences in earnings. In software publishers, earnings of all wage and salary workers averaged $1,342 a week in 2004, while in food service and drinking places, earnings of all wage and salary workers averaged only $194 weekly. The difference is large primarily because software publishing establishments employ more higher-skilled, full-time workers, while food services and drinking places employ many lower-skilled workers on a part-time basis. In addition, most workers in software publishing are paid an annual salary, while many workers in food service and drinking places are paid a low hourly wage that is supplemented with money the workers receive as tips. Table 9 highlights the fields with the highest and lowest average weekly earnings.

Table 9. Average weekly earnings of production or nonsupervisory workers on private nonfarm payrolls, selected fields, 2004

Field	Earnings
All fields	$529
Fields with high earnings	
Software publishers	1,342
Computer systems design and related services	1,136
Aerospace product and parts manufacturing	1,019
Scientific research and development services	1,006
Motor vehicle and parts manufacturing	925
Mining	909
Fields with low earnings	
Food manufacturing	510
Grocery stores	332
Arts, entertainment, and recreation	313
Hotels and other accommodations	302
Child day care services	299
Food services and drinking places	194

Employee benefits, once a minor addition to wages and salaries, continue to grow in diversity and cost. In addition to traditional benefits—paid vacations, life and health insurance, and pensions—many employers now offer various benefits to accommodate the needs of a changing labor force. Such benefits sometimes include childcare; employee assistance programs that provide counseling for personal problems; and wellness programs that encourage exercise, stress management, and self-improvement. Benefits vary among occupational groups, full- and part-time workers, public and private sector workers, regions, unionized and nonunionized workers, and small and large establishments. Data indicate that full-time workers and those in medium-sized and large establishments—those with 100 or more workers—usually receive better benefits than do part-time workers and those in smaller establishments.

Union representation of the workforce varies widely by field, and it also may play a role in determining earnings and benefits. In 2004, about 13.8 percent of workers throughout the nation were union members or covered by union contracts. As table 10 demonstrates, union affiliation of workers varies widely by field. Fully 50.0 percent of the workers in air transportation were union members, the highest rate of all the fields, followed by 37.6 percent in educational services and 33.0 percent in iron and steel mills and steel product manufacturing. Fields with the lowest unionization rate include computer systems design and related services, 1.3 percent; food services and drinking places, 1.7 percent; and advertising and related services, 1.7 percent.

Table 10. Union members and other workers covered by union contracts as a percent of total employment, selected fields, 2004

Field	Percent union members or covered by union contract
All fields	13.8
Fields with high unionization rates	
Air transportation	50.0
Educational services	37.6
Iron and steel mills and steel product manufacturing	33.0
Motor vehicles and motor vehicle equipment manufacturing	30.2
Fields with low unionization rates	
Banking and related activities	1.9
Advertising and related services	1.7
Food services and drinking places	1.7
Computer systems design and related services	1.3

Outlook

Total employment in the United States is projected to increase by about 14 percent over the 2004–2014 period. Employment growth, however, is only one source of job openings. The total number of openings in any field also depends on the field's current employment level and its need to replace workers who leave their jobs. Throughout the economy, replacement needs will create more job openings than will employment growth. Employment size is a major determinant of job openings—larger fields generally have larger numbers of workers who must be replaced and provide more openings. The occupational composition of a field is another factor. Fields with high concentrations of professional, technical, and other jobs that require more formal education—occupations in which workers tend to leave their jobs less frequently—generally have fewer openings resulting from replacement needs. On the other hand, more replacement openings generally occur in fields with high concentrations of service, laborer, and other jobs that require little formal education and have lower wages because workers in these jobs are more likely to leave their occupations.

Employment growth is determined largely by changes in the demand for the goods and services provided by a field, worker productivity, and foreign competition. Each field is affected by a different set of variables that determines the number and composition of jobs that will be available. Even within a field, employment may grow at different rates in different occupations. For example, changes in technology, production methods, and business practices in a field might eliminate some jobs while creating others. Some fields may be growing rapidly overall, yet opportunities for workers in certain occupations could be stagnant or even declining because they are adversely affected by technological change. Similarly, employment of some occupations may be declining in the economy as a whole, yet may be increasing in a rapidly growing field.

As shown in table 4, employment growth rates over the next decade will vary widely among fields. Agriculture and natural resources is the only sector in which all of the fields are expected to experience employment declines. Consolidation of farmland, increasing worker productivity, and depletion of wild fish stocks should continue to decrease employment in agriculture, forestry, and fishing. Employment in mining is expected to decline due to labor-saving technology while jobs in oil and gas extraction are expected to decrease with the continued reliance on foreign sources of energy.

Employment in manufacturing, construction, and utilities is expected to remain nearly unchanged as growth in construction is partially offset by declines in utilities and selected manufacturing fields. Growth in construction employment will stem from new factory construction as existing facilities are modernized; from new school construction, reflecting growth in the school-age population; and from infrastructure improvements, such as road and bridge construction. Employment declines are expected in chemical manufacturing, except drugs; machinery manufacturing; computer and electronic product manufacturing; printing; steel manufacturing; and textile, textile product, and apparel manufacturing. Textile, textile product, and apparel manufacturing is projected to lose about 321,200 jobs over the 2004–2014 period—more than any other manufacturing field—due primarily to increasing imports replacing domestic products.

Employment gains are expected in some manufacturing fields. Small employment gains in food manufacturing are expected as a growing and ever more diverse population increases the demand for manufactured food products. Employment growth in pharmaceutical and medicine manufacturing is expected as sales of pharmaceuticals increase with growth in the population, particularly among the elderly, and with the introduction of new medicines to the market. Both food and pharmaceutical and medicine manufacturing also have growing export markets. Aerospace product and parts manufacturing and motor vehicle and parts manufacturing are both expected to have modest employment increases.

Growth in overall employment will result primarily from growth in service-providing fields over the 2004–2014 period, almost all of which are expected to have increasing employment. Job growth is expected to be led by health services and educational services—the two largest fields discussed in this book—with large numbers of new jobs also in employment services, food services and drinking places, state and local government, and wholesale trade. When combined, these sectors will account for almost half of all new wage and salary jobs across the nation. Employment growth is expected in many other service-providing fields discussed in this book, but they will result in far fewer numbers of new jobs.

Health services will account for the most new wage and salary jobs, about 3.6 million over the 2004–2014 period. Population growth, advances in medical technologies that increase the number of treatable diseases, and a growing share of the population in older age groups will drive employment growth. Offices of physicians, the largest health care field group, is expected to account for about 760,000 of these new jobs as patients seek more health care outside of the traditional inpatient hospital setting.

The educational services field is expected to grow by nearly 17 percent over the 2004–2014 period, adding about 2.1 million new jobs. A growing emphasis on improving education and making it available to more children and young adults will be the primary factors contributing to employment growth. Employment growth at all levels of education is expected, particularly at the postsecondary level, as children of the baby boomers continue to reach college age and as more adults pursue continuing education to enhance or update their skills.

Employment in one of the nation's fastest-growing fields—employment services—is expected to increase by more than 45 percent, adding another 1.6 million jobs over the 2004–2014 period. Employment will increase, particularly in temporary help services and professional employer organizations, as businesses seek new ways to make their workforces more specialized and responsive to changes in demand.

The food services and drinking places field is expected to add almost 1.5 million new jobs over the 2004–2014 projection period. Increases in population, dual-income families, and dining sophistication will contribute to job growth. In addition, the increasing diversity of the population will contribute to job growth in food services and drinking places that offer a wider variety of ethnic foods and drinks.

Over 890,000 new jobs are expected to arise in state and local government, adding over 11 percent over the 2004–2014 period. Job growth will result primarily from growth in the population and its demand for public services. Additional job growth will result as state and local governments continue to receive greater responsibility for administering federally funded programs from the federal government.

Wholesale trade is expected to add almost 480,000 new jobs over the coming decade, reflecting growth both in trade and in the overall economy. Most new jobs will be for sales representatives at the wholesale and manufacturing levels. However, field consolidation and the growth of electronic commerce using the Internet are expected to limit job growth to 8.4 percent over the 2004–2014 period, less than the 14 percent projected for all fields.

Continual changes in the economy have far-reaching and complex effects on employment in each of the fields covered in this book. Jobseekers should be aware of these changes, keeping alert for developments that can affect job opportunities in fields and the variety of occupations that are found in each field. For more detailed information on specific occupations, consult the 2006–2007 edition of the *Occupational Outlook Handbook* or the online resource CareerOINK (http://www.careeroink.com), both of which provide information on hundreds of occupations.

Agriculture and Natural Resources

Agriculture, Forestry, and Fishing

- Annual Earnings: $19,090
- Job Growth: –10.7%
- Size of Workforce: 438,250
- Self-Employed: 41.7%
- Part-Time: 20.3%

Significant Points

- Although farms generating over $250,000 per year in sales make up less than 10 percent of all farms, they supply three-quarters of all agricultural output.

- Self-employed workers—mostly farmers and fishers—account for 42 percent of the field's workforce.

- Employment in agriculture, forestry, and fishing is projected to decline, especially among self-employed farmers and ranchers.

Nature of the Field

The agriculture, forestry, and fishing field plays a vital role in our economy and our lives. It supplies us and many other countries with a wide variety of food products and non-food products such as fibers, lumber, and nursery items. It contributes positively to our foreign trade balance, and it remains one of the nation's larger fields in terms of total employment. However, technology continues to enable us to produce more of these products with fewer workers, even in the face of stagnant prices for output, resulting in fewer farms and farmworkers.

Establishments in this field include farms, ranches, dairies, greenhouses, nurseries, orchards, and hatcheries.

But production also takes place in the country's natural habitats and on government-owned lands and waterways, as in the case of logging, cattle-grazing, and fishing. The vast majority of farms, ranches, and fishing companies are small enterprises owned and operated by families as their primary or secondary source of income. Although large family farms (those generating more than $250,000 per year in gross annual sales) and corporate farms comprise less than 10 percent of the establishments in the field, they produce over three-fourths of all agricultural output. Increasingly, these large farms are being operated for the benefit of large agribusiness firms, which buy most of the product.

The agriculture sector of this field is divided into two major segments, *animal production* and *crop production*. Animal production includes establishments that raise livestock, such as beef cattle, sheep, and hogs; dairy farms; poultry and egg farms; and animal specialty farms, such as apiaries (bee farms) and aquaculture (fish farms). Crop production includes the growing of grains, such as wheat, corn, and barley; field crops, such as cotton and tobacco; vegetables and melons; fruits and nuts; and horticultural specialties, such as flowers and ornamental plants. Of course, many farms have both crops and livestock, such as those that grow their own animal feed, or have diverse enterprises.

Production of some types of crops and livestock tends to be concentrated in particular regions of the country based on growing conditions and topography. For example, the warm climates of Florida, California, Texas, and Arizona are well suited for citrus fruit production, while northern states are better suited to growing blueberries, maple syrup, and apples. Grains, potatoes, hogs, and range-fed cattle are major products in the plains states, where cattle feedlots also are numerous. In the Southwest and West, ranchers raise beef cattle. Poultry and dairy farms tend to be found in most areas of the country.

The nature of agricultural work varies, depending on the crops grown, the animals being raised, and the size of the farm. Although much of the work is now highly mechanized, large numbers of people still are needed to plant and harvest some crops on the larger farms. During the planting, growing, and harvesting seasons, farmers and employed workers are busy for long hours plowing, disking, harrowing, seeding, fertilizing, and harvesting. Vegetables generally are still harvested manually by groups of migrant farmworkers, although new machines have been developed to replace manual labor for some fruit crops. Vegetable growers on large farms of approximately 100 acres or more usually practice "monoculture," large-scale cultivation of one crop on each division of land. Fieldwork on large grain farms—consisting of hundreds, sometimes thousands, of acres—often is done using massive, global positioning system (GPS)–controlled tractors and other modern agricultural equipment.

Workers on farms that raise other products, particularly those raising animals, have work that must be done all year long. On dairy farms, for example, the cows must be milked and fed every day and their stalls must be cleaned. Cows may then be taken outside for exercise and grazing. Dairy workers also may plant, harvest, and store crops, such as corn or hay, to feed the cattle through the cold of winter or the drought of summer.

Though the nature of the work on large livestock ranches in the West and Southwest still entails the kind of activities—such as branding and herding—often seen in western movies, the use of modern equipment and technology has changed the way the work is done. Branding and vaccinating of herds, for example, are largely mechanized, and the use of trucks, portable communications gear, and geopositioning equipment now is common and saves valuable time for ranchers. The work on such establishments still tends to be seasonal and to take place largely outdoors. Common activities include raising feed crops, rotating cattle from one pasture to another, and keeping fences in good repair.

Most poultry and egg farms are large operations resembling production lines. Although free-range farms allow fowl some time outside during the day for exercise and sunlight, most poultry production involves mainly indoor work, with workers repeatedly performing a limited number of specific tasks. Because of increased mechanization, poultry growers can raise chickens by the thousands—sometimes by the hundreds of thousands—under one roof. Eggs still are collected manually in some small-scale hatcheries, but eggs tumble down onto conveyor belts in larger hatcheries. Machines then wash the eggs, sort them, and pack them into individual cartons. Workers place the cartons into boxes and stack the boxes onto pallets for shipment.

Aquaculture farmers raise fish and shellfish in salt, brackish, or fresh water, depending on the requirements of the particular species. Farms usually use ponds, floating net pens, raceways, or recirculating systems, but larger fish farms are actually in the sea, relatively close to shore. Workers on aquaculture farms stock, feed, protect, and otherwise manage aquatic life to be sold for consumption or used for recreational fishing.

Horticulture farms raise ornamental plants, bulbs, shrubbery, sod, and flowers. Although much of the work takes place outdoors, in climates with cold seasons, substantial production also takes place in greenhouses or hothouses. On such farms, the work can be year-round.

Although most agricultural establishments sell their products to food processing, textile, and food retailing companies, some cater directly to the public. For example, some fruit and vegetable growers use the marketing strategy of "pick-your-own" produce, set up roadside stands, or sell at farmers' markets. Nurseries and greenhouses, which grow everything from flowers to tree seedlings, provide products to lawn and garden centers and other retailers, landscaping contractors, and other businesses; some also sell directly to individual consumers.

Workers employed in the forestry and logging sector grow and harvest timber on a long production cycle of 10 years or more and specialize in different stages of the production cycle. Those engaged in reforestation handle seedlings in specialized nurseries. Workers in timber production remove diseased or damaged trees from timberland, as well as brush and debris that could pose a fire hazard. Besides commercial timberland, they may also work in natural forests or other suitable areas of land that remain available for production over a long duration. Logging workers harvest the timber in order for it to become lumber for construction, wood products, or paper products. They cut down the trees, remove their tops and branches, and cut their trunks into logs of specified length. They usually use a variety of specialized machinery to move the logs to loading areas and load them on trucks for transport to paper mills and sawmills.

People employed in fishing harvest fish and shellfish from their natural habitat in fresh water and in tidal areas and the ocean and depend for their livelihood on a naturally replenishing supply of fish, lobster, shellfish, or other edible marine life. Some full-time and many part-time fishers work on small boats in relatively shallow waters, often in sight of land. Crews are small—usually only one or two people collaborate on all aspects of the fishing operation. Others fish hundreds of miles offshore on large commercial fishing vessels. Navigation and communication are essential for safety of all of those who work on the water, but particularly for those who work far from shore. Large boats, capable of hauling a catch of tens of thousands of pounds of fish, require a crew that includes a captain, or "skipper," a first mate and sometimes a second mate, a boatswain (called a deckboss on some smaller boats), and deckhands to operate the fishing gear, sort and load the catch when it is brought to the deck, and aid in the general operation of the vessel.

The agriculture, forestry, and fishing field also includes companies that provide support activities to this field. On farms that primarily grow crops, these activities may include farm management services, soil preparation, and planting and cultivating services, as well as crop harvesting and post-harvesting services. It also includes farm labor contractors who specialize in supplying labor for agricultural and production services. Typically, such support services are provided to the larger farms that are run more like businesses. As farms get larger, it becomes more economical as well as necessary to hire specialists to perform a range of farm services, from pest management to animal breeding. Farm management services establishments manage farms on a contract or fee basis. As more farms are owned by absentee landowners and corporations, farm managers are being hired to run the farms. They make decisions about planting and harvesting as well as do most of the hiring of farmworkers and specialists. Farm labor contractors provide and manage temporary farm laborers—often migrant workers—who usually work during peak harvesting times. Contractors may place bids with farmers to harvest labor-intensive crops such as fruit, nuts, or vegetables or perform other short-term tasks. Once the bid is accepted, the contractor, or crew leader, organizes and supervises the laborers as they harvest, load, move, and store the crops. Other support services companies provide aerial dusting and spraying of pesticides over a large number of acres. They may also perform post-harvesting tasks to prepare crops for market, including shelling, fumigating, cleaning, grading, grinding, and packaging agricultural products.

Establishments that supply support activities for animal production perform services that may include breeding, pedigree record services, boarding horses, livestock spraying, and sheep dipping and shearing. Workers in establishments providing breeding services monitor herd condition and nutrition, evaluate the quality and quantity of forage, recommend adjustments to feeding when necessary, identify the best cattle or other livestock for breeding and calving, advise on livestock pedigrees, inseminate cattle artificially, and feed and care for sires.

The agriculture, forestry, and fishing field is being transformed by the implementation of science and technology in almost every phase of the agricultural process. From the planting of bioengineered crops to the use of GPS in planting and harvesting and the latest in the science of genetics to reproduce animals with specific characteristics, the agriculture field is rapidly changing.

Working Conditions

Agriculture, forestry, and fishing attract people who enjoy working with animals, living an independent lifestyle, or working outdoors on the land. For many, the wide-open physical expanse, the variability of day-to-day work, and the rural setting provide benefits that offset the sometimes hard labor and the risks associated with unseasonable or extreme weather and shifting outlook for revenues.

Although the working conditions vary by occupation and setting, there are some characteristics common to most agriculture, forestry, and fishing jobs. Work hours generally vary and the jobs often require longer than an 8-hour day and a 5-day, 40-hour week; work cannot be delayed when crops must be planted and harvested or when animals must be sheltered and fed. Weekend work is common, and farmers, agricultural managers, crew leaders, farm-equipment operators, and agricultural workers may work a 6- or 7-day week during planting and harvesting seasons. Graders and sorters may work evenings or weekends because of the perishable nature of the products. Almost 1 out of 4 employees in this field work variable schedules, compared with fewer than 1 in 10 workers in all fields combined. Because much of the work is seasonal in nature, many farmworkers must cope with periods of unemployment or obtain short-term jobs in other fields when the farms have no work. Migrant farmworkers, who move from location to location to harvest crops as they ripen, live an unsettled lifestyle, which can be stressful.

Much of the work on farms and ranches takes place outdoors, in all kinds of weather, and is physical in nature. Harvesting some types of vegetables, for example, requires manual labor and workers do a lot of bending, stooping, and lifting. Living conditions of contract laborers are often modest, although there are regulations to assure minimum standards. The year-round nature of much livestock production work means that ranch workers must be out in the heat of summer as well as the cold of winter. Those who work directly with animals risk being bitten or kicked.

Farmers, farm managers, and agricultural workers in crop production risk exposure to pesticides and other potentially hazardous chemicals that are sprayed on crops or plants. Those who work on mechanized farms must take precautions when working with tools and heavy equipment in order to avoid injury.

Forestry and logging jobs are physically demanding and often dangerous, although machinery has eliminated some of the heavy labor. Most logging occupations involve lifting, climbing, and other strenuous activities. Loggers work under unusually hazardous conditions. Falling trees and branches are a constant menace, as are the dangers associated with log-handling operations and the use of sawing equipment, especially delimbing devices. Special care must be taken during strong winds, which can even halt operations. Slippery or muddy ground and hidden roots or vines not only reduce efficiency but also present a constant danger, especially in the presence of moving vehicles and machinery. Workers may encounter poisonous plants, brambles, insects, snakes, and heat and humidity. If safety precautions are not taken, the high noise level of sawing and skidding operations over long periods may impair hearing. If workers are to avoid injury, their experience, exercise of caution, and use of proper safety measures and equipment—such as hardhats, eye and ear protection, and safety clothing and boots—are extremely important.

Logging sites are often far from population centers and require long commutes. Some lumber companies set up bunkhouses or camps for employees to stay in overnight.

Fishing operations are conducted under various environmental conditions, depending on the region of the country and the kind of species sought. Storms, fog, and wind may hamper the work of fishing vessels. People employed in fishing work under conditions that can quickly turn from pleasant to wet and hazardous, and help is often not readily available. Work must be performed on decks that are wet and slippery as the result of fish processing operations or ice formation in the winter. Workers must be constantly on guard against entanglement in fishing nets and gear, sudden breakage or malfunction of fishing gear, or being swept overboard. Malfunctioning navigation or communication equipment may lead to collisions with underwater hazards or other vessels and even shipwrecks. Also, when injuries occur, medical treatment beyond simple first aid usually is not available until the vessel can reach port.

Most workers employed in fishing return to their homes every evening. However, workers on vessels that range far from port may be at sea for days or even weeks. While newer vessels of this type have improved living quarters and amenities, such as television and shower stalls, crews still experience the aggravations of confined conditions, continuous close personal contact, and the absence of family.

Some component fields making up agriculture, forestry, and fishing have some of the highest incidences of illnesses and injuries of any field. In 2003, the overall field had 6.2 injuries and illnesses per 100 full-time workers, compared with a nongovernment average of 5.0. Those working with livestock had significantly higher incidences of work-related illness and injury than those working with crops.

Table 1. Distribution of wage and salary employment in agriculture, forestry, and fishing by detailed field, 2004 (Employment in thousands)

Field	Employment	Percent
Total, all fields	1,149	100.0
Crop production	530	46.1
Animal production	406	35.3
Logging	68	5.9
Fishing, hunting, and trapping	30	2.6
Forestry	12	1.0
Support activities for agriculture and forestry	103	9.0

Important Characteristics of the Field

Skills: Repairing; Management of Material Resources; Management of Personnel Resources; Science; Management of Financial Resources; Equipment Maintenance. **Abilities:** Static Strength; Dynamic Flexibility; Dynamic Strength; Extent Flexibility; Spatial Orientation; Explosive Strength. **Work-Related Values:** Authority; Creativity; Variety; Moral Values.

Employment

In 2004, agriculture, forestry, and fishing employed a total of about 2.1 million workers, including self-employed and unpaid family workers, making it one of the largest fields in the nation. This field is unusual in that self-employed and unpaid family workers account for nearly 50 percent of its workforce, of whom the vast majority—about 9 out of 10—were employed in the agricultural products subsector of this field. Among all workers in the agriculture, forestry and fishing field, more than 1.1 million were wage and salary workers (see table 1), while slightly less than 1 million were self-employed and unpaid family workers.

Agriculture, forestry, and fishing is one of the few remaining areas of the economy in which unpaid family workers remain a significant part of the workforce. Most unpaid family workers assist with the farm work or fishing, but a small number do bookkeeping; purchase supplies; or arrange the sale of crops, livestock, or the daily catch.

Workers in agriculture, forestry, and fishing tend to be older than workers in other fields. In 2004, 30 percent of workers were aged 55 or older, compared with about 16 percent of all workers in all fields.

Most individual agricultural-production establishments employ fewer than 5 workers (see chart).

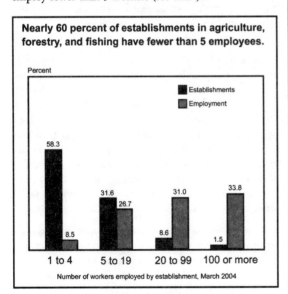

Nearly 60 percent of establishments in agriculture, forestry, and fishing have fewer than 5 employees.

Percent

■ Establishments
■ Employment

	1 to 4	5 to 19	20 to 99	100 or more
Establishments	58.3	31.6	8.6	1.5
Employment	8.5	26.7	31.0	33.8

Number of workers employed by establishment, March 2004

Occupations in the Field

Agriculture, forestry, and fishing employs many occupational specialties—from bookkeepers, accountants, and auditors to mechanics and repairers (table 2). Among wage and salary workers, the single most common occupation was that of *farmworkers*, who made up about 46 percent of the entire field. The majority of self-employed workers were farmers and ranchers, but many also worked as fishers. Along with farm managers, farmworkers, farmers, and ranchers comprise the overwhelming majority of workers.

Farmers and ranchers are the self-employed owner-operators of establishments that produce agricultural output. Their work encompasses numerous tasks, both production-related and management-related. Along with planting, cultivating, harvesting their crops, and feeding and raising their livestock, farmers and ranchers must perform numerous bookkeeping activities. They keep records of their animals' health, crop rotation, operating expenses, major purchases, bills paid, and income due, as well as pay bills and file taxes. If the farm or ranch has paid employees, its owner or operator may keep all of the paperwork needed to satisfy legal requirements, including payroll records and state and federal tax records. Computer literacy has become as necessary for farmers as it has for many other occupations. Farmers also hire, train, and manage the schedules and supervise the work of farmworkers or farm labor contractors. They assign, monitor, and assess individuals' work day in and day out.

Farmers and ranchers must have additional skills to keep a farm or ranch operating. Basic understanding and working knowledge of mechanics, carpentry, plumbing, and electricity are helpful, if not essential, for running an agricultural establishment. Increasingly, farmers are becoming more involved in marketing, too, especially in "direct marketing" where they sell their products directly to the consumer.

Farmers who work large farms make decisions as much as a year in advance about which crop to grow. Therefore, a farmer must be aware of commodity prices in national and international markets to use for guidance while tracking the costs associated with each particular crop. When dealing in hundreds or thousands of acres of one crop, even small errors in judgment are magnified, so the impact can be substantial. Thus, large-scale farmers strive to keep costs to a minimum in every phase of the operation. Furthermore, risk management of portfolios—the practice of juggling stocks, buying and selling futures, and engaging in other paper deals such as bond trading—is now becoming more important for owner-operators of large commercial farms.

Farm, ranch, and other agricultural managers operate farms, ranches, nurseries, timber tracts, and aquaculture operations on a daily basis for the owners. Agricultural managers perform many of the same tasks as that of farmers and ranchers. Large commercial farms may have a manager for different operations within the establishment. On smaller farms, one manager may oversee all operations. Managers are responsible for purchasing machinery, seed, fertilizers, herbicides and pesticides, fuel, and labor. They must be aware of any laws that govern the use of such inputs in the farm's locality. Agricultural managers must be knowledgeable about crop rotation, soil testing, and various types of capital improvements necessary to maximize crop yields.

Agricultural workers include occupations that perform a whole spectrum of daily chores involved in crop and livestock production. *Graders and sorters* ensure the quality of the agricultural commodities that reach the market. They grade, sort, or classify unprocessed food and other agricultural products by size, weight, color, or condition. *Farmworkers and laborers, crop, nursery, and greenhouse* manually plant, maintain, and harvest food crops; apply pesticides, herbicides, and fertilizer to crops; and cultivate plants used to beautify landscapes. They prepare nursery acreage or greenhouse beds for planting; water, weed, and spray trees, shrubs, and plants; cut, roll, and stack sod; stake trees; tie, wrap, and pack flowers, plants, shrubs, and trees to fill orders; and dig up or move field-grown and containerized shrubs and trees. Additional duties include planting seedlings, transplanting saplings, and watering and trimming plants. Lastly, *animal breeders* select and breed animals according to their genealogy, characteristics, and offspring. Usually, these workers need knowledge of the techniques of artificial insemination. Often, they keep the records of these animals' birth cycles and pedigree.

Farmworkers, farm and ranch animals care for farm, ranch, or aquaculture animals that may include cattle, sheep, swine, goats, horses, poultry, finfish, shellfish, and bees. They also tend to animals raised for animal products, such as meat, fur, skins, feathers, eggs, milk, and honey. Duties may include feeding, watering, herding, grazing, castrating, branding, debeaking, weighing, catching, and loading animals. These farmworkers also

may maintain records on animals; examine animals to detect diseases and injuries; and assist in birth deliveries and administer medications, vaccinations, or insecticides, as appropriate. Daily duties include cleaning and maintaining animal housing areas. These workers also may repair farm buildings and fences and haul livestock products to market. On dairy farms, they may operate milking machines and other dairy-processing equipment.

Forest and conservation workers perform a variety of tasks to reforest and conserve timberlands and maintain forest facilities, such as roads and campsites. They may plant tree seedlings to reforest timberland areas, remove diseased or undesirable trees, and spray trees with insecticides. They also may clear away brush and debris from trails, roadsides, and camping areas. Other forest and conservation workers work in forest nurseries, sorting out tree seedlings and discarding those that do not meet prescribed standards of root formation, stem development, and foliage condition.

Foresters manage forested lands for economic, recreational, and conservation purposes. They inventory the type, amount, and location of standing timber; determine the timber's worth; negotiate with purchasers for the timber; and draw up contracts for tree removal and procurement. Foresters determine how to conserve wildlife habitats, creekbeds, water quality, and soil stability and how best to comply with environmental regulations. They also devise plans for planting and growing trees, monitor the trees' growth, and determine the best time for harvesting.

Forest and conservation technicians, under the direction of foresters, compile data on the size, content, and condition of forest land tracts. These workers travel through sections of forest to gather basic information, such as species and population of trees, disease and insect damage, tree seedling mortality, and conditions that may cause fire danger. Forest and conservation technicians also train and lead forest and conservation workers in seasonal activities, such as planting tree seedlings, putting out forest fires, and maintaining recreational facilities.

Fishers and related fishing workers use nets, fishing rods, or other equipment to catch and trap various types of marine life for human consumption, animal feed, bait, and other uses. Fishing boat captains plan and oversee fishing operations—the fish to be sought, the location of the best fishing grounds, the method of capture, the duration of the trip, and the sale of the catch. *First mates*—captains' assistants, who must be familiar with navigation requirements and the operation of the vessel and all of its electronic equipment—assume control of the vessel when the captain is off duty. *Boatswains*, highly experienced deckhands with supervisory responsibilities, direct the *deckhands* as they carry out the sailing and fishing operations.

Table 2. Employment of wage and salary workers in agriculture, forestry, and fishing by occupation, 2004 and projected change, 2004–2014 (Employment in thousands)

Occupation	Employment, 2004		Percent change, 2004–2014
	Number	Percent	
Total, all occupations	1,149	100.0	–5.2
Management, business, and financial occupations	214	18.6	3.3
Top executives	14	1.2	–9.1
Farm, ranch, and other agricultural managers	189	16.4	4.9
Professional and related occupations	14	1.2	–0.1
Agricultural and food science technicians	3	0.2	–5.8
Service occupations	49	4.3	–4.2
Landscaping and groundskeeping workers	18	1.6	–7.9
Animal trainers	10	0.9	12.7
Nonfarm animal caretakers	4	0.4	8.6
Sales and related occupations	12	1.0	–11.9
Office and administrative support occupations	53	4.6	–18.7
Bookkeeping, accounting, and auditing clerks	18	1.5	–19.9
Information and record clerks	5	0.5	–18.7
Secretaries and administrative assistants	15	1.3	–16.2
Farming, fishing, and forestry occupations	690	60.1	–6.2
Supervisors, farming, fishing, and forestry workers	36	3.1	–2.2
Agricultural inspectors	1	0.1	–1.4
Animal breeders	2	0.1	–4.9
Graders and sorters, agricultural products	13	1.1	–3.1
Agricultural equipment operators	48	4.2	–0.7
Farmworkers and laborers, crop, nursery, and greenhouse	487	42.4	–6.6
Farmworkers, farm and ranch animals	42	3.7	–9.8
Fishers and related fishing workers	17	1.5	–22.2
Forest and conservation workers	4	0.3	–11.4
Fallers	9	0.8	–14.2
Logging equipment operators	22	1.9	8.9
Installation, maintenance, and repair occupations	23	2.0	–9.5
Heavy vehicle and mobile equipment service technicians and mechanics	11	0.9	–9.2
Production occupations	22	1.9	–11.1
Transportation and material moving occupations	64	5.6	–7.8
Truck drivers, heavy and tractor-trailer	19	1.6	–7.3
Truck drivers, light or delivery services	7	0.7	–8.2
Laborers and freight, stock, and material movers, hand	10	0.9	–18.3
Packers and packagers, hand	13	1.1	–1.9

Note: May not add to totals due to omission of occupations with small employment

Agriculture and Natural Resources

Training, Other Qualifications, and Advancement

The agriculture, forestry, and fishing field is characterized by a large number of workers with relatively low levels of educational attainment. Almost 29 percent of this field's workforce does not have a high school diploma, compared with only 11 percent of all workers in all fields combined. The proportion of workers without a high school diploma is particularly high in the crop-producing agricultural sector, where there are more labor-intensive establishments employing migrant farmworkers.

Training and education requirements for general farmworkers are few. Some experience in farm work or ranch work is beneficial, but most tasks are learned fairly quickly on the job. Advancement for farmworkers is somewhat limited. Motivated and experienced farmworkers may become crew leaders or farm-labor contractors. Because firsthand knowledge of farm produce is good preparation for grading, sorting, and inspecting, some farmworkers may become agricultural graders and sorters or inspectors. Farmworkers who wish to become independent farmers or ranchers first must buy or lease a plot of land, which can be a substantial financial commitment if one buys instead of leases.

Becoming a farmer generally does not require formal training or credentials. However, knowledge of and expertise in agricultural production are essential to success for prospective farmers. The traditional method for acquiring such knowledge is through growing up on a farm, but this background is becoming less and less common as the percentage of the U.S. population raised on farms continues to dwindle. But even with a farming background, a person considering farming would benefit from a formal postsecondary agricultural education offered by either the land-grant universities in many of the states or community colleges. Programs usually incorporate hands-on training to complement the academic subjects. Typical coursework covers the agricultural sciences (crop, dairy, and animal) and business subjects such as accounting, marketing, and farm management. Also, there are some private organizations that help people gain farming skills, particularly if they are interested in more "alternative" types of farming.

Experience and some formal education are necessary for agricultural managers. A bachelor's degree in business with a concentration in agriculture provides a good background. Work experience in the various aspects of farm or ranch operations enhances knowledge and develops decision-making skills, which further qualifies prospective agricultural managers. The experience of having performed tasks on other farming establishments as a farmworker may save managers valuable time in forming daily or monthly work plans and help them to avoid pitfalls that could result in financial burdens for the farm.

Whether it is gained through experience or formal education, both farmers and agricultural managers need enough technical knowledge of crops, growing conditions, and plant diseases to make sound scientific and business decisions. A rudimentary knowledge of veterinary science, as well as animal husbandry, is important for dairy and livestock farmers, ranchers, and agricultural managers.

It also is crucial for farmers, ranchers, and agricultural managers to stay abreast of the latest developments in agricultural production. They may do this by reviewing agricultural journals that publish information about new cost-cutting procedures, new forms of marketing, or improved production using new techniques. County cooperative extension agencies serve as a link between university and government research programs on the one hand and farmers and farm managers on the other, providing the latest information on numerous agriculture-related subjects. County cooperative extension agents may demonstrate new animal-breeding techniques or more environmentally safe methods of fertilizing, for example. Other organizations provide information—through journals, newsletters, and the Internet—on agricultural research and the results of implementing innovative methods and ideas.

Some private organizations are helping to make farmland available and affordable for new farmers through a variety of institutional innovations. Land Link programs, coordinated by the National Farm Transition Network, operate in 19 states. They help match up young farmers with farmers approaching retirement so that arrangements can be made to pass along their land to young farmers wishing to keep the land under cultivation. Often a beginning farmer will lease some or all of his or her farmland. Sometimes a new farmer will work on a farm for a few years while the farm owner gradually transfers ownership to the new farmer.

Most forest, conservation, and logging workers develop skills and learn to operate the complex machinery through on-the-job training with instruction coming primarily from experienced workers and the logging companies themselves. Some trade associations also offer special training programs. Safety training is a vital part of instruction for all logging workers.

Many state forestry and logging associations provide training sessions for fallers, whose jobs require more skill and experience than other positions on the logging team. Sessions may take place in the field, where trainees, under the supervision of an experienced logger, have the opportunity to practice various felling techniques. Fallers learn how to manually cut down extremely large or expensive trees safely and with minimal damage to the felled or surrounding trees. They also may receive training in best management practices, safety, endangered species preservation, reforestation, and business management. Some programs lead to logger certification.

Workers in the fishing field usually acquire occupational skills on the job, many as members of families involved in fishing activities. No formal academic requirements exist. Operators of large commercial fishing vessels are required to complete a Coast Guard–approved training course. Students can expedite their entrance into these occupations by enrolling in 2-year vocational-technical programs offered by secondary schools. In addition, some community colleges and universities offer fishery technology and related programs that include courses in seamanship, vessel operations, marine safety, navigation, vessel repair and maintenance, health emergencies, and fishing gear technology. Courses include hands-on experience. Secondary and postsecondary programs are normally offered in or near coastal areas.

Fishers must be in good health and possess physical strength. Good coordination, mechanical aptitude, and the ability to work under difficult or dangerous conditions are necessary to operate, maintain, and repair equipment and fishing gear. On large vessels, they must be able to work as members of a team. Fishers must be patient, yet always alert, to overcome the boredom of long watches when their vessel is not engaged in fishing operations. The ability to assume any deckhand's functions on short notice is important. As supervisors, mates must be able to assume all duties, including the captain's, when necessary. The captain must be highly experienced, mature, and decisive and must possess the business skills needed to run business operations.

On fishing vessels, most workers begin as deckhands. Deckhands who acquire experience and whose interests are in ship engineering—maintenance and repair of ship engines and equipment—can eventually become licensed chief engineers on large commercial vessels after meeting the Coast Guard's experience, physical, and academic requirements. Experienced, reliable deckhands who display supervisory qualities may become boatswains. Boatswains may, in turn, become second mates, first mates, and, finally, captains. Almost all captains become self-employed, and the overwhelming majority eventually own, or have an interest in, one or more fishing vessels. Some may choose to run a sport or recreational fishing operation. When their seagoing days are over, experienced individuals may work in or, with the necessary capital, own stores selling fishing and marine equipment and supplies.

Outlook

Employment for paid and unpaid workers in the agriculture, forestry, and fishing field is projected to decline 11 percent over the 2004–2014 period. Low agricultural prices and increasing imports of lumber and fish will cause many workers to leave this field. In addition, fishers face growing restrictions on where they can fish and how much they can harvest because many fisheries (fish habitats) have been depleted due to years of overfishing.

Numerous farms are expected to go out of business over the next decade because prices for many agricultural goods are low, a situation that has many causes. First, U.S. farms continue to produce more than is needed to meet domestic and export requirements. Increasing productivity means that it takes less farm labor to produce crops and livestock than in the past. In addition, market pressures on the family farm will continue to drive consolidation in the field as farms become bigger and more likely to be controlled by large corporations. The decline in employment will be fastest, at 21 percent, among self-employed and unpaid family workers, most of whom are farmers and their families. Employment of wage and salary workers is expected to decline by 5 percent compared with 14 percent growth for all fields combined.

Employment on many farms will most likely continue to be characterized by low wages and lack of benefits. Employment of farmers and ranchers is projected to decrease, but it is expected to increase for agricultural managers. The number of farmworkers is expected to decline as technology replaces some manual labor. The same is true for the occupation of graders and sorters.

Employment in aquaculture has been growing steadily over the past 12 years in response to growth in the demand for fish. However, competition from imported fish and an unsettled regulatory environment that is placing restrictions on some fish farms may slow the growth of this sector of agriculture.

Employment declines, however are being moderated by other changes taking place in agriculture. New developments in the marketing of milk and other agricultural produce through farmer-owned and -operated cooperatives hold promise for some dairy and other farms. Furthermore, demand is growing for organic farm produce—grown to a large extent on small to medium-sized farms. The production of crops without the use of pesticides and certain chemicals is allowing farms of small acreage, which only 12 years ago appeared to have almost no future as working farms, to remain economically viable. Also, some federal, state, and local government programs provide assistance targeted at small farms. For example, some programs allow farmers to sell the development rights to their property to nonprofit organizations that have pledged to preserve green space. This immediately lowers the market value of the land—and the property taxes levied on it—making farming more affordable.

Employment in forestry is also expected to decline as the sector moves towards greater mechanization, replacing many lower-skilled workers with more machinery tended by a few operators. In addition, imports of wood and wood products are expected to continue to grow. Other countries—particularly Canada—have invested more heavily in their lumber and paper mills than has the United States, enabling them to keep prices low. The best job opportunities will be for those forestry workers with more skills, such as technicians and foresters.

In the fishing sector, increases in imports and efforts to revive fisheries by limiting fishing activity in them will continue to lead to employment declines. Although certain areas of the country, such as Alaska, will continue to harvest massive amounts of fish and remain relatively prosperous, the nation's fisheries are a delicate resource. To the extent that they are damaged by such factors as coastal pollution or overfishing, there will be fewer jobs for fishers.

Earnings

In 2004, median earnings for workers in the agriculture, forestry, and fishing field were $417 a week, with a wide range from less than $248 a week for the lowest 10 percent to more than $915 a week for the highest 10 percent. Lower–than-average earnings are due in part to the low level of skill required for many of the jobs in the field and to the seasonal nature of the work. Median weekly earnings of prominent occupations in the field are as follows:

Table 3. Median weekly earnings of the largest occupations in agriculture, forestry, and fishing, 2004

Occupation	Agriculture, forestry, and fishing
Farm, ranch, and other agricultural managers	$621
Welding, soldering, and brazing workers	606
Logging workers	465
Sawing machine setters, operators, and tenders, wood	444
Forest and conservation workers	415
Fishers and related fishing workers	398
Grounds maintenance workers	372
Packers and packagers, hand	349
Farmers and ranchers	300

Sources of Additional Information

For general information about starting out in farming, contact

- United States Department of Agriculture, Cooperative State, Research, Education, and Extension Service, 1400 Independence Avenue SW, Stop 2201, Washington, DC 20250-2201. Internet: http://www.csrees.usda.gov/ProgView.cfm

- Growing New Farmers Consortium, c/o New England Small Farm Institute, P.O. Box 11, Belchertown, MA 01007.

For information about organic farming, horticulture, and internships, contact

- ATTRA, National Sustainable Agriculture Information Service, P.O. Box 3657, Fayetteville, AR 72702. Internet: http://attra.ncat.org

For information on a wide range of topics in agriculture, contact

- The National Agricultural Library, AFSIC, 10301 Baltimore Ave., Room 132, Beltsville, MD 20705-2351. Internet: http://agricola.nal.usda.gov/

For information on a career as a farm manager, contact

- American Society of Farm Managers and Rural Appraisers, 950 South Cherry St., Suite 508, Denver, CO 80246-2664. Internet: http:://www.asfmra.org

For information on Land Link programs, contact

- The National Farm Transition Network, ISU Extension Outreach Center, 2020 DMACC Boulevard, Ankeny, IA 50021. Internet: http://www.extension.iastate.edu/nftn//netwpart.html

For information about state agencies involved in the purchases of development rights of farmland, contact

- American Farmland Trust, 1200 18th St. NW, Washington, DC 20036. Internet: http://www.farmland.org
- For information about careers and education resources in agriculture, contact
- National FFA Organization, The National FFA Center, Attention: Career Information Requests, P.O. Box 68690, Indianapolis, IN 46268-0960. Internet: http://www.ffa.org

Information on licensing of fishing vessel captains and mates, and requirements for merchant mariner documentation, is available from the U.S. Coast Guard Marine Inspection Office or Marine Safety Office in your state, or

- Licensing and Evaluation Branch, National Maritime Center, 4200 Wilson Blvd., Suite 630, Arlington, VA 22203-1804.

Schools of forestry at states' land-grant colleges or universities also should be able to provide useful information.

Mining

- ◎ Annual Earnings: $36,380
- ◎ Job Growth: –12.9%
- ◎ Size of Workforce: 207,490
- ◎ Self-Employed: 1.6%
- ◎ Part-Time: 2.3%

Significant Points

- Employment is projected to decline; however, job opportunities should be favorable for construction and extraction and for production workers in coal mining and nonmetallic mineral mining.
- While most mining jobs can be entered directly from high school, the increasing sophistication of equipment and machinery requires a higher level of technical skill.
- Earnings are higher than the average for all fields.

Nature of the Field

Mining has played an important role in the development of the United States. In the past, the discovery of minerals such as gold and silver resulted in population shifts and economic growth. Extraction of minerals and coal continues to provide the foundation for local economies in some parts of the country. Products of this field are used as inputs for consumer goods, processes, and services provided by all other fields, including agriculture, manufacturing, transportation, utilities, communication, and construction. Uses of mined materials include coal for energy, copper for wiring, gold for satellites and sophisticated electronic components, and a variety of other minerals as ingredients in medicines and household products.

Besides mining coal and metallic and nonmetallic minerals, employers in this field explore for minerals and develop new mines and quarries. *Metallic minerals* include ores, such as bauxite (from which aluminum is extracted), copper, gold, iron, lead, silver, and zinc. *Nonmetallic minerals* include stone; sand; gravel; clay; and other minerals such as lime and soda ash, used as chemicals and fertilizers. This field also includes initial mineral processing and preparation activities because processing plants usually operate together with mines or quarries as part of the extraction process. (A separate section in this book covers careers in oil and gas extraction.)

Mining is the process of digging into the earth to extract naturally occurring minerals. There are two kinds of mining, *surface mining* and *underground mining*. Surface mining, also called open-pit mining or strip mining, is undertaken if the mineral is near the earth's surface. This method usually is more cost-effective and requires fewer workers to produce the same quantity of ore than does underground mining. In surface mining, after blasting with explosives, workers use huge earthmoving equipment, such as power shovels or draglines, to scoop off the layers of soil and rock covering the mineral bed. Once the mineral is exposed, smaller shovels are used to lift it from the ground and load it into trucks. The mineral also can be broken up using explosives if necessary. In quarrying operations, workers use machines to extract stone used primarily as a building material. Stone, such as marble, granite, limestone, and sandstone, is quarried by splitting blocks of rock from a massive rock surface.

Underground mining is used when the mineral deposit lies deep below the surface of the earth. When developing an underground mine, miners first must dig two or more openings, or tunnels, deep into the earth near the place where they believe coal or minerals are located. Depending on where the vein of ore is in relation to the surface, tunnels may be vertical, horizontal, or sloping. One opening allows the miners to move in and out of the mine with their tools and also serves as a path for transporting the mined rock by small railroad cars or by conveyor belts to the surface. The other opening is used for ventilation.

Entries are constructed so that miners can get themselves and their equipment to the ore and carry it out while allowing fresh air to enter the mine. Once dug to the proper depth, a mine's tunnels interconnect with a network of passageways going in many directions. Long steel bolts and pillars of unmined ore support the roof of the tunnel. Using the room-and-pillar method, miners remove half of the ore as they work the ore seams from the tunnel entrance to the edge of the mine property, leaving columns of ore to support the ceiling. This process is then reversed, and the remainder of the ore is extracted as the miners work their way back out. In the case of longwall mining of coal, self-advancing roof supports made of hydraulic jacks and metal plates are moved ahead, allowing the ceiling in the mined area to cave in as the miners work back towards the tunnel entrance.

Once all the minerals or coal have been extracted, the mine and its surrounding environment must be restored to the condition that existed before mining began. In surface mining, the layers of topsoil, or overburden, that were removed in order to reach the mineral are used to fill in the mine and reshape the land. This ensures that native plants and animals will be able to thrive once again. Underground mining does not require as extensive a reclamation process; however, mine operators and environmental engineers still must ensure that groundwater remains uncontaminated and that abandoned mines will not collapse. The reclamation process is highly regulated by federal, state, and local laws, and reclamation plans often must be approved before mining permits will be granted.

During the 1990s, production of both minerals and coal increased. Given the more volatile price of metal, its production fluctuated more than that of nonmetallics. However, employment in both sectors declined significantly as new technology and more sophisticated mining techniques increased productivity, allowing growth in output while employing fewer workers. Most mining machines and control rooms are now automatic or computer-controlled, requiring fewer, if any, human operators. Many mines also operate with other sophisticated technology such as lasers and robotics, which further decrease the number of workers needed to mine materials.

Working Conditions

The average production worker in the mining field worked 45.8 hours a week in 2004, although schedules can vary widely. Some mines operate 24 hours a day 7 days a week, creating the opportunity for some mining workers to work long shifts several days in a row and then have 4 to 5 days off. Work environments vary by occupation. Scientists and technicians work in office buildings and laboratories, while miners and mining engineers spend much of their time in the mine. Geologists who specialize in the exploration of natural resources may have to travel for extended periods to remote locations, in all types of climates, in order to locate mineral or coal deposits.

Agriculture and Natural Resources

Working conditions in mines and quarries can be unusual and sometimes dangerous. Underground mines are damp and dark, and some can be very hot and noisy. At times, several inches of water may cover tunnel floors. Although underground mines have electric lights, only the lights on miners' caps illuminate many areas. Workers in mines with very low roofs may have to work on their hands and knees, backs, or stomachs in confined spaces. In underground mining operations, dangers include the possibility of an explosion or cave-in, electric shock, or exposure to harmful gases.

Workers in surface mines and quarries are subject to rugged outdoor work in all kinds of weather and climates. Some surface mines shut down in the winter because snow and ice covering the minesite makes work too difficult. Physical strength and stamina are necessary because the work involves lifting, stooping, and climbing. Surface mining, however, usually is less hazardous than underground mining.

In 2003, the rate of work-related injury and illness was 3.7 per 100 full-time workers in metal mining, 3.7 in nonmetallic minerals, and 6.2 in coal mining, compared with 5.0 for the entire private sector. Mining illnesses and injuries have steadily declined over the years because of stricter safety laws and improvements in mining machinery and practices. Although mine health and safety conditions have improved dramatically, dust generated by drilling in mines still places miners at risk of developing either of two serious lung diseases: pneumoconiosis, also called "black lung disease," from coal dust, or silicosis from rock dust. The Federal Coal Mine Health and Safety Act of 1969 regulates dust concentrations in coal mines, and respirable dust levels are closely monitored. Dust concentrations in mines have declined as a result. Underground miners have the option to have their lungs X-rayed when starting a job, with a mandatory follow-up X ray 3 years later, in order to monitor any development of respiratory illness. Additional X rays are given every 5 years on a voluntary basis. Workers who develop black lung disease or silicosis may be eligible for federal aid.

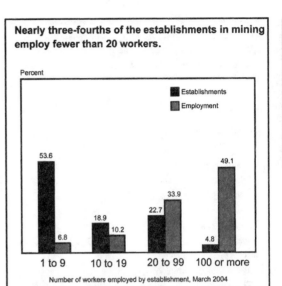

Nearly three-fourths of the establishments in mining employ fewer than 20 workers.

Percent

- Establishments
- Employment

	1 to 9	10 to 19	20 to 99	100 or more
Establishments	53.6	18.9	22.7	4.8
Employment	6.8	10.2	33.9	49.1

Number of workers employed by establishment, March 2004

Important Characteristics of the Field

Skills: Operation and Control; Repairing; Equipment Maintenance; Operation Monitoring; Installation; Troubleshooting. **Abilities:** Static Strength; Reaction Time; Response Orientation; Explosive Strength; Rate Control; Multilimb Coordination. **Work-Related Values:** Supervision, Technical; Compensation; Independence.

Employment

There were approximately 207,000 wage and salary jobs in the mining field in 2004; around 72,000 in coal mining; 27,000 in metal mining; and 108,000 in nonmetallic mineral mining. According to the Energy Information Administration, there were around 1,400 coal mining operations in 26 states in 2003. Over half of all coal mines are in three states—Kentucky, Pennsylvania, and West Virginia. Other states employing large numbers of coal miners are Alabama, Illinois, Indiana, Virginia, and Wyoming. Metal mining is more prevalent in the West and Southwest, particularly in Arizona, Colorado, Nevada, New Mexico, and Utah. Nonmetallic mineral mining is the most widespread, as quarrying of nonmetallic minerals, such as stone, clay, sand, and gravel, is done in nearly every state. In many rural areas, mining operations are the main employer. About 73 percent of mining establishments employ fewer than 20 workers (chart 1).

Table 1. Employment of wage and salary workers in mining by occupation, 2004 and projected change, 2004–2014. (Employment in thousands)

Occupation	Employment, 2004		Percent change, 2004–2014
	Number	Percent	
Total, all occupations	207	100.0	–12.9
Management, business, and financial occupations	10	5.0	–10.5
Top executives	5	2.2	–9.7
Professional and related occupations	8	3.7	–15.2
Mining and geological engineers, including mining safety engineers	2	0.8	–22.0
Office and administrative support occupations	14	6.8	–17.0
Office clerks, general	3	1.3	–14.2
Construction and extraction occupations	69	33.4	–13.8
First-line supervisors/ managers of construction trades and extraction workers	8	3.9	–14.0
Operating engineers and other construction equipment operators	21	10.2	–9.9
Electricians	5	2.4	–19.8
Earth drillers, except oil and gas	2	1.0	–14.9
Explosives workers, ordnance handling experts, and blasters	1	0.6	–14.9
Mining machine operators	13	6.1	–12.9
Continuous mining machine operators	7	3.6	–14.2
Mine cutting and channeling machine operators	3	1.6	–13.6
Rock splitters, quarry	2	1.1	–0.5
Roof bolters, mining	4	2.1	–29.9
Helpers—extraction workers	6	3.0	–16.1
Installation, maintenance, and repair occupations	27	13.2	–14.6
First-line supervisors/ managers of mechanics, installers, and repairers	3	1.3	–16.9
Mobile heavy equipment mechanics, except engines	7	3.3	–15.3
Industrial machinery mechanics	3	1.5	–16.0
Maintenance and repair workers, general	7	3.5	–12.4
Maintenance workers, machinery	3	1.3	–14.5
Production occupations	26	12.5	–9.2
First-line supervisors/ managers of production and operating workers	3	1.6	–9.7
Welders, cutters, solderers, and brazers	3	1.3	–12.0
Separating, filtering, clarifying, precipitating, and still machine setters, operators, and tenders	3	1.3	–13.4
Crushing, grinding, and polishing machine setters, operators, and tenders	7	3.3	–7.1
Transportation and material moving occupations	50	24.0	–11.6
Truck drivers, heavy and tractor-trailer	15	7.1	–5.5
Conveyor operators and tenders	3	1.4	–10.5
Excavating and loading machine and dragline operators	11	5.2	–9.0
Loading machine operators, underground mining	3	1.4	–14.2
Industrial truck and tractor operators	3	1.6	–4.3
Laborers and freight, stock, and material movers, hand	5	2.6	–19.1
Shuttle car operators	3	1.3	–45.9

Note: May not add to totals due to omission of occupations with small employment

Occupations in the Field

The mining field requires many kinds of workers. In 2004, 7 out of 10 workers were in *construction and extraction, production,* or *transportation and material moving* occupations (table 1).

Mining occupations. The majority of jobs in the mining field are in construction and extraction occupations. Though most of these jobs can be entered into directly from high school or after acquiring some experience and on-the-job training in an entry-level position, the increasing sophistication of equipment and machinery used in mining means that a higher level of technical skill is now required for many positions.

Underground mining primarily includes three methods—conventional, continuous, and longwall mining. Conventional mining, which is being phased out, is the oldest method, requiring the most workers and procedures. In this method, a strip or "kerf" is cut underneath the ore seam to control the direction in which the ore falls after it has been blasted. *Cutting-machine operators* use a huge electric chain saw with a cutter from 6 to 15 feet long to cut the kerf. Next, *drilling-machine operators* drill holes in the ore where the *shot firers* place explosives. This potentially dangerous work requires workers to follow safety procedures, such as making sure everyone is clear of the area before the explosives are detonated. After the blast, *loading-machine operators* scoop up the material and dump it into small rubber-tired cars run by *shuttle-car operators,* who bring the coal or ore to a central location for transportation to the surface.

The continuous mining method eliminates the drilling and blasting operations of conventional mining through the use of a machine called a continuous miner. Traditionally, a *continuous-mining machine operator* sits or lies in a machine's cab and operates levers that cut or rip out ore and load it directly onto a conveyor or shuttle car. However, the use of remote-controlled continuous mining machines—which have increased safety considerably—now allows an operator to control the machine from a distance.

In longwall mining, which is similar to continuous mining, *longwall-machine operators* run large machines with rotating drums that automatically shear ore and load it on a conveyor. At the same time, hydraulic jacks reinforce the roof of the tunnel. As ore is cut, the jacks are hydraulically winched forward, supporting the roof as they move along.

Many other workers are needed to operate safe and efficient underground mines. Before miners are allowed underground, a *mine safety inspector* checks the work area for such hazards as loose roofs, dangerous gases, and inadequate ventilation. If safety standards are not met, the inspector prohibits the mine from producing until conditions are made safe. *Rock-dust machine operators* spray the mine walls and floor to hold down dust, which can interfere with breathing.

Roof bolters operate the machines that automatically install roof support bolts to prevent roof cave-ins, the biggest cause of mining injuries. *Brattice builders* construct doors, walls, and partitions in tunnel passageways to force air into the work areas. *Shift bosses* oversee all operations at the worksite.

In surface mining, most miners operate huge machines that either remove the earth above the ore deposit or dig and load the ore onto trucks. The number of workers required to operate a surface mine depends on the amount of overburden, or earth, above the ore seam. In many surface mines, the overburden is first drilled and blasted. *Overburden stripping operators* or *dragline operators* then scoop the earth away to expose the coal or metal ore. Some draglines are among the largest land machines on earth.

Next, *loading-machine operators* rip the exposed ore from the seam and dump it into trucks to be driven to the preparation plant. *Tractor operators* use bulldozers to move earth and ore and to remove boulders or other obstructions. *Truck drivers* haul ore to railroad sidings or to preparation plants and transport supplies to mines.

Construction, maintenance, and *repair occupations.* Other workers who are not directly involved in the extraction process work in and around mines and quarries. For example, skilled *mechanics* are needed to repair and maintain the wide variety of mining machinery, and skilled *electricians* are needed to check and install electrical wiring. Mechanical and electrical repair work has become increasingly complex as machinery and other equipment have become computerized. *Carpenters* construct and maintain benches, bins, and stoppings (barricades to prevent airflow through a tunnel). These workers generally need specialized training to work under the unusual conditions found in mines. Mechanics, for example, may have to repair machines while on their knees with only their headlamps to illuminate the working area.

Quarrying occupations. Workers at quarries have duties similar to those of miners. Using jackhammers and wedges, *rock splitters* remove pieces of stone from a rock mass. *Dredge operators* and *dipper tenders* operate power-driven dredges, or dipper sticks of dredges, to mine sand, gravel, and other materials from beneath the surfaces of lakes, rivers, and streams. Using power-driven cranes with dragline buckets, *dragline operators* excavate or move sand, gravel, and other materials.

Processing-plant occupations. Processing plants often are located next to mines or quarries. In these plants, rocks and other impurities are removed from the ore, which is then washed, crushed, sized, or blended to meet buyer specifications. Methods for physically separating the ore from surrounding material also include more complex processes, such as leaching—mixing the ore with chemical solutions or other liquids in order to separate materials. Most processing plants are highly mechanized and require only a few workers for the washing, separating, and crushing operations. *Processing-plant supervisors* oversee all operations. In plants that are not heavily mechanized, *washbox attendants* operate equipment that sizes and separates impurities from ore, and *shake tenders* monitor machinery that further cleans and sizes ore with a vibrating screen. Most jobs in the processing plant are repetitive and, as a result of highly computerized mechanization, are becoming more automated.

Management, business, and financial and *professional and related occupations* also are important to the mining field. Administrative workers include *top executives*, who are responsible for making policy decisions. Staff specialists (such as *accountants*, *attorneys*, and *market researchers*) provide information and advice for policymakers.

Professional and related workers in mining include engineering, scientific, and technical personnel. *Environmental scientists* and *geoscientists* search for locations likely to yield coal or mineral ores in sufficient quantity to justify extraction costs. Using sophisticated technologies and equipment, such as the Global Positioning System (GPS)—a satellite system that locates points on the earth using radio signals transmitted by satellites—*surveyors* help to map areas for mining. *Mining and geological engineers* examine seams for depth and purity; determine the type of mine to build; and supervise the construction, maintenance, and operation of mines. *Mechanical engineers* oversee the installation of equipment, such as heat and water systems; *electrical engineers* oversee the installation and maintenance of electrical equipment; *civil engineers* oversee the building and construction of minesites, plants, roads, and other infrastructure; *safety engineers* direct health and safety programs; *chemical engineers* develop the chemical processes for transforming mined products into consumer goods, such as medications and fertilizers; and *materials engineers* determine the usefulness of mined ore and also develop processes for transforming the minerals into products.

Environmental engineers play an increasingly important role in mining, given environmental concerns and stringent federal, state, and local regulations imposed on all operations. Restrictions imposed by environmental regulations make obtaining permits for new mine development projects increasingly difficult. Mine owners and operators face substantial penalties should they fail to abide by current regulations. In addition, both federal regulations, such as the Surface Mining Control and Reclamation Act (SMCRA), and state laws require that land reclamation be part of the mining process. Reclamation plans usually must be approved by both government officials and local interest groups. When a mining operation is closed, the land must be restored to its pre-mine condition, which can include anything from leveling soil and removing waste to replanting vegetation.

Training, Other Qualifications, and Advancement

Workers in mining production occupations usually must be at least 18 years old, in good physical condition, and able to work in confined spaces. A high school diploma is not necessarily required. Most workers start as helpers to experienced workers and learn skills on the job; however, formal training is becoming more important as more technologically advanced machinery and mining methods are used. Some employers prefer to hire recent graduates of high school vocational programs in mining or graduates of junior college or technical school programs in mine technology. Such programs usually are found only at schools in mining areas.

Mining companies must offer formal training in either classrooms or training mines for a few weeks before new miners actually begin work. The Federal Mine Safety and Health Act of 1977 mandates that each U.S. mine have an approved worker training program in health and safety issues. Each plan must include at least 40 hours of basic safety training for new miners with no experience in underground mines and 24 hours for new miners in surface mines. In addition to new miner training, each miner must receive at least 8 hours of refresher safety training a year, and miners assigned to new jobs must receive safety training relating to their new task. The U.S. Mine Safety and Health Administration (MSHA) also conducts classes on health, safety, and mining methods, and some mining machinery manufacturers offer courses in machine operation and maintenance as well. The MSHA has recently put interactive training materials on its Web site and also has translated many of the training materials into Spanish. Increasingly, mines are employing more high-tech tools for miner training, such as machinery simulators and virtual reality simulators. By simulating actual mine conditions and emergencies, mine workers are better prepared and companies can instantly assess a mineworker's progress and skills.

As production workers gain more experience, they can advance to higher-paying jobs requiring greater skill. A mining machine operator's helper, for example, might become an operator. When vacancies occur, announcements are posted, and all qualified workers can bid for the job. Positions are filled on the basis of seniority and ability. Miners with significant experience or special training also can become mine safety, health, and compliance officers, whose duties include mine safety inspection. According to MSHA, a mine safety, health, and compliance officer needs at least 5 years' experience as a miner or a degree in mining engineering.

For professional and managerial positions in mining, a master's degree in engineering, one of the physical sciences, or business administration, is preferred. A number of colleges and universities have mining schools or departments and programs in mining or minerals. Environmental positions require regulatory knowledge and a strong natural science background or a background in a technical field, such as environmental engineering or hydrology. To date, most environmental professionals have been drawn from the ranks of engineers and scientists who have had experience in the mining field.

Universities and mining schools have introduced more environmental coursework into their programs, and mining firms are hiring professionals from existing environment-related disciplines and training them to meet their companies' needs. Additionally, specialized mine technology programs are offered by a few colleges. Enrollment in these programs can lead to a certificate in mine technology after 1 year, an associate degree after 2 years, or a bachelor's degree after 4 years. Courses cover areas such as mine ventilation, roof bolting, and machinery repairs.

Outlook

Wage and salary employment in mining is expected to decline by 13 percent through the year 2014, compared with 14 percent growth projected for the entire economy. This continuing long-term decline is due to increased productivity resulting from technological advances in mining operations and larger mining equipment, consolidation, international competition, and stringent environmental regulations. Employment is expected to decline substantially in coal and metal ore mining, but only slightly in nonmetallic mineral mining.

Advances in mining technology will adversely affect employment in mining as new machinery and processes increase worker productivity. New mining machines that operate remotely by computer and self-diagnose mechanical problems require fewer workers for operation and maintenance. Advances in longwall and surface mining, which are less labor intensive, also have increased productivity, as have improvements in transportation and processing. Additionally, innovations such as roof bolting, self-advancing roof supports, and continuous mining machinery have led to safer, more efficient operations.

In the past, low commodity prices caused domestic production to decline, but as prices for metals increase due to increasing demand from China and India, domestic production is picking up and moderating the loss of mining jobs. Worldwide demand is expected to continue to increase, which is expected to result in more exploration and greater domestic production.

Environmental concerns will continue to affect mining operations. Increasingly, government regulations are restricting access to land and restricting the type of mining that is performed in order to protect native plants and animals and decrease the amount of water and air pollution. As population growth expands further into the countryside, new developments are competing for land with mine operators, and residents are increasing their opposition to nearby mining activities.

The products of the coal mining field are used to produce electricity and steel products, so demand for coal should remain high. Although production of coal is expected to increase, employment will decline by about 23 percent through 2014 as more efficient and automated production operations require less labor. Increased competition should lead to further consolidation in the field.

The long-term outlook for coal depends on how electric utility companies—the major consumers of coal—respond to provisions of the Clean Air Act Amendments of 1990, which attempt to limit the emission of sulfur dioxide and other harmful pollutants caused by the burning of coal. Compliance involves the installation of costly cleaning and monitoring equipment or increased use of low-sulfur coal. As energy plants seek cleaner-burning fuel, many new power plants are being built to run on natural gas. If the demand for coal contracts as a result of stricter environmental regulations, employment in mines will decline further as mine operators are forced to decrease production. However, recent increases in the price of natural gas have caused some electricity producers to delay the conversion to natural gas, which is helping to retain coal production.

Despite the trend towards cleaner-burning fuel, the United States still is highly dependent on coal as a source of energy. Coal accounts for half of the electricity production in this country because it is the cheapest and most abundant fossil fuel. The rising demand for cleaner-burning fuel has resulted in regional shifts in coal production and markets. Because of this, lower-sulfur Western coal now accounts for an increasing share of output. This trend is resulting in a gradual regional shift in employment from the eastern states to the west. Improvements in clean coal technologies also may help the field cope with increasingly restrictive regulations through projects such as the Integrated Gasification Combined Cycle (IGCC). This technology combines traditional coal gasification with gas-turbine and steam power to generate electricity more efficiently and reduce carbon and sulfur dioxide emissions.

As in coal mining, continuing productivity increases and field consolidation are expected to cause employment in the metal ore mining field to decline through 2014. Because metals are used primarily as raw materials by other fields, such as telecommunications and steel, chemical, drug, aerospace, and automobile manufactur-

ing, the strength of the metal ore mining field is greatly affected by the strength of the fields that consume its products. Metal ore mining is also the sector most vulnerable to international competition. Many nations have mineral resources and, for some developing countries especially, mineral resources are one of the few goods they export. However, increasing worldwide demand for metals is causing metals prices to increase and production to rise.

Employment in nonmetallic mineral mining should decline slightly—2 percent—because of continued demand for crushed stone, cement, and gravel used in construction activities. Like the metal mining field, the nonmetallic mineral mining field is influenced by the strength of the fields that use nonmetals in the manufacture of their products; these are fields in which employment is impacted by swings in the economy. Nonmetallic minerals are used to make concrete and agricultural chemicals and also are used as materials in residential, nonresidential, and maintenance construction. The nonmetallic mineral mining field experienced slight employment growth over the past decade, largely attributable to construction. The demand for crushed stone and gravel should remain strong over the next few years because of demand for residential housing, roads, and airports, but productivity increases should keep employment relatively unchanged. Worker separation rates are high in nonmetallic mineral mining because most mines are small and operate only during warm months; many workers laid off during the winter find jobs in other fields and must be replaced when the mines reopen. Jobs in nonmetallic mineral mining attract many migrant workers and those looking for summer employment.

Despite declining employment, job opportunities should be favorable for construction, extraction, and production workers in coal mining and nonmetallic mineral mining. Many miners are approaching retirement age and younger miners will need to be hired to replace the retirees. Job opportunities for professional workers, such as scientists and engineers, should be good as many of these workers are also nearing retirement age.

Earnings

Average wage and salary earnings in mining were significantly higher than the average for all fields. In 2004, production workers earned $21.57 an hour in coal mining,

$22.91 an hour in metal mining, and $17.74 an hour in nonmetallic minerals mining compared to the non-government average of $15.67 an hour (table 2). Workers in underground mines spend time traveling from the mine entrance to their working areas, so their paid workday is slightly longer than that of surface mine workers: 8-hour versus 7 1/4-hour shifts. Earnings in selected occupations in specified mining fields appear in table 3.

Table 2. Average earnings of nonsupervisory workers in mining, except oil and gas, 2004

Field segment	Weekly	Hourly
Total, nongovernment	$529	$15.67
Mining	909	19.85
Coal mining	1,030	21.57
Metal ore mining	1,034	22.91
Nonmetallic mineral mining and quarrying	791	17.74

About 24 percent of mineworkers are union members or are covered by union contracts, compared with about 14 percent of nongovernment workers. About 27.5 percent of workers in coal mining and 18.6 percent in non-metallic mineral mining were union members in 2004, compared with about 13.9 percent of workers in metal mining. Union coal miners are primarily represented by the United Mine Workers of America (UMWA). The United Steelworkers of America, the International Union of Operating Engineers, and other unions also represent miners.

Workers covered by UMWA contracts receive 11 paid holidays, 12 days of paid vacation each year, 4 additional floating holidays, and 5 days of sick leave. However, coal miners generally must take their vacations during 1 of 3 regular vacation periods to assure a continuous supply of coal. As length of service increases, UMWA miners get up to 13 extra vacation days after 18 years of continuous employment. Union workers also receive benefits from a welfare and retirement fund.

Table 3. Median hourly earnings of the largest occupations in coal mining and nonmetallic minerals, except fuels, May 2004

Occupation	Mining, except oil and gas	All fields
First-line supervisors/managers of construction trades and extraction workers	$27.66	$24.25
Mobile heavy equipment mechanics, except engines	19.15	18.34
Continuous mining machine operators	18.35	17.87
Operating engineers and other construction equipment operators	16.39	17.00
Truck drivers, heavy and tractor-trailer	15.01	16.11
Excavating and loading machine and dragline operators	15.20	15.37
Maintenance and repair workers, general	18.04	14.77
Crushing, grinding, and polishing machine setters, operators, and tenders	15.07	12.96
Helpers—extraction workers	14.89	12.66
Laborers and freight, stock, and material movers, hand	13.38	9.67

Sources of Additional Information

For additional information about careers and training in the mining field, contact

- American Geological Institute, 4220 King St., Alexandria, VA 22302. Internet: http://www.agiweb.org
- Mine Safety and Health Administration, 1100 Wilson Blvd., Arlington, VA 22209-3939. Internet: http://www.msha.gov
- National Mining Association, 101 Constitution Ave. NW, Suite 500 East, Washington, DC 20001. Internet: http://www.nma.org
- Society for Mining, Metallurgy, and Exploration, Inc., 8307 Shaffer Parkway, Littleton, CO 80127. Internet: http://www.smenet.org
- United Mine Workers of America, 8315 Lee Highway, Fairfax, VA 22031. Internet: http://www.umwa.org

Agriculture and Natural Resources

Oil and Gas Extraction

- Annual Earnings: $39,973
- Job Growth: –6.1%
- Size of Workforce: 313,510
- Self-Employed: 3.3%
- Part-Time: 3.2%

Significant Points

- Most establishments employ fewer than 5 workers.
- About 71 percent of the onshore oil and gas extraction workforce is concentrated in California, Louisiana, Oklahoma, and Texas.
- Although technological innovations have expanded exploration and development worldwide, employment is expected to decline; however, workers with experience in oilfield operations are in demand.
- Earnings are relatively high.

Nature of the Field

Oil and natural gas furnish about three-fifths of our energy needs, fueling our homes, workplaces, factories, and transportation systems. In addition, they constitute the raw materials for plastics, chemicals, medicines, fertilizers, and synthetic fibers. Petroleum, commonly referred to as oil, is a natural fuel formed from the decay of plants and animals buried beneath the ground, under tremendous heat and pressure, for millions of years. Formed by a similar process, natural gas often is found in separate deposits and is sometimes mixed with oil. Finding, developing, and extracting oil and gas are the primary functions of the oil and gas extraction field. While some of these functions are done by the large oil companies, most are done by contractors working in the support activities for mining subsector, which is included in this field.

Using a variety of methods, on land and at sea, small crews of specialized workers search for geologic formations that are likely to contain oil and gas. Sophisticated equipment and advances in computer technology have increased the productivity of exploration. Maps of potential deposits now are made using remote-sensing satellites. Seismic prospecting—a technique based on measuring the time it takes sound waves to travel through underground formations and return to the surface—has revolutionized oil and gas exploration. Computers and advanced software analyze seismic data to provide three-dimensional models of subsurface rock formations. This technique lowers the risk involved in exploring by allowing scientists to locate and identify structural oil and gas reservoirs and the best locations to drill. Four-D, or "time-lapsed," seismic technology tracks the movement of fluids over time and enhances production performance even further. Another method of searching for oil and gas is based on collecting and analyzing core samples of rock, clay, and sand in the earth's layers.

After scientific studies indicate the possible presence of oil, an oil company selects a well site and installs a derrick—a tower-like steel structure—to support the drilling equipment. A hole is drilled deep into the earth until oil or gas is found or until the company abandons the effort. Similar techniques are employed in offshore drilling, except that the drilling equipment is part of a steel platform that either sits on the ocean floor or floats on the surface and is anchored to the ocean floor.

In rotary drilling, a rotating bit attached to a length of hollow drill pipe bores a hole in the ground by chipping and cutting rock. As the bit cuts deeper, more pipe is added. A stream of drilling "mud"—a mixture of clay, chemicals, and water—is continuously pumped through the drill pipe and through holes in the drill bit. Its purpose is to cool the drill bit, plaster the walls of the hole to prevent cave-ins, carry crushed rock to the surface, and prevent "blowouts" by equalizing pressure inside the hole. When a drill bit wears out, all drill pipe must be removed from the hole a section at a time, the bit replaced, and the pipe returned to the hole. New materials and better designs have advanced drill bit technology, permitting faster, more cost-effective drilling for longer periods.

Advancements in directional or horizontal drilling techniques, which allow increased access to potential reserves, have had a significant impact on drilling capabilities. Drilling begins vertically, but the drill bit can be turned so that drilling can continue at an angle of up to 90 degrees. This technique extends the drill's reach, enabling it to reach separate pockets of oil or gas. Because constructing new platforms is costly, this technique commonly is employed by offshore drilling operations.

When oil or gas is found, the drill pipe and bit are pulled from the well and metal pipe (casing) is lowered into the hole and cemented in place. The casing's upper end is fastened to a system of pipes and valves called a wellhead, or "Christmas tree," through which natural pressure forces the oil or gas into separation and storage tanks. If natural pressure is not great enough to force the oil to the surface, pumps may be used. In some cases, water, steam, or gas may be injected into the oil-producing formation to improve recovery.

Crude oil is transported to refineries by pipeline, ship, barge, truck, or railroad. Natural gas usually is transported to processing plants by pipeline. While oil refineries may be many thousands of miles away from the producing fields, gas processing plants typically are near the fields so that impurities—water, sulfur, and natural gas liquids—can be removed before the gas is piped to customers. The oil refining field is considered a separate field, and its activities are not covered here, even though many oil companies both extract and refine oil.

The oil and gas extraction field has experienced both "booms" and "busts" over the years, illustrating the cyclical relationship between the price of oil and employment. During periods of high oil and gas prices, the field expands exploration and production and hires more workers. The opposite occurs during periods of low prices.

Working Conditions

Working conditions in the field vary significantly by occupation. Roustabout jobs and jobs in other construction and extraction occupations may involve rugged outdoor work in remote areas in all kinds of weather. For these jobs, physical strength and stamina are necessary. This work involves standing for long periods, lifting moderately heavy objects, and climbing and stooping to work with tools that often are oily and dirty. Executives generally work in office settings, as do most administrators and clerical workers. Geologists, engineers, and managers may split their time between the office and the jobsites, particularly while involved in exploration work.

Opportunities for part-time work in this field are rare. In fact, a higher percentage of workers in oil and gas extraction work overtime than in all fields combined. The average nonsupervisory worker in the oil and gas extraction field worked 43.5 hours per week in 2004, compared

with 33.7 hours for all nonsupervisory workers on private nonfarm payrolls.

Oil and gas well drilling and servicing can be hazardous. However, in 2003 the rate of work-related injury and illness in the oil and gas extraction field was 1.8 per 100 full-time workers and 2.7 for workers in support activities for mining, somewhat lower than the 5.0 for the entire private sector. Improvements in drilling technology and oil rig operations, such as remote-controlled drills, have led to fewer injuries.

Drilling rigs operate continuously. On land, drilling crews usually work 6 days in a row, 8 hours a day, and then have a few days off. In offshore operations, workers can work 14 days in a row, 12 hours a day, and then have 14 days off. If the offshore rig is located far from the coast, drilling crew members live on ships anchored nearby or in facilities on the platform itself. Workers on offshore rigs are always evacuated in the event of a storm. Most workers in oil and gas well operations and maintenance or in natural gas processing work 8 hours a day, 5 days a week.

Many oilfield workers are away from home for weeks or months at a time. Exploration field personnel and drilling workers frequently move from place to place as work at a particular field is completed. In contrast, well operation and maintenance workers and natural gas processing workers usually remain in the same location for extended periods.

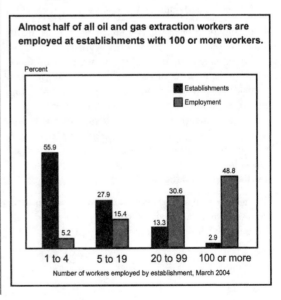

Almost half of all oil and gas extraction workers are employed at establishments with 100 or more workers.

Percent

- ■ Establishments
- ■ Employment

| 1 to 4 | 5 to 19 | 20 to 99 | 100 or more |
Establishments: 55.9 | 27.9 | 13.3 | 2.9
Employment: 5.2 | 15.4 | 30.6 | 48.8

Number of workers employed by establishment, March 2004

Important Characteristics of the Field

Skills: Operation Monitoring; Mathematics; Troubleshooting; Operation and Control; Management of Financial Resources; Equipment Maintenance. **Abilities:** Mathematical Reasoning; Rate Control; Category Flexibility; Number Facility; Problem Sensitivity; Selective Attention. **Work-Related Values:** Supervision, Human Relations; Supervision, Technical; Advancement; Compensation; Company Policies and Practices; Security.

Employment

The oil and gas extraction field employed about 316,000 wage and salary workers in 2004. Of these, only 4 in 10 workers were employed directly by the oil and gas extraction companies. The rest worked as contractors in the support activities for mining sector, which also included workers who extract coal and minerals on a contract basis. Although onshore oil and gas extraction establishments are found in 42 states, almost 3 out of 4 of the field's workers in 2004 were located in just four states—California, Louisiana, Oklahoma, and Texas. While most workers are employed on land, many work at offshore sites. Although they are not included in employment figures for this field, many Americans are employed by oil companies at locations in Africa, the North Sea, the Far East, the Middle East, South America, and countries of the former Soviet Union.

While slightly more than 50 percent of establishments employ fewer than 5 workers, the vast majority of workers are employed in establishments with 20 or more workers (chart 1). As more large domestic oilfields and gas fields are depleted, major oil companies are focusing their exploration and production activity in foreign countries. Consequently, smaller companies with less capital for foreign exploration and production are drilling an increasing share of domestic oil and gas. Technology also has significantly decreased the risk and cost for smaller producers.

Relatively few oil and gas extraction workers are in their teens or early 20s. About 56 percent of the workers in this field are between 35 and 54 years of age.

Table 1. Employment of wage and salary workers in oil and gas extraction by occupation, 2004 and projected change, 2004–2014 (Employment in thousands)

Occupation	Employment, 2004		Percent change, 2004–2014
	Number	Percent	
Total, all occupations	316	100.0	–6.1
Management, business, and financial occupations	38	12.0	–6.3
Top executives	11	3.6	–6.0
Accountants and auditors	7	2.2	–9.0
Professional and related occupations	43	13.6	–5.3
Computer specialists	6	1.8	–2.6
Marine engineers and naval architects	1	0.3	–10.5
Mining and geological engineers, including mining safety engineers	1	0.3	–10.4
Petroleum engineers	9	2.9	–3.6
Drafters, engineering, and mapping technicians	3	0.9	–1.7
Geoscientists, except hydrologists and geographers	6	2.0	–11.1
Geological and petroleum technicians	5	1.6	–5.7
Office and administrative support occupations	34	10.8	–16.2
First-line supervisors/ managers of office and administrative support workers	2	0.7	–14.3
Bookkeeping, accounting, and auditing clerks	7	2.1	–16.6
Executive secretaries and administrative assistants	5	1.6	–12.4
Secretaries, except legal, medical, and executive	6	2.0	–20.5
Office clerks, general	7	2.1	–16.5
Construction and extraction occupations	118	37.4	–1.7

Occupation	Employment, 2004		Percent change, 2004–2014
	Number	Percent	
First-line supervisors/ managers of construction trades and extraction workers	12	3.9	–2.2
Construction equipment operators	4	1.2	–0.4
Operating engineers and other construction equipment operators	4	1.2	–0.4
Derrick operators, oil and gas	14	4.5	–1.1
Rotary drill operators, oil and gas	13	4.2	–1.1
Service unit operators, oil, gas, and mining	15	4.9	–1.8
Earth drillers, except oil and gas	2	0.7	0.0
Explosives workers, ordnance handling experts, and blasters	1	0.2	0.0
Continuous mining machine operators	1	0.1	–2.7
Mine cutting and channeling machine operators	1	0.1	0.0
Roustabouts, oil and gas	28	8.8	–1.9
Helpers—extraction workers	13	4.1	–0.7
Extraction workers, all other	6	1.9	–0.3
Production occupations	28	8.9	–6.6
Gas plant operators	2	0.5	–11.8
Petroleum pump system operators, refinery operators, and gaugers	14	4.4	–8.2
Transportation and material moving occupations	32	10.1	–14.1
Truck drivers, heavy and tractor-trailer	7	2.3	–0.9
Gas compressor and gas pumping station operators	2	0.6	–25.3
Pump operators, except wellhead pumpers	3	1.0	–27.0
Wellhead pumpers	10	3.0	–26.1

Note: May not add to totals due to omission of occupations with small employment

Occupations in the Field

People with many different skills are needed to explore for oil and gas, drill new wells, maintain existing wells, and process natural gas. The largest group, construction and extraction workers, account for about 37 percent of field employment. Professional and related workers account for about 14 percent of field employment, and managerial, business, and financial workers account for about 12 percent. Transportation and material moving workers make up about 10 percent, and production workers about 9 percent (table 1).

A *petroleum geologist* or a *geophysicist*, who is responsible for analyzing and interpreting the information gathered, usually heads exploration operations. Other geological specialists also may be involved in exploration activities, including *paleontologists*, who study fossil remains to locate oil; *mineralogists*, who study physical and chemical properties of mineral and rock samples; *stratigraphers*, who determine the rock layers most likely to contain oil and natural gas; and *photogeologists*, who examine and interpret aerial photographs of land surfaces. Additionally, exploration parties may include *surveyors* and *drafters*, who assist in surveying and mapping activities.

Some geologists and geophysicists work in district offices of oil companies or contract exploration firms, where they prepare and study geological maps and analyze seismic data. These scientists also may analyze samples from test drillings.

Other workers involved in exploration are *geophysical prospectors*. They lead crews consisting of *gravity* and *seismic prospecting observers*, who operate and maintain electronic seismic equipment; *scouts*, who investigate the exploration, drilling, and leasing activities of other companies to identify promising areas to explore and lease; and *lease buyers*, who make business arrangements to obtain the use of the land or mineral rights from its owners.

Petroleum engineers are responsible for planning and supervising the actual drilling operation once a potential drill site has been located. These engineers develop and implement the most efficient recovery method in order to achieve maximum profitable recovery. They also plan and supervise well operation and maintenance. *Drilling superintendents* serve as supervisors of drilling crews, overseeing one or more drilling rigs.

Rotary drilling crews usually consist of four or five workers. *Rotary drillers* supervise the crew and operate machinery that controls drilling speed and pressure. *Rotary-rig engine operators* are in charge of engines that provide the power for drilling and hoisting. Second in charge, *derrick operators* work on small platforms high on rigs to help run pipe in and out of well holes and operate the pumps that circulate mud through the pipe. *Rotary-driller helpers*, also known as *roughnecks*, guide the lower ends of pipe to well openings and connect pipe joints and drill bits.

Though not necessarily part of the drilling crew, *roustabouts*, or general laborers, do general oilfield maintenance and construction work, such as cleaning tanks and building roads.

Pumpers and their helpers operate and maintain motors, pumps, and other surface equipment that forces oil from wells and regulate the flow according to a schedule set up by petroleum engineers and production supervisors. In fields where oil flows under natural pressure and does not require pumping, *switchers* open and close valves to regulate the flow. *Gaugers* measure and record the flow, taking samples to check quality. *Treaters* test the oil for water and sediment and remove these impurities by opening a drain or using special equipment. In most fields, pumping, switching, gauging, and treating operations are automatic.

Other skilled oilfield workers include *oil well cementers*, who mix and pump cement into the space between the casing and well walls to prevent cave-ins; *acidizers*, who pump acid down the well and into the producing formation to increase oil flow; *perforator operators*, who use subsurface "guns" to pierce holes in the casing to make openings for oil to flow into the well bore; *sample-taker operators*, who take samples of soil and rock formations from wells to help geologists determine the presence of oil; and *well pullers*, who remove pipes, pumps, and other subsurface devices from wells for cleaning, repairing, and salvaging.

Many other skilled workers—such as *welders*, *pipefitters*, *electricians*, and *machinists*—also are employed in maintenance operations to install and repair pumps, gauges, pipes, and other equipment.

In addition to the types of workers required for onshore drilling, crews at offshore locations also need radio operators, cooks, ships' officers, sailors, and pilots. These workers make up the support personnel who work on or operate drilling platforms, crewboats, barges, and helicopters.

Most workers involved in gas processing are operators. *Gas treaters* tend automatically controlled treating units that remove water and other impurities from natural gas. *Gas-pumping-station operators* tend compressors that raise the pressure of gas for transmission in pipelines. Both types of workers can be assisted by *gas-compressor operators*.

Training, Other Qualifications, and Advancement

Workers can enter the oil and gas extraction field with a variety of educational backgrounds. The most common entry-level field jobs, such as roustabouts or roughnecks, usually require little or no previous training or experience. Applicants for these routine laborer jobs must be physically fit and able to pass a physical examination. Companies also may administer aptitude tests and screen prospective employees for drug use. Basic skills usually can be learned over a period of days through on-the-job training. However, previous work experience or formal training in petroleum technology that provides knowledge of oilfield operations and familiarity with computers and other automated equipment can be beneficial. In fact, given the increasing complexity of operations and the sophisticated nature of technology used today, employers now demand a higher level of skill and adaptability, including the ability to work with computers and other sophisticated equipment.

Other entry-level positions, such as engineering technician, usually require at least a 2-year associate degree in engineering technology. Professional jobs, such as geologist, geophysicist, or petroleum engineer, require at least a bachelor's degree, but many companies prefer to hire candidates with a master's degree and may require a Ph.D. for those involved in petroleum research. For well operation and maintenance jobs, companies generally prefer applicants who live nearby, have mechanical ability, and possess knowledge of oilfield processes. Because this work offers the advantage of a fixed locale, members of drilling crews or exploration parties who prefer not to travel may transfer to well operation and maintenance jobs. Training is acquired on the job.

Promotion opportunities for some jobs may be limited due to the general decline of the domestic petroleum field. Advancement opportunities for oilfield workers remain best for those with skill and experience. For example, roustabouts may move up to become switchers, gaugers, and pumpers. More experienced roughnecks may advance to derrick operators and, after several years, to drillers. Drillers may advance to tool pushers. There should continue to be some opportunities for entry-level field crew workers to acquire the skills that qualify them for higher-level jobs within the field. Due to the critical nature of the work, offshore crews, even at the entry level, generally are more experienced than land crews. Many companies will not employ someone who has no knowledge of oilfield operations to work on an offshore rig, so workers who have gained experience as part of a land crew might advance to offshore operations.

As workers gain knowledge and experience, U.S. or foreign companies operating in other countries also may hire them. Although this can be a lucrative and exciting experience, it may not be suitable for everyone, because it usually means leaving family and friends and adapting to different customs and living standards.

Experience gained in many oil and gas extraction jobs also has application in other fields. For example, roustabouts can move to construction jobs, while machinery operators and repairers can transfer to other fields with similar machinery. Geologists and engineers may become involved with environmental activities, especially those related to this field.

Outlook

Although worldwide demand for oil and gas is expected to grow, overall U.S. wage and salary employment in the oil and gas extraction field is expected to decline by 6 percent through the year 2014, compared to an employment increase of about 14 percent in all fields combined.

In general, the level of future crude petroleum and natural gas exploration and development and, therefore, employment opportunities in this field remains contingent upon the size of accessible reserves available and the going prices for oil and gas. Stable and favorable prices are needed to allow companies enough revenue to expand exploration and production projects to keep pace with growing global energy demand, particularly by India and China. Rising worldwide demand for oil and gas is likely to cause higher long-term prices and generate the needed incentive to continue exploring and developing oil and gas in this country, at least in the short run. Over the moderate term, fewer reserves of oil and gas in

the U.S. will cause a decline in domestic production unless new oil and gas fields are found and developed.

Environmental concerns, accompanied by strict regulation and limited access to protected federal lands, also continue to have a major impact on this field. Restrictions on drilling in environmentally sensitive areas and other environmental constraints should continue to limit exploration and development, both onshore and offshore. However, changes in policy could expand exploration and drilling for oil and natural gas in currently protected areas, especially in Alaska.

In addition, environmental emissions standards already in place or planned for the future are expected to significantly limit the amount of sulfur and carbon dioxide levels that can be emitted by power plants. Employment in the natural gas exploration and production field normally would grow with the increasing demand for cleaner-burning fuels, such as natural gas. However, recent high natural gas prices are limiting demand and causing some planned future power plants to return to coal as a power source, which could hurt the long-term natural gas outlook.

While some new oil and gas deposits are being discovered in this country, companies increasingly are moving to more lucrative foreign locations. As companies expand into other areas around the globe, the need for employees in the United States is reduced. However, advances in technology have increased the proportion of exploratory wells that yield oil and gas, enhanced offshore exploration and drilling capabilities, and extended the production of existing wells. As a result, more exploration and development ventures are profitable and provide employment opportunities that otherwise would have been lost.

Despite an overall decline in employment in the oil and gas extraction field, job opportunities in most occupations should be good. The need to replace workers who transfer to other fields, retire, or leave the workforce will be the major source of job openings as more workers in this field approach retirement age and others seek more stable employment opportunities in other fields. Employment opportunities will be best for those with previous experience and with technical skills, especially qualified professionals and extraction workers who have significant experience in oilfield operations and who can work with new technology. More workers will be needed who are capable of using new technologies—such as 3-D and 4-D seismic exploration methods, horizontal and

Agriculture and Natural Resources

directional drilling techniques, and deepwater and sub-sea technologies—as employers develop and implement sophisticated new equipment.

Earnings

Average wage and salary earnings in the oil and gas extraction field were significantly higher than the average for all fields. The average hourly earnings of nonsupervisory workers in the oil and gas extraction sector and of workers in support activities for mining were $18.58 and $16.92, respectively, compared with $15.67 for all non-government workers. Due to the working conditions, employees at offshore operations generally earn higher wages than do workers at onshore oilfields. College-educated workers and technical school graduates in professional and technical occupations usually earn the most. Earnings in selected occupations in oil and gas extraction and support services appear in table 2.

Few field workers belong to unions. In fact, only about 5 percent of workers were union members or were covered by union contracts in 2004, compared with about 14 percent of all nongovernment workers.

Table 2. Median hourly earnings of the largest occupations in oil and gas extraction and support activities for mining, May 2004

Occupation	Oil and gas extraction	Support activities for mining	All fields
General and operations managers	$49.93	$37.57	$37.22
Petroleum engineers	47.24	36.68	42.55
First-line supervisors/managers of construction trades and extraction workers	27.44	24.90	24.25
Petroleum pump system operators, refinery operators, and gaugers	23.52	22.12	24.27
Wellhead pumpers	16.73	14.82	16.31
Rotary drill operators, oil and gas	16.17	17.34	17.11
Service unit operators, oil, gas, and mining	15.87	14.58	14.75
Derrick operators, oil and gas	15.26	16.18	16.11
Roustabouts, oil and gas	12.60	11.89	11.94
Helpers—extraction workers	11.58	12.77	12.66

Sources of Additional Information

Information on training and career opportunities for petroleum engineers or geologists is available from

- American Association of Petroleum Geologists, Communications Department, P.O. Box 979, Tulsa, OK 74101. Internet: http://www.aapg.org
- American Geological Institute, 4220 King St., Alexandria, VA 22302. Internet: http://www.agiweb.org
- American Petroleum Institute, 1220 L Street NW, Washington, DC 20005-4070 Internet: http://www.energyprofessions.org
- Society of Petroleum Engineers, P.O. Box 833836, Richardson, TX 75083. Internet: http://www.spe.org

Manufacturing, Construction, and Utilities

Aerospace Product and Parts Manufacturing

- Annual Earnings: $53,270
- Job Growth: 8.2%
- Size of Workforce: 439,130
- Self-Employed: 0.0%
- Part-Time: 1.9%

Significant Points

- Skilled production, professional, and managerial jobs account for the largest share of employment.
- Employment is projected to grow more slowly in this field than in fields generally.

- During slowdowns in aerospace manufacturing, production workers are vulnerable to layoffs, while professional workers enjoy more job stability.

- Earnings are substantially higher, on average, than in most other manufacturing fields.

Nature of the Field

The aerospace field comprises companies producing aircraft, guided missiles, space vehicles, aircraft engines, propulsion units, and related parts. Aircraft overhaul, rebuilding, and conversion also are included.

Firms producing transport aircraft make up the largest segment of the civil (nonmilitary) aircraft portion of the field. Civil transport aircraft are produced for air transportation businesses such as airlines and cargo transportation companies. These aircraft range from small turboprops to wide-body jets and are used to move people and goods all over the world. Another segment of civil aircraft is general aviation aircraft. General aviation aircraft range from the small two-seaters designed for leisure use to corporate jets designed for business transport. Civil helicopters, which make up one of the smallest segments of civil aircraft, are commonly used by police departments, emergency medical services, and businesses such as oil and mining companies that need to transport people to remote worksites.

Aircraft engine manufacturers, not the aircraft manufacturers, produce the engines used in civil and military aircraft. These manufacturers design and build engines according to the aircraft design and performance specifications of the aircraft manufacturers. Aircraft manufacturers may use engines designed by different companies on the same type of aircraft.

Military aircraft and helicopters are purchased by governments to meet national defense needs, such as delivering weapons to military targets and transporting troops and equipment around the globe. Some of these aircraft are specifically designed to deliver or guide a powerful array of ordnance to military targets with tremendous maneuverability and low detectability. Other aircraft, such as unmanned aerial vehicles, are produced to gather defense intelligence such as radio signals or to monitor movement on the ground.

Firms producing guided missiles and missile propulsion units sell primarily to military and government organizations. Although missiles are viewed predominantly as offensive weapons, improved guidance systems have led to their increased use as defensive systems. This part of the field also produces space vehicles and the rockets for launching them into space. Consumers of spacecraft include the National Aeronautics and Space Administration (NASA), the U.S. Department of Defense (DOD), telecommunications companies, television networks, and news organizations. Firms producing space satellites are discussed with the computer and electronic product manufacturing field in this book because satellites are primarily electronic products.

In 2004, about 2,800 establishments made up the aerospace field. In the aerospace parts field, most establishments were subcontractors that manufacture parts and employ fewer than 100 workers. Nevertheless, 63 percent of the jobs in aerospace manufacturing were in large establishments that employed 1,000 or more workers (chart 1).

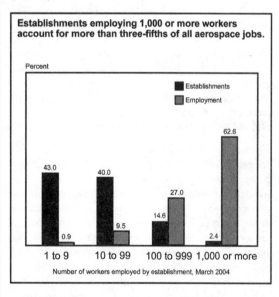

Establishments employing 1,000 or more workers account for more than three-fifths of all aerospace jobs.

Percent

Number of workers employed by establishment, March 2004

The federal government traditionally has been the aerospace field's biggest customer. The vast majority of government contracts to purchase aerospace equipment are awarded by DOD. NASA also is a major purchaser of the field's products and services, mainly for space vehicles and launch services.

The aerospace field is dominated by a few large firms that contract to produce aircraft with government and

Manufacturing, Construction, and Utilities

private businesses, usually airline and cargo transportation companies. These large firms, in turn, subcontract with smaller firms to produce specific systems and parts for their vehicles. Government purchases are largely related to defense. Typically, DOD announces its need for military aircraft or missile systems, specifying a multitude of requirements. Large firms specializing in defense products subsequently submit bids, detailing proposed technical solutions and designs, along with cost estimates, hoping to win the contract. Firms also may research and develop materials, electronics, and components relating to their bid, often at their own expense, to improve their chances of winning the contract. Following a negotiation phase, a manufacturer is selected and a prototype is developed and built and then tested and evaluated. If approved by DOD, the craft or system enters production. This process usually takes many years.

Commercial airlines and private businesses typically identify their needs for a particular model of new aircraft based on a number of factors, including the routes they fly. After specifying requirements such as range, size, cargo capacity, type of engine, and seating arrangements, the airlines invite manufacturers of civil aircraft and aircraft engines to submit bids. Selection ultimately is based on a manufacturer's ability to deliver reliable aircraft that best fit the purchaser's stated market needs at the lowest cost and at favorable financing terms.

The way in which commercial and military aircraft are designed, developed, and produced continues to undergo significant change in response to the need to cut costs and deliver products faster. Firms producing commercial aircraft have reduced development time drastically through computer-aided design (CAD), which allows firms to design and test an entire aircraft, including the individual parts, by computer; the drawings of these parts can be sent electronically to subcontractors who use them to program their machinery. Increasingly, firms bring together teams composed of customers, engineers, and production workers to pool ideas and make decisions concerning the aircraft at every phase of product development. Additionally, the military has changed its design philosophy, using commercially available off-the-shelf technology when appropriate, rather than developing new customized components.

Working Conditions

The average aerospace products and parts production employee worked 42.6 hours a week in 2004, compared with 40.8 hours a week for all manufacturing workers and 33.7 hours a week for workers in all fields. Working conditions in aerospace manufacturing facilities vary. Many new plants, in contrast to older facilities, are spacious, well lit, and modern. Specific work environments usually depend on occupation and the age of the production line. Engineers, scientists, and technicians frequently work in office settings or laboratories, although production engineers may spend much of their time with production workers on the factory floor. Production workers, such as welders and other assemblers, may have to cope with high noise levels. Oil, grease, and grime often are present, and some workers may face exposure to volatile organic compounds found in solvents, paints, and coatings. Heavy lifting is required for many production jobs.

The rate of work-related injury and illness in the aerospace products and parts field was 4.7 per 100 full-time workers in 2003. In comparison, cases of work-related injury and illness throughout the private sector averaged 5.0 per 100 workers.

Important Characteristics of the Field

Skills: Quality Control Analysis; Installation; Troubleshooting; Science; Systems Analysis; Technology Design. **Abilities:** Visualization; Mathematical Reasoning; Problem Sensitivity; Information Ordering; Inductive Reasoning; Explosive Strength. **Work-Related Values:** Ability Utilization; Responsibility; Social Status; Compensation; Creativity; Recognition.

Employment

Aerospace manufacturing provided 444,000 wage and salary jobs in 2004. The largest numbers of aerospace jobs were in Washington and California, although many also were located in Kansas, Texas, Connecticut, and Arizona.

Employment data in this description do not include aerospace R&D-related workers who work in separate establishments. Under the North American Field Classification System (NAICS), workers in research and development establishments that are not part of a manufacturing facility are included in a separate field—research and development in the physical, engineering, and life sciences. This field is covered in the description of Scientific Research and Development Services elsewhere in Part II. Given the importance of R&D work to the aerospace manufacturing field, however, aerospace-related R&D occupations and issues are discussed in the following sections, even though much of their employment is not included in the employment data in this description.

Occupations in the Field

The design and manufacture of the technologically sophisticated products of the aerospace field require the input and skills of various workers. Skilled production, professional and related, and managerial jobs make up the bulk of employment. Those employed in managerial and administrative support occupations manage the design process and factory operations, coordinate the hundreds of thousands of parts that are assembled into an aircraft, and ensure compliance with federal record-keeping regulations. The aerospace field has a larger proportion of workers with education beyond high school than the average for all fields.

The aerospace field is on the leading edge of technology, constantly striving to create new products and improve existing ones. The field invests a great deal of time and money in research and development of aerospace products, and much of the work is performed by professional and related workers, who made up 34 percent of the aerospace workforce in 2004 (table 1). In addition, as mentioned in the previous section, many more aerospace-related professionals work in the scientific research and development services field. A bachelor's degree in a specialized field, such as engineering, is required for many of these jobs; a master's or doctoral degree is preferred for a few. For many technician occupations, 2 years of technical training after high school are favored.

Professionals and technicians develop new designs and make improvements to existing designs. *Aerospace engineers* are integral members of the teams that research, design, test, and produce aerospace vehicles. Some specialize in areas such as structural design, guidance, navigation and control, and instrumentation and communication. Electrical and electronics, industrial, and mechanical engineers also contribute to the research

for and development and production of aerospace products. For example, *mechanical engineers* help design mechanical components and develop the specific tools and machines needed to produce aircraft, missile, and space vehicle parts, or they may design jet and rocket engines. *Engineering technicians* assist engineers, both in the research and development laboratory and on the manufacturing floor. They may help build prototype versions of newly designed products, run tests and experiments, and perform a variety of other technical tasks. One of the earliest users of computer-aided design, the aerospace field continues to use the latest computer technology. *Computer scientists and systems analysts, database administrators, computer software engineers, computer programmers, computer support specialists;* and *network and computer systems administrators* are responsible for the design, testing, evaluation, and setup of computer systems that are used throughout the field for design and manufacturing purposes.

Management, business, and financial occupations accounted for 18 percent of field employment in 2004. Many advance to these jobs from professional occupations. Many managers in the aerospace field have a technical or engineering background and supervise teams of engineers in activities such as testing and research and development. *Industrial production managers* oversee all workers and lower-level managers in a factory. They also coordinate all activities related to production. In addition to technical and production managers, *financial managers; purchasing managers, buyers, and purchasing agents; cost estimators;* and *accountants and auditors* are needed to negotiate with customers and subcontractors and to track costs.

Of all aerospace workers, 37 percent are employed in production; installation, maintenance, and repair; and transportation and material moving occupations. Many of these jobs are not specific to aerospace and can be found in other manufacturing fields. Many production jobs are open to persons with only a high school education; however, special vocational training after high school is preferred for some of the more highly skilled jobs.

Aircraft structure, surfaces, rigging, and systems assemblers usually specialize in one assembly task; hundreds of different assemblers may work at various times on producing a single aircraft. Assemblers may put together parts of airplanes, such as wings or landing gear, or install parts and equipment into the airplane itself. Those involved in assembling aircraft or systems must be skilled in reading and interpreting engineering specifications and instructions.

Machinists make parts that are needed in numbers too small to mass-produce. Machinists follow blueprints and specifications and are highly skilled with machine tools and metalworking. *Tool and die makers* are responsible for constructing precision tools and metal forms, called dies, which are used to shape metal. Increasingly, as individual components are designed electronically, these highly skilled workers must be able to read electronic blueprints and set up and operate computer-controlled machines.

Inspectors, testers, sorters, samplers, and weighers perform numerous quality-control and safety checks on aerospace parts throughout the production cycle. Their work is vital to ensure the safety of the aircraft.

The remaining jobs in the field are in office and administrative support, service, and sales occupations. Most of these jobs can be entered without education beyond high school. Workers in office and administrative support occupations help coordinate the flow of materials to the worksite, draw up orders for supplies, keep records, and help with all of the other paperwork associated with keeping a business functioning. Those in service occupations are employed mostly as guards and janitors and other cleaning and maintenance workers. Sales workers are mostly wholesale and manufacturing sales representatives and sales workers' supervisors.

Table 1. Employment of wage and salary workers in aerospace manufacturing by occupation, 2004 and projected change, 2004–2014 (Employment in thousands)

Occupation	Employment, 2004 Number	Percent	Percent change, 2004–2014
Total, all occupations	444	100.0	8.2
Management, business, and financial occupations	78	17.6	9.6
Industrial production managers	5	1.1	7.8
Engineering managers	9	2.0	9.0
Purchasing agents, except wholesale, retail, and farm products	9	2.0	7.8
Management analysts	10	2.3	7.8
Business operation specialists, all other	9	2.0	18.6
Accountants and auditors	4	1.0	7.8
Professional and related occupations	150	33.8	11.2
Computer software engineers	13	2.9	29.1
Computer systems analysts	6	1.3	18.6
Aerospace engineers	45	10.2	5.6
Industrial engineers	12	2.7	19.9
Mechanical engineers	13	3.0	9.0
Engineers, all other	7	1.6	9.1
Drafters, engineering, and mapping technicians	23	5.3	8.5
Aerospace engineering and operations technicians	5	1.2	7.8
Engineering technicians, except drafters, all other	7	1.6	9.0
Sales and related occupations	5	1.2	8.6
Office and administrative support occupations	36	8.0	–3.0
Material recording, scheduling, dispatching, and distributing occupations	14	3.1	–1.9
Secretaries and administrative assistants	7	1.6	–0.3
Office clerks, general	6	1.3	–4.0
Installation, maintenance, and repair occupations	35	8.0	19.7
Avionics technicians	5	1.0	20.8
Aircraft mechanics and service technicians	15	3.5	30.9
Maintenance and repair workers, general	5	1.1	7.8

Occupation	Employment, 2004		Percent change, 2004–2014
	Number	Percent	
Production occupations	121	27.2	4.1
First-line supervisors/ managers of production and operating workers	9	2.0	7.8
Aircraft structure, surfaces, rigging, and systems assemblers	16	3.6	7.8
Team assemblers	8	1.8	7.8
Computer-controlled machine tool operators, metal and plastic	5	1.2	7.8
Machine tool cutting setters, operators, and tenders, metal and plastic	11	2.5	–4.4
Machinists	16	3.6	7.8
Miscellaneous metalworkers and plastic workers	5	1.2	–5.9
Inspectors, testers, sorters, samplers, and weighers	14	3.1	–1.9

Note: May not add to totals due to omission of occupations with small employment

Training, Other Qualifications, and Advancement

Because employers need well-informed, knowledgeable employees who can keep up with the rapid technological advancements in aerospace manufacturing, the field provides substantial support for the education and training of its workers. Firms provide onsite job-related training to upgrade the skills of technicians, production workers, and engineers. Classes teaching computer skills and blue-print reading are common. Some firms reimburse employees for educational expenses at colleges and universities, emphasizing 4-year degrees and postgraduate studies.

Professionals, such as engineers and scientists, require a bachelor's degree in a specialized field. For some jobs, particularly in research and development, a master's or doctoral degree may be preferred.

Production workers may enter the aerospace field with minimal skills. Mechanical aptitude and good hand-eye coordination usually are necessary. A high school diploma or equivalent is required, and some vocational training in electronics or mechanics also is favored.

Unskilled production workers typically start by being shown how to perform a simple assembly task. Through experience, on-the-job instruction provided by other workers, and brief formal training sessions, they expand their skills. Their pay increases as they advance into more highly skilled or responsible jobs. For example, machinists may take additional training to become numerical tool and process control programmers or tool and die makers. Inspectors usually are promoted from assembly, machine operation, and mechanical occupations.

Because of the reliance on computers and computer-operated equipment, classes in computer skills are common. With training, production workers may be able to advance to supervisory or technician jobs.

To enter some of the more highly skilled production occupations, workers must go through a formal apprenticeship. Machinists and electricians complete apprenticeships that can last as long as 4 years. Apprenticeships usually include classroom instruction and shop training.

Entry-level positions for technicians usually require a degree from a technical school or junior college. Companies sometimes retrain technicians to upgrade their skills or to teach different specialties. They are taught traditional as well as new production technology skills, such as computer-aided design and manufacturing and statistical process control methods.

Outlook

Wage and salary employment in the aerospace product and parts manufacturing field is expected to grow by 8 percent over the 2004–2014 period, slower than the 14-percent growth projected for all fields combined. Employment in the aerospace field has declined in recent years as a result of a drastic reduction in commercial transport aircraft orders, but a modest increase in orders is expected over the projection period. The decline in orders was caused by the reduction in air travel that resulted from the terrorist attacks on the United States and severe financial problems that many of the nation's airlines have experienced. However, an increase in air traffic and the improving financial health of the nation's airlines are beginning to reverse the trend.

Manufacturing, Construction, and Utilities

The outlook for the military aircraft and missiles portion of the field is better. Concern for the nation's security has increased the need for military aircraft and military aerospace equipment. Although new employment opportunities in the defense-related sector of the aerospace field may not reach levels previously attained during the Cold War, employment in this sector is expected to rise.

Because of past reductions in defense expenditures and competition in the commercial aircraft sector, there have been and may continue to be mergers in the field, resulting in layoffs. Even though the number of large firms performing final assembly of aircraft has been reduced, hundreds of smaller manufacturers and subcontractors will remain in this field.

In addition to some growth in employment opportunities for professional workers in the field, there should be job openings arising from replacement needs, especially for aerospace engineers. Many engineers who entered the field in the 1960s are approaching retirement. Among those in the aerospace manufacturing field, professionals typically enjoy more job stability than do other workers. During slowdowns in production, companies prefer to keep technical teams intact to continue research and development activities in anticipation of new business. Production workers, on the other hand, are particularly vulnerable to layoffs during downturns in the economy, when aircraft orders decline.

Earnings

Production workers in the aerospace field earn higher pay than the average for all fields. Weekly earnings for production workers averaged $1,019 in aerospace product parts manufacturing in 2004, compared with $659 in all manufacturing and $529 in all nongovernment settings. Above-average earnings reflect, in part, the high levels of skill required by the field and the need to motivate workers to concentrate on maintaining high quality standards in their work. Nonproduction workers, such as engineering managers, engineers, and computer specialists, generally command higher pay because of their advanced education and training (table 2).

Table 2. Median hourly earnings of the largest occupations in aerospace product and parts manufacturing, May 2004

Occupation	Aerospace product and parts manufacturing	All fields
Engineering managers	$49.79	$46.94
Aerospace engineers	36.43	38.03
Mechanical engineers	33.84	31.88
Industrial engineers	31.85	31.26
Management analysts	30.78	30.51
First-line supervisors/ managers of production and operating workers	27.78	21.51
Aircraft mechanics and service technicians	20.60	21.77
Inspectors, testers, sorters, samplers, and weighers	18.58	13.66
Aircraft structure, surfaces, rigging, and systems assemblers	18.29	17.79
Machinists	17.78	16.33

Sources of Additional Information

For additional information about the aerospace product and parts manufacturing field, contact

- Aerospace Industries Association, 1000 Wilson Blvd., Suite 1700, Arlington, VA 22209. Internet: http://www.aia-aerospace.org

- American Institute of Aeronautics and Astronautics, 1801 Alexander Bell Dr., Suite 500, Reston, VA 20191. Internet: http://www.aiaa.org

- Federal Aviation Administration, 800 Independence Ave. SW, Room 810, Washington, DC 20591. Internet: http://www.faa.gov/education

Chemical Manufacturing, Except Drugs

- ⊚ Annual Earnings: $38,869
- ⊚ Job Growth: −14.4%
- ⊚ Size of Workforce: 593,550
- ⊚ Self-Employed: 0.7%
- ⊚ Part-Time: 3.8%

Significant Points

- Employment is projected to decline.
- Workers involved in production and in installation, maintenance, and repair hold over half of all jobs.
- Earnings are higher than average.

Nature of the Field

Vital to fields such as construction, motor vehicles, paper, electronics, transportation, agriculture, and pharmaceuticals, chemicals are an essential component of manufacturing. Although some chemical manufacturers produce and sell consumer products such as soap, bleach, and cosmetics, most chemical products are used as intermediate products for other goods.

Chemical manufacturing is divided into seven segments, six of which are covered here: basic chemicals; synthetic materials, including resin, synthetic rubber, and artificial and synthetic fibers and filaments; agricultural chemicals, including pesticides, fertilizer, and other agricultural chemicals; paint, coating, and adhesives; cleaning preparations, including soap, cleaning compounds, and toilet preparations; and other chemical products. The seventh segment, pharmaceutical and medicine manufacturing, is described elsewhere in Part II.

The basic chemicals segment produces various petrochemicals, gases, dyes, and pigments. Petrochemicals contain carbon and hydrogen and are made primarily from petroleum and natural gas. The production of both organic and inorganic chemicals occurs in this segment. Organic chemicals are used to make a wide range of products, such as dyes, plastics, and pharmaceutical products; however, the majority of these chemicals are used in the production of other chemicals. Industrial inorganic chemicals usually are made from salts, metal compounds, other minerals, and the atmosphere. In addition to producing solid and liquid chemicals, firms involved in inorganic chemical manufacturing produce industrial gases such as oxygen, nitrogen, and helium. Many inorganic chemicals serve as processing ingredients in the manufacture of chemicals, but do not appear in the final products because they are used as catalysts—chemicals that speed up or otherwise aid a reaction.

The synthetic materials segment produces a wide variety of finished products as well as raw materials, including common plastic materials such as polyethylene, polypropylene, polyvinyl chloride (PVC), and polystyrene. Among products into which these plastics can be made are loudspeakers, toys, PVC pipes, and beverage bottles. Motor vehicle manufacturers are particularly large users of such products. Plastic materials used for mixing and blending resins on a custom basis also are produced in this field segment.

The agricultural chemical segment, which employs the fewest workers in the chemical field, supplies farmers and home gardeners with fertilizers, herbicides, pesticides, and other agricultural chemicals. The segment also includes companies involved in the formulation and preparation of agricultural and household pest control chemicals.

The paint, coating, and adhesive products segment includes firms making paints, varnishes, putties, paint removers, sealers, adhesives, glues, and caulking. The construction and furniture fields are large customers of this segment. Other customers range from individuals refurbishing their homes to businesses needing anticorrosive paints that can withstand high temperatures.

The cleaning preparations segment is the only segment in which much of the production is geared directly toward consumers. The segment includes firms making soaps, detergents, and cleaning preparations. Cosmetics and toiletries, including perfume, lotion, and toothpaste, also are produced in this segment. Households and businesses use these products in many ways, cleaning everything from babies to bridges.

The other chemical products segment includes manufacturers of explosives, printing ink, film, toners, matches, and other miscellaneous chemicals. These products are used by consumers or in the manufacture of other products.

Chemicals generally are classified into two groups: commodity chemicals and specialty chemicals. Commodity chemical manufacturers produce large quantities of basic and relatively inexpensive compounds in large plants, often built specifically to make one chemical. Most of these basic chemicals are utilized to make more highly refined chemicals used in the production of everyday consumer goods by other fields. Specialty chemical manufacturers produce smaller quantities of more expensive chemicals that are used less frequently. Specialty chemical manufacturers often supply larger chemical companies on a contract basis. Many traditional commodity chemical manufacturers are divided into two separate entities, one focused on commodities and the other on specialty chemicals.

The diversity of products produced by the chemical field also is reflected in its component establishments. For example, firms producing synthetic materials operated relatively large plants in 2004. The segment had 10 percent of reporting establishments in the chemical manufacturing field, yet had 18 percent of all jobs in the field. By contrast, manufacturers of paints, coatings, and adhesive products had a greater number of establishments, each employing a much smaller number of workers. This segment made up 13 percent of the establishments in the chemical field, yet employed only 11 percent of all workers.

The chemical field segments vary in the degree to which their workers are involved in production activities, administration and management, and research and development. Fields that make products such as cosmetics or paints that are ready for sale to the final consumer employ more administrative and marketing personnel. Fields that market their products mostly to industrial customers generally employ a greater proportion of precision production workers and a lower proportion of unskilled labor.

Chemical firms are concentrated in areas that are abundant with other manufacturing businesses, such as the Great Lakes region, near the automotive field, or the West Coast, near the electronics field. Chemical plants also are located near the petroleum and natural-gas production centers along the Gulf Coast in Texas and Louisiana. Because chemical production processes often use water and chemicals are primarily exported by ship all over the world, major industrial ports are another common location of chemical plants. California, Illinois, New Jersey, New York, Ohio, Pennsylvania, South Carolina, Tennessee, and Texas had about 50 percent of the establishments in the field in 2004.

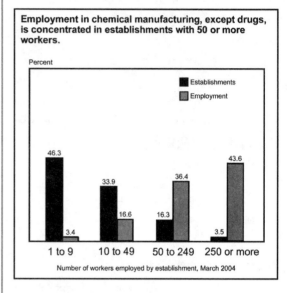

Employment in chemical manufacturing, except drugs, is concentrated in establishments with 50 or more workers.

Percent

- Establishments
- Employment

	1 to 9	10 to 49	50 to 249	250 or more
Establishments	46.3	33.9	16.3	3.5
Employment	3.4	16.6	36.4	43.6

Number of workers employed by establishment, March 2004

Working Conditions

Manufacturing chemicals usually is a continuous process; this means that, once a process has begun, it cannot be stopped when it is time for workers to go home. Split, weekend, and night shifts are common, and workers on such schedules usually are compensated with higher rates of pay. As a result, the average workweek in the chemical field was 42.8 hours in 2004, 2.8 hours longer than the average for nondurable-manufacturing fields and 9.1 hours longer than the average for all nongovernment fields. The field employs relatively few part-time workers.

Most jobs in chemical manufacturing are in large establishments. The largest 20 percent of establishments, those that employed 50 or more workers in 2004, had 80 percent of the field's jobs (chart 1). The plants usually are clean, although the continually running machines sometimes are loud and the interior of many plants can be hot. Hardhats and safety goggles are mandatory and worn throughout the plant.

Hazards in the chemical field can be substantial, but they generally are avoided through strict safety procedures. Workers are required to have protective gear and extensive knowledge of the dangers associated with the chemicals being handled. Body suits with breathing devices designed to filter out any harmful fumes are mandatory for work in dangerous environments.

In spite of the hazards associated with working with chemicals, extensive worker training in handling hazardous chemicals and chemical company safety measures have resulted in injury and illness rates for some segments of the chemical field that are much lower than the average for the manufacturing sector. The chemical field (including pharmaceuticals) reported just 3.4 cases of work-related injury or illness per 100 workers, compared with an average of 6.8 cases for all manufacturing fields in 2003.

Important Characteristics of the Field

Skills: Operation Monitoring; Operation and Control; Science; Quality Control Analysis; Equipment Maintenance; Troubleshooting. **Abilities:** Reaction Time; Control Precision; Response Orientation; Information Ordering; Rate Control; Selective Attention. **Work-Related Values:** Supervision, Technical; Moral Values; Advancement; Company Policies and Practices; Supervision, Human Relations; Activity.

Employment

The chemical and allied products field employed about 596,000 wage and salary workers in 2004, about 4 percent of the total employed in manufacturing. Most segments of the field had substantial numbers of jobs, as shown in table 1.

Table 1. Distribution of wage and salary employment in chemical manufacturing, except pharmaceutical and medicine manufacturing, by detailed field, 2004 (Employment in thousands)

Field	Employment	Percent
Total, all fields	596.1	100.0
Basic chemical manufacturing	156.1	25.9
Soap, cleaning compound, and toilet preparation manufacturing	114.4	19.0
Resin, synthetic rubber, and artificial synthetic fibers and filaments manufacturing	108.8	18.0
Paint, coating, and adhesive manufacturing	68.2	11.3
Pesticide, fertilizer, and other agricultural chemical manufacturing	41.1	6.8
Other chemical product and preparation manufacturing	107.5	19.0

Under the North American Field Classification System (NAICS), workers in research and development (R&D) establishments that are not part of a manufacturing facility are included in a separate field: research and development in the physical, engineering, and life sciences. However, due to the importance of R&D work to the chemical manufacturing field, chemical-related R&D workers are discussed in this description even though a large proportion of those workers is not included in the employment data.

Occupations in the Field

About 52 percent of those employed in the field work in production and in installation, maintenance, and repair occupations. Another 9 percent worked in transportation and material moving occupations. Approximately 21 percent worked in management, business, and financial occupations and in office and administrative support occupations, and about 12.5 percent worked in professional and related occupations (table 2).

Production. Workers in production occupations operate and fix plant machinery, transport raw materials, and monitor the production process. Improvements in technology gradually are increasing the level of plant automation, reducing the number of jobs in production occupations. Although high school graduates qualify for most entry-level production jobs, advancement into better-paying jobs requiring higher skills or more responsibility usually is possible only with on-the-job training and work experience or through additional vocational training at a 2-year technical college.

Manufacturing, Construction, and Utilities

Chemical plant and system operators monitor the entire production process. From chemical ingredient ratios to chemical reaction rates, the operator is responsible for the efficient operation of the chemical plant. Chemical plant operators generally advance to these positions after having acquired extensive experience and technical training in chemical production processes. Experienced operators sometimes advance to senior supervisory positions.

Table 2. Employment of wage and salary workers in chemical manufacturing, except drugs, by occupation, 2004 and projected change, 2004–2014 (Employment in thousands)

Occupation	Employment, 2004 Number	Percent	Percent change, 2004–2014
Total, all occupations	596	100.0	–14.4
Management, business, and financial occupations	58	9.7	–11.8
Top executives	13	2.1	–12.7
Industrial production managers	8	1.3	–12.4
Professional and related occupations	74	12.5	–13.0
Chemical engineers	7	1.2	–10.6
Industrial engineers, including health and safety	7	1.1	–5.8
Chemists	13	2.2	–15.7
Materials scientists	1	0.1	–16.8
Chemical technicians	17	2.9	–16.7
Sales and related occupations	20	3.3	–9.7
Sales representatives, wholesale and manufacturing	16	2.7	–9.3
Office and administrative support occupations	67	11.2	–19.2
Bookkeeping, accounting, and auditing clerks	7	1.2	–17.6
Customer service representatives	7	1.2	–8.6
Production, planning, and expediting clerks	6	1.0	–10.8
Shipping, receiving, and traffic clerks	10	1.7	–17.6
Secretaries and administrative assistants	12	1.9	–21.1
Office clerks, general	6	1.0	–21.3
Installation, maintenance, and repair occupations	50	8.4	–15.1
Electrical and electronics repairers, commercial and industrial equipment	5	0.9	–11.8
Industrial machinery mechanics	11	1.9	–16.0
Maintenance and repair workers, general	20	3.4	–14.5
Production occupations	260	43.6	–14.7
First-line supervisors/ managers of production and operating workers	24	4.1	–13.7
Team assemblers	19	3.2	–4.0
Molding, coremaking, and casting machine setters, operators, and tenders, metal and plastic	6	0.9	–12.7
Extruding and forming machine setters, operators, and tenders, synthetic and glass fibers	4	0.7	–31.4
Chemical plant and system operators	51	8.5	–22.0
Chemical equipment operators and tenders	25	4.2	–19.8
Separating, filtering, clarifying, precipitating, and still machine setters, operators, and tenders	4	0.7	–15.3
Mixing and blending machine setters, operators, and tenders	36	6.0	–6.6
Inspectors, testers, sorters, samplers, and weighers	12	2.1	–14.4
Packaging and filling machine operators and tenders	23	3.9	–12.0
Helpers—production workers	9	1.5	–9.0

Occupation	Employment, 2004		Percent change, 2004–2014
	Number	Percent	
Transportation and material moving occupations	56	9.4	–12.6
Truck drivers, heavy and tractor-trailer	6	1.0	–18.6
Laborers and freight, stock, and material movers, hand	13	2.2	–16.3
Packers and packagers, hand	12	2.0	–1.8

Note: May not add to totals due to omission of occupations with small employment

Industrial machinery mechanics and *machinery maintenance workers* repair equipment, install machines, or practice preventive maintenance in the plant. Workers advance to these jobs through apprenticeships, through formal vocational training, or by completing in-house training courses.

Inspectors, testers, sorters, samplers, and weighers ensure that the production process runs efficiently and that products meet quality standards. They refer problems to plant operators or managers.

Packaging and filling machine operators and tenders wrap products and fill boxes to prepare the final product for shipment or sale to the wholesaler or consumer. More than half of these jobs are in the soap and cosmetics field, due to the amount of packaging needed for this field's consumer products.

Transportation and material moving workers use industrial trucks to move materials around the plant or to deliver finished products to customers. For these jobs, employers seek experienced workers with knowledge of chemical hazards, safety procedures, and regulations governing the transport of hazardous chemicals. Learning to operate an industrial truck or tractor can be effected with on-the-job training, but previous experience driving a truck and a commercial driver's license generally are required to operate a tractor-trailer carrying chemicals. Some jobs in transportation and material movement are open to workers without experience. Workers in these jobs move raw materials and finished products through the chemical plant and assist motor vehicle operators in loading and unloading raw materials and chemicals.

They learn safe ways to handle chemicals on the job and develop skills that enable them to advance to other occupations.

Research and development. Most workers in research and development have at least a college degree, and many have advanced degrees.

Chemists and materials scientists carry out research over a wide range of activities, including analyzing materials; preparing new materials or modifying existing ones; studying process chemistry pathways for new or existing products; and formulating cosmetics, household care products, or paints and coatings. They also try to develop new chemicals for specific applications and new applications for existing chemicals. The most senior chemists sometimes advance to management positions. Although chemical companies hire some chemists with bachelor's degrees, a master's or doctoral degree is becoming more important for chemist jobs.

Chemical engineers design equipment and develop processes for manufacturing chemicals on a large scale. They conduct experiments to learn how processes behave and to discover new chemical products and processes. A bachelor's degree is essential for all of these jobs, and a master's degree may be preferred or required for some.

Engineering and *science technicians* assist chemists and engineers in research activities and may conduct some research independently. Those with bachelor's degrees in chemistry or graduates of 2-year technical institutes usually fill these positions. Some graduates of engineering programs start as technicians until an opportunity to advance into an engineering position arises.

Administration and management. Most managers need a 4-year college degree in addition to experience in the field. As in other highly technical fields, top managerial positions often are held by those with substantial technical experience. Employment in administrative support and managerial occupations is expected to decline as companies merge and consolidate operations.

Engineering managers conduct cost estimations, perform plant design feasibility studies, and coordinate daily operations. These jobs require a college degree in a technical discipline, such as chemistry or chemical engineering, as well as experience in the field. Some employees advance from research and development positions to management positions.

Manufacturing, Construction, and Utilities

Advertising, marketing, promotions, public relations, and *sales managers* promote sales of chemical products by informing customers of company products and services. A bachelor's degree in marketing, chemistry, or chemical engineering usually is required for these jobs.

Training, Other Qualifications, and Advancement

Despite recent reductions in the workforce, the chemical field offers career opportunities for persons with varying levels of experience and education. Training and advancement differ for the three major categories of occupations.

Production workers may start as laborers or in other unskilled jobs and, with experience and training, advance into better-paying positions that require greater skills or have greater responsibility. Substantial advancement is possible even within a single occupation. For example, chemical plant operators may move up through several levels of responsibility until they reach the highest-paying operator job. Advancement in production occupations usually requires mastery of advanced skills, generally acquired by a combination of on-the-job training and formal training provided by the employer. Some workers advance into supervisory positions.

Most jobs in research and development require substantial technical education after high school, but opportunities exist for persons with degrees ranging from a 2-year associate's degree up to a doctorate. Developing a new product or being awarded a patent brings an increase in pay and prestige but, after a point, advancement may require moving from research and development into management. Researchers usually are familiar with company objectives and production methods, which, combined with college education, equips them with many of the tools necessary for management positions.

Managerial jobs usually require a 4-year college degree, though some may require only a 2-year technical degree. Managers can advance into higher-level jobs without additional formal training outside the workplace, although competition is keen. In general, advancement into the highest management ranks depends on one's experience and proven ability to handle responsibility in several functional areas. Among larger, multinational firms, international experience is important for career advancement. Also, field restructuring has left fewer lay-ers of management, intensifying competition for promotions.

Outlook

Although output is expected to grow, wage and salary employment in the chemical manufacturing field, excluding pharmaceuticals and medicine, is projected to decline by 14 percent over the 2004–2014 period, compared with 14-percent growth projected for the entire economy. The expected decline in employment can be attributed to trends affecting the U.S. and global economies. A number of factors will influence chemical field employment, such as more efficient production processes, increased plant automation, the state of the national and world economy, company mergers and consolidation, increased foreign competition, the shifting of production activities to foreign countries, and environmental health and safety concerns and legislation. Another trend in the chemical field is the rising demand for specialty chemicals. Chemical companies are finding that, in order to remain competitive, they must differentiate their products and produce specialty chemicals, such as advanced polymers and plastics designed for customer-specific uses—for example, a durable body panel on an automobile.

Improvements in production technology have reduced the need for workers in production; installation, maintenance, and repair; and material moving occupations, which account for large proportions of jobs in the chemical field. Both the application of computerized controls in standard production and the growing manufacture of specialty chemicals requiring precise, computer-controlled production methods will reduce the need for workers to monitor or directly operate equipment. Although production facilities will be easier to run with the increased use of computers, the new production methods will require workers with a better understanding of the systems.

Foreign competition has been intensifying in most fields, and the chemical field is no exception. Globalization—the increase in international trade and rapidly expanding foreign production capabilities—should intensify competition. Pressure to reduce costs and streamline production will result in mergers and consolidations of companies both within the United States and abroad. Mergers and consolidations are allowing chemical companies to increase profits by eliminating duplicate tasks and departments and shifting operations to locations in which costs are lowest. U.S. companies are expected to move some production activities to developing countries—in East Asia and Latin America, for example—to take advantage of rapidly expanding markets.

The chemical field invests billions of dollars yearly in technology to reduce pollution and clean up waste sites. Concerns about waste remediation and hazardous chemicals and their effects on the environment may spur producers to create chemicals with fewer or less-dangerous byproducts or with byproducts that can be recycled or disposed of cleanly.

The factors influencing employment in the chemical manufacturing field will affect different segments of the field to varying degrees. Only one segment—cleaning preparations, including soap, cleaning compounds, and toilet preparations—is projected to grow, with an increase of about 5,600 jobs. Three segments—other chemical products, basic chemical manufacturing, and synthetic materials—are projected to lose jobs: about 11,000, 46,000, and 23,000, respectively.

Earnings

Earnings in the chemical field are higher than average. Weekly earnings for all production workers in chemical manufacturing averaged $820 in May 2004, compared with $659 in all manufacturing fields and $529 throughout nongovernment fields. The higher earnings were due, in part, to the chemical field's practice of assigning more overtime and weekend work, which commands higher hourly rates.

Wages of workers in the chemical field vary according to occupation, the specific field segment, and the size of the production plant. Earnings by major occupation group are shown in table 3.

Table 3. Median hourly earnings of the largest occupations in chemical manufacturing, May 2004

Occupation	Chemical manufacturing	All fields
Chemists	$27.91	$26.95
First-line supervisors/managers of production and operating workers	25.41	21.51

Occupation	Chemical manufacturing	All fields
Chemical plant and system operators	21.47	21.55
Maintenance and repair workers, general	19.75	14.77
Chemical technicians	19.75	18.35
Chemical equipment operators and tenders	19.16	18.69
Inspectors, testers, sorters, samplers, and weighers	14.98	13.66
Mixing and blending machine setters, operators, and tenders	14.37	13.51
Packaging and filling machine operators and tenders	12.52	10.67
Team assemblers	11.09	11.42

Sources of Additional Information

Additional information on training and careers in the chemical manufacturing field is available from either of the following organizations:

- American Chemical Society, 1155 16th St. NW, Washington, DC 20036. Internet: http://www.acs.org
- American Institute of Chemical engineers, 3 Park Ave., New York, NY 10016-5991. Internet: http://www.aiche.org

Computer and Electronic Product Manufacturing

- Annual Earnings: $47,070
- Job Growth: -7.1%
- Size of Workforce: 1,314,920
- Self-Employed: 0.2%
- Part-Time: 2.8%

Significant Points

- Employment is projected to decline 7 percent over the 2004–2014 period due to productivity improvements, imports, and the movement of some jobs to lower-wage countries.

- The field is characterized by significant research and development activity and rapid technological change.

- Professional and related personnel account for 1 out of 3 workers.

Nature of the Field

The computer and electronic product manufacturing field produces computers; computer-related products, including printers; communications equipment; and home electronic equipment, as well as a wide range of goods used for both commercial and military purposes. In addition, many electronics products or components are incorporated into other fields' products, such as cars, toys, and appliances.

Products manufactured in this field include computers and computer storage devices, such as DVD drives, and computer peripheral equipment, such as printers and scanners; communications equipment—wireless telephones and telephone switching equipment; consumer electronics, such as televisions and audio equipment; and military electronics—for example, radar, communications equipment, guidance for "smart" bombs, and electronic navigation equipment. The field also includes the manufacture of semiconductors—silicon or computer "chips," or integrated circuits—which constitute the heart of computers and many other advanced electronic products. Two of the most significant types of computer chips are microprocessors, which make up the central-processing system of computers, and memory chips, which store information. Technological innovation characterizes this field more than most others and, in fact, drives much of the field's production. Many new products, such as digital cameras and hand-held devices that permit wireless Internet access, reflect a convergence of technologies.

The computer and electronic product manufacturing field differs from other manufacturing fields in that production workers account for a much lower proportion of all workers. The unusually rapid pace of innovation and technological advancement requires a high proportion of engineers, engineering technicians, and other highly technical workers to continually develop and produce new products. Likewise, the importance of promoting and selling the products manufactured by the various segments of field requires knowledgeable marketing and sales workers. American companies manufacture and assemble many products abroad because of lower production costs and new trade agreements.

Companies producing intermediate components and finished goods frequently locate near each other because doing so allows easier access to recent innovations. Electronic products contain many components—and sometimes even major parts, such as integrated circuits—that often are purchased from other manufacturers. As a result of having the skilled workforce that fosters product improvement, some areas of the country have become centers of the electronics field. The most prominent of these centers is Silicon Valley, a concentration of integrated circuit, software, and computer firms in California's Santa Clara Valley, near San Jose; however, there are electronics-manufacturing plants throughout the country.

To a large extent, electronics manufacturing has become truly global, and it is difficult to characterize many companies and their products as American or foreign. The movement of foreign companies to manufacture some goods in the United States does not change the fact that many products are being designed in one country, manufactured in another, and assembled in a third. Highly sensitive and sophisticated products such as semiconductors and computers are being designed and tested in the United States, for example, but it remains likely that other parts of final products, such as the keyboards and outer casings, are made somewhere else and shipped to yet another site for final assembly.

Although some of the companies in this field are very large, most are small. The history of innovation in the field explains the startup of many small firms. Some companies are involved in design or research and development (R&D), whereas others may simply manufacture components, such as computer chips, under contract for others. Often, an engineer or a physicist will have an innovative idea and set up a new company to develop the associated product. Although electronic products can be quite sophisticated, it has been possible to manufacture many electronic products or components (not necessarily finished products) with a relatively small investment. Furthermore, investors often are willing to put their money behind new companies in this field because of the history of large paybacks from some successful companies. Success always will depend on innovation, and although investment costs are rising, there should continue to be opportunities to develop good ideas.

The rapid pace of innovation in electronics technology makes for a constant demand for newer and faster products and applications. This demand puts a greater emphasis on R&D than is typical in most manufacturing operations. Being the first firm to market a new or better product can mean success for both the product and the firm. Even for many relatively commonplace items, R&D continues to result in better, cheaper products with more desirable features. For example, a company that develops a new kind of computer chip to be used in many brands of computers can earn millions of dollars in sales until a competitor is able to copy the technology or develop a better chip. Many employees, therefore, are research scientists, engineers, and technicians whose job it is to continually develop and improve products.

The product design process includes not only the initial design, but also development work, which ensures that the product functions properly and can be manufactured as inexpensively as possible. When a product is manufactured, the components are assembled, usually by soldering them to a printed circuit board by means of automated equipment. Hand assembly of small parts requires both good eyesight and coordination, but because of the cost and precision involved, assembly and packaging are becoming highly automated.

Working Conditions

In general, those working in computer and electronics manufacturing—even production workers—enjoy relatively good working conditions. In contrast to those in many other manufacturing fields, production workers in this field usually work in clean and relatively noise-free environments. Computer chips are manufactured in "clean rooms," in which the air is filtered and workers wear special garments to prevent any dust from getting into the air. A speck of dust will ruin a computer chip.

In 2003, the rate of work-related injuries and illnesses per 100 full-time workers was 2.4 in the computer and electronic parts manufacturing field, lower than the average of 5.0 for the private sector. However, some jobs in the field may present risks. For example, some workers who fabricate integrated circuits and other components

may be exposed to hazardous chemicals, and working with small parts may cause eyestrain.

About half of all employees work regular 40-hour weeks, but pressure to develop new products ahead of competitors may result in some R&D personnel working extensive overtime to meet deadlines. The competitive nature of the field makes for an exciting, but sometimes stressful, work environment—especially for those in technical and managerial occupations.

Important Characteristics of the Field

Skills: Installation; Quality Control Analysis; Technology Design; Troubleshooting; Science; Programming. **Abilities:** Mathematical Reasoning; Visual Color Discrimination; Perceptual Speed; Visualization; Finger Dexterity; Inductive Reasoning. **Work-Related Values:** Social Status; Ability Utilization; Working Conditions; Responsibility; Advancement; Authority.

Employment

The computer and electronic product manufacturing field employed 1.3 million wage and salary workers in 2004 (table 1). Few workers were self-employed.

Table 1. Distribution of wage and salary employment in computer and electronic product manufacturing by field segment, 2004 (Employment in thousands)

Field segment	Employment	Percent
Total, computer and electronic product manufacturing	1,327	100.0
Semiconductor and other electronic components	453	34.1
Navigational, measuring, electro-medical, and control instruments	432	32.6
Computer and peripheral equipment	212	16.0
Communications equipment	151	11.4
Manufacturing and reproducing magnetic and optical media	47	3.5
Audio and video equipment	32	2.4

The field comprised about 20,000 establishments in 2004, many of which were small, employing only one or

Manufacturing, Construction, and Utilities

a few workers. Large establishments of 250 or more workers employed the majority—61 percent—of the field's workforce (chart 1).

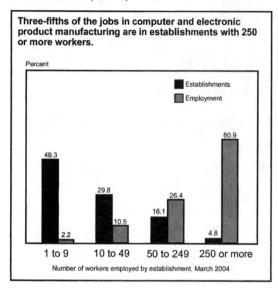

Three-fifths of the jobs in computer and electronic product manufacturing are in establishments with 250 or more workers.

Percent

- Establishments
- Employment

1 to 9	10 to 49	50 to 249	250 or more
49.3 / 2.2	29.8 / 10.5	16.1 / 26.4	4.8 / 60.9

Number of workers employed by establishment, March 2004

Under the North American Field Classification System (NAICS), workers in R&D establishments that are not part of a manufacturing facility are included in a separate field—research and development in the physical, engineering, and life sciences. However, due to the importance of R&D work to the computer and electronic product manufacturing field, computer and electronic product–related R&D is discussed in this description even though a large proportion of the associated workers are not included in the employment data.

Occupations in the Field

Given the importance of R&D to the field, it is not surprising that a large proportion—about 1 in 3—of all workers are in professional and related occupations (table 2). About 14 percent of those workers are engineers—predominantly *electrical and electronics engineers* and *computer hardware engineers*, but also many *industrial* and *mechanical engineers*. These workers develop new products and devise better, more efficient production methods. Engineers may coordinate and lead teams developing new products. Others may work with customers to help them make the best use of the products. *Computer systems analysts, database administrators, and computer scientists* are employed throughout the field, becoming more dispersed with the increasing computer-

ization of development and production methods. Other professionals include *mathematical* and *physical scientists* and *technical writers*.

About 6 percent of workers are *engineering technicians*, many of whom work closely with engineers. Engineering technicians help develop new products; work in production areas; and sometimes assist customers in installing, maintaining, and repairing equipment. They also may test new products or processes to make sure that everything works correctly.

Despite the relatively high proportion of professional and technical workers in electronics manufacturing, more than 3 out of 10 employees are production workers. Many are assemblers, who place and solder components on circuit boards or assemble and connect the various parts of electronic devices. *Semiconductor processors* initiate and control the many automated steps in the process of manufacturing integrated circuits or computer chips. *Electrical and electronic equipment assemblers* are responsible for putting together products such as computers and appliances, telecommunications equipment, and even missile control systems. Some assemblers are highly skilled and use their significant experience and training to assemble major components. A skilled assembler may put together an entire subassembly or even an entire product, especially when products are made in relatively small numbers. Other, less skilled assemblers often work on a production line, attaching one or a few parts and continually repeating the same operation. Increasingly, as production work becomes more automated, assemblers and other production workers are monitoring the machinery that actually does the assembly work. *Inspectors, testers, sorters, samplers, and weighers* use sophisticated testing machinery to ensure that devices operate as designed.

About 16 percent of workers in the field are in management, business, and financial operations occupations. In this field, top management is much more likely to have a technical background than are its counterparts in other fields. This is especially true in smaller companies, which often are founded by engineers, computer scientists, or other technical professionals.

About 14 percent of workers in the field hold office and administrative support or sales and related jobs. Sales positions require technical knowledge and abilities; as a result, engineers and technicians often may find opportunities in sales or sales support.

Table 2. Employment of wage and salary workers in computer and electronic product manufacturing by occupation, 2004 and projected change, 2004–2014 (Employment in thousands)

Occupation	Employment, 2004 Number	Percent	Percent change, 2004–2014
Total, all occupations	1,326	100.0	–7.1
Management, business, and financial occupations	206	15.5	–7.9
Top executives	24	1.8	–10.3
Marketing and sales managers	18	1.4	–9.1
Engineering managers	28	2.1	0.1
Business operations specialists	57	4.3	–7.8
Financial specialists	25	1.9	–10.5
Professional and related occupations	454	34.2	0.9
Computer specialists	142	10.7	2.8
Computer hardware engineers	33	2.5	–3.6
Electrical and electronics engineers	72	5.4	1.8
Industrial engineers, including health and safety	27	2.1	10.6
Mechanical engineers	23	1.7	4.5
Drafters, engineering, and mapping technicians	92	6.9	–1.5
Sales and related occupations	41	3.1	–8.8
Sales representatives, wholesale and manufacturing	26	2.0	–10.3
Office and administrative support occupations	137	10.4	–18.4
Customer service representatives	15	1.2	–7.6
Shipping, receiving, and traffic clerks	17	1.3	–18.4
Secretaries and administrative assistants	25	1.9	–16.4
Office clerks, general	14	1.0	–21.2
Installation, maintenance, and repair occupations	38	2.8	–7.8
Other installation, maintenance, and repair occupations	22	1.7	–9.4
Industrial machinery installation, repair, and maintenance workers	19	1.4	–10.2
Production occupations	414	31.2	–10.9
First-line supervisors/ managers of production and operating workers	30	2.3	–9.8
Assemblers and fabricators	225	17.0	–10.3
Metal workers and plastic workers	56	4.2	–11.2
Inspectors, testers, sorters, samplers, and weighers	35	2.6	–14.0
Semiconductor processors	42	3.2	–10.2
Miscellaneous production workers	15	1.1	–17.3
Transportation and material moving occupations	26	1.9	–14.3
Laborers and material movers, hand	20	1.5	–15.7

Note: May not add to totals due to omission of occupations with small employment

Training, Other Qualifications, and Advancement

Workers with different levels of education find employment opportunities in the computer and electronic product manufacturing field. Entry to engineering occupations generally requires at least a bachelor's degree in engineering, although those with 4-year degrees in physical science, computer science, or another technical area sometimes qualify as well. Some positions, however, may require a master's degree or higher or relevant work experience. Computer systems analysts or scientists usually need a degree in computer science or a related field, and in many cases they also must have considerable programming experience. Because companies often are founded by professionals with technical backgrounds,

Manufacturing, Construction, and Utilities

opportunities for advancement into executive or managerial positions may arise for experienced workers who keep up with rapid changes in technology and who possess the business expertise necessary to succeed in a fast-changing economy. Likewise, due to the rapid pace of technological development, employees often need to continue to update their skills and knowledge base to stay abreast. Also, due to the global nature of computer and electronic product manufacturing, knowledge of another language or culture is emerging as a desired qualification for workers in this field.

Training for engineering technicians is available from a number of sources. Although most employers prefer graduates of 2-year postsecondary training schools—usually technical institutes or junior colleges—training in the U.S. Armed Forces or through proprietary schools also may meet employer requirements. Engineering technicians should have an aptitude for math and science. Entry-level technicians may begin working with a more experienced technician or engineer. Advancement opportunities for experienced technicians may include supervisory positions or movement into other production and inspection operations.

Although assembly workers generally need only a high school diploma, assemblers in the computer and electronic product manufacturing field may need more specialized training or experience than do workers in other manufacturing fields. Precision assembly work can be extremely sophisticated and complex, and some jobs may even require formal technical training. A 1-year certificate in semiconductor technology is good preparation for semiconductor processor operator positions; for more highly skilled technician positions, an associate's degree in electronics technology or a related field is necessary. Again, advancement opportunities depend not only on work experience, but also on the level of technical training and the ability to keep up with changing technology.

Outlook

Wage and salary employment in the computer and electronic product manufacturing field is expected to decline by 7 percent between 2004 and 2014, compared with a projected increase of 14 percent in all fields. Although the output of this field is projected to increase more rapidly than that of any other field, employment will still decline as a result of continued rapid productivity

growth—the ability of the field to produce more and better products with fewer employees. Employment also will be adversely affected by continued increases in imports of electronic and computer products and by a more recent trend: outsourcing of some professional functions, such as computer programming and engineering, to lower-wage countries. While much of the design of computer and electronic products is done domestically, most of the mass manufacturing of these products occurs abroad. Despite the overall projected decrease in employment, the technological revolutions taking place in computers, semiconductors, and telecommunications, as well as the need to replace the many workers who leave the field due to retirement or other reasons, should continue to provide many employment opportunities in the field, especially in research and development. The products of this field—especially powerful computer chips—will continue to enhance productivity in all areas of the economy.

The projected change in employment over the 2004–2014 period varies by field segment (table 3). Although demand for computers should remain relatively strong worldwide, employment is expected to decline 17 percent in computers and peripheral equipment and 12 percent in semiconductor and other electronic component manufacturing, due to both the introduction of new technology and automated manufacturing processes and a slowdown in the growth of output in these segments from previously high levels. Further, these segments will continue to face strong import competition. Employment in navigational, measuring, electromedical, and control instruments manufacturing is expected to increase 4 percent due to recent heavy investments in defense electronics. In addition, employment in audio and video equipment manufacturing is expected to decrease by 22 percent, due largely to continued import competition as well as improvements in productivity. Employment in communications equipment manufacturing is also expected to decrease by 10 percent due to automation and consolidation among firms in the field. Employment in the manufacturing and reproduction of magnetic and optical media is expected to decrease by less than 1 percent because of higher productivity and more efficient production processes.

Table 3. Projected employment change in computer and electronic product manufacturing by field segment, 2004–2014

Field segment	Percent change
Total, computer and electronic product manufacturing	–7.1
Computer and peripheral equipment	–17.5
Communications equipment	–10.3
Audio and video equipment	–21.6
Semiconductor and other electronic components	–11.7
Navigational, measuring, electromedical, and control instruments	4.2
Manufacturing and reproducing magnetic and optical media	–0.2

There should be a smaller decrease in employment among professional and related occupations than among most other occupations in the computer and electronic product manufacturing field. However, the use of the Internet and other new forms of communication makes it possible for engineers and similar professionals working in other countries to perform work that previously was done in this country. Some of these workers are directly employed by U.S. companies, while others work for contractors hired by foreign companies. Because the earnings of professional workers in many countries are much less than earnings in the United States, the trend toward hiring foreign workers will accelerate, especially as companies gain more experience and confidence in the use of these workers. While this trend undoubtedly will have a detrimental impact on U.S. professional worker employment, there still will be numerous jobs in this country that cannot be exported.

The computer and electronic product manufacturing field is characterized by rapid technological advances and has grown faster than most other fields over the past several decades, although rising costs, imports, and the rapid pace of innovation continue to pose challenges. Certain segments of the field and individual companies often experience problems. For example, the field occasionally undergoes severe downturns, and individual companies—even those in segments of the field doing well—can run into trouble because they have not kept up with the latest technological developments or because they have erred in deciding which products to manufacture. Such uncertainties can be expected to continue. In addition, the intensity of foreign competition and the future role of imports remain difficult to project. Import competition has wiped out major parts of the domestic consumer electronics field, and future effects of such competition depend on trade policies and market forces. The field is likely to continue to encounter strong competition from imported electronic goods and components from countries throughout Asia and Europe.

Because defense expenditures are expected to increase, sales of military electronics, an important segment of the field, will likely pick up. Furthermore, firms will continue to develop new products, creating large new markets, as they have in the past. Smaller, more powerful computer chips are constantly being developed and incorporated into an even wider array of products, and the semiconductor content of all electronic products will continue to increase. The growth of digital technology, artificial intelligence, and nanotechnology, as well as the expansion of the Internet and the increasing demand for global information networking, will continue to create new opportunities.

Earnings

In general, earnings in the computer and electronic product manufacturing field are high, although this is partly because many of the lower-wage production jobs have been automated or exported to other countries. Average weekly earnings of all production or nonsupervisory workers in the field were $698, higher than the average of $529 for all fields in 2004 (table 4).

Table 4. Average earnings of nonsupervisory workers in the computer and electronic product manufacturing field, 2004

Field segment	Weekly	Hourly
Total, nongovernment	$529	$15.67
Computer and electronic products manufacturing	698	17.28
Computer and peripheral equipment	841	20.56
Search, detection, and navigation instruments	829	20.90
Electronic instruments	691	17.37
Semiconductors and electronic components	654	16.24

Field segment	Weekly	Hourly
Communications equipment	698	16.86
Audio and video equipment	733	18.32

Earnings in selected occupations in several components of the computer and electronic product manufacturing field in 2004 appear in table 5.

Table 5. Median hourly earnings of the largest occupations in computer and electronic product manufacturing, May 2004

Occupation	Computer and electronic product manufacturing	All fields
Computer hardware engineers	$41.29	$39.02
Computer software engineers, systems software	41.09	38.34
Computer software engineers, applications	39.72	36.05
Electronics engineers, except computer	36.71	36.43
Electrical engineers	35.91	34.43
Electrical and electronic engineering technicians	20.23	22.26
Inspectors, testers, sorters, samplers, and weighers	13.94	13.66
Semiconductor processors	13.84	13.85
Electrical and electronic equipment assemblers	11.70	11.68
Team assemblers	11.40	11.42

Sources of Additional Information

Information on the electronics field, including publications, salary surveys, and education and training, is available from

- American Electronics Association, The Center for Workforce Excellence, 5201 Great America Pkwy., Suite 520, Santa Clara, CA 95054. Internet: http://www.aeanet.org

For information on technology and other aspects of the electronics field, contact

- The Electronic Industries Alliance, 2500 Wilson Blvd., Arlington, VA 22201. Internet: http://www.eia.org

Construction

- Annual Earnings: $35,060
- Job Growth: 11.4%
- Size of Workforce: 7,037,380
- Self-Employed: 15.9%
- Part-Time: 8.7%

Significant Points

- Job opportunities are expected to be excellent for experienced workers.
- Workers in construction have relatively high hourly earnings.
- Almost 2 out of 3 establishments in the field employ fewer than 5 people.
- Construction has a very large number of self-employed workers.

Nature of the Field

Houses, apartments, factories, offices, schools, roads, and bridges are only some of the products of the construction field. This field's activities include the building of new structures as well as additions and modifications to existing ones. The field also includes maintenance, repair, and improvements on these structures.

The construction field is divided into three major segments. *Construction of buildings contractors*, or *general contractors*, build residential, industrial, commercial, and other buildings. *Heavy and civil engineering construction contractors* build sewers, roads, highways, bridges, tunnels, and other projects. *Specialty trade contractors* perform specialized activities related to construction such as carpentry, painting, plumbing, and electrical work.

Construction usually is done or coordinated by general contractors, who specialize in one type of construction such as residential or commercial building. They take full responsibility for the complete job, except for specified portions of the work that may be omitted from the general contract. Although general contractors may do a portion of the work with their own crews, they often subcontract most of the work to heavy construction or specialty trade contractors.

Specialty trade contractors usually do the work of only one trade, such as painting, carpentry, or electrical work, or of two or more closely related trades, such as plumbing and heating. Beyond fitting their work to that of the other trades, specialty trade contractors have no responsibility for the structure as a whole. They obtain orders for their work from general contractors, architects, or property owners. Repair work is almost always done on direct order from owners, occupants, architects, or rental agents.

Working Conditions

Most employees in this field work full time, and many work over 40 hours a week. In 2004, about 1 in 5 construction workers worked 45 hours or more a week. Construction workers may sometimes work evenings, weekends, and holidays to finish a job or take care of an emergency. Construction workers who work outdoors often must contend with the weather. Rain, snow, or wind may halt construction work, causing workers to go home or not report to work.

Workers in this field need physical stamina because the work frequently requires prolonged standing, bending, stooping, and working in cramped quarters. They also may be required to lift and carry heavy objects. Exposure to weather is common because much of the work is done outside or in partially enclosed structures. Construction workers often work with potentially dangerous tools and equipment amidst a clutter of building materials; some work on temporary scaffolding or at great heights and in bad weather. Consequently, they are more prone to injuries than are workers in other jobs. In 2003, cases of work-related injury and illness were 6.8 per 100 full-time construction workers, which is significantly higher than the 5.0 rate for the entire private sector. Workers who are employed by foundation, structure, and building exterior contractors experienced the highest injury rates. In response, employers increasingly emphasize safe working conditions and work habits that reduce the risk of injuries. To avoid injury, employees wear safety clothing,

such as gloves and hardhats, and devices to protect their eyes, mouth, or hearing as needed.

Table 1. Distribution of wage and salary employment in construction by field, 2004 (Employment in thousands)

Field	Employment	Percent
Total, all fields	6,964	100.0
Construction of buildings	1,632	23.4
Residential building	894	12.8
Nonresidential building construction	738	10.6
Heavy and civil engineering construction	903	13.0
Utility system construction	370	5.3
Highway, street, and bridge construction	348	5.0
Land subdivision	86	1.2
Other heavy and civil engineering construction	99	1.4
Specialty trade contractors	4,430	63.6
Building equipment contractors	1,863	26.7
Foundation, structure, and building exterior contractors	1,006	14.4
Building finishing contractors	926	13.3
Other specialty trade contractors	636	9.1

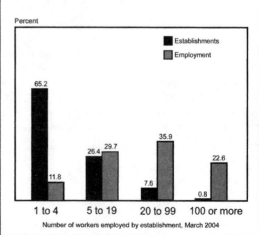

Chart 1. Nine-tenths of establishments in construction employ fewer than 20 workers.

Important Characteristics of the Field

Skills: Installation; Repairing; Equipment Maintenance; Technology Design; Equipment Selection; Troubleshooting. **Abilities:** Static Strength; Dynamic Strength; Gross Body Equilibrium; Extent Flexibility; Stamina; Manual Dexterity. **Work-Related Values:** Moral Values; Compensation; Variety; Supervision, Technical; Co-workers.

Employment

Construction, with 7.0 million wage and salary jobs and 1.9 million self-employed and unpaid family workers in 2004, was one of the nation's largest fields. Almost 2 out of 3 wage and salary jobs in construction were with specialty trade contractors—primarily plumbing, heating, and air conditioning; electrical; and masonry contractors. Around 1 out of 4 jobs were with building contractors, mostly in residential and nonresidential construction. The rest were with heavy and civil engineering construction contractors (table 1). Employment in this field is distributed geographically in much the same way as the nation's population.

There were about 818,000 construction establishments in the United States in 2004: 247,000 were building construction contractors, 57,000 were heavy and civil engineering construction or highway contractors, and 514,000 were specialty trade contractors. Most of these establishments tend to be small, the majority employing fewer than 5 workers (chart 1). About 1 out of 9 workers are employed by small contractors.

Construction offers more opportunities than most other fields for individuals who want to own and run their own business. The 1.9 million self-employed and unpaid family workers in 2004 performed work directly for property owners or acted as contractors on small jobs, such as additions, remodeling, and maintenance projects. The rate of self-employment varies greatly by individual occupation in the construction trades (chart 2).

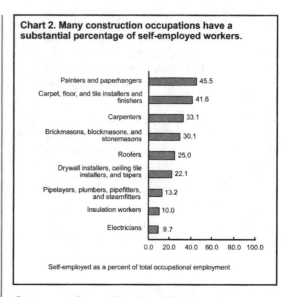

Chart 2. Many construction occupations have a substantial percentage of self-employed workers.

Occupation	Value
Painters and paperhangers	45.5
Carpet, floor, and tile installers and finishers	41.6
Carpenters	33.1
Brickmasons, blockmasons, and stonemasons	30.1
Roofers	25.0
Drywall installers, ceiling tile installers, and tapers	22.1
Pipelayers, plumbers, pipefitters, and steamfitters	13.2
Insulation workers	10.0
Electricians	9.7

Self-employed as a percent of total occupational employment

Occupations in the Field

Construction offers a great variety of career opportunities. People with many different talents and educational backgrounds—managers, clerical workers, engineers, truck drivers, trades workers, and construction helpers—find job opportunities in the construction field (table 2).

Most of the workers in construction are *construction trades workers*, which include both skilled and apprentice craftsworkers, *construction managers*, and *construction laborers*. Most construction trades workers are classified as either structural, finishing, or mechanical workers, with some performing activities of more than one type. *Structural workers* build the main internal and external framework of a structure and can include *carpenters; construction equipment operators; brickmasons, blockmasons, and stonemasons; cement masons and concrete finishers;* and *structural and reinforcing iron and metal workers.* *Finishing workers* perform the tasks that give a structure its final appearance and may include carpenters; *drywall and ceiling tile installers; plasterers and stucco masons; segmental pavers; terrazzo workers; painters and paperhangers; glaziers; roofers; carpet, floor, and tile installers and finishers;* and *insulation workers.* *Mechanical workers* install the equipment and material for basic building operations and may include *pipelayers, plumbers, pipefitters, and steamfitters; electricians; sheet metal workers;* and *heating, air-conditioning, and refrigeration mechanics and installers.*

Construction trades workers are employed in a large variety of occupations that are involved in all aspects of the construction field. *Boilermakers* make, install, and repair boilers, vats, and other large vessels that hold liquids and gases. *Brickmasons, blockmasons, and stonemasons* build and repair walls, floors, partitions, fireplaces, chimneys, and other structures with brick, precast masonry panels, concrete block, stone, and other masonry materials. *Carpenters* construct, erect, install, or repair structures and fixtures made of wood, such as framing walls and partitions, putting in doors and windows, building stairs, laying hardwood floors, and hanging kitchen cabinets. *Carpet, floor, and tile installers and finishers* lay floor coverings, apply tile and marble, and sand and finish wood floors in a variety of buildings. *Cement masons, concrete finishers, segmental pavers, and terrazzo workers* smooth and finish poured concrete surfaces and work with cement to create sidewalks, curbs, roadways, or other surfaces. *Construction equipment operators* use machinery that moves construction materials, earth, and other heavy materials and applies asphalt and concrete to roads and other structures. *Drywall installers, ceiling installers, and tapers* fasten drywall panels to the inside framework of residential houses and other buildings and prepare these panels for painting by taping and finishing joints and imperfections. *Electricians* install, connect, test, and maintain building electrical systems, which also can include lighting, climate control, security, and communications. *Glaziers* are responsible for selecting, cutting, installing, replacing, and removing all types of glass. Insulation workers line and cover structures with insulating materials. *Painters and paperhangers* stain, varnish, and apply other finishes to buildings and other structures and apply decorative coverings to walls and ceilings. *Pipelayers, plumbers, pipefitters, and steamfitters* install, maintain, and repair many different types of pipe systems. They may also install heating and cooling equipment and mechanical control systems. *Plasterers and stucco masons* apply plaster, cement, stucco, and similar materials to interior and exterior walls and ceilings. *Roofers* repair and install roofs made of tar or asphalt and gravel, rubber or thermoplastic, or metal or shingles made of asphalt, slate, fiberglass, wood, tile, or other material. Sheet metal workers fabricate, assemble, install, and repair products and equipment made out of sheet metal, such as duct systems, roofs, siding, and drainpipes. *Structural and reinforcing iron and metal workers* place and install iron or steel girders, columns, and other structural members to form completed structures or frameworks of buildings, bridges, and other structures.

Lastly, *construction laborers* perform a wide range of physically demanding tasks at building and highway construction sites, such as tunnel and shaft excavation, hazardous waste removal, environmental remediation, and demolition. Many trades workers perform their services with the assistance of *helpers*. These people assist trades workers and perform duties of lesser skill.

Table 2. Employment of wage and salary workers in construction by occupation, 2004 and projected change, 2004–2014 (Employment in thousands)

Occupation	Employment, 2004		Percent change, 2004–2014
	Number	Percent	
Total, all occupations	6,964	100.0	11.4
Management, business, and financial occupations	540	7.8	15.2
Construction managers	152	2.2	14.0
Cost estimators	116	1.7	21.1
Professional and related occupations	92	1.3	15.2
Architecture and engineering occupations	70	1.0	14.8
Sales and related occupations	137	2.0	11.3
Office and administrative support occupations	667	9.6	1.4
Bookkeeping, accounting, and auditing clerks	140	2.0	2.4
Secretaries and administrative assistants	188	2.7	–1.3
Construction and extraction occupations	4,645	66.7	11.7
First-line supervisors/ managers of construction trades and extraction workers	425	6.1	13.8
Brickmasons and blockmasons	100	1.4	14.8
Carpenters	737	10.6	13.1
Carpet installers	26	0.4	13.2
Tile and marble setters	38	0.5	25.1

Occupation	Employment, 2004		Percent change, 2004–2014
	Number	Percent	
Cement masons and concrete finishers	179	2.6	15.9
Construction laborers	700	10.0	2.0
Paving, surfacing, and tamping equipment operators	43	0.6	13.3
Operating engineers and other construction equipment operators	226	3.2	13.1
Drywall and ceiling tile installers	112	1.6	6.5
Electricians	430	6.2	14.2
Glaziers	33	0.5	15.0
Insulation workers, floor, ceiling, and wall	35	0.5	2.8
Painters, construction and maintenance	195	2.8	12.7
Pipelayers	39	0.6	12.8
Plumbers, pipefitters, and steamfitters	341	4.9	16.7
Plasterers and stucco masons	54	0.8	7.7
Roofers	115	1.7	18.6
Sheet metal workers	128	1.8	16.6
Structural iron and steel workers	63	0.9	15.2
Helpers, construction trades	388	5.6	10.3
Elevator installers and repairers	20	0.3	14.9
Installation, maintenance, and repair occupations	471	6.8	17.8
Heating, air conditioning, and refrigeration mechanics and installers	143	2.1	27.4
Line installers and repairers	65	0.9	12.7
Transportation and material moving occupations	262	3.8	10.5
Truck drivers, heavy and tractor-trailer	96	1.4	13.3
Crane and tower operators	15	0.2	13.9
Excavating and loading machine and dragline operators	40	0.6	11.5

Note: May not add to totals due to omission of occupations with small employment

The construction field employs a number of other workers apart from the construction trades. *Elevator installers and repairers* assemble, install, and replace elevators, escalators, moving walkways, and similar equipment in new and old buildings. *Heating, air-conditioning, and refrigeration mechanics and installers* install systems that control the temperature, the humidity, and the total air quality in residential, commercial, industrial, and other buildings. *Material-moving occupations* use machinery to move construction materials, earth, petroleum products, and other heavy materials or manually handle freight, stock, or other materials; clean vehicles, machinery, and other equipment; feed materials into or remove materials from machines or equipment; and pack or package products and materials.

First-line supervisors and managers of construction trades and extraction workers oversee trades workers and helpers and ensure that work is done well, safely, and according to code. They plan the job and solve problems as they arise. Those with good organizational skills and exceptional supervisory ability may advance to construction management occupations, including project manager, constructor, field manager, or superintendent. These workers are responsible for getting a project completed on schedule by working with the architect's plans, making sure materials are delivered on time, assigning work, overseeing craft supervisors, and ensuring that every phase of the project is completed properly and expeditiously. They also resolve problems and see to it that work proceeds without interruptions.

The construction field employs nearly all of the workers in some construction craft occupations. In other construction craft occupations, large numbers also work in other fields (table 3). Other fields employing large numbers of construction workers include transportation equipment manufacturing; transportation, communication, and utilities; real estate; wholesale and retail trade; educational services; and state and local government.

Table 3. Percent of wage and salary workers in construction craft occupations employed in the construction field, 2004

Occupation	Percent
Plasterers and stucco masons	90.6
Cement masons, concrete finishers, and terrazzo workers	88.9
Structural iron and steel workers	86.4
Insulation workers	81.1
Drywall installers, ceiling tile installers, and tapers	76.2
Roofers	71.4
Pipelayers, plumbers, pipefitters, and steamfitters	67.9
Glaziers	66.2
Electricians	65.5
Brickmasons, blockmasons, and stonemasons	64.6
Carpenters	54.6
Carpet, floor, and tile installers and finishers	43.9
Painters and paperhangers	41.4

Training, Other Qualifications, and Advancement

Persons can enter the construction field through a variety of educational and training backgrounds. Those entering construction out of high school usually start as laborers, helpers, or apprentices. While some laborers and helpers can learn their job in a few days, the skills required for many of the trades worker jobs take years to learn and are usually learned through some combination of classroom instruction and on-the-job training. In a few cases, skills can be learned entirely through informal on-the-job training, but the more education received, generally the more skilled workers become. Skilled workers such as carpenters, bricklayers, plumbers, and other construction trade specialists most often get their formal instruction by attending a local technical or trade school or through an apprenticeship or other employer-provided training program. In addition, they learn their craft by working with more experienced workers. Most construction trades workers' jobs require proficiency in reading and mathematics. Safety training is also required for most jobs, and English skills are essential for workers to advance within their trade.

Laborers and helpers advance to the more skilled trades occupations by acquiring experience and skill in various phases of the craft. As they demonstrate their ability to perform tasks they are assigned, they move to progressively more challenging work. As they broaden their skills, they are allowed to work more independently, and responsibilities and earnings increase. They may qualify for jobs in related, more highly skilled occupations. For example, after several years of experience, painters' helpers may become skilled painters.

Many persons enter the construction trades through apprenticeship programs. Apprenticeships administered by local employers, trade associations, and trade unions provide the most thorough training. Apprenticeships usually last between 3 and 5 years and consist of on-the-job training and 144 hours or more of related classroom instruction each year. However, a number of apprenticeship programs are now using competency standards in place of time requirements, making it possible to complete a program in a shorter time. Those who enroll in apprenticeship programs usually are at least 18 years old and in good physical condition. Those who enter construction from technical or vocational schools also may go through apprenticeship training; however, they progress at a somewhat faster pace because they already have had courses such as mathematics, mechanical drawing, and woodworking.

To develop their skills further, construction trades workers can work on different projects, such as housing developments, office and industrial buildings, or road construction. Flexibility and a willingness to adopt new techniques, as well as the ability to get along with people, are essential for advancement. Those who are skilled in all facets of the trade and who show good leadership qualities may be promoted to supervisor or construction manager. Construction managers may advance to superintendent of larger projects or go into the business side of construction. Some go into business for themselves as contractors. Those who plan to rise to supervisory positions should have basic Spanish language skills to communicate basic safety and work instructions.

Outside of the construction field, skilled trades workers may transfer to jobs such as construction building inspector, purchasing agent, sales representative for building supply companies, or technical or vocational school instructor. In order to advance to a management position, additional education and training is recommended.

Managerial personnel usually have a college degree or considerable experience in their specialty. Individuals who enter construction with college degrees usually start as management trainees or construction managers' assistants. Those who receive degrees in construction science often start as field engineers, schedulers, or cost estimators. College graduates may advance to positions such as assistant manager, construction manager, general superintendent, cost estimator, construction building inspector, general manager or top executive, contractor, or consultant. Although a college education is not always required, administrative jobs usually are filled by people with degrees in business administration, finance, accounting, or similar fields.

Opportunities for workers to form their own firms are better in construction than in many other fields. Construction workers need only a moderate financial investment to become contractors, and they can run their businesses from their homes, hiring additional construction workers only as needed for specific projects. The contract construction field, however, is very competitive, and the rate of business turnover is high. Taking courses in business helps to improve the likelihood of success.

Outlook

Job opportunities are expected to be excellent in the construction field, especially for skilled trades workers, due to the large number of retirements of these workers anticipated over the next decade as well as fewer people with the right education or experience entering the skilled trades.

The number of wage and salary jobs in the construction field is expected to grow about 11 percent through the year 2014, compared with the 14 percent projected for all fields combined. Employment in this field depends primarily on the level of construction and remodeling activity, which is expected to increase over the coming decade.

Although household growth is expected to slow slightly over the coming decade, the increase will create demand for residential construction, especially in the fastest growing areas in the South and West. Rising numbers of immigrants, as well as the children of the baby boomers, will generate demand for homes and rental apartments. In addition, a desire for larger homes with more amenities will fuel demand for move-up homes as well as the renovation and expansion of older homes. Townhouses and condominiums in conveniently located suburban and urban settings also are increasingly desired types of properties.

Employment is expected to grow faster in nonresidential construction over the decade. Replacement of many industrial plants has been delayed for years, and a large number of structures will have to be replaced or remodeled. Construction of nursing homes and other residential homes for the elderly, as well as all types of healthcare facilities, will be needed to meet the need for more medical treatment facilities, especially by the growing elderly population. Construction of schools will continue to be needed, especially in the South and West where the population is growing the fastest. In other areas, however, replacing and renovating older schools will create jobs.

Employment in heavy and civil engineering construction is projected to increase due to growth in new highway, bridge, and street construction as well as in maintenance and repairs to prevent further deterioration of the nation's existing highways and bridges. Voters and legislators in most states and localities continue to approve spending on road construction, which will create jobs over the next decade.

Employment in specialty trades contracting, the largest segment of the field, will grow the fastest as demand grows for subcontractors in building and heavy construction and as more workers are needed to repair and remodel existing homes, which specialty trade contractors are more likely to perform. Home improvement and repair construction is expected to continue to grow faster than new home construction. Remodeling should be the fastest-growing sector of housing construction because of a growing stock of old residential and nonresidential buildings. Many older, smaller homes will be remodeled to appeal to more-affluent space- and amenity-hungry buyers. Remodeling tends to be more labor-intensive than new construction. In addition, the construction field, as well as all types of businesses and institutions, are increasingly contracting out the services of specialty trades workers instead of keeping these workers on their own payrolls.

The number of job openings in construction may fluctuate from year to year. New construction is usually cut back during periods when the economy is not expanding or interest rates are high. However, it is rare that all segments of the construction field are down at the same time, allowing workers to switch from building houses to working on office building construction, depending on demand.

Employment growth will differ among various occupations in the construction field. Employment of construction managers is expected to grow as a result of the increasing complexity of construction work that needs to be managed, including the need to deal with the proliferation of laws dealing with building construction, worker safety, and environmental issues. Also, the growth of self-employment in this field is leading to a larger number of managers that own small construction businesses. An especially favorable job outlook is expected for those who have a bachelor's degree in construction science, with an emphasis on construction management, and people with related work experience in construction management services firms. Employment growth of administrative support occupations will be limited by increased office automation.

Although employment in construction trades as a whole is expected to grow about as fast as the field average, the rate of growth will vary by trade. Employment of tile and marble setters; construction and building inspectors; and heating, air-conditioning, and refrigeration mechanics and installers is projected to grow faster than the field average because their specialized services will be in greater demand. On the other hand, employment of carpet installers, construction laborers, floor sanders and finishers, insulation workers, paperhangers, plasters and stucco masons, and tapers are expected to grow more slowly than that of the construction field as a whole because either their specialty is not in as great demand or they are becoming more productive.

Table 4. Average earnings of nonsupervisory workers in construction, 2004

Field segment	Weekly	Hourly
Total, nongovernment	$529	$15.67
Construction field	736	19.23
Construction of buildings	706	18.73
Industrial building	767	19.49
Nonresidential building	793	20.18
Commercial building	801	20.41
Residential building	631	17.38
Heavy and civil engineering construction	811	19.18
Highway, street, and bridge construction	844	19.82
Other heavy construction	781	18.71
Specialty trade contractors	730	19.40
Electrical contractors	831	21.38
Plumbing and HVAC contractors	777	20.14
Flooring contractors	716	19.41
Building finishing contractors	677	18.66
Masonry contractors	629	18.55
Painting and wall covering contractors	607	16.47
Roofing contractors	610	17.36

Earnings

Earnings in construction are higher than the average for all fields (table 4). In 2004, production or nonsupervisory workers in construction averaged $19.23 an hour, or about $736 a week. In general, the higher-skilled trades workers, such as electricians and plumbers, get paid more than less-skilled trades workers, laborers, and helpers. Earnings also vary by the worker's education and experience, the type of work, the complexity of the construction project, and the geographic location. Earnings of construction workers are often affected when poor weather prevents them from working, because they usually do not get paid if they do not work. Traditionally, winter is the slack period for construction activity, especially in colder parts of the country, but there is a trend toward more year-round construction even in colder areas. Construction trades are dependent on one another to complete specific parts of a project—especially on large projects—so work delays in one trade can delay or stop the work of another trade. Earnings in 2004 of selected occupations in construction appear in table 5.

About 17 percent of construction trades workers were union members or covered by union contracts, compared with about 14 percent of all nongovernment workers. In general, union workers are paid more than nonunion workers and have better benefits. Many different unions represent the various construction trades and form joint apprenticeship committees with local employers to supervise apprenticeship programs.

Table 5. Median hourly earnings of the largest occupations in construction, May 2004

Occupation	Construction of buildings	Heavy and civil engineering construction	Specialty trade contractors	All fields
First-line supervisors/ managers of construction trades and extraction workers	$24.43	$24.45	$24.44	$24.25
Plumbers, pipefitters, and steamfitters	21.29	19.13	19.77	19.85
Operating engineers and other construction equipment operators	19.38	18.53	17.93	17.00
Electricians	19.09	23.73	19.76	20.33
Carpenters	17.11	18.17	16.90	16.78
Cement masons and concrete finishers	16.06	14.80	15.14	15.10
Heating, air conditioning, and refrigeration mechanics and installers	15.09	15.26	16.79	17.43
Painters, construction and maintenance	15.06	14.44	14.41	14.55
Bookkeeping, accounting, and auditing clerks	14.84	15.23	14.31	13.74
Construction laborers	12.50	12.82	12.13	12.10
Office clerks, general	10.56	10.89	10.74	10.95

Sources of Additional Information

Information about apprenticeships and training can be obtained from local construction firms and employer associations, the local office of the state employment service or apprenticeship agency, or the Bureau of Apprenticeship and Training, U.S. Department of Labor.

For additional information on jobs in the construction field, contact

- Associated Builders and Contractors, Workforce Development Department, 9th Floor, 4250 North Fairfax Dr., Arlington, VA 22203. Internet: http://www.trytools.org

- Associated General Contractors of America, Inc., 2300 Wilson Boulevard, Suite 400, Arlington, VA 22201. Internet: http://www.agc.org

- National Association of Home Builders, Home Builders Institute, 1201 15th St. NW, Washington, DC 20005-2800. Internet: http://www.hbi.org

- National Center for Construction Education and Research, P.O. Box 141104, Gainesville FL, 32614. Internet: http://www.nccer.org

Food Manufacturing

- Annual Earnings: $24,180
- Job Growth: 3.8%
- Size of Workforce: 1,485,240
- Self-Employed: 1.8%
- Part-Time: 9.0%

Significant Points

- This field has one of the highest incidences of injury and illness among all fields; animal slaughtering plants have the highest incidence among all food manufacturing fields.

- Production workers account for 53 percent of all jobs.

- Most production jobs require little formal education or training; many can be learned in a few days.

- Automation and increasing productivity will limit employment growth, but unlike many other fields, food manufacturing is not highly sensitive to economic conditions.

Nature of the Field

Workers in the food manufacturing field link farmers and other agricultural producers with consumers. They do this by processing raw fruits, vegetables, grains, meats, and dairy products into finished goods ready for the grocer or wholesaler to sell to households, restaurants, or institutional food services.

Food manufacturing workers perform tasks as varied as the many foods we eat. For example, they slaughter, dress, and cut meat or poultry; process milk, cheese, and other dairy products; can and preserve fruits, vegetables, and frozen specialties; manufacture flour, cereal, pet foods, and other grain mill products; make bread, cookies, cakes, and other bakery products; manufacture sugar and candy and other confectionery products; process shortening, margarine, and other fats and oils; and prepare packaged seafood, coffee, potato and corn chips, and peanut butter. Although this list is long, it is not exhaustive: Food manufacturing workers also play a part in delivering numerous other food products to our tables.

Quality control and quality assurance are vital to this field. The U.S. Department of Agriculture (USDA) oversees all aspects of food manufacturing. In addition, other food safety programs have been adopted recently as issues of chemical contamination and the growing number of new food-borne pathogens remain a public health concern. For example, by applying science-based controls from raw materials to finished products, a program called Hazard Analysis and Critical Control Point (HACCP) focuses on identifying hazards and preventing them from contaminating food.

Thirty-four percent of all food manufacturing workers are employed in plants that slaughter and process animals, and another 19 percent work in establishments that make bakery goods (table 1). Seafood product preparation and packaging, the smallest sector of the food manufacturing field, accounts for only 3 percent of all jobs.

Table 1. Distribution of wage and salary employment in food manufacturing by field segment, 2004 (Employment in thousands)

Field segment	Employment, 2004	Percent change, 2004–2014
Total employment	1497.5	3.81
Animal slaughtering and processing	505.3	12.82
Bakeries and tortilla manufacturing	287.8	3.79
Fruit and vegetable preserving and specialty food manufacturing	181.7	−1.49
Other food manufacturing	154.1	6.42
Dairy product manufacturing	132.0	−10.61
Sugar and confectionery product manufacturing	83.7	−4.42
Grain and oilseed milling	60.6	−6.60
Animal food manufacturing	50.7	−4.93
Seafood product preparation and packaging	41.6	−3.85

Working Conditions

Many production jobs in food manufacturing involve repetitive, physically demanding work. Food manufacturing workers are highly susceptible to repetitive-strain injuries to their hands, wrists, and elbows. This type of injury is especially common in meat-processing and poultry-processing plants. Production workers often stand for long periods and may be required to lift heavy objects or use cutting, slicing, grinding, and other dangerous tools and machines. To deal with difficult working conditions, ergonomic programs have been introduced to cut down on work-related accidents and injuries.

In 2003, there were 8.6 cases of work-related injury or illness per 100 full-time food manufacturing workers, much higher than the rate of 5.0 cases for the private sector as a whole. Injury rates vary significantly among specific food manufacturing fields, ranging from a low of 1.8 per 100 workers in retail bakeries to 12.9 per 100 in animal slaughtering plants, the highest rate in food manufacturing.

Manufacturing, Construction, and Utilities

In an effort to reduce occupational hazards, many plants have redesigned equipment, increased the use of job rotation, allowed longer or more frequent breaks, and developed training programs in safe work practices. Furthermore, meat and poultry plants must comply with a wide array of Occupational Safety and Health Administration (OSHA) regulations ensuring a safer work environment. Although injury rates remain high, training and other changes have reduced those rates. Some workers wear protective hats, gloves, aprons, and shoes. In many fields, uniforms and protective clothing are changed daily for reasons of sanitation.

Because of the considerable mechanization in the field, most food manufacturing plants are noisy, with limited opportunities for interaction among workers. In some highly automated plants, "hands-on" manual work has been replaced by computers and factory automation, resulting in less waste and higher productivity. While much of the basic production—such as trimming, chopping, and sorting—will remain labor intensive for many years to come, automation is increasingly being applied to various functions, including inventory management, product movement, and quality control issues such as packing and inspection.

Working conditions also depend on the type of food being processed. For example, some bakery employees work at night or on weekends and spend much of their shifts near ovens that can be uncomfortably hot. In contrast, workers in dairies and meat-processing plants typically work daylight hours and may experience cold and damp conditions. Some plants, such as those producing processed fruits and vegetables, operate on a seasonal basis, so workers are not guaranteed steady, year-round employment and occasionally travel from region to region seeking work. These plants are increasingly rare, however, as the field continues to diversify and manufacturing plants produce alternative foods during otherwise inactive periods.

Important Characteristics of the Field

Skills: Equipment Maintenance; Operation and Control; Operation Monitoring; Repairing; Programming. **Abilities:** Static Strength; Dynamic Strength; Stamina; Extent Flexibility; Manual Dexterity; Trunk Strength. **Work-Related Values:** Supervision, Technical; Moral Values; Supervision, Human Relations.

Employment

In 2004, the food manufacturing field provided 1.5 million jobs. Almost all employees were wage and salary workers, but a few food manufacturing workers were self-employed and unpaid family workers. In 2004, about 29,000 establishments manufactured food, with 89 percent employing fewer than 100 workers (chart 1). Nevertheless, establishments employing 500 or more workers accounted for 36 percent of all jobs.

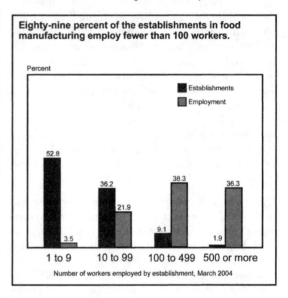

Eighty-nine percent of the establishments in food manufacturing employ fewer than 100 workers.

Percent

- Establishments
- Employment

1 to 9	52.8 / 3.5
10 to 99	36.2 / 21.9
100 to 499	9.1 / 38.3
500 or more	1.9 / 36.3

Number of workers employed by establishment, March 2004

The employment distribution in this field varies widely. Animal slaughtering and processing employs the largest proportion of workers. Economic changes in livestock farming and slaughtering plants have changed the field. Increasingly, fewer but larger farms are producing the vast majority of livestock in the United States. Similarly, there are now fewer, but much larger, meat-processing plants owned by fewer companies—a development that has tended to concentrated employment in a few locations.

Food manufacturing workers are found in all states, although some sectors of the field are concentrated in certain parts of the country. For example, in 2004, California, Illinois, Iowa, Pennsylvania, and Texas employed 24 percent of all workers in animal slaughtering and processing. That same year, Wisconsin employed 33 percent of all cheese manufacturing workers, and California accounted for 20 percent of fruit and vegetable preserving and specialty food manufacturing workers.

Occupations in the Field

The food manufacturing field employs many different types of workers. More than half are production workers, including skilled precision workers and less-skilled machine operators and laborers (table 2). Production jobs require manual dexterity, good hand-eye coordination, and, in some sectors of the field, strength.

Red-meat production is the most labor-intensive food-processing operation. Animals are not uniform in size, and *slaughterers and meatpackers* must slaughter, skin, eviscerate, and cut each carcass into large pieces. They usually do this work by hand, using large, suspended power saws. They also clean and salt hides and make sausage. *Meat, poultry, and fish cutters and trimmers* use hand tools to break down the large primary cuts into smaller sizes for shipment to wholesalers and retailers. These workers use knives and other hand tools to eviscerate, split, and bone chickens and turkeys.

Bakers mix and bake ingredients according to recipes to produce breads, cakes, pastries, and other goods. Bakers produce goods in large quantities, using mixing machines, ovens, and other equipment.

Many food manufacturing workers use their hands or small hand tools to do their jobs. *Cannery workers* perform a variety of routine tasks—such as sorting, grading, washing, trimming, peeling, or slicing—in the canning, freezing, or packing of food products. *Hand food decorators* apply artistic touches to prepared foods. *Candy molders and marzipan shapers* form sweets into fancy shapes by hand.

With increasing levels of automation in the food manufacturing field, a growing number of workers are operating machines. For example, *food batchmakers* operate equipment that mixes, blends, or cooks ingredients used in manufacturing various foods, such as cheese, candy, honey, and tomato sauce. *Dairy processing equipment operators* process milk, cream, cheese, and other dairy products. *Cutting and slicing machine operators* slice bacon, bread, cheese, and other foods. *Mixing and blending machine operators* produce dough batter, fruit juices, or spices. *Crushing and grinding machine operators* turn raw grains into cereals, flour, and other milled-grain products, and they produce oils from nuts or seeds. *Extruding and forming machine operators* produce molded food and candy, and *casing finishers and stuffers* make sausage links and similar products. *Bottle packers and bot-tle fillers* operate machines that fill bottles and jars with preserves, pickles, and other foodstuffs.

Food cooking machine operators and tenders steam, deep-fry, boil, or pressure-cook meats, grains, sugar, cheese, or vegetables. *Food and tobacco roasting, baking, and drying machine operators and tenders* operate equipment that roasts grains, nuts, or coffee beans and tend ovens, kilns, dryers, and other equipment that removes moisture from macaroni, coffee beans, cocoa, and grain. *Baking equipment operators* tend ovens that bake bread, pastries, and other products. Some foods—ice cream, frozen specialties, and meat, for example—are placed in freezers or refrigerators by *cooling and freezing equipment operators*. Other workers tend machines and equipment that clean and wash food or food-processing equipment. Some machine operators also clean and maintain machines and perform duties such as checking the weight of foods.

Many other workers are needed to keep food manufacturing plants and equipment in good working order. *Industrial machinery mechanics* repair and maintain production machines and equipment. *Maintenance repairers* perform routine maintenance on machinery, such as changing and lubricating parts. Specialized mechanics include *heating, air-conditioning, and refrigeration mechanics, farm equipment mechanics*, and *diesel engine specialists*.

Still other workers directly oversee the quality of the work and of final products. *Supervisors* direct the activities of production workers. *Graders and sorters* of agricultural products, *production inspectors*, and *quality control technicians* evaluate foodstuffs before, during, or after processing.

Food may spoil if not packaged properly or delivered promptly, so packaging and transportation employees play a vital role in the field. Among these are *freight, stock, and material movers*, who manually move materials; *hand packers and packagers*, who pack bottles and other items as they come off the production line; and *machine feeders and offbearers*, who feed materials into machines and remove goods from the end of the production line. *Industrial truck and tractor operators* drive gasoline or electric-powered vehicles equipped with forklifts, elevated platforms, or trailer hitches to move goods around a storage facility. *Truck drivers* transport and deliver livestock, materials, or merchandise and may load and unload trucks. *Driver/sales workers* drive company vehicles over established routes to deliver and sell goods, such as bakery items, beverages, and vending-machine products.

The food manufacturing field also employs a variety of managerial and professional workers. Managers include *top executives,* who make policy decisions; *industrial production managers,* who organize, direct, and control the operation of the manufacturing plant; and *advertising, marketing, promotions, public relations, and sales managers,* who direct advertising, sales promotion, and community relations programs.

Engineers, scientists, and technicians are becoming increasingly important as the food manufacturing field implements new automation and food safety processes. These workers include *industrial engineers,* who plan equipment layout and workflow in manufacturing plants, emphasizing efficiency and safety. Also, *mechanical engineers* plan, design, and oversee the installation of tools, equipment, and machines. *Chemists* perform tests to develop new products and maintain the quality of existing products. *Computer programmers and systems analysts* develop computer systems and programs to support management and scientific research. *Food scientists and technologists* work in research laboratories or on production lines to develop new products, test current ones, and control food quality, including minimizing foodborne pathogens.

Finally, many sales workers, including *sales representatives, wholesale and manufacturing,* are needed to sell the manufactured goods to wholesale and retail establishments. *Bookkeeping, accounting, and auditing clerks* and *procurement clerks* keep track of the food products going into and out of the plant. *Janitors and cleaners* keep buildings clean and orderly.

Table 2. Employment of wage and salary workers in food manufacturing by occupation, 2004 and projected change, 2004–2014 (Employment in thousands)

Occupation	Employment, 2004		Percent change, 2004–2014
	Number	Percent	
Total, all occupations	1,498	100.0	3.8
Management, business, and financial occupations	66	4.4	6.3
Top executives	18	1.2	4.8
Marketing and sales managers	5	0.3	6.4
Industrial production managers	10	0.7	5.7
Purchasing agents and buyers, farm products	1	0.1	5.7
Professional and related occupations	25	1.6	9.2
Computer specialists	5	0.3	13.4
Agricultural engineers	1	0.0	3.5
Food scientists and technologists	4	0.2	7.9
Agricultural and food science technicians	4	0.3	3.7
Service occupations	61	4.1	6.3
Cooks and food preparation workers	11	0.7	6.9
Food and beverage serving workers	17	1.1	5.9
Building cleaning workers	25	1.6	7.9
Sales and related occupations	57	3.8	2.1
Retail sales workers	29	2.0	0.0
Sales representatives, wholesale and manufacturing	20	1.3	5.2
Office and administrative support occupations	105	7.0	–6.6
Financial clerks	21	1.4	–5.2
Information and record clerks	15	1.0	–5.0
Shipping, receiving, and traffic clerks	19	1.3	–4.1
Secretaries and administrative assistants	9	0.6	–4.1
Office clerks, general	12	0.8	–5.5
Farming, fishing, and forestry occupations	19	1.3	11.6

Occupation	Employment, 2004		Percent change, 2004–2014
	Number	Percent	
Installation, maintenance, and repair occupations	86	5.8	6.2
Industrial machinery installation, repair, and maintenance workers	71	4.7	6.3
Production occupations	789	52.7	5.2
First-line supervisors/ managers of production and operating workers	50	3.4	7.1
Bakers	48	3.2	6.8
Butchers and other meat, poultry, and fish processing workers	249	16.6	13.9
Miscellaneous food processing workers	105	7.0	2.9
Packaging and filling machine operators and tenders	107	7.1	–10.2
Miscellaneous production workers	107	7.2	3.6
Transportation and material moving occupations	284	19.0	1.2
Motor vehicle operators	56	3.7	4.5
Industrial truck and tractor operators	40	2.7	0.4
Laborers and material movers, hand	168	11.2	0.2

Note: May not add to totals due to omission of occupations with small employment

Training, Other Qualifications, and Advancement

Most production jobs in food manufacturing require little formal education or training. Graduation from high school is preferred, but not always required. In general, inexperienced workers start as helpers to experienced workers and learn skills on the job. Many of these entry-level jobs can be learned in a few days. Typical jobs include operating a bread-slicing machine, washing fruits and vegetables before processing begins, hauling carcass-es, and packing bottles as they come off the production line. Even though it may not take long to learn to operate a piece of equipment, employees may need several years of experience to enable them to keep the equipment running smoothly, efficiently, and safely.

Some food manufacturing workers need specialized training and education. Inspectors and quality control workers, for example, are trained in food safety and usually need a certificate to be employed in a food manufacturing plant. Often, USDA-appointed plant inspectors possess a bachelor's degree in agricultural or food science. Formal educational requirements for managers in food manufacturing plants range from 2-year degrees to master's degrees. Those who hold research positions, such as food scientists, usually need a master's or doctoral degree.

In addition to participating in specialized training, a growing number of workers receive broader training to perform a number of jobs. The need for flexibility in more automated workplaces has meant that many food manufacturing workers are learning new tasks and being trained to work effectively in teams. Some specialized training is provided for bakers and some other positions.

Advancement may come in the form of higher earnings or more responsibility. Helpers usually progress to jobs as machine operators, but the speed of this progression can vary considerably. Some workers who perform exceptionally well on the production line, or those with special training and experience, may advance to supervisory positions. Plant size and the existence of formal promotion tracks may influence advancement opportunities.

Requirements for other jobs are similar to requirements for the same types of jobs in other fields. Employers usually hire high school graduates for secretarial and other clerical work. Graduates of 2-year associate degree or other postsecondary programs often are sought for science technician and related positions. College graduates or highly experienced workers are preferred for middle-management or professional jobs in personnel, accounting, marketing, or sales.

Outlook

Overall wage and salary employment in food manufacturing is expected to increase by 4 percent over the 2004–2014 period, compared with 14 percent employment growth projected for the entire economy. Despite the rising demand for manufactured food products by a

Manufacturing, Construction, and Utilities

growing population, automation and increasing productivity are limiting employment growth. Nevertheless, numerous job openings will arise in many segments of food manufacturing as experienced workers transfer to other fields, retire, or leave the labor force for other reasons.

Job growth will vary by occupation but will be concentrated among food manufacturing workers—the largest group of workers in the field. Because many of the cutting, chopping, and eviscerating tasks performed by these workers have proven difficult to automate, employment among handworkers will rise along with the growing demand for food products, especially beef. Hand-working occupations include slaughterers and meat packers and meat, poultry, and fish cutters and trimmers, whose employment will rise as the consumption of meat, poultry, and fish climbs and more processing takes place at the manufacturing level. Other production workers also will benefit from the shift in food processing from retail establishments to manufacturing plants.

Although automation has had little effect on most handworkers, it is having a broader impact on numerous other occupations in the field. Fierce competition has led food manufacturing plants to invest in technologically advanced machinery to be more productive. The new machines have been applied to tasks as varied as packaging, inspection, and inventory control. As a result, employment will not increase as rapidly among some machine operators, such as packaging machine operators, as for industrial machinery mechanics who repair and maintain the new machinery. Computers also are being widely implemented throughout the field, reducing employment growth of some mid-level managers and resulting in decreased employment for administrative support workers, but increasing the demand for workers with excellent technical skills. Taken as a whole, automation will continue to have a significant impact on workers in the field as competition becomes even more intense in coming years.

Food manufacturing firms will be able to use this new automation to better meet the changing demands of a growing and increasingly diverse population. As convenience becomes more important, consumers increasingly demand highly processed foods such as pre-marinated pork loins, peeled and cut carrots, microwaveable soups, or "ready-to-heat" dinners. Such a shift in consumption will contribute to the demand for food manufacturing workers and will lead to the development of thousands of new processed foods. Domestic producers also will attempt to market these goods abroad as the volume of international trade continues to grow. The increasing size and diversity of the American population has driven demand for a greater variety of foods, including more ethnic foods. The combination of expanding export markets and shifting and increasing domestic consumption will help employment among food manufacturing workers to rise over the next decade and will lead to significant changes throughout the food manufacturing field.

Unlike many other fields, food manufacturing is not highly sensitive to economic conditions. Even during periods of recession, the demand for food is likely to remain relatively stable.

Earnings

Table 3 shows that production workers in food manufacturing averaged $12.98 an hour, compared with $15.67 per hour for all nongovernment workers in May 2004. Weekly earnings among food manufacturing workers were lower than average, $510 compared with $529 for all nongovernment workers in May 2004. Food manufacturing workers averaged about 39.3 hours a week, compared with only 33.7 for all workers in the private sector. Weekly earnings ranged from $408 in seafood product preparation and packaging plants to $832 in grain and oilseed milling plants. Hours worked play a large part in determining earnings. For example, grain-milling and oilseed-milling workers, who averaged 41.4 hours a week, had higher hourly and weekly earnings than did workers in bakeries and tortilla manufacturing companies, who averaged 37.3 hours a week. Earnings in selected occupations in food manufacturing appear in table 4.

Table 3. Average earnings of production or non-supervisory workers in food manufacturing by field segment, 2004

Field segment	Weekly	Hourly
Total, nongovernment	$529	$15.67
Food manufacturing	510	12.98
Grain and oilseed milling	832	19.27
Beverages	735	18.70

Field segment	Weekly	Hourly
Dairy products	680	16.60
Sugar and confectionery products	580	15.34
Fruit and vegetable preserving and specialty	512	12.86
Other food products	494	12.90
Bakeries and tortilla manufacturing	472	12.64
Animal slaughtering and processing	458	11.53
Seafood product preparation and packaging	408	10.69

Table 4. Median hourly earnings of the largest occupations in food manufacturing, May 2004

Occupation	Food manufacturing	All fields
First-line supervisors/managers of production and operating workers	$19.71	$21.51
Maintenance and repair workers, general	16.25	14.77
Packaging and filling machine operators and tenders	11.41	10.67
Food batchmakers	11.01	10.62
Bakers	10.62	10.26
Laborers and freight, stock, and material movers, hand	10.23	9.67
Helpers—production workers	10.10	9.70
Slaughterers and meat packers	10.04	10.03
Packers and packagers, hand	9.20	8.25
Meat, poultry, and fish cutters and trimmers	8.96	9.09

Sources of Additional Information

For information on job opportunities in food manufacturing, contact individual manufacturers, locals of the unions listed in the section on earnings, and state employment service offices.

Machinery Manufacturing

- Annual Earnings: $35,000
- Job Growth: –12.8%
- Size of Workforce: 1,140,720
- Self-Employed: 1.0%
- Part-Time: 3.7%

Significant Points

- High productivity growth is expected to keep employment growth low, but many openings will result from the need to replace workers who retire.

- Production workers, who account for over half of all jobs in the field, increasingly need training beyond the high school level.

- Machinery manufacturing has some of the most highly skilled—and highly paid—production jobs in manufacturing.

- Job prospects should be favorable for skilled production workers.

Nature of the Field

The development and implementation of machinery was responsible for one of the great advances in human history, the industrial revolution. Machinery encompasses a vast range of products, ranging from huge industrial machines costing millions of dollars to the common lawn mower, but all machinery has one common defining feature: it either reduces or eliminates the amount of human work required to accomplish a task. Machinery plays a key role in the production of much of the country's goods and services because nearly every workplace in every field uses some form of machinery. From the oil derrick that pumps out oil to the commercial refrigerator in use by your favorite restaurant, machinery is mainly responsible for the way we live today. Thus, while most people never use or even see the machinery that makes their lifestyle possible, they use the products it makes every day.

The machinery manufacturing field sector contains seven more detailed field segments, as shown in table 1.

Manufacturing, Construction, and Utilities

Three of these make machinery designed for a particular field–called special-purpose machinery: agriculture, construction, and mining machinery manufacturing; industrial machinery manufacturing; and commercial and service machinery manufacturing. The other four segments make machinery used by many different fields–called general-purpose machinery: ventilation, heating, air-conditioning, and commercial refrigeration equipment manufacturing; metalworking machinery manufacturing; engine, turbine, and power transmission equipment manufacturing; and other general-purpose machinery manufacturing.

The metalworking machinery field makes machinery that forms metal when it is in its molten state as well as machinery that cuts or shapes it when it is a solid. Although the growth of plastics has reduced the prevalence of metals, an enormous variety of products have some metal parts in them, all of which have to be precisely formed from the raw metal. The same properties that make metal a desirable component—its strength and durability—also make it a difficult material to form. The specialized drills, grinders, molds, presses, and rollers needed to form metal are made in this field, as are the accessories used by these machines. Metalworking machinery manufacturing has a disproportionate share of the establishments that make up the machinery manufacturing field because many are small, averaging fewer than 20 workers.

The agriculture, construction, and mining machinery manufacturing field is made up of much larger establishments that produce some of the largest and most sophisticated machines, as well as some common household equipment. Examples of machines produced in this segment are farm combines, which are large self-propelled machines that both harvest and thresh grains at the same time; bulldozers and backhoes; equipment used for both surface and underground mining; and oil and gas field drilling machinery and derricks. This segment also makes lawn mowers, leaf blowers, and other lawn and garden outdoor power equipment intended for residential as well as commercial use.

The ventilation, heating, air-conditioning, and commercial refrigeration equipment manufacturing field makes machinery that provides climate control for residential and commercial buildings. In addition to heating and cooling equipment, this field makes air purification equipment, which is increasingly common in new construction, as well as commercial refrigeration equipment, which is used primarily for food storage.

The machinery used by firms in the service sector of the economy is made by the commercial and service machinery manufacturing field. Machinery produced here includes the commercial versions of common household appliances such as laundry equipment, coffee makers, microwave ovens, and vacuum cleaners. Other large components of this field are manufacturers of automatic vending machines; non-electronic office machinery, such as typewriters and mail sorters; non-digital cameras; photocopiers; and machinery used to make optical lenses.

The industrial machinery manufacturing field makes machinery used in the production of finished goods from raw materials. Wood, plastics, rubber, paper, textiles, food, glass, and oil are among the materials processed by the machinery made by this segment. It also makes machinery used in printing and bookbinding as well as in the manufacturing of semiconductors and circuit boards.

The engine, turbine, and power transmission equipment manufacturing segment includes a variety of machines that transfer one type of work into another. Turbines use the energy from the motion of steam, gas, water, or wind to create mechanical power by turning a drive shaft, which with the use of gears, speed changers, clutches, drive chains, and pulleys—all also made in this segment—puts assembly lines and other industrial machinery in motion. Turbines also can create electrical power when attached to a generator. This field segment also produces diesel and other internal combustion engines and their components that are used to power portable generators, air compressors, pumps, and other equipment. Aircraft and motor vehicle engines are made by the Aerospace Product and Parts Manufacturing and Motor Vehicle and Parts Manufacturing fields, respectively, which appear elsewhere in Part II.

The last segment—other general-purpose machinery manufacturing—includes manufacturers of miscellaneous machines used primarily by manufacturing fields, including pumps and compressors, welding and soldering equipment, and packaging machinery. It also makes a variety of materials handling equipment used in manufacturing but also by a wide variety of fields, including industrial trucks and tractors, overhead cranes and hoists, conveyors, and many types of equipment that use hydraulics. This field segment also manufactures other machinery that consumers are likely to encounter, such as scales and balances; power-driven hand tools; and elevators, escalators, and moving walkways.

The machinery manufacturing field also includes companies that specialize in making parts for larger manufacturers. Some of these parts manufacturers specialize in creating parts that require particular skill to make and then selling them to a wide variety of other manufacturers. Companies contract with these parts manufacturers because they can often provide parts cheaper than if they made them themselves. Cost is a primary selling point for these parts manufacturers and many of their parts are generally small and easy to transport, so these companies are particularly threatened by foreign competition.

The wide range of products made in the machinery manufacturing field means that it includes establishments of all sizes. In general, however, the larger and more complicated the machinery is, the larger the manufacturing facility must be to produce it. Thus the agriculture, construction, and mining machinery and the ventilation, heating, air-conditioning, and commercial refrigeration equipment sectors tend to have large establishments, while the metalworking machinery segment has the most small ones.

Large firms involved in manufacturing machinery tend to have a multistage production process. Separate teams of individuals are responsible for the design and testing stages, the manufacture of parts, and the final assembly of the finished product. Workers in different parts of the process still work closely together, however. Design offices are often located near the factory floor to facilitate interaction with production workers. Small establishments, in contrast, may have a handful of workers responsible for the entire production process.

The machinery manufacturing field, like all U.S. manufacturers, continues to evolve to adopt new technologies and techniques to lower costs and raise the productivity of its workforce. Growing pressures from domestic and foreign competition are increasingly forcing machinery manufacturers to turn to high-technology production techniques, including robots, computers, and programmable equipment. Productivity gains resulting from these more efficient production techniques maximize the utilization of available equipment and workers, allowing reductions in the number of unskilled workers needed in the production process.

Pressures to reduce costs and maximize profits have also caused manufacturers in the field to adopt new business practices. One common change is the contracting out of support functions, such as janitorial and security jobs, and increasingly some administrative services and warehouse and shipping jobs. Rather than employ workers directly for these jobs, a manufacturer will often contract with another company that specializes in providing these services. Not only does this reduce costs by forcing service providers to compete for the work, it allows the manufacturer to focus on what it does best—design and production. It also makes the manufacturer more flexible, allowing them to add and subtract contract workers more easily than they could hire and fire employees.

These changes have had a profound effect on the machinery manufacturing workforce. By automating many of the production processes and outsourcing many of the administrative and support functions, it has reduced the need for many less-skilled workers and increased the skill level required for the remaining workers. These changes are allowing the field to remain competitive and meet the demand for machinery that other fields rely on.

Table 1. Percent distribution of establishments and wage and salary employment in machinery manufacturing by detailed field, 2004

Field segment	Employment	Establishments
Total	100.0	100.0
Metalworking machinery manufacturing	17.6	35.0
Agriculture, construction, and mining machinery manufacturing	17.0	10.7
Ventilation, heating, air-conditioning, and commercial refrigeration equipment manufacturing	13.4	6.6
Industrial machinery manufacturing	10.6	13.3
Commercial and service machinery manufacturing	10.1	9.2
Engine, turbine, and power transmission equipment manufacturing	8.2	3.4
Other general-purpose machinery manufacturing	23.2	21.8

Working Conditions

Production workers in the machinery manufacturing field generally encounter conditions that are much improved from the past. New facilities in particular tend to be clean, well lighted, and temperature controlled. Noise can still be a factor, however, especially in larger production facilities. Most of the labor-intensive work is now automated, though some heavy lifting may still be required of workers. Some workers may also have to work with oil and grease or chemicals that require special handling. Certain types of machinery also require particular care in their use. Nevertheless, injuries are rare when proper safety procedures are observed. In 2003, the rate of work-related injuries and illnesses per 100 workers was 6.9, compared with 6.8 for all manufacturing fields. The rate for the private sector as a whole was 5.0.

Most workers in machinery manufacturing work 8-hour shifts 5 days a week. Overtime can be common, though, especially during periods of peak demand. About 34 percent of workers averaged more than 40 hours a week in 2004. Some plants are capable of operating 24 hours a day, but some shifts are able to operate with a reduced workforce due to the automated nature of the production process.

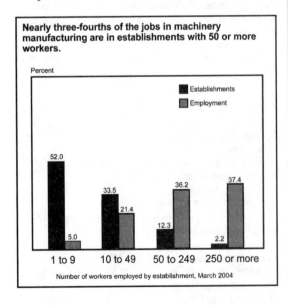

Nearly three-fourths of the jobs in machinery manufacturing are in establishments with 50 or more workers.

Percent

- Establishments
- Employment

52.0
33.5
21.4
5.0
12.3
36.2
2.2
37.4

1 to 9   10 to 49   50 to 249   250 or more

Number of workers employed by establishment, March 2004

Important Characteristics of the Field

Skills: Operation Monitoring; Installation; Equipment Maintenance; Operation and Control; Quality Control Analysis; Repairing. **Abilities:** Rate Control; Arm-Hand Steadiness; Control Precision; Manual Dexterity; Reaction Time; Multilimb Coordination. **Work-Related Values:** Moral Values; Activity; Supervision, Technical; Company Policies and Practices; Supervision, Human Relations; Independence.

Employment

The machinery manufacturing field provided 1.1 million wage and salary jobs in 2004. Employment was relatively evenly distributed among all segments of the field (table 1). There were about 32,000 establishments in the field; more than half employed fewer than 10 workers (chart 1). However, 37 percent of workers were employed in large establishments of 250 workers or more.

Although machinery manufacturing jobs are located throughout the country, certain states account for the greatest numbers of jobs. About a third of all jobs were located in the midwestern states of Illinois, Indiana, Michigan, Ohio, and Wisconsin. Populous states such as California, Texas, New York, and Pennsylvania also had large numbers of jobs.

Table 2. Employment of wage and salary workers in machinery manufacturing, by occupation, 2004 and projected change, 2004–2014 (Employment in thousands)

Occupation	Employment, 2004 Number	Employment, 2004 Percent	Percent change, 2004–2014
Total, all occupations	1,142	100.0	–12.8
Management, business, and financial occupations	112	9.8	–11.2
General operations managers	19	1.7	–13.2
Industrial production managers	12	1.0	–11.7
Buyers and purchasing agents	14	1.3	–11.8

Occupation	Employment, 2004		Percent change, 2004–2014
	Number	Percent	
Professional and related occupations	128	11.2	–7.2
Computer specialists	18	1.6	–8.6
Electrical and electronics engineers	10	0.9	–6.8
Industrial engineers	14	1.2	0.7
Mechanical engineers	30	2.6	–7.6
Mechanical drafters	15	1.3	–7.7
Engineering technicians, except drafters	20	1.8	–6.5
Sales and related occupations	40	3.5	–12.3
Office and administrative support occupations	127	11.1	–21.0
Bookkeeping, accounting, and auditing clerks	14	1.2	–20.7
Production, planning, and expediting clerks	12	1.1	–11.0
Shipping, receiving, and traffic clerks	18	1.6	–20.0
Construction and extraction occupations	19	1.7	–10.1
Installation, maintenance, and repair occupations	48	4.2	–11.3
Industrial machinery mechanics	11	0.9	–10.5
Maintenance and repair workers, general	17	1.5	–10.9
Production occupations	618	54.1	–12.8
First-line supervisors/ managers of production and operating workers	41	3.6	–11.3
Assemblers and fabricators	193	17.0	–10.0
Computer-controlled machine tool operators	30	3.2	–10.9
Machine tool cutting setters, operators, and tenders, metal and plastic	74	6.5	–22.8
Machinists	69	6.0	–11.6
Molders and molding machine setters, operators, and tenders, metal and plastic	12	1.0	–18.0
Multiple machine tool setters, operators, and tenders, metal and plastic	12	1.0	–11.8
Tool and die makers	29	2.5	–12.8
Welding, soldering, and brazing workers	64	5.6	–8.4
Inspectors, testers, sorters, samplers, and weighers	23	2.0	–16.4
Transportation and material moving occupations	42	3.7	–14.2
Laborers and material movers, hand	23	2.0	–17.6

Note: May not add to totals due to omission of occupations with small employment

Occupations in the Field

It takes a wide variety of occupations to create and produce a machine (table 2). Before any work can begin on the production of a particular piece of machinery, an extensive process to create and test the design must be completed. This process can take up to several years, depending on the complexity of the machinery.

The design process takes place under the oversight of *engineering managers*. Much of the design work is done by *engineers*, who first develop a concept of what a new machine could do or how an existing one could be improved. Starting with this concept, they use computer modeling and simulating software to design the machine and test it for performance, cost, reliability, ease of use, and other factors important to both producers and consumers of the final product. *Mechanical engineers* design the moving parts of the machine, such as the gears, levers, and pistons in engine and hydraulic systems. They also direct the work of *mechanical engineering technicians*, who run tests on materials and parts before they are assembled into the final product. For machines with complicated electric or electronic systems, *electrical and electronics engineers* also assist in the design and testing

Manufacturing, Construction, and Utilities

process. *Industrial engineers* determine how best to allocate the resources of the factory—both workers and equipment—for optimal production.

Once a design is finalized and testing complete, *mechanical drafters* create the plans that production workers use in the assembly of the machine. They provide specifications and diagrams for each part required as well as assembly instructions for the final product.

The production process is directed by *industrial production managers,* who watch over all activities on the factory floor. Production workers account for over half of all jobs in the machinery manufacturing field. *First-line supervisors and managers of production and operating workers* oversee all workers in the production process and ensure that equipment and supplies are available when needed. *Metal workers and plastic workers* create all the various parts that are needed in the production and assembly processes. As the production process becomes more automated, the jobs of most metal and plastic workers are more complex than in the past. Fewer workers are simply operating machines; most are now also responsible for programming and performing minor repairs on the machine tools.

Among the most skilled metal and plastic workers are *tool and die makers,* and machinery manufacturing has about 30 percent of the nation's jobs for these workers. *Machine tool cutting setters, operators, and tenders, metal and plastic* set up and operate machines that make parts out of the raw materials. As most machines now operate automatically, the role of the machine tool operator is mainly to monitor the machine and perform minor repairs as needed.

Computer control programmers and operators manage the automatic metalworking machines that can mass-produce individual parts. They also write programs based upon the specifications of the part that define what operation the machine should perform. *Machinists* produce precision parts that require particular skill or that are needed in quantities too small to require the use of automated machinery. *Welding, soldering, and brazing workers* operate machines that join two or more pieces of metal together; they may also perform welding work manually.

Once all of the parts have been made, it is the responsibility of *assemblers and fabricators* to put them all together to finish the product. Some assemblers specialize in one particular stage of the process, while others, such as

team assemblers, work as a group and may contribute to an entire subassembly process. While there has been increased automation of the assembly process, many parts of the products still have to be put together and fastened by hand. When assembly is complete, *painting workers* apply paint or a protective coating to the exterior of the machine.

While quality control is a responsibility of all production workers, it is the primary focus of *inspectors, testers, samplers, and weighers.* They monitor the entire production stage, making sure that individual parts as well as the finished product meet the standards set by the company.

Other occupations in the field provide support to production activities. *Industrial machinery installation, repair, and maintenance workers* are skilled mechanics that make sure that all the machines and other equipment used in the production process are regularly serviced and function properly. *Production, planning, and expediting clerks* produce records and reports related to various aspects of production, such as materials and parts used, products produced, and defects encountered. They also make sure customer orders are completed, deliveries are scheduled, and shipments are made on time. *Purchasing agents* use the data provided by production, planning, and expediting clerks to procure supplies needed in production.

Training, Other Qualifications, and Advancement

The composition of the machinery manufacturing labor force continues to evolve as labor intensive tasks are automated, increasing the proportion of production work that requires additional skills. Nearly all jobs now require at least a high school diploma. Employers also want workers with good communication and problem-solving skills, since new manufacturing processes, such as lean manufacturing, require workers to be able to perform many different tasks depending on where they are most needed. Strong basic mathematical skills are also essential.

Skilled production workers, such as tool and die makers and machinists, are usually hired on the basis of previous experience or after completion of a training program at a local college. Some companies also train workers entering the field in apprenticeship programs that can last between 1 and 5 years, depending on the specialty. These programs combine on-the-job training with classroom instruction, either within the company or at local technical schools. Topics covered in the apprenticeship include mechanical drawing, tool designing, programming of computer-controlled machines, blueprint reading, mathematics, hydraulics, and electronics. Workers also learn about company policies on quality control, safety, and communications.

Experienced workers can advance into the more highly skilled positions within their field or into supervisory positions. Because advancement is based on experience and merit, even those workers who enter in low-skilled positions can advance to significantly higher-skilled jobs if they work to improve their skills.

Management and professional occupations generally require a bachelor's degree in the particular field, though some management positions are filled by experienced production workers. Most engineer jobs in the field require a degree in mechanical or electrical engineering or one of their specialties. Because engineers tend to be familiar with both design and production issues within the company, it is possible for them to advance into the upper levels of management.

Table 3. Employment in machinery manufacturing by field segment, 2004 and projected change, 2004–2014 (Employment in thousands)

Field segment	2004 Employment	Percent change 2004–2014
Machinery manufacturing, total	1,142	–12.83
Metalworking machinery manufacturing	202	–16.21
Agriculture, construction, and mining machinery manufacturing	195	–2.56
Ventilation, heating, air-conditioning, and commercial refrigeration equipment manufacturing	152	–8.79
Industrial machinery manufacturing	119	–12.53
Commercial and service field machinery manufacturing	115	–26.02
Engine, turbine, and power transmission equipment manufacturing	93	–15.95
Other general-purpose machinery manufacturing	266	–13.47

Outlook

Wage and salary employment in the machinery manufacturing field is expected to decrease 13 percent over the 2004–2014 period, compared with a 14 percent increase for all fields combined. As shown in table 3, all segments of the field are expected to experience some employment declines.

Despite the decline in employment projected for this sizeable field, a significant numbers of job openings will become available because of the need to replace workers who retire or move to jobs outside of the field. However, not all jobs that are vacated will be filled because attrition is one of the main ways that establishments reduce the number of employees. It is also a way the establishments upgrade the skill mix of their workforce. Machinery manufacturing establishments will be seeking to hire more highly skilled workers, especially persons with good basic educational skills that make the good candidates to be trained for the high-skilled job of twenty-first century manufacturing.

The main factor affecting the level of employment in the machinery manufacturing field is the high rate of productivity growth. Increases in productivity allow companies to produce more with the same number of workers. Even though output in machinery manufacturing is expected to increase significantly, firms will be able to meet the increase by increasing the productivity of existing workers, rather than by creating new jobs.

A second factor expected to cause employment declines in machinery manufacturing is growth of parts imports. This field is less likely to lose a large part of its output to imports from other countries than some other manufacturing fields. The large size and complexity of many of the types of machinery made by this field and the relatively skilled workforce it requires is an advantage that many manufacturing fields do not share. However, while

Manufacturing, Construction, and Utilities

most finished machines are made in the U.S., it is increasingly common for manufacturers to have some parts of the final product made in other countries and then shipped to the U.S. for final assembly. While still expected to account for only a small part of the total process, this increased offshoring of production will limit machinery manufacturing employment growth.

Demand for machinery is expected to remain strong. Machinery is important for all fields because it boosts their productivity, and advances in technology will make machinery even more efficient and thus more desirable. Demand for machinery is highly sensitive to cyclical swings in the economy, however, causing employment in machinery manufacturing to fluctuate. During periods of economic prosperity, companies invest in new equipment, such as machinery, in order to boost production. When economic growth slows, however, many companies are reluctant to purchase new machinery. These changes in demand cause machinery manufacturers to replace fewer workers who leave or even lay off some workers.

Although overall employment in the machinery manufacturing field is expected to decline, the outlook for occupations will vary; some will experience larger declines than others, while some will even experience growth instead. Increased automation and more efficient production processes will cause employment declines in assembler and fabricator occupations. Office and administrative support workers will also experience declines as a result of increased automation and contracting out. Employment in professional and management occupations will experience smaller declines relative to other occupations in the field; engineers in particular will experience very good employment opportunities, as they are responsible for increasing innovation and competitiveness in the field.

Earnings

The earnings of workers in the machinery manufacturing field are relatively high, primarily because of the high productivity of workers in this field. Median weekly earnings in 2004 for production workers in machinery manufacturing were $700, compared with $659 for the manufacturing sector as a whole and $529 for all fields. Earnings vary by detailed field segment of the field (table 4). They also vary based upon a worker's particular occupation, experience, and the size of the company employ-

ing them. Earnings of the largest occupations in machinery manufacturing appear in table 5.

Table 4. Average earnings of production or nonsupervisory workers in machinery manufacturing by field segment, 2004

Field segment	Weekly	Hourly
Total, nongovernment	$529	$15.67
Machinery manufacturing	700	16.68
Metalworking machinery manufacturing	754	17.80
Agriculture, construction, and mining machinery manufacturing	639	15.16
Ventilation, heating, air-conditioning, and commercial refrigeration equipment manufacturing	613	14.82
Commercial and service field manufacturing	748	18.36
Industrial machinery manufacturing	728	17.37
Engine, turbine, and power transmission equipment manufacturing	762	18.04
Other general-purpose machinery manufacturing	698	16.55

In 2004, about 11 percent of workers in machinery manufacturing were union members or were covered by union contracts, slightly less than the proportion for both the manufacturing field as a whole and all fields combined. Major unions include the International Association of Machinists and Aerospace Workers of America; the International Brotherhood of Electrical Workers; and the United Automobile, Aerospace, and Agricultural Implement Workers of America.

Table 5. Median hourly earnings of the largest occupations in machinery manufacturing, May 2004

Occupation	Machinery manufacturing	All fields
General and operations managers	$45.38	$37.22
Mechanical engineers	28.68	31.88
First-line supervisors/managers of production and operating workers	23.18	21.51

Occupation	Machinery manufacturing	All fields
Tool and die makers	19.82	20.55
Machinists	16.70	16.33
Computer-controlled machine tool operators, metal and plastic	15.96	14.75
Inspectors, testers, sorters, samplers, and weighers	15.58	13.66
Welders, cutters, solderers, and brazers	14.55	14.72
Cutting, punching, and press machine setters, operators, and tenders, metal and plastic	13.04	12.45
Team assemblers	12.73	11.42

Sources of Additional Information

Information on employment and training opportunities in the machinery manufacturing field is available from state employment service offices, employment offices of machinery manufacturing firms, and locals of the unions listed in the previous section.

Motor Vehicle and Parts Manufacturing

- Annual Earnings: $38,011
- Job Growth: 5.6%
- Size of Workforce: 1,120,800
- Self-Employed: 0.2%
- Part-Time: 1.7%

Significant Points

- Although 22 percent of jobs are located in Michigan, especially in the Detroit area, plants and jobs are increasingly being located in other parts of the country.
- Average earnings are very high compared with those of workers in the same occupations in other fields.

- Employment is highly sensitive to cyclical swings in the economy.
- Employment is expected to grow more rapidly in firms that manufacture motor vehicle parts, bodies, and trailers than in firms that make complete vehicles.

Nature of the Field

The motor vehicle is an intricate series of systems, subsystems, and components assembled into a final product. Each manufactured part or component is integrated into the vehicle; none is developed to exist separately. Vehicles are constantly changing as new technology or reengineered components are incorporated and as new and updated models are designed in response to changing consumer preferences. Motor vehicle and parts manufacturers must continually evolve to maximize efficiency and provide products that consumers want in a highly competitive market.

Motor vehicles—passenger cars, sport utility vehicles (SUVs), pickup trucks and vans, heavy-duty trucks, buses, and other special-purpose motor vehicles ranging from limousines to garbage trucks—play a central role in our society. Most U.S. residents rely on them daily to travel to work or school, shop, or visit family and friends. Businesses depend on motor vehicles to transport people and goods. The United States is the world's largest marketplace for motor vehicles because of the size and affluence of its population. According to the U.S. Department of Transportation, almost 230 million motor vehicles—nearly 136 million automobiles, 95 million trucks, and 777,000 buses—were registered in the United States in 2003. The number of light trucks—including vans, pickup trucks, and SUVs—has shown especially steady growth since the mid- to late 1980s.

Making the vehicles we drive is only a small part of the story in the motor vehicle and parts manufacturing field. In 2004, about 9,400 establishments manufactured motor vehicles and parts; these ranged from small parts plants with only a few workers to huge assembly plants that employ thousands. Table 1 shows that about 7 out of 10 establishments in the field manufactured motor vehicle parts—including electrical and electronic equipment; gasoline engines and parts; brake systems; seating and interior trim; steering and suspension components; transmission and power train parts; air conditioners; and motor vehicle stampings, such as fenders, tops, body parts, trim, and molding. Other establishments specialized in manufacturing truck trailers; motor homes; travel trailers; campers; and car, truck, and bus bodies placed on separately purchased chassis.

Table 1. Percent distribution of establishments and employment in motor vehicle and parts manufacturing by detailed field sector, 2004

Field sector	Establishments	Employment
Total	100.0	100.0
Motor vehicle parts manufacturing	68.9	62.1
Motor vehicle body and trailer manufacturing	25.9	14.9
Motor vehicle manufacturing	5.1	23.1

The motor vehicle and parts manufacturing field in the United States has become increasingly integrated into the international economy. In fact, "domestic" vehicles often are produced using the components, manufacturing plants, and distribution methods of other nations around the world, as U.S. and foreign manufacturers of motor vehicles benefit from strategic alliances in the design, production, and distribution of vehicles and parts. Collaboration in manufacturing practices has dramatically increased productivity and improved efficiency. These cooperative practices also have resulted in manufacturers from the United States, Europe, and the Pacific Rim working closely with parts suppliers and locating production plants in the countries in which they plan to sell their vehicles to reduce distribution time and costs. Foreign motor vehicle and parts makers with production sites in the United States are known as "domestic internationals" and account for a growing share of U.S. production and employment.

Globalization of the field has boosted competition among U.S. motor vehicle manufacturers, prompting innovations in product design and in the manufacturing process. Manufacturers have rapidly designed and produced new models aimed at niches in the market. Firms also must be fast and flexible in implementing new production techniques, such as replacing traditional assembly lines with modern systems using computers, robots, and interchangeable platforms. Plants designed for production flexibility put resources in the right place at the right time, allowing manufacturers to shift to new models quickly and efficiently.

Motor vehicle and parts manufacturers have a major influence on other fields in the economy. As major consumers of steel, rubber, plastics, glass, and other basic materials, they create jobs in fields that produce those materials. The production of motor vehicles also spurs employment growth in other fields, including automobile and other motor vehicle dealers; automotive repair and maintenance shops; gasoline stations; highway construction companies; and automotive parts, accessories, and tire stores.

Working Conditions

In 2004, about 33 percent of workers in the motor vehicle and parts manufacturing field worked, on average, more than 40 hours per week. Overtime is especially common during periods of peak demand. Most employees, however, typically work an 8-hour shift: either from 7 a.m. to 3:30 p.m. or from 4 p.m. to 12:30 a.m., with two breaks per shift and a half-hour for meals. A third shift often is reserved for maintenance and cleanup.

Although working conditions have improved in recent years, some production workers still are subject to uncomfortable conditions. Heat, fumes, noise, and repetition are not uncommon in this field. In addition, many workers come into contact with oil and grease and may have to lift and fit heavy objects. Employees also may operate powerful, high-speed machines that can be dangerous. Accidents and injuries usually are avoided when protective equipment and clothing are worn and safety practices are observed.

Newer plants are more automated and have safer, more comfortable conditions. For example, these plants may have ergonomically designed work areas and job tasks that accommodate the worker's physical size and eliminate awkward reaching and bending and unnecessary heavy lifting. Workers typically function as part of a team, doing more than one job and thus reducing the repetitiveness of assembly line work.

Workers in this field experience higher rates of injury and illness than do workers in most other fields. In 2003, cases of work-related injury and illness averaged 15.2 per 100 full-time workers in motor vehicle manufacturing, 12.2 in motor vehicle body and trailer manufacturing, and 9.0 in motor vehicle parts manufacturing

—compared with 6.8 in all manufacturing fields and 5.0 in the entire private sector.

As in other fields, professional and managerial workers normally have clean, comfortable offices and are not subject to the hazards of assembly line work. Improved ergonomics help office and administrative support workers avoid repetitive strain injuries, but employees using computer terminals for long periods may develop eye strain and fatigue.

Important Characteristics of the Field

Skills: Operation Monitoring; Installation; Quality Control Analysis; Equipment Maintenance; Operation and Control; Repairing. **Abilities:** Rate Control; Control Precision; Manual Dexterity; Multilimb Coordination; Arm-Hand Steadiness; Reaction Time. **Work-Related Values:** Supervision, Technical; Moral Values; Activity; Company Policies and Practices; Supervision, Human Relations; Independence.

Employment

Motor vehicle and parts manufacturing was among the largest of the manufacturing fields in 2004, providing 1.1 million jobs. The majority of jobs, about 62 percent, were in firms that make motor vehicle parts. About 23 percent of workers in the field were employed in firms assembling complete motor vehicles, while about 15 percent worked in firms producing truck trailers; motor homes; travel trailers; campers; and car, truck, and bus bodies placed on separately purchased chassis.

Although motor vehicle and parts manufacturing jobs are scattered throughout the nation, certain states account for the greatest numbers of jobs. Michigan, for example, accounts for 22 percent of all jobs. Combined, Michigan, Ohio, and Indiana include 46 percent of all the jobs in this field. Other states that account for significant numbers of jobs include California, Tennessee, Texas, Kentucky, and Missouri.

Employment is concentrated in a relatively small number of very large establishments. About 73 percent of motor vehicle and parts manufacturing jobs were in establishments employing 250 or more workers (chart 1). Motor vehicle manufacturing employment, in particular, is concentrated in large establishments, whereas many motor

vehicle parts manufacturing jobs are found in small and medium-sized establishments.

Employment data in this description do not include workers related to automotive research and development (R&D) who work in separate establishments. Under the North American Field Classification System (NAICS), workers in R&D establishments that are not part of a manufacturing facility are included in a separate field— research and development in the physical, engineering, and life sciences. This field is covered in the description of Scientific Research and Development Services elsewhere in Part II. However, given the importance of R&D work to the motor vehicle and parts manufacturing field, occupations and issues related to R&D are discussed in the following sections even though some of their employment is not included in the employment data in this description. Many of these jobs are located in Michigan.

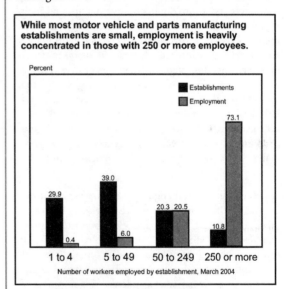

While most motor vehicle and parts manufacturing establishments are small, employment is heavily concentrated in those with 250 or more employees.

Number of workers employed by establishment, March 2004

Occupations in the Field

Prior to assembling components in the manufacturing plant, extensive design, engineering, testing, and production planning go into the manufacture of motor vehicles. These tasks often require years to complete and cost millions of dollars.

Using artistic talent; computers; and information on product use, marketing, materials, and production methods, *commercial and industrial designers* create designs they hope will make the vehicle competitive in the marketplace. Designers use sketches and computer-aided design techniques to create computer models of proposed vehicles. These computer models eliminate the need for physical body mockups in the design process because they give designers complete information on how each piece of the vehicle will work with others. Workers may repeatedly modify and redesign models until the models meet engineering, production, and marketing specifications. Designers working in parts production increasingly collaborate with manufacturers in the initial design stages to integrate motor vehicle parts into the design specifications for each vehicle.

Engineers—who form the largest professional contingent in the field—play an integral role in all stages of motor vehicle manufacturing. They oversee the building and testing of the engine, transmission, brakes, suspension, and other mechanical and electrical components. Using computers and assorted models, instruments, and tools, engineers simulate various parts of the vehicle to determine whether each part meets cost, safety, performance, and quality specifications. *Mechanical engineers* design improvements for engines, transmissions, and other working parts. *Electrical and electronics engineers* design the vehicle's electrical and electronic systems, as well as industrial robot control systems used to assemble the vehicle. *Industrial engineers* concentrate on plant layout, including the arrangement of assembly line stations, material-moving equipment, work standards, and other production matters.

Under the direction of engineers, *engineering technicians* prepare specifications for materials, devise and run tests to ensure product quality, and study ways to improve manufacturing efficiency. For example, testing may reveal how metal parts perform under conditions of heat, cold, and stress and whether emissions-control equipment meets environmental standards. Finally, prototype vehicles incorporating all the components are built and tested on test tracks, on road simulators, and in test chambers that can duplicate almost every driving condition, including crashes.

Computer systems analysts work with computer systems to improve manufacturing efficiency. After working out the many details involved, computer specialists help put in place the machinery and tools required for assembly line production of the vehicle.

Management workers establish guidelines for the design of motor vehicles to provide direction for the teams of experts in engineering, design, marketing, sales, finance, and production. From the earliest stages of planning and design, these specialists help assess whether the vehicle will satisfy consumer demand, meet safety and environmental regulations, and prove economically practical to make. These executives also serve as public representatives for the company; they are the face of the company.

Industrial production managers oversee *first-line supervisors and managers of production and operating workers*. These supervisors oversee inspectors, precision workers, machine setters and operators, assemblers, fabricators, and plant and system operators. They coordinate a variety of manufacturing processes and production activities, including scheduling, staffing, equipment, quality control, and inventory control.

Production workers account for about 64 percent of motor vehicle and parts manufacturing jobs (table 2). *Assemblers and fabricators* and *metal workers and plastic workers* put together various parts to form subassemblies and then put the subassemblies together to build a complete motor vehicle. Most assemblers in this field are *team assemblers*, who may work on a variety of tasks as needed. Some may perform other routine tasks such as mounting and inflating tires; adjusting brakes; and adding gas, oil, brake fluid, and coolant. Metal parts are welded, plastic and glass parts are molded and cut, seat cushions are sewn, and many parts are painted. Many manufacturing processes are highly automated; robots, computers, and programmable devices are an integral part of motor vehicle manufacturing. Throughout the manufacturing process, "statistical process control" (teamwork and quality control) is emphasized. From initial planning and design to final assembly, numerous tests and inspections ensure that vehicles meet quality and safety standards. Modern manufacturing facilities integrate interchangeable tools on the assembly line so that they can quickly be changed to meet the needs of various models and specifications.

Although robots perform most of the welding, *welding, soldering, and brazing workers* still are needed for some welding and for maintenance and repair duties. *Machinists* produce precision metal parts that are made in numbers too small to produce with automated machinery. *Tool and die makers* produce tools, dies, and special guiding and holding devices used in machines.

Computer-controlled machine tool operators use computer-controlled machines or robots programmed to manufacture parts of different dimensions automatically.

Workers in other production occupations run various machines that produce an array of motor vehicle bodies and parts. These workers set up and operate machines and make adjustments according to their instructions. In computer-controlled systems, they monitor computers controlling the machine processes and may have little interaction with the machinery or materials. Some workers specialize in one type of machine; others operate more than one type.

Grinding and polishing workers use hand tools or handheld power tools to sand and polish metal surfaces, and *painting workers* paint surfaces of motor vehicles. *Sewing machine operators* sew together pieces of material to form seat covers and other parts.

Throughout the manufacturing process, *inspectors, testers, sorters, samplers, and weighers* ensure that motor vehicles and parts meet quality standards. They inspect raw materials, check parts for defects, check the uniformity of subassemblies, and test-drive vehicles. *Helpers* supply or hold materials or tools and clean work areas and equipment.

Motor vehicle operators and material moving workers are essential to keeping the plant running smoothly. *Industrial truck and tractor operators* carry components, equipment, and other materials from factory warehouse and outdoor storage areas to assembly areas. *Truck drivers* carry raw materials to plants, components and materials between plants, and finished motor vehicles to dealerships for sale to consumers. *Laborers and hand freight, stock, and material movers* manually move materials to and from storage areas, loading docks, delivery vehicles, and containers. *Machine feeders and offbearers* feed materials into, or remove materials from, machines or equipment on the assembly line, and *hand packers and packagers* manually package or wrap materials.

Workers in construction, installation, maintenance, and repair occupations set up, maintain, and repair equipment. *Electricians* service complex electrical equipment. *Industrial machinery mechanics and machinery maintenance workers* maintain machinery and equipment to prevent costly breakdowns and, when necessary, perform repairs. *Millwrights* install and move machinery and heavy equipment according to the factory's layout plans.

Automotive service technicians and mechanics fix bodies, engines, and other parts of motor vehicles, industrial trucks, and other mobile heavy equipment.

Table 2. Employment of wage and salary workers in motor vehicle and parts manufacturing by occupation, 2004 and projected change, 2004–2014

Occupation	Employment, 2004		Percent change, 2004–2014
	Number	Percent	
Total, all occupations	1,109	100.0	5.6
Management, business, and financial occupations	70	6.3	12.0
Top executives	9	0.8	8.9
Business operation specialists, all other	15	1.4	19.1
Professional and related occupations	84	7.6	14.1
Industrial engineers	18	1.6	21.5
Mechanical engineers	12	1.0	14.1
Engineers, all other	18	1.6	9.6
Engineering technicians, except drafters, all other	11	1.0	11.9
Construction and extraction occupations	33	3.0	8.5
Electricians	18	1.6	8.5
Installation, maintenance, and repair occupations	74	6.7	8.9
Electrical and electronics installers and repairers, transportation equipment	1	0.1	9.7
Electronic equipment installers and repairers, motor vehicles	1	0.1	9.0
Recreational vehicle service technicians	1	0.1	9.0
Industrial machinery mechanics	13	1.1	9.4
Maintenance and repair workers, general	22	2.0	9.1
Millwrights	9	0.9	8.7

Manufacturing, Construction, and Utilities

Occupation	Employment, 2004		Percent change, 2004–2014
	Number	Percent	
Production occupations	705	63.5	4.4
First-line supervisors/ managers of production and operating workers	37	3.3	9.3
Engine and other machine assemblers	16	1.5	8.5
Team assemblers	204	18.4	9.6
Assemblers and fabricators, all other	67	6.0	–0.1
Computer-controlled machine tool operators, metal and plastic	15	1.3	10.2
Forging machine setters, operators, and tenders, metal and plastic	7	0.6	–0.1
Machine tool cutting setters, operators, and tenders, metal and plastic	63	5.6	–6.2
Machinists	25	2.2	10.0
Model makers, metal and plastic	2	0.2	1.4
Molding, coremaking, and casting machine setters, operators, and tenders, metal and plastic	16	1.4	–0.5
Multiple machine tool setters, operators, and tenders, metal and plastic	19	1.7	10.2
Tool and die makers	21	1.9	9.6
Welders, cutters, solderers, and brazers	35	3.2	9.5
Welding, soldering, and brazing machine setters, operators, and tenders	12	1.1	10.0
Metal workers and plastic workers, all other	12	1.1	–13.9
Inspectors, testers, sorters, samplers, and weighers	36	3.2	–0.7
Painting workers	16	1.5	6.3
Production workers, all other	37	3.3	–14.5
Transportation and material moving occupations	69	6.2	1.1
Industrial truck and tractor operators	24	2.2	1.5
Laborers and material movers, hand	33	3.0	0.1

Note: May not add to totals due to omission of occupations with small employment

Training, Other Qualifications, and Advancement

Faced with technological advances and the continued need to cut costs, manufacturers increasingly emphasize continuing education and cross-train many workers—that is, they train workers to do more than one job. This has led to a change in the profile of the field's workers. Standards for new hires are higher now than in the past. Employers increasingly require at least a high school diploma as the number of unskilled jobs declines, and most motor vehicle manufacturers administer lengthy examinations when hiring assemblers. Manual dexterity will continue to be necessary for many production jobs, but employers also look for employees with good communication and math skills as well as an aptitude for computers, problem solving, and critical thinking. Because many plants now emphasize the team approach, employees interact more with co-workers and supervisors to determine the best way to get the job done. They are expected to work with much less supervision than in the past and to be responsible for ensuring that their work conforms to guidelines.

Opportunities for training and advancement vary considerably by occupation, plant size, and sector. Training programs in larger auto and light truck assembly plants usually are more extensive than those in smaller parts, truck trailer, and motor home factories. Production workers receive most of their training on the job or through more formal apprenticeship programs. Training normally takes from a few days to several months and may combine classroom instruction with on-the-job training under the guidance of more experienced workers. Attaining the highest level of skill in some production jobs requires several years, however. Training often includes courses in health and safety, teamwork, and quality control. With advanced training and experience, production workers can advance to inspector or to more skilled production, craft, operator, or repair jobs.

Skilled production workers—such as tool and die makers, millwrights, machinists, pipefitters, and electricians—normally are hired on the basis of previous experience and, in some cases, a competitive examination. Alternatively, the company may train inexperienced workers in apprenticeship programs that last up to 5 years and combine on-the-job training with classroom instruction. Typical courses include mechanical drawing, tool designing and programming, blueprint reading, shop mathematics, hydraulics, and electronics. Training also includes courses on health and safety, teamwork, quality control, computers, and diagnostic equipment. With training and experience, workers who excel can advance to become supervisors or managers.

Motor vehicle manufacturers provide formal training opportunities to all workers regardless of educational background. Manufacturers offer some classes themselves and may pay tuition for workers who enroll in colleges, trade schools, or technical institutes. Workers sometimes can get college credit for training received on the job. Subjects of company training courses range from communication skills to computer science. Formal educational opportunities at postsecondary institutions range from courses in English, basic mathematics, electronics, and computer programming languages to work-study programs leading to associate, bachelor's, and graduate degrees in engineering and technician specialties, management, and other fields.

Outlook

Overall wage and salary employment in the motor vehicle and parts manufacturing field is expected to increase by 6 percent over the 2004–2014 period, compared with 14 percent for all fields combined. While employment in motor vehicle manufacturing is expected to grow very slowly, firms manufacturing motor vehicle parts, bodies, and trailers are expected to add more jobs. Employment is expected to increase by only 2 percent in motor vehicle manufacturing, with increases of 6 percent in motor vehicle parts manufacturing and 8 percent in motor vehicle body and trailer manufacturing.

Growth in firms that manufacture motor vehicle parts, bodies, and trailers will generate many job openings, as will the departure of workers who retire or transfer to jobs in other fields. Not all of the motor vehicle manufacturing workers who leave the field will be replaced, however, and many of the new workers will be hired for occupations different from those vacated by departing employees.

Employment in the motor vehicle and parts manufacturing field is expected to grow with demand for motor vehicles and parts, but jobs will be lost due to productivity increases. The growing intensity of international and domestic competition has increased cost pressures on manufacturers. In response, they have sought to improve productivity and quality with high-technology production techniques, including computer-assisted design, production, and testing. Increasing productivity should meet much of the demand created by the increasing output of the motor vehicle and parts manufacturing field, resulting in slow job growth. Moreover, the field is increasingly turning to contract employees in an effort to reduce costs. Contract workers are less costly to hire and lay off than are permanent employees; contract jobs also serve as a screening tool for candidates for permanent jobs that are more complex and require more skills.

Growth in demand for domestically manufactured motor vehicles could be limited by a number of factors, such as improvements in vehicle quality and durability, which extend longevity, and more stringent safety and environmental regulations, which increase the cost of producing and operating motor vehicles. Continued efforts to reduce costs also may drive some manufacturers to import parts. However, manufacturing output is expected to continue to grow over the projection period to replace existing vehicles and meet the demand for new vehicles as the driving population grows.

Employment in motor vehicle and parts manufacturing is highly sensitive to cyclical swings in the economy. During periods of economic prosperity, consumers are more willing and able to purchase expensive goods such as motor vehicles, which may require large down payments and extended loan payments. During recessions, however, consumers are more likely to delay such purchases. Motor vehicle manufacturers respond to these changes in demand by hiring or laying off workers.

Expanding factory automation, robotics, efficiency gains, and the need to cut costs are expected to keep employment from growing as fast as output. Increases in efficiency and automation will cause employment declines in some occupations, particularly in production occupations. Employment of office and administrative support workers will decline due to expanding office and warehouse automation. Automation and continued global competition, however, are expected to produce job growth for industrial engineers, industrial production managers, business operations specialists, and computer specialists. Manufacturers will increasingly turn to these

Manufacturing, Construction, and Utilities

workers for further innovation in reducing costs and enhancing competitive advantage.

Earnings

Average weekly earnings of production or nonsupervisory workers in the motor vehicle and parts manufacturing field are relatively high. At $1,217 per week, earnings of production workers in establishments that manufacture complete motor vehicles were among the highest in the nation in 2004. Workers in establishments that make motor vehicle parts averaged $872 weekly, and those in motor vehicle body and trailer manufacturing earned $690 per week, compared with $659 for workers in all manufacturing fields and $529 for those in the entire private sector. Earnings in selected occupations in transportation equipment manufacturing, which comprises motor vehicle and parts manufacturing and aerospace product and parts manufacturing, appear in table 3.

Table 3. Median hourly earnings of the largest occupations in transportation equipment manufacturing, May 2004

Occupation	Transportation equipment manufacturing	All fields
Industrial engineers	$31.15	$31.26
Production workers, all other	24.12	11.38
First-line supervisors/managers of production and operating workers	24.10	21.51
Assemblers and fabricators, all other	23.85	11.90
Maintenance and repair workers, general	19.66	14.77
Inspectors, testers, sorters, samplers, and weighers	18.51	13.66
Machinists	17.56	16.33
Welders, cutters, solderers, and brazers	15.55	14.72
Team assemblers	13.79	11.42
Cutting, punching, and press machine setters, operators, and tenders, metal and plastic	13.46	12.45

These hourly earnings may increase during overtime or special shifts. Workers generally are paid 1.5 times their normal wage rate for working more than 8 hours a day or more than 40 hours a week or for working on Saturdays. They may receive double their normal wage rate for working on Sundays and holidays. The largest manufacturers and suppliers often offer other benefits, including paid vacations and holidays; life, accident, and health insurance; education allowances; nonwage cash payment plans, such as performance and profit-sharing bonuses; and pension plans. Some laid-off workers in the motor vehicle and parts manufacturing field have access to supplemental unemployment benefits, which can provide them with nearly full pay and benefits for up to several years, depending on the worker's seniority.

Sources of Additional Information

Information on employment and training opportunities in the motor vehicle and parts manufacturing field is available from local offices of state employment services, employment offices of motor vehicle and parts manufacturing firms, and locals of the unions mentioned earlier.

Pharmaceutical and Medicine Manufacturing

- Annual Earnings: $44,420
- Job Growth: 26.1%
- Size of Workforce: 287,150
- Self-Employed: 0.7%
- Part-Time: 3.6%

Significant Points

- This field ranks among the fastest-growing manufacturing fields.
- More than 6 out of 10 workers have a bachelor's, master's, professional, or Ph.D. degree—twice the proportion for all fields combined.

- Fifty-nine percent of all jobs are in large establishments employing more than 500 workers.

- Earnings are much higher than in other manufacturing fields.

Nature of the Field

The pharmaceutical and medicine manufacturing field has produced a variety of medicinal and other health-related products undreamed of by even the most imaginative apothecaries of the past. These drugs save the lives of millions of people from various diseases and permit many ill people to lead normal lives.

Thousands of medications are available today for diagnostic, preventive, and therapeutic uses. In addition to aiding in the treatment of infectious diseases such as pneumonia, tuberculosis, malaria, influenza, and sexually transmitted diseases, these medicines also help prevent and treat cardiovascular disease, asthma, diabetes, hepatitis, cystic fibrosis, and cancer. For example, antinausea drugs help cancer patients endure chemotherapy, clot-buster drugs help stroke patients avoid brain damage, and psychoactive drugs reduce the severity of mental illness for many people. Antibiotics and vaccines have virtually wiped out such diseases as diphtheria, syphilis, and whooping cough. Discoveries in veterinary drugs have controlled various diseases, some of which are transmissible to humans.

Advances in biotechnology and information technology are transforming drug discovery and development. Within biotechnology, scientists have learned a great deal about human genes, but the real work—translating that knowledge into viable new drugs—has only recently begun. So far, millions of people have benefited from medicines and vaccines developed through biotechnology, and several hundred new biotechnologically-derived medicines are currently in the pipeline. These new medicines, all of which are in human clinical trials or awaiting FDA approval, include drugs for cancer, infectious diseases, autoimmune diseases, neurologic disorders, and HIV/AIDS and related conditions.

Many new drugs are expected to be developed in the coming years. Advances in technology and the knowledge of how cells work will allow pharmaceutical and medicine manufacturing makers to become more efficient in the drug discovery process. New technology allows life scientists to test millions of drug candidates far more rapidly than in the past. Other new technology, such as regenerative therapy using stem cell research, also will allow the natural healing process to work faster or to enable the regrowth of missing or damaged tissue.

There is a direct relationship between gene discovery and identification of new drugs—the more genes identified, the more paths available for drug discovery. Discovery of new genes also can lead to new diagnostics for the early detection of disease. Among other uses, new genetic technology is being explored to develop vaccines to prevent or treat diseases that have eluded traditional vaccines, such as AIDS, malaria, tuberculosis, and cervical cancer.

The pharmaceutical and medicine manufacturing field consists of about 2,500 places of employment located throughout the country. These include establishments that make pharmaceutical preparations or finished drugs; biological products, such as serums and vaccines; bulk chemicals and botanicals used in making finished drugs; and diagnostic substances such as pregnancy and blood glucose kits.

The U.S. pharmaceutical field has achieved worldwide prominence through research and development (R&D) work on new drugs and spends a relatively high proportion of its funds on R&D compared with other fields. Each year, pharmaceutical field testing involves tens of thousands of new substances, yet may eventually yield fewer than 100 new prescription medicines.

For the majority of firms in this field, the actual manufacture of drugs is the last stage in a lengthy process that begins with scientific research to discover new products and to improve or modify existing ones. The R&D departments in pharmaceutical and medicine manufacturing firms start this process by seeking and rapidly testing libraries of thousands to millions of new chemical compounds with the potential to prevent, combat, or alleviate symptoms of diseases or other health problems. Scientists use sophisticated techniques, including computer simulation, combinatorial chemistry, and high-throughput screening (HTS), to hasten and simplify the discovery of potentially useful new compounds.

Most firms devote a substantial portion of their R&D budgets to applied research, using scientific knowledge to develop a drug targeted to a specific use. For example, an R&D unit may focus on developing a compound that will effectively slow the advance of breast cancer. If the discovery phase yields promising compounds, technical teams then attempt to develop a safe and effective product based on the discoveries.

To test new products in development, a research method called "screening" is used. To screen an antibiotic, for example, a sample is first placed in a bacterial culture. If the antibiotic is effective, it is next tested on infected laboratory animals. Laboratory animals also are used to study the safety and efficacy of the new drug. A new drug is selected for testing on humans only if it promises to have therapeutic advantages over drugs already in use or is safer. Drug screening is an incredibly risky, laborious, and costly process—only 1 in every 5,000 to 10,000 compounds screened eventually becomes an approved drug.

After laboratory screening, firms conduct clinical investigations, or "trials," of the drug on human patients. Human clinical trials normally take place in three phases. First, medical scientists administer the drug to a small group of healthy volunteers to determine and adjust dosage levels and monitor for side effects. If a drug appears useful and safe, additional tests are conducted in two more phases, each phase using a successively larger group of volunteers or carefully selected patients, sometimes upwards of 10,000 individuals.

After a drug successfully passes animal and clinical tests, the U.S. Food and Drug Administration's (FDA) Center for Drug Evaluation and Research (CDER) must review the drug's performance on human patients before approving the substance for commercial use. The entire process, from the first discovery of a promising new compound to FDA approval, can take over a decade and cost hundreds of millions of dollars.

After FDA approval, problems of production methods and costs must be worked out before manufacturing begins. If the original laboratory process of preparing and compounding the ingredients is complex and too expensive, pharmacists, chemists, chemical engineers, packaging engineers, and production specialists are assigned to develop a manufacturing process economically adaptable to mass production. After the drug is marketed, new production methods may be developed to incorporate new technology or to transfer the manufacturing operation to a new production site.

In many production operations, pharmaceutical manufacturers have developed a high degree of automation. Milling and micronizing machines, which pulverize substances into extremely fine particles, are used to reduce bulk chemicals to the required size. These finished chemicals are combined and processed further in mixing machines. The mixed ingredients may then be mechanically capsulated, pressed into tablets, or made into solutions. One type of machine, for example, automatically fills, seals, and stamps capsules. Other machines fill bottles with capsules, tablets, or liquids and seal, label, and package the bottles.

Quality control and quality assurance are vital in this field. Many production workers are assigned full time to quality control and quality assurance functions, whereas other employees may devote part of their time to these functions. For example, although pharmaceutical company sales representatives, often called detailers, work primarily in marketing, they engage in quality control when they assist pharmacists in checking for outdated products.

Working Conditions

Working conditions in pharmaceutical plants are better than those in most other manufacturing plants. Much emphasis is placed on keeping equipment and work areas clean because of the danger of contamination. Plants usually are air-conditioned, well lighted, and quiet. Ventilation systems protect workers from dust, fumes, and disagreeable odors. Special precautions are taken to protect the relatively small number of employees who work with infectious cultures and poisonous chemicals. With the exception of work performed by material handlers and maintenance workers, most jobs require little physical effort. In 2003, the incidence of work-related injury and illness was 2.8 cases per 100 full-time workers, compared with 6.8 per 100 for all manufacturing fields and 5.0 per 100 for the entire private sector.

Only about 3 percent of the workers in the pharmaceutical and medicine manufacturing field are union members or are covered by a union contract, compared with about 14 percent of all nongovernment workers.

Important Characteristics of the Field

Skills: Quality Control Analysis; Operation Monitoring; Science; Troubleshooting; Equipment Maintenance; Operation and Control. **Abilities:** Control Precision; Perceptual Speed; Reaction Time; Rate Control;

Response Orientation; Selective Attention. **Work-Related Values:** Independence; Supervision, Technical; Company Policies and Practices; Activity; Advancement; Moral Values.

Employment

Pharmaceutical and medicine manufacturing provided 291,000 wage and salary jobs in 2004. Pharmaceutical and medicine manufacturing establishments typically employ many workers. Nearly 60 percent of this field's jobs in 2004 were in establishments that employed more than 500 workers (chart 1). Most jobs are in California, Illinois, Texas, Indiana, New Jersey, New York, North Carolina, and Pennsylvania.

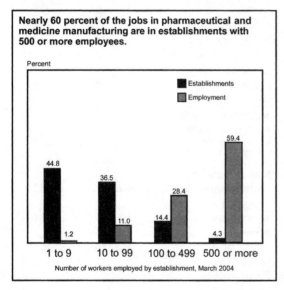

Nearly 60 percent of the jobs in pharmaceutical and medicine manufacturing are in establishments with 500 or more employees.

Under the North American Field Classification System (NAICS), workers in research and development (R&D) establishments that are not part of a manufacturing facility are included in a separate field—research and development in the physical, engineering, and life sciences. However, due to the importance of R&D work to the pharmaceutical and medicine manufacturing field, drug-related R&D is discussed in this description even though a large proportion of pharmaceutical field-related R&D workers are not included in the employment data.

Occupations in the Field

About 29 percent of all jobs in the pharmaceutical and medicine manufacturing field are in professional and related occupations, mostly scientists and science technicians; about 18 percent are in management occupations; another 12 percent are in office and administrative support; and 3 percent are in sales and related occupations. About 1 out of 4 jobs in the field are in production occupations, including both low-skilled and high-skilled jobs (table 1).

Scientists, engineers, and technicians conduct research to develop new drugs. Others work to streamline production methods and improve environmental and quality control. Life scientists are among the largest scientific occupations in this field. Most of these scientists are *biological* and *medical scientists* who produce new drugs using biotechnology to recombine the genetic material of animals or plants. Biological scientists normally specialize in a particular area. *Biologists* and *bacteriologists* study the effect of chemical agents on infected animals. *Biochemists* study the action of drugs on body processes by analyzing the chemical combination and reactions involved in metabolism, reproduction, and heredity. *Microbiologists* grow strains of microorganisms that produce antibiotics. *Physiologists* investigate the effect of drugs on body functions and vital processes. *Pharmacologists* and *zoologists* study the effects of drugs on animals. *Virologists* grow viruses and develop vaccines and test them in animals. *Botanists*, with their special knowledge of plant life, contribute to the discovery of botanical ingredients for drugs. Other biological scientists include *pathologists*, who study normal and abnormal cells or tissues, and *toxicologists*, who are concerned with safety, dosage levels, and the compatibility of different drugs. *Medical scientists*, who also may be physicians, conduct clinical research, test products, and oversee human clinical trials.

The work of physical scientists, particularly *chemists*, also is important in the development of new drugs. *Combinatorial* and *computational chemists* create molecules and test them rapidly for desirable properties. *Organic chemists*, often using combinatorial chemistry, then combine new compounds for biological testing. *Physical chemists* separate and identify substances, determine molecular structure, help create new compounds, and improve manufacturing processes. *Radiochemists* trace the course of drugs through body organs and tissues. *Pharmaceutical chemists* set standards and specifications for the form of products and for storage conditions; they also see that drug labeling and literature meet the requirements of state and federal laws. *Analytical chemists* test raw and intermediate materials and finished products for quality.

Science technicians, such as *biological* and *chemical technicians*, play an important part in research and development of new medicines. They set up, operate, and maintain laboratory equipment; monitor experiments; analyze data; and record and interpret results. Science technicians usually work under the supervision of scientists or engineers.

Although engineers account for a small fraction of scientific and technical workers, they make significant contributions toward improving quality control and production efficiency. *Chemical engineers* design equipment and devise manufacturing processes. *Bioprocess engineers*, who are similar to chemical engineers, design fermentation vats and various bioreactors for microorganisms that will produce a given product. *Industrial engineers* plan equipment layout and workflow to maintain efficient use of plant facilities.

Table 1. Employment of wage and salary workers in pharmaceutical and medicine manufacturing by occupation, 2004 and projected change, 2004–2014 (Employment in thousands)

Occupation	Employment, 2004		Percent change, 2004–2014
	Number	Percent	
Total, all occupations	291	100.0	26.1
Management, business, and financial occupations	53	18.2	31.7
Top executives	4	1.5	27.8
Marketing and sales managers	4	1.3	34.1
Industrial production managers	4	1.3	28.9
Natural sciences managers	5	1.6	28.9
Managers, all other	5	1.6	28.9
Business operation specialists, all other	7	2.3	41.8
Accountants and auditors	3	1.0	28.9
Professional and related occupations	85	29.3	31.7
Computer systems analysts	4	1.3	41.7
Industrial engineers, including health and safety	3	1.0	28.4
Industrial engineering technicians	3	0.9	29.1
Biochemists and biophysicists	4	1.2	28.9
Microbiologists	3	1.0	28.9
Medical scientists, except epidemiologists	10	3.5	41.8
Chemists	14	5.0	23.6
Biological technicians	8	2.8	28.2
Chemical technicians	5	1.6	28.9
Sales and related occupations	9	3.0	27.9
Sales representatives, wholesale and manufacturing, technical and scientific products	6	2.0	28.9
Office and administrative support occupations	34	11.6	14.5
Bookkeeping, accounting, and auditing clerks	2	0.8	16.0
Customer service representatives	3	0.9	32.0
Production, planning, and expediting clerks	3	1.0	27.6
Shipping, receiving, and traffic clerks	3	1.1	16.7
Executive secretaries and administrative assistants	5	1.7	22.2
Secretaries, except legal, medical, and executive	5	1.7	8.5
Installation, maintenance, and repair occupations	13	4.5	28.8
Industrial machinery installation, repair, and maintenance workers	10	3.5	28.9

Occupation	Employment, 2004		Percent change, 2004–2014
	Number	Percent	
Production occupations	79	27.0	21.6
First-line supervisors/ managers of production and operating workers	7	2.5	28.9
Team assemblers	5	1.6	28.9
Chemical plant and system operators	3	1.0	28.9
Chemical equipment operators and tenders	8	2.6	28.9
Separating, filtering, clarifying, precipitating, and still machine setters, operators, and tenders	6	2.0	28.9
Mixing and blending machine setters, operators, and tenders	8	2.7	28.9
Inspectors, testers, sorters, samplers, and weighers	8	2.7	16.3
Packaging and filling machine operators and tenders	22	7.6	9.8
Transportation and material moving occupations	13	4.4	20.2
Laborers and material movers, hand	10	3.6	18.2

Note: May not add to totals due to omission of occupations with small employment

At the top of the managerial group are executives who make policy decisions concerning matters of finance, marketing, and research. Other managerial workers include *natural sciences managers* and *industrial production managers.*

Office and administrative support employees include *secretaries and administrative assistants, general office clerks,* and others who keep records on personnel, payroll, raw materials, sales, and shipments.

Sales representatives, wholesale and manufacturing, describe their company's products to physicians, pharmacists, dentists, and health services administrators. These sales representatives serve as lines of communication between their companies and clients.

Most plant workers fall into 1 of 2 occupational groups: production workers who operate drug-producing equipment, inspect products, and install, maintain, and repair production equipment and transportation and material moving workers who package and transport the drugs.

Workers among the larger of the production occupations, *assemblers and fabricators,* perform all of the assembly tasks assigned to their teams, rotating through the different tasks rather than specializing in a single task. They also may decide how the work is to be assigned and how different tasks are to be performed.

Other production workers specialize in one part of the production process. *Chemical processing machine setters, operators, and tenders,* such as *pharmaceutical operators,* control machines that produce tablets, capsules, ointments, and medical solutions. Included among these operators are *mixing and blending machine setters, operators, and tenders,* who tend milling and grinding machines that reduce mixtures to particles of designated sizes. *Extruding, forming, pressing, and compacting machine setters, operators, and tenders* tend tanks and kettles in which solutions are mixed and compounded to make up creams, ointments, liquid medications, and powders. *Crushing, grinding, polishing, mixing, and blending workers* operate machines that compress ingredients into tablets. *Coating, painting, and spraying machine setters, operators, and tenders,* often called capsule coaters, control a battery of machines that apply coatings that flavor, color, preserve, or add medication to tablets or control disintegration time. Throughout the production process, *inspectors, testers, sorters, samplers, and weighers* ensure consistency and quality. For example, *ampoule examiners* inspect ampoules for discoloration, foreign particles, and flaws in the glass. *Tablet testers* inspect tablets for hardness, chipping, and weight to assure conformity with specifications. After the drug is prepared and inspected, it is bottled or otherwise packaged by *packaging and filling machine operators and tenders.*

Training, Other Qualifications, and Advancement

Training requirements for jobs in the pharmaceutical and medicine manufacturing field range from a few hours of on-the-job training to years of formal education plus job experience. More than 6 out of 10 of all workers have a bachelor's, master's, professional, or Ph.D. degree—twice

Manufacturing, Construction, and Utilities

the proportion for all fields combined. The field places a heavy emphasis on continuing education for employees, and many firms provide classroom training in safety, environmental and quality control, and technological advances.

For production occupations, manufacturers usually hire inexperienced workers and train them on the job; high school graduates generally are preferred. Beginners in production jobs assist experienced workers and learn to operate processing equipment. With experience, employees may advance to more skilled jobs in their departments.

Many companies encourage production workers to take courses related to their jobs at local schools and technical institutes or to enroll in correspondence courses. College courses in chemistry and related areas are particularly encouraged for highly skilled production workers who operate sophisticated equipment. Some companies reimburse workers for part, or all, of their tuition. Skilled production workers with leadership ability may advance to supervisory positions.

For science technician jobs in this field, most companies prefer to hire graduates of technical institutes or community colleges or those who have completed college courses in chemistry, biology, mathematics, or engineering. Some companies, however, require science technicians to hold a bachelor's degree in a biological or chemical science. In many firms, newly hired workers begin as laboratory helpers or aides, performing routine jobs such as cleaning and arranging bottles, test tubes, and other equipment.

The experience required for higher-level technician jobs varies from company to company. Usually, employees advance over a number of years from assistant technician to technician to senior technician and then to technical associate, or supervisory technician.

For most scientific and engineering jobs, a bachelor of science degree is the minimum requirement. Scientists involved in research and development usually have a master's or doctoral degree. A doctoral degree is generally the minimum requirement for medical scientists, and those who administer drug or gene therapy to patients in clinical trials must have a medical degree. Because biotechnology is not one discipline but the interaction of several disciplines, the best preparation for work in biotechnology is training in a traditional biological sci-

ence, such as genetics, molecular biology, biochemistry, virology, or biochemical engineering. Individuals with a scientific background and several years of industrial experience may eventually advance to managerial positions. Some companies offer training programs to help scientists and engineers keep abreast of new developments in their fields and to develop administrative skills. These programs may include meetings and seminars with consultants from various fields. Many companies encourage scientists and engineers to further their education; some companies provide financial assistance or full reimbursement of expenses for this purpose. Publication of scientific papers also is encouraged.

Pharmaceutical manufacturing companies prefer to hire college graduates, particularly those with strong scientific backgrounds. In addition to a 4-year degree, most newly employed pharmaceutical sales representatives complete rigorous formal training programs revolving around their company's product lines.

Outlook

The number of wage and salary jobs in pharmaceutical and medicine manufacturing is expected to increase by about 26 percent over the 2004–2014 period, compared with 14 percent for all fields combined. Pharmaceutical and medicine manufacturing ranks among the fastest-growing manufacturing fields. Demand for this field's products is expected to remain strong. Even during fluctuating economic conditions, there will be a market for over-the-counter and prescription drugs, including the diagnostics used in hospitals, laboratories, and homes; the vaccines used routinely on infants and children; analgesics and other symptom-easing drugs; antibiotics and other drugs for life-threatening diseases; and "lifestyle" drugs for the treatment of non–life-threatening conditions.

Although the use of drugs, particularly antibiotics and vaccines, has helped to eradicate or limit a number of deadly diseases, many others, such as cancer, Alzheimer's, and heart disease, continue to elude cures. Ongoing research and the manufacture of new products to combat these diseases will continue to contribute to employment growth.

Because so many of the pharmaceutical and medicine manufacturing field's products are related to preventive or routine healthcare, rather than just illness, demand is expected to increase as the population expands. The growing number of older people who will require more healthcare services will further stimulate demand—along with the growth of both public and private health insurance programs, which increasingly cover the cost of drugs and medicines.

Another factor propelling demand is the increasing popularity of "lifestyle" drugs that treat symptoms of chronic non–life-threatening conditions resulting from aging or genetic predisposition and can enhance one's self-confidence or physical appearance. Other factors expected to increase the demand for drugs include greater personal income and the rising health consciousness and expectations of the general public.

Despite the increasing demand for drugs, drug producers and buyers are expected to place more emphasis on cost effectiveness due to concerns about the cost of healthcare, including prescription drugs. Growing competition from the producers of generic drugs also may exert cost pressures on many firms in this field, particularly as brand-name drug patents expire. In addition, the average time for the FDA to review "nonpriority" drug applications is becoming longer, further delaying the time a drug comes to market. These factors, combined with continuing improvements in manufacturing processes, are expected to result in slower employment growth over the 2004–2014 period than occurred during the previous 10-year period.

Strong demand is anticipated for professional occupations—especially for life and physical scientists engaged in R&D, the backbone of the pharmaceutical and medicine manufacturing field. Much of the basic biological research done in recent years has resulted in new knowledge, including the successful identification of genes. Life and physical scientists will be needed to take this knowledge to the next stage, which is to understand how certain genes function so that gene therapies can be developed to treat diseases. Computer specialists such as systems analysts, biostatisticians, and computer support specialists also will be in demand as disciplines such as biology, chemistry, and electronics continue to converge and become more interdisciplinary, creating demand in rapidly emerging fields such as bioinformatics and nanotechnology. Strong demand also is projected for production occupations. Employment of office and administrative support workers is expected to grow more slowly than the field as a whole as companies streamline operations and increasingly rely on computers. In an

effort to curb research and technological development costs, many companies have merged. As companies consolidate and grow in size, so do their marketing and sales departments. Despite substantial increases over the past decade, sales forces at pharmaceutical and medicine manufacturing firms should continue to experience strong growth as companies promote and sell their products to doctors at hospitals and private clinics.

Unlike many other manufacturing fields, the pharmaceutical and medicine manufacturing field is not highly sensitive to changes in economic conditions. Even during periods of high unemployment, work is likely to be relatively stable in this field.

Earnings

Earnings of workers in the pharmaceutical and medicine manufacturing field are higher than the average for all manufacturing fields. In May 2004, production or non-supervisory workers in this field averaged $892 a week, while those in all manufacturing fields averaged $659 a week. Earnings in selected occupations in pharmaceutical and medicine manufacturing appear in table 2.

Some employees work in plants that operate around the clock—three shifts a day, 7 days a week. In most plants, workers receive extra pay when assigned to the second or third shift. Because drug production is subject to little seasonal variation, work is steady.

Table 2. Median hourly earnings of the largest occupations in pharmaceutical and medicine manufacturing, May 2004

Occupation	Pharmaceutical and medicine manufacturing	All fields
Medical scientists, except epidemiologists	$36.92	$10.67
Sales representatives, wholesale and manufacturing, technical and scientific products	30.69	26.95
Chemists	27.43	29.48
Business operations specialists, all other	26.76	15.97
First-line supervisors/managers of production and operating workers	25.46	13.66

Occupation	Pharmaceutical and medicine manufacturing	All fields
Biological technicians	18.62	13.51
Chemical equipment operators and tenders	15.80	18.69
Inspectors, testers, sorters, samplers, and weighers	15.08	21.51
Mixing and blending machine setters, operators, and tenders	14.14	25.70
Packaging and filling machine operators and tenders	12.89	28.17

Sources of Additional Information

For additional information about careers in pharmaceutical and medicine manufacturing and the field in general, write to the personnel departments of individual pharmaceutical and medicine manufacturing companies.

For information about careers in biotechnology, contact

- Biotechnology Industry Organization, 1625 K St. NW, Suite 1100, Washington, DC 20006. Internet: http://www.bio.org

For information on careers in pharmaceutical and medicine manufacturing, contact

- Pharmaceutical Research and Manufacturers of America (PHRMA), 1100 15th St. NW, Washington, DC 20005. Internet: http://www.phrma.org

Printing

- ◎ Annual Earnings: $30,210
- ◎ Job Growth: –9.8%
- ◎ Size of Workforce: 658,740
- ◎ Self-Employed: 4.2%
- ◎ Part-Time: 8.6%

Significant Points

- Employment is expected to decline in the face of increasing computerization, growing imports of some printed materials, and the expanding use of the Internet.

- Computerization has eliminated many prepress and production jobs but has also provided new job opportunities for digital typesetters, desktop publishers, and other computer-related occupations.

- Though employment is concentrated in firms that employ 50 or more workers, most firms are small: 7 out of 10 employ fewer than 10 people.

Nature of the Field

The printing field prints products ranging from newspapers, magazines, and books to brochures, labels, newsletters, postcards, memo pads, business order forms, checks, maps, T-shirts, and packaging. The field also consists of establishments that provide related services to printers, such as embossing, binding, finishing, and prepress services. Commercial lithographic printing establishments, which print a wide variety of products, including newspaper inserts, catalogs, pamphlets, and advertisements, make up the largest segment of the field, accounting for about 31 percent of employment and about 39 percent of total establishments. Establishments offering primarily digital printing, which is the most technologically advanced method of printing, constitute the smallest segment of the field—about 4 percent of total employment. Much of the work of this segment is characterized by low volume and is often done by very small shops. Another segment of the printing field is quick printing. Quick-printing establishments generally provide short-run printing and copying with fast turnaround times.

Printing is a large field composed of many shops that vary in size. About 7 of every 10 printing shops employ 10 or fewer workers. (See chart.)

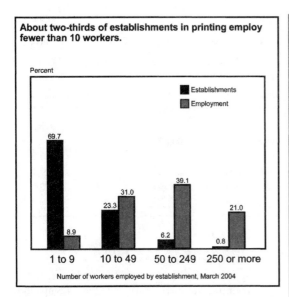

About two-thirds of establishments in printing employ fewer than 10 workers.

Percent

	Establishments	Employment
1 to 9	69.7	8.9
10 to 49	23.3	31.0
50 to 249	6.2	39.1
250 or more	0.8	21.0

Number of workers employed by establishment, March 2004

There are five printing methods that use plates or some other form of image carrier—lithography, flexography, gravure, screen printing, and letterpress. Plateless or non-impact processes, such as electronic, electrostatic, or inkjet or "toner-based" printing, are used mainly for copying, duplicating, and specialty printing and are being used more and more throughout the field.

Lithography, which uses the basic principle that water repels oil, is the most widely used printing process in the field. Lithography lends itself to computer composition and the economical use of color, accounting for its dominance. Flexography produces vibrant colors with little ruboff, qualities valued for newspapers, directories, and books, which are its biggest markets. Gravure's high-quality reproduction, flexible pagination and formats, and consistent print quality have won it a significant share of packaging and product printing and a growing share of periodical printing. Screen printing prints designs on clothes and other fabric items, such as caps or napkins. Where letterpress is still used, it prints images from the raised surfaces on which ink sits; the sunken surfaces do not show up on the paper. The raised surfaces are generated by means of casting, acid etching, or photoemulsion.

The printing field, like many other fields, continues to undergo technological changes as computers and technology alter the manner in which work is performed. Many of the processes that were once done by hand are becoming more automated. Technology's influence can be seen in all three stages of printing: *Prepress*, preparation of materials for printing; *press* or *output*, the actual printing process; and *postpress* or *finishing*, the folding, binding, and trimming of printed sheets into final form. The most notable changes have occurred in the prepress stage. Instead of cutting and pasting articles by hand, workers now produce entire publications on a computer, complete with artwork and graphics. Columns can be displayed and arranged on the computer screen exactly as they will appear in print and then be printed. Nearly all prepress work is becoming computerized, and prepress workers need more training in computers and graphic communications software. Technology has also affected the printing process. In response to environmental concerns, printers increasingly use alcohol-free solutions, water-based inks, and recycled paper.

Most commercial printers now do some form of digital printing. Printing processes today use scanners and digital cameras to input images and computers to manipulate and format the graphic images prior to printing. Digital printing also is transforming prepress operations as well as the printing process. It eliminates much of the lengthy process in transferring print files to the printing press by directly transferring digital files to an electronically driven output device, bypassing traditional prepress operations.

Working Conditions

The average nonsupervisory worker in the printing and related support activities field worked 38.4 hours per week in 2004, compared with 40.8 hours per week across all manufacturing fields. Workers in the field generally put in an 8-hour day, but overtime is often required to meet production deadlines. Larger companies tend to have shift work. There is a fair amount of variability with shift schedules and overtime, which are based largely on seniority.

Working conditions vary by occupation. For example, press operators who work with large web presses or pieces of bindery equipment wear ear protectors. On the other hand, prepress technicians and related workers usually work in quiet, clean, air-conditioned offices. Fortunately, with the advanced technology in machinery, there is not as much strain on the eyes as in the past. Most printing work involves dealing with fine detail, which can be tiring both mentally and physically.

Manufacturing, Construction, and Utilities

Even with more safety-enhanced machinery, some workers still are subject to occupational hazards. Platemakers, for example, may work with toxic chemicals that can cause skin irritations, and press operators work with rapidly moving machinery that can cause injuries. In recent years, working conditions have become less hazardous as the field has become more automated. Also, companies are using fewer chemicals and solutions than in the past and are experiencing fewer equipment-related accidents.

Important Characteristics of the Field

Skills: Operation and Control; Operation Monitoring; Equipment Maintenance; Quality Control Analysis. **Abilities:** Visual Color Discrimination; Manual Dexterity; Control Precision; Dynamic Flexibility; Rate Control; Wrist-Finger Speed. **Work-Related Values:** Moral Values; Supervision, Technical; Independence; Supervision, Human Relations; Activity; Company Policies and Practices.

Employment

In 2004, the printing field had about 665,000 wage and salary jobs in addition to 33,000 self-employed and unpaid family workers, ranking it among the larger manufacturing fields. About 9 percent of wage and salary jobs were in establishments employing fewer than 10 workers. (See chart.) About 31 percent were in the largest field sector—commercial lithographic printing (table 1). Printing plants are widely dispersed throughout the country; however, more specialized types of printing tend to be regionally concentrated. For example, the printing of financial documents is concentrated in New York City.

Table 1. Percent distribution of establishments and wage and salary employment in printing by detailed field, 2004

Field segment	Establish- ments	Employ- ment
Total	100.0	100.0
Commercial lithographic printing	31.3	39.5
Commercial gravure printing	1.0	2.6
Commercial flexographic printing	3.9	6.2

Field segment	Establish- ments	Employ- ment
Commercial screen printing	12.7	9.9
Quick printing	26.3	10.5
Digital printing	3.7	3.0
Manifold business forms printing	2.4	6.0
Book printing	1.5	5.0
Blank book and looseleaf binder manufacturing	0.6	1.6
Other commercial printing	8.6	7.1
Trade binding and related work	2.7	3.7
Prepress services	5.2	4.8

Occupations in the Field

Printing occupations range in skill from those found in quick printing to specialized production occupations rarely found in other fields (table 2). Production occupations make up 53 percent of field employment with printing machine operators accounting for the most employment of any single occupation in the field at 14 percent.

Prepress technicians and workers basically prepare material for printing presses: They take what clients send to them and make it printworthy. Increasingly, prepress technicians receive the material for the pages as electronic computer files, which they load into their computers, and use digital imaging software to lay out the pages. In very small shops or shops with small format digital equipment, prepress technicians can also do design for those clients who need it. "Preflight" technicians examine and edit the pages to ensure that the design, format, settings, quality, and all other aspects of the automated desktop work are acceptable and that the finished product will be completed according to the client's specifications before it is printed.

Printing plants that use older technology and employ people in older, manual occupations, such as film strippers, lithographic dot etchers, and platemakers, are disappearing. However, because of digitization, new computerized occupations have arisen. *Scanner operators,* for example, employ electronic or computerized scanning equipment to produce and screen film separations of photographs or art to use in lithographic printing plates. *Desktop publishers* and *digital typesetters* perform typesetting and page layout on personal computers and make sure that the files submitted by the customers are in the right format. *Illustrators* create drawings, charts, graphs, or full-color artwork to complement the text, while *graphic designers* use their creativity and computer skills to lay out advertising material, brochures, and other print items that artfully bring together text, photos, and illustrations to create the kind of visual impact desired by clients.

When the material is ready, *printing machine operators* install and adjust the printing plate on the press, mix fountain solution, adjust pressure, ink the printing presses, load paper, and adjust the press to the paper size. Operators also must correct any problems that might occur during a press run. *Job printers,* who usually work in small print shops, perform the prepress work as well as operate the press.

Table 2. Employment of wage and salary workers in printing by occupation, 2004 and projected change, 2004–2014 (Employment in thousands)

Occupation	Employment, 2004 Number	Percent	Percent change, 2004–2014
Total, all occupations	665	100.0	–9.8
Management, business, and financial occupations	45	6.7	–2.8
Top executives	14	2.2	–4.7
Industrial production managers	5	0.8	–3.9
Cost estimators	6	0.8	2.2
Professional and related occupations	29	4.3	–5.3
Computer specialists	8	1.2	–1.9
Graphic designers	14	2.1	–9.1
Sales and related occupations	37	5.5	–4.5
Sales representatives, wholesale and manufacturing, except technical and scientific products	21	3.1	–3.9
Office and administrative support occupations	131	19.7	–14.2
Bookkeeping, accounting, and auditing clerks	10	1.6	–13.5

Occupation	Employment, 2004 Number	Percent	Percent change, 2004–2014
Customer service representatives	26	4.0	–1.8
Production, planning, and expediting clerks	7	1.0	–4.9
Shipping, receiving, and traffic clerks	13	2.0	–13.0
Secretaries and administrative assistants	9	1.4	–14.8
Desktop publishers	8	1.3	2.6
Office clerks, general	11	1.6	–14.5
Installation, maintenance, and repair occupations	12	1.8	–4.0
Production occupations	354	53.2	–10.0
First-line supervisors/ managers of production and operating workers	27	4.1	–3.9
Bindery workers	56	8.4	–23.3
Bookbinders	6	0.9	–7.4
Job printers	39	5.8	–4.1
Prepress technicians and workers	44	6.6	–18.2
Printing machine operators	93	14.0	–3.9
Cutting and slicing machine setters, operators, and tenders	10	1.5	–10.3
Inspectors, testers, sorters, samplers, and weighers	7	1.1	–13.7
Packaging and filling machine operators and tenders	5	0.8	–9.1
Paper goods machine setters, operators, and tenders	9	1.4	–3.9
Helpers—production workers	25	3.7	–4.1
Transportation and material moving occupations	53	8.0	–10.7
Truck drivers, light or delivery services	6	0.9	–3.9
Laborers and freight, stock, and material movers, hand	9	1.4	–13.5
Machine feeders and offbearers	14	2.1	–23.1
Packers and packagers, hand	14	2.1	–3.9

Note: May not add to totals due to omission of occupations with small employment

Manufacturing, Construction, and Utilities

During the binding or postpress stage, the printed sheets are transformed into products such as books, catalogs, magazines, or directories. *Bookbinders* assemble books from large, flat, printed sheets of paper. They cut, saw, and glue parts to bind new books and perform other finishing operations, such as decorating and lettering, often using hand tools.

A small number of bookbinders work in hand binderies. These highly skilled workers design original or special bindings for publications with limited editions or restore and rebind rare books. In many other shops, *bindery workers* fold and fasten groups of sheets together, often using a machine stapler, to make "signatures." They then feed the signatures into various machines for stitching or gluing. More of these workers are now using computers on the job and consequently must learn new skills to operate the more complex machinery.

Training, Other Qualifications, and Advancement

Workers enter the printing field with various educational backgrounds. Helpers generally have a high school or vocational school background, while management trainees usually have a college background. In general, job applicants must be high school graduates with mathematical, verbal, and written communication skills and be computer literate.

Formal graphic communications programs, offered by community and junior colleges and some 4-year colleges, provide good preparation for entering the field. Two-year programs provide technical skills, while bachelor's degree programs in graphic arts prepare persons who want to obtain advanced skills or who want to enter management.

As the field continues to become more computerized, most workers will need a working knowledge of computers. Courses in electronics and computer technology are beneficial for anyone entering the field, and some employers will offer tuition assistance or continuing education classes. Training in desktop publishing is also becoming more important.

Workers generally are trained informally on the job. The length of on-the-job training needed to learn skills varies by occupation and shop. For example, press operators begin as helpers and can advance to press operator positions after years of training. Bindery workers begin by doing simple tasks such as moving paper from cutting machines to folding machines. Workers learn how to operate more complicated machinery within a few months. Training often is given under the close supervision of an experienced or senior employee. Through experience and training, workers may advance to more responsible positions. Workers usually begin as helpers, advance to skilled craft jobs, and eventually may be promoted to supervisor.

Opportunities for advancement depend on the specific plant or shop. Technological changes will continue to introduce new types of computerized equipment or dictate new work procedures. Workers with computer and mechanical aptitude are especially in demand, so proper training or retraining will be essential to careers in printing.

Outlook

Wage and salary employment in the printing and related support activities field is projected to decline 10 percent over the 2004–2014 period, compared with the 14 percent growth projected for the economy as a whole. This decline reflects the increasing computerization of the printing process; growing imports of some types of printed products; and the expanding use of the Internet, which reduces the need for printed materials. Some small and medium-size firms are also consolidating in order to afford the investment in new technology, which is expected to lead to a drop in employment. Despite the projected downturn in overall employment, retirements and turnover will continue to generate job openings in this field throughout the decade, especially for the most skilled.

While most subsectors of the printing field will decline, employment in commercial flexographic and digital printing should increase. Employment in manifold business forms should continue to decrease as firms take customers' orders over the Internet, allowing companies to process customer orders without printed forms. Declining employment in printing of blank books and looseleaf binders, printing of books, and other commercial printing will reflect increased imports of some types of printed products with ample "lead times." In response, more companies in the field are expanding the services they offer to include "ancillary services," such as performing inventory and database management for clients; if these other lines of business become the main source of revenue for some companies, they will become members of other non-printing fields.

Employment growth or decline will differ among the various occupations in the printing field, largely because of technological advances. Processes currently performed manually are being computerized, causing a shift from production occupations to computer-related occupations that perform the same function. For example, employment of desktop publishers is expected to grow slowly within the field over the 2004–2014 period as layout and design are performed electronically and transmitted to the printing press without the need to make a plate manually. In contrast, demand for prepress technicians and workers who perform these tasks manually—paste-up workers, photoengravers, camera operators, film strippers, and platemakers—is expected to decline. Although the concepts and principles behind page layout and design are unchanged, these prepress technicians will have to learn how to perform their work using new tools.

Growth in mechanization should result in declines in the employment of bookbinders and bindery workers. The increasing sophistication of printing presses is similarly expected to lead to a slight decline in the employment of printing machine operators within the field as well.

New technology and equipment will require workers to update their skills to remain competitive in the job market. This should translate into good career opportunities for those who obtain the education to work with this new technology, especially in the field of electronic prepress.

Earnings

In 2004, average weekly earnings for production workers in the printing field were $604, compared with $659 for all production workers in manufacturing. Weekly wages in the printing field can vary significantly by field sector, but in commercial lithographic, the field's largest activity, median weekly wages are $671. Median hourly earnings of the largest occupations in the field also vary, as shown in table 3.

The principal union in this field is the Graphic Communications Conference of the International Brotherhood of Teamsters. About 6 percent of printing field employees are union members or are covered by a union contract, compared with 14 percent of workers throughout the economy, but this proportion varies greatly from city to city.

Table 3. Median hourly earnings of the largest occupations in printing, May 2004

Occupation	Printing	All fields
Sales representatives, wholesale and manufacturing, except technical and scientific products	$25.20	$21.83
First-line supervisors/managers of production and operating workers	22.77	21.51
Prepress technicians and workers	15.91	15.30
Graphic designers	15.79	18.28
Job printers	15.67	15.41
Printing machine operators	15.16	14.38
Customer service representatives	14.86	12.99
Bindery workers	11.60	11.31
Machine feeders and offbearers	11.12	10.68
Helpers—production workers	10.17	9.70

Sources of Additional Information

For general information on careers and training programs in printing, contact

- NPES, The Association for Suppliers of Printing, Publishing, and Converting Technologies, 1899 Preston White Dr., Reston, VA 20191-4367. Internet: http://www.npes.org/

- Printing Industries of America/Graphic Arts Technical Foundation, 200 Deer Run Rd., Sewickley, PA 15143-2600. Internet: http://www.gain.net

- Graphic Communications Conference of the International Brotherhood of Teamsters, 1900 L St. NW, Washington, DC 20036-5007. Internet: http://www.gciu.org

- National Association for Printing Leadership, 75 W. Century Rd., Paramus, NJ 07652-1408. Internet: http://www.napl.org

Manufacturing, Construction, and Utilities

Steel Manufacturing

- Annual Earnings: $36,599
- Job Growth: –13.4%
- Size of Workforce: 155,870
- Self-Employed: 1.4%
- Part-Time: 2.4%

Significant Points

- Employment is expected to continue to decline due to consolidation and further automation of the steelmaking process.
- Employers staffing production jobs increasingly prefer individuals with 2-year degrees in mechanical or electrical technology.
- Opportunities will be best for engineers, computer scientists, business majors, and skilled production workers.

Nature of the Field

Faced with international competition, the U.S. steel field continues to respond by modernizing its manufacturing processes and consolidating businesses to increase productivity. Despite successful efforts to reduce costs and an improving competitive position, steel manufacturing firms still face stiff competition. Investment in modern equipment and worker training has transformed the U.S. steel field from one of the nation's most moribund to one of the world's leaders in worker productivity and the lowest-cost producer for some types of steel. Over the past 25 to 30 years, steel producers have, in some cases, reduced the number of man-hours required to produce a ton of steel by ninety percent.

Establishments in this field produce steel by melting iron ore, scrap metal, and other additives in furnaces. The molten metal output is then solidified into semifinished shapes before it is rolled, drawn, cast, and extruded to make sheet, rod, bar, tubing, and wire. Other establishments in the field make finished steel products directly from purchased steel.

The least costly method of making steel uses scrap metal as its base. Steel scrap from many sources—such as old bridges, refrigerators, and automobiles—and other additives are placed in an electric arc furnace, where the intense heat produced by carbon electrodes and chemical reactions melts the scrap, converting it into molten steel. Establishments that use this method of producing steel are called electric arc furnace (EAF) mills, or minimills. While EAFs are sometimes small, some are large enough to produce 400 tons of steel at a time. The growth of EAFs has been driven by the technology's smaller initial capital investment and lower operating costs. Moreover, scrap metal is found in all parts of the country, so EAFs are not tied as closely to raw material deposits as are integrated mills and can be placed closer to consumers. EAFs now account for over half of American steel production, and their share is expected to continue to grow in coming years.

The growth of EAFs comes partly at the expense of integrated mills. Integrated mills reduce iron ore to molten pig iron in blast furnaces. The iron is then sent to the oxygen furnace, where it is combined with scrap to make molten steel. The steel produced by integrated mills generally is considered to be of higher quality than steel from EAFs but, because the production process is more complicated and consumes more energy, it is more costly.

During the final phase of the steel manufacturing process, semi-finished steel from either EAFs or integrated mills is converted into finished products. Some of the goods produced in finishing mills are steel wire, pipe, bars, rods, and sheets. Products also may be coated with chemicals, paints, or other metals that give the steel desired characteristics for various fields and consumers. Also involved in steel manufacturing are firms that produce alloys by adding materials such as silicon and manganese to the steel. Varying the amounts of carbon and other elements contained in the final product can yield thousands of different types of steel, each with specific properties suited for a particular use.

Steel mills employ sophisticated technology. Taking several forms, this technology has improved both product quality and worker productivity. Computers are essential to most technological advances in steel production, from production scheduling and machine control to metallurgical analysis. Computerized systems change the nature of many jobs, while they eliminate or reduce the numbers of others.

For workers, modernization of integrated and EAF steel mills often has meant learning new skills to operate sophisticated equipment. Competition also has resulted in increasing specialization of steel production as various producers attempt to capture different niches in the market. With these changes has come a growing emphasis on flexibility and adaptability for both workers and production technology. As strong international and domestic competition continue for U.S. steel producers, the nature of the field and the jobs of its workers are expected to continue to change.

Working Conditions

Steel mills evoke images of strenuous, hot, and potentially dangerous work. While many dangerous and difficult jobs remain in the steel field, modern equipment and facilities have helped to change this. The most strenuous tasks were among the first to be automated. For example, computer-controlled machinery helps to monitor and move iron and steel through the production processes, reducing the need for heavy labor. In some cases, workers now monitor and control the equipment from air-conditioned rooms.

Nevertheless, large machinery and molten metal can be hazardous unless safety procedures are observed. Hardhats, safety shoes, protective glasses, earplugs, and protective clothing are required in most production areas.

The rates of occupational injury and illness per 100 full-time workers in 2003 were 7.0 in iron and steel mills and 10.5 in steel product manufacturing, higher than the rate of 5.0 per 100 workers for the entire private sector and 6.8 per 100 for all of manufacturing.

The expense of plant and machinery and significant production startup costs force most mills to operate around the clock, 7 days a week. Workers averaged 44.5 hours per week in 2004 in iron and steel mills and 41.7 hours in steel product manufacturing, and only about 3 percent of workers are employed part time. Workers typically work varying shifts, switching between working days one week and nights the next. Some mills operate two 12-hour shifts, while others operate three 8-hour shifts. Overtime work during peak production periods is common.

Important Characteristics of the Field

Skills: Operation Monitoring; Installation; Operation and Control; Equipment Maintenance; Repairing;

Quality Control Analysis. **Abilities:** Static Strength; Extent Flexibility; Manual Dexterity; Dynamic Strength; Control Precision; Multilimb Coordination. **Work-Related Values:** Supervision, Technical; Moral Values; Activity; Supervision, Human Relations; Company Policies and Practices; Independence.

Employment

Employment in the steel field declined to about 156,000 wage and salary jobs in 2004. The steel field traditionally has been located in the eastern and midwestern regions of the country, where iron ore, coal, or one of the other natural resources required for steel are found. Even today, about 44 percent of all steelworkers are employed in Pennsylvania, Ohio, and Indiana. The growth of EAFs has allowed steelmaking to spread to virtually all parts of the country, although many firms find lower-cost rural areas the most attractive. Large firms employ most workers in the steel field. About 62 percent of the jobs in 2004 were in establishments employing at least 250 workers (chart 1).

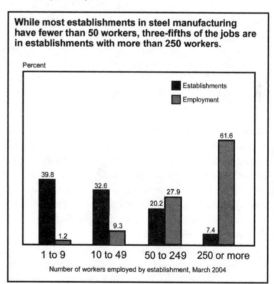

While most establishments in steel manufacturing have fewer than 50 workers, three-fifths of the jobs are in establishments with more than 250 workers.

Percent

- Establishments
- Employment

1 to 9: 39.8 / 1.2
10 to 49: 32.6 / 9.3
50 to 249: 20.2 / 27.9
250 or more: 7.4 / 61.6

Number of workers employed by establishment, March 2004

Occupations in the Field

Opportunities exist in steel manufacturing in a variety of occupations, but the largest group of workers—48 percent—is employed in production occupations (table 1). Other large groups of workers are installation, maintenance, and repair workers and transportation and material-moving workers.

Although the steelmaking process varies with the type of furnace used, the jobs associated with the various processes are similar. Most jobs in steel mills can be classified into 1 of 3 types: operators, maintenance and repair workers, and supervisors and managers. In addition, significant numbers of electricians, engineers, inspectors and testers, and material-moving workers are needed to assist in the production process and repair of equipment. Workers generally are assigned to work in a particular sector of the production line, such as the blast furnace or rolling mill areas, and their titles reflect the types of machines they work on.

At integrated mills, production begins when *material-moving workers* use robots and cranes to load iron ore, coke, and limestone into the top of a blast furnace. As the materials are heated, a chemical reaction frees the iron from other elements in the ore. *Metal-refining furnace operators and tenders*, also known as *blowers* and *melters*, use automated and computer controls to manage the overall operation of the furnace to melt and refine metal before casting or to produce specific types of steel. They gather information on the characteristics of the raw materials they will use and the type and quality of steel they are expected to produce. They direct the loading of the furnace with raw materials and supervise the taking of samples to ensure that the steel has the desired qualities. They may also coordinate the loading and melting of raw materials with the steel molding or casting operation to avoid delays in production.

Generally, either a basic oxygen or an electric arc furnace is used to make steel. Operators and tenders use controls to tilt the furnace to receive the raw materials. Once they have righted the furnace, they use levers and buttons to control the flow of oxygen and other materials into the furnace. During the production process, *testers* routinely take samples to be analyzed. Based on this analysis, operators determine how much longer they must process the steel or what materials they must add to meet specifications. Operators also pay close attention to conditions within the furnace and correct any problems that arise during the production process.

Metal pourers and casters tend machines that release the molten steel from the ladle at a controlled rate into water-cooled molds, where it solidifies into semifinished shapes. This process is called "continuous casting." These shapes are then cut to desired lengths as they emerge from the caster. During this process, operators monitor

the flow of raw steel and the supply of water to the mold.

The "rolling" method is used to shape most steel processed in steel mills. In this method, hot steel is squeezed between two cylinders, or "rollers," which flatten or shape the steel. *Rolling machine operators* operate the rolling mills that produce the finished product; the quality of the product and the speed at which the work is completed depend on the operator's skills. Placing the steel and positioning the rollers are very important, for they control the product's final shape. Improperly adjusted equipment may damage the rolling mill or gears.

Extruding and drawing machine operators control equipment that extrudes, or draws, metal materials into tubes, rods, hoses, wire, bars, or structural shapes. *Cutting, punching, and press machine operators* operate machines that saw, cut, shear, slit, punch, crimp, notch, bend, or straighten metal. *Welding, soldering, and brazing workers* join metal components or fill holes, indentations, or seams of fabricated metal products. *Multiple machine tool operators* are skilled in the operation of more than one type of cutting or forming machine tool or robot.

Team assemblers and leaders work as part of a team responsible for assembling an entire product or component of a product. Team assemblers can perform all tasks conducted by the team in the assembly process and rotate through all or most of them rather than being assigned to a specific task on a permanent basis. They may participate in making management decisions affecting the work. *Machinists* operate a variety of machine tools to produce precision parts and instruments. They may fabricate and modify parts to make or repair machine tools or maintain industrial machines. *Inspectors, testers, sorters, samplers, and weighers* check parts or products for defects, wear, and deviations from specifications.

Millwrights are employed to install and maintain much of the sophisticated machinery in steel mills. As the technology becomes more advanced, they work more closely with *electricians*, who help repair and install electrical equipment such as computer controls for machine tools.

Engineers, chemists, and computer specialists are playing an increasing role at steel mills, helping to address a variety of issues. *Metallurgical engineers* work with the metals and ores that go into steel in order to change or improve its properties or to find new applications for steel. They make adjustments to the steel-making process in response to quality control issues. *Industrial engineers* work in process control with engineers from other specialties to make plants more productive and energy efficient by designing and installing the latest technology. *Mechanical engineers* often are found in supervisory or management jobs, helping to solve mechanical problems on the production line. *Environmental engineers* design environmental control systems to maintain water and air quality standards or to clean up old sites.

Additionally, as with most companies, there are accountants, sales agents, various managers, and administrative and clerical workers who perform company administrative tasks and market the product.

Table 1. Employment of wage and salary workers in steel manufacturing by occupation, 2004 and projected change, 2004–2014 (Employment in thousands)

Occupation	Employment, 2004		Percent change, 2004–2014
	Number	Percent	
Total, all occupations	156	100.0	–13.4
Management, business, and financial occupations	8	5.4	–8.8
Top executives	2	1.2	–9.3
Industrial production managers	2	1.0	–10.0
Professional and related occupations	7	4.6	–3.9
Engineers	4	2.3	–0.6
Sales and related occupations	3	1.6	–8.5
Sales representatives, wholesale and manufacturing, except technical and scientific products	2	1.2	–7.9
Office and administrative support occupations	13	8.3	–17.5
Production, planning, and expediting clerks	4	2.3	–12.8
Shipping, receiving, and traffic clerks	2	1.2	–18.1

Occupation	Employment, 2004		Percent change, 2004–2014
	Number	Percent	
Construction and extraction occupations	8	5.1	–12.5
Electricians	4	2.7	–12.0
Installation, maintenance, and repair occupations	19	12.0	–11.6
First-line supervisors/managers of mechanics, installers, and repairers	2	1.3	–11.9
Industrial machinery mechanics	3	2.1	–11.6
Maintenance and repair workers, general	8	4.9	–11.0
Millwrights	3	1.7	–12.4
Production occupations	75	47.9	–14.0
First-line supervisors/managers of production and operating workers	7	4.3	–9.9
Team assemblers	3	2.0	–5.8
Forming machine setters, operators, and tenders, metal and plastic	13	8.5	–16.2
Machine tool cutting setters, operators, and tenders, metal and plastic	12	7.7	–19.7
Machinists	3	1.6	–10.1
Metal-refining furnace operators and tenders	4	2.4	–13.1
Pourers and casters, metal	2	1.5	–13.5
Molders and molding machine setters, operators, and tenders, metal and plastic	2	1.2	–13.1
Welding, soldering, and brazing workers	4	2.7	–9.3
Heat treating equipment setters, operators, and tenders, metal and plastic	2	1.4	–10.1
Inspectors, testers, sorters, samplers, and weighers	4	2.8	–15.2
Helpers—production workers	5	3.4	–10.1

Manufacturing, Construction, and Utilities

Occupation	Employment, 2004		Percent change, 2004–2014
	Number	Percent	
Transportation and material moving occupations	22	14.4	–15.9
Crane and tower operators	6	3.6	–12.2
Industrial truck and tractor operators	4	2.4	–9.4
Laborers and freight, stock, and material movers, hand	6	3.7	–18.9
Machine feeders and offbearers	2	1.2	–28.2
Packers and packagers, hand	2	1.0	–9.5

Note: May not add to totals due to omission of occupations with small employment

Training, Other Qualifications, and Advancement

Many jobs in steel manufacturing require only a high school diploma. However, machinery continues to become more complex, and growing numbers of operating and maintenance positions are highly skilled, so employers increasingly prefer to hire graduates from formal postsecondary technical and trade schools. Two-year degrees in mechanical or electrical technology or 2- to 4-year apprenticeships are recommended for persons seeking to advance into the best production jobs.

After production workers are hired, they receive specific training on the job. New workers entering the production process as lower-skilled operators and maintenance personnel generally assist more experienced workers, beginning with relatively simple tasks. As workers acquire experience, they specialize in a particular process and acquire greater skill in that area. The time required to become a skilled worker depends upon individual abilities, acquired skills, and available job openings. It generally takes at least 2 to 5 years, and sometimes longer, to advance to a skilled position. At times, workers change their specialization to increase their opportunities for advancement. Workers are continuously trained to perform a variety of tasks and provide more flexibility to the firm as company needs change. Computers have become important as companies have modernized. Workers must learn to operate computers and other advanced equipment.

To work as an engineer or scientist, or in some other technical occupations in the steel field, a college education is necessary. Many workers in administrative and managerial occupations have degrees in business or possess a combination of technical and business degrees. A master's degree may give an applicant an advantage in getting hired or help an employee advance. Managers need strong problem-solving, planning, and supervisory skills.

Outlook

Employment in the steel field is expected to decline 13 percent over the 2004–2014 period, primarily due to increasing consolidation in the field as companies are bought by other companies in the field and their operations merge. As larger companies create more-efficient mills, the result will be fewer workers but a more productive field that will be better able to meet foreign competition.

EAF mills, with their leaner workforce and lower cost structure, are expected to benefit from the field's transformation and will continue to gain market share. They now produce more than 50 percent of the country's steel, up from 25 percent two decades ago. They are also attempting to improve the quality of the steel they make by melting pig iron along with the scrap. In this way, they can more effectively compete with integrated mills in markets that demand higher-quality steel. Thus, as EAFs continue to grow in relation to integrated mills, job opportunities will be better at these mills.

Automation, computerization, and changes in business practices that have led to a leaner workforce have reduced the number of man-hours needed to produce a ton of steel and raised productivity enormously in the last few decades. These productivity improvements, which were a leading cause of employment declines in the past, are not expected to be as powerful a factor in the future, as some companies have automated the process as much as they can. Technological improvements, however, will continue to be made, impacting the number and type of workers hired. Low-skilled jobs will continue to be automated and the jobs that remain will require more education and training.

Employment in the steel field varies with overall economic conditions and the demand for goods produced with steel. Much of the demand for steel is derived from the demand for products that consume large amounts of steel. Fields that are significant users of steel include manufacturers of structural metal products used in construction, motor vehicle parts and equipment (a typical car uses about a ton of steel), and household appliances. As many of these goods require large outlays, consumers, businesses, and governments are more likely to purchase them in good economic times.

Currently, strong economic growth in some developing countries is driving up both the global demand for and prices of steel. These developing countries are requiring large amounts of steel to be used in the construction of buildings, bridges, and other infrastructure. In addition, as these countries grow more wealthy, their citizens are purchasing more automobiles, appliances and other steel products. Because economic growth in developing countries has been driving the global demand for steel, their continued economic growth will greatly impact the worldwide demand and production of steel.

Despite the projected decline, job openings are expected to be very good or favorable for a number of occupations. Demand for all types of engineers, including mechanical, metallurgical, industrial, electrical, and civil, is expected to be very good. Companies report great difficulty in hiring these highly skilled professionals. Also, computer scientists and business majors should be in great demand. For skilled production jobs, workers with associate degrees in technology will be highly sought after to operate computer-controlled machines and to repair equipment. Among persons without postsecondary training, those who have good math and computer skills will have better opportunities to be hired and trained for skilled production jobs. Those without a degree must be flexible and willing to go through extensive classroom and on-the-job training. Keen competition can be expected for low-skilled material handling and machine operator jobs, for which employment is expected to decline. Despite the declines in employment, many workers will need to be hired to replace those who leave the field or retire. A large number of workers are expected to retire over the next decade.

Table 2. Median hourly earnings of the largest occupations in steel manufacturing, May 2004

Occupation	Iron and steel mills and ferroalloy manufacturing	Steel product manufacturing from purchased steel	All fields
First-line supervisors/ managers of production and operating workers	$24.34	$22.55	$21.51
Electricians	22.44	20.75	20.33
Maintenance and repair workers, general	17.91	17.57	14.77
Rolling machine setters, operators, and tenders, metal and plastic	17.39	15.87	14.33
Inspectors, testers, sorters, samplers, and weighers	17.39	14.87	13.66
Crane and tower operators	16.63	15.57	17.99
Extruding and drawing machine setters, operators, and tenders, metal and plastic	15.66	15.03	13.18
Laborers and freight, stock, and material movers, hand	14.69	11.87	9.67
Cutting, punching, and press machine setters, operators, and tenders, metal and plastic	14.22	13.06	12.45
Helpers—production workers	10.88	11.97	9.70

Earnings

Earnings in the steel manufacturing field vary by type of production and occupation but are higher than average nongovernment earnings. Average weekly earnings of nonsupervisory production workers in 2004 were $1,028 in iron and steel mills and $727 in establishments making steel products from purchased steel, compared with $659 in all manufacturing and $529 throughout nongovernment fields. Earnings in selected occupations in steel manufacturing appear in table 2.

Manufacturing, Construction, and Utilities

Union membership, geographic location, and plant size affect earnings and benefits of workers. In most firms, earnings or bonuses are linked to output. Workers receive standard benefits, including health insurance, paid vacation, and pension plans.

Sources of Additional Information

For additional information about employers and training in the steel field, contact

- American Iron and Steel Institute, 1140 Connecticut Ave. NW, Suite 705, Washington, DC 20036. Internet: http://www.steel.org
- Steel Manufacturers Association, 1150 Connecticut Ave. NW, Suite 715, Washington, DC 20036. Internet: http://www.steelnet.org

Textile, Textile Product, and Apparel Manufacturing

- ◎ Annual Earnings: $23,912
- ◎ Job Growth: −44.6%
- ◎ Size of Workforce: 456,740
- ◎ Self-Employed: 4.0%
- ◎ Part-Time: 9.4%

Significant Points

- Employment is expected to decline because of technological advances and imports of apparel and textiles from lower-wage countries.
- Extensive on-the-job training is required to operate new high-technology machinery.
- Production workers account for almost 2 out of 3 jobs.
- About 1 out of 3 jobs are in three states—North Carolina, South Carolina, and Georgia.

Nature of the Field

This description covers closely related fields: textiles and apparel. The *textile mills and products field* comprises establishments that produce yarn, thread, and fabric and a wide variety of other textile products for use by individuals and businesses, but not including apparel. Some of the items made in this field include household items, such as carpets and rugs; towels, curtains, and sheets; cord and twine; furniture and automotive upholstery; and industrial belts and fire hoses. Because the process of converting raw fibers into finished nonapparel textile products is complex, most textile mills specialize.

Textile mills take natural and synthetic fibers such as cotton and polyester and transform them into yarn, thread, or webbing. Yarns are strands of fibers in a form ready for weaving, knitting, or otherwise intertwining to form a textile fabric. They form the basis for most textile production and commonly are made of cotton, wool, or a synthetic fiber such as polyester. Yarns also can be made of thin strips of plastic, paper, or metal. To produce spun yarn, natural fibers such as cotton and wool must first be processed to remove impurities and give products the desired texture and durability as well as other characteristics. After this initial cleaning stage, the fibers are spun into yarn.

Fabric and textile products are mostly produced by means of weaving, knitting, or tufting. Workers in weaving mills use complex, automated looms to transform yarns into cloth, a process that has been known for centuries. Looms weave or interlace two yarns so they cross each other at right angles to form fabric. Knitting uses automated sewing machines to interlock a series of loops of one or more yarns to form goods such as sweaters, socks, and underwear. Tufting, used by carpeting and rug mills, is a process by which a cluster of soft yarns is drawn through a backing fabric.

At any time during the production process, a number of processes, called finishing, may be performed on the fabric. These processes, which include dyeing, bleaching, and stonewashing, among others, may be performed by the textile mill or at a separate finishing mill. Finishing encompasses chemical or mechanical treatments performed on fiber, yarn, or fabric to improve appearance, texture, or performance.

The *apparel manufacturing field* transforms fabrics produced by textile manufacturers into clothing and accessories that fill the nation's retail stores. By cutting and sewing fabrics or other materials, such as leather, rubberized fabrics, plastics, and furs, workers in this field help to keep consumers warm, dry, and in style.

The apparel field traditionally has consisted mostly of production workers who performed the cutting and sewing functions in an assembly line. This field remains labor-intensive, despite advances in technology and workplace practices. Although many workers still perform this work in the United States, the field increasingly contracts out its production work to foreign suppliers to take advantage of lower labor costs in other countries. In its place, a growing number of apparel manufacturers are performing only the entrepreneurial functions involved in apparel manufacturing, such as buying raw materials, designing clothes and accessories and preparing samples, arranging for the production and distribution of the apparel, and marketing the finished product.

Many of the remaining production workers work in teams. For example, sewing machine operators are organized into production "modules." Each operator in a module is trained to perform nearly all of the functions required to assemble a garment. Each module is responsible for its own performance, and individuals usually receive compensation based on the team's performance.

The textile and apparel manufacturing fields are rapidly modernizing as new investments in automation and information technology have been made necessary by growing international competition. Firms also have responded to competition by developing new products and services. For example, some manufacturers are producing textiles developed from fibers made from recycled materials. These innovations have had a wide effect across the field. Advanced machinery is boosting productivity levels in textiles, costing some workers their jobs while fundamentally changing the nature of work for others. New technology also has led to increasingly technical training for workers throughout the field. Computers and computer-controlled equipment aid in many functions, such as design, patternmaking, and cutting. Wider looms, more computerized equipment, and the increasing use of robotics to move material within the plant are other technologies recently designed to make the production plant more efficient. Despite these changes, however, the apparel field—especially its sewing function—has remained significantly less automated than many other manufacturing fields.

One advantage the domestic field has is its closeness to the market and its ability to react to changes in fashion more quickly than its foreign competitors can. Also, as retailers consolidate and become more cost conscious, they require more apparel manufacturers to move toward a just-in-time delivery system, in which purchased apparel items are quickly replaced by the manufacturer rather than from a large inventory kept by the retailer. Through electronic data interchange—mainly using barcodes—information is quickly communicated to the manufacturers, providing information not only on inventory, but also about the desires of the public for fashion items.

Some apparel firms have responded to growing competition by merging with other apparel firms and by moving into the retail market. They also are contracting out functions in addition to the production of garments—for example, warehousing and order fulfillment functions—to concentrate on their strengths: design and marketing. Such changes may help the apparel manufacturing field meet the growing competition and continue to supply the nation's consumers with garments at an acceptable cost.

Working Conditions

Working conditions vary greatly. Production workers, including frontline managers and supervisors, spend most of their shift on or near the production floor. Some factories are noisy and can have airborne fibers and odors, but most modern facilities are relatively clean, well lit, and ventilated.

In 2003, work-related injuries and illnesses in textile mills averaged 5.0 per 100 full-time workers, compared with 6.8 percent for all manufacturing and 5.0 percent for the entire private sector. Work-related injuries and illnesses in textile product mills averaged 5.5 per 100 full-time workers, and in apparel manufacturing, the rate was 3.6 per 100 full-time workers.

When appropriate, the use of protective shoes, clothing, facemasks, and earplugs is required. Also, new machinery is designed with additional protection, such as noise shields. Still, many workers in textile production occupations must stand for long periods while bending over machinery, and noise and dust still are a problem in some plants. Apparel manufacturing operators often sit for long periods and lean over machines. New ergonomically designed chairs and machines that allow workers to stand during their operation are some of the means that

Manufacturing, Construction, and Utilities

firms use to minimize discomfort for production workers. Another concern for workers is injuries caused by repetitive motions. The implementation of modular units and specially designed equipment reduces potential health problems by lessening the stress of repetitive motions. Workers sometimes are exposed to hazardous situations that could produce cuts or minor burns if proper safety practices are not observed. Also, some workers are occasionally exposed to the fumes and odors of coolants and lubricants used in machines.

Because many factories run 24 hours a day as the cost of new machinery continues to increase, production workers may work evenings and weekends. Many operators work on rotating schedules, which can cause sleep disorders and other stress from constant changes in work hours. Overtime is common for these workers during periods of peak production. Managerial and administrative support personnel typically work a 5-day, 40-hour week in an office setting, although some of these employees also may work significant overtime. Travel is an important part of the job for many managers and designers, who oversee the design and production of the apparel. As more production moves abroad, foreign travel is becoming more common. Quality-control inspectors and other workers also may need to travel to other production sites, especially if working for large companies.

The movement away from traditional piecework systems in apparel manufacturing often results in a significant change in working conditions. Modular manufacturing involves teamwork, increased responsibility, and greater interaction among co-workers than on traditional assembly lines.

Important Characteristics of the Field

Skills: Operation Monitoring; Operation and Control; Equipment Maintenance; Repairing; Quality Control Analysis; Installation. **Abilities:** Manual Dexterity; Arm-Hand Steadiness; Rate Control; Control Precision; Wrist-Finger Speed; Dynamic Flexibility. **Work-Related Values:** Moral Values; Supervision, Technical; Activity; Independence; Supervision, Human Relations; Company Policies and Practices.

Employment

In 2004, 416,000 workers were employed by the textile mills and textile product fields, while 285,000 worked in the apparel manufacturing field (table 1). Most of the wage and salary workers employed in the textile mills, textile product, and apparel manufacturing fields in 2004 were found in southeastern states. North Carolina accounted for about 15 percent of these jobs. South Carolina and Georgia combined to provide employment for another 18 percent of the workers in this field. The remaining jobs primarily were found in California and the Northeast.

Table 1. Percent distribution of establishments and wage and salary employment in textile, textile product, and apparel manufacturing by detailed field, 2004

Field segment	Establishments	Employment
Total	100.0	100.0
Textile mills	18.3	34.1
Fiber, yarn, and thread mills	2.2	7.7
Fabric mills	7.0	16.5
Textile and fabric finishing and fabric coating mills	9.1	9.9
Textile product mills	31.8	25.3
Textile furnishings mills	12.3	14.5
Other textile product mills	19.5	10.8
Apparel manufacturing	49.9	40.8
Apparel knitting mills	2.7	6.0
Cut and sew apparel manufacturing	43.7	31.6
Apparel accessories and other apparel manufacturing	3.5	3.2

Most apparel and textile production is concentrated in large mills. In fact, establishments employing 20 persons or more accounted for 87 percent of all apparel and textile workers (chart 1).

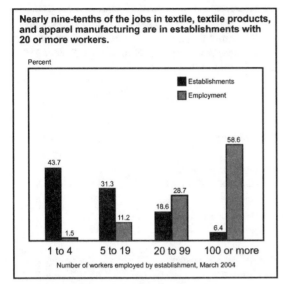

Nearly nine-tenths of the jobs in textile, textile products, and apparel manufacturing are in establishments with 20 or more workers.

Percent

Establishments
Employment

1 to 4: 43.7, 1.5
5 to 19: 31.3, 11.2
20 to 99: 18.6, 28.7
100 or more: 6.4, 58.6

Number of workers employed by establishment, March 2004

Occupations in the Field

The textile field offers employment opportunities in a variety of occupations, but production occupations accounted for 64 percent of all jobs. Some of these production occupations are unique to the field (table 2). Additional opportunities also exist in material-moving, administrative support, maintenance, repair, management, and professional occupations. The field also employs a small number of workers in service and sales occupations.

Many workers enter the textile field as *machine setters and operators*, the largest occupational group in the field. They are responsible for setting each machine and monitoring its operation. They inspect their machines to determine if they need repairs or adjustments. They may clean and oil their machines and repair or replace worn parts. Additionally, they must diagnose problems when the machinery stops and must restart it as soon as possible to reduce costly machine idle time. Textile machine setters and operators also install, level, and align components such as gears, chains, dies, cutters, and needles.

Textile machine setters and operators thread yarn, thread, or fabric through guides, needles, or rollers. Extruding machine operators load chemicals or wood pulp into their machines. They adjust the controls for proper tension, speed, and heat; for electronically controlled equipment, they program controls or key in instructions using a computer keyboard. Operators then start the machines and monitor their operation, observing control panels and gauges to detect problems.

Skilled production occupations also include quality-control inspectors, who use precision measuring instruments and complex testing equipment to detect product defects, wear, or deviations from specifications.

Among installation, maintenance, and repair occupations, *industrial machinery mechanics* account for about 2 percent of field employment. They inspect machines to make sure they are working properly. They clean, oil, and grease parts and tighten belts on a regular basis. When necessary, they make adjustments or replace worn parts and put the equipment back together. Mechanics are under pressure to fix equipment quickly because breakdowns usually stop or slow production. In addition to making repairs, mechanics help install new machines. They may enter instructions for computer-controlled machinery and demonstrate the equipment to machine operators.

Plant workers who do not operate or maintain equipment mostly perform a variety of other material-moving tasks. Some drive industrial trucks or tractors to move materials around the plant, load and unload trucks and railroad cars, or package products and materials by hand.

Engineers and *engineering technicians*, although a vital part of the textile and apparel fields, account for less than 1 percent of employment in the field. Some engineers are *textile engineers*, who specialize in the design of textile machinery, the study of fibers, and textile production. The field also employs other types of engineers, particularly *industrial* and *mechanical engineers*.

Fashion designers are the artists of the apparel field. They create ideas for a range of products, including coats, suits, dresses, hats, and underwear. Fashion designers begin the process by making rough sketches of garments or accessories, often using computer-assisted design (CAD) software. This software prints detailed designs from a computer drawing. It can also store fashion styles and colors that can be accessed and easily changed. Designers then create the pattern pieces that will be used to construct the finished garment. They measure and draw pattern pieces to actual size on paper. Then, they use these pieces to measure and cut pattern pieces in a sample fabric. Designers sew the pieces together and fit them on a model. They examine the sample garment and make changes until they get the effect they want. Some

Manufacturing, Construction, and Utilities

designers use assistants to cut and sew pattern pieces to their specifications.

Before sewing can begin, pattern pieces must be made, layouts determined, and fabric cut. *Fabric and apparel patternmakers* create the "blueprint" or pattern pieces for a particular apparel design. This often involves "grading," or adjusting the pieces for different-sized garments. Grading once was a time-consuming job, but now it is quickly completed with the aid of a computer. *Markers* determine the best arrangement of pattern pieces to minimize wasted fabric. Traditionally, markers judged the best arrangement of pieces by eye; today, computers quickly help determine the best layout.

The layout arrangement is then given to *cutters*. In less automated companies, cutters may use electric knives or cutting machines to cut pattern pieces. In more automated facilities, markers electronically send the layout to a computer-controlled cutting machine, and *textile cutting machine setters, operators, and tenders* monitor the machine's work.

Sewing machine operators assemble or finish clothes. Most sewing functions are specialized and require the operator to receive specific training. Although operators specialize in one function, the trend toward cross-training requires them to broaden their skills. *Team assemblers* perform all of the assembly tasks assigned to their team, rotating through the different tasks rather than specializing in a single task. They also may decide how the work is to be assigned and how tasks are to be performed.

Pressers receive a garment after it has been assembled. Pressers eliminate wrinkles and give shape to finished products. Most pressers use specially formed, foot-controlled pressing machines to perform their duties. Some pressing machines now have the steam and pressure controlled by computers. *Inspectors, testers, sorters, samplers, and weighers* inspect the finished product to ensure consistency and quality.

Table 2. Employment of wage and salary workers in textile, textile product, and apparel manufacturing by occupation, 2004 and projected change, 2004–2014 (Employment in thousands)

Occupation	Employment, 2004		Percent change, 2004–2014
	Number	Percent	
Total, all occupations	701	100.0	–45.8
Management, business, and financial occupations	34	4.8	–36.9
Top executives	12	1.7	–36.8
Industrial production managers	5	0.8	–36.5
Professional and related occupations	17	2.5	–38.0
Designers	8	1.1	–43.8
Sales and related occupations	21	2.9	–38.7
Retail salespersons	5	0.7	–39.1
Sales representatives, wholesale and manufacturing	12	1.7	–37.4
Office and administrative support occupations	76	10.8	–43.5
First-line supervisors/ managers of office and administrative support workers	4	0.6	–42.3
Bookkeeping, accounting, and auditing clerks	7	1.0	–43.4
Customer service representatives	6	0.9	–34.9
Shipping, receiving, and traffic clerks	15	2.2	–44.3
Stock clerks and order fillers	6	0.9	–49.6
Office clerks, general	11	1.6	–42.3
Installation, maintenance, and repair occupations	33	4.8	–36.1
Industrial machinery mechanics	12	1.7	–37.4
Maintenance and repair workers, general	11	1.5	–36.4

Occupation	Employment, 2004 Number	Percent	Percent change, 2004–2014
Production occupations	450	64.2	–49.5
First-line supervisors/ managers of production and operating workers	26	3.7	–36.0
Team assemblers	17	2.4	–26.4
Pressers, textile, garment, and related materials	9	1.3	–53.9
Sewing machine operators	159	22.7	–57.6
Sewers, hand	6	0.9	–48.1
Tailors, dressmakers, and custom sewers	4	0.6	–54.9
Textile bleaching and dyeing machine operators and tenders	19	2.7	–51.9
Textile cutting machine setters, operators, and tenders	15	2.2	–47.2
Textile knitting and weaving machine setters, operators, and tenders	42	6.0	–59.4
Textile winding, twisting, and drawing out machine setters, operators, and tenders	46	6.6	–49.9
Extruding and forming machine setters, operators, and tenders, synthetic and glass fibers	7	1.0	–45.5
Fabric and apparel pattern-makers	5	0.8	–52.6
Textile, apparel, and furnishings workers, all other	9	1.3	–53.6
Cutters and trimmers, hand	6	0.8	–32.7
Inspectors, testers, sorters, samplers, and weighers	26	3.7	–40.6
Packaging and filling machine operators and tenders	7	1.0	–36.4
Helpers—production workers	16	2.2	–33.9
Transportation and material moving occupations	60	8.6	–37.2
Industrial truck and tractor operators	10	1.4	–28.8
Laborers and freight, stock, and material movers, hand	19	2.7	–42.3
Packers and packagers, hand	19	2.7	–34.1

Note: May not add to totals due to omission of occupations with small employment

Training, Other Qualifications, and Advancement

As the textile field becomes increasingly automated, production workers need to be prepared. A high school diploma or GED may be necessary for many entry-level positions, and extensive postsecondary training is required for more technical jobs. This training may be obtained at technical schools and community colleges. More often, job applicants are screened through the use of tests to ensure that they have the necessary skills. Most apparel production workers are trained on the job. Although a high school diploma is not required, some employers prefer it. Basic math and computer skills are important for computer-controlled machine operators.

Extensive on-the-job training has become an integral part of working in today's textile mills. Technical training is designed to help workers understand complex automated machinery, recognize problems, and restart machinery when the problem is solved.

Installation, maintenance, and repair workers, such as industrial machinery mechanics, also require extensive training. Training may help experienced workers advance to more skilled jobs or even supervisory positions.

Increasingly, training is offered to enable people to work well in a team-oriented environment. Many firms have established training centers or hosted seminars that encourage employee self-direction and responsibility and the development of interpersonal skills. Because of the emphasis on teamwork and the small number of management levels in modern textile mills, firms place a premium on workers who show initiative and communicate effectively.

Cutters and pressers are trained on the job, while patternmakers and markers usually have technical or trade school training. All of these workers must understand textile characteristics and have a good sense of three-dimensional space. Traditional cutters need exceptional hand-eye coordination. Computers are becoming a standard tool for these occupations because patternmakers and markers increasingly design pattern pieces and layouts on a computer screen. New entrants seeking these jobs should learn basic computer skills. Those running automatic cutting machines could need technical training, which is available from vocational schools.

Manufacturing, Construction, and Utilities

Sewing machine operators must have good hand-eye coordination and dexterity as well as an understanding of textile fabrics. They normally are trained on the job for a period of several weeks to several months, depending on their previous experience and the function for which they are training. Operators usually begin by performing simple tasks, working their way up to more difficult assemblies and fabrics as they gain experience.

Modular manufacturing requires operators to perform more than one function, so they usually are trained to perform several duties. In addition to this functional training, workers in a modular system may also be offered courses in the interpersonal and communication skills necessary to work as part of a team. Further, the added responsibility of self-managing their modules may lead these workers to receive training in problem-solving and management.

Advancement for sewing machine operators, however, is limited. Advancement often takes the form of higher wages as workers become more experienced. Experienced operators who have good people and organizational skills may become supervisors. Operators with a high school diploma and some vocational school training have more chances for advancement.

Designers need a good sense of color, texture, and style. In addition, they must understand the construction and characteristics of specific fabrics, such as durability and stiffness. Many employers seek designers who know how to use computer-assisted design. This specialized training usually is obtained through a university or design school that offers 4-year or 2-year degrees in art, fine art, or fashion design. Many schools do not allow entry into a bachelor's degree program until a student has completed a year of basic art and design courses. Applicants may be required to submit drawings and other examples of their artistic ability. Formal training also is available in 2- and 3-year fashion design schools that award certificates or associate degrees. Graduates of 2-year programs generally qualify as assistants to designers.

Beginning designers usually receive on-the-job training. They normally need 1 to 3 years of training before they advance to higher-level positions, such as assistant technical designer, pattern designer, or head designer. Sometimes fashion designers advance by moving to bigger firms. Some designers choose to move into positions in business or merchandising.

Engineering applicants generally need a bachelor's or advanced degree in a field of engineering or production management. Degrees in mechanical or industrial engineering are common, but concentrations in textile-specific areas of engineering are especially useful. For example, many applicants take classes in textile engineering, textile technology, textile materials, and design. These specialized programs usually are found in engineering and design schools in the South and Northeast. As in other fields, a technical degree with an advanced degree in business can lead to opportunities in management.

Outlook

Wage and salary employment in the apparel and textile field is expected to decline by 45 percent through 2014, compared with a projected increase of 14 percent for all fields combined. Declining employment will result from growth in imports and from technological advances. Nevertheless, some job openings will arise as experienced workers transfer to other fields or retire or leave the workforce for other reasons.

Changing trade regulations are the single most important factor influencing future employment patterns. Because the apparel field is labor intensive, it is especially vulnerable to import competition from nations in which workers receive lower wages. In 2005, quotas for apparel and textile products were lifted among members of the World Trade Organization, including most U.S. trading partners and, in particular, China. Although some bilateral quotas have been re-imposed between the United States and China, the lifting of many import restrictions allows for more apparel and textile products to be imported into the United States. Because many U.S. firms will continue to move their assembly operations to low-wage countries, this trend is likely to affect the jobs of lower-skilled machine operators most severely. It does not, however, have as adverse an effect on the demand for some of the pre-sewing functions, such as designing, because much of the apparel will still be designed in the United States.

Some segments of the textile field, like industrial fabrics, carpets, and specialty yarns, are highly automated, innovative, and competitive on a global scale, so they will be able to expand exports as a result of more open trade. Other sectors, such as fabric for apparel, will be negatively impacted as a number of apparel manufacturers relocate production to other countries. Textile mills are likely to lose employment as a result. The expected increase in apparel imports will adversely affect demand for domestically produced textiles.

Increasing investment in technology by textile firms, and the resulting increase in labor productivity, is another major reason for the projected decline in employment in the textile field. Wider looms, robotics, new methods for making textiles that do not require spinning or weaving, and the application of computers to various processes are resulting in fewer workers needed to produce the same amount of textile products. Companies are also continuing to open new, more modern plants, which use fewer workers, while closing inefficient ones. As this happens, overall demand for textile machine operators and material handlers will continue to decline, but demand for those who have the skills to operate the more high-technology machines will grow.

New technology will increase the apparel field's productivity, but unlike other fields, the apparel field is likely to remain labor-intensive. The variability of cloth and the intricacy of the cuts and seams of the assembly process have been difficult to automate. Machine operators, therefore, will continue to perform most sewing tasks, and automated sewing will be limited to simple functions. In some cases, however, computerized sewing machines will increase the productivity of operators and reduce required training time.

Technology also is increasing the productivity of workers who perform other functions, such as designing, marking, cutting, and pressing. Computers and automated machinery will continue to raise productivity and reduce the demand for workers in these areas, but the decline will be moderated by growth in demand for the services of these workers generated by offshore assembly sites. The rapid rate at which fashions change also will boost demand for workers employed in U.S.-based firms that have quick-response capabilities.

Continuing changes in the market for apparel goods will exert cost-cutting pressures that affect all workers in the textile and apparel fields: Consumers are becoming more price conscious, retailers are gaining bargaining power over apparel producers, and increasing competition is limiting the ability of producers to pass on costs to consumers. Apparel firms are likely to respond by relying more on foreign production and boosting productivity through investments in technology and new work structures. These responses will adversely affect employment of U.S. apparel workers.

The trend today is for apparel firms to merge or consolidate to remain competitive. This trend continues to drive down the number of firms in this field. In the future, the apparel field will be dominated by highly efficient, profitable organizations that have developed their dominance through well-recognized strategies that enable them to be among the lowest-cost producers of apparel. Consolidation and mergers are likely to result in layoffs of some workers.

Technology also has its bright side. The United States is leading the world in discovering new fibers and finding new uses for high-technology textiles. For example, biotechnology research is expected to lead to new sources of fibers, such as corn, and to improvements in existing fibers. Some fibers currently being introduced have built-in memories of color and shape, and some have antibacterial qualities. As these technologies and engineering advancements in textile production are implemented, the need will arise for more highly skilled workers who can work in an increasingly high-technology environment.

Earnings

Average weekly earnings of nonsupervisory textile production workers were $487 in textile mills and $443 in textile product mills in 2004, compared with $659 for production workers in all manufacturing and $529 for workers throughout nongovernment fields. Wages within the textile field depend upon skill level and type of mill. In addition to typical benefits, employees often are eligible for discounts in factory merchandise stores.

Average weekly earnings for apparel production workers were $351 in 2004, significantly lower than the overall $659 per week in manufacturing and $529 in the entire private sector.

Earnings in selected occupations in textile and apparel manufacturing appear in table 3. Traditionally, sewing machine operators are paid on a piecework basis determined by the quantity of goods they produce. Many companies are changing to incentive systems based on group performance that consider both the quantity and the quality of the goods produced. A few companies pay production workers a salary.

Manufacturing, Construction, and Utilities

Table 3. Median hourly earnings of the largest occupations in textile, textile product, and apparel manufacturing, May 2004

Occupation	Textile mills	Textile product mills	Apparel manufacturing	All fields
First-line supervisors/ managers of production and operating workers	$19.35	$18.49	$15.23	$21.51
Textile knitting and weaving machine setters, operators, and tenders	11.91	11.77	9.68	11.48
Inspectors, testers, sorters, samplers, and weighers	10.87	10.50	8.62	13.66
Textile bleaching and dyeing machine operators and tenders	10.80	10.59	9.82	10.56
Textile winding, twisting, and drawing out machine setters, operators, and tenders	10.54	11.74	9.55	10.87
Team assemblers	10.40	11.45	9.07	11.42
Laborers and freight, stock, and material movers, hand	10.09	9.22	8.60	9.67
Helpers—production workers	9.83	9.30	8.00	9.70
Sewing machine operators	9.35	9.08	8.08	8.61
Packers and packagers, hand	9.30	8.55	8.46	8.25

Sources of Additional Information

Information about job opportunities in textile, apparel, and furnishings occupations is available from local employers and local offices of the state employment service. Information about job opportunities in technical and design occupations in the apparel field can be obtained from colleges offering programs in textile and apparel engineering, production, and design.

Utilities

◉ Annual Earnings: $51,760
◉ Job Growth: −1.3%
◉ Size of Workforce: 563,780
◉ Self-Employed: 0.0%
◉ Part-Time: 3.2%

Significant Points

● Employment in water and sewage systems is projected to grow, while other segments of the field are projected to decline.

● Persons with college training in advanced technology will have the best opportunities.

● Skills developed in one segment of the field may not be transferable to other segments because the utilities field consists of many different companies and products.

● Earnings for production workers are significantly higher than in most other fields.

Nature of the Field

The simple act of walking into a restroom, turning on the light, and washing your hands uses the products of perhaps four different utilities. Electricity powers the light, water supply systems provide water for washing, wastewater treatment plants treat the sewage, and natural gas or electricity heats the water. Some government establishments do the same work and employ a significant number of workers; however, information about them is not included in this description. Information concerning government employment in utilities is included in this book in descriptions of Federal Government and State and Local Government, Except Education and Health. Each of the various segments within the utilities sector is distinctly different.

Electric power generation, transmission, and distribution. This segment includes firms engaged in the generation, transmission, and distribution of electric power. Electric plants harness highly pressurized steam or some force of nature to spin the blades of a turbine, which is attached to an electric generator. Coal is the dominant fuel used to generate steam in electric power plants, followed by natural gas, petroleum, nuclear power, and other energy sources. Hydroelectric generators are powered by the release of the tremendous pressure of water existing at the bottom of a dam or near a waterfall. Scientists also are conducting considerable research into renewable sources of electric power—including geothermal, wind, and solar energy.

Legislative changes and field competition have created new classes of firms that generate and sell electricity. Some industrial plants have their own electricity-generating facilities, capable of producing more power than they require. Those that sell their excess power to utilities or to other industrial plants are called nonutility generators (NUGs). A type of NUG, termed an independent power producer, is an electricity-generating plant designed to take advantage of both field deregulation and the latest generating technology to compete directly with utilities for industrial and other wholesale customers.

Transmission or high-voltage lines supported by huge towers connect generating plants with industrial customers and substations. At substations, the electricity's voltage is reduced and made available for household and small business use via distribution lines, which usually are carried by telephone poles.

Natural gas distribution. Natural gas, a clear odorless gas, is found underground, often near or associated with crude oil reserves. Exploration and extraction of natural gas is part of the Oil and Gas Extraction field, covered elsewhere in Part II. Once found and brought to the surface, it is transported throughout the United States, Canada, and Mexico by gas transmission companies using pressurized pipelines. Local distribution companies take natural gas from the pipeline, depressurize it, add its odor, and operate the system that delivers the gas from transmission pipelines to industrial, residential, and commercial customers. Industrial customers, such as chemical and paper manufacturing firms, account for more than a third of natural gas consumption. Residential customers who use gas for heating and cooking, electric utilities, and commercial businesses—such as hospitals and restaurants—account for most of the remaining consumption.

Water, sewage, and other systems. Water utilities provide about 100 gallons of fresh, treated water every day for each person in this country, or close to 40 billion gallons per day nationwide. Water is collected from various sources, such as rivers, lakes, and wells. After collection, water is filtered, treated, and sold for residential, industrial, agricultural, commercial, and public use. Depending on the population served by the water system, the utility may be a small plant in a rural area that requires the occasional monitoring of a single operator or a huge system of reservoirs, dams, pipelines, and treatment plants, requiring the coordinated efforts of hundreds of people. Sewage treatment facilities operate sewer systems or plants that collect, treat, and dispose of waste from homes and fields. Other utilities include steam and air-conditioning supply utilities, which produce and sell steam, heated air, and cooled air.

Utilities and the services they provide are so vital to everyday life that they are considered "public goods" and are typically heavily regulated. Formerly, utility companies operated as "regulated monopolies," meaning that in return for having no competition, they were subject to control by public utility commissions that ensured utilities acted in the public interest and regulated the rates they were allowed to charge. However, legislative changes in recent years have established and promoted competition in the utilities field. The electric utilities field, for example, is currently restructuring in an effort to promote efficiency, lower costs to customers, and provide users with an increased number of service options.

Many utility companies are municipally owned. In the natural gas field, for example, a large majority of the distribution companies in the United States are municipally owned. However, they serve just a fraction of the nationwide customers. In general, utilities serving large cities have sufficient numbers of customers to justify the large expenditures necessary for building plants and are operated by private, investor-owned companies. In rural areas, where the small number of customers in need of services would not provide an adequate return for private investors, the state or local government funds the plant construction and operates the utility.

The various segments of the utilities field vary in the degree to which their workers are involved in production activities, administration and management, or research and development. Fields such as water supply that employ relatively few workers employ more production workers and plant operators. On the other hand, electric utilities generally operate larger plants using very expensive, high-technology equipment and thus employ more professional and technical personnel.

Manufacturing, Construction, and Utilities

A unique feature of the utilities field is that urban areas with many inhabitants generally have relatively few utility companies. For instance, there were about 52,800 community water systems in the United States in 2004 serving more than 272 million people. The 30,000 smallest water systems served only 5 million people while the 3,900 largest systems served more than 220 million. Alaska, with a 2004 population about 12 percent of that of Maryland, had almost 3 times more electric generating plants than Maryland. These examples show that economies of scale in the utilities field allow one or two large companies to serve large numbers of customers in metropolitan areas more efficiently than many smaller companies. In fact, some utility companies, predominately serving large metropolitan areas, offer more than one utility to their customers.

Unlike most fields, the utilities field imports and exports only a small portion of its product. In the natural gas field, for example, this reflects the fact that the country has a sizable, proven resource base that can be used economically to meet the country's needs. This is the result of a national policy that utilities should be self-sufficient, without dependence on imports for the basic services our country requires. However, easing trade restrictions, increased pipeline capacity, and shipping natural gas in liquefied form have made importing and exporting natural gas more economical. In 2004, about 19 percent of the natural gas consumed was imported, mostly from Canada. A small portion of natural gas is exported in liquefied form, primarily to Japan.

Working Conditions

Electricity, gas, and water are produced and used continuously throughout each day. As a result, split, weekend, and night shifts are common for utility workers. The average workweek for production workers in utilities was 40.9 hours in 2004, compared with 33.5 hours for all trade, transportation, and utilities fields and 33.7 hours for all nongovernment fields. Employees often must work overtime to accommodate peaks in demand and to repair damage caused by storms, cold weather, accidents, and other occurrences. The field employs relatively few part-time workers.

The hazards of working with electricity, natural gas, treatment chemicals, and wastes can be substantial, but generally are avoided by following rigorous safety procedures. Protective gear such as rubber gloves with long

sleeves, nonsparking maintenance equipment, and body suits with breathing devices designed to filter out any harmful fumes are mandatory for work in dangerous environs. Employees also undergo extensive training on working with hazardous materials and utility company safety measures.

In 2003, the utilities field reported 4.4 cases of work-related injury or illness per 100 full-time workers, compared with an average of 5.0 cases for all nongovernment fields.

Important Characteristics of the Field

Skills: Repairing; Troubleshooting; Equipment Maintenance; Installation; Operation Monitoring; Operation and Control. **Abilities:** Reaction Time; Wrist-Finger Speed; Extent Flexibility; Spatial Orientation; Glare Sensitivity; Sound Localization. **Work-Related Values:** Supervision, Technical; Supervision, Human Relations; Moral Values; Security; Independence; Company Policies and Practices.

Employment

Utilities employed about 570,000 workers in 2004. Electric power generation, transmission, and distribution provided about 7 in 10 jobs, as shown in table 1.

Table 1. Distribution of wage and salary employment in nongovernment utilities, 2004 (Employment in thousands)

Field	Employment	Percent
Total, all utilities	570	100.0
Electric power generation, transmission, and distribution	412	72.3
Natural gas distribution	112	19.6
Water, sewage, and other systems	46	8.1

The diversity of production processes in the utilities field was reflected in the size of the establishments that made up the field. For example, the electric power and natural gas distribution sectors consisted of relatively large plants. In 2004, electric power generation, transmission, and distribution plants employed an average of about 51 workers per establishment. On the other hand, the water, sewage, and other systems sector employed an average of only 8 workers per establishment (table 2).

Table 2. Nongovernment establishments in utilities and average employment per establishment, 2004

Field	Number of establishments	Employment per establishment
Total, all utilities	16,400	34
Electric power generation, transmission, and distribution	8,000	51
Natural gas distribution	2,700	40
Water, sewage, and other systems	5,700	8

Although many establishments are small, most utilities jobs were in establishments with 50 or more workers (chart 1).

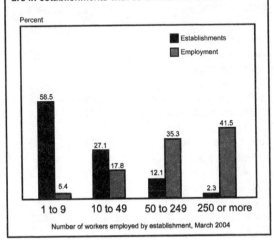

About 85 percent of the utilities industry establishments have fewer than 50 workers, but three-fourths of the jobs are in establishments with 50 workers or more.

Percent

- Establishments
- Employment

58.5
27.1
17.8
12.1
35.3
5.4
2.3
41.5

1 to 9   10 to 49   50 to 249   250 or more

Number of workers employed by establishment, March 2004

Occupations in the Field

About 223,000 jobs—about 39 percent of all wage and salary jobs in the utilities field—were in production or installation, maintenance, and repair occupations in 2004 (table 3). About 22 percent of jobs were in office and administrative support occupations; 14 percent were in professional and related occupations; and 13 percent were in management, business, and financial occupations. The remaining jobs were in construction, transportation, sales, and service occupations.

Workers in production and installation, maintenance, and repair occupations install and maintain pipelines and powerlines, operate and fix plant machinery, and monitor treatment processes. For example, *electrical powerline installers and repairers* install and repair cables or wires used in electrical power or distribution systems. They install insulators, wooden poles, and light-duty or heavy-duty transmission towers. *First-line supervisors and managers* directly supervise and coordinate the activities of production and repair workers. These supervisors ensure that workers use and maintain equipment and materials properly and efficiently to maximize productivity.

Production occupations include *power plant operators, power distributors and dispatchers,* and *water and liquid waste treatment plant operators. Power plant operators* control or operate machinery, such as stream-driven turbine generators, to generate electric power, often using control boards or semi-automatic equipment. *Power distributors and dispatchers* coordinate, regulate, or distribute electricity or steam in generating stations, over transmission lines to substations, and over electric power lines. *Water and liquid waste treatment plant and system operators* control the process of treating water or wastewater, take samples of water for testing, and may perform maintenance of treatment plants.

Industrial machinery mechanics install, repair, and maintain machinery in power generating stations, gas plants, and water treatment plants. They repair and maintain the mechanical components of generators, waterwheels, water-inlet controls, and piping in generating stations; steam boilers, condensers, pumps, compressors, and similar equipment in gas manufacturing plants; and equipment used to process and distribute water for public and industrial uses.

Manufacturing, Construction, and Utilities

General maintenance and repair workers perform work involving a variety of maintenance skills to keep machines, mechanical equipment, and the structure of an establishment in repair. Generally found in small establishments, these workers have duties that may involve pipefitting, boilermaking, electrical work, carpentry, welding, and installing new equipment.

Office and administrative support occupations account for about a quarter of jobs in the utilities field. *Customer service representatives* interview applicants for water, gas, and electric service. They talk with customers by phone or in person and receive orders for installation, turn-on, discontinuance, or change in service. *General office clerks* may do bookkeeping, typing, stenography, office machine operation, and filing. *Utilities meter readers* read electric, gas, water, or steam consumption meters visually or remotely, using radio transmitters, and record the volume used by residential and industrial customers. Financial clerks, such as *bookkeeping, accounting, and auditing clerks*, compute, classify, and record numerical data to keep financial records complete. They perform any combination of routine calculating, posting, and verifying duties to obtain primary financial data for use in maintaining accounting records.

Professional and related occupations in this field include *engineers* and *computer specialists*. *Engineers* develop technologies that allow, for example, utilities to produce and transmit gas and electricity more efficiently and water more cleanly. They also may develop improved methods of landfill or wastewater treatment operations in order to maintain compliance with government regulations. *Computer specialists* develop computer systems to automate utility processes; provide plant simulators for operator training; and improve operator decision making. *Engineering technicians* assist engineers in research activities and may conduct some research independently.

Managers and administrators in the utilities field plan, organize, direct, and coordinate management activities. They often are responsible for maintaining an adequate supply of electricity, gas, water, steam, or sanitation service.

Table 3. Employment of wage and salary workers in utilities by occupation, 2004 and projected change, 2004–2014. (Employment in thousands)

Occupation	Employment, 2004		Percent change, 2004–2014
	Number	Percent	
Total, all occupations	570	100.0	–1.3
Management, business, and financial occupations	72	12.6	2.3
Top executives	12	2.1	2.4
Engineering managers	4	0.7	0.6
Management analysts	5	0.9	–0.4
Business operation specialists, all other	9	1.6	9.8
Accountants and auditors	8	1.4	1.1
Professional and related occupations	83	14.5	4.7
Computer systems analysts	5	0.9	9.6
Electrical engineers	11	1.9	8.5
Nuclear engineers	7	1.1	7.0
Electrical and electronic engineering technicians	7	1.3	–1.3
Nuclear technicians	3	0.5	–0.4
Office and administrative support occupations	127	22.3	–13.2
Supervisors, office and administrative support workers	8	1.5	–6.4
Bill and account collectors	4	0.7	–2.9
Billing and posting clerks and machine operators	5	0.8	–13.0
Bookkeeping, accounting, and auditing clerks	7	1.2	–4.9
Customer service representatives	32	5.7	3.1
Dispatchers	4	0.7	–10.3
Meter readers, utilities	22	3.8	–49.8
Stock clerks and order fillers	4	0.7	–23.5
Secretaries and administrative assistants	16	2.8	–6.5
Office clerks, general	11	1.9	–8.0

Occupation	Employment, 2004		Percent change, 2004–2014
	Number	Percent	
Construction and extraction occupations	36	6.4	3.0
Construction equipment operators	5	0.8	2.4
Operating engineers and other construction equipment operators	5	0.8	2.4
Electricians	9	1.6	0.0
Plumbers, pipefitters, and steamfitters	10	1.8	4.6
Installation, maintenance, and repair occupations	150	26.2	0.1
Supervisors of installation, maintenance, and repair workers	15	2.7	0.7
Electrical and electronics repairers, powerhouse, substation, and relay	15	2.6	–4.2
Vehicle and mobile equipment mechanics, installers, and repairers	7	1.2	0.5
Control and valve installers and repairers	18	3.2	0.6
Industrial machinery mechanics	9	1.6	1.5
Maintenance and repair workers, general	12	2.0	3.7
Electrical power-line installers and repairers	54	9.5	–0.5
Miscellaneous installation, maintenance, and repair workers	10	1.8	1.8
Production occupations	73	12.8	5.0
Supervisors, production workers	11	2.0	3.2
Nuclear power reactor operators	4	0.6	–1.8
Power distributors and dispatchers	5	0.8	–1.4
Power plant operators	23	4.0	–1.6
Water and liquid waste treatment plant and system operators	9	1.7	34.5

Occupation	Employment, 2004		Percent change, 2004–2014
	Number	Percent	
Gas plant operators	5	0.8	17.6
Transportation and material moving occupations	14	2.4	–3.0

Note: May not add to totals due to omission of occupations with small employment

Training, Other Qualifications, and Advancement

Utilities provide career opportunities for persons with varying levels of experience and education. However, because the utilities field consists of many different companies and products, skills developed in one segment of the field may not be transferable to other segments.

High school graduates qualify for many entry-level production jobs. In some cases, however, new safety and security regulations have led to stricter requirements for employment, such as documented proof of the skills and abilities necessary to complete the work. As a result, a degree from a college, university, or technical school may be required. Production workers may start as laborers or in other unskilled jobs and, by going through an apprenticeship program and gaining on-the-job experience, advance into better-paying positions that require greater skills or have greater responsibility. Substantial advancement is possible even within a single occupation. For example, power plant operators may move up through several levels of responsibility until they reach the highest-paying operator jobs. Advancement in production occupations generally requires mastery of advanced skills on the job, usually with some formal training provided by the employer or through additional vocational training at a 2-year technical college.

Most computer, engineering, and technician jobs require technical education after high school, although opportunities exist for persons with degrees ranging from an associate degree to a doctorate. These workers are usually familiar with company objectives and production methods, which, when combined with college education, equip them with many of the tools necessary for advancement to management positions. Graduates of

Manufacturing, Construction, and Utilities

2-year technical institutes usually fill technician positions. Sometimes, graduates of engineering programs will start as technicians until an opportunity to advance into an engineering position arises.

Managerial jobs generally require a 4-year college degree, although a 2-year technical degree may be sufficient in smaller plants. Managers usually can advance into higher-level management jobs without additional formal training outside the workplace. Competition is expected to be keen for management positions, as field restructuring is forcing utility companies to shed excess layers of management to improve productivity and competitiveness in the new deregulated environment.

Outlook

Wage and salary employment in utilities is expected to decline 1 percent between 2004 and 2014, compared with an increase of about 14 percent for all fields combined. Projected employment change varies by field segment, as shown in table 4. Although electric power and natural gas are essential to everyday life, employment declines will result from improved production methods and technology, energy conservation by consumers and more efficient appliances, and a more competitive regulatory environment. However, this decline in employment may be tempered by an increasing demand for safety and security workers to help ensure the protection of the nation's power plants and the safe transportation and storage of its hazardous materials.

Table 4. Projected employment growth in nongovernment utilities by field segment, 2004–2014

Field segment	Percent change
Total, all nongovernment utilities	−1.32
Electric power generation, transmission and distribution	−2.96
Natural gas distribution	−4.48
Water, sewage and other systems	20.95

Reorganization of electric and gas utilities has increased competition and provided incentives for improved efficiency. For example, nonutility generators of electricity, such as a major industrial plant operating its own power generators, are permitted to sell their excess electricity to utilities at competitive rates. Also, independent power producers can build electric power–generating plants for the sole purpose of selling their power to utilities. These producers generally build gas-turbine generating plants, which have lower construction and environmental costs, employ fewer workers, and—depending on fuel costs—usually can sell electric power more cheaply than the coal-powered, steam-turbine generator plants.

In the gas transmission and distribution field, regulatory changes now allow wholesale buyers to purchase gas at competitive rates from any producer and to use the gas pipeline transmission network to transport the gas. This process also is occurring at the distribution level. These changes have caused an increase in gas and electric utility mergers, workforce reductions, and the redesign and reallocation of job duties in a process that will continue through the 2004–2014 projection period.

New and continuing energy policies also provide investment tax credits for research and development of renewable sources of energy and ways to improve the efficiency of equipment used in electric utilities. As a result, electric utilities will continue to increase the productivity of their plants and workers, resulting in a slowdown in employment opportunities. This slowdown will lead to keen competition for some jobs in the field. However, highly trained technical personnel with the education and experience to take advantage of new developments in electric utilities should face good prospects for employment.

In the water and sewage systems fields, regulatory changes have had the opposite impact. Regulations in these fields have not been designed to increase competition, but to increase the number of contaminants that must be monitored and treated and to tighten the environmental impact standards of these fields, resulting in increased employment.

Water and sewage systems services are projected to be the only growing segment of utilities, with employment projected to increase 21 percent from 2004 to 2014. This segment is expected to grow as a result of an increase in the amount of waste generated from a growing population. Also, newly constructed housing developments are more likely to have community water supplies and waste treatment facilities, increasing demand for these services.

Technology and automation will adversely affect natural gas distribution utilities employment. Although natural gas is an increasingly popular choice among homeowners, businesses, and electric utilities, the efficiency of natural gas furnaces has increased considerably, thereby reducing average home consumption. These energy-conserving technologies will likely continue to minimize the relative use of natural gas by most fields and by individual homes. In addition, utilities in colder climates have increasingly automated their meter reading and billing procedures. Combined, these developments are projected to result in a decrease in employment in natural gas distribution services.

In general, persons with college training in advanced technology will have the best opportunities in utilities fields. Computer systems analysts and network systems and data communications analysts are expected to be among the fastest-growing occupations in the professional and related occupations group as plants emphasize automation and productivity. Some office and administrative support workers, such as utilities meter readers and bookkeeping, accounting, and auditing clerks, are among those adversely affected by increasing automation. Technologies including radio-transmitted meter reading and computerized billing procedures are expected to decrease employment.

Earnings

Overall, production workers in the utilities field had average weekly earnings of $1,049 in 2004. Earnings varied by field segment within utilities (table 5). Average weekly earnings for production workers were highest in natural gas distribution and in electric power generation, $1,089 and $1,074 respectively, and lowest in water, sewage, and other systems, $714.

Table 5. Average earnings and hours of production workers in nongovernment utilities by field segment, 2004

Field segment	Earnings	Weekly hours	Hourly
Total, nongovernment	$529	$15.67	33.7
Nongovernment utilities	1049	25.62	40.9
Natural gas distribution	1089	25.32	43.0
Electric power generation, transmission, and distribution	1074	26.49	40.5
Water, sewage, and other systems	714	18.30	39.0

Earnings in utilities were generally higher than earnings in other fields. The hourly earnings for production workers in utilities averaged $25.62 in 2004, compared with $15.67 in all nongovernment fields. This was due in part to more overtime and weekend work—as utility plant operations must be monitored 24 hours a day—which commands higher hourly rates. Earnings in selected occupations in utilities appear in table 6.

Table 6. Median hourly earnings of the largest occupations in utilities, May 2004

Occupation	Utilities	All fields
Electrical engineers	$35.60	$34.43
First-line supervisors/managers of production and operating workers	33.29	21.51
First-line supervisors/managers of mechanics, installers, and repairers	31.70	24.20
Electrical and electronics repairers, powerhouse, substation, and relay	26.33	25.86
Power plant operators	25.94	25.26
Electrical power-line installers and repairers	25.17	23.61
Control and valve installers and repairers, except mechanical door	24.44	21.01
Maintenance and repair workers, general	22.29	14.77
Customer service representatives	16.60	12.99
Meter readers, utilities	15.90	14.15

Sources of Additional Information

General information on the utilities field and employment opportunities is available from local utilities and from

- American Water Works Association, 6666 West Quincy, Denver, CO 80235. Internet: http://www.awwa.org

- International Brotherhood of Electrical Workers, 1125 15th St. NW, Washington, DC 20005.

- American Public Gas Association, 201 Massachusetts Ave. NE, Suite C-4, Washington, DC 20002. Internet: http://www.apga.org

- American Public Power Association, 2301 M St. NW, Washington, DC 20037-1484. Internet: http://www.appanet.org

Manufacturing, Construction, and Utilities

Trade

Automobile Dealers

- Annual Earnings: $33,270
- Job Growth: 12.2%
- Size of Workforce: 1,258,720
- Self-Employed: 4.1%
- Part-Time: 8.8%

Significant Points

- About half of all workers in this field have no formal education beyond high school.
- Employment is expected to grow, but will remain sensitive to downturns in the economy.
- Opportunities should be plentiful in vehicle maintenance and repair occupations, especially for persons who complete formal automotive service technician training.
- Earnings in this field are relatively high.

Nature of the Field

Automobile dealers are the bridge between automobile manufacturers and the U.S. consumer. *New car dealers* are primarily engaged in retailing new cars, sport utility vehicles (SUVs), and passenger and cargo vans. New car dealers employ 9 out of 10 workers in the field. Most new car dealers combine vehicle sales with other activities, such as providing repair services, retailing used cars, and selling replacement parts and accessories. These dealers offer one-stop shopping for customers who wish to buy, finance, and service their next vehicle. On the other hand, stand-alone *used car dealers* specialize in used vehicle sales and account for only 1 out of 10 jobs in the field.

Sales of new cars, trucks, and vans depend on changing consumer tastes, the popularity of the manufacturer's vehicle models, and the intensity of competition with other dealers. The business cycle greatly affects automobile sales: When the economy of the nation is declining,

car buyers may postpone purchases of new vehicles, and conversely, when the economy is growing and consumers feel more financially secure, vehicle sales increase. Consumers are also highly sensitive to the cost of borrowing. Automotive dealers are more likely to offer generous incentives, rebates, and financing deals during slow periods to maintain high sales volumes and to reduce inventories.

According to the National Automobile Dealers Association, new vehicle sales account for more than half of total sales revenue at franchised new car and new truck dealers. These sales generate additional revenue in other departments of new car dealers. By putting new vehicles on the road, dealers can count on aftermarket additions, new repair and service customers, and future trade-ins of used vehicles.

The aftermarket sales department in a new car dealer sells additional services and merchandise after the vehicle salesperson has closed a deal. Aftermarket sales workers sell service contracts and insurance to buyers of new and used cars and arrange financing for their purchases. Representatives offer extended warranties and additional services, such as undercoat sealant and environmental paint protection packages, to increase the revenue generated for each vehicle sold.

Leasing a car or truck is another financing option for consumers. Leasing services have grown in recent years to accommodate changing consumer purchasing habits. As vehicles have become more costly, growing numbers of consumers are unable or reluctant to make a long-term investment in a new car or truck purchase. Leasing provides an alternative to high initial investment costs while typically yielding lower monthly payments.

Service departments in automobile dealers provide automotive repair services and sell accessories and replacement parts. Most departments service only cars and light trucks, but some service heavy trucks, buses, and tractor-trailers. Some dealers also have body shops to do collision repair, refinishing, and painting. The work of the service department has a major influence on customers' satisfaction and willingness to purchase future vehicles from the dealer.

The used car sales department of new car dealers sells trade-ins as well as cars, trucks, and vans that were formerly rented and leased. Improvements in technology continue to increase the durability and longevity of new cars, raising the number of high-quality used cars. In recent years, the sale of used cars has become a major source of profits for many new car dealers in the wake of decreasing margins for new cars. In fact, some luxury vehicle manufacturers promote "certified pre-owned" vehicles to customers who may be unable to afford new vehicles of a particular make. In economic downturns, the relative demand for these and other used cars often increases as sales of new cars decline.

Stand-alone used car dealers range from small, one-location stores to large, nationwide superstores, which have increased in popularity over the last decade. Like the used car departments of new car dealers, they capitalize on increased demand for used cars and relatively large profits on sales of previously owned cars, trucks, and vans. Some of the larger stores offer low-hassle sales on large inventories of these popular vehicles. Such dealers typically contract out warranty and other service-related work to other dealers or to satellite service facilities. Growth in leasing agreements and rental companies will continue to provide quality vehicles to these dealers, thus providing for future employment growth in the used car market.

Automobile dealers increasingly use the Internet to market new and used cars. Through Web sites, consumers can easily access vehicle reviews; view pictures of vehicles; and compare models, features, and prices. Many Web sites also allow consumers to research insurance, financing, leasing, and warranty options. As a result, consumers are generally better informed and spend less time meeting with salespersons.

Working Conditions

Employees in automobile dealers work longer hours than do those in most other fields. Eighty-four percent of automobile dealer employees worked full time in 2004, and 38 percent worked more than 40 hours a week. To satisfy customer service needs, many dealers provide evening and weekend service. The 5-day, 40-hour week usually is the exception, rather than the rule, in this field.

Because most automobile salespersons and administrative workers spend their time in dealer showrooms, individual offices are a rarity. Multiple users share limited office space that may be cramped and sparsely equipped. The competitive nature of selling is stressful to automotive salespersons as they try to meet company sales quotas and personal earnings goals. Compared with that for

all occupations in general, the proportion of workers who transfer from automotive sales jobs to other occupations is relatively high.

Service technicians and automotive body repairers generally work indoors in well-ventilated and well-lighted repair shops. However, some shops are drafty and noisy. Technicians and repairers frequently work with dirty and greasy parts and in awkward positions. They often lift heavy parts and tools. Minor cuts, burns, and bruises are common, but serious accidents are avoided when shops are kept clean and orderly and safety practices are observed. Despite hazards, precautions taken by dealers to prevent injuries have kept the workplace relatively safe. In 2003, there were 5.1 cases of work-related injuries and illnesses per 100 full-time workers in the automobile dealers field, close to the national average of 5.0 cases.

Important Characteristics of the Field

Skills: Repairing; Troubleshooting; Equipment Maintenance; Instructing; Installation; Critical Thinking. **Abilities:** Extent Flexibility; Trunk Strength; Multilimb Coordination; Speech Recognition; Manual Dexterity; Gross Body Coordination. **Work-Related Values:** Supervision, Technical; Social Service; Advancement; Variety; Co-workers; Working Conditions.

Employment

Automobile dealers provided about 1.3 million wage and salary jobs in 2004. An additional 55,000 self-employed and unpaid family workers were employed in this field. Sales, installation, maintenance, and repair workers accounted for 63 percent of wage and salary employment. Management, office and administrative support, and transportation and material moving occupations made up another 35 percent.

Since 1950, the trend in this field has been toward consolidation. Franchised dealers have decreased in number, while their sales volume has increased. Larger dealers can offer more services, typically at lower costs to both dealer and customer. About 55 percent of jobs in automobile dealers were in establishments employing between 20 and 99 workers (chart 1). On average, automobile dealers had 25 employees per establishment, compared with

Trade

an average of 14 employees per establishment among all retail businesses.

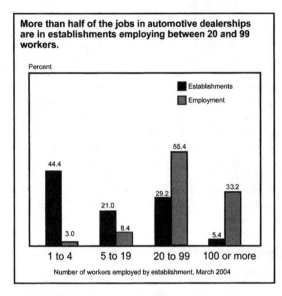

More than half of the jobs in automotive dealerships are in establishments employing between 20 and 99 workers.

Percent

Legend: ■ Establishments ▨ Employment

1 to 4: 44.4, 3.0
5 to 19: 21.0, 8.4
20 to 99: 29.2, 55.4
100 or more: 5.4, 33.2

Number of workers employed by establishment, March 2004

Occupations in the Field

The number of workers employed by automobile dealers varies significantly depending on dealer size, location, makes of vehicles handled, and distribution of sales among departments. Table 1 indicates that the majority of workers in this field were in sales occupations; installation, maintenance, and repair occupations; and office and administrative support occupations.

Sales and related occupations are among the most important occupations in automobile dealers and account for 36 percent of field employment. Sales workers' success in selling vehicles and services determines the success of the dealer. Automotive *retail salespersons* usually are the first to greet customers and determine their interests through a series of questions. Before entering the dealer, many customers use the Internet to research and compare vehicle prices, features, and options. Salespersons then explain and demonstrate the vehicle's features in the showroom and on the road. Working closely with automotive *sales worker supervisors* and the customers, salespersons negotiate the final terms and price of the sale. Automotive salespersons must be tactful, well groomed, and able to express themselves well. Their success in sales depends on their ability to win the respect and trust of prospective customers.

Installation, maintenance, and repair occupations are another integral part of automobile dealers, constituting 27 percent of field employment. *Automotive service technicians and mechanics* service, diagnose, adjust, and repair automobiles and light trucks, such as vans, pickups, and SUVs. *Automotive body and related repairers* repair and finish vehicle bodies, straighten bent body parts, remove dents, and replace crumpled parts that are beyond repair. *Shop managers* usually are among the most experienced service technicians. They supervise and train other technicians to make sure that service work is performed properly. *Service managers* oversee the entire service department and are responsible for the department's reputation, efficiency, and profitability. Increasingly, service departments use computers to increase productivity and improve service workflow by scheduling customer appointments, troubleshooting technical problems, and locating service information and parts.

Service advisors handle the administrative and customer relations part of the service department. They greet customers, listen to their description of problems or service desired, write repair orders, and estimate the cost and time needed to do the repair. They also handle customer complaints, contact customers when technicians discover new problems while doing the work, and explain to customers the work performed and the charges associated with the repairs.

In support of the service and repair department, *parts salespersons* supply vehicle parts to technicians and repairers. They also sell replacement parts and accessories to the public. *Parts managers* run the parts department and keep the automotive parts inventory. They display and promote sales of parts and accessories and deal with garages and other repair shops seeking to purchase parts.

Office and administrative support workers handle the paperwork of automobile dealers and make up about 15 percent of employment in the field. *Bookkeeping, accounting, and auditing clerks; general office clerks;* and *secretaries and administrative assistants* prepare reports on daily operations, inventory, and accounts receivable. They gather, process, and record information and perform other administrative support and clerical duties. *Office managers* organize, supervise, and coordinate administrative operations. Many office managers also are responsible for collecting and analyzing information on each department's financial performance.

Transportation and material moving occupations account for about 12 percent of jobs in automobile dealers. *Cleaners of vehicles and equipment* prepare new and used cars for display in the showroom or parking lot and for delivery to customers. They may wash and wax vehicles by hand and perform simple services such as changing a tire or a battery. *Truck drivers* typically operate light delivery trucks to pick up and deliver automotive parts; some drive tow trucks that bring damaged vehicles to the dealer for repair.

Management jobs often are filled by promoting workers with years of related experience. For example, most *sales managers* start as automotive salespersons. *Sales managers* hire, train, and supervise the dealer's sales force. They are the lead negotiators in all transactions between sales workers and customers. Most advance to their positions after success as salespersons. They review market analyses to determine consumer needs, estimate volume potential for various models, and develop sales campaigns.

General and operations managers are in charge of all dealer operations. They need extensive business and management skills, usually acquired through experience as a manager in one or more of the dealer departments. Dealer performance and profitability ultimately are up to them. General managers sometimes have an ownership interest in the dealer.

Table 1. Employment of wage and salary workers in automobile dealers by occupation, 2004 and projected change, 2004–2014 (Employment in thousands)

Occupation	Employment, 2004		Percent change, 2004–2014
	Number	Percent	
Total, all occupations	1,254	100.0	12.2
Management, business, and financial occupations	92	7.4	18.6
General and operations managers	27	2.2	16.5
Sales managers	22	1.7	26.0
Financial managers	9	0.7	18.0
Accountants and auditors	7	0.6	17.7
Service occupations	15	1.2	15.2

Occupation	Employment, 2004		Percent change, 2004–2014
	Number	Percent	
Sales and related occupations	454	36.2	12.9
Supervisors, sales workers	54	4.3	8.4
Cashiers, except gaming	22	1.8	6.0
Counter and rental clerks	30	2.4	23.6
Parts salespersons	66	5.3	–5.8
Retail salespersons	269	21.5	17.7
Office and administrative support occupations	193	15.4	2.9
Supervisors, office and administrative support workers	15	1.2	6.7
Switchboard operators, including answering service	13	1.1	–11.7
Bookkeeping, accounting, and auditing clerks	35	2.8	6.0
Customer service representatives	14	1.1	20.6
Receptionists and information clerks	14	1.1	12.2
Shipping, receiving, and traffic clerks	6	0.5	6.6
Stock clerks and order fillers	5	0.4	–9.8
Secretaries and administrative assistants	13	1.0	3.6
Office clerks, general	36	2.9	4.8
Installation, maintenance, and repair occupations	337	26.8	15.9
First-line supervisors/ managers of mechanics, installers, and repairers	35	2.8	17.7
Automotive body and related repairers	42	3.4	3.2
Automotive service technicians and mechanics	227	18.1	17.7
Bus and truck mechanics and diesel engine specialists	8	0.6	17.7
Helpers—installation, maintenance, and repair workers	14	1.1	17.7

Trade

Occupation	Employment, 2004		Percent change, 2004–2014
	Number	Percent	
Transportation and material moving occupations	153	12.2	9.1
Truck drivers, light or delivery services	19	1.5	18.0
Taxi drivers and chauffeurs	9	0.7	18.0
Cleaners of vehicles and equipment	81	6.4	6.7
Laborers and freight, stock, and material movers, hand	15	1.2	6.0

Note: May not add to totals due to omission of occupations with small employment

Training, Other Qualifications, and Advancement

Requirements for many jobs vary from dealer to dealer. To find out exactly how to qualify for a specific job, ask the dealer or manager in charge. Many jobs require no postsecondary education; about half of all workers in the field have no formal education beyond high school. In today's competitive job market, however, nearly all dealers demand a high school diploma. Courses in automotive technology are important for service jobs, as is a basic background in business, electronics, mathematics, computers, and science. Sales workers require strong communication skills to deal with the public because they represent the dealer.

Most new salespersons receive extensive on-the-job training, beginning with mentoring from sales managers and experienced sales workers. In large dealers, beginners receive several days of classroom training to learn the models for sale, methods for approaching prospective customers, negotiation techniques, and ways to close sales. Some manufacturers furnish training manuals and other informational materials for sales workers. Managers continually guide and train sales workers, both on the job and at periodic sales meetings.

Some service technicians and mechanics may begin as apprentices or trainees, helpers, or lubrication workers. They work under close supervision of experienced technicians, repairers, and service managers. Even though beginners may be able to perform routine service tasks and make simple repairs after a few months on the job, they usually need 1 to 2 years of experience to acquire enough skills to become certified service technicians.

Automotive technology is rapidly increasing in sophistication, and dealers prefer to hire graduates of postsecondary automotive training programs for trainee positions. Graduates of such programs often earn promotion to the journey level after only a few months on the job. Most community and junior colleges and vocational and technical schools offer postsecondary automotive training programs leading to an associate degree in automotive technology or auto body repair. They generally provide intense career preparation through a combination of classroom instruction and hands-on practice. Good reading and basic math skills also are required to study technical manuals, keep abreast of new technology, and learn new service and repair techniques.

Various automotive manufacturers and their participating dealers sponsor 2-year associate degree programs at postsecondary schools across the nation. Students in these programs typically spend alternate 10- to 12-week periods attending classes full time and working full time in the service departments of sponsoring dealers. Dealers increasingly send experienced technicians to factory training centers to receive special training in the repair of components such as electronic fuel injection or air-conditioning. Factory representatives also visit many shops to conduct short training sessions.

Workers need years of experience in sales, service, or administration to advance to management positions in dealers. Employers increasingly prefer persons with 4-year college degrees in business administration and marketing, particularly in dealers that are larger, more competitive, and more efficient. Some motor vehicle manufacturers offer management training classes and seminars.

Outlook

Wage and salary jobs in automobile dealers are projected to increase 12 percent over the 2004–2014 period, compared with projected growth of 14 percent for all fields combined. Job growth in automobile dealers strongly reflects consumer confidence and purchasing habits. The strength of the nation's economy and trends in consumer preferences will heavily influence the employment outlook for this field.

Through 2014, population growth will increase demand for passenger cars and boost employment in automobile dealers. Growth of the labor force and in the number of families in which both spouses need vehicles to commute to work will contribute to increased vehicle sales and employment in this field. As personal incomes continue to grow, more people will be able to afford the luxury of owning multiple vehicles, a factor that also should increase sales. However, the trend for the public to keep vehicles longer than in the past may have a dampening effect on motor vehicle sales. New and used car dealers may also face increasing competition from online electronic auctions that facilitate consumer-to-consumer and business-to-consumer trade in new and used goods, including vehicles.

Any future dealer consolidation should have a minimal effect on the field because of continued demand for vehicles and related services. Dealers will always need well-qualified people to work in the various departments of the dealer. In an effort to achieve greater financial and operational efficiency and flexibility, greater emphasis will be placed on aftermarket services, such as financing and vehicle service and repair.

Growth in leasing agreements and rental companies will continue to provide quality vehicles to the used car market, thus providing for future employment growth. Some large used car dealers offer low-hassle sales on large inventories of popular vehicles. Such dealers typically contract out warranty and other service-related work to other dealers or to satellite service facilities, reducing the demand for workers in these departments.

While the need to replace workers who retire or transfer to other occupations will result in many job openings for sales workers in automobile dealers, consumers' increasing use of the Internet to research automobile purchases will limit employment growth among sales occupations. As consumers become more knowledgeable and demand more of sales workers, dealers will seek more highly educated salespersons. Those who have a college degree and previous sales experience should have the best opportunities. If alternative sales techniques and compensation systems, such as using salaried rather than commissioned sales professionals, become more common, the greater income stability may lead to less turnover of sales jobs.

Opportunities in vehicle maintenance and repair should be plentiful, especially for persons who complete formal automotive service technician training. The growing complexity of automotive technology increasingly requires highly trained automotive service technicians and mechanics to service vehicles. Most persons who enter maintenance and repair occupations in this field may expect steady work because changes in economic conditions have little effect on this part of the dealer's business.

Opportunities in management occupations will be best for persons with college degrees and those with considerable field experience. However, consolidation of dealers will slow the growth of managerial jobs. Competition for managerial positions will remain relatively keen.

Earnings

Average weekly earnings of nonsupervisory workers in automobile dealers were $634 in 2004, substantially higher than the average for retail trade ($371), as well as that for all nongovernment fields ($529). Earnings vary depending on occupation, experience, and the dealer's geographic location and size. Earnings in selected occupations in automobile dealers appear in table 2.

Most automobile sales workers are paid on commission. Commission systems vary, but dealers often guarantee new salespersons a modest salary for the first few months until they learn how to sell vehicles. Many dealers also pay experienced, commissioned sales workers a modest weekly or monthly salary to compensate for the unstable nature of sales. Dealers, especially larger ones, also pay bonuses and have special incentive programs for exceeding sales quotas. With increasing customer service requirements, some dealers and manufacturers have adopted a sales force paid entirely by salary.

Most automotive service technicians and mechanics receive a commission related to the labor cost charged to the customer. Their earnings depend on the amount of work available and completed.

In 2004, relatively few workers in automobile dealers, 4 percent, were union members or were covered by union contracts, compared with 14 percent of workers in all fields.

Trade

Table 2. Median hourly earnings of the largest occupations in automobile dealers, May 2004

Occupation	Automobile dealers	All fields
First-line supervisors/managers of retail sales workers	$31.80	$15.73
First-line supervisors/managers of mechanics, installers, and repairers	25.22	24.20
Retail salespersons	18.61	8.98
Automotive service technicians and mechanics	18.30	15.60
Counter and rental clerks	17.87	8.79
Automotive body and related repairers	17.73	16.68
Parts salespersons	15.16	12.32
Bookkeeping, accounting, and auditing clerks	12.93	13.74
Office clerks, general	10.55	10.95
Cleaners of vehicles and equipment	8.98	8.41

Sources of Additional Information

For more information about work opportunities, contact local automobile dealers or the local offices of the state employment service. The latter also may have information about training programs.

For additional information about careers and training in the automobile dealers field, write to

- National Automobile Dealers Association, 8400 Westpark Dr., McLean, VA 22102. Internet: http://www.nada.org

- Automotive Aftermarket Industry Association, 4600 East-West Hwy, Suite 300, Bethesda, MD 20814. Internet: http://www.aftermarket.org

Clothing, Accessory, and General Merchandise Stores

- Annual Earnings: $18,360
- Job Growth: 10.1%
- Size of Workforce: 4,338,110
- Self-Employed: 3.9%
- Part-Time: 31.8%

Significant Points

- Sales and administrative support jobs account for 83 percent of employment in the field.

- Most jobs do not require formal education; many people get their first jobs in this field.

- Clothing, accessory, and general merchandise stores offer many part-time jobs, but earnings are relatively low.

- Despite relatively slow employment growth, turnover will produce numerous job openings in this large field.

Nature of the Field

Clothing, accessory, and general merchandise stores are some of the most-visited establishments in the country. Whether shopping for an item of clothing, a piece of jewelry, a household appliance, or even food, you will likely go to one of these stores to make your purchase or compare selections with other retail outlets. Composed of department stores (including discount department stores), supercenters, and warehouse club stores, general merchandise stores in particular sell a large assortment of items. Also included among general merchandise stores are dollar stores that sell a wide variety of inexpensive merchandise.

Department stores sell an extensive selection of merchandise, with no one line predominating. As the name suggests, these stores generally are arranged into departments, each headed by a manager. The various departments can sell apparel, furniture, appliances, home furnishings, cosmetics, jewelry, paint and hardware, electronics, and sporting goods. They also may sell services such as optical, photography, and pharmacy services. Discount department stores typically have fewer sales workers, relying more on self-service features, and have centrally located cashiers. Department stores that sell bulk items, like major appliances, usually provide delivery and installation services. Upscale department stores may offer tailoring for their clothing lines and more personal service.

Warehouse club stores and supercenters, the fastest-growing segment of this field, sell an even more eclectic mix of products and services in fixed quantities and at low prices. These stores typically include an assortment of food items, often sold in bulk, along with an array of household and automotive goods, clothing, and services that may vary over time. Often, such stores require that shoppers purchase a membership that entitles them to shop there. They offer very little service and usually require the customer to take the item home.

Compared with department stores, clothing and accessory stores sell a much narrower group of items that include apparel for all members of the family as well as shoes, luggage, leather goods, lingerie, jewelry, uniforms, and bridal gowns. Stores in this sector may sell a relatively broad range of these items or concentrate on a few. They often are staffed with knowledgeable salespersons who can help in the selection of sizes, styles, and accessories. Many of these stores are located in shopping malls across the country and have significantly fewer workers than department stores.

Working Conditions

Most employees in clothing, accessory, and general merchandise stores work under clean, well-lighted conditions. Many jobs are part time, with the most employees working during peak selling times, including nights, weekends, and holidays. Because weekends are busy days in retailing, almost all employees work at least one of these days and have a weekday off. During busy periods, such as holidays and the back-to-school season, longer-than-normal hours may be scheduled, and vacation time is limited for most workers, including buyers and managers.

Retail salespersons and cashiers often stand for long periods, and stock clerks may perform strenuous tasks, such as moving heavy, cumbersome boxes. Sales representatives and buyers often travel to visit clients and may be

away from home for several days or weeks at a time. Those who work for large manufacturers and retailers may travel outside of the country.

The incidence of work-related illnesses and injuries varies greatly among segments of the field. In 2003, workers in clothing and accessory stores had 2.8 cases of injury and illness per 100 full-time workers, while those in general merchandise stores had 7.2 cases per 100 full-time workers. These figures compare with an average of 5.0 throughout nongovernment fields.

Important Characteristics of the Field

Skills: Social Perceptiveness. **Abilities:** Trunk Strength; Extent Flexibility; Stamina; Static Strength; Gross Body Equilibrium; Gross Body Coordination. **Work-Related Values:** Supervision, Technical; Co-workers; Advancement; Supervision, Human Relations; Working Conditions; Social Service.

Employment

Clothing, accessory, and general merchandise stores—one of the largest employers in the nation—had about 4.2 million wage and salary jobs in 2004. Department stores accounted for most jobs in the field, but only about 7 percent of establishments. In 2004, about 7 of

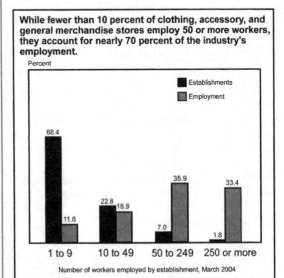

While fewer than 10 percent of clothing, accessory, and general merchandise stores employ 50 or more workers, they account for nearly 70 percent of the industry's employment.

Number of workers employed by establishment, March 2004

10 workers were employed in clothing, accessory, and general merchandise stores having more than 50 workers (chart 1). In contrast to many fields, this field employs workers in all sections of the country, from the largest cities to the smallest towns.

Many of the field's workers are young—31 percent were under 24 years old in 2004, compared with 14 percent for all fields. About 29 percent of the workers were employed part time.

Occupations in the Field

Sales and related occupations accounted for 65 percent of workers in this field in 2004 (table 1). Retail salespersons, who make up 43 percent of employment in the field, help customers select and purchase merchandise. A salesperson's primary job is to interest customers in the merchandise and to answer any questions the customers may have. In order to do this, the worker may describe the product's various models, styles, and colors or demonstrate its use. To sell expensive and complex items, workers need extensive knowledge of the products.

In addition to selling, most retail salespersons register the sale electronically on a cash register or terminal; receive cash, checks, and charge payments; and give change and receipts. Depending on the hours they work, they may open or close their cash registers or terminals. Either of these operations may include counting the money in the cash register; separating charge slips, coupons, and exchange vouchers; and making deposits at the cash office. Salespersons are held responsible for the contents of their register, and repeated shortages often are cause for dismissal.

Salespersons may be responsible for handling returns and exchanges of merchandise, wrapping gifts, and keeping their work areas neat. In addition, they may help stock shelves or racks, arrange for mailing or delivery of a purchase, mark price tags, take inventory, and prepare displays. They also must be familiar with the store's security practices to help prevent theft of merchandise. *Cashiers* total bills, receive money, make change, fill out charge forms, and give receipts. Retail salespersons and cashiers often have similar duties.

Office and administrative support occupations make up the next largest group of employees, accounting for 19 percent of total employment in the field. *Stock clerks and order fillers* bring merchandise to the sales floor and stock shelves and racks. They also may mark items with identifying codes or prices so that they can be recognized quickly and easily, although many items today arrive preticketed. *Customer service representatives* investigate and resolve customers' complaints about merchandise, service, billing, or credit ratings. The field also employs administrative occupations found in most fields, such as general office clerks and bookkeepers.

Management and business and financial operations occupations accounted for 2 percent of field employment. (Only managers located at the individual stores are counted in this field. Higher-level managers for national or regional chain stores with multiple locations typically are employed at the stores' headquarters and are classified in the management of companies and enterprises field, which is not covered in this book.) *Department managers* oversee sales workers in a department or section of the store. They set the work schedule, supervise employee performance, and are responsible for the overall sales and profitability of their departments. They also may be called upon to settle a dispute between a customer and a salesperson.

Buyers purchase merchandise for resale from wholesalers or manufacturers. Using historical records, market analysis, and their sense of consumer demand, they buy merchandise, keeping in mind their customers' demand for style, quality, and low price. Wrong decisions mean that the store will mark down slow-selling merchandise, thus losing profits. Buyers for larger stores or chains usually buy one classification of merchandise, such as casual menswear or home furnishings; those working for smaller stores may buy all the merchandise sold in the store. They also plan and implement sales promotion plans for their merchandise, such as arranging for advertising and ensuring that the merchandise is displayed properly.

Merchandise managers are in charge of a group of buyers and department managers; they plan and supervise the purchase and marketing of merchandise in a broad area, such as women's apparel or appliances. In department store chains, with numerous stores, many of the buying and merchandising functions are centralized in one location. Some local managers might decide which merchandise, among that bought centrally, would be best for their own stores.

Department store managers direct and coordinate the activities in these stores. They may set pricing policies to maintain profitability and notify senior management of concerns or problems. Department store managers usually directly supervise department managers and indirectly oversee other department store workers.

Clothing and accessory store managers—often the only managers in smaller stores—combine many of the duties of department managers, department store managers, and buyers. *Retail chain store area managers* or *district managers* oversee the activities of clothing and accessory store managers in an area. They hire managers, ensure that company policies are carried out, and coordinate sales and promotional activities.

Various other store-level occupations in this diversified field include pharmacists, hairdressers, material moving workers, food preparation and serving workers, and security guards.

Table 1. Employment of wage and salary workers in clothing, accessory, and general merchandise stores by occupation, 2004 and projected change, 2004–2014 (Employment in thousands)

Occupation	Employment, 2004		Percent change, 2004–2014
	Number	Percent	
Total, all occupations	4,205	100.0	10.1
Management, business, and financial occupations	102	2.4	16.6
General and operations managers	47	1.1	14.7
Professional and related occupations	87	2.1	31.5
Merchandise displayers and window trimmers	19	0.5	11.6
Opticians, dispensing	11	0.3	0.9
Service occupations	205	4.9	14.1
Security guards	28	0.7	1.2
Counter attendants, cafeteria, food concession, and coffee shop	11	0.3	18.6
Janitors and cleaners, except maids and housekeeping cleaners	44	1.1	18.2
Locker room, coatroom, and dressing room attendants	11	0.3	12.6

Occupation	Employment, 2004		Percent change, 2004–2014
	Number	Percent	
Entertainment attendants and related workers, all other	26	0.6	18.7
Sales and related occupations	2,720	64.7	11.6
First-line supervisors/ managers of retail sales workers	265	6.3	5.8
Cashiers, except gaming	601	14.3	5.9
Retail salespersons	1,795	42.7	14.3
Demonstrators and product promoters	15	0.4	15.4
Office and administrative support occupations	778	18.5	0.6
First-line supervisors/ managers of office and administrative support workers	56	1.3	7.0
Customer service representatives	64	1.5	20.6
Information and record clerks, all other	24	0.6	–5.1
Shipping, receiving, and traffic clerks	71	1.7	6.3
Stock clerks and order fillers	429	10.2	–3.8
Office clerks, general	27	0.7	3.4
Installation, maintenance, and repair occupations	43	1.0	13.4
Watch repairers	2	0.1	–0.9
Production occupations	100	2.4	6.9
Tailors, dressmakers, and custom sewers	12	0.3	14.7
Jewelers and precious stone and metal workers	12	0.3	21.0
Transportation and material moving occupations	170	4.0	9.5
Laborers and freight, stock, and material movers, hand	124	2.9	6.4

Note: May not add to totals due to omission of occupations with small employment

Trade

Training, Other Qualifications, and Advancement

There are no formal educational requirements for most sales and administrative support jobs; in fact, many people get their first jobs in this field. A high school education is preferred, especially by larger employers. Because many of the new workers in the field are recent immigrants, employers may require proficiency in English and may even offer language training to employees.

Salespersons should enjoy working with people. Among other desirable characteristics are a pleasant personality, a neat appearance, and the ability to communicate clearly. Because of the trend toward providing more service, it is becoming increasingly important for salespersons to be knowledgeable about the products and merchandise that are available. Some employers may conduct a background check of applicants, especially of those seeking work selling high-priced items.

In most small stores, an experienced employee or the manager instructs newly hired sales personnel on making out sales checks and operating the cash register. In larger stores, training programs are more formal and usually are conducted over several days. Some stores provide periodic training seminars to refresh and improve the customer service and selling skills of their sales workers. Initially, trainees are taught how to make cash, check, and charge sales; eventually, they are instructed on how to deal with returns and special orders. Other topics usually covered are customer service, security, and store policies and procedures. Depending on the type of product they are selling, sales workers may be given specialized training in their area. For example, those working in cosmetic sales receive instruction on the types of products that are available and the types of customers to whom those products would be most beneficial.

Some salespersons are hired for a particular department, whereas others are placed after they have completed training. Placement usually is based on where positions are available. Some salespersons, often called "floaters," are not assigned to a particular department; instead, they work where they are needed.

Advancement opportunities for salespersons vary. As those who work full time gain experience and seniority, they usually move to positions of greater responsibility or to positions with potentially higher commissions. Salespersons who are paid on a commission basis—that is, they earn a percentage of the value of what they sell—may advance to selling more expensive items. The most experienced and highest-paid salespersons sell big-ticket items. This work requires the most knowledge of the product and the greatest talent for persuasion. In some establishments, advancement opportunities are limited because one person, often the owner, is the only manager, but sales experience may be useful in finding a higher-level job elsewhere. Retail selling experience is an asset when one is applying for sales positions with larger retailers or in other kinds of sales, such as sales of motor vehicles, financial services, or wholesale merchandise.

Traditionally, capable salespersons with good leadership skills, yet without a college degree, could advance to management positions; however, a college education is becoming increasingly important for managerial positions such as department manager, store manager, or buyer. Computer skills are extremely important in all parts of the field, especially in areas such as inventory control, human resources, sales forecasting, and electronic commerce. Many retailers prefer to hire persons with associate's or bachelor's degrees in marketing, merchandising, or business as management trainees or assistant managers. As of 2004, more than 150 colleges and universities offered educational programs in retail management, retail merchandising, retail marketing, retail sales, and fashion and apparel merchandising.

The National Retail Federation offers the National Professional Certification in Customer Service for customer service and sales-related occupations. Certification is voluntary and is earned by passing an exam and applying for certification.

Outlook

Numerous job openings will result from turnover in this large field. Jobs will be available for young workers; first-time jobseekers; persons with limited job experience; senior citizens; and people seeking part-time work, such as those with young children or those who wish to supplement their income from other jobs. Persons with a college degree or computer skills will be sought for managerial positions.

Overall, the number of wage and salary jobs in clothing, accessory, and general merchandise stores is expected to increase 10 percent over the 2004–2014 period, compared with the 14 percent increase projected for all fields combined. The relatively slow growth is due mainly to limited job growth in clothing and accessory stores as discount department stores and supercenters account for a greater share of apparel sales. Also limiting employment growth is the popularity of supercenters and warehouse stores that stress self-service and are, consequently, less labor intensive than traditional retailers. Employment in full-service department stores will grow the slowest, as more people buy from discounters.

Alternative retail outlets such as mail-order companies, home shopping, and the Internet will continue to take customers away from traditional retail stores, thereby limiting job growth. However, the negative effects on employment resulting from this trend will be minimized as traditional retailers increase their presence in these outlets. In addition, although online sales are expected to grow rapidly, sales at traditional retail stores are projected to continue to account for a major portion of total retail sales. Also, although electronic commerce is expected to limit the growth of some retail jobs, it is increasing opportunities for other occupations, such as Internet sales managers, Webmasters, technical support workers, and other related workers.

Some companies are moving toward obtaining goods directly from the manufacturer, bypassing the wholesale level completely and thereby reducing costs and increasing profits. This trend may further limit job growth in the field, particularly among administrative and managerial workers. In addition, many of these stores, particularly clothing and accessory stores, are highly sensitive to changes in the economy and to changing tastes of consumers. Guessing wrong on upcoming trends, especially several years in a row, or being unable to weather a recession can cause even large, well-established stores to go bankrupt or out of business. As a result, changes in employment can be volatile and may include periods of rapid increases and decreases in the number of jobs.

Job growth also will be limited as retailers try to lower costs by contracting out some of the activities typically performed by retail workers. For example, retailers will use temporary workers to stock and order products and to perform customer service.

Worker productivity is increasing because of technological advances, particularly among clerks, managers, and buyers. For example, computerized systems allow companies to streamline purchasing and obtain customer information and preferences, reducing the need for buyers. However, because direct customer contact also will

remain important, employment of sales workers who interact personally with customers will be less affected by technological advances.

Earnings

Hourly earnings of nonsupervisory workers in clothing, accessory, and general merchandise stores are well below the average for all workers in nongovernment fields. This reality reflects both the high proportion of part-time and less experienced workers in these stores and the fact that even experienced workers receive relatively low pay compared with experienced workers in many other fields (table 2). Earnings in selected occupations in clothing, accessory, and general merchandise stores appear in table 3.

Table 2. Average earnings of nonsupervisory workers in clothing, accessory, and general merchandise stores, 2004

Field segment	Weekly	Hourly
Total, nongovernment	$529	$15.67
Total, general merchandise stores	301	10.32
Warehouse clubs and supercenters	328	9.94
Other general merchandise stores	317	9.93
Discount department stores	307	9.93
Department stores	290	10.67
Total, clothing and clothing accessory stores	268	10.55
Men's clothing stores	376	13.06
Family clothing stores	237	9.57
Shoe stores	241	9.46
Women's clothing stores	236	11.19

Many employers permit workers to buy merchandise at a discount. Smaller stores usually offer limited employee benefits. In larger stores, benefits are more comparable with those offered by employers in other fields and can include vacation and sick leave, health and life insurance, profit sharing, and pension plans.

Unionization in this field is limited. Only about 3 percent of workers were union members or covered by union contracts, compared with 14 percent in all fields.

Trade

Table 3. Median hourly earnings of the largest occupations in clothing, accessory, and general merchandise stores, May 2004

Occuaption	General merchandise stores	Apparel and accessory stores	All fields
General and operations managers	$23.50	$27.65	$37.22
First-line supervisors/ managers of office and administrative support workers	18.41	11.21	19.72
First-line supervisors/ managers of retail sales workers	15.04	15.18	15.73
Security guards	11.61	9.86	9.77
Customer service representatives	10.54	9.80	12.99
Shipping, receiving, and traffic clerks	10.15	8.89	11.73
Laborers and freight, stock, and material movers, hand	9.12	8.38	9.67
Stock clerks and order fillers	8.56	8.70	9.66
Retail salespersons	8.26	8.44	8.98
Cashiers, except gaming	7.76	7.87	7.81

Sources of Additional Information

General information on careers in retail establishments is available from either of the following organizations:

- National Retail Federation, 325 7th St. NW, Suite 1100, Washington, DC 20004.
- International Council of Shopping Centers, 665 5th Ave., New York, NY 10022. Internet: http://www.icsc.org

Grocery Stores

- Annual Earnings: $18,270
- Job Growth: 6.6%
- Size of Workforce: 2,447,100
- Self-Employed: 2.1%
- Part-Time: 35.3%

Significant Points

- Numerous job openings—many of them part time and relatively low paying—should be available due to the field's large size and high rate of turnover.
- Many grocery store workers are young: People who are 16 to 24 years old hold 32 percent of the jobs.
- Cashiers and stock clerks and order fillers account for 49 percent of all jobs.
- College graduates will fill most new management positions.

Nature of the Field

Grocery stores, also known as supermarkets, are familiar to everyone. They sell an array of fresh and preserved foods, primarily for preparation and consumption at home. They also often sell prepared food, such as hot entrees or salads, for takeout meals. Stores range in size from "supercenters," which may employ hundreds of workers, provide a variety of consumer services, and sell numerous food and nonfood items, to traditional supermarkets to convenience stores with small staffs and limited selections.

Convenience stores, however, also often sell fuel, including gasoline, diesel fuel, kerosene, and propane. Recently, many convenience stores have expanded their scope of services by providing automatic teller machines; money orders; and a more comprehensive selection of products, including food for immediate consumption and an assortment of nonfood items.

(Specialty grocery stores—meat and fish markets; fruit and vegetable markets; candy, nut, and confectionery stores; dairy product stores; retail bakeries; and health and dietetic food stores, for example—are not covered in this section. Food services and drinking places that sell food and beverages for consumption on the premises are also excluded. The latter are discussed elsewhere in Part II.)

Grocery stores are found everywhere, although the size of the establishment and the range of goods and services offered vary. Traditionally, inner-city stores are small and offer a limited selection, although larger stores, including specialty grocers and a few supercenters, are now being built in many urban areas; suburban stores are predominantly large supermarkets and supercenters with a more diverse stock. Most supermarkets include several specialty departments that offer the products and services of seafood stores, bakeries, delicatessens, pharmacies, or florist shops. Household goods, health and beauty care items, automotive supplies, pet products, greeting cards, and clothing also are among the nonfood items that can be found at large supermarkets. Some of the largest supermarkets, including wholesale clubs, even have cafeterias or food courts, and a few feature convenience stores, automotive services, and full-service banks. In addition, most grocery stores may offer basic banking services and automatic teller machines, postal services, onsite film processing, dry cleaning, video rentals, and catering services.

Working Conditions

Working conditions in most grocery stores are pleasant, with clean, well-lighted, climate-controlled surroundings. Work can be hectic, and dealing with customers can be stressful.

Grocery stores are open more hours and days than most work establishments, so workers are needed for early morning, late night, weekend, and holiday work. With employees working 30.8 hours a week, on average, these jobs are particularly attractive to workers who have family or school responsibilities or another job.

Most grocery store workers wear some sort of uniform, such as a jacket or an apron, that identifies them as store employees and keeps their personal clothing clean. Health and safety regulations require some workers, such as those who work in the delicatessen or meat department, to wear head coverings, safety glasses, or gloves.

In 2003, cases of work-related injury and illness averaged 7.2 per 100 full-time workers in grocery stores, compared with 5.0 per 100 full-time workers in the entire private sector. Some injuries occur while workers trans-

port or stock goods. Persons in food-processing occupations, such as butchers and meat cutters, as well as cashiers working with computer scanners or traditional cash registers, may be vulnerable to cumulative trauma and other repetitive motion injuries.

Important Characteristics of the Field

Skills: Social Perceptiveness; Management of Personnel Resources; Learning Strategies; Service Orientation. **Abilities:** Extent Flexibility; Stamina; Trunk Strength; Static Strength; Gross Body Coordination; Manual Dexterity. **Work-Related Values:** Supervision, Technical; Co-workers; Supervision, Human Relations; Independence; Moral Values.

Employment

Grocery stores ranked among the largest fields in 2004, providing 2.4 million wage and salary jobs. About 31 percent of all grocery store employees worked part time, and the average workweek of nonsupervisory workers was 30.8 hours. Some self-employed workers also worked in grocery stores, mostly in smaller establishments.

In 2004, there were 85,000 grocery stores throughout the nation. Most grocery stores are small; 80 percent employ fewer than 50 workers. Most jobs, however, are

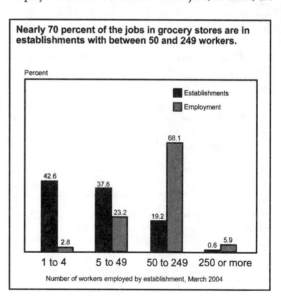

Nearly 70 percent of the jobs in grocery stores are in establishments with between 50 and 249 workers.

Percent

■ Establishments
■ Employment

1 to 4	5 to 49	50 to 249	250 or more
42.6 / 2.8	37.6 / 23.2	19.2 / 68.1	0.6 / 5.9

Number of workers employed by establishment, March 2004

Trade

found in the largest stores. Seventy-four percent of workers were employed in grocery stores with more than 50 workers (chart 1).

Many grocery store workers are young: People who are 16 to 24 years old hold 32 percent of the jobs. This reflects the large number of jobs in this field open to young workers who have little or no work experience.

Occupations in the Field

Grocery store workers stock shelves on the sales floor; prepare food and other goods; assist customers in locating, purchasing, and understanding the content and uses of various items; and provide support services to the establishment. However, 49 percent of all grocery store employees are cashiers or stock clerks and order fillers.

Cashiers make up the largest occupation in grocery stores, accounting for 34 percent of all workers (table 1). They scan the items being purchased by customers, total the amount due, accept payment, make change, fill out charge forms, and produce a cash register receipt that shows the quantity and price of the items. In most supermarkets, the cashier passes the Universal Product Code, or UPC, on the item's label across a computer scanner that identifies the item and its price, which is automatically relayed to the cash register. In some grocery stores, customers themselves scan and bag their purchases and pay using an automatic payment terminal, a system known as self-checkout. Cashiers verify that the items have been paid for before the customer leaves, and if needed, assist the customer in completing the transaction. In other grocery stores, the cashier reads a hand-stamped price on each item and keys that price directly into the cash register. Cashiers then place items in bags for customers; accept cash, personal checks, credit cards, or electronic debit card payments; and make change. When cashiers are not needed to check out customers, they sometimes assist other workers.

Stock clerks and order fillers are the second-largest occupation in grocery stores, accounting for 15 percent of workers. They fill the shelves with merchandise and arrange displays to attract customers. In stores without computer-scanning equipment, stock clerks and order fillers may have to manually mark prices on individual items and count stock for inventory control.

Table 1. Employment of wage and salary workers in grocery stores by occupation, 2004 and projected change, 2004–2014 (Employment in thousands)

Occupation	Employment, 2004		Percent change, 2004–2014
	Number	Percent	
Total, all occupations	2,447	100.0	6.6
Management, business, and financial occupations	59	2.4	21.4
General and operations managers	31	1.3	20.5
Professional and related occupations	46	1.9	54.2
Floral designers	8	0.3	23.3
Pharmacists	18	0.7	60.0
Pharmacy technicians	17	0.7	69.3
Service occupations	316	12.9	18.0
Pharmacy aides	5	0.2	32.5
First-line supervisors/ managers of food preparation and serving workers	24	1.0	21.8
Cooks	18	0.7	15.6
Food preparation workers	103	4.2	21.8
Combined food preparation and serving workers, including fast food	98	4.0	15.1
Counter attendants, cafeteria, food concession, and coffee shop	28	1.2	10.1
Janitors and cleaners, except maids and housekeeping cleaners	18	0.7	21.8
Sales and related occupations	1,021	41.7	0.9
First-line supervisors/ managers of retail sales workers	129	5.3	12.0
Cashiers, except gaming	824	33.7	–2.6
Retail salespersons	47	1.9	21.8

Occupation	Employment, 2004 Number	Employment, 2004 Percent	Percent change, 2004–2014
Office and administrative support occupations	539	22.0	–0.6
First-line supervisors/ managers of office and administrative support workers	23	1.0	10.3
Bookkeeping, accounting, and auditing clerks	22	0.9	9.6
Customer service representatives	58	2.4	24.6
Stock clerks and order fillers	373	15.2	–6.7
Other office and administrative support workers	25	1.0	3.4
Production occupations	196	8.0	14.8
Bakers	45	1.8	21.7
Butchers and meat cutters	88	3.6	9.6
Meat, poultry, and fish cutters and trimmers	19	0.8	21.8
Transportation and material moving occupations	258	10.6	11.2
Laborers and freight, stock, and material movers, hand	46	1.9	9.6
Packers and packagers, hand	195	8.0	11.0

Note: May not add to totals due to omission of occupations with small employment

Many office clerical workers—such as *secretaries and administrative assistants*; *general office clerks*; and *bookkeeping, accounting, and auditing clerks*—prepare and maintain the records necessary to keep grocery stores running smoothly.

Butchers and other meat-, poultry-, and fish-processing workers prepare meat, poultry, and fish for purchase by cutting up and trimming carcasses and large sections into smaller pieces, which they package, weigh, price, and place on display. They also prepare ground meat from other cuts and fill customers' special orders. These workers also may prepare ready-to-heat foods by filleting or cutting meat, poultry, or fish into bite-sized pieces, preparing and adding vegetables, or applying sauces or breading. While most butchers work in the meat section

of grocery stores, many other meat-, poultry-, and fish-processing workers are employed at central processing facilities, from which smaller packages are sent to area stores.

Some specialty workers prepare food for sale in the grocery store but work in kitchens that may not be located in the store. *Bakers* produce breads, rolls, cakes, cookies, and other baked goods. *Chefs and head cooks* direct the preparation, seasoning, and cooking of salads, soups, fish, meats, vegetables, desserts, or other foods. Some plan and price menu items, order supplies, and keep records and accounts. *Cooks and food preparation workers* make salads—such as coleslaw or potato, macaroni, or chicken salad—and other entrees and prepare ready-to-heat foods—such as burritos, marinated chicken breasts, or chicken stir-fry—for sale in the delicatessen or in the gourmet food or meat department. Other food preparation workers arrange party platters or prepare various vegetables and fruits that are sold at the salad bar.

Demonstrators and product promoters may offer samples of various products to entice customers to purchase them.

In supermarkets that serve food and beverages for consumption on the premises, *food and beverage serving workers* take orders and serve customers at counters. They may prepare short-order items, such as salads or sandwiches, to be taken out and consumed elsewhere. *Building cleaning workers* keep the stores clean and orderly.

In the warehouses and stockrooms of large supermarkets, *hand laborers and freight, stock, and material movers* move stock and goods in storage and deliver them to the sales floor; they also help load and unload delivery trucks. *Hand packers and packagers*, also known as courtesy clerks or baggers, perform a variety of simple tasks, such as bagging groceries, loading parcels in customers' cars, and returning unpurchased merchandise from the checkout counter to shelves.

First-line managers of retail sales workers supervise mostly entry-level employees in the grocery, produce, meat, and other specialty departments. These managers train employees and schedule their hours; oversee ordering, inspection, pricing, and inventory of goods; monitor sales activity; and make reports to store managers. *General and operations managers* are responsible for the efficient and profitable operation of grocery stores. Working through their department managers, general and operations managers may set store policy, hire and train employees, develop merchandising plans, maintain

Trade

good customer and community relations, address customer complaints, and monitor the store's profits or losses.

Purchasing managers plan and direct the task of purchasing goods for resale to consumers. Purchasing managers must thoroughly understand grocery store foods, other items, and each store's customers. They must select the best suppliers and maintain good relationships with them. Purchasing managers evaluate their store's sales reports to determine what products are in demand and plan purchases according to their budget.

Training, Other Qualifications, and Advancement

Most grocery store jobs are entry-level and can be learned in a short time. Employers generally prefer high school graduates for occupations such as cashier, stock clerk and order filler, or food preparation worker. In large supermarket chains, prospective employees are matched with available jobs, hours, and locations and are usually trained onsite. Cashiers are often trained in a few days, and many larger retailers offer formal Web-based and computer-based classroom training to familiarize workers with company guidelines and the equipment with which they will work. Cashiers may require slightly more in-house training in order to supervise and oversee the smooth operation of multiple self-checkout stations. Meat cutters and bakers can attend training courses provided by trade schools and field associations, but they can also learn the necessary skills on the job.

College graduates will fill most new management positions. Employers increasingly seek graduates of college and university, junior and community college, and technical institute programs in food marketing, food management, and supermarket management. Many supermarket chains place graduates of these programs, or of bachelor's or master's degree programs in business administration, in various professional positions or management training programs in areas such as logistics, supply chain, marketing, replenishment, food safety, human resources, and strategic planning. Management trainees start as assistant or department managers and, depending on experience and performance, may advance to positions of greater responsibility. It is not unusual for managers to supervise a large number of employees early in their careers.

Courtesy clerks or baggers sometimes advance to work as delicatessen service clerks, stock clerks, order fillers, or perhaps cashiers. Sometimes, workers rotate assignments in a supermarket; for example, a stock clerk might occasionally weigh and give out delicatessen meats. Union contracts, however, often have strict occupational definitions in some stores, making movement among departments difficult.

Grocery store management has become increasingly complex and technical. Managers of some large supermarkets are responsible for millions of dollars in yearly revenue and for hundreds of employees. They use sophisticated software to manage budgets, schedule work, track and order products, price goods, control inventory, manage shelf space, and assess product profitability. Entry-level workers may advance to management positions, depending on experience and performance. Stores that promote from within have established tracks by which workers move from department to department, gaining broad experience, until they are considered ready for an entry-level management position. Opportunities for advancement to management jobs exist in both large supermarket chains and in small, independent grocery stores.

Grocery store jobs call for various personal attributes. Almost all workers must be in good physical condition. Because managers, cashiers, stock clerks and order fillers, and other workers on the sales floor constantly deal with the public, a neat appearance and a pleasant, businesslike manner are important. Cashiers and stock clerks and order fillers must be able to do repetitive work swiftly and accurately. Cashiers need basic arithmetic skills, good hand-eye coordination, and manual dexterity. Stock clerks and order fillers, especially, must be in good physical condition because of the lifting, crouching, and climbing that they do. For managers, good communication skills as well as the ability to solve problems quickly and to perform well under pressure are important. In addition, personal qualities such as initiative, attention to detail, and leadership ability are essential for managers.

Outlook

Wage and salary employment in grocery stores is expected to increase about 7 percent by the year 2014, compared with the 14 percent growth projected for all fields combined. Many additional job openings will arise from the need to replace workers who transfer to jobs in other fields, retire, or stop working for other reasons. Replacement needs are particularly significant due to the field's large size and the high turnover rate among cashiers and other workers who do not choose to pursue long-term grocery field careers.

Employment will grow as the population increases and as more grocery stores offer a wider array of goods and services that include prescription drugs, dry cleaning, film developing, flowers, liquor, and carryout food, as well as banking, postal, and catering services. Grocery stores are adding and enhancing delicatessens, bakeries, and meat and seafood departments to accommodate the trend toward eating away from home; stores are also adding ready-to-eat-meals to compete with fast-food restaurants. The trend toward opening supercenters, where a myriad of products and services are available at a single location, is increasingly popular. These expansions are expected to create many new jobs.

Some technological advances—such as computer-scanning cash registers and automated warehouse equipment—have boosted productivity, but these innovations are not expected to adversely affect employment levels. In fact, past technological improvements like scanners and electronic data interchange are expected to improve opportunities in areas such as category management and distribution.

Increasing competition from large discount department stores and supercenters will either force smaller independent grocery stores to sell out to larger ones or, at a minimum, encourage the field to become more efficient by adopting new technologies and procedures that eliminate redundancies, especially in the supply chains.

Increasingly, many stores let customers process their own transactions with almost no interaction with a cashier. The growing use of self-checkout machines at grocery stores may have an adverse effect on employment of cashiers. This trend, however, will depend largely on the public's acceptance of automated checkouts. Thus far, self-checkouts have been popular, but the popularity is concentrated among individuals who purchase only a few items or who seek to minimize the length of time spent in stores.

Another technology which may also impact employment of cashiers is radio frequency identification (RFID). This technology allows universal bar codes to be replaced with microchips on individual items, thereby allowing entire shopping carts to be instantaneously scanned, fully automating the checkout process. Such automation, however, would initially appear only at larger supermarkets due to the cost and is years away from being implemented.

On the other hand, many other tasks, such as stocking shelves on the sales floor or helping a customer find a product, cannot be performed effectively by machines. In addition, many consumers have demonstrated their strong desire for personal services. For example, consumers want managers to answer questions about store policy and services; they want cashiers and courtesy clerks to answer questions, bag goods, or help them bring groceries to their cars; and they want workers in specialty departments to advise them on their purchases and fill personal orders by providing custom cuts of meat, fish, or poultry.

Projected growth for some grocery store occupations differs from the 7 percent growth projected for the field as a whole. For example, employment of bakers and workers in food preparation and serving related occupations is expected to grow faster than the field because of the popularity of freshly baked breads and pastries, carryout food, and catering services. With cost cutting in mind, however, some supermarkets may outsource bakery services to small specialty bakeries, thus shifting demand from large chain supermarkets to specialty bakery shops.

Electronic shopping currently is gaining in popularity across the country. Growth of online grocery shopping, however, should remain modest as a result of several factors, including logistical complications, particularly in rural areas, and the expense of delivering perishable goods in a timely manner.

Unlike many other fields, the grocery field is not highly sensitive to changes in economic conditions. Even during periods of recession, demand for food is likely to remain relatively stable.

Earnings

Average weekly earnings in grocery stores are considerably lower than the average for all fields, reflecting the large proportion of entry-level, part-time jobs. In May 2004, nonsupervisory workers in grocery stores averaged $332 a week, compared with $529 a week for all workers in the private sector. Earnings in selected occupations in grocery stores appear in table 2.

Managers receive a salary, and often a bonus, based on store or department performance. Managers in highly profitable stores generally earn more than those in less-profitable stores.

Full-time workers generally receive typical benefits, such as paid vacations, sick leave, and health and life insurance. Part-time workers who are not unionized may receive few benefits. Unionized part-time workers sometimes receive partial benefits. Grocery store employees may receive a discount on purchases.

Over 22 percent of all employees in grocery stores belong to a union or are covered by union contracts, compared with 14 percent in all fields. Workers in chain stores are more likely to be unionized or covered by contracts than workers in independent grocery stores. In independent stores, wages often are determined by job title, and increases are tied to length of job service and to job performance. The United Food and Commercial Workers International Union is the primary union representing grocery store workers.

Table 2. Median hourly earnings of the largest occupations in grocery stores, May 2004

Occupation	Grocery stores	All fields
First-line supervisors/managers of retail sales workers	$15.08	$15.73
Butchers and meat cutters	13.00	12.45
Retail salespersons	9.24	8.98
Stock clerks and order fillers	8.94	9.66
Customer service representatives	8.69	12.99
Combined food preparation and serving workers, including fast food	8.59	7.06
Food preparation workers	8.54	8.03
Laborers and freight, stock, and material movers, hand	8.25	9.67
Cashiers	7.90	7.81
Packers and packagers, hand	7.07	8.25

Sources of Additional Information

For information on job opportunities in grocery stores, contact individual stores or the local office of the state employment service.

General information on careers in grocery stores is available from

- United Food and Commercial Workers International Union, Education Office, 1775 K St. NW, Washington, DC 20006-1502.
- Food Marketing Institute, 655 15th St. NW, Suite 700, Washington, DC 20005. Internet: http://www.fmi.org
- National Association of Convenience Stores, 1605 King St., Alexandria, VA 22314.

Wholesale Trade

- Annual Earnings: $33,170
- Job Growth: 8.4%
- Size of Workforce: 5,676,170
- Self-Employed: 4.6%
- Part-Time: 7.5%

Significant Points

- Most workplaces are small, employing fewer than 50 workers.
- About 7 in 10 work in office and administrative support, sales, or transportation and material moving occupations.
- While some jobs require a college degree, a high school education is sufficient for most jobs.
- Consolidation and new technology should slow employment growth in some occupations, but many new jobs will be created in other occupations.

Nature of the Field

When consumers purchase goods, they usually buy them from a retail establishment, such as a supermarket, department store, gas station, or Internet site. When retail establishments, other businesses, governments, or institutions—such as universities or hospitals—need to purchase goods for their own use—such as equipment, motor vehicles, office supplies, or any other items—or for resale to consumers, they normally buy them from wholesale trade establishments.

The size and scope of firms in the wholesale trade field vary greatly. Wholesale trade firms sell any and every type of good. Customers of wholesale trade firms buy goods for use in making other products, as in the case of a bicycle manufacturer that purchases steel tubing, wire cables, and paint. Customers also may purchase items for use in the course of daily operations, as when a corporation buys office furniture, paper clips, or computers, or for resale to the public, as does a department store that purchases socks, flatware, or televisions. Wholesalers may offer only a few items for sale, perhaps all made by one manufacturer, or they may offer thousands of items produced by hundreds of different manufacturers. Some wholesalers sell only a narrow range of goods, such as very specialized machine tools, while others sell a broad range of goods, such as all the supplies necessary to open a new store, including shelving, light fixtures, wallpaper, floor coverings, signs, cash registers, accounting ledgers, and perhaps even some merchandise for resale.

Wholesale trade firms are essential to the economy. They simplify product, payment, and information flows by acting as intermediaries between the manufacturer and the final customer. They may store goods that neither manufacturers nor retailers can store until consumers require them. In so doing, they fill several roles in the economy. They provide businesses a nearby source of goods made by many different manufacturers; they provide manufacturers with a manageable number of customers while allowing their products to reach a large number of users; and they allow manufacturers, businesses, institutions, and governments to devote minimal time and resources to transactions by taking on some sales and marketing functions—such as customer service, sales contact, order processing, and technical support—that manufacturers otherwise would have to perform.

There are two main types of wholesalers: merchant wholesalers and wholesale electronic markets, agents, and brokers. Merchant wholesalers generally take title to the goods that they sell; in other words, they buy and sell goods on their own account. They deal in either durable or non-durable goods. Durable goods are new or used items that generally have a normal life expectancy of 3 years or more. Establishments in this sector of wholesale trade are engaged in wholesaling goods such as motor vehicles, furniture, construction materials, machinery and equipment (including household appliances), metals and minerals (except petroleum), sporting goods, toys and hobby goods, recyclable materials, and parts. Non-durable goods are items that generally have a normal life expectancy of less than 3 years. Establishments in this sector of wholesale trade are engaged in wholesaling goods such as paper and paper products, chemicals and chemical products, drugs, textiles and textile products, apparel, footwear, groceries, farm products, petroleum and petroleum products, alcoholic beverages, books, magazines, newspapers, flowers and nursery stock, and tobacco products. The merchant wholesale sector also includes the individual sales offices and sales branches (but not retail stores) of manufacturing and mining enterprises that are specifically set up to perform the sales and marketing of their products.

Firms in the *wholesale electronic markets, and agents, and brokers* subsector arrange for the sale of goods owned by others, generally on a fee or commission basis. They act on behalf of the buyers and sellers of goods, but generally do not take ownership of the goods. This sector includes agents and brokers as well as business-to-business electronic markets that use electronic means, such as the Internet or Electronic Data Interchange (EDI), to facilitate wholesale trade.

Only firms that sell their wares to businesses, institutions, and governments are considered part of wholesale trade. As a marketing ploy, many retailers that sell mostly to the general public present themselves as wholesalers. For example, "wholesale" price clubs, factory outlets, and other organizations are retail establishments, even though they sell their goods to the public at "wholesale" prices.

Besides selling and moving goods to their customers, merchant wholesalers may provide other services to clients, such as the financing of purchases, customer service and technical support, marketing services such as advertising and promotion, technical or logistical advice, and installation and repair services. After customers buy equipment, such as cash registers, copiers, computer workstations, or various types of industrial machinery, assistance may be needed to integrate the products into the customer's workplace. Wholesale trade firms often employ workers to visit customers, install or repair equipment, train users, troubleshoot problems, or advise on how to use the equipment most efficiently.

Trade

Working Conditions

Working conditions and physical demands of wholesale trade jobs vary greatly. Moving stock and heavy equipment can be strenuous, but freight, stock, and material movers may make use of forklifts in large warehouses. Workers in some automated warehouses use computer-controlled storage and retrieval systems that further reduce labor requirements. Employees in refrigerated meat warehouses work in a cold environment and those in chemical warehouses often wear protective clothing to avoid harm from toxic chemicals. Outside sales workers are away from the office for much of the workday and may spend a considerable amount of time traveling. On the other hand, most management, administrative support, and marketing staff work in offices.

Overall, work in wholesale trade is relatively safe. In 2003, there were 4.7 work-related injuries or illnesses per 100 full-time workers, comparable with the rate of 5.0 per 100 for the entire private sector. Not all wholesale trade sectors are equally safe, however. Occupational injury and illness rates were considerably higher than the national average for wholesale trade workers who dealt with lumber and construction materials (7.1 per 100 workers); motor vehicle and motor vehicle parts and supplies (6.2 per 100 workers); groceries (7.5 per 100 workers); and beer, wine, and distilled beverages (10.9 per 100 workers).

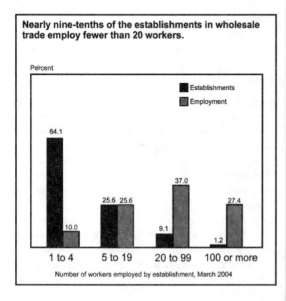

Nearly nine-tenths of the establishments in wholesale trade employ fewer than 20 workers.

Percent

- Establishments
- Employment

64.1 | 10.0 | 25.6 25.6 | 37.0 | 9.1 | 27.4 | 1.2

1 to 4   5 to 19   20 to 99   100 or more

Number of workers employed by establishment, March 2004

Most workers put in long shifts, particularly during peak times, and others, such as produce wholesalers, work unusual hours. Produce wholesalers must be on the job before dawn to receive shipments of vegetables and fruits, and they must be ready to begin delivering goods to local grocers in the early morning.

Important Characteristics of the Field

Skills: Service Orientation; Management of Financial Resources; Negotiation; Persuasion; Time Management; Social Perceptiveness. **Abilities:** Speech Recognition; Stamina; Extent Flexibility; Glare Sensitivity; Peripheral Vision; Multilimb Coordination. **Work-Related Values:** Supervision, Technical; Supervision, Human Relations; Independence; Compensation; Company Policies and Practices; Advancement.

Employment

Wholesale trade accounted for about 5.7 million wage and salary jobs in 2004. More than 193,000 workers in the wholesale trade field were self-employed. About 90 percent of the establishments in the field are small, employing fewer than 20 workers, and they have about 36 percent of the field's jobs (chart 1). Although some large firms employ many workers, wholesale trade is characterized by a large number of relatively small establishments when compared with other fields. Wholesale trade workers are spread throughout the country, have relatively low union membership, and are more likely to work full time than are workers in most other fields.

Table 1. Employment of wage and salary worker in wholesale trade by occupation, 2004 and projected change, 2004–2014 (Employment in thousands)

Occupation	Employment, 2004		Percent change, 2004–2014
	Number	Percent	
Total, all occupations	5,655	100.0	8.4
Management, business, and financial occupations	538	9.5	14.6
General and operations managers	136	2.4	11.8
Marketing and sales managers	70	1.2	19.5

Occupation	Employment, 2004		Percent change, 2004–2014
	Number	Percent	
Buyers and purchasing agents	77	1.4	8.9
Accountants and auditors	51	0.9	13.6
Professional and related occupations	313	5.5	21.6
Computer specialists	153	2.7	23.8
Designers	36	0.6	13.8
Sales and related occupations	1,442	25.5	11.7
First-line supervisors/ managers of non-retail sales workers	109	1.9	5.5
Retail sales workers	182	3.2	2.0
Sales representatives, wholesale and manufacturing, except technical and scientific products	814	14.4	13.9
Sales engineers	26	0.5	13.1
Office and administrative support occupations	1,320	23.3	–0.9
First-line supervisors/ managers of office and administrative support workers	77	1.4	3.0
Bookkeeping, accounting, and auditing clerks	145	2.6	1.1
Customer service representatives	150	2.6	17.9
Order clerks	74	1.3	–25.8
Shipping, receiving, and traffic clerks	161	2.8	3.4
Stock clerks and order fillers	177	3.1	–12.6
Secretaries, except legal, medical, and executive	74	1.3	–4.8
Office clerks, general	170	3.0	0.6
Installation, maintenance, and repair occupations	395	7.0	11.3
Computer, automated teller, and office machine repairers	58	1.0	7.8
Bus and truck mechanics and diesel engine specialists	40	0.7	13.4

Occupation	Employment, 2004		Percent change, 2004–2014
	Number	Percent	
Mobile heavy equipment mechanics, except engines	37	0.7	10.4
Maintenance and repair workers, general	62	1.1	11.9
Production occupations	356	6.3	10.5
Assemblers and fabricators	109	1.9	14.1
Packaging and filling machine operators and tenders	42	0.7	3.0
Transportation and material moving occupations	1,176	20.8	7.1
Driver/sales workers	112	2.0	11.3
Truck drivers, heavy and tractor-trailer	202	3.6	8.3
Truck drivers, light or delivery services	185	3.3	12.9
Industrial truck and tractor operators	107	1.9	7.5
Laborers and freight, stock, and material movers, hand	373	6.6	1.3
Packers and packagers, hand	76	1.3	13.2

Note: May not add to totals due to omission of occupations with small employment

Occupations in the Field

Many occupations are involved in wholesale trade, but not all are represented in every type of wholesale trade firm. Merchant wholesalers, by far, make up the largest part of the field. The activities of these wholesale trade firms commonly center on storing, selling, and transporting goods. As a result, the three largest occupational groups in the field are *office and administrative support workers*, many of whom work in inventory management; *sales and related workers*; and workers in *transportation and material moving occupations*, most of whom are truck drivers and material movers. In 2004, 70 percent of wholesale trade workers were concentrated in these three groups (table 1).

Most office and administrative support workers need to have at least a high school diploma, and some related

Trade

experience or additional schooling is an asset. As in most fields, many *secretaries and administrative assistants; bookkeeping, accounting and auditing clerks*; and *general office clerks* are employed in wholesale trade. Most of the other administrative support workers are needed to control inventory. *Shipping, receiving, and traffic clerks* check the contents of all shipments, verifying condition, quantity, and sometimes shipping costs. They may use computer terminals or barcode scanners and, in small firms, may pack and unpack goods. *Order clerks* handle order requests from customers or from the firm's regional branch offices in the case of a large, decentralized wholesaler. These workers take and process orders and route them to the warehouse for packing and shipment. Often, they must be able to answer customer inquiries about products and monitor inventory levels or record sales for the accounting department. *Stock clerks and order fillers* code or price goods and store them in the appropriate warehouse sections. They also retrieve from stock the appropriate type and quantity of goods ordered by customers. In some cases, they also may perform tasks similar to those performed by shipping and receiving clerks.

Like office and administrative support workers, sales and related workers typically do not need postsecondary training, but many employers seek applicants with prior sales experience. Generally, workers in marketing and sales occupations try to interest customers in purchasing a wholesale firm's goods and assist them in buying the goods. There are three primary types of sales people in wholesale firms: inside sales workers, outside sales workers, and sales worker supervisors.

Inside sales workers generally work in sales offices taking sales orders from customers. They are also increasingly performing duties such as problem solving, solicitation of new and existing customers, and handling complaints. Outside sales workers, also called *sales representatives* or *sales engineers*, are the most skilled workers and one of the largest occupations in wholesale trade. They travel to places of business—whether manufacturers, retailers, or institutions—to maintain contact with current customers or to attract new ones. They make presentations to buyers and management or may demonstrate items to production supervisors. In the case of complex equipment, sales engineers often need a great deal of highly technical knowledge, often obtained through postsecondary training. As more customers gather information and complete orders through the Internet, outside sales workers are devoting more time to developing prospec-

tive clients and offering services to existing clients such as installation, maintenance, and advice on the most efficient use of purchases. Sales representatives and sales engineers also may be known as manufacturers' representatives or agents in some wholesale trade firms. *Sales worker supervisors* monitor and coordinate the work of the sales staff and often do outside sales work themselves. *Counter clerks* wait on customers who come to the firm to make a purchase.

Transportation and material-moving workers move goods around the warehouse, pack and load goods for shipment, and transport goods to buyers. *Laborers and freight, stock, and material movers* manually move goods to or from storage and help to load delivery trucks. *Hand packers and packagers* also prepare items for shipment. *Industrial truck and tractor operators* use forklifts and tractors with trailers to transport goods within the warehouse, to outdoor storage facilities, or to trucks for loading. *Truck drivers* transport goods between the wholesaler and the purchaser or between distant warehouses. Drivers of medium and heavy trucks need a state Commercial Driver's License (CDL). *Driver/sales workers* deliver goods to customers, unload goods, set up retail displays, and take orders for future deliveries. They are responsible for maintaining customer confidence and keeping clients well-stocked. Sometimes these workers visit prospective clients in hopes of generating new business.

Management and business and financial operations workers direct the operations of wholesale trade firms. *General and operations managers* and *chief executives* supervise workers and ensure that operations meet standards and goals set by top management. Managers with ownership interest in smaller firms often also have some sales responsibilities. *First-line supervisors* oversee warehouse workers—such as clerks, material movers, and truck drivers—and see that standards of efficiency are maintained.

In order to provide manufactured goods to businesses, governments, or institutional customers, merchant wholesalers employ large numbers of *wholesale buyers* and *purchasing managers*. Wholesale buyers purchase goods from manufacturers for resale, based on price and what they think customers want. Purchasing managers coordinate the activities of buyers and determine when to purchase what types and quantities of goods.

Training, Other Qualifications, and Advancement

Although some workers need a college degree, most jobs in wholesale trade can be entered without education beyond high school. New workers usually receive training after they begin work—for example, in operation of inventory management databases, online purchasing systems, or electronic data interchange systems. Technological advances and market forces are rapidly altering this field. Even workers in small firms need to keep informed about new selling techniques, management methodologies, and information systems. In addition, technological advances affect the skill requirements for occupations across the entire field—from warehouse workers to truck drivers to managers. As a result, numerous firms devote significant resources to worker training.

Many firms offer on-the-job training. However, as providing training is becoming more costly and complex, the field is increasingly using third-party training organizations and trade associations to reduce this burden. To increase productivity, many companies make their employees responsible for more than one function and cross-train them by familiarizing them with many aspects of the company.

Wholesale trade has historically offered good advancement opportunities from the least-skilled jobs up through management positions. For example, unskilled workers can start in the warehouse or stockroom. After they become familiar with the products and procedures of the firm, workers may be promoted to counter sales or even to inside sales positions. Others may be trained to install, service, and repair the products sold by the firm. Eventually, workers may advance to outside sales positions or to managerial positions. Wholesale trade firms often emphasize promotion from within, especially in the numerous small businesses in the field. Even in some of the largest firms, it is not uncommon to find top executives who began as part-time warehouse help.

As the wholesale trade field changes in the coming years, advancement opportunities could become more limited. Increasing use of the Internet and other electronic means of communication, as well as changing sales techniques, are placing increasing demands on managers, so it will become more difficult to promote less-educated workers from within the firm. However, consolidation among wholesale trade firms has resulted in larger companies with more advancement opportunities for those with the appropriate skills. Currently, several large firms in this field have formal management training programs that train college graduates for management positions, and the number of these programs will probably grow. There are also a growing number of industrial distribution programs at universities, providing students with both business and technical training. All workers should expect to periodically take classes and seminars to learn new skills as the field adapts to new technology and business practices.

In addition to advancement opportunities within a firm, there also are opportunities for self-employment. For example, because brokers match buyers with sellers and never actually own goods, individuals with the proper connections can establish wholesale brokerage businesses with only a small investment—perhaps working out of their home. Moreover, establishing a wholesale distribution business can be easier than establishing many other kinds of businesses. Wholesalers that get exclusive distribution rights to popular items can become profitable quickly; although wholesale distribution firms usually require a substantial investment, obtaining rights to a successful product can be the foundation of a successful new business.

Outlook

Over the 2004–2014 period, wage and salary employment in wholesale trade is projected to grow by 8 percent, versus 14 percent growth for all fields combined. Consolidation and the spread of new technology are the main reasons for employment to be slower than average. Employment in the field, however, still depends primarily on overall levels of consumption of goods, which should grow with the economy. Growth will vary, however, depending on the products and sectors of the economy with which individual wholesale trade firms are involved. For example, due to the nation's aging population, growth is expected to be higher than average for wholesale trade firms that distribute pharmaceuticals and medical devices. Additionally, a large number of job openings will arise as people retire or leave the field for other reasons.

The trend towards consolidation of wholesale trade firms into fewer and larger companies is likely to remain strong. Globalization and cost pressures are likely to continue to force wholesale distributors to merge with other

Trade

firms or to acquire smaller firms. As retail firms grow, the demand for large national wholesale distributors to supply them will increase. The differences between large and small firms will become more pronounced as they compete less for the same customers and instead emphasize their area of expertise. The resulting consolidation of wholesale trade into fewer, larger firms will reduce demand for some workers, especially office and administrative support workers, as merged companies eliminate redundant staff.

New technologies are constantly changing the shape and scope of the workforce in wholesale trade. The Internet, e-commerce, and Electronic Data Interchange (EDI) have allowed wholesalers and their customers to better gather price data, track deliveries, obtain product information, and market products. This technology will increasingly allow customers of wholesale firms to purchase goods and track deliveries electronically, thus limiting the growth of sales and customer service workers, who would normally perform these functions. Further automation of recordkeeping, ordering, and processing will result in slower growth for office and administrative support occupations. Customers frequently order and pay for goods electronically; therefore, fewer bookkeeping, accounting, and auditing clerks will be needed as fewer paper transactions are conducted.

New radio frequency identification (RFID) technology has the potential to streamline the inventory and ordering process further and replace the need for manual barcode scans and eliminate most counting and packing errors. As RFID spreads, it may lessen demand for administrative workers, particularly order; stock; and shipping, receiving, and traffic clerks. Not all wholesalers will implement this technology, though, as it may not be cost effective for some firms, and workers will still be needed to maintain these new systems.

This twenty-first-century supply chain will create a strong demand for computer specialists in the wholesale trade field. Those computer specialists with knowledge of information technologies have the best chances for employment. Wholesalers' presence in e-commerce and the uses of electronic data interchanges (EDI) will require more computer specialists to develop, maintain, and update these systems. Computer specialists will also be needed to install and develop radio frequency identification systems for those firms that adopt it and to troubleshoot any problems these systems encounter.

With these new technologies making it easier for firms to bypass the wholesaler and order directly from the manufacturer or supplier, wholesale firms are putting greater emphasis on customer service to differentiate themselves from these other suppliers. Thus, wholesale firms are offering more services such as installation, maintenance, assembly, and repair work and creating many jobs for people that perform these functions. Sales workers will also be in demand to more aggressively develop prospective clients, including demonstrating new products and offering improved customer service to clients.

Earnings

Nonsupervisory wage and salary workers in wholesale trade averaged $667 a week in 2004, higher than the average of $529 a week for the entire workforce. Earnings varied greatly among specialties in wholesale trade. For example, in the area with the highest earnings—commercial equipment—workers averaged $872 a week, but in the area with the lowest earnings—farm-product raw materials—workers made $469 a week. Earnings in selected occupations in wholesale trade appear in table 2.

Part of the earnings of some workers is based on performance, especially in the case of outside sales workers, who frequently receive commissions on their sales. Although many sales workers receive a base salary in addition to commission, some receive compensation based solely on sales revenue. Performance-based compensation may become more common among other occupations as wholesaling firms attempt to offer more competitive compensation packages.

Like earnings, benefits vary widely from firm to firm. Some small firms offer few benefits. Larger firms may offer common benefits such as life insurance, health insurance, and a pension. Only about 5 percent of workers in the wholesale trade field were union members or were covered by union contracts in 2004, compared with about 14 percent of the entire workforce.

Table 2. Median hourly earnings of the largest occupations in wholesale trade, May 2004

Occupation	Merchant wholesalers, durable goods	Merchant wholesalers, nondurable goods	Wholesale electronic markets and agents and brokers	All fields
General and operations managers	$42.90	$41.91	$47.92	$37.22
Sales representatives, wholesale and manufacturing, technical and scientific products	26.53	28.14	31.73	28.17
Sales representatives, wholesale and manufacturing, except technical and scientific products	21.31	21.34	24.37	21.83
Truck drivers, heavy and tractor-trailer	14.67	16.37	15.78	16.11
Customer service representatives	14.53	13.67	14.85	12.99
Bookkeeping, accounting, and auditing clerks	14.09	13.37	14.20	13.74
Shipping, receiving, and traffic clerks	11.84	12.08	11.72	11.73
Office clerks, general	11.06	10.66	10.96	10.95
Stock clerks and order fillers	11.04	10.83	11.59	9.66
Truck drivers, light or delivery services	11.00	11.90	11.78	11.80
Laborers and freight, stock, and material movers, hand	10.36	10.22	9.91	9.67

Sources of Additional Information

Information on careers for manufacturers' representatives and agents is available from

- Manufacturers' Agents National Association, 1 Spectrum Pointe, Suite 150, Lake Forest, CA 92360. Internet: http://www.manaonline.org

- Manufacturers' Representatives Educational Research Foundation, 8329 Cole Street, Arvada, CO 80005 Internet: http://www.mrerf.org

Transportation

Air Transportation

- Annual Earnings: $42,810
- Job Growth: 8.8%
- Size of Workforce: 513,280
- Self-Employed: 0.5%
- Part-Time: 12.9%

Significant Points

- Although flight crews—pilots and flight attendants—are the most visible occupations, the vast majority of the field's employees work in ground occupations.

- Senior pilots for major airlines are among the highest-paid workers in the nation.

- A bachelor's degree is increasingly required or preferred for most pilot and flight attendant jobs.

- Job prospects generally are better in regional and low-fare carriers than in major airlines, where competition for many jobs is keen; a unique benefit—free or reduced-fare transportation for airline employees and their immediate families—attracts many jobseekers.

Nature of the Field

Air travel in the United States grew at a rapid pace until 2001, expanding from 172 million passengers in 1970 to nearly 642 million in 2003. However, over the next 3 years, a combination of factors—including the events of September 11, 2001, and an economic recession—combined to reduce traffic to 1996 levels. Nevertheless, air travel remains one of the most popular modes of transportation.

Airlines transport passengers and freight over regularly scheduled routes or on routes called "charters,"

Transportation

specifically designed for a group of travelers or a particular cargo. Several classes of airlines function in the United States. As of 2004, there were 15 major airlines—12 passenger and 3 all-cargo—which the U.S. Department of Transportation defines as having operating revenues of more than $1 billion. The largest of these, often called the Big Six, generally have a "hub" and also fly internationally. A hub is a centrally located airport designated by an airline to receive a large number of its flights from many locations and at which passengers can transfer to flights to any of the locations served by the airline's system. In this way, the greatest number of passengers, from as many locations as possible, can be served in the most efficient way with a given set of resources.

In competition with the Big Six are low-cost, low-fare carriers. These carriers have traditionally not used hub and spoke systems and have offered flights between limited numbers of cities. They primarily have focused on flying shorter routes (400 miles or less) and on serving leisure travelers. But some low-fare carriers are expanding their routes to include longer transcontinental and non-stop flights. These moves have helped low-fare carriers expand their customer base to include more business travelers.

Another type of passenger airline carrier is the commuter or regional carrier. As of 2004, there were approximately 75 of these carriers. Regional airlines operate short- and medium-haul scheduled airline service connecting smaller communities with larger cities and with hubs. Some of the largest regional carriers are subsidiaries of the major airlines, but most are independently owned, often contracting their services to the majors. The regional airlines' fleet consists primarily of smaller 19- to 68-seat turbo-prop and 40- to 70-seat jet aircraft. The regional airlines are the fastest-growing segment of commercial aviation, with 1 out of every 7 domestic airline passengers flying on a regional airline during at least part of his or her trip.

Air cargo is another sector of the airline field. Cargo can be carried in cargo holds of passenger airlines or on aircraft designed exclusively to carry freight. Cargo carriers in this field do not provide door-to-door service. Instead, they provide only air transport from an airport near the cargo's origin to an airport near the cargo's destination. Companies that provide door-to-door delivery of parcels either across town or across the continent are classified in the couriers and messengers field.

Most sectors of the airline field were in a downturn in 2002, with several passenger airlines having declared bankruptcy and others on the verge of doing so. After 6 relatively successful years in the late 1990s, fueled by an increase in passenger volume and a booming economy, the growth in airline passenger traffic began to slow in 2001, coinciding with the economic recession. After the tragic events of September 11, 2001, passenger traffic dropped steeply, causing airlines to cut flights, lay off workers, and park surplus aircraft. Although passenger volume has since recovered somewhat, the growth rate in the field will likely continue to be depressed for several years.

As the low-fare airlines continue to compete and gain market share over the higher-cost major airlines and as passenger traffic remains lower, managing costs has become more critical to the survival of some airlines. Labor costs are the airlines' largest cost component—amounting to over 40 percent of some airlines' operating costs—and reducing these costs is a key part of the recovery plans of several major airlines. Reducing costs usually involves getting their constituent labor groups to restructure their wages, benefits, and work rules while continuing to improve labor productivity.

The airline field faces many challenges in the future. Airlines must focus on cost control, cash preservation, and cautious growth. The goal of the field is to be prepared to respond quickly to economic recovery. Passenger volume should slowly improve, but it will take longer for rapid employment growth to return to the air transportation field.

Working Conditions

Working conditions in air transportation vary widely, depending on the occupation. Most employees work in fairly comfortable surroundings, such as offices, terminals, or airplanes. However, mechanics and others who service aircraft are subject to excessive noise, dirt, and grease and sometimes work outside in bad weather.

In 2003, the air transportation field had 11.0 injuries and illnesses per 100 full-time workers, compared with 5.0 throughout nongovernment fields. Virtually all work-related fatalities resulted from transportation accidents.

Airlines operate flights at all hours of the day and night. As a result, many workers have irregular hours or variable work schedules. Flight and ground personnel, including mechanics and reservation and transportation ticket agents, may have to work at night or on weekends or holidays. Flight personnel may be away from their home bases frequently. When they are away from home, the airlines provide them with hotel accommodations, transportation between the hotel and airport, and an allowance for meals and expenses. Flight attendants typically fly from 65 to 85 hours a month. In addition to flight time, they have about 50 hours a month of duty time between flights.

Flight crews, especially those on international routes, often suffer jet lag—disorientation and fatigue caused by flying into different time zones. Because employees must report for duty well rested, they must allow ample time to rest during their layovers.

Important Characteristics of the Field

Skills: Service Orientation. **Abilities:** Spatial Orientation; Wrist-Finger Speed; Night Vision; Response Orientation; Auditory Attention; Peripheral Vision. **Work-Related Values:** Social Service; Supervision, Human Relations; Supervision, Technical; Company Policies and Practices; Co-workers; Compensation.

Employment

The air transportation field provided 515,000 wage and salary jobs in 2004. Most employment is found in larger establishments—2 out of 3 jobs are in establishments with 1,000 or more workers. However, 86 percent of all establishments employ fewer than 50 workers (chart 1).

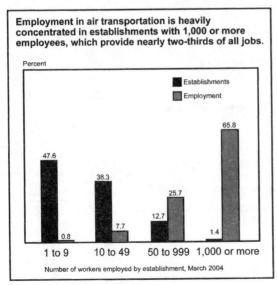

Employment in air transportation is heavily concentrated in establishments with 1,000 or more employees, which provide nearly two-thirds of all jobs.

Percent

Establishments
Employment

	1 to 9	10 to 49	50 to 999	1,000 or more
Establishments	47.6	38.3	12.7	1.4
Employment	0.8	7.7	25.7	65.8

Number of workers employed by establishment, March 2004

Most air transportation jobs are at large airports that are located close to cities and that serve as hubs for major airlines.

Occupations in the Field

Although pilots and flight attendants are the most visible occupations in this field, two-thirds of all employees in air transportation work in ground occupations (table 1). Two of the largest ground occupations are *aircraft mechanics and service technicians* and *reservation and transportation ticket agents and travel clerks.*

Aircraft mechanics and service technicians service, inspect, and repair planes. They may work on several different types of aircraft, such as jet transports, small propeller-driven airplanes, or helicopters. Many mechanics and technicians specialize, working on the airframe (the body of the aircraft) or the powerplant (the engines) or avionics (the parts of an aircraft that depend on electronics, such as navigation and communication equipment). In small, independent repair shops, they usually inspect and repair many different types of aircraft.

Some mechanics and technicians specialize in scheduled maintenance required by the Federal Aviation Administration (FAA). Following a schedule based on the number of hours flown, calendar days, cycles of operation, or a combination of these factors, mechanics inspect the engines, landing gear, instruments, and other parts of aircraft and perform necessary maintenance and repairs.

A *reservation and transportation ticket agent* is most often the first employee that passengers meet after entering the airport. Ticket agents work at airport ticket counters and boarding gates and use computers to provide customer service to incoming passengers. They can make and confirm reservations, sell tickets, and issue boarding passes. They also may work in call centers, answering phone inquiries about flight schedules and fares, verifying reservations, issuing tickets, and handling payments. *Customer service representatives* assist passengers, check tickets when passengers board or disembark from an airplane, and check luggage at the reception area and ensure that it is placed on the proper carrier. They assist elderly or handicapped persons and unaccompanied children in claiming personal belongings and baggage and in getting on and off the plane. They also may provide assistance to passengers who become ill or injured.

Transportation

Other ground occupations include *airplane cargo agents, baggage handlers,* and *aircraft cleaners. Airplane cargo agents* take orders from shippers and arrange for transportation of their goods. *Baggage handlers,* classified under *laborers and freight, stock, and material movers, hand,* are responsible for loading and unloading passengers' baggage. They stack baggage on specified carts or conveyors to see that it gets to the proper destination and also return baggage to passengers at airline terminals. *Aircraft cleaners* clean aircraft interiors after each flight.

Flight crewmembers make up 33 percent of air transportation employment and include pilots and flight attendants. *Airline pilots, copilots, and flight engineers* are highly trained professionals who fly and navigate jet and turboprop airplanes. Generally, the most experienced pilot, or captain, is in command and supervises all other crewmembers. The pilot and copilot split flying and other duties, such as communicating with air traffic controllers and monitoring the instruments. Some aircraft have a third pilot in the cockpit—the *flight engineer* or second officer—who assists the other pilots by monitoring and operating many of the instruments and systems and watching for other aircraft. Most new aircraft are designed to be flown without a flight engineer. Small aircraft and helicopters that transport passengers and cargo and perform activities such as crop-dusting, monitoring traffic, firefighting, and rescue missions are flown and navigated by *commercial pilots.*

Airline flights must have one or more *flight attendants* on board, depending on the number of passengers. The attendants' most important function is assisting passengers in the event of an emergency. This may range from reassuring passengers during occasional encounters with strong turbulence to opening emergency exits and inflating escape chutes. More routinely, flight attendants instruct passengers in the use of safety and emergency equipment. Once in the air, they serve meals and snacks, answer questions about the flight, distribute magazines and pillows, and help care for small children and elderly and disabled persons. They also may administer first aid to passengers who become ill.

Table 1. Employment of wage and salary workers in air transportation by occupation, 2004 and projected change, 2004–2014 (Employment in thousands)

Occupation	Employment, 2004 Number	Employment, 2004 Percent	Percent change, 2004–2014
Total, all occupations	515	100.0	8.8
Management, business, and financial occupations	24	4.7	18.4
General and operations managers	3	0.5	21.6
Transportation, storage, and distribution managers	2	0.4	15.6
Training and development specialists	3	0.5	17.2
Professional and related occupations	9	1.8	16.7
Computer specialists	4	0.8	17.7
Engineers	2	0.4	16.2
Service occupations	119	23.2	15.1
Personal care and service occupations	116	22.5	15.2
Baggage porters and bellhops	10	2.0	3.4
Flight attendants	101	19.5	16.4
Transportation attendants, except flight attendants and baggage porters	3	0.7	15.8
Sales and related occupations	5	1.1	12.0
Office and administrative support occupations	163	31.7	–2.5
First-line supervisors/ managers of office and administrative support workers	10	2.0	2.7
Bookkeeping, accounting, and auditing clerks	3	0.7	6.0
Customer service representatives	14	2.7	16.8

Occupation	Employment, 2004		Percent change, 2004–2014
	Number	Percent	
Reservation and transportation ticket agents and travel clerks	97	18.9	–6.3
Cargo and freight agents	14	2.8	–9.9
Production, planning, and expediting clerks	4	0.8	12.3
Installation, maintenance, and repair occupations	62	12.1	7.4
First-line supervisors/ managers of mechanics, installers, and repairers	6	1.1	15.0
Avionics technicians	3	0.5	14.3
Aircraft mechanics and service technicians	42	8.1	4.1
Maintenance and repair workers, general	8	1.5	13.0
Transportation and material moving occupations	129	25.1	15.2
Aircraft cargo handling supervisors	3	0.5	16.9
Airline pilots, copilots, and flight engineers	70	13.6	19.4
Commercial pilots	7	1.4	19.6
Transportation workers, all other	21	4.1	13.4
Cleaners of vehicles and equipment	4	0.8	8.8
Laborers and freight, stock, and material movers, hand	10	2.0	4.5
Material moving workers, all other	8	1.5	–10.0

Note: May not add to totals due to omission of occupations with small employment

Training, Other Qualifications, and Advancement

The skills and experience needed by workers in the air transportation field differ by occupation. Some jobs may be entered directly from high school, while others require specialized training. Most positions in the airline field involve extensive customer service contact, requiring strong interpersonal and communication skills. Mechanics and pilots require specialized formal training and must be certified by the FAA. Skills for many other air transportation occupations can be learned on the job or through company-sponsored training.

Pilots must have a commercial pilot's license with an instrument rating, must have a medical certificate, and must be certified to fly the types of aircraft that their employer operates. For example, helicopter pilots must hold a commercial pilot's certificate with a helicopter rating. Pilots receive their flight training from the military or from civilian flying schools. Physical requirements are strict. A medical exam, from an FAA-designated physician, must be taken to get a medical certificate. With or without glasses, pilots must have 20/20 vision and good hearing and be in excellent health. In addition, airlines generally require 2 years of college and increasingly prefer or require a college degree. Pilots who work for smaller airlines may advance to flying for larger companies. They also can advance from flight engineer to copilot to captain and, by becoming certified, to flying larger planes.

Applicants for flight attendant jobs must be in excellent health. Employers increasingly prefer applicants who have a college degree and experience in dealing with the public. Speaking a foreign language also is an asset. Airlines operate flight attendant training programs on a continuing basis. Training usually lasts from 4 to 8 weeks, depending on the size and the type of carrier, and may include crew resource management, which emphasizes teamwork and safety. Courses also are provided in personal grooming and weight control. After completing initial training, flight attendants must go through additional training and pass an FAA safety exam each year in order to continue flying. Advancement opportunities are limited, although some attendants become customer service directors, instructors, or recruiting representatives.

When hiring aircraft mechanics, employers prefer graduates of aircraft mechanic trade schools, particularly those who gained experience in the military and are certified. Additionally, employers prefer mechanics who are in good physical condition and able to perform a variety of tasks. After being hired, aircraft mechanics must keep up to date on the latest technical changes and improvements in aircraft and associated systems. Most mechanics remain in the maintenance field, but they may advance to lead mechanic and, sometimes, to crew chief or shop supervisor.

A good speaking voice and a pleasant personality are essential for reservation and transportation ticket agents and customer service representatives. Airlines prefer applicants with experience in sales or in dealing with the public, and most require a high school education, although some college is preferred. Formal company training is required to learn how to operate airline computer systems, issue tickets, and plan trips. Agents and service representatives usually are promoted through the ranks. For example, an experienced ticket agent may advance to lead worker on the shift. Agents who obtain additional skills, experience, and training improve their chances for advancement, although a college degree may be required for some administrative positions.

Some entry-level jobs in this field, such as baggage handler and aircraft cleaner, require little or no previous training. The basic tasks associated with many of these jobs are learned in less than a week, and most newly hired workers are trained on the job under the guidance of an experienced employee or a manager. However, advancement opportunities for many ground occupations are limited because of the narrow scope of duties and specialized skills necessary for other occupations. Some may advance to supervisor or to another administrative position.

Outlook

Wage and salary jobs in the air transportation field are projected to increase by 9 percent over the 2004–2014 period, compared with 14 percent for all fields combined. However, the number of job openings may vary from year to year because the demand for air travel—particularly pleasure travel, a discretionary expense—fluctuates with ups and downs in the economy. In the long run, passenger and cargo traffic is expected to continue expanding in response to increases in population, income, and business activity. Job prospects generally are better in regional and low-fare carriers than in major airlines, where competition for many jobs is keen.

Despite a recent slowdown in passenger air travel, demographic and income trends indicate favorable conditions for leisure travel in the United States and abroad over the next decade. The aging of the population, in combination with growth of disposable income among older peo-

ple, should increase the demand for air transportation services. Also, business travel should improve as the U.S. economy and world trade expand, companies continue to go global, and the economies in many foreign countries become more robust. However, as businesses also try to reduce costs, they are resorting to cheaper alternatives to flying and finding new ways to communicate. Many business travelers are using other means of transportation—for example, driving or using the railway system—and are conducting more business by phone, e-mail, and better-quality and lower-cost videoconferencing technologies.

International cargo traffic is expected to increase with the economy and growing world trade. It should also be stimulated by the development of global electronic commerce and manufacturing trends such as just-in-time delivery, which requires materials to be shipped rapidly. Growth of domestic air cargo traffic is not expected to increase as much as international cargo, primarily because of the rise of time-definite trucking. Increasingly, shipments will be sent via trucks, as opposed to aircraft, because trucks are reliable, trackable through GPS technology, and more cost effective.

Job opportunities in the air transportation field are expected to vary depending on the occupation. Employment of pilots and flight attendants is projected to grow through 2014 as the economy and passenger traffic rebound from the severe field downturn. In the near term, the best opportunities will be with the faster-growing regional and low-fare carriers. College graduates and former military pilots can expect to have the best job prospects. In addition to growth, turnover among flight attendants will produce job openings as many in this occupation leave for more stable work schedules or better salaries.

The number of reservation and transportation ticket agents will grow more slowly than the overall field as more airlines phase out paper tickets and allow passengers to purchase electronic tickets over the Internet. However, the safety and security responsibilities of these jobs will continue, thereby preventing job declines. Competition for ticket agent and customer service representative jobs will continue to be keen as many more people are likely to apply for these jobs than there are openings, in part because of the travel benefits.

Opportunities should be excellent for aircraft and avionics equipment mechanics and service technicians. The likelihood of fewer entrants from the military and a large number of retirements indicates excellent opportunities for students just beginning technician training. Most job openings are likely to be at smaller airlines since these airlines typically pay less than major airlines, leading to fewer applicants. Competition for jobs is expected to be stiff at major airlines; applicants with experience should have the best job prospects.

Opportunities also are expected to be good for those seeking unskilled, entry-level positions, such as baggage handler and aircraft cleaner, because many workers leave these jobs and need to be replaced.

Earnings

Senior pilots for major airlines are among the highest-paid workers in the nation. Earnings in selected occupations in air transportation appear in table 2.

Table 2. Median annual earnings of the largest occupations in air transportation, May 2004

Occupation	Air transportation	All fields
Airline pilots, copilots, and flight engineers	$137,160	$129,250
Aircraft mechanics and service technicians	54,890	45,290
First-line supervisors/managers of office and administrative support workers	47,450	41,030
Flight attendants	43,470	43,440
Baggage porters and bellhops	38,600	17,760
Transportation workers, all other	37,790	32,170
Cargo and freight agents	36,700	34,250
Reservation and transportation ticket agents and travel clerks	31,450	27,750
Customer service representatives	28,420	27,020
Laborers and freight, stock, and material movers, hand	21,570	20,120

Most employees in the air transportation field receive standard benefits, such as paid vacation and sick leave, life and health insurance, and often profit-sharing and retirement plans. Some airlines provide allowances to employees for purchasing and cleaning their company uniforms. A unique benefit—free or reduced-fare

transportation for airline employees and their immediate families—attracts many jobseekers.

Sources of Additional Information

Information about specific job opportunities and qualifications required by a particular airline may be obtained by writing to personnel managers of the airlines.

For further information on how to apply for a job in the air transportation field, contact

- Federal Aviation Administration, 800 Independence Ave. SW, Washington, DC 20591. Internet: http://www.faa.gov

Truck Transportation and Warehousing

- Annual Earnings: $32,152
- Job Growth: 14.0%
- Size of Workforce: 1,924,450
- Self-Employed: 12.1%
- Part-Time: 6.7%

Significant Points

- Truck drivers hold 45 percent of all jobs in the field.
- Job opportunities are expected to be especially good for truck drivers and diesel service technicians.
- Opportunities are prone to rise and fall with in the movements of the economy.
- Many jobs require only a high school education.

Nature of the Field

Firms in the truck transportation and warehousing field provide a link between manufacturers and consumers. Businesses, and occasionally individuals, contract with trucking and warehousing companies to pick up, transport, store, and deliver a variety of goods. The field

Transportation

includes general freight trucking, specialized freight trucking, and warehousing and storage.

General freight trucking uses motor vehicles, such as trucks and tractor-trailers, to provide over-the-road transportation of general commodities. This field segment is further subdivided based on distance traveled. Local trucking establishments carry goods primarily within a single metropolitan area and its adjacent non-urban areas. Long-distance trucking establishments carry goods between distant areas.

Local trucking comprised 27,000 trucking establishments in 2004. The work of local trucking firms varies with the products transported. Produce truckers usually pick up loaded trucks early in the morning and spend the rest of the day delivering produce to many different grocery stores. Lumber truck drivers, on the other hand, make several trips from the lumberyard to one or more construction sites. Some local truck transportation firms also take on sales and customer relations responsibilities in addition to delivering the firm's products. Some local trucking firms specialize in garbage collection and trash removal or hauling dirt and debris.

Long-distance trucking comprises establishments engaged primarily in providing long-distance trucking between distant areas and sometimes between the United States and Canada or Mexico. Numbering 39,000 establishments, these firms handle every kind of commodity.

Specialized freight trucking provides over-the-road transportation of freight that, because of size, weight, shape, or other inherent characteristics, requires specialized equipment, such as flatbeds, tankers, or refrigerated trailers. This field sector also includes the moving field—that is, the transportation of used household, institutional, and commercial furniture. Like general freight trucking, specialized freight trucking is subdivided into local and long-distance components. The specialized freight trucking sector contained 46,000 establishments in 2004.

Some goods are carried cross country using intermodal transportation to save time and money. Intermodal transportation encompasses any combination of transportation by truck, train, plane, or ship. Typically, trucks perform at least one leg of the trip. For example, a shipment of cars from an assembly plant begins its journey when they are loaded onto rail cars. Next, trains haul the cars across country to a depot, where the shipments are broken into smaller lots and loaded onto tractor-trailers,

which drive them to dealerships. Each of these steps is carefully orchestrated and timed so that the cars arrive just in time to be shipped on their next leg of their journey. Goods can be transported at lower cost this way, but they cannot be highly perishable—like fresh produce—or have strict delivery schedules. Trucking dominates the transportation of perishable and time-sensitive goods.

Warehousing and storage facilities comprised 13,000 establishments in 2004. These firms are engaged primarily in operating warehousing and storage facilities for general merchandise and refrigerated goods. They provide facilities to store goods; self-storage mini-warehouses that rent to the general public also are included in this segment of the field.

The deregulation of interstate trucking in 1980 encouraged many firms to add a wide range of customer-oriented services to complement trucking and warehousing services and led to innovations in the distribution process. Increasingly, trucking and warehousing firms are providing logistical services encompassing the entire transportation process. Firms that offer these services are called third-party logistics providers. Logistical services manage all aspects of the movement of goods between producers and consumers. Among their value-added services are sorting bulk goods into customized lots, packaging and repackaging goods, controlling and managing inventory, order entering and fulfillment, labeling, performing light assembly, and marking prices. Some full-service companies even perform warranty repair work and serve as local parts distributors for manufacturers. Some of these services, such as maintaining and retrieving computerized inventory information on the location, age, and quantity of goods available, have helped to improve the efficiency of relationships between manufacturers and customers.

Many firms are relying on new technologies and the coordination of processes to expedite the distribution of goods. Voice control software allows a computer to coordinate workers through audible commands—telling workers what items to pack for which orders—helping to reduce errors and increase efficiency. Voice control software also can be used to perform inventory checks and reordering. Some firms use Radio Frequency Identification Devices (RFID) to track and manage incoming and outgoing shipments. RFID simplifies the receiving process by allowing entire shipments to be scanned without unpacking a load to manually compare it against a bill of lading. Just-in-time shipping is a process whereby goods arrive just before they are needed, saving recipients money by reducing their need to carry large inventories. These technologies and processes reflect two major trends in warehousing: supply chain integration, whereby firms involved in production, transportation, and storage all move in concert so as to act with the greatest possible efficiency, and ongoing attempts to reduce inventory levels and increase inventory accuracy.

Working Conditions

In 2004, workers in the truck transportation field averaged 41.3 hours a week, compared with an average of 37.4 hours in warehousing and storage and 33.7 in all nongovernment fields.

The U.S. Department of Transportation governs work hours and many other working conditions of truck drivers engaged in interstate commerce. Long-distance drivers are not permitted to drive after having worked for 60 hours in the past 7 days or 70 hours in the past 8 days unless they have taken at least 34 consecutive hours off duty. Drivers are required to document their time in logbooks. Many drivers, particularly on long runs, work close to the maximum time permitted because employers usually compensate them on the basis of the number of miles or hours they drive. Drivers frequently travel at night, on holidays, and on weekends to avoid traffic delays so that they can deliver their cargo on time.

Truck drivers must cope with a variety of working conditions, including variable weather and traffic conditions, boredom, and fatigue. Many truck drivers enjoy the independence and working without direct supervision found in long-distance driving. Local truck drivers often have regular routes or assignments that allow them to return home in the evening.

Improvements in roads and trucks are reducing stress and increasing the efficiency of long-distance drivers. Many advanced trucks are equipped with refrigerators, televisions, and beds for their drivers' convenience. Included in some of these state-of-the-art vehicles are satellite links with their company's headquarters so that drivers can get directions, weather and traffic reports, and other important communications in a matter of seconds. In the event of bad weather or mechanical problems, truckers can communicate with dispatchers to discuss delivery schedules and courses of action. Satellite links allow dispatchers to track the location of the truck and monitor fuel consumption and engine performance.

Vehicle and mobile equipment mechanics, installers, and repairers usually work indoors, although they occasionally make repairs on the road. Minor cuts, burns, and bruises are common, but serious accidents typically can be avoided if the shop is kept clean and orderly and if safety practices are observed. Service technicians and mechanics handle greasy and dirty parts and may stand or lie in awkward positions to repair vehicles and equipment. They usually work in well-lighted, heated, and ventilated areas, but some shops are drafty and noisy.

Laborers and hand freight, stock, and material movers usually work indoors, although they may do occasional work on trucks and forklifts outside. These occupations often require a great deal of physical labor, including heavy lifting.

Safety is a major concern for the truck transportation and warehousing field. The operation of trucks, forklifts, and other technically advanced equipment can be dangerous without proper training and supervision. Efforts are underway to standardize training programs to make drivers more efficient and effective truck operators. Truck drivers already must adhere to federally mandated certifications and regulations requiring them to submit to drug and alcohol tests as a condition of employment. Employers are required to perform random on-the-job checks for drugs and alcohol.

In 2003, work-related injuries and illnesses per 100 full-time workers averaged 6.8 in the truck transportation field and 10.1 in warehousing and storage, compared with a rate of 5.0 for the entire private sector. More than 8 out of 10 on-the-job fatalities in the truck transportation field resulted from transportation-related incidents.

Important Characteristics of the Field

Skills: Equipment Maintenance; Operation and Control; Repairing; Operation Monitoring. **Abilities:** Static Strength; Reaction Time; Response Orientation; Spatial Orientation; Rate Control; Explosive Strength. **Work-Related Values:** Compensation; Independence; Supervision, Technical; Company Policies and Practices; Supervision, Human Relations.

Transportation

Employment

The truck transportation and warehousing field provided 1.9 million wage and salary jobs in 2004. About 45 percent of the salaried jobs in the field, 857,000, were for truck drivers. Other transportation and material moving jobs accounted for 24 percent of field employment, while various office and administrative support occupations employed another 17 percent. Management, business, and financial occupations held 4 percent of all jobs in the field; vehicle and mobile equipment mechanics, installers, and repairers 3 percent; and sales and related workers 2 percent. In addition to the wage and salary workers, there were an estimated 282,000 self-employed and unpaid family workers in the field.

Most employees in the truck transportation and warehousing field work in small establishments. About 86 percent of trucking and warehousing establishments employ fewer than 20 workers (chart 1). Consolidation in the field has reduced the number of small, specialized firms.

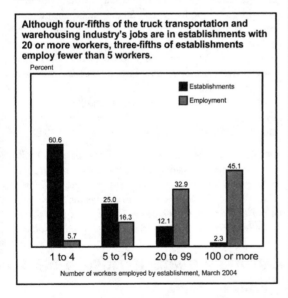

Although four-fifths of the truck transportation and warehousing industry's jobs are in establishments with 20 or more workers, three-fifths of establishments employ fewer than 5 workers.

Percent

- Establishments
- Employment

	1 to 4	5 to 19	20 to 99	100 or more
Establishments	60.6	25.0	12.1	2.3
Employment	5.7	16.3	32.9	45.1

Number of workers employed by establishment, March 2004

Trucking and warehousing establishments are found throughout the United States, with a higher concentration around the major interstate highways and in heavily industrialized regions of the country, such as California, New Jersey, and Texas.

Occupations in the Field

Transportation and material moving occupations account for 68 percent of all jobs in the field (table 1). *Truck drivers and driver/sales workers,* who hold 45 percent of all trucking and warehousing jobs, transport goods from one location to another. They ensure the safe delivery of cargo to a specific destination, often by a designated time. Drivers also perform some minor maintenance work on their vehicles and make routine safety checks.

The length of trips varies with the type of merchandise and its final destination. Local drivers provide regular service while other drivers make intercity and interstate deliveries that take longer and may vary from job to job. The driver's responsibilities and assignments change according to the time spent on the road and the type of payloads transported.

Local drivers typically have regular schedules and return home at the end of the day. They may deliver goods to stores or homes or haul away dirt and debris from excavation sites. Many local drivers cover the same routes daily or weekly. Long-distance truck drivers often are on the road for long stretches of time. Their trips vary from an overnight stay to a week or more. On longer trips, drivers sometimes sleep in bunks in their cabs or share the driving with another driver.

Laborers and hand freight, stock, and material movers help load and unload freight and move it around warehouses and terminals. Often, these unskilled employees work together in groups of three or four. They may use conveyor belts, handtrucks, pallet jacks, or forklifts to move freight. They may place heavy or bulky items on wooden skids or pallets and have industrial truck and tractor operators move them.

Office and administrative support workers perform the daily recordkeeping operations for the truck transportation and warehousing field. *Dispatchers* coordinate the movement of freight and trucks and provide the main communication link that informs the truck drivers of their assignments, schedules, and routes. Dispatchers frequently receive new shipping orders on short notice and must juggle drivers' assignments and schedules to accommodate a client. *Shipping, receiving, and traffic clerks* keep records of shipments arriving and leaving. They verify the contents of trucks' cargo against shipping records. They also may pack and move stock. *Billing and posting clerks and machine operators* maintain company records of the shipping rates negotiated with customers and shipping charges incurred; they also prepare customer invoices.

Workers in installation, maintenance, and repair occupations generally enter these jobs only after acquiring experience in related jobs or after receiving specialized training. Most *vehicle and mobile equipment mechanics, installers, and repairers* require special vocational training. Service technicians and mechanics in trucking and warehousing firms perform preventive safety checks as well as routine service and repairs. Service technicians and mechanics sometimes advance to parts manager positions. *Parts managers* maintain the supply of replacement parts needed to repair vehicles. Parts managers monitor the parts inventory using a computerized system and purchase new parts to replenish supplies. These employees need mechanical knowledge and must be familiar with computers and purchasing procedures.

Sales and related workers sell trucking and warehousing services to shippers of goods. They meet with prospective buyers, discuss the customers' needs, and suggest appropriate services. Travel may be required, and many analyze sales statistics, prepare reports, and handle some administrative duties.

Managerial staff provides general direction to the firm. They staff, supervise, and provide safety and other training to workers in the various occupations. They also resolve logistical problems such as forecasting the demand for transportation, mapping out the most efficient traffic routes, ordering parts and equipment service support, and scheduling the transportation of goods.

Table 1. Employment of wage and salary workers in truck transportation and warehousing by occupation, 2004 and projected change, 2004–2014 (Employment in thousands)

Occupation	Employment, 2004		Percent change, 2004–2014
	Number	Percent	
Total, all occupations	1,907	100.0	14.0
Management, business, and financial occupations	84	4.4	22.0
General and operations managers	27	1.4	18.3
Transportation, storage, and distribution managers	13	0.7	20.9
Accountants and auditors	6	0.3	21.4
Professional and related occupations	17	0.9	34.7
Sales and related occupations	42	2.2	21.8
Office and administrative support occupations	324	17.0	7.9
Bookkeeping, accounting, and auditing clerks	19	1.0	6.1
Customer service representatives	23	1.2	25.6
Dispatchers, except police, fire, and ambulance	34	1.8	2.1
Shipping, receiving, and traffic clerks	39	2.1	21.5
Stock clerks and order fillers	51	2.7	4.6
Secretaries and administrative assistants	23	1.2	4.1
Office clerks, general	44	2.3	5.2
Installation, maintenance, and repair occupations	85	4.4	17.4
Bus and truck mechanics and diesel engine specialists	46	2.4	13.4
Maintenance and repair workers, general	15	0.8	26.2
Production occupations	32	1.7	28.9
Transportation and material moving occupations	1,300	68.2	13.8
First-line supervisors/ managers of helpers, laborers, and material movers, hand	23	1.2	6.1
First-line supervisors/ managers of transportation and material-moving machine and vehicle operators	38	2.0	17.0

Occupation	Employment, 2004		Percent change, 2004–2014
	Number	Percent	
Truck drivers, heavy and tractor-trailer	765	40.1	13.2
Truck drivers, light or delivery services	82	4.3	16.1
Industrial truck and tractor operators	101	5.3	18.2
Laborers and freight, stock, and material movers, hand	212	11.1	13.6
Packers and packagers, hand	36	1.9	13.7

Note: May not add to totals due to omission of occupations with small employment

Training, Other Qualifications, and Advancement

Many jobs in the truck transportation and warehousing field require only a high school education, although an increasing number of workers have at least some college education. College education is most important for those seeking positions in management. Increasing emphasis on formal education stems from the increasing use of technology in the field. Nearly all operations involve computers and information management systems. Many occupations—especially those involved in scheduling, ordering, and receiving—require detail-oriented people with computer skills. A growing number of employers recommend some form of formal training. Some companies provide such training in-house. Other sources of training include trade associations, unions, and vocational schools. Many companies have specific curricula on safety and procedural issues as well as on occupational duties.

Whereas many states allow those who are 18 years old to drive trucks within their borders, the U.S. Department of Transportation establishes minimum qualifications for truck drivers engaged in interstate commerce. Federal Motor Carrier Safety Regulations require truck drivers to be at least 21 years old, have at least 20/40 vision and good hearing, and be able to read and speak English. They also must have good driving records and a commercial driver's license, which they obtain by passing a written examination and a skills test in which they oper-

ate the type of vehicle they will be driving. Commercial driver's licenses are issued by the individual states. Companies often have additional requirements that applicants must meet.

Some enter the occupation by attending training schools for truck drivers. Schools vary greatly in the quality of training they provide, but they are becoming more standardized. Many employers and a number of states support these programs.

Some large trucking companies have formal training programs that prospective drivers attend. Other companies assign experienced drivers to teach and mentor newer drivers. Local trucking firms often start drivers as truck driver helpers. Experienced and reliable truck drivers with good driving records receive better pay as well as more desirable routes, schedules, or loads. Because of increased competition for experienced drivers, some larger companies are luring these drivers with higher wages, signing bonuses, and preferred assignments. Some trucking firms hire only experienced drivers.

Some long-distance truck drivers purchase trucks and go into business for themselves. Although many of these owner-operators are successful, some fail to cover expenses and eventually go out of business. Owner-operators should have good business sense as well as truck-driving experience. Courses in accounting, business, and business mathematics are helpful, and knowledge of truck mechanics can enable owner-operators to perform their own routine maintenance and minor repairs. Some trucking companies engage in franchising, providing drivers with the means to purchase a truck while also lining up loads for them to haul.

Unskilled employees may work as helpers, laborers, and material movers in their first jobs. They must be in good physical condition because the work often involves a great deal of physical labor and heavy lifting. They acquire skills on the job and can advance to more skilled jobs, such as industrial truck operator, truck driver, shipping and receiving clerk, or supervisor.

Office and administrative support jobs in the truck transportation and warehousing field require familiarity with computers. Shipping and receiving clerks watch and learn the skills of the trade from more experienced workers while on the job. Stock clerks may advance to dispatcher positions after becoming familiar with company operations and procedures.

While some vehicle and mobile equipment mechanics, installers, and repairers learn the trade on the job, most employers prefer to hire graduates of programs in diesel mechanics offered by community and junior colleges or vocational and technical schools. Those with no training often start as helpers to mechanics, doing basic errands and chores, such as washing trucks or moving them to different locations. Experience as an automotive service technician is helpful because many of the skills relate to diesel technology. Experienced technicians may advance to shop supervisor or parts manager positions.

For managerial jobs in the truck transportation and warehousing field, employers prefer persons with bachelor's degrees in business, marketing, accounting, industrial relations, or economics. Good communication, problem-solving, and analytical skills are valuable in entry-level jobs. Since trucking and warehousing firms may rely heavily on computer technology to aid in the distribution of goods, knowledge of information systems also is helpful for advancement. Although most managers must learn logistics through extensive training on the job, several universities offer graduate and undergraduate programs in logistics. These programs emphasize the tools necessary to manage the distribution of goods and may be associated with the business departments of schools. Managers hired for entry-level positions sometimes advance to top-level managerial jobs.

Marketing and sales workers must be familiar with their firm's products and services and have strong communication skills.

Outlook

The number of wage and salary jobs in the truck transportation and warehousing field is expected to grow 14 percent from 2004 through 2014, compared with projected growth of 14 percent for all fields combined. Growth will result in many job openings because the field is so large. There also will be openings due to replacement needs for the large number of workers who will transfer to other fields or retire. Job opportunities should be especially good for truck drivers and diesel service technicians and mechanics.

One of the main factors influencing the growth of the truck transportation and warehousing field is the state of the national economy. Growth in the field parallels the movements of the national economy. As the national economy grows and the production and sales of goods increases, there is an increase in the demand for transportation services to move goods from their producers to consumers. During economic downturns, the truck transportation and warehousing field is one of the first to slow down as orders for goods and shipments decline. Competition in truck transportation is intense, both among trucking companies and, in some long-haul truckload segments, with the railroad field. Nevertheless, trucking accounts for the bulk of freight transportation. Warehousing is expected to grow faster than the rest of the field, although many midsized firms are being purchased by others in attempts to consolidate.

Additional employment growth will result from manufacturers' willingness to concentrate more on their core competencies—producing goods—while outsourcing their distribution functions to trucking and warehousing companies which can perform these tasks for less money. As firms in other fields increasingly employ the field's logistical services, such as inventory management and just-in-time shipping, many new jobs will be created. Also, as more consumers and businesses make purchases over the Internet, the expansion of electronic commerce will continue to increase demand for the transportation, logistical, and value-added services offered by the truck transportation and warehousing field.

Opportunities for truck drivers are expected to be favorable. In some areas, companies have experienced difficulties recruiting adequately skilled drivers. Many people leave the career because of the lengthy periods away from home, the long hours of driving, and the negative public image that drivers face. Employment opportunities should be better among truckload carriers than among less-than-truckload (LTL) carriers because many workers prefer the working conditions of LTL carriers. Stricter requirements for obtaining—and keeping—a commercial driver's license also make truck driving a less attractive career. New restrictions on who can obtain or renew their hazardous-material endorsement should increase opportunities for those able to pass the criminal background checks now required. Opportunities for diesel service technicians and mechanics also are expected to be favorable, especially for applicants with formal postsecondary training.

Growth in the truck transportation and warehousing field should prompt an increase in office and administrative support employment. More dispatchers, stock clerks, and shipping, receiving, and traffic clerks will be needed to support expanded logistical services across the

Transportation

country. However, fewer secretaries, bookkeepers, and file clerks will be needed because computers and other automated equipment will make workers in these occupations more efficient and productive. Opportunities for those with information technology skills will be excellent.

Earnings

In 2004, average earnings in the truck transportation and warehousing field were higher than the average for all nongovernment fields, as shown in table 2. The average wage in the trucking sector of the field was higher than the average wage in warehousing. Earnings in selected occupations in truck transportation and warehousing appear in table 3.

Table 2. Average earnings of nonsupervisory workers in truck transportation and warehousing, 2004

Field segment	Weekly	Hourly
All nongovernment fields	$529	$15.67
Truck transportation	686	16.61
General freight trucking	714	17.14
Specialized freight trucking	620	15.28
Warehousing and storage	558	14.90
Refrigerated warehousing and storage	595	15.84
Miscellaneous warehousing and storage	596	15.07
General warehousing and storage	558	14.90

Most employers compensate truck drivers with an hourly rate, a rate per mile, or a percentage of their loads' revenue. Benefits, including performance-related bonuses, health insurance, and sick and vacation leave, are common in the trucking field.

The major union in the truck transportation and warehousing field is the International Brotherhood of Teamsters. About 11 percent of trucking and warehousing workers are union members or are covered by union contracts, compared with approximately 14 percent of workers in all fields combined. Since union drivers tend to make more than nonunion drivers, some trucking companies use "double breasting"—employing union as well as nonunion operating divisions in an attempt to lower labor costs. Other companies use graduated pay

scales and pay lower wages for new hires. Many give pay increases after predetermined periods to those with safe driving records. Some deal exclusively with owner-operators in order to offset the cost of owning and maintaining a fleet of vehicles.

Table 3. Median hourly earnings of the largest occupations in truck transportation and warehousing, May 2004

Occupation	Truck transportation	Warehousing and storage	All fields
First-line supervisors/ managers of transportation and material-moving machine and vehicle operators	$21.93	$20.52	$21.54
Bus and truck mechanics and diesel engine specialists	16.15	17.47	17.20
Truck drivers, heavy and tractor-trailer	17.00	17.46	16.11
Industrial truck and tractor operators	14.25	12.64	12.78
Truck drivers, light or delivery services	13.76	12.12	11.80
Shipping, receiving, and traffic clerks	12.83	12.47	11.73
Office clerks, general	10.85	11.71	10.95
Laborers and freight, stock, and material movers, hand	11.36	11.39	9.67
Stock clerks and order fillers	11.46	12.32	9.66
Packers and packagers, hand	9.71	9.75	8.25

Sources of Additional Information

For additional information about careers and training in the truck transportation and warehousing field, write to any of the following organizations:

- American Trucking Associations, 2200 Mill Rd., Alexandria, VA 22314-4677.

- International Association of Refrigerated Warehouses, 1500 King St., Suite 201, Alexandria, VA 22314.

- International Brotherhood of Teamsters, 25 Louisiana Ave. NW, Washington, DC 20001.

- Professional Truck Driver Institute, 2200 Mill Rd., Alexandria, VA 22314. Internet: http://www.ptdi.org

- Warehousing Education and Research Council, 1100 Jorie Blvd., Suite 170, Oak Brook, IL 60523-4413. Internet: http://werc.org

Information

Broadcasting

- Annual Earnings: $36,238
- Job Growth: 10.7%
- Size of Workforce: 324,560
- Self-Employed: 2.4%
- Part-Time: 8.6%

Significant Points

- Keen competition is expected for many jobs, particularly in large metropolitan areas, because of the large number of jobseekers attracted by the glamour of this field.

- Job prospects will be best for applicants with a college degree in broadcasting or a related field and relevant experience, such as work at college radio and television stations or internships at professional stations.

- In this highly competitive field, broadcasters are less willing to provide on-the-job training and instead seek candidates who can perform the job immediately.

- Many entry-level positions are at smaller broadcast stations; consequently, workers often must change employers, and sometimes relocate, in order to advance.

Nature of the Field

The broadcasting field consists of radio and television stations and networks that create content or acquire the right to broadcast taped television and radio programs. Networks transmit their signals from broadcasting studios via satellite signals to local stations or cable distributors. Broadcast signals then travel over cable television lines, satellite distribution systems, or the airwaves from a station's transmission tower to the antennas of televisions and radios. Anyone in the signal area with a radio or television can receive the programming. Most Americans receive their television broadcasts through cable and other pay television providers. Although cable television stations and networks are included in this description, cable and other pay television distributors are classified in the telecommunications field. (See the description of Telecommunications elsewhere in Part II.)

Radio and television stations and networks broadcast a variety of programs, such as national and local news, talk shows, music programs, movies, other entertainment, and advertisements. Stations produce some of these programs, most notably news programs, in their own studios; however, much of the programming is produced outside the broadcasting field. Establishments that produce filmed or taped programming for radio and television stations and networks—but do not broadcast the programming—are in the motion picture field. Many television networks own production companies that produce their many shows. (A description of the Motion Picture and Video field appears elsewhere in Part II.)

Cable and other program distributors compensate local television stations and cable networks for rebroadcast rights. For popular cable networks and local television stations, distributors pay a fee per subscriber and/or agree to broadcast a less popular channel owned by the same network. Revenue for radio and television stations and networks also comes from the sale of advertising time. The rates paid by advertisers depend on the size and characteristics (age, gender, and median income, among others) of a program's audience. Educational and noncommercial stations generate revenue primarily from donations by individuals, foundations, government, and corporations. These stations generally are owned and managed by public broadcasting organizations, religious institutions, or school systems.

Changes in federal government regulation and communication technology have affected the broadcast field.

Information

The Telecommunications Act of 1996 relaxed ownership restrictions, an action that has had a tremendous impact on the field. Instead of owning only one radio station per market, companies can now purchase up to eight radio stations in a single large market. These changes have led to a large-scale consolidation of radio stations. In some areas, five FM and three AM radio stations are owned by the same company and share the same offices. The ownership of commercial radio stations is increasingly concentrated. In television, owners are permitted two stations in larger markets and are restricted in the total number of stations nationwide (in terms of percent of all viewers).

The U.S. Federal Communications Commission (FCC) is a proponent of digital television (DTV), a technology that uses digital signals to transmit television programs. Digital signals consist of pieces of simple electronic code that can carry more information than conventional analog signals. This code allows for the transmission of better-quality sound and higher-resolution pictures, often referred to as high-definition television (HDTV). FCC regulations require all stations to broadcast digital signals as well as conventional analog signals. The current goal of the FCC is to have all stations stop broadcasting analog signals by 2007. However, because of the number of viewers who do not yet own television sets that are compatible with DTV, full implementation of the change from analog to digital broadcasting may take longer. After the switch is complete, any viewers using an analog TV and over-the-air signals will need a converter box to change the signal from digital to analog. Most television stations are currently broadcasting digital signals in response to FCC regulations. Many digital cable systems and satellite television providers already broadcast all their channels digitally, with some channels in high definition.

The transition to HDTV broadcasting has also accelerated the conversion of other aspects of television and radio production from analog to digital. Many stations have replaced specialized hardware with less-specialized computers equipped with software that performs the same functions. Stations may use digital cameras, edit with computers, and store video on computer servers. Many major network shows now use HDTV cameras and editing equipment.

The transition to digital broadcasting also is occurring in radio. Most stations already store music, edit clips, and broadcast their analog signals with digital equipment. Satellite radio services, which offer 100 channels of digital sound, operate on a subscription basis, like pay television services. To compete, some radio stations are embedding a digital signal into their analog signals. With a specially equipped radio, these digital services offer better-quality sound and display some limited text, such as the title of the song and the artist.

Working Conditions

Most employees in this field work in clean, comfortable surroundings in broadcast stations and studios. Some employees work in the production of shows and broadcasting while other employees work in advertising, sales, promotions, and marketing.

Television news teams made up of reporters, camera operators, and technicians travel in electronic news–gathering vehicles to various locations to cover news stories. Although such location work is exciting, some assignments, such as reporting on military conflicts or natural disasters, may be dangerous. These assignments may also require outdoor work under adverse weather conditions.

Camera operators working on such news teams must have the physical stamina to carry and set up their equipment. Broadcast technicians on electronic news–gathering trucks must ensure that the mobile unit's antenna is correctly positioned for optimal transmission quality and to prevent electrocution from power lines. Field service engineers work on outdoor transmitting equipment and may have to climb poles or antenna towers; their work can take place under a variety of weather conditions. Broadcast technicians who maintain and set up equipment may have to do heavy lifting. Technological changes have enabled camera operators also to fulfill the tasks of broadcast technicians, operating the transmission and editing equipment on a remote broadcasting truck. News operations, programming, and engineering employees work under a great deal of pressure in order to meet deadlines. As a result, these workers are likely to experience varied or erratic work schedules, often working on early-morning or late-evening news programs.

Sales workers may face stress meeting sales goals. Aside from sometimes erratic work schedules, management and administrative workers typically find themselves in an environment similar to any other office.

For many people, the excitement of working in broadcasting compensates for the demanding nature of the work. Although this field is noted for its high pressure and long hours, the work is generally not hazardous.

Important Characteristics of the Field

Skills: Speaking; Management of Personnel Resources; Negotiation; Time Management; Social Perceptiveness; Writing. **Abilities:** Speech Clarity; Speech Recognition; Oral Expression; Originality; Fluency of Ideas; Written Expression. **Work-Related Values:** Creativity; Variety; Recognition; Authority; Ability Utilization; Working Conditions.

Employment

Broadcasting provided about 327,000 wage and salary jobs in 2004. Although more than half of all establishments employed fewer than 10 people, most jobs were in large establishments; about 73 percent of all jobs were in establishments with at least 50 employees (chart 1). Broadcasting establishments are found throughout the country, but jobs in larger stations are concentrated in large cities.

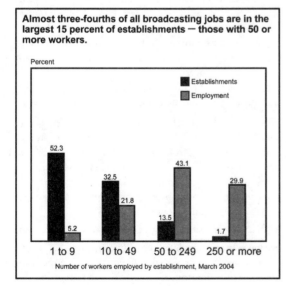

Almost three-fourths of all broadcasting jobs are in the largest 15 percent of establishments — those with 50 or more workers.

Percent

- Establishments
- Employment

52.3	32.5	13.5	1.7
5.2	21.8	43.1	29.9
1 to 9	10 to 49	50 to 249	250 or more

Number of workers employed by establishment, March 2004

Occupations in the Field

Occupations at large broadcast stations and networks fall into five general categories: program production, news-related, technical, sales, and general administration. At small stations, jobs are less specialized, and employees often perform several functions. Although on-camera or on-air positions are the most familiar occupations in broadcasting, the majority of employment opportunities are behind the scenes (table 1).

Program production occupations. Most television programs are produced by the motion picture and video field; actors, directors, and producers working on these prerecorded programs are not employed by the broadcasting field. Employees in program production occupations at television and radio stations create programs such as news, talk, and music shows.

Assistant producers provide clerical support and background research; assist with the preparation of musical, written, and visual materials; and time productions to make sure that they do not run over schedule. Assistant producers also may operate cameras and other audio and video equipment.

Video editors select and assemble pretaped video to create a finished program, applying sound and special effects as necessary. Conventional editing requires assembling pieces of videotape in a linear fashion to create a finished product. The editor first assembles the beginning of the program and then works sequentially towards the end. Newer computerized editing allows an editor to electronically cut and paste video segments. This electronic technique is known as nonlinear editing because the editor is no longer restricted to working sequentially; a segment may be moved at any time to any location in the program.

Producers plan and develop live or taped productions, determining how the show will look and sound. They select the script, talent, sets, props, lighting, and other production elements. Producers also coordinate the activities of on-air personalities, production staff, and other personnel. *Web site* or *Internet producers*, a relatively new occupation in the broadcasting field, plan and develop Internet sites that provide news updates, program schedules, and information about popular shows. These producers decide what will appear on the Internet sites and design and maintain them.

Information

Announcers read news items and provide other information, such as program schedules and station breaks for commercials or public service information. Many radio announcers are referred to as disc jockeys; they play recorded music on radio stations. Disc jockeys may take requests from listeners; interview guests; and comment on the music, weather, or traffic. Most stations now have placed all of their advertisements, sound bites, and music on a computer, which is used to select and play or edit the items. Technological advances have simplified the monitoring and adjusting of the transmitter, leaving disc jockeys responsible for most of the tasks associated with keeping a station on the air. Traditional tapes and CDs are used only as backups in case of a computer failure. Announcers and disc jockeys need a good speaking voice; the latter also need a significant knowledge of music.

Program directors are in charge of on-air programming in radio stations. Program directors decide what type of music will be played, supervise on-air personnel, and often select the specific songs and the order in which they will be played. Considerable experience, usually as a disc jockey, is required, as well as a thorough knowledge of music.

News-related occupations. News, weather, and sports reports are important to many television stations because these reports attract a large audience and account for a large proportion of revenue. Many radio stations depend on up-to-the-minute news for a major share of their programming. Program production staff, such as producers and announcers, also work on the production of news programs.

Reporters gather information from various sources, analyze and prepare news stories, and present information on the air. *Correspondents* report on news occurring in U.S. and foreign cities in which they are stationed. *Newswriters* write and edit news stories from information collected by reporters. Newswriters may advance to positions as reporters or correspondents.

Broadcast news analysts, also known as news anchors, analyze, interpret, and broadcast news received from various sources. News anchors present news stories and introduce videotaped news or live transmissions from on-the-scene reporters. Newscasters at large stations may specialize in a particular field. Weathercasters, also called weather reporters, report current and forecasted weather conditions. They gather information from national satellite weather services, wire services, and local and region-al weather bureaus. Some weathercasters are trained *atmospheric scientists* and can develop their own weather forecasts. Sportscasters, who are responsible for reporting sporting events, usually select, write, and deliver the sports news for each newscast.

Assistant news directors supervise the newsroom; they coordinate wire service reports, tape or film inserts, and stories from individual newswriters and reporters. *Assignment editors* assign stories to news teams, sending the teams on location if necessary.

News directors have overall responsibility for the news team made up of reporters, writers, editors, and newscasters as well as studio and mobile unit production crews. This senior administrative position entails responsibilities that include determining what events to cover, and how and when they will be presented in a news broadcast.

Technical occupations. Employees in these occupations operate and maintain the electronic equipment that records and transmits radio or television programs. The titles of some of these occupations use the terms "engineer," "technician," and "operator" interchangeably.

Radio operators manage equipment that regulates the signal strength, clarity, and range of sounds and colors of broadcasts. They also monitor and log outgoing signals and operate transmitters. *Audio and video equipment technicians* operate equipment to regulate the volume, sound quality, brightness, contrast, and visual quality of a broadcast. *Broadcast technicians* set up and maintain electronic broadcasting equipment. Their work can extend outside the studio, as when they set up portable transmitting equipment or maintain stationary towers.

Television and video camera operators set up and operate studio cameras, which are used in the television studio, and electronic news–gathering cameras, which are mobile and used outside the studio when a news team is pursuing a story at another location. Camera operators need training in video production as well as some experience in television production.

Master control engineers ensure that all of the radio or television station's scheduled program elements, such as on-location feeds, prerecorded segments, and commercials, are smoothly transmitted. They also are responsible for ensuring that transmissions meet FCC requirements.

Technical directors direct the studio and control room technical staff during the production of a program. They need a thorough understanding of both the production and technical aspects of broadcasting; this knowledge often is acquired by working as a lighting director or camera operator or as another type of broadcast worker.

Network and computer systems administrators and *network systems and data communications analysts* design, set up, and maintain systems of computer servers. These servers store recorded programs, advertisements, and news clips.

Assistant chief engineers oversee the day-to-day technical operations of the station. *Chief engineers* or *directors of engineering* are responsible for all of the station's technical facilities and services. These workers need a bachelors' degree in electrical engineering, technical training in broadcast engineering, and years of broadcast engineering experience.

Table 1. Employment of wage and salary workers in broadcasting by occupation, 2004 and projected change, 2004–2014 (Employment in thousands)

Occupation	Employment, 2004		Percent change, 2004–2014
	Number	Percent	
Total, all occupations	327	100.0	10.7
Management, business, and financial occupations	34	10.5	13.8
General and operations managers	9	2.8	10.2
Sales managers	4	1.3	8.8
Accountants and auditors	3	0.8	13.5
Professional and related occupations	159	48.6	5.4
Computer support specialists	2	0.7	39.4
Network and computer systems administrators	2	0.6	48.7
Electronics engineers, except computer	2	0.5	12.0
Electrical and electronic engineering technicians	2	0.7	20.2
Producers and directors	21	6.5	10.0
Radio and television announcers	39	11.9	–7.3
Broadcast news analysts	6	1.8	2.4
Reporters and correspondents	11	3.3	2.2
Public relations specialists	3	1.0	6.7

Occupation	Employment, 2004		Percent change, 2004–2014
	Number	Percent	
Editors	4	1.3	7.0
Writers and authors	3	0.9	7.2
Broadcast and sound engineering technicians and radio operators	29	8.8	5.2
Audio and video equipment technicians	4	1.2	5.9
Broadcast technicians	22	6.9	5.2
Sound engineering technicians	2	0.7	5.8
Photographers	4	1.1	0.1
Camera operators, television, video, and motion picture	9	2.9	5.3
Film and video editors	4	1.1	10.7
Sales and related occupations	46	14.0	7.0
First-line supervisors/ managers of non-retail sales workers	3	0.9	–0.3
Advertising sales agents	32	9.7	2.7
Sales representatives, services, all other	4	1.1	36.2
Office and administrative support occupations	61	18.6	13.2
First-line supervisors/ managers of office and administrative support workers	5	1.4	9.7
Bookkeeping, accounting, and auditing clerks	4	1.3	0.6
Customer service representatives	14	4.2	48.4
Receptionists and information clerks	3	1.0	3.3
Dispatchers, except police, fire, and ambulance	2	0.6	31.8
Production, planning, and expediting clerks	2	0.7	16.1
Executive secretaries and administrative assistants	6	1.8	10.0
Secretaries, except legal, medical, and executive	4	1.1	–8.5
Office clerks, general	9	2.9	3.7

Information

Occupation	Employment, 2004		Percent change, 2004–2014
	Number	Percent	
Installation, maintenance, and repair occupations	23	7.1	42.7
Telecommunications equipment installers and repairers, except line installers	4	1.4	47.2
Telecommunications line installers and repairers	11	3.4	46.9

Note: May not add to totals due to omission of occupations with small employment

Sales, promotions, and marketing occupations. Most workers in this category are *advertising sales agents*, sometimes known as *account executives.* They sell advertising time to sponsors, advertising agencies, and other buyers. Sales representatives must have a thorough knowledge of the size and characteristics of their network's or station's audience, including income levels, gender, age, and consumption patterns.

Sales work has expanded beyond the traditional role of simply selling advertising to a wide range of marketing efforts. For instance, stations earn additional revenue by broadcasting from a business, such as a dance club. Businesses also sponsor concerts or other promotions that are organized by a station. In return for sponsorship, the businesses are usually allowed to set up a booth or post large signs at the event.

Continuity directors schedule and produce commercials. Continuity directors carefully schedule commercials, taking into account both the timeslot in which a commercial is to be played and competing advertisements. For example, two car dealership advertisements should not be played during the same commercial break. Continuity directors also create and produce advertisements for clients who do not produce their own.

Large stations and networks generally have several workers who spend all of their time handling sales. *Sales worker supervisors*, who may handle a few large accounts personally, supervise these workers. In small stations, part-time sales personnel or announcers often handle sales responsibilities during hours when they are not on the air.

Training, Other Qualifications, and Advancement

Professional, management, and sales occupations generally require a college degree; technical occupations often do not. It is easier to obtain employment and gain promotions with a degree, especially in larger, more competitive markets. Advanced schooling generally is required for supervisory positions—including technical occupations—having greater responsibility and higher salaries.

Entry-level jobs in news or program production increasingly require a college degree and some broadcast experience. More than 1,200 institutions offer programs in communications, journalism, and related programs. As of 2004, there were 104 schools accredited by the Accrediting Council on Education in Journalism and Mass Communications (ACEJMC). Some community colleges offer 2-year programs in broadcasting. Broadcast trade schools offer courses that last 6 months to a year and teach radio and television announcing, writing, and production.

Individuals pursuing a career in broadcasting often gain initial experience through work at college radio and television stations or through internships at professional stations. Although these positions usually are unpaid, they sometimes provide college credit or tuition. More importantly, they provide hands-on experience and a competitive edge when applying for jobs. In this highly competitive field, broadcasters are less willing to provide on-the-job training and instead seek candidates who can perform the job immediately.

Some technical positions require only a high school diploma. However, many broadcast stations seek individuals with training in broadcast technology, electronics, or engineering from a technical school, community college, or 4-year college. An understanding of computer networks and software will become increasingly important as field use of digital technology expands. Supervisory technical positions and jobs in large stations generally require a college degree.

The Society of Broadcast Engineers (SBE) issues certification to technicians who pass a written examination. Several classes of certification are available, requiring increasing levels of experience and knowledge for eligibility. The Telecommunications Act of 1996 mandated that the FCC drop its licensing requirements for transmitter maintenance; SBE certification has filled the void left by the elimination of this license.

Employees in the radio and television broadcasting field often find their first job in broadcast stations that serve smaller markets. Competition for positions in large metropolitan areas is stronger, and stations in these areas usually seek highly experienced personnel. Because many radio and television stations are small, workers in this field often must change employers to advance. Relocation to other parts of the country frequently is necessary for advancement.

Outlook

Employment in broadcasting is expected to increase 11 percent over the 2004–2014 period, more slowly than the 14 percent projected for all fields combined. Factors contributing to the relatively slow rate of growth include field consolidation, introduction of new technologies, and competition from other media outlets. Keen competition is expected for many jobs, particularly in large metropolitan areas, because of the large number of job-seekers attracted by the glamour of this field. Job prospects will be best for applicants with a college degree in broadcasting, journalism, or a related field as well as relevant work experience.

Consolidation of individual broadcast stations into large networks, especially in radio, has increased as the result of relaxed ownership regulations. This trend will continue to limit employment growth as networks use workers more efficiently. For example, a network can run eight radio stations from one office, producing news programming at one station and then using the programming for broadcast from other stations, thus eliminating the need for multiple news staffs. Similarly, technical workers, upper-level management, and marketing and advertising sales workers are pooled to work for several stations simultaneously. In the consolidation of the radio field, several major companies have purchased numerous stations nationwide. These companies plan to achieve cost savings through consolidation and economies of scale, limiting employment growth.

The introduction of new technology also is slowing employment growth. Conventional broadcast equipment used to be relatively specialized; each piece of equipment served a separate function and required an operator with specialized knowledge. Newer computerized equipment often combines the functions of several

older pieces of equipment and does not require specialized knowledge for operation. This reduces the need for certain types of workers, including those responsible for editing, recording, and creating graphics. In addition, increased use of remote monitoring equipment allows technical workers in one location to operate and monitor transmissions at a remote station.

Job growth also is being constrained by the use of radio and television programming created by services outside the broadcasting field. These establishments provide prepared programming, including music, news, weather, sports, and professional announcer services. The services can easily be accessed through satellite connections and reduce the need for program production and news staff at radio and television stations.

Radio broadcasters expect continued growth in revenues as national media companies that own multiple cable stations, network television stations, and/or radio stations use their combined marketing power to include radio advertising packages with other marketing deals. The new national scope of radio networks allows radio to more effectively sell advertising to large national advertisers to better compete with television networks. The major threats to the radio field, especially smaller, marginal stations, are from car CD (compact disc) players and from satellite radio, which functions like cable television with subscribers paying a monthly fee.

Earnings

Weekly earnings of nonsupervisory workers in broadcasting averaged $703 in 2004, higher than the average of $529 for all nongovernment fields. As a common rule, earnings of broadcast personnel are highest in large metropolitan areas. Earnings in selected occupations in broadcasting for May 2004 appear in table 2.

Table 2. Median hourly earnings of the largest occupations in broadcasting, May 2004

Occupation	Broadcasting, except Internet	All fields
General and operations managers	$42.73	$37.22
Producers and directors	21.58	25.40
Advertising sales agents	19.08	19.37
Telecommunications line installers and repairers	17.35	19.39

Information

Occupation	Broadcasting, except Internet	All fields
Reporters and correspondents	16.37	15.06
Camera operators, television, video, and motion picture	14.60	18.08
Customer service representatives	14.00	12.99
Broadcast technicians	12.35	13.47
Office clerks, general	12.15	10.95
Radio and television announcers	10.51	10.64

Sources of Additional Information

For a list of schools with accredited programs in broadcast journalism, send a request to

- Accrediting Council on Education in Journalism and Mass Communications, University of Kansas, School of Journalism, Stauffer-Flint Hall, Lawrence, KS 66045-7575. Internet: http://www.ku.edu/~acejmc

For career information and links to employment resources, contact

- National Association of Broadcast Employees and Technicians, Communications Workers of America, 501 Third St. NW, Washington, DC 20001. Internet: http://www.nabetcwa.org

For information on broadcasting education and scholarship resources, contact

- National Association of Broadcasters, Career Center, 1771 N St. NW, Washington, DC 20036. Internet: http://www.nab.org

For descriptions of occupations in the cable field and links to employment resources, contact

- National Cable and Telecommunications Association, 1724 Massachusetts Ave. NW, Washington, DC 20036.

Internet Service Providers, Web Search Portals, and Data Processing Services

- Annual Earnings: $48,370
- Job Growth: 27.8%
- Size of Workforce: 383,540
- Self-Employed: 8.2%
- Part-Time: 10.4%

Significant Points

- Projected employment growth varies by field sector, but all segments should grow faster than the economy as a whole.
- About a third of all jobs are in computer occupations; another third are in office and administrative support occupations.
- About 2 out of 5 jobs are in California, Texas, Florida, Virginia, and New York.

Nature of the Field

The ability to quickly transmit information over long distances has become an important part of modern life. The Internet has changed the way people find and use information to communicate, work, shop, learn, and live. Internet service providers, Web search portals, and data processing services provide the information backbone of the Internet and World Wide Web. They connect people with information and relay information from people.

Internet service providers (ISPs) directly connect people, businesses, and organizations to the Internet by routing data being sent and received to the desired location. Unlike individual users of the Internet, ISPs must develop and maintain the physical, technical, and contractual connections and agreements with other ISPs to enable the transmission of data. There is no single connection point for the Internet, so ISPs typically need many bilateral and multilateral peering agreements to exchange data through peering points, which are physical connections between the computer equipment of service providers for the purpose of allowing other service providers access to their network of connections. These points-of-presence between ISPs provide a nearly unlimited number of potential connection pathways between data and end users.

In addition to connecting to other ISPs to form the infrastructure of the Internet, service providers must also connect with clients. These clients may range from individual homes to large office buildings. To allow end users to access their networks, establishments in the field may provide customers with proprietary software, user identification names, e-mail addresses, or equipment. Like telephone or electric service, ISPs offer access to customers on a subscription basis. They may also provide related services beyond Internet access, such as Web hosting, Web page design, and consulting services related to networking software and hardware.

While ISPs connect clients to the Internet by switching and routing data, the physical connections that carry the information to end users are often the wires or cables of telecommunications establishments. The Telecommunications field is covered in a separate Part II description.

Web search portals canvas the Web to create databases of content and corresponding Internet addresses in a format that is easy to search. These databases can then be searched by typing keywords into a prompt on the search portal's Web site. By using search engines to collect the data and then present it in a usable format, these sites enable users to sort through the huge amount of information on the Internet quickly. The search engines that find content on the Web automatically follow every link on a Web page to find new pages to catalogue and then store their location along with text that can be searched at a later point. Because the Internet offers such a vast array of sites, advanced algorithms must be developed to rank the results of a search according to their relevance. Some Web search portals also offer additional services, such as news, e-mail, translation of Web sites, and local business directories. The key distinction of Web search portals is that the information is gathered automatically from across the Web rather than manually edited and entered into a predetermined directory. Even though the databases are automatically generated, they must be constantly refreshed as new Web sites emerge and existing ones update their content.

Data processing, hosting, and related services are involved primarily in handling large amounts of data for businesses, organizations, and individuals. Data hosting often takes the form of Web hosting, in which Web site content is placed on a server that allows it to be accessed by users over the Internet. While establishments in this field host Web sites, the content is typically produced by someone else and then made accessible through the Web hosting service. Other data hosting services allow clients to place electronic data, such as streaming music and video or company databases, onto servers that can be accessed directly through specialized computer programs. An additional service provided by this field is to simply store old data for archival purposes with no Internet access to it.

Data processing covers a broad range of data services, including data entry, conversion, and analysis. Organizations with large quantities of data on paper may turn to data processing services to enter the data into a computer database by hand or by using optical scanners. Similarly, clients may want old data files or several databases converted to a single, more easily accessible format. Aside from converting data to another format, data processing services also produce reports that summarize the data for better analysis by their clients. While most data hosting companies sell subscription services, data processing services companies often work on projects of defined scope.

The Internet is constantly expanding and evolving, and so are the fields associated with it. Due to constantly changing technology and the relatively low additional cost of most new services, companies are frequently upgrading their existing services and offering new ones to attract or retain customers.

Working Conditions

In 2004, workers in Internet service providers, Web search portals, and data processing services averaged 37.6 hours per week, compared with 33.7 for all fields. The average in Internet service providers and Web search portals was 38.2, while the average in data processing, hosting, and related services was 37.4.

Most workers in this field work in quiet offices, sitting at computer monitors most of the time. While most usually work a standard 40-hour workweek, there are numerous exceptions. Customer service representatives may work weekends, evenings, or holidays to support

Information

customers. As a result, the occupation is well suited to flexible work schedules. Some computer specialists may be required to work unusual or long hours at times to fix problems or perform routine maintenance. In order to minimize the disruptive impact of scheduled maintenance and updates, many Internet service providers and data hosting services perform major work at night or on the weekends. Even though major projects are typically tested before implementation if possible, there may be periods of stress and long work hours before and after implementation deadlines. Similarly, long hours and intense work may be required to fix unexpected problems arising from system upgrades, viruses, or malicious attacks by computer hackers. The very popularity of Web search portals has made them particularly attractive targets for hackers.

Important Characteristics of the Field

Skills: Programming; Troubleshooting; Systems Analysis; Technology Design; Systems Evaluation; Operations Analysis. **Abilities:** Speech Recognition; Written Comprehension; Mathematical Reasoning; Written Expression; Deductive Reasoning; Inductive Reasoning. **Work-Related Values:** Working Conditions; Creativity; Advancement; Ability Utilization; Authority; Autonomy.

Employment

Internet service providers, Web search portals, and data processing services provided 388,000 wage and salary jobs in 2004. Data processing, hosting, and related services accounted for about 70 percent of the jobs, with the other 30 percent in ISPs and Web search portals. Due to the relatively low capital costs of equipment for data hosting services and the geographic distribution of ISPs, 87 percent of establishments have fewer than 20 workers (chart 1). For the same reasons, self-employed workers make up a larger proportion of employment than in most fields.

While this field can be found in every state, employment is concentrated in a few areas. Just five states—California, Texas, Florida, Virginia, and New York—account for about 40 percent of employment in the field.

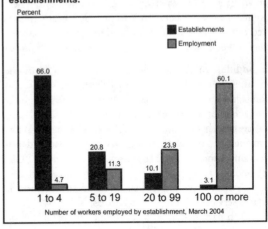

Two-thirds of the establishments in the Internet service providers, Web search portals, and data processing services industry employ fewer than 5 workers, but three-fifths of the jobs are in the largest 3 percent of establishments.

Number of workers employed by establishment, March 2004

Occupations in the Field

In order to provide Internet and data services, this field employs a wide range of occupations. *Computer specialists* are the largest group and account for approximately 34 percent of wage and salary employment in the field. With nearly the same employment, *office and administrative support occupations* make up about 34 percent of jobs. An additional 18 percent of workers are in *management, business, and financial occupations*, with other occupations accounting for about 14 percent (table 1).

Computer specialists work to develop and maintain the computer equipment and software programs that form the basis of the Internet. *Computer programmers* write, test, and customize the detailed instructions, called programs or software, that computers follow to perform various functions such as connecting to the Internet or displaying a Web page. Programmers break down tasks into a logical series of simple commands for the computer to implement, using programming languages such as C++ or Java. *Computer software engineers*, often simply called *computer engineers*, analyze user needs to formulate software specifications and then design, develop, test, and evaluate programs to meet these requirements. While computer software engineers must possess strong programming skills, they generally focus on developing logical instructions that are coded by computer programmers.

Computer systems analysts develop customized systems to process data for clients. They work with organizations to solve problems by designing or tailoring computer systems to meet unique requirements and then implementing these solutions. By customizing systems to specific tasks, they help their clients to maximize the benefit from investment in hardware, software, and other resources. *Computer support specialists* provide technical assistance and advice to customers or users experiencing problems. Within this field, they may provide support either to other employees or to customers by analyzing problems with automated diagnostic programs and through the use of their technical knowledge. These troubleshooters identify problems and provide technical support for hardware, software, and systems primarily through telephone calls and e-mail messages.

Office and administrative support occupations are involved primarily with the continuation of business processes such as billing, recordkeeping, and customer service. *Customer service representatives* interact with customers to provide information in response to inquiries and to handle complaints—typically by telephone, by e-mail, or in person. Some customer service representatives handle general questions and complaints, whereas others specialize in a particular area. In ISPs, they help new customers set up or discontinue Internet service, but their primary function is not sales. *Data entry keyers* input lists of items, numbers, or other data into computers using keyboards or scanners. They also may manipulate existing data, edit current information, or proofread new entries to a database for accuracy. Nearly all data entry keyers in this field are employed in data processing, hosting, and related services; relatively few work for ISPs or Web search portals.

Financial, information and record, and general office clerks account for about 16 percent of office and administrative support employment in this field, or about 1 out of 6 workers. *Financial clerks* keep track of money, recording all amounts coming into or leaving a company. They perform a wide variety of financial recordkeeping duties, from preparing bills and invoices to computing wages for payroll records. *Information and record clerks* focus on maintaining, updating, and processing a variety of records, ranging from payrolls to information on the receipt of goods. Customer service representatives are included in this occupational group. *General office clerks* often have daily responsibilities that change with the needs of the job. They may enter data at a computer terminal; operate photocopiers, fax machines, and other office equipment; prepare mailings; proofread copies; and answer telephones and deliver messages.

Computer and information systems managers are the largest of the management, business, and financial occupations, due to the nature of the field. They plan, coordinate, and direct the activities of computer specialists to ensure that the internal and external computer systems meet the needs of users or clients. Because the field is primarily engaged in facilitating data transmission over the Internet, these managers work closely with top executives or clients to set schedules for implementing Web sites, performing system maintenance, or installing new hardware and software.

Table 1. Employment of wage and salary workers in Internet service providers, Web search portals, and data processing services by occupation, 2004 and projected change, 2004–2014

Occupation	Employment, 2004		Percent change, 2004–2014
	Number	Percent	
Total, all occupations	388	100.0	27.8
Management, business, and financial occupations	69	17.7	32.6
Top executives	10	2.6	27.9
Marketing managers	3	0.7	26.6
Sales managers	4	1.0	30.7
Computer and information systems managers	12	3.1	36.8
Financial managers	4	1.0	32.5
Human resources, training, and labor relations specialists	5	1.2	35.6
Management analysts	7	1.7	34.5
Accountants and auditors	5	1.2	30.5
Professional and related occupations	152	39.3	39.5
Computer and information scientists, research	1	0.3	35.4
Computer programmers	22	5.6	8.4
Computer software engineers, applications	19	5.0	56.4

Information

Occupation	Employment, 2004		Percent change, 2004–2014
	Number	Percent	
Computer software engineers, systems software	18	4.7	56.5
Computer support specialists	22	5.5	27.9
Computer systems analysts	19	4.8	47.6
Database administrators	4	1.1	47.8
Network and computer systems administrators	13	3.2	50.4
Network systems and data communications analysts	9	2.3	69.2
Computer specialists, all other	4	1.1	30.4
Operations research analysts	3	0.9	14.7
Engineers	4	1.0	32.6
Sales and related occupations	22	5.7	21.4
Sales representatives, services	8	2.1	25.1
Sales representatives, wholesale and manufacturing	7	1.9	29.2
Telemarketers	3	0.8	–8.6
Office and administrative support occupations	131	33.8	13.3
Supervisors, office and administrative support workers	8	2.1	20.0
Bill and account collectors	3	0.7	25.5
Bookkeeping, accounting, and auditing clerks	8	2.0	19.0
Customer service representatives	27	6.9	31.5
Material recording, scheduling, dispatching, and distributing occupations	5	1.2	22.1
Secretaries and administrative assistants	10	2.5	22.3
Computer operators	8	2.1	–23.9
Data entry and information processing workers	20	5.3	5.4
Mail clerks and mail machine operators, except postal service	5	1.2	–29.8
Office clerks, general	14	3.5	20.3
Office machine operators, except computer	7	1.8	–9.8

Note: May not add to totals due to omission of occupations with small employment

Training and Advancement

The occupations in Internet service providers, Web search portals, and data processing services require a variety of educational levels and specialized training. About 45 percent of workers held college degrees in 2004, while 36 had some college education and another 15 percent held high school diplomas. Entry-level computer and management positions in the field often require a bachelor's degree in a computer-related field.

Educational requirements have been less rigid for computer specialists than for most other occupations. In the early days of the Internet and Web, many employers struggled to meet ballooning demand for technical workers. However, the growing number of qualified workers and the reduction of demand for computer specialists in recent years have led employers to look for more education and experience when hiring. While employers may seek workers with high-demand skills regardless of formal training in the short term, such conditions are unlikely to last long if they do arise. The general trend has been toward greater demand for workers with computer-related college degrees and more experience. Those with bachelor's degrees in computer-related fields also enjoy greater opportunities for advancement to managerial positions.

Computer programmers typically hold a bachelor's degree in computer science, mathematics, or information systems. Those without bachelor's degrees or with degrees in other fields generally take additional courses in computer programming methods and languages. The needs of employers vary extensively and change over time, so a 2-year degree or certificate may be sufficient for some positions if the workers possess the right programming knowledge. Entry-level programmers usually start by updating existing code and advance to more difficult programming. Computer programmers with general business experience may become systems analysts.

Computer software engineers usually have at least a bachelor's degree in computer science, software engineering, or computer information systems. Experience working with a broad range of computer systems is highly valued by employers. Educational requirements vary, with some workers holding advanced degrees in technical fields and others simply completing computer training programs leading to certifications offered by systems software vendors. Because computer software engineers often work closely with computer programmers, communications skills are important in this occupation.

Computer systems analysts and database administrators typically hold a bachelor's degree in computer science, information science, or management information systems (MIS). Many computer systems analysts hold advanced degrees in business administration or technical fields, and becoming certified in various types of systems software may provide a competitive advantage. Relevant work experience also is very important and can be obtained by participating in internship or co-op programs or by working in related occupations. Systems analysts may begin working on one aspect of a system and advance to more complex systems with experience.

Computer support specialists usually need only an associate degree in a computer-related field and experience with computer systems. They must possess strong problem-solving and analytical skills, as well as excellent communication skills, because troubleshooting and helping others are such a vital part of the job. Technical support specialists may advance by developing expertise in a particular area, with job promotions typically depending more on performance than on formal education. Some become applications developers, using their troubleshooting experience to design products to be more reliable and user-friendly.

As technological advances in the computer field continue, all computer specialists must keep abreast of developing technologies to remain competitive. Obtaining technical certification is a way in which workers can demonstrate their competency to employers. Certification can be obtained voluntarily through many organizations, and many vendors now offer certification to professionals who work with their products.

Office and administrative support occupations generally require only a high school diploma, but this may vary by occupation and firm. Although some positions may require previous experience in the occupation or field, many of these jobs are entry level. Some workers in these occupations are college graduates who accept entry-level clerical positions to get into the field or a particular company. Most companies fill office and administrative support supervisory and managerial positions by promoting individuals within their organization, so those who acquire additional skills, experience, and training improve their opportunities for advancement. However, a college degree is often required for advancement to management ranks.

Customer service representatives typically need only a high school diploma or its equivalent. Because they constantly interact with customers, they need good interpersonal skills for success in this occupation. Strong problem-solving abilities and basic computer knowledge also are important. Verbal or written communications skills may be more important, depending on whether inquiries will be addressed by telephone, in person, through e-mail, or by letter. Because customer service representatives represent the companies for which they work, employers place great emphasis on a friendly and professional demeanor, as well as the ability to remain patient when dealing with difficult or angry customers. Nearly all employers provide training in basic customer service skills and company-specific services, policies, and systems.

Data entry keyers usually hold high school diplomas or their equivalent and are hired largely based on their keyboarding speed. Familiarity with basic computer operations and with word processing, spreadsheet, and database software is highly desirable. The skills required by data entry keyers can be developed by taking high school, community college, or business school courses; by working for temporary help agencies; and by making use of self-teaching aids. Attention to detail is important in this occupation, as are spelling, punctuation, and grammar skills.

Financial, information and record, and general office clerks typically need at least a high school diploma. For financial clerks, particularly in the fields of bookkeeping and accounting, an associate degree is often required. While basic computer knowledge and general office skills are required for all clerks, a professional appearance and demeanor are particularly important for those whose work involves frequent interaction with the public. Nearly all financial, information and record, and general office clerks receive some training on the job. Under the guidance of a supervisor or other senior workers, new employees learn company procedures. With experience and training, clerks may be promoted to supervisory or specialist positions.

Computer and information systems managers typically have a bachelor's degree and several years of experience in computer occupations, particularly as computer systems analysts. However, many employers prefer those with advanced degrees in business administration (MBA) or information systems management. In addition to

Information

technical knowledge, they must possess strong communications skills and business acumen.

Outlook

Internet service providers, Web search portals, and data processing services are expected to experience 28 percent growth in wage and salary employment between 2004 and 2014, faster than the 14 percent projected for the economy as a whole. This growth will vary by field sector, with Internet service providers and Web search portals growing 16 percent and data processing, hosting, and related services growing 33 percent.

As the number of people connecting to the Internet continues to increase, ISPs will enjoy growing demand for their services. While the percent of the population connecting to the Internet is unlikely to continue rising at the pace of the 1990s, there should still be a considerable increase stemming from population growth. Changes in the way in which people access the Internet also should drive growth as the demand for wireless connectivity, broadband service, and more points of connection increases. Despite their differences, both urban and rural areas should benefit from this growth, with urban areas expanding wireless networks and rural areas expanding broadband connectivity. The rapid pace of technological advancement in this field also should generate growth as networks are continuously upgraded to improve performance.

However, consolidation of Internet service providers should temper employment growth in this field sector, as will the growth of cable and telephone service providers offering Internet access through their networks. When Internet access is coupled with another service, the related employment may be counted as part of another field, such as the telecommunications field.

Every day, new content is added to the Web. Sorting through this data and organizing it for search portals is an unending task, and the number of pages grows exponentially. In addition, there are numerous pages that are not accurately catalogued due to the technical difficulties associated with them. The need to keep up with all this content should ensure strong growth for Web search portals over the next decade. Further growth should come from an increase in the number and scope of additional services beyond simple search functions as Web search portals compete for users and look for additional sources of revenue.

As the number of Internet users has grown, so has the number of businesses, organizations, and individuals providing information and services primarily through Web sites. This can range from simple text to retail or subscription music services. Whatever the content, the continuing growth in the number of such sites should drive strong employment growth in data processing, hosting, and related services. Increasing concerns over security also will require more advanced technical solutions, resulting in further job growth within the field. Both data hosting services and data processing centers also should experience employment growth as the result of the continued need to input paper records into computer files and to convert older archived data to newer formats.

In ISPs and Web search portals, job opportunities should be best for computer specialists, such as computer software engineers and network systems and data communications analysts. There should be strong continuing demand for these and other computer specialists to maintain and upgrade the systems that keep users connected and the search engines that make the Web navigable. As companies in this field continue to add services and content, they will need these workers to implement the changes. Demand for computer specialists also should experience solid growth in data processing, hosting, and related services, particularly in Web hosting services.

Earnings

In 2004, nonsupervisory workers in Internet service providers, Web search portals, and data processing services earned $769 per week on average, compared with the $529 average for all fields. Workers in Internet service providers and Web search portals earned more, with $824 as the average. Those in data processing, hosting, and related services earned less, on average, at $745 per week.

Like those of the entire workforce, earnings also varied considerably by occupation, with workers in professional occupations earning more than those in office and administrative support occupations. For example, customer service representatives and computer programmers—the two largest occupations in the field—had median hourly earnings of $13.88 and $31.39, respectively. As in other fields, managers had higher earnings because they have greater responsibilities and are more experienced than their staffs. Median hourly earnings for specific occupations within the field are shown in table 2.

Table 2. Median hourly earnings of the largest occupations in Internet service providers, Web search portals, and data processing services, May 2004

Occupations	Internet service providers, Web search portals, and data processing services	All fields
Computer and information systems managers	$47.09	$44.51
Computer software engineers, systems software	36.16	38.34
Computer software engineers, applications	35.63	36.05
Computer systems analysts	33.01	31.95
Computer programmers	31.39	30.24
Network and computer systems administrators	28.57	27.98
Computer support specialists	18.20	19.44
Customer service representatives	13.88	12.99
Office clerks, general	10.98	10.95
Data entry keyers	9.96	11.18

Sources of Additional Information

Individual Internet service providers; Web search portals; and data processing, hosting, and related services companies can provide detailed information about job openings and qualifications.

Motion Picture and Video Fields

- Annual Earnings: $26,210
- Job Growth: 17.1%
- Size of Workforce: 369,950
- Self-Employed: 10.8%
- Part-Time: 27.1%

Significant Points

- Keen competition is expected for the more glamorous jobs—writers, actors, producers, and directors—but better job prospects are expected for multimedia artists and animators, film and video editors, and others skilled in digital filming and computer generated imaging.
- Although many films are shot on location, employment is centered in several major cities, particularly New York and Los Angeles.
- Many workers have formal training, but experience, talent, creativity, and professionalism are the factors that are most important in getting many jobs in this field.

Nature of the Field

The U.S. motion picture field produces much of the world's feature films and many of its recorded television programs. The field is dominated by several large studios, based mostly in Hollywood. However, with the increasing popularity and worldwide availability of cable television, digital video recorders, computer graphics and editing software, and the Internet, many small and medium-sized independent filmmaking companies have sprung up to fill the growing demand. In addition to producing feature films and filmed television programs, the field produces made-for-television movies, music videos, and commercials. Establishments engaged primarily in operating motion picture theaters and exhibiting motion pictures or videos at film festivals also are included in this field. Other establishments provide postproduction services to the motion picture field, such as editing, film and tape transfers, titling and subtitling, credits, closed captioning, computer-produced graphics, and animation and special effects.

Some motion picture and video companies produce films for limited, or specialized, audiences. Among these films are documentaries, which use film clips and interviews to chronicle actual events with real people, and educational films ranging from "do-it-yourself" projects to exercise films. In addition, the field produces business, industrial, and government films that promote an organization's image, provide information on its activities or products, or aid in fundraising or worker training. Some of these films are short enough to release to the public through the Internet; many offer an excellent training ground for beginning filmmakers.

Information

Making a movie can be a difficult yet rewarding experience. However, it is also a very risky one. Although thousands of movies are produced each year, only a small number of them account for most box office receipts. Indeed, most films do not make a full return on their investment from domestic box office revenues, so filmmakers rely on profits from other markets, such as broadcast and cable television, videocassette and DVD sales and rentals, and foreign distribution. In fact, major film companies are receiving a growing portion of their revenue from abroad. These cost pressures have reduced the number of film production companies to the current seven major studios, who produce most of the filmed television programs as well as the movies released nationally. Smaller and independent filmmakers often find it difficult to finance new productions and pay for a film's distribution because they must compete with large motion picture production companies for talent and available movie screens. However, digital technology is lowering production costs for some small-budget films, enabling more independents to succeed in getting their films released nationally.

Although studios and other production companies are responsible for financing, producing, publicizing, and distributing a film or program, the actual making of the film often is done by hundreds of small businesses and independent contractors hired by the studios on an as-needed basis. These companies provide a wide range of services, such as equipment rental, lighting, special effects, set construction, and costume design, as well as much of the creative and technical talent that go into producing a film. The field also contracts with a large number of workers in other fields that supply support services to the crews while they are filming, such as truck drivers, caterers, electricians, and makeup artists. Many of these workers, particularly those in Los Angeles, depend on the motion picture field for their livelihood.

Most motion pictures are still made on film. However, digital technology and computer-generated imaging are rapidly making inroads and are expected to transform the field. Making changes to a picture is much easier with digital techniques. Backgrounds can be inserted after the actors perform on a sound stage, or locations can be digitally modified to reflect the script. Even actors can be created digitally. Independent filmmakers will continue to benefit from this technology as reduced costs improve their ability to compete with the major studios.

Digital technology also makes it possible to distribute movies to theaters through the use of satellites or fiber-optic cable, although relatively few theaters are capable of receiving them in that manner right now. In the future, however, more theaters will be capable of receiving films digitally, and the costly process of producing and distributing bulky films will be sharply reduced.

Working Conditions

Most individuals in this field work in clean, comfortable surroundings. Filming, or "shooting," outside the studio or "on location," however, may require working in adverse weather and under unpleasant and sometimes dangerous conditions. Actors, producers, directors, cinematographers, and camera operators also need stamina to withstand the heat of studio and stage lights, long and irregular hours, and travel.

Directors and producers often work under stress as they try to meet schedules, stay within budget, and resolve personnel and production problems. Actors, producers, directors, cinematographers, and camera operators face the anxiety of rejection and intermittent employment. Writers and editors must deal with criticism and demands to restructure and rewrite their work many times until the producer and director are finally satisfied. All writers must be able to withstand such criticism and disappointment; freelance writers are under the added

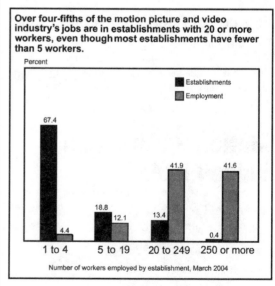

Over four-fifths of the motion picture and video industry's jobs are in establishments with 20 or more workers, even though most establishments have fewer than 5 workers.

Number of workers employed by establishment, March 2004

pressure of always looking for new jobs. In spite of these difficulties, many people find that the glamour and excitement of filmmaking more than compensate for the frequently demanding and uncertain nature of careers in motion pictures.

Important Characteristics of the Field

Skills: Social Perceptiveness; Management of Personnel Resources; Speaking; Persuasion; Negotiation; Active Listening. **Abilities:** Speech Clarity; Speech Recognition; Hearing Sensitivity; Time Sharing; Gross Body Coordination; Oral Expression. **Work-Related Values:** Co-workers; Social Service; Working Conditions; Variety; Authority; Creativity.

Employment

In 2004, there were about 368,000 wage and salary jobs in the motion picture and video fields. Most of the workers were in motion picture and video production. They are involved in casting, acting, directing, editing, film processing, and motion picture and videotape reproduction. Although seven major studios produce most of the motion pictures released in the United States, many small companies are used as contractors throughout the process. Most motion picture and video establishments employ fewer than 5 workers (chart 1).

Many additional individuals work in the motion picture and video fields on a freelance, contract, or part-time basis, but accurate statistics on their numbers are not available. Numerous people in the film field are self-employed, selling their services to anyone who needs them and often working on productions for many different companies during the year. Competition for these jobs is intense, and many people are unable to earn a living solely from freelance work.

Employment in the production of motion pictures and other films for television is centered in Los Angeles and New York City. Studios also are located in Chicago; Orlando; Irving, Texas; and Wilmington, North Carolina. In addition, many films are shot on location throughout the United States and abroad.

Table 1. Employment of wage and salary workers in motion picture and video fields by occupation, 2004 and projected change, 2004–2014 (Employment in thousands)

Occupation	Employment, 2004		Percent change, 2004–2014
	Number	Percent	
Total, all occupations	368	100.0	17.1
Management, business, and financial occupations	27	7.4	24.2
General and operations managers	9	2.6	17.6
Operations specialties managers	4	1.0	27.1
Accountants and auditors	2	0.6	26.3
Professional and related occupations	148	40.3	26.7
Computer specialists	6	1.7	38.1
Multi-media artists and animators	7	2.0	39.5
Graphic designers	2	0.6	26.7
Actors	30	8.0	19.1
Producers and directors	13	3.6	26.5
Entertainers and performers, sports and related workers, all other	43	11.8	27.3
Audio and video equipment technicians	8	2.2	27.7
Sound engineering technicians	4	1.0	28.2
Camera operators, television, video, and motion picture	7	1.9	26.4
Film and video editors	10	2.7	27.3
Service occupations	107	29.2	8.5
First-line supervisors/ managers of food preparation and serving workers	3	0.8	5.2
Combined food preparation and serving workers, including fast food	7	1.8	4.7
Counter attendants, cafeteria, food concession, and coffee shop	33	8.9	23.0

Information

Occupation	Employment, 2004 Number	Employment, 2004 Percent	Percent change, 2004–2014
Janitors and cleaners, except maids and housekeeping cleaners	4	1.2	9.7
First-line supervisors/ managers of personal service workers	4	1.2	4.4
Motion picture projectionists	9	2.5	–16.4
Ushers, lobby attendants, and ticket takers	42	11.3	4.2
Sales and related occupations	36	9.9	2.3
First-line supervisors/ managers of retail sales workers	3	0.8	–2.7
Cashiers, except gaming	22	6.1	–5.7
Office and administrative support occupations	34	9.1	13.6
Bookkeeping, accounting, and auditing clerks	4	1.2	12.7
Customer service representatives	4	1.1	29.3
Shipping, receiving, and traffic clerks	3	0.7	15.2
Executive secretaries and administrative assistants	5	1.3	19.3
Office clerks, general	5	1.3	10.0
Production occupations	5	1.2	7.1
Transportation and material moving occupations	8	2.1	16.5
Laborers and freight, stock, and material movers, hand	6	1.6	14.6

Note: May not add to totals due to omission of occupations with small employment

Occupations in the Field

The length of the credits at the end of most feature films and television programs gives an idea of the variety of workers involved in producing and distributing films. The motion picture field employs workers in every major occupational group. Professionals and related workers account for about 4 in 10 salaried jobs in the field. Approximately 3 in 10 salaried workers hold jobs in service occupations (table 1).

Jobs in the field can be broadly classified according to the three phases of filmmaking: preproduction, production, and postproduction. Preproduction is the planning phase, which includes budgeting, casting, finding the right location, set and costume design and construction, and scheduling. Production is the actual making of the film. The number of people involved in the production phase can vary from a few, for a documentary film, to hundreds, for a feature film. It is during this phase that the actual filming is done. Postproduction activities take place in editing rooms and recording studios, where the film is shaped into its final form.

Some individuals work in all three phases. *Producers*, for example, are involved in every phase from beginning to end. These workers look for ideas that they believe can be turned into lucrative film projects or television shows. They may see many films, read hundreds of manuscripts, and maintain numerous contacts with literary agents and publishers. Producers are also responsible for all of the financial aspects of a film, including finding financing for its production. The producer works closely with the director on the selection of the script, the principal members of the cast, and the filming locations because these decisions greatly affect the cost of a film. Once financing is obtained, the producer works out a detailed budget and sees to it that the production costs stay within that budget. In a large production, the producer also works closely with *production managers*, who are in charge of crews, travel, casting, and equipment. For television shows, much of this process requires especially tight recording deadlines.

Directors interpret the script and develop its thematic and visual images for the film. They also are involved in every stage of production. They may supervise hundreds of people, from screenwriters to costume, lighting, and set designers. Directors are in charge of all technical and artistic aspects of the film or television show. They conduct auditions and rehearsals and approve the location, scenery, costumes, choreography, and music. In short, they direct the entire cast and crew during shooting. *Assistant directors* (or *first and second assistants*) help them with such details as handling the transportation of equipment, arranging for food and accommodations, and hiring performers who appear in the film but have no lines.

Some directors assume multiple roles, such as *director-producer* or *writer-producer-director*. Successful directors must know how to hire the right people and create effective teams.

Preproduction occupations. Before a film or a television program moves into the production phase, it begins with an idea. Anyone can pitch an idea to a studio executive or an independent producer, but usually an agent representing an actor, writer, or director will have the best opportunity—the best access—to someone who can give the green light to a project.

Once a project is approved, whether developed from an original idea or taken from an existing literary work, *screenwriters* will be brought in to turn that idea into a screenplay or a script for a television pilot (a sample episode of a proposed television series). Screenwriters work closely with producers and directors. Sometimes they prepare a treatment, a synopsis of the story and how a few scenes will play out, but no dialogue. Before filming or taping can begin, screenwriters will prepare a "shooting script," which has instructions pertaining to shots, camera angles, and lighting. Frequently, screenwriters make changes to reflect the directors' and producers' ideas and desires. The work, therefore, requires not only creativity, but also an ability to collaborate with others and to write and rewrite many versions of a script under pressure. Although the work of feature film screenwriters generally ends when shooting begins, writing for a television series usually continues throughout the television season with a new script required for every episode.

Art directors design the physical environment of the film or television set to create the mood called for by the script. Television art directors may design elaborate sets for use in situation comedies or commercials. They supervise many different people, including *illustrators, scenic designers, model makers, carpenters, painters, electricians, laborers, set decorators, costume designers,* and *makeup and hairstyling artists.* These positions can provide an entry into the motion picture field. Many start in such jobs in live theater productions and then move back and forth between the stage, film, and television.

Production occupations. Actors entertain and communicate with the audience through their interpretation of dramatic or comedic roles. Only a small number achieve recognition in motion pictures or television. Many are cast in supporting roles or as walk-ons. Some start as background performers with no lines to deliver. Also called "extras," these are the people in the background—crowds on the street, workers in offices, or dancers at a ball. Others perform stunts, such as driving cars in chase scenes or falling from high places. Although a few actors find parts in feature films straight out of drama school, most support themselves by working for many years outside of the field. Most acting jobs are found through an agent, who finds auditions that may lead to acting assignments.

Cinematographers, camera operators, and gaffers work together to capture the scenes in the script on film. *Cinematographers* compose the film shots to reflect the mood the director wishes to create. They do not usually operate the camera; instead, they plan and coordinate the actual filming. *Camera operators* handle all camera movements and perform the actual shooting. *Assistant camera operators* check the equipment, load and position cameras, run the film to a lab or darkroom, and take care of the equipment. *Commercial camera operators* specialize in shooting commercials. This experience translates easily into filming documentaries or working on smaller-budget independent films. *Gaffers,* or lighting technicians, set up the different kinds of lighting needed for filming. They work for the *director of photography,* who plans all lighting needs. *Sound engineering technicians, film recordists,* and *boom operators* record dialogue, sounds, music, and special effects during the filming. Sound engineering technicians are the "ears" of the film, supervising all sound generated during filming. They select microphones and the level of sound from mixers and synthesizers to assure the best sound quality. Recordists help to set up the equipment and are in charge of the individual tape recorders. Boom operators handle long booms with microphones that are moved from one area of the set to another. One person often performs many of these functions because more filming is done on location and the equipment has become compact, lighter, and simpler to operate.

Multimedia artists and animators create the movie "magic." Through their imagination, creativity, and skill, they can create anything required by the script, from talking animals to flaming office buildings and earthquakes. Many begin as stage technicians or scenic designers. They not only need a good imagination, but also must be part carpenter, plumber, electrician, and electronics expert. These workers must be familiar with many ways of achieving a desired special effect because

Information

each job requires different skills. Computer skills have become very important in this field. Some areas of television and film production, including animation and visual effects, now rely heavily on computer technology. Although there was a time when elaborate computer animation was restricted to blockbuster movies, much of the three-dimensional work being generated today occurs in small to midsized companies. Some specialists create "synthespians"—realistic digital humans—which appear mainly in science fiction productions. These digital images are often used when a stunt or scene is too dangerous for an actor.

Many individuals get their start in the field by running errands, moving things on the set, controlling traffic, and helping with props. *Production assistants* and *grips* (stagehands) are often used in this way.

Postproduction occupations. One of the most important tasks in filmmaking and television production is editing. After a film is shot and processed, *film and video editors* study footage, select the best shots, and assemble them in the most effective way. Their goal is to create dramatic continuity and the right pace for the desired mood. Editors first organize the footage and then structure the sequence of the film by splicing and resplicing the best shots. They must have a good eye and understand the subject of the film and the director's intentions. The ability to work with digital media also is becoming increasingly important. Strong computer skills are mandatory for most jobs. However, few field-wide standards exist, so companies often look for people with skills in the hardware or software they are currently using.

Assistant editors or *dubbing editors* select the soundtrack and special sound effects to produce the final combination of sight and sound as it appears on the screen. *Editing room assistants* help with splicing, patching, rewinding, coding, and storing film. Some television networks have *film librarians*, who are responsible for organizing, filing, cataloging, and selecting footage for the film editors. There is no one way of entering the occupation of editor, but experience as a film librarian, camera operator, sound editor, or assistant editor—plus talent and perseverance—usually help.

Sound effects editors or *audio recording engineers* perform one of the final jobs in postproduction: adding prerecorded and live sound effects and background music by manipulating various elements of music, dialogue, and background sound to fit the picture. Their work is

becoming increasingly computer driven as electronic equipment replaces conventional tape-recording devices. The best way to gain experience in sound editing is through work in radio stations, with music groups, or in music videos or by adding audio to Internet sites.

Even before the film or television show starts production, *marketing personnel* develop the marketing strategy for the release. They estimate the demand for the film or show and the audience to whom it will appeal, develop an advertising plan, and decide where and when to release the work. They also may follow the filming or review film looking for images to use in movie trailers and advertising. *Advertising workers*, or "unit publicists," write press releases and short biographies of actors and directors for newspapers and magazines. They may also set up interviews or television appearances for the stars or director to promote a film or television series. *Sales representatives* sell the finished product. Many production companies hire staff to distribute, lease, and sell their films and made-for-television programs to theater owners and television networks. The best way to enter sales is to start by selling advertising time for television stations.

Training, Other Qualifications, and Advancement

Formal training can be a great asset to workers in filmmaking and television production, but experience, talent, creativity, and professionalism usually are the most important factors in getting a job. Many entry-level workers start out by working on documentary, business, educational, industrial, or government films or in the music video field. This kind of experience can lead to more advanced jobs.

Actors usually are required to have formal dramatic training or acting experience. Training can be obtained in acting conservatories, university programs, theatre-sponsored training programs, and independent dramatic arts schools. The National Association of Schools of Theatre accredits 135 colleges and universities that offer bachelor's or higher degrees in dramatic and theater arts. However, many reputable studio programs offer training on a course-by-course basis that do not lead to a formal degree. Many professional actors who are between acting jobs obtain additional advanced training through private sessions with an acting coach or by participating in a master class to focus on a particular challenge or to broaden their skills.

Training in singing, dancing, or stage combat or experience in modeling, stand-up comedy, or acting in commercials is especially useful and helps an actor stand out among the many resumes being considered. But actual performance credits, even those for performing in local and regional theater productions, can be the most useful in getting into an audition. Many actors begin their careers by performing in smaller markets and commercials and working as extras. Most professional actors rely on agents or managers to find auditions for them.

There are no specific training requirements for producers and directors. Talent, experience, and business acumen are very important. An ability to deal with many different kinds of people while under stress also is essential. Producers and directors come from varied backgrounds. Many start as assistant directors; others gain field experience first as actors, writers, film editors, or business managers. Formal training in directing and producing is available at some colleges and universities. Individuals interested in production management who have a bachelor's degree or 2 years of on-the-set experience in motion picture or television production may qualify for the Assistant Directors Training Program offered jointly by the Directors Guild of America and the Alliance of Motion Picture and Television Producers. Training is given in New York City and Los Angeles. To enroll in this highly competitive program, individuals must take a written exam and go through a series of assessments.

Although many screenwriters have college degrees, talent and creativity are even more important determinants of success in the field. Screenwriters need to develop creative-writing skills, a mastery of film language, and a basic understanding of filmmaking. Self-motivation, perseverance, and an ability to take criticism also are valuable. Feature-film writers usually have many years of experience and work on a freelance basis. Many start as copywriters in advertising agencies and as writers for educational film companies, government audiovisual departments, or in-house corporate film divisions. These jobs not only serve as a good training ground for beginners, but also have greater job security than freelancing has.

Cinematographers, camera operators, and sound engineers usually have either a college or technical school education or they go through a formal training program. Computer skills are required for many editing, special-effects, and cinematography positions.

In addition to colleges and technical schools, many independent centers offer training programs on various aspects of filmmaking, such as screenwriting, film editing, directing, and acting. For example, the American Film Institute offers training in directing, production, cinematography, screenwriting, and production design.

The educational background of managers and top executives varies widely, depending on their responsibilities. Most managers have a bachelor's degree in liberal arts or business administration. Their majors often are related to the departments they direct. For example, a degree in accounting or finance, or in business administration with an emphasis on accounting or finance, is suitable academic preparation for financial managers.

For top-level positions in marketing, promotions, or general or human resources management, employers prefer individuals with an undergraduate degree in a field related to the department in which they will work, such as degrees in marketing, advertising, or business administration. Experience in retail and print advertising also is helpful. A high school diploma and retail or telephone sales experience are beneficial for sales jobs.

Promotion opportunities for many jobs are extremely limited because of the narrow scope of the duties and skills of the occupations. Thousands of jobs are also temporary, intermittent, part time, or on a contract basis, making advancement difficult. Individual initiative is very important for advancement in the motion picture field.

Screenwriters usually have had writing experience as freelance writers or editors or in other employment settings. As they build a reputation in their career, demand for their screenplays or teleplays increases, and their earnings grow. Some become directors or producers. Film and video editors often begin as camera operators or editing room assistants, cinematographers usually start as assistant camera operators, and sound recordists often start as boom operators and gradually progress to become sound engineers. Computer courses in digital sound and electronic mixing often are important for upward mobility.

General managers may advance either to top executive positions, such as executive or administrative vice president, in their own firm or to similar positions in a larger firm. Top-level managers may advance to chief operating officer and chief executive officer. Financial, marketing, and other managers may be promoted to top

Information

management positions or may transfer to closely related positions in other fields. Some may start their own businesses.

Outlook

Wage and salary employment in the motion picture and video industries is projected to grow 17 percent between 2004 and 2014, which is faster than the 14 percent growth projected for wage and salary employment in all industries combined. Job growth will result from the explosive growth of demand for programming needed to fill an increasing number of cable and satellite television channels, both in the United States and abroad. Also, more films will be needed to meet in-home demand for videos, DVDs, and films over the Internet. Responding to an increasingly fragmented audience will create many opportunities to develop films. The international market for U.S.–made films is expected to continue growing as more countries and foreign individuals acquire the ability to view our films. As the industry registers employment growth, many more job openings will arise through people leaving the industry, mainly for more stable employment.

There is concern in the motion picture industry over the number of films that are being made abroad. Tax breaks offered chiefly by English-speaking countries, especially Canada, have induced U.S. filmmakers to increasingly move the production of films abroad. Production of many lower-budget films, such as made-for-television movies, and commercials has been moved abroad to reduce production costs. In addition, more feature films are being made abroad, but mostly for artistic reasons. When film production leaves, it takes away large numbers of jobs that are filled at the site of the filming—most of the noncritical supporting actors and behind-the-scenes workers, caterers, drivers, and production assistants. To address this issue, several cities and states have initiated tax breaks and other incentives to encourage filmmakers to make movies in their locales. Also, the U.S. Congress has considered legislation that offers tax incentives for filmmakers to stay in the United States.

The motion picture industry is also concerned about piracy of its work, which can occur in several ways. For example, as the power and speed of the Internet grows, more movies are being downloaded directly into homes, causing declines in theatre attendance and losses in revenue from ticket sales. The industry has launched an anti-piracy initiative in order to combat this trend, which potentially could have an adverse affect on employment. Digital transmission of motion pictures from studios directly to movie houses for exhibition will be able to prevent some piracy problems, but it also has high start-up costs—expensive digital projectors and costs to install transmission and distribution technology and security software.

Opportunities will be better in some occupations than in others. Computer specialists; multimedia artists and animators; film and video editors; and others skilled in digital filming, editing, and computer-generated imaging should have the best job prospects. There also will be opportunities for broadcast and sound engineering technicians and other specialists, such as gaffers and set construction workers. In contrast, keen competition can be expected for the more glamorous high-paying jobs in the industry—writers, actors, producers, and directors—as many more people seek a lesser number of these jobs. Small or independent filmmakers may provide the best job prospects because they are likely to grow more quickly as digital technology cuts production costs.

Table 2. Median hourly earnings of the largest occupations in motion picture and video industries, May 2004

Occuaption	Motion picture and video industries	All industries
General and operations managers	$44.49	$37.22
Producers and directors	36.16	25.40
Film and video editors	21.50	20.96
Entertainers and performers, sports and related workers, all other	17.44	16.73
Audio and video equipment technicians	16.19	15.66
Actors	9.27	11.28
Motion picture projectionists	8.05	8.32
Cashiers	7.14	7.81
Ushers, lobby attendants, and ticket takers	6.77	7.30
Counter attendants, cafeteria, food concession, and coffee shop	6.67	7.53

Earnings

Earnings of workers in the motion picture and video fields vary, depending on education and experience, type of work, union affiliation, and duration of employment. In 2004, median weekly earnings of wage and salary workers in the motion picture and video fields were $592, compared with $529 for wage and salary workers in all fields combined.

On the basis of a union contract negotiated in July 2003, motion picture and television actors who are members of the Screen Actors Guild earn a minimum daily rate of $716, or $2,483 for a 5-day week. They also receive additional compensation for reruns. Annual earnings for many actors are low, however, because employment is intermittent. Many actors supplement their incomes from acting with earnings from other jobs outside the field. Some established actors get salaries well above the minimums, and earnings of the few top stars are astronomical.

Salaries for directors vary widely. Producers seldom have a set salary; they get a percentage of a show's earnings or ticket sales. Earnings in selected occupations in the motion picture and video fields appear in table 2.

Sources of Additional Information

For general information on employment as an actor, contact either of the following organizations:

- Screen Actors Guild, 5757 Wilshire Blvd., Los Angeles, CA 90036-3600. Internet: http://www.sag.org
- American Federation of Television and Radio Artists—Screen Actors Guild, Suite 204, 4340 East-West Hwy., Bethesda, MD 20814. Internet: http://www.aftra.org

For general information about arts education and a list of accredited college-level programs, contact

- National Office for Arts Accreditation in Higher Education, 11250 Roger Bacon Dr., Suite 21, Reston, VA 22091. Internet: http://www.arts-accredit.org

Publishing, Except Software

- Annual Earnings: $33,630
- Job Growth: 6.5%
- Size of Workforce: 672,890
- Self-Employed: 4.3%
- Part-Time: 23.8%

Significant Points

- Strong communication skills and the ability to meet tight deadlines are crucial for many jobs in this field.
- Mergers and computerization will make firms more productive and limit employment growth.
- Writers and editors face keen competition for jobs as this field attracts a large number of applicants, especially at nationally known publications.
- Technological advances will result in a decline in employment of some workers, such as prepress technicians.

Nature of the Field

The publishing field produces a variety of publications, including magazines, books, newspapers, and directories. It also produces greeting cards, databases, calendars, and other published material, excluding software (table 1). Although mostly producing printed materials, the publishing field is increasingly producing its material in other formats, such as audio, CD-ROM, or other electronic media.

Newspapers employ the largest number of workers in the publishing field. With a staff of reporters and correspondents, newspapers report on events taking place locally and around the world. Despite the local nature of most newspaper reporting, the newspaper field is dominated by several large corporations that own most of the newspapers in the country. It also is becoming common for companies to buy several newspapers in a single region, called "clustering." In this way, newspapers can be produced more efficiently. For example, advertising sales

Information

agents can now sell advertising space for multiple newspapers, which also share the same printing plant.

Book publishing is also dominated by a few very large companies, primarily based in New York City. However, some mid-size and small publishers across the country are thriving, particularly those that specialize in certain subjects. Textbooks and technical, scientific, and professional books provide nearly half of the revenues of the book publishing field. The other half consists of adult trade—which is what is typically found in a bookstore—and juvenile, religious, paperback, mail-order, book club, and reference books.

Magazine, or periodical, publishers run the gamut from small one- or two-person shops to large media conglomerates that may publish dozens of magazines. There are two types of magazines—business-to-business, called "trade," and consumer magazines. Trade magazines serve a particular field, profession, or service, while consumer magazines are written for general audiences.

Directory publishers produce collections of residential and business customers covering a specific regional area. Directories are designed for the purpose of assisting calling parties in locating correct telephone numbers, as well as providing a means of locating businesses and their products. Directories are typically split into two major categories: white pages and yellow pages. White pages consist of complementary phone and address listings from the local telephone service provider given to their customers. The yellow pages are a collection of listings, typically of businesses, that are paid advertisements and sorted by the type of business.

Although the content and formats may vary, most publishers follow similar steps to produce their publishable material. First, editorial departments must acquire the content, or material, to be published. Some publishers have a staff of writers, reporters, and editors who research and write articles, stories, and other text for the publications. Photographers and artists are also brought in to supplement the stories with photos and illustrations as needed. Other publishers purchase their material, which may also include photos and artwork from outside sources, mainly independent "freelance" writers, photographers, or artists. When this is done, the publishers obtain the legal right to publish the material from the content providers prior to publication. After the story or article is written, the manuscript is reviewed to check that the information it contains is accurate and then edited to ensure that it uses correct grammar and a writing style that is clear and interesting. Editors and publishers develop captions and headlines and design the pages and the covers.

The sale of advertisements, including classified advertising, is the major source of revenue for magazines, newspapers, and directories, such as the telephone Yellow Pages. Advertising sales agents work with clients and advertising agencies to sell space in the publication. While most commercial advertisements are produced by advertising agencies, small advertisers may require the help of the copywriters and graphic artists of the publisher's advertising department staff to create an advertisement.

When complete, all of the content—manuscript; photos and captions; and illustrations and any other artwork, including advertisements—is collected at one location and, with the help of desktop publishing software, the pages are laid out. Most newspapers and many magazines have art and design staffs that perform this "prepress" operation; other publishers usually contract out their prepress to companies in the printing field, along with the actual printing of the publication.

Newspaper publishers usually own the printing plants that print their newspapers. Over the years, this type of printing operation has become highly automated and the skills needed to produce a newspaper are changing with the technology. The dominant printing process used to produce newspapers is lithography. The process involves putting the pages of the newspaper on film and then "burning" the images from the film onto a thin aluminum plate, which is then installed on a press. In the plant, rolls of paper are brought in from the warehouse, the plates are treated with chemicals, ink is mixed, and presses move the paper along the rotating inked plates at very high rates of speed.

Publishers' publicity, marketing, and circulation departments are responsible for promoting a publication and increasing sales and circulation. Book publishers, in particular, promote new books by creating elaborate publicity campaigns involving book signings and public appearances by the author.

Getting the publication to the readers is a function of the distribution department. Major book publishers often have large warehouse operations where books are stored and from which they are delivered as needed.

Newspapers and magazines, however, distribute each issue only once. Immediately after they are printed, newspapers are folded, filled with inserts, bundled, and wrapped. The newspapers are then transported to distributors, who deliver the newspapers to newsstands and individual carriers. Another major function of the department in newspapers is making sure that the newspaper is delivered on time at readers' doorsteps. Magazines are mailed to subscribers after printing or shipped to retail distributors. Many magazines and some newspapers contract out their distribution.

Much of the publishing field is venturing online. Newspapers, in particular, and some magazines have extensive Web sites that are updated around the clock as news breaks. These Web sites may have their own writers and editors to supply content, but, for the most part, they reformat material developed by the print publication's regular staff. Books are also beginning to be reproduced electronically so that they can be read on hand-held "readers" or on computers.

Computerization, in particular digital technology, is having a significant impact on the publishing field. Digital photography eliminates the need for film processing and allows for easy manipulation of images. Electronic mail also allows advertisers to send their ads directly to the publisher's production department for insertion. In the latest print technologies, computers use lasers to burn images and text into the printing plate, eliminating the need to produce a film negative of each page.

Table 1. Establishments and wage and salary employment in publishing, except software, by detailed field, 2004

Field segment	Establishments	Employment
Total	100.0	100.0
Newspapers	36.9	55.8
Periodicals	33.8	21.0
Book publishing	15.0	11.9
Directory and mailing lists	8.3	7.0
Other publishers	6.1	4.3

Working Conditions

Meeting deadlines is one of the primary conditions of employment in this field. Magazines and newspapers, in particular, are published on a very tight schedule and workers must be prepared to meet these deadlines. This can often make for a very chaotic and stressful environment, and employees frequently may be required to work overtime. Working nights, weekends, and holidays also is common, especially for those working on newspapers. The average nonsupervisory worker in newspaper publishing worked 34.1 hours per week in 2004, compared with 33.7 hours per week across all fields. Within periodical publishing, nonsupervisory workers worked an average of 33.5 hours per week, and they worked an average of 39.5 hours per week in book publishing. Part-time employment is significant in this field, with 20 percent working part time. Newspaper distributors and drivers usually work 5 to 6 hours a day, often in the middle of the night. Also, some telephone advertising and classified sales representatives work part time.

Writers, editors, reporters, and correspondents have the most varied working conditions. Many work from home, particularly in book publishing, sending manuscripts back and forth using electronic mail. For most writers and reporters, travel is required to perform research and conduct interviews. News correspondents for large metropolitan newspapers or national news publications may be stationed in cities around the world, reporting on events in their territory.

Many advertising sales agents also travel in order to meet with potential customers, although some sell over the telephone. Rejection by clients and the need to meet quotas can be stressful for some agents. Although the hours are long and often irregular, most agents have the freedom to determine their own schedule.

At headquarters, many in publishing work in comfortable, private offices, while others—particularly at newspapers—work in large, noisy, cubicle-filled rooms. Classified advertising clerks and customer service representatives increasingly work in call-center environments, manning telephones much of the day. Newspaper pressrooms are manufacturing plants that can be noisy and dangerous if safety procedures are not followed, but computerization of the machines has reduced injuries. In 2003, occurrences of work-related injury and illness in the publishing field ranged from an average of 1.1 per 100 full-time workers in periodical publishing to 3.8 per

Information

100 full-time workers in newspaper publishing, lower than the average of 5.0 per 100 full-time workers for all nongovernment fields.

Important Characteristics of the Field

Skills: Operation and Control. **Abilities:** Visual Color Discrimination; Near Vision; Night Vision; Dynamic Flexibility; Speech Recognition; Rate Control. **Work-Related Values:** Advancement; Independence; Working Conditions; Creativity; Recognition; Supervision, Human Relations.

Employment

The publishing field provided 671,000 wage and salary jobs in 2004. In addition, there were 37,000 self-employed workers. The field does not include independent (or "freelance") writers, artists, journalists, or photographers, whose jobs are included in the arts, entertainment, and recreation field, but who contribute a significant amount of content material to this field.

Newspaper publishing companies employ the largest number of people in this field because they write much of their own material and typically print, and sometimes distribute, their newspapers. While newspaper publishing is done throughout the country, magazine and book publishers are based mostly in large cities. The largest

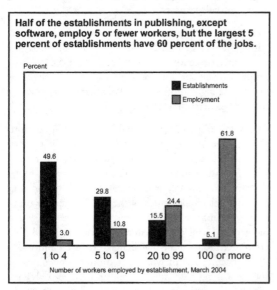

Half of the establishments in publishing, except software, employ 5 or fewer workers, but the largest 5 percent of establishments have 60 percent of the jobs.

Percent

Number of workers employed by establishment, March 2004

concentration of publishers is in New York City. Although most establishments in this field are small, most employees work at the largest ones (chart 1).

Occupations in the Field

Most occupations in the publishing field fall into 1 of 4 categories: writing and editing; production; advertising sales and marketing; and general administration (table 2). However, variations in the number and type of workers employed occur by type of publication. For example, most book publishing companies employ few writers because most of their content is acquired from freelance writers and photographers. In contrast, newspapers employ a number of writers and reporters, who supply the content for the paper. Also, newspapers generally perform their own printing, whereas most books and magazines are printed by companies in the printing field. Differences also exist depending on the size of the company and the variety of media in which the company publishes.

Writing and editing occupations. Everything that is published in this field must first be written. *Writers and authors* and *reporters and correspondents* write the articles, stories, and other text that end up in publications. Writers are assigned stories to write by *editors.* At newspapers and news magazines, reporters usually specialize in certain categories, or "beats," such as education, crime, sports, or world news. Writers and reporters gather information on their topic by performing Internet and library research and by interviewing people either in person or by telephone. They must then organize their material and write it down in a coherent manner that will interest and entertain readers. Copywriters, who write advertising copy, also are common in this field.

Editors are essential to a publication. They review, rewrite, and edit the work of writers. They may also do original writing, such as producing editorials for newspapers or columns for magazines. In book publishing, they oversee the acquisition and selection of material, often working directly with the authors to achieve the final product. Most publishing companies employ several types of editors. The executive editor generally has the final say about what will be published and how it will be covered and presented. The managing editor is responsible for the day-to-day operation of the editorial department and makes sure that material produced conforms to guidelines and that deadlines are met. Associate and assistant editors give assignments to writers and reporters, oversee projects, and do much of the editing of text. Copy editors review manuscripts or reporters' copy for accuracy, content, grammar, and style. They also are performing more layout design and prepress functions as computerization moves these jobs from the production department to the editorial department.

Other occupations that work closely with the editorial department are *art and design workers* and *photographers*, whose work often complements the written material. They illustrate children's books, photograph news events, design book jackets and magazine covers, and lay out every page of publications. The *art director* determines the overall look of the publication, overseeing placement of text, artwork and photographs, and any advertising on the page and selecting type sizes and styles, or fonts.

Production occupations. *Industrial production managers,* with the help of *production and planning clerks,* oversee the production of the publication. They set up production schedules and see that deadlines are met. They also try to keep printing costs under control while maintaining quality. The production manager also determines how much it will cost to produce, for example, a 300-page textbook or an advertising insert in a magazine. In newspaper publishing, the production manager also oversees and controls the entire production operation.

Other production occupations found mainly in newspaper printing plants are *prepress technicians* and *printing machine operators.* Prepress technicians scan images and do page layout and camera work. They then process the film and make plates from it. Printing machine operators set up and run the printing presses and work with the inks. *Driver/sales workers* deliver the newspapers to newsstands and residential customers.

Sales, promotion, and marketing occupations. Magazines, newspapers, and directories, in particular, employ many *advertising sales agents,* who generate most of the revenue for these publications. Using demographic data produced by the market research department, they make presentations to potential clients promoting the use of their publication for advertising purposes. Increasingly, advertising agents sell integrated packages that include advertisements to be placed online or with a broadcast subsidiary, along with additional promotional tie-ins. This job can require substantial travel for some, while others may sell advertising over the telephone.

Classified advertising sales are handled by *telemarketers* or *customer service representatives,* depending on who is making the call. *Advertising and promotions managers,* called circulation directors at some magazines and newspapers, study trends and devise promotion campaigns to generate new readers. They also work with the driver/sales workers to ensure that the publications are delivered on time.

Because books do not have advertising, book publishers generate sales through the use of publicity campaigns and a sales force. *Public relations specialists* promote books by setting up media interviews with authors and book signings and by placing advertisements in relevant publications. *Sales representatives* go to places such as libraries, schools, and bookstores to promote the sale of their books. They also are responsible for finding additional sources of profit for a title, including book clubs, paperback editions, audio, e-books, and foreign rights for publishing the title in other languages.

General administration occupations. The publishing field, as with most fields, has a variety of *general managers, accountants,* and administrative support staff who help to run the company. There are also *computer specialists* to keep the computer systems running and to implement new technologies. Others work as Internet site developers, who work with the design, editorial, and production departments in order to implement content changes and redesigns of Web sites operated by the publication. But the field also has other occupations that are unique or important to its operations. For example, publishers are the *chief executives* of the company. Publishers are in charge of the business side of the organization and are responsible for implementing company policies. Subsidiary rights and permissions personnel are *business operations specialists,* who negotiate the copyrights for material and also license to others the right to reproduce or reprint copyrighted material. *Stock clerks and order fillers* and *customer service representatives* keep track of books in publishers' warehouses and respond to customer inquiries. Lastly, as publications, particularly books, are published in more than one format, workers are needed to develop the new formats. Audio books, for example, require *sound engineering technicians* to transfer the books to tape.

Information

Table 2. Employment of wage and salary workers in publishing, except software by occupation, 2004 and projected change, 2004–2014 (Employment in thousands)

Occupation	Employment, 2004		Percent change, 2004–2014
	Number	Percent	
Total, all occupations	671	100.0	6.5
Management, business, and financial occupations	63	9.4	15.3
General and operations managers	12	1.7	12.3
Advertising and promotions managers	4	0.6	13.5
Sales managers	5	0.7	12.2
Accountants and auditors	6	0.9	14.8
Professional and related occupations	184	27.4	12.3
Computer programmers	4	0.6	–5.6
Computer software engineers	5	0.8	41.0
Graphic designers	21	3.2	16.0
Reporters and correspondents	39	5.7	4.2
Editors	59	8.8	12.1
Writers and authors	11	1.6	10.3
Photographers	6	1.0	–5.1
Sales and related occupations	97	14.4	8.9
First-line supervisors/ managers of non-retail sales workers	8	1.2	1.4
Advertising sales agents	48	7.1	15.7
Sales representatives, whole-sale and manufacturing, except technical and scientific products	11	1.6	14.5
Telemarketers	14	2.1	–13.7
Office and administrative support occupations	162	24.1	–2.2
First-line supervisors/ managers of office and administrative support workers	10	1.6	1.8
Bookkeeping, accounting, and auditing clerks	12	1.8	0.2
Customer service representatives	20	3.0	15.1
Order clerks	8	1.1	–28.2
Production, planning, and expediting clerks	5	0.7	13.4
Executive secretaries and administrative assistants	10	1.5	8.5
Data entry and information processing workers	7	1.1	–15.2
Desktop publishers	13	2.0	21.0
Mail clerks and mail machine operators, except postal service	11	1.6	–44.3
Office clerks, general	19	2.9	–1.8
Production occupations	81	12.1	5.6
First-line supervisors/ managers of production and operating workers	7	1.1	9.6
Bindery workers	7	1.0	14.2
Job printers	9	1.3	8.1
Prepress technicians and workers	18	2.6	–3.2
Printing machine operators	18	2.7	8.0
Other production occupations	19	2.8	5.7
Miscellaneous production workers	13	1.9	9.1
Helpers—production workers	9	1.3	11.1
Transportation and material moving occupations	72	10.7	1.4
Driver/sales workers	10	1.4	4.2
Truck drivers, light or delivery services	14	2.0	4.9
Laborers and freight, stock, and material movers, hand	15	2.2	–0.3
Machine feeders and offbearers	12	1.8	–14.7
Packers and packagers, hand	12	1.8	8.6

Note: May not add to totals due to omission of occupations with small employment

Training, Other Qualifications, and Advancement

The ability to communicate well is one of the most important skills needed to enter the publishing field. Although it is especially critical for those in the editorial and sales departments, it is also required for those in production, who may be called upon to compose text. Computer literacy also is becoming a requirement for almost everyone seeking work in this field. And finally, the ability to meet tight deadlines is a must for most workers.

Writers, reporters, and editors generally need a bachelor's degree. Most people in these occupations majored in English, communication, or journalism. Some publishers, however, prefer graduates with liberal arts degrees or specific subject knowledge if the person will be writing about a certain topic or doing technical writing. For the most part, writers and editors need to be able to express ideas clearly and logically and to write under pressure. Familiarity with desktop publishing software is helpful.

Writers and editors often start as assistants, performing fact-checking, doing research, or copy editing along with clerical tasks. News reporters often start by covering local community events or criminal cases and advance to reporting regional or national news. Writers and reporters can advance to editorial positions, but some choose to continue writing and advance by becoming nationally known experts in their field.

A college degree is preferred for most advertising, sales, and marketing positions in which meeting with clients is required. Courses in marketing, communication, business, and advertising are helpful. For those who sell over the telephone, a high school degree may be sufficient. However, more important for success are excellent communication and interpersonal skills. Those in advertising and sales must be able to get along with others as well as be self-motivated, well-organized, persistent, independent, and able to handle rejection. Enthusiasm and a sense of humor also help. One advances in these fields by taking on bigger, more important clients or by going into management.

Most prepress technicians and printing machine operators learn on the job by working alongside experienced craftworkers. Although a high school education is sufficient to get a job, taking classes in printing techniques or getting an associate degree at a postsecondary institution will enhance one's credentials and make it easier to get a job and to advance. Computer skills and familiarity with publishing software packages are important because prepress work and printing are increasingly computerized. Training on new machines will be needed throughout one's career. Advancement usually comes by working on more complex printing jobs or by becoming a supervisor.

Most professional jobs in this field require experience, especially if one wants to work for a top newspaper, magazine, or book publishing company. Experience can be obtained by working for a school newspaper or by performing an internship with a publishing company. However, most people start by working for small publishing companies or newspapers in smaller cities and towns and work their way up to better-paying jobs with larger newspapers or publishers. Others break into the field by doing freelance work.

Earnings

In 2004, average weekly earnings for workers in the publishing field varied by type of publication. Average weekly earnings were $726 in periodical publishing, $651 in book publishing, and $570 in newspaper publishing, compared with $529 for all fields. Writers, editors, and reporters working on major metropolitan newspapers or those with technical expertise writing for specialized magazines usually have the highest salaries. Advertising sales representatives usually earn a base salary plus an amount based on sales. Earnings in selected occupations in publishing appear in table 3.

The Newspaper Guild is the major union representing most nonsupervisory employees in the newspaper field.

Table 3. Median hourly earnings of the largest occupations in publishing, except software, May 2004

Occupations	Publishing, except software	All fields
Editors	$20.97	$21.10
Advertising sales agents	16.87	19.37
Printing machine operators	16.46	14.38
Graphic designers	15.57	18.28
Reporters and correspondents	14.46	15.06
Prepress technicians and workers	14.22	15.30

Information

Occupations	Publishing, except software	All fields
Customer service representatives	13.13	12.99
Office clerks, general	10.96	10.95
Telemarketers	10.11	9.82
Laborers and freight, stock, and material movers, hand	9.46	9.67

Sources of Additional Information

For information about careers in book publishing, write to

- Association of American Publishers, 71 Fifth Ave., 2nd Floor, New York, NY 10003. Internet: http://www.publishers.org

For information about careers in newspaper publishing, write to

- Newspaper Association of America, 1921 Gallows Rd., Suite 600, Vienna, VA 22182. Internet: http://www.naa.org

For information about careers in periodical or magazine publishing, write to

- Magazine Publishers of America, 810 Seventh Ave., 24th Floor, New York, NY 10019 Internet: http://www.magazine.org

Software Publishers

- ☺ Annual Earnings: $71,170
- ☺ Job Growth: 67.6%
- ☺ Size of Workforce: 235,130
- ☺ Self-Employed: 2.8%
- ☺ Part-Time: 4.4%

Significant Points

- Employment is projected to increase 68 percent between 2004 and 2014, ranking software publishers as the third-fastest-growing field in the economy.

- Computer specialists account for 52 percent of all workers.

- Job opportunities will be excellent for most workers; professional workers enjoy the best prospects, reflecting continuing demand for higher-level skills needed to keep up with changes in technology.

Nature of the Field

All organizations today rely on computer and information technology to conduct business and operate more efficiently. Computer software is needed to run and protect computer systems and networks. Some 10,000 establishments are engaged primarily in computer software publishing or publishing and reproduction. Software publishing establishments carry out the functions necessary for producing and distributing computer software, such as designing, providing documentation, assisting in installation, and providing support services to software purchasers. The term *publishing* often implies the production and distribution of information in printed form. The software publishing field also produces and distributes information, but usually it "publishes" or distributes its information by other methods, such as by CD-ROMs, via the sale of new computers already preloaded with software, or through distribution over the Internet rather than in printed form. These establishments may design, develop, and publish or publish only. Establishments providing access to software for clients from a central host site, designing custom software to meet the needs of specific users, or involved in mass duplication of software are classified elsewhere. (For more information, see the description of Computer Systems Design and Related Services found elsewhere in Part II.)

Software publishing establishments that design and publish prepackaged software may develop operating system software as well as word processing and spreadsheet packages, games and graphics packages, data storage software, and Internet-related software tools such as search engines and Web browsers—the software that permits browsing, retrieval, and viewing of content from the Internet. Some establishments may install the software package on a user's system and provide customer support.

Software is often divided into two main categories—applications software and systems software. Applications software includes individual programs for computer users—such as programs for word processing or for developing and maintaining spreadsheets and databases. Systems software, on the other hand, includes the operating system and all of the related programs that enable the computer to function. The Internet has vastly altered the complexion of the software field over the last decade. Much applications and system software is developed for use on the Internet and for connections to the Internet.

Organizations are constantly seeking to implement technologies which will improve efficiency. Enterprise resource planning (ERP) software is such an example. ERP consists of cross-field applications that automate a firm's business processes. Common applications include human resources, manufacturing, and financial management software. Examples of more recent applications are software to manage customer relations and a firm's sources of supply, known as customer relationship management (CRM) and supply-chain management software. Enterprise resource planning software has traditionally been implemented by large organizations with vast computer networks.

Electronic business (e-business) is any process that a business organization conducts over a computer network. Electronic commerce (e-commerce) is that part of e-business that involves the buying and selling of goods and services. With the growth of the Internet and the expansion of e-commerce, there is significant demand for e-commerce software that enables businesses to become as efficient as possible.

This widespread use of the Internet and intranets also has led to greater focus on the need for computer security. The robust growth of e-commerce increases this concern as firms seek to attract as many potential customers as possible to their Web sites. Security threats range from damaging computer viruses to online credit card fraud. As a result, organizations and individual computer users are demanding software, such as firewalls and antivirus software, that secures their computer networks or individual computer environments.

Working Conditions

Most workers in this field work in clean, quiet offices. Given the technology available today, however, more work can be done from remote locations using modems, fax machines, e-mail, and especially the Internet.

About 2 percent of the workers in software publishing firms work part time, compared with 16 percent of workers throughout all fields. For some professionals, evening or weekend work may be necessary to meet deadlines or solve problems. Professionals working for large establishments may have less freedom in planning their schedule than do consultants for very small firms, whose work may be more varied.

Employees who work at video terminals for extended periods may experience musculoskeletal strain; eye problems; stress; or repetitive motion illnesses, such as carpal tunnel syndrome.

Important Characteristics of the Field

Skills: Programming; Troubleshooting; Technology Design; Systems Analysis; Operations Analysis; Complex Problem Solving. **Abilities:** Deductive Reasoning; Inductive Reasoning; Speech Recognition; Originality; Mathematical Reasoning; Oral Comprehension. **Work-Related Values:** Creativity; Ability Utilization; Working Conditions; Authority; Social Status; Autonomy.

Employment

In 2004, there were about 239,000 wage and salary jobs in the field. While the field has both large and small firms, the average establishment in software publishing is relatively small; over half of the establishments employed fewer than 5 workers. About 75 percent of jobs, however, are found in a small number of establishments that employ 50 or more workers (chart 1). Many small establishments in the field are startup firms that hope to capitalize on a market niche.

Relative to the rest of the economy, there are significantly fewer workers 45 years of age and older in software publishing establishments; this field's workforce remains younger than most, with large proportions of workers in the 25-to-44 age range (table 1). This reflects the field's explosive growth in employment since the early 1980s. The huge increase in employment afforded numerous opportunities to younger workers possessing the latest technical skills.

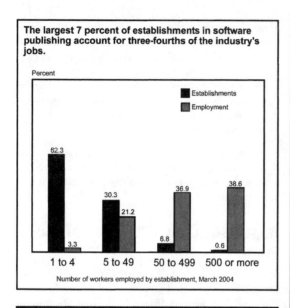

The largest 7 percent of establishments in software publishing account for three-fourths of the industry's jobs.

Percent

- ■ Establishments
- ▨ Employment

	1 to 4	5 to 49	50 to 499	500 or more
Establishments	62.3	30.3	6.8	0.6
Employment	3.3	21.2	36.9	38.6

Number of workers employed by establishment, March 2004

Table 1. Percent distribution of employment, by age group, 2004

Age group	Software publishing	All fields
Total	100.0%	100.0%
16–19	0.0	4.2
20–24	0.0	9.9
25–34	50.0	21.8
35–44	26.9	24.8
45–54	19.2	23.3
55–64	3.8	12.4
65 and older	0.0	3.5

Occupations in the Field

Providing a wide array of information services to clients requires a diverse and well-educated workforce. The majority of workers in the software publishing field are professional and related workers, such as computer software engineers and computer programmers (table 2). This major occupational group accounts for 60 percent of the jobs in the field, reflecting the emphasis on high-level technical skills and creativity. By 2014, the employment share of professional and related occupations is expected to be even greater, while the employment share of office and administrative support jobs, currently accounting for 11 percent of field employment, is projected to fall.

Programmers write, test, and maintain the detailed instructions, called programs or software, that computers must follow to perform their functions. These programs tell the computer what to do—which information to identify and access, how to process it, and what equipment to use. Programmers write these commands by breaking down each operation into a logical sequence of steps, converting the instructions for those steps into a language that the computer understands. While some still work with traditional programming languages like COBOL, object-oriented programming languages such as C++ and Java, computer-aided software engineering (CASE) tools, and artificial intelligence tools now are being used to create and maintain programs. These languages and tools allow portions of code to be reused in programs that require similar routines. Many programmers also customize purchased software or create better software to meet a client's specific needs.

Computer software engineers design, develop, test, and evaluate software programs and systems. Although programmers write and support programs in new languages, much of the design and development now is the responsibility of *software engineers* or *software developers*. Software engineers must possess strong programming skills, but are more concerned with developing algorithms and analyzing and solving programming problems than with actually writing code. These professionals develop many types of software, including operating systems software, network distribution software, and a variety of applications software. *Computer systems software engineers* coordinate the construction and maintenance of a company's computer systems and plan their future growth. They develop software systems for control and automation in manufacturing, business, and other areas. They research, design, and test operating system software, compilers—software that converts programs for faster processing—and network distribution software. *Computer applications software engineers* analyze users' needs and design, create, and modify general computer applications software or specialized utility programs. They develop software solutions. For example, video game programmers are software engineers who plan and write video game software.

Computer support specialists provide technical assistance, support, and advice to customers and users. This group of occupations includes workers with a variety of titles, such as *technical support specialists* and *help-desk technicians*. These troubleshooters interpret problems and provide technical support for software and systems. Support specialists may work either within a company or other organization or directly for a computer software vendor. They answer telephone calls, analyze problems using automated diagnostic programs, and resolve difficulties encountered by users.

Other computer specialists include a wide range of professionals who specialize in operation, analysis, education, application, or design for a particular piece of the system. Many are involved in the design, testing, and evaluation of network systems such as local area networks (LAN), wide area networks (WAN), the Internet, and other data communications systems. Specialty occupations reflect an emphasis on client-server applications and end-user support; however, occupational titles shift rapidly to reflect new developments in technology.

Table 2. Employment of wage and salary workers in software publishing by occupation, 2004 and projected change, 2004–2014 (Employment in thousands)

Occupation	Employment, 2004		Percent change, 2004–2014
	Number	Percent	
Total, all occupations	239	100.0	67.6
Management, business, and financial occupations	46	19.2	64.6
Top executives	7	2.8	59.6
Marketing managers	4	1.5	70.9
Sales managers	3	1.2	61.8
Computer and information systems managers	9	3.7	68.4
Financial managers	2	0.9	60.9
Managers, all other	2	0.9	60.8
Management analysts	4	1.7	60.8
Business operation specialists, all other	4	1.5	76.9
Accountants and auditors	3	1.4	60.8
Professional and related occupations	144	60.4	74.5
Computer and information scientists, research	2	0.7	60.8
Computer programmers	18	7.7	31.2

Occupation	Employment, 2004		Percent change, 2004–2014
	Number	Percent	
Computer software engineers, applications	39	16.5	93.0
Computer software engineers, systems software	21	8.9	91.8
Computer support specialists	19	7.8	60.8
Computer systems analysts	10	4.1	76.9
Database administrators	2	0.8	85.0
Network and computer systems administrators	4	1.8	87.0
Network systems and data communications analysts	4	1.6	114.7
Computer specialists, all other	4	1.6	60.8
Market research analysts	4	1.9	60.8
Multi-media artists and animators	3	1.1	84.7
Technical writers	3	1.4	60.8
Sales and related occupations	19	8.1	57.4
First-line supervisors/ managers of non-retail sales workers	2	0.7	48.7
Sales representatives, services, all other	2	0.9	60.9
Sales representatives, wholesale and manufacturing	12	4.8	60.8
Office and administrative support occupations	27	11.2	44.0
First-line supervisors/ managers of office and administrative support workers	2	0.7	45.8
Bookkeeping, accounting, and auditing clerks	2	0.9	44.7
Customer service representatives	5	2.0	64.7
Secretaries and administrative assistants	6	2.5	47.9
Office clerks, general	3	1.1	43.2

Note: May not add to totals due to omission of occupations with small employment

Information

Training, Other Qualifications, and Advancement

Occupations in the software publishing field require varying levels of education. The level of education and type of training required depend on the employer's needs, which often change due to changes in technology and business conditions. As demonstrated by the current demand for workers with skills related in computer security, employers often scramble to find workers capable of implementing "hot" new technologies. Another factor driving employers' needs is the timeframe within which a project must be completed.

Computer programmers commonly hold a bachelor's degree; however, there are no universal educational requirements. Some hold a degree in computer science, mathematics, or information systems, while others have taken special courses in computer programming to supplement their study in fields such as accounting, inventory control, or other areas of business. Because employers' needs are so varied, a 2-year degree or certificate may be sufficient for some positions so long as applicants possess the right technical skills.

Most computer software engineers have at least a bachelor's degree and broad knowledge and experience with computer systems and technologies. Usual degree concentrations for applications software engineers are computer science or software engineering; for systems software engineers, usual concentrations are computer science or computer information systems. Graduate degrees are preferred for some of the more complex software engineering jobs.

Persons interested in becoming a computer support specialist generally need only an associate degree in a computer-related field as well as significant hands-on experience with computers. They also must possess strong problem-solving and analytical skills as well as excellent communication skills because troubleshooting and helping others are such vital parts of the job. And because there is constant interaction on the job with other computer personnel, customers, or employees, computer support specialists must be able to communicate effectively in writing, often by e-mail, or in person. They also must possess strong writing skills when preparing manuals for employees and customers. As technology continues to improve, computer support specialists must constantly strive to stay up to date and acquire new skills if they wish to remain in the field.

The size of the firm and the local demand for workers also may influence training requirements for specific jobs. Smaller firms may be willing to train informally on the job, whereas larger organizations may pay for formal training or higher education. For example, many marketing and sales workers are able to secure entry-level jobs with little technical knowledge but quickly acquire knowledge of their company's products and services through on-the-job training. With more formal education, employees may advance to completely different jobs within the field. Education or training in a specialty area, such as information security, may provide new opportunities for the worker and allow the establishment to offer new services.

Continuing technological advances in the computer field have led to demand for workers with a higher level of skill and expertise. As information technology continues to expand into more sectors of the economy, employers are demanding workers posses some expertise in other fields. For example, a computer software engineer interested in working for a bank should have some expertise in finance as they integrate new technologies into the bank's computer system. Employers, hardware and software vendors, colleges and universities, private training institutions, and professional computing societies offer continuing education and professional development seminars. The Institute of Electrical and Electronics Engineers Computer Society, for example, recently created a certification process for software development professionals who possess a bachelor's degree and work experience that demonstrates a body of knowledge and who pass a written examination.

Software publishing offers advancement opportunities for all workers who keep up with changing technology. For example, computer support specialists may move into computer programmer positions and, later, into computer software engineer jobs. This advancement usually results from work experience and continued training and education.

Entry-level computer programmers usually start working with an experienced programmer to update existing code, generate lines of one portion of a larger program, or write relatively simple programs. They then advance to more difficult programming and may become project supervisors or move into higher management positions within the organization. Many programmers who work closely with systems analysts advance to systems analyst positions.

Computer software engineers who show leadership ability also can become project managers or advance into management positions, such as manager of information systems or even chief information officer. Technical support specialists may advance by developing expertise in a particular program or software that can lead to opportunities as a programmer or software engineer.

Many experienced workers also have opportunities to move into sales positions as they gain knowledge of specific products and services. Computer programmers who write accounting software, for example, may use their specialized knowledge to sell such products to similar firms. Also, computer support specialists providing technical support for an operating system may eventually market that product, based on their experience and knowledge of the system.

Outlook

Employment in the software publishing field has more than doubled since 1990. As firms continue to invest heavily in information technology and demand for specialized software rises, software publishing is projected to be the third-fastest-growing field in the U.S. economy over the next decade. Wage and salary employment is expected to increase by 68 percent between 2004 and 2014, almost five times the 14 percent growth projected for all fields combined. Even in difficult economic times, organizations continue to make investments in software. Software boosts productivity, increases efficiency, and, in some cases, reduces the need for workers. Growth will not be as rapid as it was during the technology boom of the 1990s, however, as the software field begins to mature and as routine work is increasingly outsourced overseas.

An increasing reliance on information technology, combined with falling prices of computers and related hardware, means that individuals and organizations will continue to invest in applications and systems software to maximize the return on their investments in equipment and to fulfill their growing computing needs. Such needs include the expansion of electronic commerce, a growing reliance on the Internet, faster and more efficient and secure internal and external communication, and the development of new technologies and applications. Given the rate at which the software publishing field is expected to grow and the increasing integration and application of software in all sectors of the economy,

job opportunities should be excellent for most workers. Professional workers should enjoy the best opportunities, reflecting employers' continuing demand for higher-level skills to keep up with changes in technology. However, employment growth may be tempered somewhat by off-shore outsourcing as companies contract out more of the routine tasks to foreign countries, where labor costs are lower, in an attempt to remain competitive.

Today, there is demand for software products ranging from educational software to assist people learning a new language to home networking software and firewalls to maintain security. Yet new growth areas will continue to arise from rapidly evolving technologies and business forces. The increasing uses of the Internet, the proliferation of Web sites, and mobile technology such as the wireless Internet have created demand for a wide variety of new software. The market for educational software and entertainment software, which includes video games, is also expected to experience robust growth over the next decade.

The way the Internet is used is constantly changing, and so is the software required to run the new and emerging computer applications. Expanding electronic commerce, for example, has changed the way companies transact business. Business-to-business commerce is automating many steps in the transaction of business between companies, allowing many firms to operate more efficiently. Businesses are moving their supply networks online and participating in and developing online marketplaces. The sustained growth of electronic commerce as well as the growing uses of intranets and extranets will drive demand for increasingly sophisticated software tools geared towards these technologies. And, as the amount of electronic information stored and accessed continues to grow, new applications and security needs will increase demand for database software. Demand for an even wider array of software applications also should increase as companies continue to expand their capabilities, integrate new technologies, and develop new applications.

One significant factor contributing to growth in software is computer security. Organizations invest heavily in software to protect their information and secure their systems from attack. And, as more individuals and organizations are conducting business electronically, the importance of maintaining computer system and network security will increase, leading to greater demand for security software.

Information

Given the increasingly widespread use of information technologies and the overall rate of growth expected for the software publishing field, most occupations should grow very rapidly, although some faster than others. The most rapid job increases will occur among computer specialists such as computer software engineers as firms continue to install sophisticated computer networks, set up Internet and intranet sites, and engage in electronic commerce and as consumers continue to explore and use vast amounts of applications software.

Earnings

Employees in the software publishing field generally command higher earnings than the national average. All production or nonsupervisory workers in the field averaged $1,342 a week in 2004, significantly higher than the average of $529 for all fields. This reflects the concentration of professionals and specialists who often are highly compensated for their skills or expertise. Given the pace at which technology advances in this field, earnings can be driven by demand for specific skills or experience. Earnings in selected occupations in software publishing appear in table 3.

Table 3. Median hourly earnings of the largest occupations in software publishing, May 2004

Occupation	Software publishers	All fields
General and operations managers	$58.13	$37.22
Computer and information systems managers	51.86	44.51
Market research analysts	41.42	26.99
Computer software engineers, systems software	40.23	38.34
Computer software engineers, applications	38.43	36.05
Sales representatives, wholesale and manufacturing, technical and scientific products	36.43	28.17
Computer programmers	35.13	30.24
Computer systems analysts	34.00	31.95
Computer support specialists	21.58	19.44
Customer service representatives	16.15	12.99

Sources of Additional Information

Further information about computer careers is available from

- Association for Computing Machinery (ACM), 1515 Broadway, New York, NY 10036. Internet: http://www.acm.org
- National Workforce Center for Emerging Technologies, 3000 Landerholm Circle SE, Bellevue, WA 98007. Internet: http://www.nwcet.org

Information on the certified software development professional program can be found at

- Institute of Electrical and Electronics Engineers Computer Society, Headquarters Office, 1730 Massachusetts Ave. NW, Washington, DC 20036-1992. Internet: http://www.computer.org/certification

Telecommunications

- Annual Earnings: $48,180
- Job Growth: –6.5%
- Size of Workforce: 1,024,840
- Self-Employed: 1.5%
- Part-Time: 3.8%

Significant Points

- Telecommunications includes voice, video, and Internet communications services.
- Employment will decline because of technological advances and consolidation.
- With rapid technological changes in telecommunications, those with up-to-date technical skills will have the best job opportunities.
- Average earnings in telecommunications greatly exceed average earnings throughout nongovernment fields.

Nature of the Field

The telecommunications field is at the forefront of the information age—delivering voice, data, graphics and video at ever-increasing speeds and in an increasing number of ways. Whereas wireline telephone communication was once the primary service of the field, wireless communication services and cable and satellite program distribution make up an increasing share of the field.

During the late 1990s, the telecommunications field experienced very rapid growth and massive investment in transmission capacity. Eventually this caused supply to significantly exceed demand, resulting in much lower prices for transmission capacity. The excess capacity and additional competition led to either declining revenues or slowing revenue growth, which has led to consolidation within the field as many companies merged or left the field.

The largest sector of the telecommunications field continues to be made up of wired telecommunications carriers. Establishments in this sector mainly provide telephone service via wires and cables that connect customers' premises to central offices maintained by telecommunications companies. The central offices contain switching equipment that routes content to its final destination or to another switching center that determines the most efficient route for the content to take. While voice used to be the main type of data transmitted over the wires, wired telecommunications service now includes the transmission of all types of graphic, video, and electronic data mainly over the Internet.

These new services have been made possible through the use of digital technologies that provide much more efficient use of the telecommunications networks. One major technology breaks digital signals into packets during transmission. Networks of computerized switching equipment, called packet-switched networks, route the packets. Packets may take separate paths to their destination and may share the paths with packets from other users. At the destination, the packets are reassembled, and the transmission is complete. Because packet switching considers alternate routes and allows multiple transmissions to share the same route, it results in a more efficient use of telecommunications capacity as packets are routed along less-congested routes.

The transmission of voice signals requires relatively small amounts of capacity on telecommunications networks.

By contrast, the transmission of data, video, and graphics requires much higher capacity. This transmission capacity is referred to as bandwidth. As the demand increases for high-capacity transmissions—especially with the rising volume of Internet data—telecommunications companies have been expanding and upgrading their networks to increase the amount of available bandwidth.

One way wired carriers are expanding their bandwidth is by replacing copper wires with fiber-optic cable. Fiber-optic cable, which transmits light signals along glass strands, permits faster, higher-capacity transmissions than traditional copper wirelines. In some areas, carriers are extending fiber-optic cable to residential customers, enabling them to offer cable television, video-on-demand, high-speed Internet, and conventional telephone communications over a single line. However, the high cost of extending fiber to homes has slowed deployment. In most areas, wired carriers are instead leveraging existing copper lines that connect most residential customers with a central office to provide digital subscriber lines (DSL) Internet service. Technologies in development will further boost the speeds available through a DSL connection.

Wireless telecommunications carriers, many of which are subsidiaries of the wired carriers, transmit voice, graphics, data, and Internet access through the transmission of signals over networks of radio towers. The signal is transmitted through an antenna into the wireline network. Other wireless services include beeper and paging services. Because wireless devices require no wireline connection, they are popular with customers who need to communicate as they travel, residents of areas with inadequate wireline service, and those who simply desire the convenience of portable communications. Increasing numbers of consumers are choosing to replace their home landlines with wireless phones.

Wireless telecommunications carriers are deploying several new technologies to allow faster data transmission and better Internet access that should make them competitive with wireline carriers. One technology is called third generation (3G) wireless access. With this technology, wireless carriers plan to sell music, videos, and other exclusive content that can be downloaded and played on phones designed for 3G technology. Wireless carriers are developing the next generation of technologies that will surpass 3G with even faster data transmission. Another

Information

technology is called "fixed wireless service," which involves connecting the telephone and/or Internet wiring system in a home or business to an antenna instead of a telephone line. The replacement of landlines with cellular service should become increasingly common because advances in wireless systems will provide data transmission speeds comparable to broadband landline systems.

Cable and other program distribution is another sector of the telecommunications field. Establishments in this sector provide television and other services on a subscription or fee basis. These establishments do not include cable networks. (Information on cable networks is included in the description of Broadcasting, which appears elsewhere in Part II.) Distributors of pay television services transmit programming through two basic types of systems. Cable systems transmit programs over fiber-optic and coaxial cables. Direct broadcasting satellite (DBS) operators constitute a growing segment of the pay television field. DBS operators transmit programming from orbiting satellites to customers' receivers, known as minidishes.

Establishments in the cable and other program distribution field generate revenue through subscriptions, special service fees—primarily installation—and advertising sales. They also charge fees for services, such as the transmission of specialty pay-per-view or video-on-demand programs; these often are popular movies or sporting events.

Some cable and satellite systems facilitate the transmission of digital television signals. Digital signals consist of simple electronic code that can carry more information than conventional television signals. Digital transmission creates higher-resolution television images and improved sound quality. It also allows the transmission of a variety of other information. Digital television also uses compression technology to expand the number of channels.

Changes in technology and regulation now allow cable television providers to compete directly with telephone companies. An important change has been the rapid increase in two-way communications capacity. Conventional pay television services provided communications only from the distributor to the customer. These services could not provide effective communications from the customer back to other points in the system due to signal interference and the limited capacity of conventional cable systems. As cable operators implement new technologies to reduce signal interference and

increase the capacity of their distribution systems by installing fiber-optic cables and improved data compression, some pay television systems now offer two-way telecommunications services, such as video-on-demand and high-speed Internet access. Cable companies are also increasing their share of the telephone communications market both through their network of conventional phone lines in some areas and their growing ability to use high-speed Internet access to provide VoIP (voice over Internet protocol).

VoIP is sometimes called Internet telephony because it uses the Internet to transmit phone calls. While conventional phone networks use packet switching to break up a call onto multiple shared lines between central offices, VoIP extends this process to the phone. A VoIP phone will break the conversation into digital packets and transmit those packets over a high-speed Internet connection. Cable companies are using the technology to offer phone services without building a conventional phone network. Wireline providers' high-speed Internet connections also can be used for VoIP, and cellular phones are being developed that use VoIP to make calls using local wireless Internet connections. All of the major sectors of the telecommunications field are or will increasingly use VoIP.

Resellers of telecommunications services are another sector of the telecommunications field. These resellers lease transmission facilities, such as telephone lines or space on a satellite, from existing telecommunications networks and then resell the service to other customers. Other sectors in the field include message communications services, such as e-mail and facsimile services, satellite telecommunications, and operators of other communication services ranging from radar stations to radio networks used by taxicab companies.

Working Conditions

The telecommunications field offers steady, year-round employment. Overtime sometimes is required, especially during emergencies such as floods or hurricanes when employees may need to report to work with little notice.

Installation, maintenance, and repair occupations account for 1 in 4 telecommunications jobs. Telecommunications line installers and repairers, one of the largest occupations, work in a variety of places, both indoors and outdoors, and in all kinds of weather. Their work involves lifting, climbing, reaching, stooping, crouching, and crawling. They must work in high places such as rooftops and telephone poles or below ground when working with buried lines. Their jobs bring them into proximity with electrical wires and circuits, so they must take precautions to avoid shocks. These workers must wear safety equipment when entering manholes and test for the presence of gas before going underground.

Telecommunications equipment installers and repairers, except line installers, generally work indoors—most often in a telecommunication company's central office or a customer's place of business. They may have to stand for long periods; climb ladders; and do some reaching, stooping, and light lifting. Adherence to safety precautions is essential to guard against work injuries such as minor burns and electrical shock.

Most communications equipment operators, such as telephone operators, work at video display terminals in pleasant, well-lighted, air-conditioned surroundings. If the worksite is not well designed, however, operators may experience eye strain and back discomfort. The rapid pace of the job and close supervision may cause stress. Some workplaces have introduced innovative practices among their operators to reduce job-related stress.

Most other telecommunications managers, administrative workers, and professionals work 40-hour weeks in comfortable offices. Customer service representatives may work in call centers where they answer customer service calls—many during evening and weekend hours.

The number of disabling injuries in telephone communications, the principal sector of the telecommunications field, has been well below the average for all fields in past years.

Important Characteristics of the Field

Skills: Installation; Troubleshooting; Repairing; Technology Design. **Abilities:** Wrist-Finger Speed; Gross Body Equilibrium; Explosive Strength; Dynamic Strength; Sound Localization; Spatial Orientation. **Work-Related Values:** Supervision, Technical; Supervision, Human Relations; Security; Advancement; Company Policies and Practices; Variety.

Employment

The telecommunications field provided 1 million wage and salary jobs in 2004. Most telecommunications employees work in large establishments. Seventy-three percent of employment is in establishments with 50 or more employees (chart 1). With continuing deregulation, however, the number of small contractors has been increasing. Telecommunications jobs are found in almost every community, but most employees work in cities that have large concentrations of industrial and business establishments.

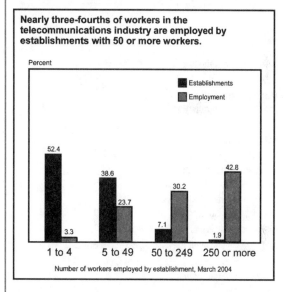

Nearly three-fourths of workers in the telecommunications industry are employed by establishments with 50 or more workers.

Percent

- Establishments
- Employment

1 to 4	52.4 / 3.3
5 to 49	38.6 / 23.7
50 to 249	7.1 / 30.2
250 or more	1.9 / 42.8

Number of workers employed by establishment, March 2004

Occupations in the Field

Although the telecommunications field employs workers in many different occupations, 55 percent of all workers are employed in either office and administrative support occupations or installation, maintenance, and repair occupations (table 1).

Telecommunications craftworkers install, repair, and maintain telephone equipment, cables and access lines, and telecommunications systems. These workers can be grouped by the type of work they perform. *Line installers and repairers* connect central offices to customers' buildings. They install poles and terminals and place wires and cables that lead to a consumer's premises. Some may install lines or equipment inside a customer's business or residence. They use power-driven equipment to dig holes and set telephone poles. Line installers climb the poles or

Information

use truck-mounted buckets (aerial work platforms) and attach the cables using various hand tools. After line installers place cables on poles or towers or in underground conduits and trenches, they complete the line connections. Some line installers, called *cable splicers*, specialize in splicing together two telecommunication lines.

Table 1. Employment of wage and salary workers in telecommunications by occupation, 2004 and projected change, 2004–2014 (Employment in thousands)

Occupation	Employment, 2004 Number	Percent	Percent change, 2004–2014
Total, all occupations	1,043	100.0	–6.5
Management, business, and financial occupations	116	11.1	–5.5
Top executives	12	1.2	–2.6
Marketing and sales managers	9	0.8	1.1
Computer and information systems managers	7	0.6	4.1
Human resources, training, and labor relations specialists	11	1.0	–3.6
Management analysts	10	1.0	–19.9
Accountants and auditors	8	0.8	–1.9
Professional and related occupations	181	17.4	–1.1
Computer software engineers	39	3.8	–2.8
Computer support specialists	12	1.2	–1.7
Computer systems analysts	14	1.4	1.3
Network and computer systems administrators	14	1.3	–0.5
Network systems and data communications analysts	14	1.3	24.3
Engineers	39	3.7	–1.9
Electrical and electronic engineering technicians	13	1.2	–4.5
Sales and related occupations	162	15.5	–7.0
Supervisors, sales workers	15	1.4	–1.9
Retail salespersons	24	2.3	12.6
Sales representatives, services, all other	53	5.1	–7.5
Sales representatives, wholesale and manufacturing	26	2.5	0.3
Telemarketers	25	2.4	–34.7
Office and administrative support occupations	307	29.5	–7.2
First-line supervisors/ managers of office and administrative support workers	24	2.3	–12.3
Telephone operators	27	2.6	–42.3
Bill and account collectors	12	1.1	–5.9
Bookkeeping, accounting, and auditing clerks	12	1.1	–14.0
Customer service representatives	133	12.7	11.3
Production, planning, and expediting clerks	13	1.2	–18.9
Secretaries and administrative assistants	16	1.6	–12.9
Office clerks, general	21	2.1	–18.8
Installation, maintenance, and repair occupations	269	25.8	–9.4
First-line supervisors/ managers of mechanics, installers, and repairers	22	2.1	–11.7
Telecommunications equipment installers and repairers	140	13.5	–17.2
Line installers and repairers	89	8.6	–0.5

Note: May not add to totals due to omission of occupations with small employment

Telecommunications equipment installers and repairers, except line installers, install, repair, and maintain the array of increasingly complex and sophisticated communications equipment and cables. Their work includes setting up, rearranging, and removing the complex switching and dialing equipment used in central offices. They may also solve network-related problems and program equipment to provide special features.

Some telecommunications equipment installers are referred to as telephone station installers and repairers. They install, service, and repair telephone systems and other communications equipment on customers' property. When customers move or request new types of service, such as a high-speed Internet connection, a fax, or an additional line, installers relocate telephones or make changes in existing equipment. They assemble equipment and install wiring. They also connect telephones to outside service wires and sometimes must climb poles or ladders to make these connections.

Cable installers travel to customers' premises to set up pay television service so that customers can receive programming. Cable service installers connect a customer's television set to the cable serving the entire neighborhood. Wireless and satellite service installers attach antennas or satellite dishes to the sides of customers' houses. These devices must be positioned to provide clear lines of sight to satellite locations. (Satellite installation may be handled by employees of retail stores that sell satellite dishes. Such workers are not employed by cable and other pay television services.)

Installers check the strength and clarity of the television signal before completing the installation. They may need to explain to the subscriber how pay television services operate. As these services expand to include telephone and high-speed Internet access, an understanding of the basic technology and computer software and an ability to communicate that knowledge are increasingly important.

Telephone operators make telephone connections, assist customers with specialized services such as reverse-charge calls, provide telephone numbers, and may provide emergency assistance.

Customer service representatives help customers understand the new and varied types of services offered by telecommunications providers. Some customer service representatives also are expected to sell services and may work on a commission basis. Other administrative support workers include *financial, information, and records clerks*; *secretaries and administrative assistants*; and *first-line supervisors/managers of office and administrative support workers*. These workers keep service records, compile and send bills to customers, and prepare statistical and other company reports, among other duties.

Seventeen percent of the field's employees are professional workers. Many of these are scientific and technical personnel such as engineers and computer specialists. *Engineers* plan cable and microwave routes, central office and PBX equipment installations, and the expansion of existing structures and solve other engineering problems. Some engineers also engage in research and development of new equipment. Many specialize in telecommunications design or voice, video, or data communications systems and integrate communications equipment with computer networks. Others research, design, and develop gas lasers and related equipment needed to send messages through fiber-optic cables. They study the limitations and uses of lasers and fiber optics; find new applications for them; and oversee the building, testing, and operations of the new applications. They work closely with clients, who may not understand sophisticated communications systems, and design systems that meet their customers' needs.

Computer software engineers and *network systems and data communications analysts* design, develop, test, and debug software products. These include computer-assisted engineering programs for schematic cabling projects; modeling programs for cellular and satellite systems; and programs for telephone options, such as voice mail, e-mail, and call waiting. Telecommunications specialists coordinate the installation of these systems and may provide follow-up maintenance and training. In addition, the field employs many other managerial, business and financial, professional, and technical workers, such as *accountants and auditors*; *human resources, training, and labor relations managers*; *engineering technicians*; and *computer programmers*.

Training, Other Qualifications, and Advancement

The telecommunications field offers employment in jobs requiring a variety of skills and training. Many jobs require at least a high school diploma or an associate degree in addition to on-the-job training. Other jobs require particular skills that may take several years of experience to learn completely. For some managerial and professional jobs, employers require a college education.

Telecommunications line installers and repairers often are hired initially as helpers, grounds workers, or tree trimmers who clear branches from lines. Because the

Information

work entails a lot of climbing, applicants should have physical stamina and be unafraid of heights. The ability to distinguish colors is important because wires and cables are coded by color. Although many line installers and repairers do not complete a formal apprenticeship, they generally receive several years of on-the-job training, which may also include some classroom or online training. Line installers may transfer to other highly skilled jobs, such as telecommunications equipment installer and repairer, or may move into other kinds of work, such as sales. Promotion to crew supervisor, technical staff, or instructor of new employees also is possible.

Most companies prefer to hire telecommunications equipment installers and repairers with postsecondary training in electronics; some choose to hire persons with experience as line installers. Training sources include 2-year and 4-year college programs in electronics or communications, trade schools, and training provided by telecommunications companies and/or equipment and software manufacturers. Telecommunications equipment installers and repairers may advance to jobs maintaining more sophisticated equipment or to engineering technician positions.

For sales jobs, individuals with sales ability enhanced by interpersonal skills and knowledge of telecommunications terminology also are sought.

Communications equipment operators should have clear speech and good hearing; computer literacy and keyboarding skills also are important. New operators learn equipment operation and procedures for maximizing efficiency. Instructors monitor both the time and quality of trainees' responses to customer requests. Formal classroom instruction and on-the-job training may last several weeks.

A bachelor's degree in engineering usually is required for entry-level jobs as electrical and electronics engineers. Continuing education is important for these engineers; those who fail to keep up with the rapid changes in technology risk technological obsolescence, which makes them more susceptible to layoffs or, at a minimum, more likely to be passed over for advancement.

While there is no universally accepted way to prepare for a job as a computer professional, most employers place a premium on some formal college education. Computer software engineers usually hold a degree in computer science or in software engineering. For systems analyst,

computer scientist, or database administrator positions, many employers seek applicants who have a bachelor's degree in computer science, information science, or management information systems.

Due to the rapid introduction of new technologies and services, the telecommunications field is among the most rapidly changing in the economy. This means workers must keep their job skills up to date. From managers to communications equipment operators, increased knowledge of both computer hardware and software is of paramount importance. Several major companies and the telecommunications unions have created a Web site that provides free training for employees, enabling them to keep their knowledge current and helping them to advance. Telecommunications field employers now look for workers with knowledge of and skills in computer programming and software design; voice telephone technology, known as telephony; laser and fiber-optic technology; wireless technology; and data compression.

Outlook

Employment in the telecommunications field is expected to decline 7 percent over the 2004–2014 period, compared with 14 percent growth for all fields combined. Field consolidation and strong price competition among telecommunications firms will decrease employment as companies try to reduce their costs. Additionally, technological improvements, such as high-speed wireless data transmission, fiber-optic lines, and advanced switching equipment, have massively increased the data transmission capacity of telecommunications networks and resulted in much higher productivity that will further reduce employment. Telecommunications equipment also is more reliable and requires less monitoring. In spite of the declining employment, a growing number of retirements and need for skilled workers will create good job opportunities for individuals with up-to-date technical skills.

The field will continue to grow despite the lower employment as people and businesses will demand ever wider ranges of telecommunications services. The growth of high-speed Internet and video services will lead to continued upgrades of telecommunications networks. Residential customers will use an increasing range of services as technology and competition lower the price of high-speed Internet access, video-on-demand, and wireless and Internet-based telephone services. Cable companies and telephone companies will both offer cable television, high-speed Internet, and phone services. Wireless carriers will compete directly with the residential wired services, providing increasingly reliable cellular communications and increasingly faster Internet service. Therefore, the lines between cable and satellite TV, wireless, and wireline telephone systems will become blurred.

Business demand will rise as companies increasingly rely on their telecommunications systems to conduct electronic commerce, ordering, record keeping, and video conferencing. In order to remain competitive, businesses will require higher-speed access to the Internet.

Technology is continuing to transform the field and will continue to bring on line a wider array of services to homes and businesses. The installation and upgrading of fiber-optic networks will bring ever faster communications to residential customers' homes. Internet telephony will blur the boundaries between telecommunications providers and Internet service providers. Wireless providers will continue to increase the capacity of their radio networks and introduce improved portable, lightweight devices capable of transmitting voice, data, e-mail, Internet access, and video. New phones will blur boundaries between phones and computers. Some wireless phones will not only function on traditional wireless networks, but also will use VoIP technology to make phone calls through local wireless Internet networks. Undersea cables and orbiting satellites are integrating wireline and wireless customers into a global system of high-speed communications.

Employment growth will differ among the various occupations in the telecommunications field, largely as a result of technological change. Employment of communications equipment operators is expected to decline due to increasing automation. Computer voice recognition technology lessens the need for central office operators as customers can obtain help with long-distance calls from automated systems. This technology, which also enables callers to request numbers from a computer instead of a person, is expected to reduce the number of directory assistance operators. The numbers of these workers will drop further as more customers use automated directory assistance resources on the Internet.

Employment of line installers and repairers is expected to decrease due to more reliable equipment and expanding applications of wireless technology. Employment of telecommunications equipment installers and repairers is

expected to decline because newer, more reliable technologies will reduce the need for equipment maintenance. Employment of these workers also will be limited by the tendency of many companies to contract out maintenance and installation work to specialized contractors that are part of the construction or retail fields. However, there still will be many openings available for individuals with the necessary technical skills.

Employment of electrical and electronics engineers and computer professionals is expected to change only slightly. The expansion of communications networks, and the need for telecommunications providers to invest in research and development, will create some job opportunities for these workers. However, the increasing standardization of telecommunications technology will limit their employment.

Earnings

Average weekly earnings of nonsupervisory workers in the telecommunications field were $853 in 2004, significantly higher than the average earnings of $529 in non-government fields. Table 2 presents earnings in selected occupations in telecommunications in 2004.

Table 2. Median hourly earnings of the largest occupations in telecommunications, May 2004

Occupation	Tele-communications	All fields
Computer software engineers, systems software	$35.46	$38.34
Electronics engineers, except computer	32.84	36.43
First-line supervisors/managers of office and administrative support workers	25.08	19.72
Telecommunications equipment installers and repairers, except line installers	24.65	23.96
Sales representatives, services, all other	24.18	22.60
Telecommunications line installers and repairers	22.78	19.39
Telephone operators	16.01	13.65
Customer service representatives	15.34	12.99
Telemarketers	14.63	9.82
Retail salespersons	12.05	8.98

Sources of Additional Information

For information about employment opportunities, contact your local telecommunications company or

- International Brotherhood of Electrical Workers, Telecommunications Department, 900 Seventh St. NW, Washington, DC 20001.
- Communications Workers of America, 501 3rd St. NW, Washington, DC 20001.

For information about certifications and courses on cable and telecommunications technology, contact

- Society of Cable and Telecommunications Engineers (SCTE), 140 Phillips Rd., Exton, PA 19341-1318. Internet: http://www.scte.org

Financial Activities

Banking

- Annual Earnings: $28,784
- Job Growth: –1.8%
- Size of Workforce: 1,774,530
- Self-Employed: 0.2%
- Part-Time: 10.6%

Significant Points

- Wage and salary employment in banking is projected to decline 2 percent over the 2004–2014 period, compared to 14 percent growth for wage and salary employment across all fields, as consolidation and automation make banks more efficient.
- Office and administrative support workers constitute 2 out of 3 jobs; tellers account for about 1 out of 4 jobs.
- Many job opportunities are expected for tellers and other office and administrative support workers because these occupations are large and have high turnover.

- Many management positions are filled by promoting experienced, technically skilled professional personnel.

Nature of the Field

Banks safeguard money and valuables and provide loans; credit; and payment services, such as checking accounts, money orders, and cashier's checks. Banks also may offer investment and insurance products, which they were once prohibited from selling. As a variety of models for cooperation and integration among finance fields have emerged, some of the traditional distinctions between banks, insurance companies, and securities firms have diminished. In spite of these changes, banks continue to maintain and perform their primary role—accepting deposits and lending funds from these deposits.

There are several types of banks, which differ in the number of services they provide and the clientele they serve. Although some of the differences between these types of banks have lessened as they begin to expand the range of products and services they offer, there are still key distinguishing traits. *Commercial banks*, which dominate this field, offer a full range of services for individuals, businesses, and governments. These banks come in a wide range of sizes, from large global banks to regional and community banks. Global banks are involved in international lending and foreign currency trading in addition to the more typical banking services. Regional banks have numerous branches and automated teller machine (ATM) locations throughout a multi-state area that provide banking services to individuals. Banks have become more oriented toward marketing and sales. As a result, employees need to know about all types of products and services offered by banks. Community banks are based locally and offer more personal attention, which many individuals and small businesses prefer. In recent years, online banks—which provide all services entirely over the Internet—have entered the market, with some success. However, many traditional banks have also expanded to offer online banking, and some formerly Internet-only banks are opting to open branches.

Savings banks and *savings and loan associations*, sometimes called thrift institutions, are the second largest group of depository institutions. They were first established as community-based institutions to finance mortgages for people to buy homes and still cater mostly to the savings and lending needs of individuals.

Credit unions are another kind of depository institution. Most credit unions are formed by people with a common bond, such as those who work for the same company or belong to the same labor union or church. Members pool their savings and, when they need money, they may borrow from the credit union, often at a lower interest rate than that demanded by other financial institutions.

Federal Reserve banks are government agencies that perform many financial services for the government. Their chief responsibilities are to regulate the banking field and to help implement our nation's monetary policy so our economy can run more efficiently by controlling the nation's money supply—the total quantity of money in the country, including cash and bank deposits. For example, during slower periods of economic activity, the Federal Reserve may purchase government securities from commercial banks, giving them more money to lend, thus expanding the economy. Federal Reserve banks also perform a variety of services for other banks. For example, they may make emergency loans to banks that are short of cash and clear checks that are drawn and paid out by different banks.

Interest on loans is the principal source of revenue for most banks, making their various lending departments critical to their success. The commercial lending department loans money to companies to start or expand a business or to purchase inventory and capital equipment. The consumer lending department handles student loans; credit cards; and loans for home improvements, debt consolidation, and automobile purchases. Finally, the mortgage lending department loans money to individuals and businesses to purchase real estate.

The money to lend comes primarily from deposits in checking and savings accounts, certificates of deposit, money market accounts, and other deposit accounts that consumers and businesses set up with the bank. These deposits often earn interest for the owner, and accounts that offer checking provide an easy method for making payments safely without using cash. Deposits in many banks are insured by the Federal Deposit Insurance Corporation, which ensures that depositors will get their money back, up to a stated limit, if a bank should fail.

Technology is having a major impact on the banking field. For example, many routine bank services that once required a teller, such as making a withdrawal or deposit, are now available through ATMs that allow people to access their accounts 24 hours a day. Also, direct deposit allows companies and governments to electronically transfer payments into various accounts. Further, debit cards, which may also used as ATM cards, instantaneously deduct money from an account when the card is swiped across a machine at a store's cash register. Electronic banking by phone or computer allows customers to pay bills and transfer money from one account to another. Through these channels, bank customers can also access information such as account balances and statement history. Some banks have begun offering online account aggregation, which makes available in one place detailed and up-to date information on a customer's accounts held at various institutions.

Advancements in technology have also led to improvements in the ways in which banks process information. Use of check imaging, which allows banks to store photographed checks on the computer, is one such example that has been implemented by some banks. Other types of technology have greatly impacted the lending side of banking. For example, the availability and growing use of credit scoring software allows loans to be approved in minutes, rather than days, making lending departments more efficient.

Other fundamental changes are occurring in the field as banks diversify their services to become more competitive. Many banks now offer their customers financial planning and asset management services, as well as brokerage and insurance services, often through a subsidiary or third party. Others are beginning to provide investment banking services that help companies and governments raise money through the issuance of stocks and bonds, also usually through a subsidiary. As banks respond to deregulation and as competition in this sector grows, the nature of the banking field will continue to undergo significant change.

Working Conditions

The average workweek for nonsupervisory workers in depository credit intermediation was 35.8 hours in 2004. Supervisory and managerial employees, however, usually work substantially longer hours. About 1 out of 10 employees in 2004, mostly tellers, worked part time.

Working conditions also vary according to where the employee works. Employees in a typical branch work weekdays, some evenings if the bank is open late, and Saturday mornings. Hours may be longer for workers in bank branches located in grocery stores and shopping malls, which are open most evenings and weekends. Branch office jobs, particularly teller positions, require continual communication with customers, repetitive tasks, and a high level of attention to security. Tellers also work for long periods in a confined space.

To improve customer service and provide greater access to bank personnel, banks are establishing centralized phone centers, staffed mainly by customer service representatives. Employees of phone centers spend most of their time answering phone calls from customers and must be available to work evening and weekend shifts.

Administrative support employees may work in large processing facilities, in the banks' headquarters, or in other administrative offices. Most support staff work a standard 40-hour week; some may work overtime. Those support staff located in the processing facilities may work evening shifts.

Commercial and mortgage loan officers often work out of the office, visiting clients, checking out loan applications, and soliciting new business. Loan officers may be required to travel if a client is out of town or to work evenings if that is the only time at which a client can meet. Financial service sales representatives also may visit clients in the evenings and on weekends to go over the client's financial needs.

The remaining employees located primarily at the headquarters or other administrative offices usually work in comfortable surroundings and put in a standard workweek. In general, banks are relatively safe places to work. In 2003, the rate of work-related injury and illness per 100 full-time workers was 3.1 in monetary authorities—central bank and 1.3 in depository credit intermediation, lower than the overall rate of 5.0 per 100 employees in the private sector.

Important Characteristics of the Field

Skills: Service Orientation; Management of Financial Resources; Speaking; Active Listening; Social Perceptiveness; Persuasion. **Abilities:** Number Facility; Mathematical Reasoning; Speech Recognition; Speech Clarity; Oral Expression; Written Expression. **Work-Related Values:** Working Conditions; Co-workers; Social Service; Advancement; Supervision, Human Relations; Supervision, Technical.

Employment

The banking field employed about 1.8 million wage and salary workers in 2004. About 7 out of 10 jobs were in commercial banks; the remainder were concentrated in savings institutions and credit unions (table 1).

Table 1. Percent distribution of employment in banking by type of institution, 2004

Field segment	Establishments	Employment
Total	100.0	100.0
Monetary authorities —central bank	0.2	1.2
Depository credit intermediation	99.8	98.8
Commercial banking	69.0	72.2
Savings institutions	15.2	13.8
Credit unions	14.5	11.8
Other depository credit intermediation	1.1	1.0

In 2004, about 83 percent of establishments in banking employed fewer than 20 workers (chart 1). However, these small establishments, mostly bank branch offices, employed 34 percent of all employees. About 66 percent

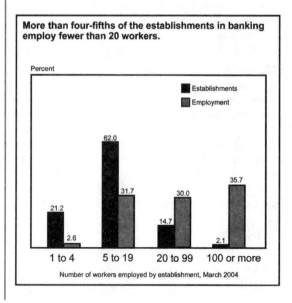

More than four-fifths of the establishments in banking employ fewer than 20 workers.

Percent

■ Establishments
■ Employment

1 to 4	5 to 19	20 to 99	100 or more
21.2 / 2.6	62.0 / 31.7	14.7 / 30.0	2.1 / 35.7

Number of workers employed by establishment, March 2004

of the jobs were in establishments with 20 or more workers. Banks are found everywhere in the United States, but most bank employees work in heavily populated states such as New York, California, Illinois, Pennsylvania, and Texas.

Occupations in the Field

Office and administrative support occupations account for 2 out of 3 jobs in the banking field (table 2). *Bank tellers*, the largest number of workers in banking, provide routine financial services to the public. They handle customers' deposits and withdrawals, change money, sell money orders and traveler's checks, and accept payment for loans and utility bills. Increasingly, tellers also are selling bank services to customers. *New accounts clerks* and *customer service representatives* answer questions from customers and help them open and close accounts and fill out forms to apply for banking services. They are knowledgeable about a broad array of bank services and must be able to sell those services to potential clients. Some customer service representatives work in a call or customer contact center environment, taking phone calls and answering e-mails from customers. In addition to responding to inquiries, these workers also help customers over the phone with routine banking transactions and handle and resolve problems or complaints.

Loan and *credit clerks* assemble and prepare paperwork, process applications, and complete the documentation after a loan or line of credit has been approved. They also verify applications for completeness. *Bill and account collectors* attempt to collect payments on overdue loans. Many *general office clerks* and *bookkeeping, accounting, and auditing clerks* are employed to maintain financial records; enter data; and process the thousands of deposit slips, checks, and other documents that banks handle daily. Banks also employ many *secretaries*, *data entry and information processing workers*, *receptionists*, and other office and administrative support workers. *Office and administrative support worker supervisors and managers* oversee the activities and training of workers in the various administrative support occupations.

Management, business, and financial occupations account for about 25 percent of employment in the banking field. *Financial managers* direct bank branches and departments, resolve customers' problems, ensure that standards of service are maintained, and administer the institutions' operations and investments. *Loan officers* evaluate loan applications, determine an applicant's ability to pay back a loan, and recommend approval of loans. They usually specialize in commercial, consumer, or mortgage lending. When loans become delinquent, loan officers, or *loan counselors*, may advise borrowers on the management of their finances or take action to collect outstanding amounts. Loan officers also play a major role in bringing in new business and spend much of their time developing relationships with potential customers. *Trust officers* manage a variety of assets that were placed in trust with the bank for other people or organizations; these assets can include pension funds, school endowments, or a company's profit-sharing plan. Sometimes, trust officers act as executors of estates upon a person's death. They also may work as accountants, lawyers, and investment managers.

Securities, commodities, and financial services sales agents, who make up the majority of sales positions in banks, sell complex banking services. They contact potential customers to explain their services and to ascertain the customer's banking and other financial needs. They also may discuss services such as deposit accounts, lines of credit, sales or inventory financing, certificates of deposit, cash management, or investment services. These sales agents also solicit businesses to participate in consumer credit card programs. At most small and medium-size banks, however, branch managers and commercial loan officers are responsible for marketing the bank's financial services. This has become a more important task in recent years.

Other occupations used widely by banks to maintain financial records and ensure the bank's compliance with federal and state regulations are *accountants and auditors* and *lawyers*. In addition, *computer specialists* are needed to maintain and upgrade the bank's computer systems and to implement the bank's entry into the world of electronic banking and paperless transactions.

Table 2. Employment of wage and salary workers in banking by occupation, 2004 and projected change, 2004–2014 (Employment in thousands)

Occupation	Employment, 2004		Percent change, 2004–2014
	Number	Percent	
Total, all occupations	1,783	100.0	–1.8
Management, business, and financial occupations	432	24.2	–0.1
Top executives	49	2.8	–1.1
General and operations managers	37	2.1	–1.3
Financial managers	78	4.4	0.3
Accountants and auditors	24	1.4	0.3
Credit analysts	14	0.8	–10.3
Financial analysts	19	1.1	19.5
Personal financial advisors	17	0.9	6.8
Financial examiners	5	0.3	–1.8
Loan counselors	6	0.4	–3.4
Loan officers	106	5.9	–5.7
Professional and related occupations	75	4.2	5.7
Computer support specialists	12	0.6	–0.3
Computer systems analysts	12	0.7	9.6
Sales and related occupations	63	3.5	3.8
Securities, commodities, and financial services sales agents	39	2.2	10.3
Office and administrative support occupations	1,193	66.9	–3.1
First-line supervisors/ managers of office and administrative support workers	108	6.0	–9.1
Bill and account collectors	22	1.2	–3.9
Bookkeeping, accounting, and auditing clerks	56	3.2	–10.3
Tellers	497	27.9	3.7
Brokerage clerks	7	0.4	–9.4
Credit authorizers, checkers, and clerks	12	0.7	–50.2
Customer service representatives	121	6.8	12.9
Loan interviewers and clerks	76	4.3	–14.0
New accounts clerks	88	4.9	–0.3
Information and record clerks, all other	12	0.7	–20.2
Secretaries and administrative assistants	59	3.3	–11.5
Data entry keyers	11	0.6	–23.0
Office clerks, general	43	2.4	–11.3
Office machine operators, except computer	10	0.6	–35.3

Note: May not add to totals due to omission of occupations with small employment

Training, Other Qualifications, and Advancement

Bank tellers and other clerks usually need only a high school education. Most banks seek people who have good basic math and communication skills, enjoy public contact, and feel comfortable handling large amounts of money. Through a combination of formal classroom instruction and on-the-job training under the guidance of an experienced worker, tellers learn the procedures, rules, and regulations that govern their jobs. Banks are offering more products and spending more on reaching out to their customers. As a result, they will need more creative and talented people to compete in the marketplace. Banks encourage upward mobility by providing access to higher education and other sources of additional training.

Some banks have their own training programs which result in teller certification. Experienced tellers qualify for certification by taking required courses and passing examinations. Experienced tellers and clerks may advance to head teller, new accounts clerk, or customer service representative. Outstanding tellers who have had some college or specialized training are sometimes promoted to managerial positions.

Workers in management, business, and financial occupations usually have at least a college degree. A bachelor's degree in business administration or a liberal arts degree with business administration courses is suitable preparation, as is a bachelor's degree in any field followed by a master's degree in business administration (MBA). Many management positions are filled by promoting experienced, technically skilled professional personnel—for example, accountants, auditors, budget analysts, credit analysts, or financial analysts—or accounting or related department supervisors in large banks.

There are currently no specific licensing requirements for loan counselors and officers working in banks or credit unions. Training and licensing requirements for loan counselors and officers who work in mortgage banks or brokerages vary by state. These criteria also may vary depending on whether workers are employed by a mortgage bank or mortgage brokerage.

Various banking-related associations and private schools offer courses and programs for students interested in lending as well as for experienced loan officers who want to keep their skills current. The Banking Administration Institute offers the Loan Review Certificate program for persons who review and approve loans. The Mortgage Banking Association (MBA) offers the Certified Mortgage Banker (CMB) program. A candidate who earns the CMB exhibits a deep understanding of the mortgage business. To obtain the CMB, one must have 3 years of experience, earn educational credits, and pass an exam. Completion of these courses and programs generally enhances one's employment and advancement opportunities.

Financial services sales agents usually need a college degree; a major or courses in finance, accounting, economics, marketing, or related fields serve as excellent preparation. Experience in sales also is very helpful. These workers learn on the job under the supervision of bank officers. Sales agents selling securities need to be licensed by the National Association of Securities Dealers, and agents selling insurance also must obtain an appropriate license.

Advancement to higher-level executive, administrative, managerial, and professional positions may be accelerated by taking additional training. Banks often provide opportunities and encourage employees to take classes offered by banking and financial management–affiliated organizations or other educational institutions. Classes often deal with a different phase of financial management and banking, such as accounting management, budget management, corporate cash management, financial analysis, international banking, and data processing systems procedures and management. Employers also sponsor seminars and conferences and provide textbooks and other educational materials. Many employers pay all or part of the costs for those who successfully complete courses.

In recent years, the banking field has been revolutionized by technological advancements in computer and data processing equipment. Learning how to apply this technology can greatly improve one's skills and advancement opportunities in the banking field.

Outlook

Wage and salary employment in banking is projected to decline by about 2 percent between 2004 and 2014, compared with the 14 percent growth projected for wage and salary employment across all fields. Employment in the banking field declined from the 1980s to the 1990s as a result of bank consolidations and technology. In addition, many consumers transferred assets from bank deposits to investment accounts offered by stock brokers and mutual funds. Also, the banking business has faced much more intense competition in the lending business from credit card companies and specialized loan carriers. In recent years, employment in the banking field has stabilized. These factors are expected to continue but at a slower pace, and banks are expected to be better able to compete with nondepository institutions in the future.

The combined effects of technology, deregulation, mergers, and population growth will continue to affect total employment growth and the mix of occupations in the banking field. The decline in some office and administrative support occupations will be offset by growth in some professional and sales occupations. Job opportunities should still be favorable for tellers and other administrative support workers because they make up a large proportion of bank employees and have high turnover.

The consolidation which resulted from bank mergers contributed significantly to employment declines throughout much of the past decade. Merger activity—at a slower pace—is expected to continue over the projection period, dampening employment growth. At the same time, banks have begun to refocus on the branch as a critical means of servicing customers, and many banks will open more branch offices in areas in which the population is growing. However, because of widespread automation of many banking services, fewer employees will be hired to staff new branches than in the past.

Advances in technology should continue to have the most significant effect on employment in the banking field. Demand for computer specialists will grow as more banks make their services available electronically and eliminate much of the paperwork involved in many banking transactions. On the other hand, these changes in technology will reduce the need for some office and administrative support occupations. Employment growth among tellers will be limited as customers increasingly use ATMs, direct deposit, debit cards, and telephone and Internet banking to perform routine transactions. Other technological improvements, such as digital imaging and computer networking, are likely to lead to a decrease or change in the nature of employment of the "back-office" clerical workers who process checks and other bank statements. Employment of customer service representatives, however, is expected to increase as banks hire more of these workers to staff phone centers and respond to e-mails.

Deregulation of the banking field allows banks to offer a variety of financial and insurance products that they were once prohibited from selling. The need to develop, analyze, and sell these new services will spur demand for securities and financial services sales representatives, financial analysts, and personal financial advisors. Demand for "personal bankers" to advise and manage the assets of wealthy clients, as well as the aging baby-boom generation, also will grow. However, banks will continue to face considerable competition—particularly in lending—from nonbank establishments, such as consumer credit companies and mortgage brokers. Companies and individuals now are able to obtain loans and credit and raise money through a variety of means other than bank loans. Therefore, some loan officers may be replaced by financial services sales representatives, who sell loans along with other bank services.

Earnings

Earnings of nonsupervisory bank employees involved in depository credit intermediation averaged $494 a week in May 2004, compared with $684 for all workers in finance and insurance fields and $529 for workers throughout the private sector. Relatively low pay in the banking field reflects the high proportion of low-paying administrative support jobs.

Earnings in the banking field vary significantly by occupation. Earnings in the largest occupations in banking appear in table 3.

Table 3. Median hourly earnings of the largest occupations in depository credit intermediation, May 2004

Occupation	Depository credit intermediation	All fields
Financial managers	$31.02	$39.37
Loan officers	21.38	23.48
First-line supervisors/managers of office and administrative support workers	17.78	19.72
Executive secretaries and administrative assistants	16.52	16.81
Loan interviewers and clerks	13.13	13.94
New accounts clerks	12.84	12.91
Customer service representatives	12.57	12.99
Bookkeeping, accounting, and auditing clerks	12.33	13.74
Office clerks, general	11.21	10.95
Tellers	10.17	10.15

In general, greater responsibilities result in a higher salary. Experience, length of service, and, especially, the location and size of the bank also are important. In addition to typical benefits, equity sharing and performance-based pay increasingly are part of compensation packages for some bank employees. As banks encourage employees to become more sales-oriented, incentives are increasingly tied to meeting sales goals, and some workers may even receive commissions for sales or referrals. As in other fields, part-time workers do not enjoy the same benefits that full-time workers do.

Sources of Additional Information

State bankers' associations can furnish specific information about job opportunities in their state. Individual banks can provide detailed information about job openings and the activities, responsibilities, and preferred qualifications of banking personnel.

For more information about career opportunities in executive search consulting, contact

- Bank Administration Institute, 1 North Franklin St., Chicago, IL 60606.

Information about careers with the Federal Reserve System is available from the Web site or human resources department of the various regional Federal Reserve Banks.

Insurance

- Annual Earnings: $38,590
- Job Growth: 9.5%
- Size of Workforce: 2,128,080
- Self-Employed: 5.6%
- Part-Time: 8.6%

Significant Points

- While corporate downsizing; productivity increases due to new technology; and increasing use of direct mail, telephone, and Internet sales will limit job growth in this large field, numerous job openings will arise from the need to replace those who leave or retire.

- Growing areas of the insurance field are medical services and health insurance and expansion into other financial services such as securities and mutual funds.

- Office and administrative occupations usually require a high school diploma, whereas employers prefer college graduates for sales, managerial, and professional jobs.

Nature of the Field

The insurance field provides protection against financial losses resulting from a variety of perils. By purchasing insurance policies, individuals and businesses can receive reimbursement for losses due to car accidents, theft of property, and fire and storm damage; medical expenses; and loss of income due to disability or death.

The insurance field consists mainly of *insurance carriers* (or *insurers*) and *insurance agencies and brokerages*. In general, insurance carriers are large companies that provide insurance and assume the risks covered by the policy. Insurance agencies and brokerages sell insurance policies for the carriers. While some of these establishments are directly affiliated with a particular insurer and sell only that carrier's policies, many are independent and are thus free to market the policies of a variety of insurance carriers. In addition to supporting these two primary components, the insurance field includes establishments that provide other insurance-related services, such as claims adjustment or third-party administration of insurance and pension funds.

Insurance carriers assume the risk associated with annuities and insurance policies and assign premiums to be paid for the policies. In the policy, the carrier states the length and conditions of the agreement, exactly which losses it will provide compensation for, and how much will be awarded. The premium charged for the policy is based primarily on the amount to be awarded in case of loss as well as the likelihood that the insurance carrier will actually have to pay. In order to be able to compensate policyholders for their losses, insurance companies invest the money they receive in premiums, building up a portfolio of financial assets and income-producing real estate which can then be used to pay off any future claims that may be brought. There are two basic types of insurance carriers: *direct* and *reinsurance*. Direct carriers are responsible for the initial underwriting of insurance policies and annuities, while reinsurance carriers assume all or part of the risk associated with the existing insurance policies originally underwritten by other insurance carriers.

Direct insurance carriers offer a variety of insurance policies. *Life insurance* provides financial protection to beneficiaries—usually spouses and dependent children—upon the death of the insured. *Disability insurance* supplies a preset income to an insured person who is unable to work due to injury or illness, and *health insurance* pays the expenses resulting from accidents and illness. *An annuity* (a contract or a group of contracts that furnishes a periodic income at regular intervals for a specified period) provides a steady income during retirement for the remainder of one's life. *Property-casualty insurance* protects against loss or damage to property resulting from hazards such as fire, theft, and natural disasters. *Liability insurance* shields policyholders from financial responsibility for injuries to others or for damage to other people's property. Most policies, such as automobile and homeowner's insurance, combine both property-casualty and liability coverage. Companies that underwrite this kind of insurance are called property-casualty carriers.

Some insurance policies cover groups of people, ranging from a few to thousands of individuals. These policies usually are issued to employers for the benefit of their employees or to unions, professional associations, or other membership organizations for the benefit of their members. Among the most common policies of this nature are group life and health plans. Insurance carriers also underwrite a variety of specialized types of insurance, such as real-estate title insurance, employee surety and fidelity bonding, and medical malpractice insurance.

A relatively recent act of Congress allows insurance carriers and other financial institutions, such as banks and securities firms, to sell one another's products. As a result, more insurance carriers now sell financial products such as securities, mutual funds, and various retirement plans. This approach is most common in life insurance companies that already sell annuities; however, property and casualty companies also are increasingly selling a wider range of financial products. In order to expand into one another's markets, insurance carriers, banks, and securities firms have engaged in numerous mergers, allowing the merging companies access to each other's client base and geographical markets.

Insurance carriers have discovered that the Internet can be a powerful tool for reaching potential and existing customers. Most carriers use the Internet simply to post company information, such as sales brochures and product information, financial statements, and a list of local agents. However, an increasing number of carriers are starting to expand their Web sites to enable customers to access online account and billing information, and a few carriers even allow claims to be submitted online. Some carriers also provide insurance quotes online based on the information submitted by customers on their Internet sites. In the future, carriers will allow customers to purchase policies through the Internet without ever speaking to a live agent.

In addition to individual carrier-sponsored Internet sites, several "lead-generating" sites have emerged. These sites allow potential customers to input information about their insurance policy needs. For a fee, the sites forward customer information to a number of insurance companies, which review the information and, if they decide to take on the policy, contact the customer with an offer.

This practice gives consumers the freedom to accept the best rate.

The insurance field also includes a number of independent organizations that provide a wide array of insurance-related services to carriers and their clients. One such service is the processing of claims forms for medical practitioners. Other services include loss prevention and risk management. Also, insurance companies sometimes hire independent claims adjusters to investigate accidents and claims for property damage and to assign a dollar estimate to the claim.

Other organizations in the field are formed by groups of insurance companies to perform functions that would result in a duplication of effort if each company carried them out individually. For example, service organizations are supported by insurance companies to provide loss statistics, which the companies use to set their rates.

Working Conditions

Many workers in the insurance field—especially those in administrative support positions—work a 5-day, 40-hour week. Those in executive and managerial occupations often put in more than 40 hours. Many insurance sales agents, claims adjusters, and investigators work irregular hours outside of office settings. Often, sales agents and adjusters arrange their own hours, scheduling evening and weekend appointments for the convenience of clients. This accommodation may result in these individuals working 50 to 60 hours per week.

Insurance sales agents often visit prospective and existing customers' homes and places of business to market new products and provide services. Claims adjusters and auto damage appraisers frequently leave the office to inspect damaged property; occasionally, claims adjusters are away from home for days, traveling to the scene of a disaster—such as a tornado, flood, or hurricane—to work with local adjusters and government officials. Insurance investigators often work irregular hours to conduct surveillance or to contact people who are not available during normal working hours.

A small, but increasing, number of insurance employees spend most of their time on the telephone working in call centers, answering questions and providing information to prospective clients or current policyholders. These jobs may include selling insurance, taking claims information, or answering medical questions. Because such centers operate 24 hours a day, 7 days a week, some of their employees must work evening and weekend shifts. The irregular business hours in the insurance field provide some workers with the opportunity for part-time work. Part-time employees make up 8 percent of the workforce. As would be expected in a field dominated by office and sales employees, the incidence of occupational injuries and illnesses among insurance workers is low. In 2003, only 1.5 cases per 100 full-time workers were reported among insurance carriers, while just 0.6 cases per 100 full-time workers were reported among agents and brokers. These figures compare with an average of 5.0 for all nongovernment fields.

Important Characteristics of the Field

Skills: Service Orientation; Persuasion; Speaking; Active Listening; Negotiation; Writing. **Abilities:** Speech Recognition; Mathematical Reasoning; Speech Clarity; Written Expression; Oral Expression; Number Facility. **Work-Related Values:** Working Conditions; Advancement; Supervision, Human Relations; Company Policies and Practices; Supervision, Technical; Social Service.

Employment

The insurance field employed about 2.3 million wage and salary workers in 2004. Insurance carriers accounted for 62 percent of jobs, while insurance agencies, brokerages, and providers of other insurance-related services accounted for 38 percent of jobs. In addition, about 151,000 workers in the field were self-employed in 2004, mostly insurance sales agents.

The majority of establishments in the insurance field were small; however, a few large establishments accounted for many of the jobs in this field. Insurance carriers tend to be large establishments, often employing 250 or more workers, whereas agencies and brokerages tend to be much smaller, frequently employing fewer than 20 workers (chart 1).

Many insurance carriers' home and regional offices are situated near large urban centers. Insurance workers who deal directly with the public—sales agents and claims adjusters—are located throughout the country. Almost all insurance sales agents work out of local company offices or independent agencies. Many claims adjusters

work for independent firms in small cities and towns throughout the country.

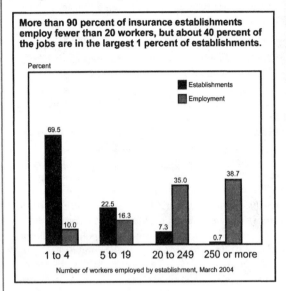

More than 90 percent of insurance establishments employ fewer than 20 workers, but about 40 percent of the jobs are in the largest 1 percent of establishments.

Percent

■ Establishments
■ Employment

69.5

22.5
16.3
10.0

35.0
7.3

38.7
0.7

1 to 4   5 to 19   20 to 249   250 or more

Number of workers employed by establishment, March 2004

Occupations in the Field

About 44 percent of insurance workers are in office and administrative support jobs found in every field, including secretaries, typists, word processors, bookkeepers, and other clerical workers (table 1). Many office and administrative support positions in the insurance field, however, require skills and knowledge unique to the field.

Customer service representatives, for example, process insurance policy applications, changes, and cancellations. They review applications for completeness, compile data on policy changes, and verify the accuracy of insurance company records. They may also process claims and sell new policies to existing clients. Nowadays, these workers are taking on increased responsibilities in insurance offices, such as handling most of the continuing contact with clients. A growing number of customer service representatives work in call centers that are open 24 hours a day, 7 days a week, where they answer clients' questions, update policy information, and provide potential clients with information regarding the types of policies the company issues.

About 28 percent of insurance workers are in management or business and financial operations occupations. *Marketing and sales managers* constitute the majority of managers in insurance carriers' local sales offices and in the insurance sales agents segment. These employees sell insurance products, work with clients, and supervise staff. Other managers who work in their companies' home offices are in charge of functions such as actuarial calculations, policy issuance, accounting, and investments.

Claims adjusters, examiners, and investigators decide whether claims are covered by the customer's policy, confirm payment, and, when necessary, investigate the circumstances surrounding a claim. Claims adjusters work for property and liability insurance carriers or for independent adjusting firms. They inspect property damage, estimate how much it will cost to repair, and determine the extent of the insurance company's liability; in some cases, they may help the claimant receive assistance quickly in order to prevent further damage and begin repairs. Adjusters plan and schedule the work required to process claims, which may include interviewing the claimant and witnesses and consulting police and hospital records. In some property-casualty companies, claims adjusters are called claims examiners, but in other companies, a claims examiner's primary job is to review claims to ensure that proper guidelines have been followed. Only occasionally—especially when disasters suddenly increase the volume of claims—do these examiners aid adjusters with complicated claims.

In the offices of life and health insurance carriers, claims examiners are the counterparts of the claims adjuster who works in a property and casualty insurance firm. Examiners in the health insurance field review health-related claims to see whether the costs are reasonable based on the diagnosis. Examiners check claim applications for completeness and accuracy, interview medical specialists, and consult policy files to verify information on a claim. Claims examiners in the life insurance field review causes of death and also may review new applications for life insurance to make sure that the applicants have no serious illnesses that would prevent them from qualifying for insurance.

Insurance investigators handle claims in which companies suspect fraudulent or criminal activity, such as suspicious fires, questionable workers' disability claims, difficult-to-explain accidents, and dubious medical treatment. Investigators usually perform database searches on suspects to determine whether they have a history of attempted or successful insurance fraud. Then, the investigators may visit claimants and witnesses to obtain a recorded statement, take photographs, inspect facilities, and conduct surveillance on suspects. Investigators often consult with legal counsel and are sometimes called to testify as expert witnesses in court cases.

Auto damage appraisers usually are hired by insurance companies and independent adjusting firms to inspect the damage to a motor vehicle after an accident and to provide unbiased estimates of repair cost. Claims adjusters and auto damage appraisers can work for insurance companies, or they can be independent or public adjusters. Insurance companies hire independent adjusters to represent their interests while assisting the insured, whereas public adjusters are hired to represent the insured's interests against insurance carriers.

Loss control representatives assess various risks faced by insurance companies. These workers inspect the business operations of insurance applicants; analyze historical data regarding workplace injuries and automobile accidents; and assess the potential for natural hazards, dangerous business practices, and unsafe workplace conditions that may result in injuries or catastrophic physical and financial loss. They might then recommend, for example, that a factory add safety equipment, that a house be reinforced to withstand environmental catastrophes, or that incentives be implemented to encourage automobile owners to install air bags in their cars or take more effective measures to prevent theft. Because the changes they recommend can greatly reduce the probability of loss, loss control representatives are increasingly important to both insurance companies and the insured.

Underwriting is another important management and business and financial occupation in insurance. *Underwriters* evaluate insurance applications to determine the risk involved in issuing a policy. They decide whether to accept or reject an application, and they determine the appropriate premium for each policy.

About 15 percent of wage and salary employees in the field are sales workers, selling policies to individuals and businesses. *Insurance sales agents*, also referred to as *producers*, may work as exclusive agents, or captive agents, selling for one company or as independent agents selling for several companies. Through regular contact with clients, agents are able to update coverage, assist with claims, ensure customer satisfaction, and obtain referrals. Insurance sales agents may sell many types of insurance, including life, annuities, property-casualty, health, and disability insurance. Many insurance sales agents are involved in "cross-selling" or "total account development," which means that, besides offering insurance, they have become licensed to sell mutual funds, annuities, and other securities. These agents usually find their own customers and ensure that the policies sold meet the specific needs of their policyholders.

The insurance field employs relatively few people in professional or related occupations, but those who are so employed are essential to company operations. For example, insurance companies' lawyers defend clients who are sued, especially when large claims may be involved. These lawyers also review regulations and policy contracts. Nurses and other medical professionals advise clients on wellness issues and on medical procedures covered by the company's managed-care plan. *Computer systems analysts, computer programmers*, and *computer support specialists* are needed to analyze, design, develop, and program the systems that support the day-to-day operations of the insurance company.

Actuaries represent a relatively small proportion of employment in the insurance field, but they are vital to the field's profitability. Actuaries study the probability of an insured loss and determine premium rates. They must set the rates so that there is a high probability that premiums paid by customers will cover claims, but not so high that their company loses business to competitors.

Table 1. Employment of wage and salary workers in insurance by occupation, 2004 and projected change, 2004–2014 (Employment in thousands)

Occupation	Employment, 2004		Percent change, 2004–2014
	Number	Percent	
Total, all occupations	2,260	100.0	9.5
Management, business, and financial occupations	642	28.4	14.1
Top executives	51	2.3	17.1
Marketing managers	9	0.4	20.9
Sales managers	13	0.6	23.1
Computer and information systems managers	15	0.7	17.4
Financial managers	21	0.9	13.5
Claims adjusters, examiners, and investigators	205	9.1	14.6
Insurance appraisers, auto damage	11	0.5	16.0
Human resources, training, and labor relations specialists	29	1.3	18.3
Management analysts	24	1.1	10.3
Business operation specialists, all other	38	1.7	22.0
Accountants and auditors	40	1.8	14.0
Financial analysts	15	0.7	12.6
Personal financial advisors	9	0.4	29.3
Insurance underwriters	87	3.8	6.0
Professional and related occupations	255	11.3	13.7
Computer programmers	24	1.0	–8.3
Computer software engineers	22	1.0	32.1
Computer systems analysts	40	1.8	20.9
Lawyers	12	0.5	11.6
Actuaries	11	0.5	10.9
Title examiners, abstractors, and searchers	22	1.0	–4.3
Registered nurses	20	0.9	11.3
Sales and related occupations	340	15.0	8.7
Supervisors, sales workers	21	0.9	9.9
Insurance sales agents	283	12.5	8.6
Office and administrative support occupations	1,002	44.3	5.8
First-line supervisors/ managers of office and administrative support workers	68	3.0	4.4
Bookkeeping, accounting, and auditing clerks	48	2.1	6.7
Correspondence clerks	7	0.3	–11.2
Customer service representatives	253	11.2	20.0
Secretaries and administrative assistants	126	5.6	4.0
Data entry and information processing workers	31	1.4	–13.8
Insurance claims and policy processing clerks	216	9.6	3.6
Office clerks, general	106	4.7	6.5
Statistical assistants	3	0.1	2.7

Note: May not add to totals due to omission of occupations with small employment

Training, Other Qualifications, and Advancement

A few jobs in the insurance field, especially in office and administrative support occupations, require no more than a high school diploma. However, employers prefer to hire workers with a college education for most jobs, including sales, managerial, and professional jobs. When specialized training is required, it usually is obtained on the job or through independent study during work or after-work hours.

Graduation from high school or a 2-year postsecondary business program is adequate preparation for most beginning office and administrative support jobs. Courses in word processing and business math are assets, and the ability to operate computers is essential. These and other special skills also help beginners advance to higher-paying positions. On-the-job training usually is provided for clerical jobs such as customer service representatives. Because representatives in call centers must be knowledgeable about insurance products in order to provide advice to clients, more states are requiring customer service representatives to become licensed.

Management, business, financial, and professional jobs require the same college training as similar jobs in other fields. Managerial positions usually are filled by promoting college-educated employees from within the company. For beginning underwriting jobs, many insurance companies prefer college graduates who have a degree in business administration or a related field. However, some companies prefer to hire liberal arts graduates at a lower cost, and many insurers send them to company schools or enroll them in outside institutes for professional training. As an underwriter's career develops, it becomes beneficial to earn one of the voluntary professional certifications in underwriting. For example, the National Association of Health Underwriters offers two certification programs. Individuals earning the Registered Health Underwriter (RHU) designation demonstrate a high level of knowledge about the principles and practices governing the disability income and health insurance business. Persons earning the Registered Employee Benefits Consultant (REBC) designation develop an understanding of the various types of group benefits and retirement plans and the practical knowledge needed for choosing and designing the best benefits package that will meet the client's needs.

The American Institute for Chartered Property-Casualty Underwriter (AICPU) offers the CPCU program, which includes courses covering a broad range of insurance, risk management, and general business topics involving both personal and commercial loss exposures. Earning the CPCU designation requires passing 10 exams, meeting a requirement of at least three years of insurance experience, and abiding by the AICPU's code of professional ethics. In conjunction with the Insurance Institute of America, the AICPCU offers 22 insurance-related educational programs, including claims, underwriting, risk management, and reinsurance.

Most companies prefer to hire college graduates for claims adjuster and examiner positions. No specific college major is required, although most workers in these positions have a business, accounting, engineering, legal, or medical background. Licensing requirements for these workers vary by state and can include prelicensing education or passing a licensing exam. In some cases, professional designations may be substituted for the exam requirement. Separate or additional requirements may apply to public adjusters. For example, some states may require public adjusters to file a surety bond. Often, claims adjusters working for companies can work under the company license and do not need to become licensed themselves. In addition, many adjusters and examiners choose to pursue certain certifications and designations to distinguish themselves. Many state licenses and professional designations require continuing education for renewal. Continuing education is important because adjusters and examiners must be knowledgeable about changes in the laws, recent court decisions, and new medical procedures. Auto damage appraisers typically begin as auto body repairers and then are hired by insurance companies or independent adjusting firms. Most companies prefer auto damage appraisers to have formal training, and many vocational colleges offer 2-year programs on how to estimate and repair damaged vehicles. Some states require them to be licensed, and certification may be required or preferred. Computer skills also are an important qualification for many auto damage appraiser positions. As with adjusters and examiners, continuing education is important for appraisers because many new car models and repair techniques are introduced each year.

Most insurance companies prefer to hire former law enforcement or private investigators as insurance investigators. Many experienced claims adjusters or examiners also can become investigators. Licensing requirements vary among states. Most employers look for individuals with ingenuity who are persistent and assertive. Investigators must not be afraid of confrontation, should communicate well, and should be able to think on their feet. Good interviewing and interrogation skills also are important and usually are developed in earlier careers in law enforcement.

For actuarial jobs, companies prefer candidates to have degrees in actuarial science, mathematics, or statistics. However, candidates with degrees in business, finance, or economics are becoming more common. Actuaries must pass a series of national examinations to become fully qualified. Completion of all the exams takes from 5 to 10 years. Some of the exams may be taken while an individual is in college, but most require extensive home study. Many companies grant study time to their actuarial students to prepare for the exams.

Although some employers hire high school graduates with potential or proven sales ability for entry-level sales positions, most prefer to hire college graduates.

All insurance sales agents must obtain licenses in the states in which they plan to sell insurance. In most states, licenses are issued only to applicants who complete specified courses and pass written examinations covering insurance fundamentals and state insurance laws. New agents receive training from their employer, either at work or at the insurance company's home office. Sometimes, entry-level employees attend company-sponsored classes to prepare for examinations. The National Alliance For Education and Research offers a wide variety of courses in health, life, and property and casualty insurance for independent insurance agents. Others study on their own and, as on-the-job training, accompany experienced agents when they meet with prospective clients. After obtaining a license, agents must earn continuing education credits throughout their careers in order to remain licensed insurance sales agents.

Insurance sales agents wishing to sell securities and other financial products must meet state licensing requirements in these areas. Specifically, they must pass an additional examination—either the Series 6 or Series 7 licensing exam, both of which are administered by the National Association of Securities Dealers (NASD). The Series 6 exam is for individuals who wish to sell only mutual funds and variable annuities; the Series 7 exam is the main NASD series license and qualifies agents as general securities representatives. To demonstrate further competency in financial planning, many agents also find it worthwhile to obtain a certified financial planner (CFP) or chartered financial consultant (ChFC) designation.

Opportunities for advancement are relatively good in the insurance field. Office and administrative support workers can advance to higher-paying claims adjusting positions and entry-level underwriting jobs. Sales workers may advance by handling greater numbers of accounts and more complex commercial insurance policies. A master's degree, particularly in business administration or a related field, is an asset for advancement into higher levels of management. Many insurance companies expect their employees to take continuing education courses to improve their professionalism and their knowledge of the field.

Outlook

Wage and salary employment in the insurance field is projected to grow about 10 percent between 2004 and 2014, compared to the 14 percent growth projected for wage and salary employment in all fields combined. While demand for insurance is expected to rise, corporate downsizing; productivity increases due to new technology; and increasing use of direct mail, telephone, and Internet sales will limit job growth. However, some job growth will result from the field's expansion into the broader financial services field, and employment in the medical service and health insurance areas is anticipated to grow. Also, thousands of openings are expected to arise in this large field to replace workers who leave the field, retire, or stop working for other reasons.

Medical service and health insurance is the fastest-growing sector of the insurance field. In recent years, increasing health insurance premiums and relatively high unemployment have left some unable to afford health insurance, but over the long term, significant growth is expected. As the share of the elderly population rises, more people are expected to buy health insurance and long-term-care insurance as well as annuities and other types of pension products sold by insurance sales agents. If legislation is passed to make health insurance affordable to more people, demand should increase further for this type of insurance. Population growth will stimulate demand for auto insurance and homeowners insurance. Population growth also will create demand for businesses to service the needs of more people, and these businesses will need insurance as well. Moreover, large liability awards are motivating growing numbers of individuals and businesses to purchase liability policies to protect against lawsuits brought by people claiming injury or damage from a product.

Many successful insurance companies will recognize the Internet's potential as a powerful marketing tool. Not only might this reduce costs for insurance companies, but it also could enable many clients to turn to the Internet first to get information on their policies, obtain quotes, or submit claims. As insurance companies begin to offer more information and services on the Internet, employment in some occupations, such as insurance sales agent, could be adversely affected.

Sales agents working in the property and casualty market, particularly in auto insurance, will be most affected by increasing reliance on the Internet. Auto policies are relatively straightforward and can be issued more easily without the involvement of a live agent. Also, auto premiums tend to cost more per year than do other types of policies, so people are more likely to shop around for the best price. The Internet makes it easier to compare rates among companies.

Insurance companies will continue to face increased competition from banks and securities firms entering the insurance markets. As more of these firms begin to sell insurance policies, increasing numbers of insurance sales agents will be employed in them rather than in insurance companies. In order to stay competitive, insurance companies have begun to expand their financial service offerings or to establish partnerships with banks or brokerage firms.

Productivity gains caused by the greater use of computer software will continue to limit the growth of certain jobs within the insurance field. For example, the use of underwriting software that automatically analyzes and rates insurance applications will limit the employment growth of underwriters. Also, computers linked directly to the databases of insurance carriers and other organizations have made communications easier among sales agents, adjusters, and insurance carriers so that all have become much more productive. Furthermore, efforts to contain costs have led to an increasing reliance on customer service representatives to deal with the day-to-day processing of policies and claims. In addition, the Internet has made insurance investigators more produc-

tive by drastically reducing the amount of time it takes to perform background checks and by allowing investigators to handle an increasing number of cases, thus limiting their employment growth.

Sales agents and adjusters still are needed to meet face-to-face with clients, many of whom prefer to talk directly with an agent, especially regarding complicated policies. Opportunities will be best for sales agents who sell more than one type of insurance or financial service. Adjusters will still be needed to inspect damage and interview witnesses, and although the number of available jobs for actuaries will be limited due to the small size of the occupation, employment opportunities should be good as stringent qualifying requirements resulting from the examination system limit the number of new entrants.

Earnings

Weekly earnings of nonsupervisory workers in the insurance field averaged $756 in May 2004, considerably higher than the average of $529 for all nongovernment fields. Earnings of the largest occupations in insurance in May 2004 appear in table 2.

Table 2. Median hourly earnings of the largest occupations in insurance, May 2004

Occupation	Insurance	All fields
General and operations managers	$49.65	$37.22
Computer systems analysts	32.09	31.95
Accountants and auditors	24.35	24.41
Insurance underwriters	23.37	23.34
First-line supervisors/managers of office and administrative support workers	23.20	19.72
Claims adjusters, examiners, and investigators	21.33	21.26
Insurance sales agents	20.14	20.06
Executive secretaries and administrative assistants	17.67	16.81
Customer service representatives	14.12	12.99
Insurance claims and policy processing clerks	14.02	14.06

Most independent sales agents own their own businesses and are paid a commission only. Sales agents who are employees of an agency may be paid a salary only, a salary plus commission, or a salary plus a bonus. An agent's earnings usually increase rapidly with experience. Many agencies also pay an agent's expenses for automobiles and transportation, travel to conventions, and continuing education.

Insurance carriers offer attractive benefits packages, as is frequently the case with large companies. Yearly bonuses, retirement investment plans, insurance, and paid vacation often are standard. Insurance agencies, which generally are smaller, offer less extensive benefits.

Sources of Additional Information

General information on employment opportunities in the insurance field may be obtained from the human resources departments of major insurance companies or from insurance agencies in local communities. Information about licensing requirements for insurance sales agents and claim adjusters may be obtained from the department of insurance in each state.

For information on the property and casualty insurance field, contact

- Insurance Information Institute, 110 William St., New York, NY 10038. Internet: http://www.iii.org
- Property Casualty Insurers Association of America, 2500 River Rd., Des Plaines, IL 60018. Internet: http://www.pciaa.net

For information about careers in the life insurance field, contact

- LIMRA International, 300 Day Hill Rd., Windsor CT 06095.

For information about the health insurance field, contact

- National Association of Health Underwriters, 2000 North 14th St., Suite 450, Arlington, VA 22201. Internet: http://www.nahu.org

For information about insurance sales careers and training, contact

- The American Institute for Chartered Property Casualty Underwriter (AICPCU) and Insurance Institute of America, 720 South Providence Rd., Malvern, PA 19355-0716. Internet: http://www.aicpcu.org

- Independent Insurance Agents of America, 127 South Peyton St., Alexandria, VA 22314. Internet: http://www.iiaa.org
- Insurance Vocational Education Student Training (InVEST), 127 South Peyton St., Alexandria, VA 22314. Internet: http://www.investprogram.org
- National Association of Professional Insurance Agents, 400 North Washington St., Alexandria, VA 22314- 2353.

For information on insurance education and training, contact

- The American College, 270 Bryn Mawr Ave., Bryn Mawr, PA 19010. Internet: http://www.theamericancollege.edu
- LOMA (Life Office Management Association), 2300 Windy Ridge Pkwy., Suite 600, Atlanta, GA 30339-8443 Internet: http://www.loma.org
- CFA Institute, P.O. Box 3668, 560 Ray C. Hunt Dr., Charlottesville, VA 22903. Internet: http://www.cfainstitute.org
- The National Alliance for Insurance Education and Research, P.O. Box 27027, Austin, TX 78755.

Securities, Commodities, and Other Investments

- Annual Earnings: $53,140
- Job Growth: 15.8%
- Size of Workforce: 768,570
- Self-Employed: 9.6%
- Part-Time: 9.4%

Significant Points

- Half of all jobs are held by securities sales agents and management, business, and financial operations workers, who generally have a college degree; office and administrative support workers hold most other jobs.

- Employment is expected to grow as a result of increasing investment in securities and commodities, along with a growing need for investment advice.

- The high earnings of successful securities sales agents and investment bankers will cause keen competition for these positions.

Nature of the Field

The securities, commodities, and other investments field is made up of a variety of firms and organizations that bring together buyers and sellers of securities and commodities, manage investments, and offer financial advice. The field has undergone substantial change because of improvements in technology, deregulation of financial services, regulatory changes, the globalization of the marketplace, and demographics. The Internet, along with high-speed computer systems, has dramatically altered the way in which securities and commodities are bought and sold, almost completely automating the transaction process. At the same time, the number of financial services being offered is rising as firms look for new ways to attract the business of an increasingly wealthy and investment-savvy public.

The Securities and Exchange Commission (SEC) and major stock exchanges have instituted accounting and corporate reforms to increase public confidence in investment markets. These new rules address conflict-of-interest issues raised by federal, state, and field investigations into overly optimistic research reports—written by analysts during the stock boom of the late 1990s—on companies that later failed or whose stock declined dramatically in value, costing investors billions of dollars. Furthermore, the securities field adopted measures to help ensure that research reports are written independently. They also require that analysts disclose details of their compensation that would make investors aware of any possible conflicts of interest. These measures also prohibit stock analysts from attending investment meetings at which investment bankers try to obtain lucrative stock and bond deals.

Also, the SEC now requires corporate chief executive officers (CEOs) to certify the reliability of their companies' financial reports. In addition, the New York Stock Exchange (NYSE) has implemented new rules to separate investment banking from company research.

One of the most important functions of the field is to facilitate the trading of securities and commodities by bringing together buyers and sellers. Brokerage firms typically provide this function. In these firms, investors place their buy and sell orders for a particular security or commodity by telephone, online by computer, or through a broker. The firm fills the order in one of three ways. If the stock or commodity is sold on an exchange, such as the NYSE or the Chicago Mercantile Exchange (CME), the firm will send the order electronically to the company's floor broker at the exchange. The floor broker will then post the order and execute the trade by finding a seller or buyer who offers the best price for the client. Alternatively, if a security is sold through a dealer network, such as Nasdaq, the broker can access a computer network that lists the prices for which dealers in that particular security are willing to buy or sell it. If a price that the client agrees with is found, then a purchase or sale is made. Large investors and brokerage firms also can buy and sell securities and commodities on "electronic communications networks," or ECNs—powerful computers that automatically list, match, and execute trades, eliminating the sales agent. ECNs commonly are used for stocks that trade frequently and in large numbers.

Brokerage firms generally are classified as full-service, discount, or online organizations. Investors who do not have time to research investments on their own will likely rely on a full-service broker to help them construct an investment portfolio, manage their investments, or make recommendations regarding which investments to buy. Full-service brokers have access to a wide range of reports and analyses from the company's large staff of financial analysts. These analysts research companies and recommend investments to people with different financial needs. Persons who prefer to select their own investments generally use a discount or online broker and pay lower commission charges. Discount firms usually do not offer advice about specific securities. Online brokerage firms make their trades over the Internet in order to keep costs down and fees low. Discount brokerage firms usually have branch offices, while online firms do not. Most brokerage firms now have call centers staffed with both licensed sales agents and customer service representatives who take orders and answer questions at all hours of the day.

Brokerage firms also provide investment banking services; that is, they act as intermediaries between those companies or governments that would like to raise money and those with money or capital to invest. Investment banking usually involves the firm buying initial stock or bond offerings from private companies or from federal, state, and local governments and, in turn, selling them to investors for a potential profit. This service can be risky, especially when it involves a new company selling stock to the public for the first time. Investment bankers must try to determine the value of the company on the basis of a number of factors, including projected growth and sales, and decide what price investors are willing to pay for the new stock. Investment bankers also advise businesses on merger and acquisition strategies and may arrange for the transfer of ownership.

Companies that specialize in providing investment advice; portfolio management; and trust, fiduciary, and custody activities also are included in this field. These companies range from very large mutual fund management companies to self-employed personal financial advisors or financial planners. Also included are managers of pension funds, commodity pools, trust funds, and other investment accounts. Portfolio or asset management companies direct the investment decisions for investors who have chosen to pool their assets in order to have them professionally managed. Many brokerage firms also provide these services. Personal financial advisors can manage investments for individuals as well, but their main objective is to be able to provide advice on a wide range of financial matters.

A relatively small number of professionals in the field work in the exchanges, where the actual trading of securities and commodities takes place. Computers and their applications have made brokers in the exchanges much more productive and capable of handling the increasing volume of trades.

Firms in this field offer a number of other services. Many offer cash management accounts that allow account holders to deposit money into a money market fund against which they can write checks, take out margin loans, or use a debit card. Some brokerage firms offer mortgages and other types of loans and lines of credit. They also may offer trust services and help businesses set up benefit plans for their employees. Finally, firms in the field may sell annuities and other life insurance products.

The securities, commodities, and other investments field has invested heavily in technology, allowing firms to handle larger volumes of trades with fewer people. The growth of online trading in particular has produced a number of online trading firms. In order to compete, many full-service brokerage firms offer online trading to their customers. This explosion in technology is changing the nature of many of the jobs and the mix of people employed by securities firms. Some companies are more likely to resemble information technology companies than securities firms, with most of the employees working in computer-related occupations. Across the field, computer professionals are accounting for a greater proportion of the workforce. Moreover, with so much business now being conducted online and through call centers, traditional sales agents are spending less time processing orders and more time seeking out new clients and offering detailed advice.

Employment in each of the segments of the securities, commodities, and other investments field is directly affected by the activity of the stock market and futures market and the savings and investment goals of individuals. Because these factors are determined largely by the strength of the economy, the field prospers during good economic times but is much more adversely affected by downturns than are many other fields.

Working Conditions

Most people in this field work in comfortable offices; however, long hours, including evenings and weekends, are common. About 24 percent of employees worked 50 or more hours per week in 2004. Even when not working, professionals in the field must keep abreast of events that may affect the markets in which they specialize. Opportunities for part-time work are limited—only about 8 percent worked part time, compared to 16 percent of workers in all fields combined. In 2003, the incidence of work-related injury and illness was only 0.5 cases per 100 full-time workers, much lower than the 5.0 cases per 100 workers for the entire private sector. Working conditions vary by occupation.

Securities sales agents who deal mostly with individual investors and small businesses often work in branch offices of regional or national brokerage firms or for a small brokerage or financial planning firm. New sales agents work long hours, mostly soliciting customers. During the day they are on the phone continually with prospective customers, while at night they may attempt to generate new business by giving classes or seminars or by attending community functions. New sales agents also spend many hours studying to pass a variety of tests that will qualify them to sell other investment products, such as commodities or insurance. Although established agents work more regular hours, all agents meet with clients in the evenings and on weekends, as needed.

Sales agents who actually perform the buying and selling of securities and commodities may have one of the most hectic jobs of any profession. Often called traders, market makers, dealers, or floor brokers, they work on the floors of exchanges or at a computer that is linked to other traders. They not only take orders from clients and try to get the best price for them, but also must constantly keep an eye on market activity and stay in touch with other traders and brokers to know what prices are being offered.

Increasingly, sales agents for many of the brokerage and mutual fund companies work in call centers, opening accounts for individuals, entering trades, and providing advice over the phone on different investment products. Although many simply respond to inquiries and do not actively solicit customers, others may be required to contact potential clients. Call centers also employ a large number of customer service representatives, who answer questions for current clients about their accounts and make any needed changes or transfers. All workers in call centers must maintain a professional and courteous attitude, work well under pressure, and be able to speak for long periods of time. Many call centers operate 24 hours a day, 7 days a week, and employees may be required to work evenings and weekends.

Jobs in investment banking, including those of financial managers, analysts, or assistants, generally require the longest hours—often 70 to 80 hours per week—in addition to extensive travel. In this area, there is a great deal of pressure to meet deadlines and acquire new business. Researchers, financial analysts, and investment managers working for brokerage and mutual fund firms also work long hours researching and evaluating companies and their markets. Frequent travel to visit companies is common.

Personal financial advisors work in offices or out of their homes. Most work regular business hours, but many accommodate clients by visiting them at their homes in the evenings or on weekends. Office and administrative support workers usually work a 40-hour week, but overtime may be necessary during times of heavy trading.

Important Characteristics of the Field

Skills: Management of Financial Resources; Persuasion; Service Orientation; Speaking; Negotiation; Active Listening. **Abilities:** Mathematical Reasoning; Speech Recognition; Number Facility; Speech Clarity; Written Expression; Oral Expression. **Work-Related Values:** Working Conditions; Recognition; Compensation; Social Service; Social Status; Advancement.

Employment

The securities, commodities, and other investments field employed 767,000 wage and salary workers in 2004. With their extensive networks of retail sales representatives located in branch offices throughout the country, the large nationally known brokerage companies operate the majority of establishments in this field. About three-fourths of the establishments in the field employ fewer than 5 workers (chart 1). However, many of the field's jobs are in the headquarters of these firms—where most executives and administrative support personnel are employed—many of which are located in the New York City area. Many people also work for mutual fund management companies and smaller regional brokerage firms. As a consequence of deregulation, banks have become a factor in this field, either acquiring securities

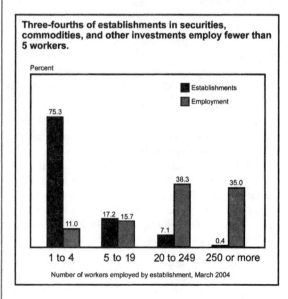

Three-fourths of establishments in securities, commodities, and other investments employ fewer than 5 workers.

Number of workers employed by establishment, March 2004

firms or adding securities and commodities business to their list of services. Personal financial advisors work for financial planning firms, many of them small in size. A relatively small number of employees work at securities or commodities exchanges—primarily the NYSE, the Chicago Board of Trade, the CME, and a number of regional exchanges.

Occupations in the Field

Securities, commodities, and financial services sales agents account for 1 in 5 wage and salary jobs in this field (table 1). Although the occupation encompasses a variety of job titles and activities, all of them involve placing orders or buying and selling securities, commodities, or other financial services. The most common types of sales agents deal directly with the public and often are called retail brokers, account executives, registered representatives, or financial consultants. Securities brokers typically buy and sell stocks, bonds, mutual funds, and other financial services, while commodities brokers deal primarily with futures contracts on metals, energy supplies, agricultural products, and financial instruments.

When a client places an order for one of these items, brokers relay the order through the firm's computers to the floor of an exchange, to a dealer, or to an ECN. Upon confirmation of the trade, the broker notifies clients of the final price. As part of their job, brokers often provide advice to clients about possible investments, taking into consideration the client's financial situation, tolerance for risk, and savings needs. Because sales is one of their major responsibilities, brokers also spend a considerable amount of time soliciting new business.

A small number of sales agents deal exclusively with large investors, such as insurance companies, pension funds, and mutual funds. These agents typically are called institutional representatives or institutional brokers, and they provide many of the same services as a retail broker, but on a larger scale.

Sales agents referred to as traders, market makers, or floor brokers actually make the trades on the floor of the exchange or over the computer. These agents match buyers and sellers of a particular security or commodity, sometimes using their own or their firm's money to close the deal.

Keeping track of transactions and paperwork constitutes a large portion of the work in this field, which is why its largest occupational group is office and administrative support workers. *Brokerage clerks*, the largest occupation in this category, handle much of the day-to-day operations within a brokerage firm. The largest group of brokerage clerks, called sales assistants, takes calls from brokers' clients, writes up order tickets and enters them into the computer, handles the paperwork for new accounts, informs clients of stock prices, and performs other tasks as needed. Some sales assistants obtain licenses to sell securities, allowing them to call brokers' clients with recommendations from the broker regarding specific investments. Other brokerage clerks may compute transfer taxes and dividends and keep daily records of transactions and holdings. At some companies, a number of brokerage clerk positions are considered entry level, with promotion potential to securities sales agent jobs or other higher-level jobs.

Because more clients are choosing to trade without the use of sales agents or brokers, *customer service representatives* are playing a larger role in securities firms. While some may have licenses to sell securities or other financial products, most are not in the business of sales or offering advice but mainly take questions from current customers. Customer service representatives usually work in central call centers, where they handle account transfers, redemptions, and address changes; answer tax questions; and help clients navigate the Web, among other services.

Management, business, and financial occupations account for about 30 percent of total employment, a larger proportion than in most fields. This category includes a myriad of people with expertise in finance and investment policy; *accountants and auditors*, who prepare the firm's financial statements; and *general and operations managers*, who run the business. *Financial analysts* generally work in the research and investment banking departments, reviewing financial statements of companies, evaluating economic and market trends, and making recommendations concerning the potential profits from investments in specific companies. Financial analysts also may attempt to determine fair market values for companies wishing to trade their stocks publicly or for those firms involved in mergers or acquisitions. Analysts in large firms usually specialize in a certain field sector, such as finance, transportation, or utilities, or in a market, such as government financing.

Personal financial advisors, also called financial planners, provide advice to both individuals and businesses on a broad range of financial subjects, such as investments, retirement planning, tax management, estate planning, and employee benefits. They may take a comprehensive approach to the client's financial needs or address only a specific issue. Advisors also may buy and sell financial products, such as stocks, bonds, mutual funds, and insurance, for their clients.

Financial managers are employed throughout the field, preparing financial documents for the regulatory authorities or directing a firm's investment policies. In many departments, managers act as senior advisors and oversee teams of junior analysts or brokers while continuing to be actively involved in working out deals with clients. Portfolio managers and commodity trading advisors are responsible for making investment decisions for clients with large sums of money to invest. These clients include mutual funds, pension funds, trust funds, commodity pools, and individuals with high net worth. Portfolio managers must know the investment goals of their clients and ensure that the investments they make meet those goals.

The increasingly computerized environment in this field requires the expertise of *computer software engineers, computer programmers*, and other computer specialists to develop and operate the communications networks that provide online trading.

Table 1. Employment of wage and salary workers in securities, commodities, and other investments by occupation, 2004 and projected change, 2004–2014 (Employment in thousands)

Occupation	Employment, 2004		Percent change, 2004–2014
	Number	Percent	
Total, all occupations	767	100.0	15.8
Management, business, and financial occupations	235	30.6	23.6
Top executives	22	2.9	21.8
Marketing and sales managers	9	1.2	24.6
Computer and information systems managers	7	0.9	27.5
Financial managers	27	3.6	17.4
Management analysts	7	0.9	23.2
Accountants and auditors	19	2.5	23.4

Occupation	Employment, 2004		Percent change, 2004–2014
	Number	Percent	
Financial analysts	39	5.1	19.0
Personal financial advisors	56	7.3	30.2
Professional and related occupations	69	9.0	30.0
Computer programmers	7	0.9	–1.1
Computer software engineers	14	1.9	45.1
Computer support specialists	7	0.9	22.0
Computer systems analysts	8	1.0	34.1
Market research analysts	7	0.9	22.0
Sales and related occupations	178	23.3	9.5
First-line supervisors/ managers of non-retail sales workers	7	0.9	11.7
Securities, commodities, and financial services sales agents	161	20.9	9.4
Office and administrative support occupations	278	36.2	9.6
First-line supervisors/ managers of office and administrative support workers	19	2.5	10.7
Bookkeeping, accounting, and auditing clerks	19	2.5	10.7
Brokerage clerks	58	7.6	9.4
Customer service representatives	36	4.7	24.0
Receptionists and information clerks	7	0.9	16.9
Secretaries and administrative assistants	61	8.0	8.3
Office clerks, general	39	5.1	8.5

Note: May not add to totals due to omission of occupations with small employment

Training, Other Qualifications, and Advancement

The securities, commodities, and other investments field has one of the most highly educated and skilled workforces of any field. About 2 out of 3 workers have a bachelor's or higher degree. The requirements for entry are high—even brokerage clerks often have a college degree. The most successful workers at all levels have an aptitude for numbers and a keen interest in investing. In addition, most people in the field are required to be licensed by the National Association of Securities Dealers (NASD) before they can sell securities or recommend specific investments. To be licensed, brokers and assistants must pass an examination that tests their knowledge of investments. Various licenses are available for different investment products; however, the one most brokers and broker's assistants receive is the "Series 7" license, which requires a passing score on the General Securities Registered Representative Examination administered by the NASD. Since 1995, the NASD also has required all registered persons with licenses to undergo a continuing education program approximately every 3 years in order to retain their licenses. Classes consist of computer-based training in regulatory matters and training on new investment products.

A number of professionals in this field begin their careers as brokerage clerks. Depending on the actual job, brokerage clerks can be high school or college graduates. Positions dealing with the public, such as broker's or sales assistant, and those dealing with more complicated financial records are increasingly being held by college graduates. In addition, these jobs require good organizational ability, phone skills, and attention to detail. A Series 7 brokerage license can make a clerk more valuable to the broker because it gives the assistant the ability to answer more of a client's questions and to pass along securities recommendations from the broker. Clerks may be promoted to sales representative positions or other professional positions. Some of the larger firms have training programs, especially for their college graduates, that provide clerks with the skills they need for advancement.

A college education, although not essential, is increasingly important for securities, commodities, and financial services sales agents because it helps them to understand economic conditions and trends. In fact, the overwhelming majority of entrants to this occupation are

college graduates. Still, many employers consider personal qualities and skills, such as self-motivation and the ability to handle rejection, more important than academic training. Many employers prefer persons who have been successful in other sales careers. Employers seek applicants with good communication skills, a professional appearance, and a strong desire to succeed.

Securities, commodities, and financial services sales workers must meet federal and state licensing requirements, which generally include passing an examination and a background investigation and, in some cases, furnishing a personal bond. Most of the large brokerage firms provide formal classroom training for new brokers that can last a couple of weeks to several months. Smaller firms usually rely on informal on-the-job training.

Although there are no specific licensure requirements for becoming a personal financial advisor, most advisors must be knowledgeable about economic trends, finance, budgeting, and accounting. Therefore, a college education is important. Personal financial advisors must possess excellent communication and interpersonal skills to be able to explain complicated issues to their clients. Many advisors earn a Certified Financial Planner credential, also referred to as CFP (R), issued by the CFP Board of Standards, or a Chartered Financial Consultant (ChFC) designation, offered by the American College in Bryn Mawr, Pennsylvania. To receive these designations, a person must pass a series of exams on insurance, investments, tax planning, employee benefits, and retirement and estate planning; must have the required experience in related jobs; and, in the case of the CFP (R), must agree to abide by the rules and regulations issued by the Board of Standards. The CFP (R) exam has been revised in recent years; candidates are now required to have a working knowledge of debt management, planning liability, emergency fund reserves, and statistical modeling. It may take from 2 to 3 years of study to complete these programs.

Entry-level financial analyst and other managerial support positions usually are filled by college graduates who have majored in business administration, marketing, economics, accounting, industrial relations, or finance. Many of the large companies have management training programs for college graduates in which trainees work for brief periods in various departments to get a broad picture of the field before they are assigned to a particular department. Those working as financial analysts are

Financial Activities

encouraged to obtain the Chartered Financial Analyst (CFA) designation sponsored by the CFA Institute. To qualify, applicants must have at least 3 years of qualifying experience and pass a series of rigorous essay exams requiring an extensive knowledge of many fields, including accounting, economics, and securities.

Advancement opportunities in the securities, commodities, and other investments field vary by occupation. To advance into the managerial ranks or enter some of the more lucrative and prestigious jobs on Wall Street in New York City, a master's degree is becoming essential. In investment banking, for example, most firms select the top candidates from the nation's most prestigious business schools. However, because many business schools accept master's degree candidates only if they have some job experience, many securities firms hire analysts with a bachelor's degree and provide them with the experience they need, assuming that they will eventually obtain their master's degree.

The principal basis of advancement for securities, commodities, and financial services sales agents is an increase in the number and size of the accounts they handle. Some eventually manage the assets of clients. Although beginners usually service the accounts of individual investors, a select few eventually may handle very large institutional accounts. Administrative support workers such as brokerage clerks may advance to sales agent positions or to other professional positions. Financial analysts may advance to positions in which they manage investment portfolios or negotiate investment banking deals.

Outlook

Wage and salary employment in securities, commodities, and other investments is projected to rise 16 percent from 2004 to 2014, compared to the 14 percent increase expected for wage and salary employment across all fields. Employment growth will be driven primarily by increasing levels of investment in securities and commodities in the global marketplace, as well as the growing need for investment advice. In addition to the many new job openings stemming from this growth, a large number of openings will arise as people retire or leave the field for other reasons.

Baby boomers are in the middle of their peak saving years, and many are putting money into a number of tax-favorable retirement plans, such as 401(k) programs and Roth IRAs. These plans have been one of the major caus-

es of inflows of money into the stock market and into mutual funds, and this trend towards saving for retirement is expected to continue.

Another factor contributing to projected employment growth is the "globalization" of securities and commodities markets—the extension of traditional exchange and trading boundaries into new markets in foreign countries. This extension, in turn, has provided an expanding array of investment opportunities and access to markets in which new financial products are now available to domestic investors. These new products and markets encourage trading and prompt firms to hire more workers.

Also, although online trading will grow and reduce the need for direct contact with an actual broker, the number of securities sales agents is still expected to increase as many people remain willing to pay for the advice that a full-service representative can offer. Competition for securities sales agent jobs, though, is expected to be keen because the potentially high earnings attracts a large number of qualified applicants. Job opportunities for sales agents should be best for mature individuals with successful work experience.

Employment of personal financial advisors is expected to increase rapidly. As the number of self-directed retirement plans grows, and as the number and complexity of investments rises, individuals will require more help to manage their money. Financial advisors who have either the CFP (R) or ChFC designation are expected to have the best opportunities.

Financial analysts will be needed in the investment banking field, where they help companies raise money and where they work on corporate mergers and acquisitions. However, growth in demand for financial analysts to do company research will be constrained by the implementation of reforms calling for investment firms to subsidize independent research and to separate research from investment banking. To help to contain the costs of reform, firms have eliminated some research jobs. Competition for entry-level analyst positions in investment banking typically is intense; because of the potentially high earnings, the number of applicants usually far exceeds the number of vacancies.

Due to advances in telecommunications and computer technology, the securities, commodities, and other investments field has become highly automated. On the one hand, this automation is expected to cause rapid growth in employment of computer specialists. On the other hand, automation has resulted in computerized recordkeeping of transactions, more productive office and administrative support staffs, and enhanced communications with foreign firms. Accordingly, employment of brokerage clerks will decline and employment of bookkeeping, accounting, and auditing clerks is projected to grow more slowly than the field as a whole.

Earnings

Most workers in the securities, commodities, and other investments field are paid a salary on an annual or a weekly basis. In May 2004, the average weekly earnings of nonsupervisory workers in the field were $921 compared with $529 in all fields combined. Median earnings for the largest occupations in the securities, commodities, and other investments field in May 2004 are presented in table 2.

Table 2. Median hourly earnings of the largest occupations in securities, commodities, and other investments, May 2004

Occupation	Securities, commodities, and other investments	All fields
General and operations managers	$49.65	$37.22
Computer systems analysts	32.09	31.95
Accountants and auditors	24.35	24.41
Insurance underwriters	23.37	23.34
First-line supervisors/managers of office and administrative support workers	23.20	19.72
Claims adjusters, examiners, and investigators	21.33	21.26
Insurance sales agents	20.14	20.06
Executive secretaries and administrative assistants	17.67	16.81
Customer service representatives	14.12	12.99
Insurance claims and policy processing clerks	14.02	14.06

Earnings of securities, commodities, and financial services sales agents—especially those working for full-service brokerage firms—depend on commissions from the sale or purchase of stocks, bonds, and other securities or futures contracts. Commissions are likely to be lower when there is a slump in market activity. Earnings also can be based on the amount of assets that a broker or portfolio manager has under his or her management, with the broker or portfolio manager receiving a small percentage of the value of the assets.

Personal financial advisors are compensated in a number of ways. Those who manage clients' assets usually collect a percentage of the assets as their fees. Others charge hourly fees, and some charge different rates depending on the type of plan requested. Many receive commissions based on the financial products they sell. Those who work for financial services firms may receive a salary.

Sources of Additional Information

For information on the securities field, contact

- Securities Industry Association, 120 Broadway, 35th Floor, New York, NY 10271-0080. Internet: http://www.sia.com

Professional and Business Services

Advertising and Public Relations Services

- Annual Earnings: $38,370
- Job Growth: 22.4%
- Size of Workforce: 434,080
- Self-Employed: 11.2%
- Part-Time: 16.3%

Significant Points

- Competition for many jobs will be keen because the glamour of the field traditionally attracts many more jobseekers than there are job openings.

- California and New York together account for about 1 in 5 firms and more than 1 in 4 workers in the field.

- Layoffs are common when accounts are lost, major clients cut budgets, or agencies merge.

Nature of the Field

Firms in the advertising and public relations services field prepare advertisements for other companies and organizations and design campaigns to promote the interests and image of their clients. This field also includes media representatives—firms that sell advertising space for publications, radio, television, and the Internet; display advertisers—businesses engaged in creating and designing public display ads for use in shopping malls, on billboards, or in similar media; and direct mail advertisers. A firm that purchases advertising time (or space) from media outlets, thereafter reselling it to advertising agencies or individual companies directly, is considered a media buying agency. Divisions of companies that produce and place their own advertising are not considered part of this field.

In 2004, there were about 47,000 advertising and public relations services establishments in the United States. About 4 out of 10 write copy and prepare artwork, graphics, and other creative work and then place the resulting ads on television, radio, or the Internet or in periodicals, newspapers, or other advertising media. Within the field, only these full-service establishments are known as *advertising agencies*. About 1 in 6 were public relations firms. Many of the largest agencies are international, with a substantial proportion of their revenue coming from abroad.

Most advertising firms specialize in a particular market niche. Some companies produce and solicit outdoor advertising, such as billboards and electric displays. Others place ads in buses, subways, taxis, airports, and bus terminals. A small number of firms produce aerial advertising, while others distribute circulars, handbills, and free samples.

Groups within agencies have been created to serve their clients' electronic advertising needs on the Internet. Online advertisements link users to a company's or product's Web site, where information such as new product announcements, contests, and product catalogs appears and from which purchases may be made.

Some firms are not involved in the creation of ads at all; instead, they sell advertising time or space on radio and television stations or in publications. Because these firms do not produce advertising, their staffs are mostly sales workers.

Companies often look to advertising as a way of boosting sales by increasing the public's exposure to a product or service. Most companies do not have the staff with the necessary skills or experience to create effective advertisements; furthermore, many advertising campaigns are temporary, so employers would have difficulty maintaining their own advertising staff. Instead, companies commonly solicit bids from ad agencies to develop advertising for them. Next, ad agencies offering their services to the company often make presentations. After winning an account, various departments within an agency—such as creative, production, media, and research—work together to meet the client's goal of increasing sales.

Widespread public relations services firms can influence how businesses, governments, and institutions make decisions. Often working behind the scenes, these firms have a variety of functions. In general, firms in public relations services advise and implement public exposure strategies. For example, a public relations firm might issue a press release that is printed in newspapers across the country. Firms in public relations services offer one or more resources that clients cannot provide themselves. Usually this resource is expertise in the form of knowledge, experience, special skills, or creativity, but sometimes the resource is time or personnel that the client cannot spare. Clients of public relations firms include all types of businesses, institutions, trades, and public interest groups and even high-profile individuals. Clients are large and small for-profit firms in the private sector; state, local, or federal governments; hospitals, universities, unions, and trade groups; and foreign governments or businesses.

Public relations firms help secure favorable public exposure for their clients, advise them in the case of a sudden public crisis, and design strategies to help them attain a certain public image. Toward these ends, public relations firms analyze public or internal sentiment about clients; establish relationships with the media; write speeches and coach clients for interviews; issue press releases; and organize client-sponsored publicity events, such as contests, concerts, exhibits, symposia, and sporting and charity events.

Lobbying firms, a special type of public relations firm, differ somewhat. Instead of attempting to secure favorable public opinion about their clients, they attempt to influence legislators in favor of their clients' special interests. Lobbyists often work for large businesses, field trade organizations, unions, or public interest groups.

In an effort to attract and maintain clients, advertising and public relations services agencies are diversifying their services, offering advertising as well as public relations, sales, marketing, and interactive media services. Advertising and public relations services firms have found that highly creative work is particularly suitable for their services, resulting in a better product and increasing their clients' profitability.

Working Conditions

Most employees in advertising and public relations services work in comfortable offices operating in a teamwork environment; however, long hours, including evenings and weekends, are common. There are fewer opportunities for part-time work than in many other fields; in 2004, 14 percent of advertising and public relations employees worked part time, compared with 16 percent of all workers.

Work in advertising and public relations is fast-paced and exciting, but it also can be stressful. Being creative on a tight schedule can be emotionally draining. Some workers, such as lobbyists, consultants, and public relations writers, frequently must meet deadlines and consequently may work long hours at times. Workers whose services are billed hourly, such as advertising consultants and public relations specialists, are often under pressure to manage their time carefully. In addition, frequent meetings with clients and media representatives may involve substantial travel.

Most firms encourage employees to attend employer-paid time-management classes, which help reduce the stress sometimes associated with working under strict time constraints. Also, with today's hectic lifestyle, many firms in this field offer or provide health facilities or clubs to help employees maintain good health.

In 2004, workers in the field averaged 33.8 hours per week, a little higher than the national average of 33.7.

Important Characteristics of the Field

Skills: Persuasion; Negotiation; Service Orientation; Social Perceptiveness; Management of Financial Resources; Speaking. **Abilities:** Speech Clarity; Speech Recognition; Written Expression; Oral Expression; Fluency of Ideas; Originality. **Work-Related Values:** Working Conditions; Creativity; Recognition; Ability Utilization; Advancement; Variety.

Employment

The advertising and public relations services field employed 425,000 workers in 2004. An additional 61,000 workers were self-employed.

Although advertising and public relations services firms are located throughout the country, they are concentrated in the largest states and cities. California and New York together account for about 1 in 5 firms and more than 1 in 4 workers in the field. Firms vary in size, ranging from one-person shops to international agencies employing thousands of workers. However, 68 percent of all advertising and public relations establishments employ fewer than 5 employees (chart 1).

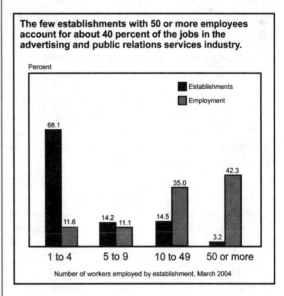

The few establishments with 50 or more employees account for about 40 percent of the jobs in the advertising and public relations services industry.

Percent

■ Establishments
■ Employment

68.1   11.6   14.2   11.1   14.5   35.0   3.2   42.3

1 to 4   5 to 9   10 to 49   50 or more

Number of workers employed by establishment, March 2004

The small size of the average advertising and public relations services firm demonstrates the opportunities for self-employment. It is relatively easy to open a small agency; in fact, many successful agencies began as one-person or two-person operations.

About 76 percent of advertising and public relations employees are 25 to 54 years of age. Very few advertising and public relations services workers are below the age of 20, which reflects the need for postsecondary training or work experience.

Occupations in the Field

Management, business, and financial workers; professionals and related workers; and sales and related workers account for more than 6 out of every 10 jobs in the field (table 1). Employees have varied responsibilities in agencies with only a few workers, and the specific job duties of each worker often are difficult to distinguish. Workers in relatively large firms specialize more, so the distinctions among occupations are more apparent.

Within advertising and public relations, the account management department links the agency and the client—it represents the agency to the client, as well as the client to the agency. Account management brings business to the agency and ultimately is responsible for the quality of the advertisement or public relations campaign. Account management workers carefully monitor the activities of the other areas to ensure that everything runs smoothly. *Account managers* and their assistants analyze competitive activity and consumer trends; report client billing; forecast agency income; and combine the talents of the creative, media, and research areas. The *creative director* oversees the copy chief, the art director, and their respective staffs. The *media director* oversees planning groups that select the communication media—for example, radio, television, newspapers, magazines, Internet, or outdoor signs—to be used to promote the organization, issue, product, or service.

In public relations firms, *public relations managers* direct publicity programs to a targeted public. They often specialize in a specific area, such as crisis management—or in a specific field, such as health care. They use every available communication medium in their effort to maintain the support of the specific group upon whom their organization's success depends, such as consumers, stockholders, or the general public. For example, public relations managers may clarify or justify the firm's point of view on health or environmental issues to community or special interest groups. *Public relations specialists* handle organizational functions such as media, community,

consumer, and governmental relations; political campaigns; interest-group representation; conflict mediation; or employee and investor relations. They prepare press releases and contact people in the media who might print or broadcast their material. Many radio or television special reports, newspaper stories, and magazine articles start on the desks of public relations specialists.

Working with an idea that account management obtains from the client, the creative department brings the idea to life. For example, an ad agency's staff works together to transform a blank piece of paper into an advertisement. As the idea takes shape, *copywriters* and their assistants write the words of ads—both the written part of print ads as well as the scripts of radio and television spots. *Art directors* and their assistants develop the visual concepts and designs of advertisements. They prepare pasteups and layouts for print ads and television storyboards, cartoon-style summaries of how an advertisement will appear. They also oversee the filming of television commercials and photo sessions. *Graphic designers* use a variety of print, electronic, and film media to create designs that meet clients' commercial needs. Using computer software, they develop the overall layout and design of print ads for magazines, newspapers, journals, corporate reports, and other publications. They also may produce promotional displays and marketing brochures for products and services, design distinctive company logos for products and businesses, and develop signs and environmental graphics—aesthetically pleasing signs that deliver a message, such as a sunset to advertise a beach resort. An increasing number of graphic designers develop material to appear on the Internet.

Workers in the research department try to understand the desires, motivations, and ideals of consumers in order to produce and place the most effective advertising or public relations campaign in the most effective media. *Research executives* compile data, monitor the progress of internal and external research, develop research tools, and interpret and provide explanations of the data gathered. Research executives often specialize in specific research areas and perform supervisory duties. *Market research analysts* are concerned with the potential sales of a product or service. They analyze statistical data on past sales to predict future sales. They provide a company's management with information needed to make decisions on the promotion, distribution, design, and pricing of products or services.

Media planners gather information on the public's viewing and reading habits and evaluate editorial content and programming to determine the potential use of media such as newspapers, magazines, radio, television, or the Internet. The media staff calculates the numbers and types of people reached by different media and how often they are reached. *Media buyers* track the media space and times available for purchase, negotiate and purchase time and space for ads, and make sure ads appear exactly as scheduled. Additionally, they calculate rates, usage, and budgets. *Advertising sales agents* sell air time on radio and television and page space in print media. They generally work in firms representing radio stations, television stations, and publications. *Demonstrators* promote sales of a product to consumers, while *product promoters* try to induce retail stores to sell particular products and market them effectively. Product demonstration is an effective technique used by both to introduce new products or promote sales of old products because it allows face-to-face interaction with potential customers.

Office and administrative support occupations accounted for 28 percent of jobs in 2004. Positions ranged from secretaries and administrative assistants to financial clerks. The occupational composition of this group varies widely among agencies. The remaining jobs in the field were in service; construction and extraction; production; transportation; and installation, maintenance, and repair occupations.

Table 1. Employment of wage and salary workers in advertising and public relations by occupation, 2004 and projected change, 2004–2014 (Employment in thousands)

Occupation	Employment, 2004		Percent change, 2004–2014
	Number	Percent	
Total, all occupations	425	100.0	22.4
Management, business, and financial occupations	66	15.6	29.1
General and operations managers	15	3.5	25.8
Advertising and promotions managers	8	1.8	30.8
Marketing managers	4	0.9	35.1
Sales managers	3	0.8	27.9

Occupation	Employment, 2004		Percent change, 2004–2014
	Number	Percent	
Public relations managers	4	0.9	36.6
Purchasing agents, except wholesale, retail, and farm products	4	0.9	27.1
Accountants and auditors	6	1.4	27.1
Professional and related occupations	105	24.6	33.0
Computer programmers	5	1.1	3.7
Market research analysts	4	0.9	27.1
Art directors	10	2.3	27.1
Multi-media artists and animators	6	1.4	39.8
Graphic designers	22	5.2	38.9
Merchandise displayers and window trimmers	4	0.9	26.2
Public relations specialists	22	5.2	39.8
Editors	3	0.8	27.1
Writers and authors	8	1.8	21.0
Sales and related occupations	95	22.4	24.0
Supervisors, sales workers	6	1.5	17.5
Advertising sales agents	43	10.2	27.2
Sales representatives, services, all other	8	2.0	27.1
Sales representatives, wholesale and manufacturing	10	2.4	27.1
Demonstrators and product promoters	19	4.4	22.4
Telemarketers	5	1.2	–1.0
Office and administrative support occupations	118	27.8	8.3
First-line supervisors/ managers of office and administrative support workers	8	1.8	15.2
Bookkeeping, accounting, and auditing clerks	11	2.6	14.4
Customer service representatives	14	3.3	30.1
Receptionists and information clerks	5	1.2	21.1

Professional and Business Services

Occupation	Employment, 2004		Percent change, 2004–2014
	Number	Percent	
Production, planning, and expediting clerks	6	1.5	25.8
Shipping, receiving, and traffic clerks	4	1.0	15.1
Secretaries and administrative assistants	18	4.3	14.9
Mail clerks and mail machine operators, except postal service	16	3.7	–34.9
Office clerks, general	13	3.1	13.1
Production occupations	17	4.0	19.6
Printers	8	1.8	18.1
Transportation and material moving occupations	13	3.1	22.0
Laborers and material movers, hand	9	2.1	19.6

Note: May not add to totals due to omission of occupations with small employment

Training, Other Qualifications, and Advancement

Most entry-level professional and managerial positions in advertising and public relations services require a bachelor's degree, preferably with broad liberal arts exposure.

Beginners in advertising usually enter the field in the account management or media department. Occasionally, entry-level positions are available in the market research or creative departments of an agency, but these positions usually require some experience. Completing an advertising-related internship while in school provides an advantage when applying for an entry-level position; in fact, internships are becoming a necessary step to obtaining permanent employment. In addition to an internship, courses in marketing, psychology, accounting, statistics, and creative design can help prepare potential entrants for careers in this field.

Assistant account executive positions—the entry-level account management occupation in most firms—require a bachelor's degree in marketing or advertising, although some firms require a master's degree in business administration.

Bachelor's degrees are not required for entry-level positions in the creative department. Assistant art directors usually need at least a 2-year degree from an art or design school. Although assistant copywriters do not need a degree, obtaining one helps to develop the superior communication skills and abilities required for this job.

Assistant media planner or assistant media buyer also are good entry-level positions, but almost always require a bachelor's degree, preferably with a major in marketing or advertising. Experienced applicants who possess at least a master's degree usually fill research positions. Often, they have a background in marketing or statistics and years of experience. Requirements for support services and administrative positions depend on the job and vary from firm to firm.

In public relations, employers prefer applicants with degrees in communications, journalism, English, or business. Some 4-year colleges and universities have begun to offer a concentration in public relations. Because there is keen competition for entry-level public relations jobs, workers are encouraged to gain experience through internships, co-op programs, or one of the formal public relations programs offered across the country. However, these programs are not available everywhere, so most public relations workers get the bulk of their training on the job. At some firms, this training consists of formal classroom education but, in most cases, workers train under the guidance of senior account executives or other experienced workers, gradually familiarizing themselves with public relations work. Entry-level workers often start as research or account assistants and may be promoted to account executive, account supervisor, vice president, and executive vice president.

A voluntary accreditation program for public relations specialists is offered by the Public Relations Society of America. The program is a recognized mark of competency in the profession and requires that workers have been employed in the field for several years.

Employees in advertising and public relations services should have good people skills, common sense, creativity, communication skills, and problem-solving ability. Foreign language skills have always been important for those wanting to work abroad for domestic firms or to represent foreign firms domestically. However, these skills are increasingly vital to reach linguistic minorities in U.S. cities, such as Los Angeles, New York, Miami, Houston, and Phoenix. New media, such as the Internet, are creating opportunities to market products, but also are increasing the need for additional training for those already employed. Keeping pace with technology is fundamental to success in the field. In addition, advertisers must keep in tune with the changing values, cultures, and fashions of the nation.

Success in increasingly responsible staff assignments usually leads to advancement to supervisory positions. As workers climb the organizational ladder, broad vision and planning skills become extremely important. Another way to get to the top in this field is to open one's own firm. In spite of the difficulty and high failure rate, many find starting their own business to be personally and financially rewarding. Among the self-employed, advancement takes the form of increasing the size and strength of the company.

Outlook

Competition for many jobs will be keen because the glamour of the advertising and public relations services field traditionally attracts many more jobseekers than there are job openings. Employment in the field is projected to grow 22 percent over the 2004–2014 period, compared with 14 percent for all fields combined. New jobs will be created as the economy expands and generates more products and services to advertise. Increased demand for advertising and public relations services also will stem from growth in the number and types of media outlets used to reach consumers, creating opportunities for people skilled in preparing material for presentation on the Internet.

On the other hand, employment growth may be tempered by the increased use of more efficient nonprint media advertising, such as Internet or radio, which could replace some workers. Employment also may be adversely affected if legislation, aimed at protecting public health and safety, further restricts advertising for specific products such as alcoholic beverages and tobacco. In addition to new jobs created over the 2004–2014 period, job openings also will arise as workers transfer to other fields or leave the workforce.

Layoffs are common in advertising and public relations services firms when accounts are lost, major clients cut budgets, or agencies merge.

Earnings

In 2004, nonsupervisory workers in advertising and public relations services averaged $633 a week—significantly higher than the $529 a week for all nonsupervisory workers in nongovernment fields. Earnings of workers in selected occupations in advertising and public relations services appear in table 2.

Table 2. Median hourly earnings of the largest occupations in advertising and public relations services, May 2004

Occupation	Advertising and public relations services	All fields
General and operations managers	$55.06	$37.22
Public relations specialists	24.25	21.07
Advertising sales agents	21.59	19.37
Graphic designers	19.23	18.28
Executive secretaries and administrative assistants	17.65	16.81
Bookkeeping, accounting, and auditing clerks	15.15	13.74
Customer service representatives	14.47	12.99
Office clerks, general	11.18	10.95
Mail clerks and mail machine operators, except postal service	9.76	10.76
Demonstrators and product promoters	8.42	9.95

In addition to a straight salary, many workers receive additional compensation, such as profit sharing, stock ownership, or performance-based bonuses.

Sources of Additional Information

For information about careers or training, contact

- American Association of Advertising Agencies, 405 Lexington Ave., New York, NY 10174. Internet: http://www.aaaa.org
- American Advertising Federation, 1101 Vermont Ave. NW, Suite 500, Washington, DC 20005. Internet: http://www.aaf.org

For more information on accreditation for public relations professionals, contact

- Public Relations Society of America, Inc., 33 Maiden Lane, New York, NY 10038-5150. Internet: http://www.prsa.org

Computer Systems Design and Related Services

- Annual Earnings: $63,320
- Job Growth: 39.5%
- Size of Workforce: 1,149,800
- Self-Employed: 8.8%
- Part-Time: 7.4%

Significant Points

- The computer systems design and related services field is expected to experience rapid growth, adding 453,000 jobs between 2004 and 2014.

- Professional and related workers enjoy the best prospects, reflecting continuing demand for higher level skills needed to keep up with changes in technology.

- Computer specialists account for 53 percent of all employees in this field.

Nature of the Field

All organizations today rely on computer and information technology to conduct business and operate more efficiently. Often, however, these institutions do not have the internal resources to effectively implement new technologies or satisfy their changing needs. When faced with these limitations, organizations turn to the computer systems design and related services field to meet their specialized needs on a contract or customer basis. Firms may enlist the services of one of 146,000 establishments in the computer systems design and related services field for help with a particular project or problem, such as setting up a secure Web site or establishing a marketplace online. Alternatively, these firms may choose to contract out one or more activities, such as the management of their onsite data center or help-desk support, to a computer services firm.

Services provided by this field include custom computer programming services; computer systems design services; computer facilities management services, including computer systems or data processing facilities support services for clients; and other computer-related services such as disaster recovery services and software installation. Computer training contractors, however, are included in the description of Educational Services, and establishments that manufacture computer equipment are included in the description of Computer and Electronic Product Manufacturing. Establishments primarily engaged in providing computer data processing services at their own facility for others are classified in the data processing, hosting, and related services field. Producers of packaged software and Internet-based software are part of the Software Publishers field, which is discussed elsewhere in Part II. Telecommunications services, including cable Internet providers, also are covered in a separate description.

Custom programming establishments write, modify, test, and support software to meet the needs of a particular customer. These service firms may be hired to code large programs or to install a software package on a user's system and customize it to the user's specific needs. Programming service firms also may update or reengineer existing systems. Systems design services firms plan and design computer systems that integrate computer hardware, software, and communications technologies. The hardware and software components of the system may be provided by the design firm as part of integrated services or may be provided by third parties or vendors. These firms often install the system and train and support its users.

Computer facilities management services usually are offered at the customer's site. Establishments offering these services provide onsite management and operation of clients' computer systems and facilities, as well as facilities support services.

Electronic business (e-business) is any process that a business organization conducts over a computer-mediated network. Electronic commerce (e-commerce) is that part of e-business that involves the buying and selling of goods and services online. With the growth of the Internet and the expansion of e-commerce, some service firms specialize in developing and maintaining sites on the World Wide Web (see below) for client companies. Others create and maintain corporate intranets or self-contained internal networks linking multiple users within an organization by means of Internet or, more recently, wireless technology. These firms design sophisticated computer networks, assist with upgrades or conversions, custom design special programming features for clients, and engage in continual maintenance. They help clients select the right hardware and software products for a particular project and then develop, install, and implement the system, as well as train the client's users. Service firms also offer consulting services for any stages of development throughout the entire process, from design and content development to administration and maintenance of site security.

The widespread use of the Internet and intranets also has resulted in an increased focus on security. The robust growth of e-commerce highlights this concern as firms seek to attract as many potential customers as possible to their Web sites. Security threats range from damaging computer viruses to online credit card fraud. Services contracted out to security consulting firms include analyzing vulnerability, managing firewalls, and providing protection against intrusion and software "viruses." Information technology (IT) security involves computer security, making software and networks safe; and homeland security, keeping track of people and information. The need for more secure Internet and intranet sites to ensure protection for individuals' personal information and to allow companies and banks to protect their funds and infrastructure has created a new demand for cyberspace security professionals.

Working Conditions

Most workers in this field work in clean, quiet offices. Those in facilities management and maintenance may work in computer operations centers. Given the technology available today, however, more work can be done from remote locations using modems, fax machines, e-mail, and especially the Internet. For example, systems analysts may work from home, with their computers linked directly to computers at a financial services firm. Although they often relocate to a customer's place of business while working on a project, programmers and consultants may actually perform work from locations offsite. Even technical support personnel can tap into a customer's computer remotely in order to identify and fix problems.

Only about 6 percent of the workers in computer systems design and related services firms work part time, compared with 16 percent of workers throughout all fields. Many workers in this field work more than the standard 40-hour workweek—about 1 in 5 work 50 or more hours a week. For many professionals and technical specialists, evening or weekend work is common to meet deadlines or solve problems. Professionals working for large establishments may have less freedom in planning their schedule than do consultants for very small firms, whose work may be more varied.

Those who work with personal computers for extended periods may experience musculoskeletal strain, eye problems, stress, or repetitive motion illnesses, such as carpal tunnel syndrome.

Important Characteristics of the Field

Skills: Programming; Troubleshooting; Systems Analysis; Technology Design; Operations Analysis; Installation. **Abilities:** Inductive Reasoning; Deductive Reasoning; Speech Recognition; Originality; Mathematical Reasoning; Written Comprehension. **Work-Related Values:** Creativity; Ability Utilization; Working Conditions; Authority; Autonomy; Social Status.

Employment

In 2004, there were about 1.1 million wage and salary jobs and an additional 132,000 self-employed and unpaid family workers. Most self-employed workers are independent consultants.

While the field has both large and small firms, the average establishment in computer systems design and related services is relatively small; about 78 percent of establishments employed fewer than 5 workers in 2004. The majority of jobs, however, are found in establishments that employ 20 or more workers (chart 1). Many small establishments in the field are startup firms that hope to capitalize on a market niche.

Compared with the rest of the economy, there are significantly fewer workers 45 years of age and older; this field's workforce remains younger than most, with large proportions of workers in the 25-to-44 age range (table 1). This reflects the field's explosive growth in employment over the last two decades. The huge increase in

Professional and Business Services

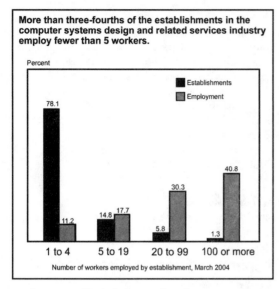

More than three-fourths of the establishments in the computer systems design and related services industry employ fewer than 5 workers.

Percent

Legend: ■ Establishments   ▨ Employment

- 1 to 4: 78.1, 11.2
- 5 to 19: 14.8, 17.7
- 20 to 99: 5.8, 30.3
- 100 or more: 1.3, 40.8

Number of workers employed by establishment, March 2004

employment afforded thousands of opportunities to younger workers possessing the newest technological skills.

Table 1. Percent distribution of employment, by age group, 2004

Age group	Computer systems design and related services	All industries
Total	100.0%	100.0%
16–19	0.5	4.2
20–24	6.3	9.9
25–34	32.4	21.8
35–44	30.8	24.8
45–54	20.8	23.3
55–64	8.6	12.4
65 and older	0.7	3.5

Occupations in the Field

Providing a wide array of information services to clients requires a diverse and well-educated workforce. The majority of workers in the computer systems design and related services field are professional and related workers—overwhelmingly computer specialists such as com-

puter systems analysts, computer software engineers, and computer programmers (table 2). This occupational group accounts for 60 percent of the jobs in the field, reflecting the emphasis on high-level technical skills and creativity. By 2014, the share of professional and related occupations is expected to be even greater, while the share of office and administrative support jobs, currently accounting for 14 percent of field employment, is projected to fall.

Programmers write, test, and maintain the detailed instructions, called programs or software, that computers must follow to perform their functions. These specialized programs tell the computer what to do—for example, which information to identify and access, how to process it, and what equipment to use. Custom programmers write these commands by breaking down each step into a logical series, converting specifications into a language that the computer understands. While some still work with traditional programming languages, such as COBOL, most programmers today use object-oriented programming languages, such as C++ and Java; computer-aided software engineering (CASE) tools; and artificial intelligence shells, which are increasingly used to create and maintain programs. These languages and tools allow portions of code to be reused in programs that require similar routines. Many programmers also customize a package to clients' specific needs or create better packages.

Computer engineers design, develop, test, and evaluate computer hardware and related equipment, software programs, and systems. Although programmers write and support programs in new languages, much of the design and development now is the responsibility of *software engineers* or *software developers*. (See the description of Software Publishers.) Software engineers in the systems design and related services field must possess strong programming skills, but are more concerned with developing algorithms and analyzing and solving programming problems for specific network systems than with actually writing code. *Computer systems software engineers* primarily write, modify, test, and develop software to meet the needs of a particular customer. They develop software systems for control and automation in manufacturing, business, and other areas.

Professionals involved in analyzing and solving problems include *systems analysts*, who study business, scientific, or engineering data-processing problems and design new flows of information. Computers need to be connected to each other and to a control server to allow communication among users, thus enhancing use of their computing power. Systems analysts tie together hardware and software to give an organization the maximum benefit from its investment in machines, personnel, and business processes. To do this, these workers may design entirely new systems or add a single new software application to harness more of the computer's power. They use data modeling, structured analysis, information engineering, and other methods. Systems analysts prepare charts for programmers to follow for proper coding and also perform cost-benefit analyses to help management to evaluate the system. These analysts also ensure that the system performs to its specifications by testing it thoroughly.

Database administrators determine ways to organize and store data and work with database management systems software. They set up computer databases and test and coordinate changes to them. Because they also may be responsible for design implementation and system security, database administrators often plan and coordinate security measures.

Computer and information scientists work as theorists, researchers, or inventors. They apply a higher level of theoretical expertise and innovation and develop solutions to complex problems relating to computer hardware and software. Computer and information scientists with advanced backgrounds in security may be employed as cyberspace security specialists in disaster recovery situations or in custom security software installation.

Computer support specialists provide technical assistance, support, and advice to customers and users. This group of occupations includes workers with a variety of titles, such as *technical support specialists* and *help-desk technicians*. These troubleshooters interpret problems and provide technical support for hardware, software, and systems. Support specialists may work either within a company or other organization or directly for a computer hardware or software vendor. They answer telephone calls, analyze problems using automated diagnostic programs, and resolve recurrent difficulties encountered by users.

Other computer specialists include a wide range of related professionals who specialize in operation, analysis, education, application, or design for a particular piece of the system. Many are involved in the design, testing, and evaluation of network systems, such as local area net-

works (LANs), wide area networks (WANs), Internet, and other data communications systems. Specialty occupations reflect an emphasis on client-server applications and end-user support; however, occupational titles shift rapidly to reflect new developments in technology.

Table 2. Employment of wage and salary workers in computer systems design and related services by occupation, 2004 and projected change, 2004–2014 (Employment in thousands)

Occupation	Employment, 2004 Number	Percent	Percent change, 2004–2014
Total, all occupations	1,147	100.0	39.5
Management, business, and financial occupations	201	17.5	38.7
Chief executives	8	0.7	35.6
General and operations managers	33	2.9	34.2
Marketing managers	9	0.8	44.1
Sales managers	8	0.7	45.1
Computer and information systems managers	36	3.1	42.0
Human resources, training, and labor relations specialists	15	1.3	41.8
Management analysts	24	2.1	35.6
Accountants and auditors	12	1.0	37.3
Professional and related occupations	688	59.9	45.5
Computer and information scientists, research	8	0.7	35.6
Computer programmers	112	9.8	10.6
Computer software engineers, applications	133	11.6	62.7
Computer software engineers, systems software	87	7.6	62.2
Computer support specialists	83	7.2	35.6
Computer systems analysts	87	7.6	49.2
Database administrators	14	1.2	56.4
Network and computer systems administrators	40	3.5	58.1
Network systems and data communications analysts	29	2.5	81.5
Computer specialists, all other	15	1.3	35.6

Occupation	Employment, 2004		Percent change, 2004–2014
	Number	Percent	
Computer hardware engineers	12	1.0	37.3
Electrical and electronics engineers	7	0.6	37.3
Multi-media artists and animators	4	0.4	35.6
Technical writers	8	0.7	35.6
Sales and related occupations	67	5.9	24.5
Sales representatives, services	20	1.8	35.5
Sales representatives, wholesale and manufacturing	30	2.6	14.8
Sales engineers	6	0.5	39.2
Office and administrative support occupations	160	13.9	22.3
First-line supervisors/ managers of office and administrative support workers	10	0.9	22.9
Bookkeeping, accounting, and auditing clerks	16	1.4	22.0
Customer service representatives	36	3.1	40.6
Secretaries and administrative assistants	29	2.5	20.7
Office clerks, general	24	2.1	20.7
Installation, maintenance, and repair occupations	20	1.7	31.3
Electrical and electronic equipment mechanics, installers, and repairers	14	1.2	29.1

Note: May not add to totals due to omission of occupations with small employment

Network systems and data communications analysts, for example, design and evaluate network systems, such as LANs, WANs, and Internet systems. They perform network modeling, analysis, and planning and may deal with the interfacing of computer and communications equipment. With the explosive growth of the Internet, this worker group has come to include a variety of occupations relating to design, development, and maintenance of Web sites and their servers. *Web developers* are responsible for day-to-day site design and creation. *Webmasters* are responsible for the technical aspects of the Web site, including performance issues such as speed of access, and for approving site content.

Network or *computer systems administrators* install, configure, and support an organization's LAN, WAN, network segment, or Internet functions. They maintain network hardware and software, analyze problems, and monitor the network to ensure availability to system users. Administrators also may plan, coordinate, and implement network security measures. In some organizations, *computer security specialists* are responsible for the organization's information security.

Computer and information systems managers direct the work of systems analysts, computer programmers, and other computer-related workers. They analyze the computer and information needs of their organization and determine personnel and equipment requirements. These managers plan and coordinate activities such as the installation and upgrading of hardware and software; programming and systems design; development of computer networks; and construction of Internet and intranet sites.

Training, Other Qualifications, and Advancement

Occupations in the computer systems design and related services field require varying levels of education. The level of education and type of training required depend on employers' needs. One factor affecting these needs is changes in technology. In the past, there has been strong demand for workers with skills related to the Internet, sending employers scrambling to find workers capable of implementing "hot" new technologies. As the job market for computer specialists has become more competitive, employers have become more selective in the hiring process. Formerly, employers might hire an applicant with less computer-related education or experience in efforts to keep up with the fast growth in this field. Growth in the number of qualified workers, as well as shrinking of the technology job market from its peak earlier in the decade, has allowed employers to become more selective, hiring those candidates with more education and more experience.

Computer programmers commonly hold a bachelor's degree; however, there are no universal educational requirements. Some hold a degree in computer science, mathematics, or information systems, while others have taken special courses in computer programming to supplement their study in fields such as accounting, inventory control, or other areas of business. Because employers' needs are so varied, a 2-year degree or certificate may be sufficient for some positions, so long as applicants possess the right technical skills.

Most computer systems analysts and computer engineers, on the other hand, usually have a bachelor's or higher degree and work experience. Many hold advanced degrees in technical fields or a master's degree in business administration (MBA) with a concentration in information systems and are specialists in their fields. For systems analyst, programmer-analyst, or even database administrator positions, many employers seek applicants who have a bachelor's degree in computer science, information science, or management information systems (MIS). For computer and information scientists, a doctoral degree generally is required due to the highly technical nature of the work. For some networks systems and data communication analysts, such as Webmasters, an associate degree or certificate generally is sufficient, although more advanced positions might require a computer-related bachelor's degree.

Persons interested in becoming a computer support specialist generally need only an associate degree in a computer-related field as well as significant hands-on experience with computers. They also must possess strong problem-solving and analytical skills as well as excellent communication skills because troubleshooting and helping others are such a vital part of the job. And because there is constant interaction on the job with other computer personnel, customers, or employees, computer support specialists must be able to communicate effectively on paper, via e-mail, or in person. They also must possess strong writing skills in order to prepare manuals for employees and customers. As technology continues to improve, computer support specialists must constantly strive to stay up to date and to acquire new skills if they wish to remain competitive in the field.

Computer and information systems managers usually require a bachelor's degree in a computer-related occupation, combined with work experience. Employers, though, often prefer a graduate degree, especially an MBA with technology as a core component.

The size of the firm and the local demand for workers also may influence training requirements for specific jobs. Smaller firms may be willing to train informally on the job, whereas larger organizations may pay for formal training or higher education. For example, many of the marketing and sales workers are able to secure entry-level jobs with little technical knowledge but quickly learn the technical knowledge necessary for their company and product. With more formal education, employees may advance to completely different jobs within the field. Education or training in a specialty area may provide new opportunities for the worker and allow the establishment to offer new services. Another factor driving employers' needs is the timeframe within which a project must be completed. Projects that have tight deadlines and involve evening and weekend work require flexible workers.

As technological advances in the computer field continue, employers in all areas demand a higher level of skill and expertise. With information technology expanding into more sectors of the economy, employers are requiring that workers possess some expertise in other fields. For example, a computer software engineer interested in working for a bank should have some expertise in finance as they integrate new technologies into the computer system of the bank. Employers, hardware and software vendors, colleges and universities, private training institutions, or professional computing societies offer continuing education and professional development seminars. Technical or professional certification is a way by which employers ensure the competency or quality of computer professionals. Certification can be obtained voluntarily, although many vendors now offer employees help in becoming certified or even require professionals who work with their products to be certified.

Voluntary certification is available through many different types of organizations. Hundreds of different certifications are available, ranging from a certified Internet Webmaster to a certified networking professional. Although professional certification is not mandatory, it may provide a jobseeker a competitive advantage. Also, government, academic institutions, and other employers increasingly seek workers with certifications in information security, reflecting the importance of keeping complex computer networks and vital electronic infrastructure safe from intruders.

Professional and Business Services

Entry-level computer programmers usually start working with an experienced programmer, updating existing code, generating lines of one portion of a larger program, or writing relatively simple programs. They then advance to more difficult programming and may become project supervisors or move into higher management positions within the organization. Many programmers who work closely with systems analysts advance to systems analyst positions.

Systems analysts may begin working with experienced analysts or may deal with only small systems or one aspect of a system. They also may move into supervisory positions as they gain further education or work experience. Systems analysts who work with one type of system, or one aspect or application of a system, can become specialty consultants or move into management positions. Computer engineers and scientists who show leadership ability also can become project managers or advance into management positions, such as manager of information systems or chief information officer. Technical support specialists may advance by developing expertise in an area that leads to other opportunities. For example, those responsible for network support may advance into network administration or network security.

Consulting is an attractive option for experienced workers who do not wish to advance to management positions or who would rather continue to work with hands-on applications or in a particular specialty. These workers may market their services on their own, under contract as specialized consultants, or with an organization that provides consulting services to outside clients. Many of the largest firms today have subsidiaries that offer specialized services to the host company and to outside clients. Large consulting and computer firms often hire inexperienced college graduates and put them through intensive, company-based programs that train them to provide such services.

Many experienced workers move into sales positions as they gain knowledge of specific products. The emergence of various forms of e-commerce has resulted in efforts by technical workers to make Web sites and content appealing to potential customers so that they become comfortable conducting transactions over the Internet. Computer programmers who adapt prepackaged software for accounting organizations may use their specialized knowledge to sell such products to similar firms.

Outlook

The computer systems design and related services field grew dramatically throughout the 1990s as employment more than doubled. And despite recent job losses in certain sectors, this remains one of the 25 fastest-growing fields in the nation. Wage and salary employment is expected to grow 40 percent by the year 2014, compared with only 14 percent growth projected for the entire economy. Given the rate at which the computer systems design and related services field is expected to grow and the increasing complexity of technology, job opportunities will be favorable for most workers. The best opportunities will be in professional and related occupations, reflecting their growth and the continuing demand for higher-level skills to keep up with changes in technology. However, employment growth will not be as robust as it was during the last decade due to increasing productivity and offshore outsourcing of some job functions to lower-wage foreign countries.

An increasing reliance on information technology, combined with falling prices of computers and related hardware, means that individuals and organizations will continue to turn to computer systems design and related services firms to maximize the return on their investments in equipment and to fulfill their growing computing needs. Such needs include the expansion of e-commerce, a growing reliance on the Internet, faster and more efficient internal and external communication, and the implementation of new technologies and applications. With increasing global competition and rising costs, organizations must be able to obtain and manage the latest information in order to make business decisions. At the same time, the computer systems design and related services field has experienced an increase in the contracting out of some of the more routine services abroad, where labor costs are lower, as companies strive to remain competitive. For example, firms have been able to cut costs by shifting more support services operations abroad to countries with highly educated workers who have strong technical skills. However, the trend toward contracting out work will adversely affect employment of only certain types of workers, such as programmers and computer support specialists, because integrating and designing systems needs to be done on site.

Within the computer systems design and related services field, projected growth varies by sector. The demand for networking and the need to integrate new hardware, software, and communications technologies will drive the demand for consulting and integration. A need for more customized applications development and for support and services to assist users will drive demand for applications development and facilities support services. And, as more individuals and organizations conduct business electronically, the importance of maintaining system and network security will increase. Recent events have made society more conscious of the vulnerability of technology and the Internet. The increasing need for security related to information technology will expand employment opportunities for individuals involved in cyberspace security services such as disaster recovery services, custom security programming, and security software installation services.

This increased need for security will help to create more jobs in the computer systems design and related services field. Security specialists will be employed more often to make judgments on a system's vulnerability. Custom programmers and designers will be asked to help develop new antivirus software, programs, and procedures as preemptive measures to keep "hackers" out and systems virus free. Therefore, employment of security analysts and of consultants with security experience and expertise should rise rapidly.

New growth areas will continue to arise as the result of rapidly evolving technologies and business forces. The expansion of the Internet, the proliferation of Web sites, and "mobile" technology such as wireless Internet have created a demand for a wide variety of new products and services, including online services, network design services, and a range of specialized consulting services. For example, the expansion of the wireless Internet, known as WiFi, brings a new aspect of mobility to information technology. This new technology will allow people to stay connected to the Internet anywhere, anytime—in restaurants, in shops, in hotels, and even on airplanes. As individuals and businesses rely more on more compact, hand-held computers and wireless Internet connections, it will be necessary to integrate the current computer systems with this more-mobile new technology. The expansion of this technology in the next 10 years will lead to an increased need for "mobility consultants" or service firms that can help companies to design and integrate computer systems so that they will be compatible with one another.

The ways in which the Internet is used are constantly changing, along with the products, services, and personnel required to support new applications. Expanding e-commerce changed the way in which companies transact business, enabling markets to expand and an increasing array of services to be provided to customers. And, as the amount of computer-stored information grows, organizations will continue to look for ways to tap the full potential of their vast stores of data. Demand for an even wider array of services should increase as companies continue to expand their capabilities, integrate new technologies, and develop new applications.

Given the increasingly widespread use of information technologies and the overall rate of growth expected for the entire field, most occupations should continue to grow rapidly, although some will do so faster than others. As firms continue to install sophisticated computer networks, set up Internet and intranet sites, and engage in e-commerce, the most rapid growth will occur among computer specialists such as systems analysts, network and computer systems administrators, computer support specialists, and computer and information systems managers. Employment of programmers should continue to expand, but more slowly than that of other occupations; the proportion of programmers will decrease in relation to those of other computer specialists as more routine programming functions are increasingly automated and as more programming is contracted out to businesses in foreign countries at a lower cost.

Earnings

Employees in the computer systems design and related services field generally command higher earnings than the national average. All production or nonsupervisory workers in the field averaged $1,136 a week in 2004, significantly higher than the average of $529 for all fields. This reflects the concentration of professionals and specialists, who often are highly compensated for their specialized skills or expertise. Given the pace at which technology advances in this field, earnings can be driven by demand for specific skills or experience. Workers in segments of the field that offer only professional services have even higher average earnings because there are fewer less-skilled, lower-paid workers in these segments. Earnings in selected occupations in computer systems design and related services appear in table 3.

As one might expect, education and experience influence earnings as well. For example, annual earnings of computer software engineers, applications ranged from less than $43,450 for the lowest-paid 10 percent to more than $118,500 for the highest-paid 10 percent in May 2004. Managers usually earn more because they have been on the job longer and are more experienced than their staffs, but their salaries, too, can vary by level and experience. Accordingly, annual earnings of computer and information systems managers ranged from less than $60,810 for the lowest-paid 10 percent to more than $145,600 for the highest-paid 10 percent in May 2004. Earnings also are affected by other factors, such as size, location, and type of establishment; hours and responsibilities of the employee; and level of sales.

Table 3. Median hourly earnings of the largest occupations in computer systems design and related services, May 2004

Occupation	Computer systems design and related services	All fields
General and operations managers	$56.60	$37.22
Computer and information systems managers	49.93	44.51
Computer software engineers, systems software	38.44	38.34
Computer software engineers, applications	36.97	36.05
Computer systems analysts	33.44	31.95
Computer programmers	32.50	30.24
Network systems and data communications analysts	30.73	29.14
Network and computer systems administrators	30.63	27.98
Computer support specialists	20.55	19.44
Customer service representatives	14.05	12.99

Sources of Additional Information

Further information about computer careers is available from

- Association for Computing Machinery, 1515 Broadway, New York, NY 10036. Internet: http://www.acm.org

- National Workforce Center for Emerging Technologies, 3000 Landerholm Circle SE, Bellevue, WA 98007. Internet: http://www.nwcet.org

Employment Services

- Annual Earnings: $21,320
- Job Growth: 45.5%
- Size of Workforce: 3,501,880
- Self-Employed: 3.2%
- Part-Time: 18.4%

Significant Points

- Employment services ranks among the fields projected to grow the fastest and to provide the most new jobs.

- Most temporary jobs in this field require only graduation from high school, while some permanent jobs may require a bachelor's or higher degree.

- Temporary jobs provide an entry into the workforce, supplemental income, and a bridge to full-time employment for many workers.

Nature of the Field

Although many people associate the employment services field with temporary employment opportunities for clerical workers, the field matches millions of people with jobs, providing both temporary and permanent employment to individuals with a wide variety of education and managerial and professional work experience. Occupations in the field range from secretary to computer systems analyst and from general laborer to nurse. In addition to temporary jobs in these occupations, permanent positions in the field include workers such as employment interviewers and marketing representatives who help assign and place workers in jobs. Nearly half of all jobs in employment services are at large establishments with 250 or more workers (chart 1).

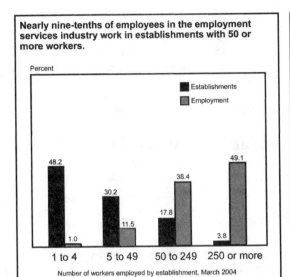

Nearly nine-tenths of employees in the employment services industry work in establishments with 50 or more workers.

Percent

- Establishments
- Employment

48.2
1.0
30.2
11.5
17.8
38.4
3.8
49.1

| 1 to 4 | 5 to 49 | 50 to 249 | 250 or more |

Number of workers employed by establishment, March 2004

The employment services field has three distinct segments. *Employment placement agencies* list employment vacancies and place permanent employees. *Temporary help services*, also referred to as temporary staffing agencies, provide employees to other organizations, on a contract basis and for a limited period, to supplement the workforce of the client. *Professional employer organizations* are engaged in providing human resources and human resources management services to staff client businesses. They also assign workers to client locations, thereby assuming responsibility as an employer while providing a cost-effective approach to the management and administration of the human resources functions of its clients on a contract basis.

The typical employment placement agency has a relatively small permanent staff, usually fewer than 10 workers, who interview jobseekers and try to match their qualifications and skills to those being sought by employers for specific job openings.

In contrast to the smaller employment agencies, temporary help agencies typically employ many more workers. Temporary help services firms provide temporary employees to other businesses to support or supplement their workforce in special situations, such as employee absences, temporary skill shortages, and varying seasonal workloads. Temporary workers are employed and paid by the temporary help services firm but are contracted out to a client for either a prearranged fee or an agreed hourly wage. Some companies choose to use temporary workers

full time on an ongoing basis rather than employ permanent staff, who typically would receive greater salaries and benefits. As a result, the overwhelming majority of workers in the temporary help services segment of the employment services field are temporary workers; relatively few are permanent staff.

Professional employer organizations specialize in performing a wide range of human resource and personnel management duties for their client businesses, including payroll processing, accounting, benefits administration, recruiting, and handling labor relations. Employee leasing establishments, which are a type of professional employer organization, typically acquire and lease back some or all of the employees of their clients and serve as the employer of the leased employees for payroll, benefits, and related purposes.

Traditionally, firms that placed permanent employees usually dealt with highly skilled applicants, such as lawyers or accountants, and those placing temporary employees dealt with less skilled workers, such as administrative support occupations. However, temporary help services firms increasingly place workers who have a range of educational backgrounds and work experience because businesses now are turning to temporary employees to fill all types of positions—from administrative to managerial, financial, professional, and production.

Working Conditions

The average annual work week in the employment services field was about 32.5 hours in 2004, compared with the average of 33.7 hours across all fields. The low average work week reflects the fact that a temporary employee could work 40 or more hours a week on a contract for an extended period and then take a few weeks off from work. Most full-time temporary workers put in 35 to 40 hours a week, while some work longer hours. Permanent employees in employment agencies usually work a standard 40-hour week, unless seasonal fluctuations require more or fewer hours.

Workers employed as permanent staff of employment agencies, temporary help services firms, or professional employer organizations usually work in offices and may meet numerous people daily. Temporary employees work in a variety of environments and often do not stay in any one place long enough to settle into a personal workspace or establish close relationships with co-workers.

Professional and Business Services

Most assignments are of short duration because temporary workers may be called to replace a worker who is ill or on vacation or to help with a short-term surge of work. However, assignments of several weeks or longer occasionally may be offered. On each assignment, temporary employees may work for a new supervisor.

Employment as a temporary is attractive to many. The opportunity for a short-term source of income while enjoying flexible schedules and an ability to take extended leaves of absence is well-suited to students, persons juggling job and family responsibilities, those exploring various careers, and those seeking permanent positions in a chosen career. Firms try to accommodate workers' preferences for particular days or hours of work and for frequency or duration of assignments. Temporary work assignments provide an opportunity to experience a variety of work settings and employers, to sharpen skills through practice, and to learn new skills. Nevertheless, many workers in temporary assignments would prefer the stability and greater benefits associated with full-time work.

The annual injury and illness rate for the employment services field as a whole was 4.4 cases for every 100 full-time workers in 2003, lower than the rate of 5.0 for the entire private sector. Temporary workers in industrial occupations often perform work that is more strenuous and potentially more dangerous, so they may have a higher rate of injury and illness.

Important Characteristics of the Field

Skills: None met the criteria. **Abilities:** Static Strength; Explosive Strength; Dynamic Strength; Trunk Strength; Extent Flexibility; Manual Dexterity. **Work-Related Values:** Supervision, Technical; Co-workers; Moral Values; Advancement; Supervision, Human Relations.

Employment

The employment services field provided 3.5 million jobs in 2004, about 2.4 million of them in temporary help services firms. Professional employer organizations employed about 815,000, and employment placement agencies employed another 262,000. Although about 37,000 of the 64,000 establishments in the field are temporary help services firms, they employ 7 out of 10 field workers.

Employment in the employment services field is distributed throughout the United States. Workers are somewhat younger than those in other fields—43 percent of employment services workers are under 35, compared with 36 percent of all workers, reflecting the large number of clerical and other entry-level positions in the field that require little formal education.

Occupations in the Field

The employment services field encompasses many fields, from office and administrative support occupations to professional and production occupations (table 1). In general, occupations in the field include the permanent staff of employment services firms and the variety of occupations supplied through the temporary help services segment of the field and the professional employer organizations.

The staff of employment service agencies is responsible for the daily operation of the firm. Many of these workers are in management, business, and financial and sales occupations, which together account for only about 8 percent of jobs in this field. *Managers* ensure that the agency is run effectively, and they often conduct interviews of potential clients and jobseekers. *Employment, recruitment, and placement specialists* recruit and evaluate applicants and attempt to match them with client firms. Most work in the personnel supply services field. *Sales workers* actively pursue new client firms and recruit qualified workers. Because of fierce competition among agencies, marketing and sales work at times can be quite stressful.

About 1 in 4 workers in this field are in office and administrative support jobs. These positions may be either temporary or permanent. Experience in office and administrative support occupations usually is preferred for these jobs, although some persons take special training to learn skills such as bookkeeping and word processing. *Receptionists* greet visitors, field telephone calls, and perform assorted office functions. *Secretaries* perform a growing range of tasks, such as keyboarding and answering the telephone, depending on the type of firm in which they work. *Medical secretaries* make appointments and need a familiarity with common medical terms and procedures; *legal secretaries* must be familiar with the format of common legal documents. *General office clerks* file documents, type reports, and enter computer data. *File clerks* classify and store office information and records. *Data entry keyers* type information into a computer database, either through a personal computer or directly into a mainframe computer. *Word processors and typists* enter and format drafts of documents using typewriters or computers. *Bookkeeping clerks* compute, classify, and record transaction data for financial records and reports.

Production occupations and transportation and material moving occupations together account for 41 percent of employment in the employment services field. Many of these jobs seldom require education beyond high school, although related work experience may be preferred for some. Others require significant experience and on-the-job training. Highly skilled *assemblers and fabricators* may assemble and connect parts of electronic devices, while those who are less skilled work on production lines, continually repeating the same operation. *Helpers* perform a variety of mostly unskilled tasks. *Laborers* and *freight, stock, and material movers* transport goods to and from storage areas in either factories, warehouses, or other businesses. *Hand packers and packagers* wrap, package, inspect, and label materials manually, often keeping records of what has been packed and shipped.

A growing number of temporary workers are specialized professional and related workers, who currently account for another 9 percent of employment. Professional and related occupations include a variety of specialists and practitioners, some of whom require many years of postsecondary education to qualify for their positions. For example, *lawyers* or *attorneys* generally need 4 years of college and 3 years of law school. They act as advisors, providing counsel on legal rights and obligations and suggesting particular courses of action in business. Computer programmers write, test, and maintain the detailed instructions, called programs or software, that computers must follow to perform their functions. Other computer specialists include computer support specialists, who provide technical assistance, support, and advice to customers and users. Licensed practical nurses provide basic bedside care to patients. Registered nurses administer medication, tend to patients, and advise patients and family members about procedures and proper care. They usually work in hospitals, but they may be assigned to private duty in patients' homes.

Service workers employed on a temporary basis also include a number of health care support occupations. *Home health aides* usually work in the home of an elder-

ly or ill patient, allowing the patient to stay at home instead of being institutionalized. Becoming a home health aide generally does not require education beyond high school. *Nursing aides* and *orderlies* also seldom need education beyond high school, but employers do prefer previous experience. These workers assist nurses with patient care in hospitals and nursing homes.

The remainder of the workers in this field includes those in farming, fishing, and forestry as well as installation, maintenance, and repair occupations.

Table 1. Employment of wage and salary workers in employment services by occupation, 2004 and projected change, 2004–2014 (Employment in thousands)

Occupation	Employment, 2004		Percent change, 2004–2014
	Number	Percent	
Total, all occupations	3,470	100.0	45.5
Management, business, and financial occupations	168	4.9	61.4
Top executives	28	0.8	62.0
Employment, recruitment, and placement specialists	51	1.5	45.2
Professional and related occupations	325	9.4	57.5
Engineers	20	0.6	56.5
Registered nurses	77	2.2	50.5
Licensed practical and licensed vocational nurses	50	1.4	55.9
Service occupations	337	9.7	56.2
Home health aides	16	0.5	52.1
Nursing aides, orderlies, and attendants	62	1.8	52.1
Food and beverage serving workers	61	1.8	50.1
Building cleaning workers	64	1.9	66.9
Landscaping and grounds-keeping workers	33	1.0	60.2
Sales and related occupations	92	2.7	50.5

Occupation	Employment, 2004		Percent change, 2004–2014
	Number	Percent	
Office and administrative support occupations	848	24.4	43.0
Bookkeeping, accounting, and auditing clerks	39	1.1	47.0
Customer service representatives	79	2.3	74.4
File clerks	27	0.8	–18.3
Receptionists and information clerks	61	1.8	55.6
Shipping, receiving, and traffic clerks	33	1.0	47.9
Stock clerks and order fillers	35	1.0	25.1
Secretaries and administrative assistants	133	3.8	41.0
Data entry keyers	51	1.5	30.7
Word processors and typists	21	0.6	11.2
Office clerks, general	182	5.2	49.3
Construction and extraction occupations	200	5.8	58.8
Construction laborers	72	2.1	66.7
Construction and related workers, all other	43	1.2	53.3
Installation, maintenance, and repair workers	50	1.5	62.9
Maintenance and repair workers, general	22	0.6	63.4
Production occupations	562	16.2	39.5
Team assemblers	122	3.5	42.9
Metal workers and plastic workers	63	1.8	47.0
Packaging and filling machine operators and tenders	72	2.1	39.1
Helpers—production workers	84	2.4	35.0
Production workers, all other	89	2.6	27.0
Transportation and material moving occupations	857	24.7	35.0
Driver/sales workers and truck drivers	69	2.0	70.2
Laborers and freight, stock, and material movers, hand	545	15.7	34.7
Packers and packagers, hand	151	4.3	19.1
Refuse and recyclable material collectors	29	0.8	8.1

Note: May not add to totals due to omission of occupations with small employment

Training, Other Qualifications, and Advancement

The employment services field offers opportunities in many occupations for workers with a variety of skill levels and experience. The majority of temporary jobs still require only graduation from high school or the equivalent, while some permanent jobs, such as those in management, may require a bachelor's or higher degree. In general, the training requirements of temporary workers mirror those for permanent employees in the economy as a whole. As the field expands to include various professional and managerial occupations, therefore, a growing number of jobs will require professional or advanced degrees.

Many temporary help services firms offer skills training to newly hired employees to make them more marketable. This training often is provided free to the temporary worker and is an economical way to acquire training in important skills such as word processing. Agency training policies vary, so persons considering temporary work should ask firms what training they offer and at what cost.

Advancement as a temporary employee usually takes the form of pay increases or greater choice of jobs. More often, temporary workers transfer to full-time jobs with other employers. Turnover among temporary workers within help supply firms usually is very high; many accept offers to work full time for clients for whom they worked as temporary workers. Some experienced temporary workers may be offered permanent jobs with help firms, either as receptionists or in positions screening or training others for temporary jobs.

Staff of employment placement agencies and permanent staff of temporary help services firms typically are employment interviewers, administrative support workers, or managers. The qualifications required of employment interviewers depend partly on the occupations that the employment placement agency or temporary help services firm specializes in placing. For example, agencies that place professionals, such as accountants or nurses, usually employ interviewers with college degrees in similar fields. Agencies specializing in placing administrative support workers, such as secretaries or word processors, are more likely to hire interviewers who have less education but have experience in those occupations. Staffs of professional employer organizations include professionals in human resources management, payroll, risk management, legal services, financial management, employment compliance, and administration.

Although administrative support occupations, such as receptionists, usually do not require formal education beyond high school, related work experience may be needed. Sometimes, staff experienced in administrative support occupations advance to employment interviewer positions. Most managers have college degrees; an undergraduate degree in personnel management or a related field is the best preparation for these jobs. Employment, recruitment, and placement specialists often advance to managerial positions, but seldom without a bachelor's degree.

Outlook

Employment services ranks among the fastest-growing fields in the nation and is expected to be among those that provide the most new jobs. The field is expected to gain about 1.6 million new jobs over the 2004–2014 projection period. Wage and salary employment in the employment services field is expected to grow 46 percent over this period, more than 3 times the 14 percent growth projected for all fields combined.

Increasing demand for flexible work arrangements and schedules, coupled with significant turnover in these positions, should create plentiful job opportunities for persons who seek jobs as temporary or contract workers through 2014. In particular, suppliers of medical personnel to hospitals and other medical facilities should continue to fare well as demand for temporary health care staffing grows to meet the needs of aging baby boomers and to supplement demand for more health care services throughout the country. In addition, businesses are expected to continue to seek new ways to make their staffing patterns more responsive to changes in demand. As a result, firms increasingly may hire temporary employees with specialized skills to reduce costs and to provide the necessary knowledge or experience in certain types of work.

Employment in professional employer organizations also is expected to grow in response to demands by businesses for changes in human resources management. The increasing complexity of employee-related laws and regulations and a desire to control costs, reduce risks, and provide more integrated services will spur more businesses to contract with professional employer organizations to handle their personnel management, health benefits, workers' compensation claims, payroll, tax compliance, and unemployment insurance claims. Businesses are expected to increasingly enter into relationships with professional employer organizations and shift these responsibilities to specialists.

Employment placement agencies are expected to continue growing, but not as fast as temporary help services or professional employer organizations. Growth in these agencies stems from employers' increasing willingness to allow outside agencies to perform the preliminary screening of candidates and the growing acceptance of executive recruitment services. However, online employment placement agencies operate without employment counselors and need fewer administrative support workers. Job postings on employer Web sites; online newspaper classified ads; and job-matching Internet sites operated by educational institutions and professional associations compete with this field, thereby limiting employment growth.

Most new jobs will arise in the largest occupational groups in this field—office and administrative support, production, and transportation and material moving occupations. However, the continuing trend toward specialization also will spur growth among professional workers, including engineers, computer specialists, and health care practitioners such as registered nurses. Managers also will see an increase in new jobs as government increasingly contracts out management functions. In addition, growth of temporary help firms and professional employer organizations—which provide human resource management, risk management, accounting, and information technology services—will provide more opportunities for professional workers within those fields. Marketing and sales representative jobs in temporary staffing firms also are expected to increase along with competition among these firms for the most-qualified workers and the best clients.

Earnings

In 2004, earnings among nonsupervisory workers in employment services firms were $12.94 per hour and $421 per week, lower than the $15.67 an hour and $529 a week for all nongovernment fields.

Earnings vary as widely as the range of skills and formal education among workers in employment services. As in other fields, managers and professionals earn more than clerks and laborers. Also, temporary workers usually earn less than workers employed as permanent staff, but some experienced temporary workers make as much as or more than workers in similar occupations in other fields. Earnings in the largest occupations in employment services appear in table 2.

Table 2. Median hourly earnings of the largest occupations in employment services, May 2004

Occupation	Employment services	All fields
Registered nurses	$30.37	$25.16
Customer service representatives	11.11	12.99
Office clerks, general	10.05	10.95
Team assemblers	8.66	11.42
Production workers, all other	8.51	11.38
Construction laborers	8.40	12.10
Packaging and filling machine operators and tenders	8.29	10.67
Laborers and freight, stock, and material movers, hand	8.14	9.67
Helpers—production workers	8.06	9.70
Packers and packagers, hand	7.80	8.25

Most permanent workers receive basic benefits; temporary workers usually do not receive such benefits unless they work a minimum number of hours or days per week to qualify for benefit plans. Only 4 percent of workers in employment services are union members or are covered by union contracts, compared with about 14 percent of workers in all fields combined.

Sources of Additional Information

For information concerning employment in temporary help services, contact

- American Staffing Association, 277 S. Washington St., Suite 200, Alexandria, VA 22314. Internet: http://www.staffingtoday.net

For information about employment placement agencies, contact

- National Association of Personnel Services, P.O. Box 2128, The Village At Banner Elk, Suite 108, Banner Elk, NC 28604. Internet: http://www.napsweb.org

For information about employer organizations, contact

- National Association of Professional Employer Organizations, 901 N. Pitt St., Suite 150, Alexandria, VA 22314. Internet: http://www.napeo.org

Management, Scientific, and Technical Consulting Services

- Annual Earnings: $46,570
- Job Growth: 60.5%
- Size of Workforce: 794,520
- Self-Employed: 24.2%
- Part-Time: 19.1%

Significant Points

- This field ranks among the fastest growing through the year 2014; however, job competition should remain keen, with the most educated and experienced workers having the best job prospects.
- This field is one of the highest paying.
- About 25 percent of all workers are self-employed.

- About 72 percent of workers have a bachelor's or higher degree; 59 percent of all jobs are in managerial, business, financial, and professional occupations.

Nature of the Field

Management, scientific, and technical consulting firms influence how businesses, governments, and institutions make decisions. Often working behind the scenes, these firms offer resources that clients cannot provide themselves. Usually, one of the resources is expertise—in the form of knowledge, experience, special skills, or creativity; another resource is time or personnel that the client cannot spare. Clients include large and small companies in the private sector; federal, state, and local government agencies; institutions, such as hospitals, universities, unions, and nonprofit organizations; and foreign governments or businesses.

The management, scientific, and technical consulting services field is diverse. Almost anyone with expertise in a given area can enter consulting. Management consulting firms advise on almost every aspect of corporate operations, including marketing; finance; corporate strategy and organization; manufacturing processes; information systems and data processing; electronic commerce (e-commerce) or business; and human resources, benefits, and compensation. Scientific and technical consulting firms provide technical advice relating to almost all nonmanagement organizational activities, including compliance with environmental and workplace safety and health regulations; the application of technology; and knowledge of sciences such as biology, chemistry, and physics.

Larger consulting firms usually provide expertise in a variety of areas, whereas smaller consulting firms generally specialize in one area of consulting. *Administrative management and general management consulting services* firms, for example, offer advice on an organization's day-to-day operations, such as budgeting, asset management, strategic and financial planning, records management, and tax strategy. A manufacturing firm building a new factory might seek the help of consultants to determine in which geographic location it would incur the lowest startup costs and how to build the equipment and design the building layout in order to increase workplace safety and reduce human error. A family opening a new restaurant might hire a consulting firm to help develop a business plan; provide tax advice; or develop occupational safety and health systems for employees, such as providing slip-resistant floors and shoes. Consulting firms also might advise clients in the implementation and use of the latest office technology or computer programs that could increase office productivity. (For information on consulting firms that are engaged primarily in developing computer systems and computer software, see the descriptions of Computer Systems Design and Related Services and Software Publishing elsewhere in Part II.) Some clients might turn to consulting firms to manage the financial aspects of their business. Consultants may provide insight into why a division of the company is not profitable or may recommend an investment strategy that meets the client's needs. (For information on firms that engage in buying and selling financial assets, see the description of Securities, Commodities, and Other Investments elsewhere in Part II.)

Effective management of a client's human capital is the primary work of consulting firms that offer *human resources consulting services*. Firms that focus on this area advise clients on effective personnel policies, employee salaries and benefits, employee recruitment and training, and employee assessment. A client with high employee turnover might seek the help of a consulting firm in improving its retention rate. Consulting firms also might be asked to help determine the appropriate level of employer and employee contributions to health care and retirement plans. Increasingly, firms are outsourcing, or contracting out, the administrative functions of their human resources division to human resources consulting firms that manage timekeeping and payroll systems and administer employee benefits.

One human resources consulting specialty is *executive search consulting*, or *executive recruiting*. Firms in this field are typically referred to as "*headhunters*." Executive search consulting firms are involved in locating the best candidates for top-level management and executive positions. Clients hire executive recruiters in order to save time and preserve confidentiality. Executive search firms keep a large database of executives' resumes and search this database for clients in order to identify candidates who would likely complement the client's corporate culture and strategic plan. Information on these candidates is then submitted to the clients for their selection. Executive search consulting firms also might conduct prescreening interviews and reference and background checks. Some executive search consulting firms specialize

Professional and Business Services

in recruiting for a particular field or geographic area, while others conduct general searches. (For information on firms that provide employment services to jobseekers at all employment levels, see the description of Employment Services, elsewhere in Part II.)

Marketing consulting services firms provide assistance to firms in areas such as developing new products and pricing, forecasting sales, planning and implementing a marketing strategy, and improving customer service. A pharmaceutical firm, for example, might seek advice as to whether it should remove a drug from the market, or a retail clothing chain might seek advice regarding the most effective way to market and sell its clothes—in a direct-mail or online catalog or over the telephone. Clients also might seek the help of a marketing consultant to set up business franchises or license their products.

Another specialty within management consulting is *process, physical distribution, and logistics consulting services*. Firms in this field specialize in the production and distribution of goods from the first stages of securing suppliers to the delivery of finished goods to consumers. Such firms give advice on improvements in the manufacturing process and productivity, product quality control, inventory management, packaging, order processing, the transportation of goods, and materials management and handling. A domestic manufacturing firm might hire a logistics consulting firm to calculate shipping rates and import duties for goods being exported or to determine the most cost-effective method of shipping products. Consulting firms in this field also advise on the latest technology that links suppliers, producers, and customers together to streamline the manufacturing process. Finally, firms in the field might suggest improvements to the manufacturing process in order to utilize inputs better, increase productivity, or decrease the amount of excess inventory.

While some management consulting firms specialize in a particular business process, others provide a range of business services specific to one field, such as health care. Many professionals—for example, doctors—lack the business expertise to manage their practice effectively. Consultants advise these clients regarding the same management issues as they do other businesses, such as staff recruitment, compensation and benefits, asset management, marketing, and other business operations. Some consultants offer advice on matters pertaining directly to the field in question—for instance, for the health care

field, compliance with biohazard removal and patient confidentiality regulations, avoidance of malpractice suits, and methods of dealing with managed care and health insurance companies. Fields such as legal services, telecommunication, and utilities also have consulting firms that specialize in specific issues.

Scientific and technical consulting services firms provide services similar to those offered by management consulting firms, but the information is not management related. One of the largest specialties in scientific and technical consulting services is *environmental consulting services*. Environmental consulting firms identify and evaluate environmental problems, such as inspecting sites for water contaminants, and offer solutions. Some firms in the field advise clients about controlling the emissions of environmental pollutants, cleaning up contaminated sites, establishing a recycling program, and complying with government environmental laws and regulations. A real estate developer, for example, might hire an environmental consulting firm to help design and develop property without damaging natural habitats, such as wetlands. A manufacturing or utilities firm might hire environmental consultants to assess whether the firm is meeting government emissions standards in order to avoid penalties before government regulators inspect the property in question. Finally, many government agencies contract work out to environmental consulting firms to assess environmental contamination in a particular geographic area or to evaluate the costs and benefits of new regulations.

Occupational safety consulting services firms provide services similar to those offered by government agencies and private businesses, identifying workplace safety hazards and ensuring that employers are in compliance with government worker safety regulations. Safety consulting firms might identify hazardous materials or systems that may cause illness or injury, assess safety risks associated with machinery, investigate accidents, and assess the likelihood of lawsuits resulting from safety code violations. Some might specialize in a particular type of hazardous material, while other consultants might specialize in a particular field's safety, such as that of construction, mining, manufacturing, health care, or food processing. As with environmental consulting firms, many government agencies contract work out to safety consulting firms for help with safety engineering, technical projects, and various kinds of assessment.

Security consulting, by contrast, seeks to ensure the safety and security of an organization's physical and human assets that may be threatened by natural or human-made disasters. Clients might hire security consulting firms to assess a building's security needs. The firms may then protect the building against theft and vandalism by installing security cameras, hiring security guards, and providing employee background checks. Other security consultants study a building's design and recommend measures to protect it from damage from fires, tornadoes, floods, earthquakes, or acts of terrorism. Security consultants also may recommend emergency evacuation procedures in the event that these disasters occur. Increasingly, clients are hiring security consulting firms to protect their confidential computer records against hackers and viruses. Most recently, government agencies have hired security consulting firms to advise them on how to protect national monuments and the national transportation, utility, and defense infrastructure—airports, bridges, nuclear reactor plants, water treatment plants, and military barracks—against terrorism.

Scientific and technical consulting firms also advise on a diverse range of issues relating to the physical and social sciences—issues having to with agriculture, biology, chemistry, economics, energy, and physics. Agricultural consulting firms might advise on different farming techniques or machinery that increases agricultural production. Economic consultants might develop forecasting models and advise clients about the potential for a recession or an increase in interest rates that could affect business decisions. Energy consultants might advise clients on how to reduce costs by implementing energy-saving machinery. Finally, biological, chemical, and physics consultants might give theoretical or applied expertise in their chosen field.

Management, scientific, and technical consulting has grown rapidly over the past several decades, with businesses increasingly using consulting services. Using consultants is advantageous because these experts are experienced; are well trained; and keep abreast of the latest technologies, government regulations, and management and production techniques. In addition, consultants are cost effective because they can be hired temporarily and can perform their duties objectively, free of the influence of company politics.

The vast majority of firms in the management, scientific, and technical consulting field are small, primarily because new firms can enter the field quite easily. Licensing, certification, and large capital outlays seldom are necessary for an individual to become a consultant, and the work can be quite lucrative for those with the right education, experience, and contacts. As a result, many wage and salary workers in management, scientific, and technical consulting services eventually leave established firms to go into business for themselves. In addition, after developing specialized expertise, people working in other fields often start their own consulting businesses, and some experienced workers perform consulting work after retiring.

Working Conditions

Working conditions in management, scientific, and technical consulting services are generally similar to those of most office workers operating in a team environment. The work is rarely hazardous, with a few exceptions—for example, environmental or safety consultants who inspect sites for contamination from hazardous materials. In 2003, the field had only 1.1 injuries and illnesses per 100 full-time workers, compared with an average of 5.0 throughout nongovernment fields.

Not all employees in this field work under identical conditions. In 2004, workers in the field averaged 35.0 hours per week, a little above the national average of 33.7. However, many consultants must meet hurried deadlines, which frequently requires working long hours in stressful environments. Consultants whose services are billed hourly often are under pressure to manage their time very carefully. Occasionally, weekend work also is necessary, depending upon the job that is being performed. In addition, some projects might require many executives and consultants to travel extensively or live away from home for extended periods of time. However, new technology—such as laptop computers with remote access to the firm's computer server and videoconferencing machines—allow some consultants to work from home or conduct meetings with clients in different locations, reducing some of the need for business travel.

Most firms encourage employees to attend employer-paid time-management classes. The classes teach participants to reduce the stress sometimes associated with working under strict time constraints. Also, with today's hectic lifestyle, many firms in this field offer or provide health facilities or clubs that employees may use to maintain good health.

Important Characteristics of the Field

Skills: Management of Financial Resources; Service Orientation; Persuasion; Negotiation; Instructing; Active Listening. **Abilities:** Speech Recognition; Written Expression; Speech Clarity; Oral Expression; Oral Comprehension; Inductive Reasoning. **Work-Related Values:** Working Conditions; Social Service; Co-workers; Advancement; Creativity; Social Status.

Employment

The management, scientific, and technical consulting services field had about 779,000 wage and salary workers in 2004; an additional 256,000 workers were self-employed and unpaid family workers, comprising 25 percent of all jobs in this field. Table 1 details how employment is broken down among the different segments of the field.

Table 1. Percent distribution of wage and salary employment in management, scientific, and technical consulting services, 2004

Establishment type	Employment
Management, scientific, and technical consulting, total 100.0	
Administrative management and general management consulting 36.8	
Marketing consulting 13.6	
Human resources and executive search consulting..12.9	
Other management consulting.....................10.8	
Process, physical distribution, and logistics consulting...9.3	
Environmental consulting 8.1	
Other scientific and technical consulting 8.5	

The vast majority of establishments in the field were fairly small, employing fewer than 5 workers (chart 1). Self-employed individuals operated many of these small firms. Despite the prevalence of small firms and self-employed workers, large firms tend to dominate the field. Approximately 54 percent of jobs are found in the 4 percent of establishments with 20 or more employees, and some of the largest firms in the field employ several thousand people.

Although employees in this field work in all parts of the country, many workers are concentrated near large urban centers.

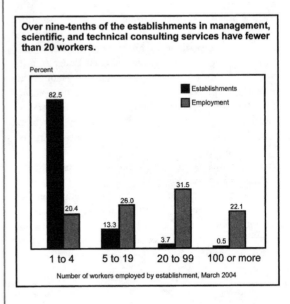

Over nine-tenths of the establishments in management, scientific, and technical consulting services have fewer than 20 workers.

Percent

Establishments
Employment

| 1 to 4 | 5 to 19 | 20 to 99 | 100 or more |

82.5, 20.4, 13.3, 26.0, 3.7, 31.5, 0.5, 22.1

Number of workers employed by establishment, March 2004

Occupations in the Field

Most management, scientific, and technical consulting services are fairly specialized; still, the field comprises a variety of occupations (table 2). Some of these occupations, such as *environmental engineers,* are specific to only one segment of the field, whereas others, such as *secretaries and administrative assistants,* can be found throughout the field.

Table 2. Employment of wage and salary workers in management, scientific, and technical consulting services by occupation, 2004 and projected change, 2004–2014 (Employment in thousands)

Occupation	Employment, 2004 Number	Percent	Percent change, 2004–2014
Total, all occupations ....779......100.0..............60.5			
Management, business, and financial occupations........258........33.1..............67.6			
Top executives ....34..........4.4..............64.8			
Marketing and sales managers ....8..........1.1..............77.2			

Occupation	Employment, 2004		Percent change, 2004–2014
	Number	Percent	
Human resources, training, and labor relations specialists	27	3.5	69.4
Management analysts	95	12.3	66.2
Accountants and auditors	15	2.0	65.6
Financial analysts and advisors	7	0.9	57.0
Professional and related occupations	202	25.9	67.3
Computer programmers	9	1.2	35.6
Computer software engineers	23	2.9	98.0
Computer support specialists	9	1.2	66.2
Computer systems analysts	13	1.6	82.9
Engineers	26	3.4	66.8
Drafters, engineering, and mapping technicians	7	0.9	67.4
Environmental scientists and specialists, including health	11	1.5	16.9
Market research analysts	13	1.7	66.2
Environmental science and protection technicians, including health	6	0.7	54.4
Designers	7	0.9	65.0
Service occupations	15	1.9	62.9
Sales and related occupations	55	7.1	55.8
Sales representatives, services	16	2.0	64.1
Sales representatives, wholesale and manufacturing	9	1.2	66.2
Telemarketers	13	1.7	30.1
Office and administrative support occupations	205	26.3	46.1
Supervisors, office and administrative support workers	14	1.7	50.7
Bookkeeping, accounting, and auditing clerks	18	2.3	49.6
Customer service representatives	27	3.4	69.6

Occupation	Employment, 2004		Percent change, 2004–2014
	Number	Percent	
Secretaries and administrative assistants	52	6.7	41.2
Data entry and information processing workers	10	1.3	22.9
Office clerks, general	36	4.7	48.0
Transportation and material moving occupations	20	2.6	57.7

Note: May not add to totals due to omission of occupations with small employment

Compared with other fields, the management, scientific, and technical consulting services field has a relatively high proportion of highly educated workers. About 42 percent have a bachelor's degree, compared with 20 percent of workers throughout the economy. Around 30 percent have a master's or higher degree, compared with 10 percent of workers throughout the economy. Certain jobs may have stringent entry requirements. For example, some management consulting firms prefer to hire only workers who have a master's degree in business administration (MBA). Other positions can be attained only after many years of related experience.

In management, scientific, and technical consulting services, workers in management and business and financial operations occupations and in professional and related occupations combined make up 59 percent of employment. These same occupational groups account for about 30 percent of workers across the entire economy. These groups of workers comprise a disproportionate share of jobs in the field because workers with education and experience in business management and workers with scientific, engineering, and other technical backgrounds conduct most of the consulting work in this field.

Top executives, the largest managerial occupation in the field, includes both the highest-level managers—such as chief executive officers and vice presidents—and many top managers with diverse duties. In consulting firms, top executives with partial ownership and profit-sharing privileges might be referred to as partners. Top-level managers or partners shape company policy, often with the help of other executives or a board of directors. They

Professional and Business Services

oversee all activities of the firm, coordinate the duties of subordinate executives and managers, and often bear ultimate responsibility for a firm's performance. Mid-level managers or partners may oversee all the activities of one department or all the activities of one or more clients.

Management analysts, also called *management consultants,* is the largest occupation in the management consulting field. Their work is quite varied, depending on the nature of the project and the client's needs. In general, consultants study and analyze business-related problems, synthesizing information from many sources, and rec-ommend solutions. The solutions can include overhaul-ing a client's computer systems, offering early retirement incentives to middle managers, recommending a switch in health plans, improving just-in-time inventory sys-tems, hiring public relations firms, or selling trouble-some parts of businesses. Because of the varied nature of these jobs, firms hire workers with diverse backgrounds, such as engineering, finance, actuarial science, chemistry, and business. Many firms require consultants to have an MBA, whereas others hire workers who have only a bachelor's degree. Many workers have experience in other fields prior to entering management consulting work.

Other management and business and financial opera-tions occupations include *administrative services man-agers,* who typically administer a consulting firm's support services. These managers oversee secretaries, data entry keyers, bookkeepers, and other clerical staff. In the management consulting services field, they also often supervise a client's clerical and support staff and do con-sulting work in that area. *Advertising, marketing, promo-tions, public relations, and sales managers* oversee the consulting firm's marketing and sales departments, researching and targeting new clients and also helping on consulting projects having to do with marketing. *Computer and information systems managers* ensure that the consulting firm's computer and network systems are fully operational and oversee other computer and techni-cal workers, such as computer support specialists. These managers might also supervise certain consulting proj-ects involving computer and information technology. *Financial managers* prepare financial statements and assess the financial health of firms. Often, they must have at least a bachelor's degree in accounting or finance. *Human resources, training, and labor relations managers and specialists* supervise the activities of a consulting

firm's human resources department, managing personnel records, payroll, benefits, and employee recruitment and training. These managers might also supervise projects for clients in the human resources consulting field. In scientific and technical consulting firms, *engineering and natural sciences managers* oversee the engineers and scien-tists working for their consulting firms. *Accountants* and *auditors* monitor firms' financial transactions and often report to financial managers. More recently, accountants and auditors have been involved in consulting projects for clients involving the preparation of financial state-ments, tax strategy, budget or retirement planning, and the implementation of accounting software.

Workers in professional and related occupations are employed mainly in the scientific and technical consult-ing portion of the field. Many of these workers are engi-neers and scientists who utilize their expertise through consulting. For example, *environmental engineers* and *environmental scientists and geoscientists* are employed by environmental consulting firms to evaluate environmen-tal damage or assess compliance with environmental laws and regulations. Other engineers, such as *agricultural, biomedical, chemical, mining and geological, nuclear,* and *petroleum engineers,* and physical and life scientists, such as *agricultural and food scientists, biological scientists, chemists, materials scientists,* and *physicists and astronomers,* are employed by consulting firms specializ-ing in their scientific disciplines. *Architects* and *civil and industrial engineers* are sometimes employed by safety and security consulting firms to assess the construction of buildings and other structures, such as bridges, and to make recommendations regarding reinforcing these structures against damage.

Other professional and related workers include *econo-mists, market and survey researchers,* and *lawyers.* Economists are employed by economic consulting firms to conduct economic research and advise clients on eco-nomic trends. Market and survey researchers are mainly employed by marketing consulting firms to conduct sur-veys and research on various topics. Lawyers are employed in virtually all management, scientific, and technical consulting fields to represent their consulting firms in case of a lawsuit and to advise the firms, as well as clients, on changes in laws and regulations pertaining to their areas of expertise.

Designers in this field are mostly *graphic designers* who use a variety of print, electronic, and film media to cre-ate designs that meet clients' commercial needs. Using computer software, these workers develop the overall lay-out and design of magazines, newspapers, journals, corporate reports, and other publications. They also may produce promotional displays and marketing brochures for products and services and may design distinctive company logos for products and businesses. An increasing number of graphic designers develop material to appear on Internet homepages.

The rapid spread of computers and information technology has generated a need for highly trained computer specialists to design and develop new hardware and software systems and to incorporate new technologies. *Systems analysts* design new computer systems or redesign old systems for new applications. They solve computer problems and enable computer technology to meet their organization's particular needs. For example, a systems analyst from a management consulting firm might be hired by a wholesale firm to implement an online inventory database. *Computer software engineers*, by contrast, can be involved in the design and development of software systems for the control and automation of manufacturing, business, and management processes. Other computer specialists include *computer support specialists*, who provide technical assistance, support, and advice to customers and users, and *database administrators*, who work with database management systems software and determine ways to organize and store data. Computer specialists such as systems analysts, computer scientists, and computer engineers sometimes are referred to simply as "consultants."

Technical workers also include *computer programmers*, who write programs and create software—often in close conjunction with systems analysts—and *engineering technicians*, who aid engineers in research and development. Like systems analysts and engineers, these workers are found primarily in the business and management consulting segments of the field.

Office and administrative support positions in management, scientific, and technical consulting services resemble those in other fields and account for 26 percent of field employment. Particularly numerous are *secretaries* and *administrative assistants* and *bookkeeping, accounting, and auditing clerks*, who record and classify financial data. The field also employs many *supervisors* and *managers of office and administrative support workers*, who oversee the support staff, often reporting to administrative services managers.

Training, Other Qualifications, and Advancement

Training and advancement opportunities vary widely within management, scientific, and technical consulting services, but most jobs in the field are similar in three respects. First, clients usually hire consulting firms on the basis of the expertise of their staffs, so proper training of employees is vital to the success of firms. Second, although employers generally prefer a bachelor's or higher degree, most jobs also require extensive on-the-job training or related experience. Third, advancement opportunities are best for workers with the highest levels of education.

Most consulting specialties provide a variety of different ways to enter the profession. Whereas very few universities or colleges offer formal programs of study in management consulting, many fields provide a suitable background. These fields include most areas of business and management, such as marketing and accounting, as well as economics, computer and information sciences, and engineering. Some schools offer programs in logistics and safety that relate directly to consulting jobs in those areas. Some college graduates with a bachelor's or master's degree and no previous work experience are hired right out of school by consulting firms and go through extensive on-the-job training. The method and extent of training can vary with the type of consulting involved and the nature of the firm. Some college students might have an advantage over other candidates if they complete an internship with a consulting firm during their studies. Other workers with related experience are hired as consultants later in their careers. For example, former military or law enforcement workers often work for security consulting firms. Similarly, some government workers with experience in enforcing regulations might join an environmental or safety consulting firm. Consultants in scientific fields often have a master's or doctoral degree, and some previously have taught at colleges and universities.

Most organizations require their employees to possess a variety of skills. To a large extent, a degree is only one desired qualification; workers also must possess proven analytical and problem-solving abilities, excellent written and verbal communications skills, experience in a particular specialty, assertiveness and motivation, strong attention to detail, and a willingness to work long hours if necessary. Consultants also must possess high ethical

Professional and Business Services

standards because most consulting firms and clients will contact references and former clients to make sure that the quality of their work was of the highest standard.

Management and leadership classes and seminars are available throughout the United States. Some are hosted by volunteer senior executives and management experts representing a variety of businesses and fields. A number of large firms invest a great deal of time and money in training programs, educating new hires in formal classroom settings over several weeks or even months, and some even have separate training facilities. Small firms often combine formal and on-the-job training.

The Institute of Management Consultants USA, Inc. (IMC USA), offers a wide range of professional development programs and resources, such as meetings and workshops that can be helpful for management consultants. The IMC USA also offers the certified management consultant (CMC) designation to those who meet minimum levels of education and experience, submit reviews from clients, and pass an interview and exam covering the IMC USA's code of ethics. Management consultants with a CMC designation must be recertified every 3 years.

Other areas of specialization, such as logistics and safety, also offer certification programs for professionals, but these programs are not necessarily designed for consultants. Still, consultants might find it beneficial to receive designations from these programs as well. Although certification is not mandatory for management consultants, it may give a jobseeker a competitive advantage.

Entry-level positions within the management consulting field involve very little responsibility at the beginning. Striving for and displaying quality work results in more responsibility. Most management consulting firms have two entry-level positions. Workers who hold bachelor's degrees usually start as research associates; those with graduate degrees generally begin as consultants. Successful workers progress through the ranks from research associate to consultant, management consultant, senior consultant, junior partner, and, after many years, senior partner. In some firms, however, it is very difficult for research associates to progress to the next level without further education. As a result, many management consulting firms offer tuition assistance, grants, or reimbursement plans so that workers can attain an MBA or some other degree.

Almost all workers in management consulting services receive on-the-job training; some have prior work experience in a related field. Most managerial and supervisory workers gain experience informally, overseeing a few workers or part of a project under the close supervision of a senior manager. Workers who advance to high-level managerial or supervisory jobs in management services firms usually have an extensive educational background. Less commonly, some large firms offer formal management training.

The management, scientific, and technical consulting services field offers excellent opportunities for self-employment. Because capital requirements are low, highly experienced workers can start their own businesses fairly easily and cheaply; indeed, every year, thousands of workers in this field go into business for themselves. Some of these workers come from established management, scientific, and technical consulting services firms, whereas others leave field, government, or academic jobs to start their own businesses. Still others remain employed in their primary organizations, but have their own consulting jobs on the side.

Outlook

Between 2004 and 2014, wage and salary employment in the management, scientific, and technical consulting services field is expected to grow by 60 percent, much faster than the 14 percent growth projected for all fields, ranking the field as the fifth-fastest-growing field in the economy. All areas of consulting should experience strong growth. Still, despite the projected growth in the field, job competition should remain keen because the prestigious and independent nature of the work and the generous salary and benefits attract more jobseekers than openings every year. Because of the high degree of competition, those with the most education and job experience will likely have the best prospects.

Projected job growth can be attributed primarily to economic growth and to the continuing complexity of business. A growing number of businesses means increased demand for advice in all areas of business planning as consultants draft business plans and budgets, develop strategy, and determine appropriate salaries and benefits for employees. The expansion of franchised restaurants and retail stores will spur demand for marketing consultants to determine the best locations and develop marketing plans. The expansion of business also will create opportunities for logistics consulting firms trying to link new suppliers with producers and get the finished goods to consumers. Finally, businesses will continue to need advice on compliance with government workplace safety and environmental laws. Clients need consultants to keep them up to date on the latest changes in legislation affecting their businesses, including changes to tax laws, environmental regulations, and policies affecting employee benefits and health care and workplace safety. As a result, firms specializing in human resources, environmental, and safety consulting should be in strong demand.

The increasing use of new technology and computer software is another major factor contributing to growth in all areas of consulting. Management consulting firms help clients implement new accounting and payroll software, whereas environmental and safety consulting firms advise clients on the use of computer technology in monitoring harmful substances in the environment or workplace. Consulting firms also might help design new computer systems or online distribution systems. One of the biggest areas upon which technology has had an impact is logistics consulting. The Internet has greatly increased the ability of businesses to link to and communicate with their suppliers and customers, increasing productivity and decreasing costs. Technology-related consulting projects have become so important that many traditional consulting firms are now merging with or setting up joint ventures with technology companies so that each firm has access to the other's resources in order to serve clients better.

The trend toward outsourcing and mergers also will create opportunities for consulting firms. In order to cut costs, many firms are outsourcing administrative and human resources functions to consultants specializing in these services. This should provide opportunities in human resources consulting for firms that manage their clients' payroll systems and benefits programs. At the same time, increasing competition has led to more business mergers, providing opportunities for consulting firms to assist in the process.

Globalization, too, will continue to provide numerous opportunities for consulting firms wishing to expand their services, or help their clients expand, into foreign markets. Consulting firms can advise clients on strategy as well as foreign laws, regarding taxes, employment, worker safety, and the environment. The growth of inter-

national businesses has created numerous opportunities for logistics consulting firms because now businesses have an international network of suppliers and consumers, which requires more coordination.

An increasing emphasis on protecting a firm's employees, facilities, and information against deliberate acts of sabotage will continue to create numerous opportunities for security consultants. These consultants provide assistance on every aspect of security, from protecting against computer viruses to reinforcing buildings against bomb blasts. Logistics consulting firms also are finding opportunities helping clients secure their supply chain against interruptions that might arise from terrorist acts, such as the disruption of shipping or railroad facilities. As security concerns grow, rising insurance costs, as well as the threat of lawsuits, are providing added incentives for businesses to protect the welfare of their employees.

Growth in management, scientific, and technical consulting services might be hampered by increasing competition from nontraditional consulting firms, such as investment banks, accounting firms, technology firms, and law firms. As consulting firms continue to expand their services, they will be forced to compete with a more diverse group of firms that provide similar services.

Economic downturns also can have an adverse effect on employment growth in consulting. As businesses are forced to cut costs, consultants may be among the first expenses that businesses eliminate. Furthermore, growth in some consulting specialties, such as executive search consulting, is directly tied to the health of the fields in which they operate. Still, some consulting firms might experience growth during recessions because as clients look to cut costs and remain competitive, they might seek the advice of consultants.

Earnings

Management, scientific, and technical consulting services is one of the highest-paying fields. Nonsupervisory wage and salary workers in the field averaged $826 a week in 2004, compared with $529 for workers throughout nongovernment fields. Medial hourly earnings in the largest occupations in management, scientific, and technical consulting appear in table 3.

Professional and Business Services

Table 3. Median hourly earnings of the largest occupations in management, scientific, and technical consulting services, May 2004

Occupation	Management, scientific, and technical consulting services	All fields
General and operations managers	$55.95	$37.22
Management analysts	34.85	30.51
Accountants and auditors	25.82	24.41
Employment, recruitment, and placement specialists	25.39	19.80
Business operations specialists, all other	25.31	25.70
Executive secretaries and administrative assistants	17.69	16.81
Bookkeeping, accounting, and auditing clerks	14.98	13.74
Customer service representatives	13.57	12.99
Secretaries, except legal, medical, and executive	13.05	12.55
Office clerks, general	11.14	10.95

The data in the table do not reflect earnings for self-employed workers, who often are paid very well. Also, both managerial workers and high-level professionals can make considerably more than the field average. According to the Association of Management Consulting Firms, the 2004 average total compensation (salary plus bonus or profit sharing) for research associates was $52,482; for entry-level consultants, $65,066; for management consultants, $89,116; for senior consultants, $123,305; for junior partners, $191,664; and for senior partners, $319,339.

According to a 2004 survey conducted by Abbot, Langer, and Associates, the median annual total cash compensation for junior consultants was $40,000; for consultants, $61,000; for senior consultants, $80,250; for principal consultants, $107,000; and for senior or executive vice presidents, $235,135.

Besides earning a straight salary, many workers receive additional compensation, such as profit sharing, stock ownership, or performance-based bonuses. In some firms, bonuses can constitute one-third, or more, of annual pay.

Sources of Additional Information

For more information about career opportunities in general management consulting, contact

- Association of Management Consulting Firms, 3580 Lexington Ave., New York, NY 10168. Internet: http://www.amcf.org

For more information about career opportunities in executive search consulting, contact

- Association of Executive Search Consultants, 500 Fifth Ave., Suite 930, New York, NY 10110. Internet: http://www.aesc.org

For more information about career opportunities in safety consulting, contact

- American Society of Safety Engineers, 1800 E. Oakton St., Des Plaines, IL 60018. Internet: http://www.asse.org

For more information about the Certified Management Consultant designation, contact

- Institute of Management Consultants USA, 2025 M St., Suite 800, Washington, DC 20036. Internet: http://www.imcusa.org

For more information about the Certified Investment Management Analyst designation, contact

- Investment Management Consultants Association, 5619 DTC Parkway, Suite 500, Greenwood Village, CO 80111. Internet: http://www.imca.org

Scientific Research and Development Services

- Annual Earnings: $58,310
- Job Growth: 11.9%
- Size of Workforce: 549,390
- Self-Employed: 3.3%
- Part-Time: 9.2%

Significant Points

- Professional and related occupations account for 57 percent of all jobs.

- More than 36 percent of workers have a master's, professional, or Ph.D. degree and almost a third have a bachelor's degree.

- Workers must continually update their knowledge to remain competitive.

- Employment growth will be greatest for computer specialists, scientists, engineers, and technicians.

Nature of the Field

From carbon nanotubes to vaccines, workers in the scientific research and development services field create today the technologies that will change the way people live and work in the future. The importance of this field is demonstrated by the considerable attention paid to it by the press, business associations, politicians, and financial markets. Major discoveries are heralded in both the technical and the popular media, and many studies monitor the pace of research and development. New technologies can quickly revolutionize business and leisure, as the Internet has.

Workers in this field conduct much but not all of the scientific research and development (R&D) in the economy. Under the North American Industrial Classification System (NAICS), each establishment is categorized by the activity in which it is primarily engaged; an establishment is defined as a single physical location where business is conducted or services performed. This means that much of the R&D conducted by companies in a wide range of fields—such as pharmaceuticals, chemicals, motor vehicles, and aerospace products—is conducted within the scientific research and development services field because many companies maintain laboratories and other R&D facilities that are located apart from production plants and other establishments characteristic of these fields. While workers in separate R&D establishments are classified in the scientific research and development services field, some R&D occurs in establishments that mainly engage in other activities, such as manufacturing or educational services. The latter type of R&D is not included within the scientific research and development services field.

R&D comprises three types of activities. Basic research is conducted to further scientific knowledge without any direct application. This sort of research typically involves a high level of theory and is very risky; many projects fail to produce conclusive or novel results. Due to the risk and broad applicability of the results, most basic research is funded by government, universities, or nonprofit organizations. Applied research is the bridge between science and business. It is directed toward solving some general problem, but may produce several viable options that all achieve some aspect of the goal. Development, which accounts for more than half of all R&D, according to the National Science Board, then refines the technologies or processes of applied research into immediately usable products. Most development is done by nongovernment fields and is generally oriented toward manufacturing. Nearly everything consumers use, from antibiotics to zoom lenses, is a product of basic research, applied research, and development.

This field includes diverse fields. The most fundamental division of the scientific research and development services field is that between R&D in the physical, engineering, and life sciences and R&D in the social sciences and humanities. Important areas of research and development in the physical, engineering, and life sciences include the biotechnology, nanotechnology, pharmaceutical, chemical and materials science, electronics, aerospace, and automotive fields. Important fields of research and development in the social sciences and humanities include economics, sociology, anthropology, and psychology.

Biotechnology is among the most active fields of research and attracts about a quarter of all funding from companies in the field, according to National Science Board data. Work in this field seeks to understand and use the fundamental processes of cellular life to develop more effective medicines, consumer products, and industrial processes. Advances in biotechnology have led to new drugs and vaccines, disease-resistant crops, more efficient enzymatic manufacturing processes, and novel methods of dealing with hazardous materials. Bioinformatics, a branch of biotechnology using information technologies to work with biological data like DNA, is a particularly vibrant new area of work. Much of the interest in biotechnology has derived from the medical applications of its basic and applied research.

Nanotechnology is perhaps even more of an emerging field than biotechnology, and they often overlap in their work on the molecular level, such as with DNA tagging. Nanotechnology is the study of new structures roughly on the same scale as individual atoms, or one millionth of a millimeter. At this size, materials behave differently and can be made into new structures such as quantum dots, which are small devices that behave like artificial atoms and can be used to tag sequences of DNA, make nanoscopic switches for electronics, or produce extremely small lasers for communications equipment. Because basic and applied research comprises the bulk of work, immediate applications of nanotechnology are still relatively few. The National Nanotechnology Initiative coordinates research funding from federal agencies and facilitates the development of new technologies resulting from this research.

Pharmaceutical R&D is involved in the discovery of new drugs, antibiotics, and vaccines to treat or prevent a wide range of health problems. This field also has benefited greatly from advances in biotechnology, nanotechnology, and chemistry, allowing better models of biochemical processes and more efficient testing. Because a great deal of time is required to develop a new treatment, most companies have several major programs running concurrently, in what is sometimes referred to as the development "pipeline." Because many projects incorporate all aspects of R&D, the pharmaceuticals field tends to do more basic research than do other fields.

Chemical and materials science R&D focuses on the design and creation of new molecules or materials with useful properties. By researching and modeling the properties of molecules under various conditions, scientists in this field can develop new chemical structures that are stable or volatile, rigid or flexible, insulating or conductive. Since chemical R&D is important to many technologies, it can include work on computer chip manufacturing, composite materials development, or pollution reduction through chemical treatment. Chemical R&D also plays a large role in both biotechnology and nanotechnology R&D.

Electronics R&D incorporates a broad range of technologies, including computer hardware, telecommunications, consumer electronics, automated control systems, medical equipment, and electronic sensing. R&D in this field leads to advances that make electronic systems faster, more reliable, more compact, more useful, more powerful, and more accessible. The development of new technologies, such as polymorphic processors for more powerful computers, and the integration of these technologies into new systems account for much of the R&D

in this field. Basic research in areas like electromagnetics and photonics also is a significant part of the work.

Aerospace R&D relates to aircraft, spacecraft, missiles, and component parts and systems. More than half of the R&D in aerospace is federally funded, with the Department of Defense and the National Aeronautics and Space Administration supporting most of the work. Civil aerospace R&D now ranges from developing more efficient passenger aircraft to designing private spacecraft to launch satellites or transport humans into space, but most is devoted to making air transportation safer and more efficient.

Automotive R&D creates new vehicles and systems that are more efficient, powerful, and reliable. While automotive R&D may be directed toward the integration of new technologies into vehicles, much research also is done on improving the individual components such as LED headlights or fuel injectors. As electronic technology has advanced, so have automotive designs. The incorporation of computer systems both for monitoring performance and as separate additional features has added a new dimension to R&D in this field. With the demand for more efficient vehicles that provide more power while using less fuel, a good deal of time and many resources are devoted to powertrain and car body R&D.

R&D in the social sciences and humanities is more closely aligned with specific occupations than it is in the physical, engineering, and life sciences. Economic research typically involves monitoring and forecasting economic trends relating to issues such as business cycles, competitiveness of markets, or international trade. Sociological research analyzes the institutions and patterns of social behavior in society, and the results are used mainly by administrators to formulate policies. Anthropological research focuses on the influence of evolution and culture on all aspects of human behavior. Psychological research studies human thought, learning, motivation, and abnormal behavior.

Working Conditions

In 2004, workers in scientific research and development services averaged 37.4 hours per week, compared with 33.7 for workers in all fields. The average for research and development in the physical, engineering, and life sciences was 38.1, while the average for research and development in the social sciences and humanities was only 32.2.

Most workers in this field work in offices or laboratories; the location and hours of work vary greatly, however, depending on the requirements of each project. Experiments may run at odd hours, require constant observation, or depend on external conditions such as the weather. In some fields, research or testing must be done in harsh environments to ensure the usefulness of the final product in a wide range of environments. Other research, particularly biomedical research, is conducted in hospitals. Workers in product development may spend much time building prototypes in workshops or laboratories, while research design typically takes place in offices.

Although there generally is little risk of injury or illness due to the working conditions, certain fields require working with potentially dangerous materials. In such cases, comprehensive safety procedures are strictly enforced.

Important Characteristics of the Field

Skills: Management of Financial Resources; Active Learning; Time Management; Reading Comprehension; Instructing; Science. **Abilities:** Mathematical Reasoning; Speech Recognition; Written Expression; Inductive Reasoning; Category Flexibility; Oral Comprehension. **Work-Related Values:** Creativity; Working Conditions; Social Status; Ability Utilization; Achievement; Recognition.

Employment

Scientific research and development services provided 548,000 jobs in 2004. Research and development in the physical, engineering, and life sciences accounted for about 88 percent of the jobs; the rest were in research and development in the social sciences and humanities. Although 82 percent of establishments have fewer than 20 workers, 53 percent of employment in the field is in establishments with more than 250 workers (chart 1).

Although scientific research and development services can be found in many places, the field is concentrated in a few areas. Just six states—California, New York, Massachusetts, Illinois, New Jersey, and Michigan—account for over half of all R&D. Michigan accounts for the vast majority of R&D in the automotive field.

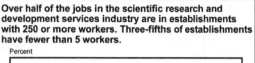

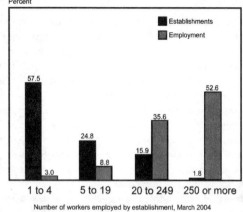

Over half of the jobs in the scientific research and development services industry are in establishments with 250 or more workers. Three-fifths of establishments have fewer than 5 workers.

Number of workers employed by establishment, March 2004

Occupations in the Field

Professional and related occupations account for over half of the employment in this field. About 40 percent of jobs are in computer and mathematical sciences, engineering occupations, and life and physical science occupations, and 3 percent of jobs are in social sciences and related occupations (table 1).

Life, physical, and social scientists form the core of the research operations in the field. *Biological scientists* conduct research to understand biological systems, develop new drugs, and work with genetic material. Most work for pharmaceutical or biotechnology companies; others perform their research in federal or academic laboratories. *Medical scientists* research the causes of health problems and diseases and then use this information to develop medical treatments and preventive measures. Their work is similar to that of biological scientists, but with a specific emphasis on disease prevention and treatment. *Chemists and materials scientists* research the nature of chemical systems and reactions, investigate the properties of materials, and develop new products or processes utilizing this knowledge. They perform research used by a broad array of fields to develop new products. Along with *physicists*, chemists and materials scientists conduct basic and applied research on nanotechnology. Social scientists, such as *economists*, *market and survey researchers*, *sociologists*, and *anthropologists*, perform research on human behavior and social interaction. *Science technicians*, sometimes called research assistants, assist scientists

Professional and Business Services

in their research and typically specialize in an area of research. They may set up and maintain lab equipment, monitor experiments, record results, or interpret collected data.

Engineers and computer specialists usually are involved in applied research or in development. *Engineers* design, produce, and evaluate solutions to problems, either by creating new products or refining existing ones. They apply the most current research findings to develop more efficient products or processes of manufacture. *Engineering technicians* assist engineers in preparing equipment for experiments, recording and calculating results, or building prototypes. Their work is similar to that of the engineers with whom they work but is more limited in scope. Computer specialists, such as *computer scientists, computer programmers,* and *computer software engineers,* develop new computer technologies, programming languages, operating systems, and programs to increase the usefulness of computers. Their work may include integrating advances in computing theory into more efficient processing techniques.

Another 19 percent of employment is in management, business, and financial occupations. *Engineering and natural science managers* accounted for a larger portion of the employment than in most fields. These managers plan, coordinate, and direct the activities of engineers, natural scientists, technicians, and support personnel to conduct research or develop new products. As with engineers and natural scientists, engineering managers tend to be involved in development, while natural science managers tend to be involved in basic research. Both use their technical expertise and business acumen to bridge the gap between goals set by top executives and the incremental work done by engineers and scientists.

Office and administrative support occupations comprise 15 percent of the field's jobs and primarily handle general business administration and clerical work. *Interviewers, except eligibility and loan,* are particularly prevalent in research and development in the social sciences and humanities, accounting for 8 percent of positions in this part of the field. They may be involved in soliciting and verifying information from individuals or groups for sociological, psychological, or market survey research, either in person or by phone. In the life sciences, they may collect and verify participant information for medical research.

Since the scientific research and development services field deals mainly in innovation and design, there are relatively few jobs in production, transportation, sales, or service occupations, which represent less than 6 percent of employment.

Table 1. Employment of wage and salary workers in scientific research and development services by occupation, 2004 and projected change, 2004–2014 (Employment in thousands)

Occupation	Employment, 2004		Percent change, 2004–2014
	Number	Percent	
Total, all occupations	548	100.0	11.9
Management, business, and financial occupations	104	19.0	12.8
Top executives	17	3.1	10.1
Marketing and sales managers	5	0.9	15.6
Computer and information systems managers	6	1.0	16.6
Engineering managers	8	1.4	12.9
Natural sciences managers	7	1.3	11.3
Management analysts	6	1.0	10.8
Accountants and auditors	6	1.2	11.1
Professional and related occupations	310	56.6	15.0
Computer and information scientists, research	4	0.6	11.2
Computer programmers	6	1.1	–9.2
Computer software engineers	28	5.1	33.4
Computer systems analysts	6	1.1	22.2
Operations research analysts	2	0.4	10.1
Statisticians	2	0.4	–0.8
Engineers	63	11.5	14.9
Engineering technicians, except drafters	19	3.4	14.0
Agricultural and food scientists	2	0.4	13.6
Biochemists and biophysicists	7	1.2	22.3
Microbiologists	3	0.5	11.5
Medical scientists	18	3.3	22.3
Physicists	5	0.9	5.6
Chemists	11	2.1	6.9

Occupation	Employment, 2004		Percent change, 2004–2014
	Number	Percent	
Environmental scientists and geoscientists	3	0.6	14.4
Economists	1	0.2	–3.9
Market and survey researchers	5	0.9	8.4
Sociologists	2	0.3	6.9
Anthropologists	1	0.2	9.3
Life, physical, and social science technicians	37	6.7	10.9
Education, training, and library occupations	11	1.9	11.3
Arts, design, entertainment, sports, and media occupations	10	1.8	10.7
Healthcare practitioners and technical occupations	11	2.0	10.9
Sales and related occupations	12	2.2	8.0
Sales representatives, wholesale and manufacturing	7	1.2	11.4
Office and administrative support occupations	80	14.7	1.3
Supervisors, office and administrative support workers	6	1.0	0.3
Financial clerks	7	1.2	0.7
Information and record clerks	16	2.9	3.9
Secretaries and administrative assistants	30	5.4	5.0
Office clerks, general	11	2.1	–1.4
Production occupations	16	2.9	8.5

Note: May not add to totals due to omission of occupations with small employment

Training, Other Qualifications, and Advancement

Scientific research and development services rely heavily on workers with extensive postsecondary education. Those with bachelor's degrees or higher held 68 percent of jobs in the field, compared with only 30 percent in all fields. The difference is particularly great for those with graduate degrees, who account for 36 percent of workers in scientific research and development services but only 10 percent of workers in all fields.

Science and engineering technicians may enter the field with a high school diploma, some college, or an associate degree, but some bachelor's degree holders begin as technicians before advancing to become researchers or pursuing additional education. Technicians usually begin working directly under a scientist, engineer, or more senior technician and advance to working with less supervision. Continuing on-the-job training is important in order to learn to use the newest equipment and methods. Some technicians become supervisors responsible for a laboratory or workshop.

For other science and engineering occupations, a bachelor's degree is generally the minimum level of education, and a master's or Ph.D. degree is typically necessary for senior scientists and engineers. Some fields require a Ph.D. even for entry-level research positions, particularly in the physical and life sciences. A bachelor's degree is sufficient for many types of work in development outside of the life sciences, but a master's degree is much more common—particularly among engineers. Continuing training is necessary for workers to keep pace with current developments in their fields. It may take the form of on-the-job training or formal training, or it may consist of attending conferences or meetings of professional societies. Workers who fail to remain current in their field and related disciplines may face unfavorable job prospects if interest in their specific area declines.

For those with a Ph.D., a period of academic research immediately after obtaining the degree—known as a "postdoc"—is increasingly preferred by employers. These postdocs may last several years with low salaries and little independence, effectively increasing the cost of doctoral degrees in time and forgone income. Once in the field, workers with doctorates typically begin as researchers, conducting and designing research projects in their field of expertise with a fair degree of autonomy. With their research training and specialized expertise, scientists or engineers with doctoral degrees design, conduct, and analyze experiments or studies. To keep current in their fields, researchers often attend conferences, read specialized journals, and confer with colleagues in field and academia.

Professional and Business Services

As scientists or engineers gain expertise in a particular field of R&D, they may advance to more senior research positions or become managers. Those who remain in technical positions may undertake more creative work, designing research or developing new technologies at a higher level. Those in science and engineering management usually coordinate work in several disciplines or components of a project. As their careers progress, they manage larger projects and ensure the work aligns with the strategic goals of their organization. Nearly all managers are responsible for some aspect of funding and for meeting deadlines.

Self-employment is uncommon in scientific research and development services because of the high cost of equipment, but opportunities to start small companies do exist. These opportunities are particularly prevalent in rapidly growing fields, partly due to the availability of investment capital. Self-employed workers in scientific R&D typically have advanced degrees and have worked in academia or other research facilities and form companies to develop commercial products resulting from prior basic or applied research.

Outlook

Wage and salary employment in scientific research and development services is projected to increase 12 percent between 2004 and 2014, compared with 14 percent employment growth for the economy as a whole. Biotechnology and nanotechnology will continue to generate employment growth. As the population ages, increased demand for medical and pharmaceutical advances also will lead to growth in these areas. While demand for new R&D is expected to continue to grow across all major fields, this field will need to digest the recent period of extremely high growth brought about, in large part, by rapid advances in computer and communication systems. Increased efficiency and the increasingly high cost of equipment also will dampen employment growth as less of each dollar spent on R&D is converted into employment.

Some of this slower job growth rate is attributable to the stagnation of the office and administrative support occupations, which are expected to see only modest employment growth as technology leads to greater efficiency in general office functions. Since similarly slow growth is expected in the other major occupational groups within the field, most new jobs will be created in professional and related occupations.

The highest growth is expected for computer specialists, scientists, and engineers—particularly those in the life and medical sciences. With the aging of the population, the demand for lifesaving new drugs and procedures to cure and prevent disease will drive this demand. Biological scientists, for example, may be employed in biotechnology or pharmaceuticals, both growing areas. Many other scientists and engineers will be employed in defense and security R&D, also a growing field. As information technology continues to be an integral component of R&D, opportunities for computer specialists are expected to grow rapidly, particularly for those with some biological science background working in bioinformatics.

Opportunities for both scientists and engineers are expected to be best for those who have doctoral degrees, which prepare graduates for research. Creativity is crucial because scientists and engineers engaged in R&D are expected to propose new research or designs. For experienced scientists and engineers, it also is important to remain current and adapt to changes in technologies that may shift interest—and employment—from one area of research to another.

Most R&D programs have long project cycles that continue during economic downturns. However, funding of R&D, particularly by nongovernment fields, is closely scrutinized during these periods. Since the federal government provides about a quarter of all R&D funding, shifts in policy also could have a marked impact on employment opportunities, particularly in basic research and aerospace.

Earnings

In 2004, nonsupervisory workers in scientific research and development services earned $1,006 per week on average, substantially higher than the $529 average for all fields. The earnings of those engaged in research and development in the physical, engineering, and life sciences differ markedly from the earnings of those in research and development in the social sciences and humanities, with respective averages of $1,041 and $741.

Earnings also varied considerably by occupation, with workers in management and professional occupations earning more. Occupations in the field with higher earnings typically require higher levels of education and experience. Hourly wages for specific occupations in the field are shown in table 2.

Table 2. Median hourly earnings of the largest occupations in scientific research and development services, May 2004

Occupation	Scientific research and development services	All fields
General and operations managers	$57.89	$37.22
Computer software engineers, systems software	43.94	38.34
Mechanical engineers	35.85	31.88
Medical scientists, except epidemiologists	31.30	29.48
Chemists	30.03	26.95
Business operations specialists, all other	28.99	25.70
Executive secretaries and administrative assistants	19.62	16.81
Biological technicians	17.56	15.97
Secretaries, except legal, medical, and executive	15.72	12.55
Office clerks, general	13.33	10.95

Sources of Additional Information

For additional information on careers in biotechnology R&D, contact

- Biotechnology Institute, 1840 Wilson Blvd., Suite 202, Arlington, VA 22201. Internet: http://www.biotechinstitute.org
- Biotechnology Industry Organization, 1225 Eye St. NW, Suite 400, Washington, DC 20005. Internet: http://www.bio.org

For additional information on careers in nanotechnology R&D, contact

- National Nanotechnology Coordination Office, 4201 Wilson Blvd., Stafford II Room 405, Arlington, VA 22230. Internet: http://www.nano.gov

For additional information on careers in pharmaceutical R&D, contact

- Pharmaceutical Research and Manufacturers of America, 1100 Fifteenth St. NW, Washington, DC 20005. Internet: http://www.phrma.org

For additional information on careers in chemical and materials science R&D, contact

- American Chemical Society, 1155 Sixteenth St. NW, Washington, DC 20036. Internet: http://www.chemistry.org

For additional information on careers in electronics R&D, contact

- Institute of Electrical and Electronics Engineers–USA, 1828 L St. NW, Suite 1202, Washington, DC 20036. Internet: http://www.ieeeusa.org

For additional information on careers in aerospace R&D, contact

- American Institute of Aeronautics and Astronautics, 1801 Alexander Bell Dr., Suite 500, Reston, VA 20191. Internet: http://www.aiaa.org
- Aerospace Industries Association, 1000 Wilson Blvd., Suite 1700, Arlington, VA 22209. Internet: http://www.aia-aerospace.org

For additional information on careers in automotive R&D, contact

- Society of Automotive Engineers, 400 Commonwealth Dr., Warrendale, PA 15096. Internet: http://www.sae.org

Education, Health Care, and Social Services

Child Day Care Services

- Annual Earnings: $18,400
- Job Growth: 38.4%
- Size of Workforce: 734,400
- Self-Employed: 28.0%
- Part-Time: 28.7%

Education, Health Care, and Social Services

Significant Points

- Preschool teachers, teacher assistants, and child care workers account for about 3 out of 4 wage and salary jobs.

- About 45 percent of all child day care workers have a high school degree or less, reflecting the minimal training requirements for most jobs.

- More than a quarter of all employees work part time, and nearly 3 out of 10 full-time employees in the field work more than 40 hours per week.

- Job openings should be numerous because dissatisfaction with benefits, pay, and stressful working conditions causes many to leave the field.

Nature of the Field

Obtaining affordable, quality child day care, especially for children under age 5, is a major concern for many parents. Child day care needs are met in different ways. Care in a child's home, care in an organized child care center, and care in a provider's home—known as family child care—are all common arrangements for preschool-aged children. Older children also may receive child day care services when they are not in school, generally through before- and after-school programs or private summer school programs. With the increasing number of households in which both parents work full time, this field has been one of the fastest growing in the U.S. economy.

The field consists of establishments that provide paid care for infants, toddlers, preschool children, or older children in before- and after-school programs. (For information on other social assistance services for children and youths, see the description of Social Assistance, Except Child Day Care.)

Two main types of child care make up the child day care services field: center-based care and family child care. Formal child day care centers include preschools, child care centers, and Head Start centers. Family child care providers care for children in their home for a fee and are the majority of self-employed workers in this field, which does not include occasional babysitters or persons who provide unpaid care in their homes for the children of relatives or friends.

The for-profit sector of this field includes centers that operate independently or as part of a local or national chain. Nonprofit child day care organizations may provide services in religious institutions, YMCAs and other social and recreation centers, colleges, public schools, social service agencies, and worksites ranging from factories to office complexes. The number of for-profit establishments has grown rapidly in response to demand for child care services. Within the nonprofit sector, there has been strong growth in Head Start, the federally funded child care program designed to provide disadvantaged children with social, educational, and health services.

Recognizing that the unavailability of child care is a barrier to the employment of many parents, especially qualified women, and that the cost of the benefits is offset by increased employee morale and reduced absenteeism, some employers offer child care benefits to their employees. Some employers sponsor child care centers in or near the workplace, while others provide direct financial assistance, vouchers, or discounts for child care or after-school or sick-child care services. Still others offer a dependent-care option in a flexible benefits plan.

Working Conditions

Helping children grow, learn, and gain new skills can be very rewarding. Preschool teachers and child care workers often improve their own communication, learning, and other personal skills by working with children. The work is sometimes routine; however, new activities and challenges mark each day. Child care can be physically and emotionally taxing, as workers constantly stand, walk, bend, stoop, and lift to attend to each child's interests and problems. Child care workers must be constantly alert, anticipate and prevent trouble, deal effectively with disruptive children, and provide fair but firm discipline.

The hours of child day care workers vary. Many centers are open 12 or more hours a day and cannot close until all of the children are picked up by their parents or guardians. Unscheduled overtime, traffic jams, and other types of emergencies can cause parents or guardians to be late. Nearly 3 out of 10 full-time employees in the child day care services field work more than 40 hours per week. Self-employed workers tend to work longer hours than do their salaried counterparts. The field also offers many opportunities for part-time work: More than a quarter of all employees worked part time in 2004.

Many child day care workers become dissatisfied with their jobs' stressful conditions, low pay, and lack of benefits and eventually leave. Turnover is generally high in the field.

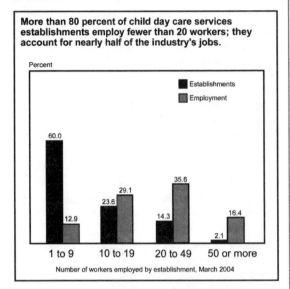

More than 80 percent of child day care services establishments employ fewer than 20 workers; they account for nearly half of the industry's jobs.

Percent

■ Establishments
■ Employment

60.0

29.1
23.6
12.9

35.6

14.3
16.4
2.1

1 to 9   10 to 19   20 to 49   50 or more

Number of workers employed by establishment, March 2004

Important Characteristics of the Field

Skills: Social Perceptiveness; Negotiation; Learning Strategies; Persuasion; Instructing; Service Orientation. **Abilities:** Speech Recognition; Originality; Stamina; Hearing Sensitivity; Fluency of Ideas; Speech Clarity. **Work-Related Values:** Social Service; Authority; Creativity; Working Conditions; Achievement; Co-workers.

Employment

Child day care services provided about 767,000 wage and salary jobs in 2004. Also, there were about 449,000 self-employed and unpaid family workers in the field, most of whom were family child care providers, although some were self-employed managers of child care centers. However, employment estimates understate the number of people working in this field because they exclude family child care provided by relatives. Also, child care workers who work in the child's home, such as nannies, are classified primarily into the private household field.

Jobs in child day care are found across the country, mirroring the distribution of the population. However, day care centers are less common in rural areas, where there are fewer children to support a separate facility. Child

day care operations vary in size, from the self-employed person caring for a few children in a private home to the large corporate-sponsored center employing a sizable staff. Almost half of all wage and salary jobs in 2004 were located in establishments with fewer than 20 employees. Nearly all establishments have fewer than 50 workers (chart 1).

Opportunities for self-employment in this field are among the best in the economy. About 37 percent of all workers in the field are self-employed and unpaid family workers, compared with only 7 percent in all fields. This disparity reflects the ease of entering the child day care business.

The median age of child day care providers is 38, compared with 44 for all workers. About 18 percent of all care providers are 24 years or younger (table 1). About 5 percent of these workers are below the age of 20, reflecting the minimal training requirements for many child day care positions.

Table 1. Percent distribution of employment, by age group, 2004

Age group	Child day care services	All fields
Total	100.0%	100.0%
16–19	4.9	4.2
20–24	12.8	9.9
25–34	24.7	21.8
35–44	23.3	24.8
45–54	20.6	23.3
55–64	10.3	12.4
65 and older	3.5	3.5

Occupations in the Field

There is far less occupational diversity in the child day care services field than in most other fields. Three occupations—*preschool teachers, teacher assistants,* and *child care workers*—account for 75 percent of all wage and salary jobs (table 2).

Preschool teachers make up the largest occupation in the child day care field, accounting for about 34 percent of wage and salary jobs. They teach pupils basic physical, intellectual, and social skills needed to enter primary school. *Teacher assistants* account for 12 percent of employment and give teachers more time for teaching by assuming a variety of tasks. For example, they may set up and dismantle equipment or prepare instructional materials.

Child care workers account for about 29 percent of wage and salary jobs, as well as a large proportion of the self-employed who care for children in their homes, known as *family child care providers*. Some parents hire *private household workers*, such as *nannies*, to care for their children in their own home. Regardless of the setting, these workers feed, diaper, comfort, and play with infants. When dealing with older children, they attend to the children's basic needs and organize activities that stimulate physical, emotional, intellectual, and social development.

Education administrators, preschool and child care center/program account for about 4 percent of wage and salary workers. They establish overall objectives and standards for their centers, provide day-to-day supervision of their staffs, and bear overall responsibility for program development as well as for marketing, budgeting, staffing, and all other administrative tasks.

In addition to hiring workers in the preceding occupations, child day care centers also employ a variety of *office and administrative support workers, building cleaning workers, cooks,* and *bus drivers*.

Table 2. Employment of wage and salary workers in child day care services by occupation, 2004 and projected change, 2004–2014 (Employment in thousands)

Occupation	Employment, 2004		Percent change, 2004–2014
	Number	Percent	
Total, all occupations	767	100.0	38.4
Management, business, and financial occupations	50	6.5	35.3
Top executives	7	0.9	39.9
Education administrators	35	4.5	32.9
Professional and related occupations	403	52.5	41.1

Occupation	Employment, 2004		Percent change, 2004–2014
	Number	Percent	
Child, family, and school social workers	9	1.1	41.2
Social and human service assistants	5	0.7	41.2
Preschool teachers, except special education	262	34.1	41.2
Kindergarten teachers, except special education	9	1.2	40.5
Elementary and middle school teachers	3	0.4	30.2
Special education teachers	2	0.3	55.1
Other teachers and instructors	3	0.4	41.1
Teacher assistants	95	12.4	41.2
Service occupations	275	35.9	36.2
Cooks, institution and cafeteria	18	2.4	12.9
Building cleaning workers	9	1.2	41.2
Supervisors, personal care and service workers	10	1.3	41.2
Child care workers	222	28.9	37.4
Recreation and fitness workers	3	0.4	39.5
Office and administrative support occupations	29	3.7	26.7
Transportation and material moving occupations	9	1.2	40.7
Bus drivers, school	7	1.0	41.2

Note: May not add to totals due to omission of occupations with small employment

Training, Other Qualifications, and Advancement

Most states do not regulate family child care providers who care for just a few children, usually up to between two and five. Providers who care for more children are required to be licensed and, in a few states, have some minimal training. Once a provider joins the field, most states require the worker to complete a number of hours of training per year. Many local governments regulate family child care providers who are not covered by state regulations. Home safety inspections and criminal background checks are usually required of an applicant.

Child care centers have staffing requirements that are imposed by states and by insurers. Although requirements vary, in most cases a minimum age of 18 years is required for teachers, and directors or officers must be at least 21. In some states, assistants may work at age 16—in several, at age 14. Most states have established minimum educational or training requirements. Training requirements are most stringent for directors, less so for teachers, and minimal for child care workers and teacher assistants. In many centers, directors must have a college degree, often with experience in child day care and specific training in early childhood development. Teachers must have a high school diploma and, in many cases, a combination of college education and experience. Assistants and child care workers usually need a high school diploma, but that is not always a requirement. Some employers prefer to hire workers who have received credentials from a nationally recognized child day care organization.

Many states also mandate other types of training for staff members, such as health and first aid, fire safety, and child abuse detection and prevention. In nearly all states, licensing regulations require criminal record checks for all child day care staff. This screening requirement protects children from abuse and reduces liability risks, making insurance more available and affordable.

State governments also have established requirements for other child care personnel—those involved in food preparation, the transportation of children, the provision of medical services, and other services. Most states have defined minimum staff-to-children ratios, which vary with the state and the age of the children involved.

Outlook

Wage and salary jobs in the child day care services field are projected to grow 38 percent over the 2004–2014 period, compared with the 14 percent employment growth projected for all fields combined. An unusually large number of job openings also will result each year from the need to replace experienced workers who leave the field. Replacement needs are substantial, reflecting the low wages and relatively meager benefits provided to most workers. Coupled with the substantial replacement

needs, faster-than-average employment growth should create numerous employment opportunities.

The rising demand for child day care services reflects in part demographic trends. Over the 2004–2014 period, the number of children under age 5 is expected to increase at a faster rate than in previous years. In addition, the labor force participation rate of women of childbearing age also is expected to increase, though only slightly. This increase likely will cause more households to have both parents working full time, increasing the demand for some form of child care arrangement. As parents continue to work during weekends, evenings, and late nights, demand for child care programs that can provide care during nontraditional hours will grow significantly. School-aged children, who generally require child care only before and after school, increasingly are being cared for in centers.

With an increasing number of parents preferring its more formal setting and believing that it provides a better foundation for children before they begin traditional schooling, center-based care should continue to expand its share of the field. However, family child care providers will continue to remain an important source of care for many young children because some parents prefer the more personal attention that such a setting provides. Demand for child care centers and preschool teachers to staff them could increase further if more states implement preschool programs for 3- and 4-year-old children as some have begun, and others are planning, to do. In addition, subsidies for children from low-income families attending child day care programs will result in more children being served in centers, as could the increasing involvement of employers in funding and operating day care centers. Legislation requiring more welfare recipients to work also could contribute to demand for child day care services.

Earnings

In 2004, hourly earnings of nonsupervisory workers in the child day care services field averaged $9.76, much less than the average of $15.67 throughout nongovernment fields. On a weekly basis, earnings in child day care services averaged only $299 in 2004, compared with the average of $529 in nongovernment fields. Weekly earnings reflect, in part, hours worked—salaried workers in child day care services averaged 30.6 hours a week, compared with about 33.7 throughout nongovernment fields. Earnings in selected occupations in child day care services in May 2004 appear in table 3.

Table 3. Median hourly earnings of the largest occupations in child day care services, May 2004

Age group	Child day care services	All fields
General and operations managers	$23.78	$37.22
Education administrators, preschool and child care center/program	16.01	17.18
Child, family, and school social workers	13.80	16.74
First-line supervisors/managers of personal service workers	11.70	14.59
Preschool teachers, except special education	9.34	10.09
Bus drivers, school	9.28	11.18
Office clerks, general	9.12	10.95
Janitors and cleaners, except maids and housekeeping cleaners	8.04	9.04
Cooks, institution and cafeteria	7.93	9.10
Child care workers	7.34	8.06

Employee benefits often are minimal as well. A substantial number of child day care centers offer no healthcare benefits to any teaching staff. Reduced day care fees for workers' children, however, are a common benefit. Wage levels and employee benefits depend in part on the type of center: Nonprofit and religiously affiliated centers generally pay higher wages and offer more generous benefits than do for-profit establishments.

Sources of Additional Information

For additional information about careers in early childhood education, contact

- National Association for the Education of Young Children, 1509 16th St. NW, Washington, DC 20036. Internet: http://www.naeyc.org

For more information about the child care workforce, contact

- Center for the Child Care Workforce, 555 New Jersey Ave. NW, Washington, DC 20001. Internet: http://www.ccw.org

For an electronic question-and-answer service on child care, information on becoming a child care provider, and other child care resources, contact

- National Child Care Information Center, 10530 Rosehaven St, Suite 400, Fairfax, VA 22030. Internet: http://www.nccic.org

For a database on licensing requirements of child care settings by state, contact

- National Resource Council for Health and Safety in Child Care, University of Colorado Health and Sciences Center at Fitzsimons, Campus Mail Stop F541, P.O. Box 6508, Aurora, CO 80045-0508. Telephone (toll free): 800-598-5437. Internet: http://nrc.uchsc.edu

For a list of colleges offering courses in early childhood education, contact

- Council for Professional Recognition, 2460 16th St. NW, Washington, DC 20009-3575. Internet: http://www.cdacouncil.org

State Departments of Human Services or Social Services can supply state regulations concerning child day care programs, child care workers, teacher assistants, and preschool teachers.

Educational Services

- Annual Earnings: $36,370
- Job Growth: 16.6%
- Size of Workforce: 12,778,104
- Self-Employed: 1.6%
- Part-Time: 21.9%

Significant Points

- With about 1 in 4 Americans enrolled in educational institutions, educational services is the second largest field, accounting for about 13 million jobs.
- Most teaching positions—which constitute almost half of all educational services jobs—require at least a bachelor's degree, and some require a master's or doctoral degree.

- Retirements in a number of education professions will create many job openings.

Nature of the Field

Education is an important part of life. The amount and type of education that individuals receive are a major influence on both the types of jobs they are able to hold and their earnings. Lifelong learning is important in acquiring new knowledge and upgrading one's skills, particularly in this age of rapid technological and economic changes. The educational services field includes a variety of institutions that offer academic education, vocational or career and technical instruction, and other education and training to millions of students each year.

Because school attendance is compulsory until at least age 16 in all 50 states and the District of Columbia, elementary, middle, and secondary schools are the most numerous of all educational establishments. They provide academic instruction to students in kindergarten through grade 12 in a variety of settings, including public schools, parochial schools, boarding and other private schools, and military academies. Some secondary schools offer a mixture of academic and career and technical instruction.

Postsecondary institutions—universities, colleges, professional schools, community or junior colleges, and career and technical institutes—provide education and training in both academic and technical subjects for high school graduates and other adults. Universities offer bachelor's, master's, and doctoral degrees, while colleges generally offer only the bachelor's degree. Professional schools offer graduate degrees in fields such as law, medicine, business administration, and engineering. The undergraduate bachelor's degree typically requires 4 years of study, while graduate degrees require additional years of study. Community and junior colleges and technical institutes offer associate degrees, certificates, or other diplomas typically involving 2 years of study or less. Career and technical schools provide specialized training and services primarily related to a specific job. They include computer and cosmetology training institutions, business and secretarial schools, correspondence schools, and establishments that offer certificates in commercial art and practical nursing.

This field also includes institutions that provide training and services to schools and students, such as curriculum development, student exchanges, and tutoring. Also

included are schools or programs that offer nonacademic or self-enrichment classes, such as automobile driving and cooking instruction, among other things.

In recent decades, the nation has focused attention on the educational system because of the growing importance of producing a trained and educated workforce. Many institutions, including government, nongovernment fields, and research organizations, are involved in improving the quality of education. The passage of the No Child Left Behind Act of 2001 established federal guidelines to ensure that all students in public elementary through secondary schools receive a high-quality education. Through this act, individual states are given more flexibility on how to spend the educational funds they are allocated. In return, the Act requires standardized testing of all students in core subject areas. In this manner, students, teachers, and all staff involved in education are held accountable for the results of testing, and teachers and teacher assistants must demonstrate that they are sufficiently qualified in the subjects or areas in which they teach. States are responsible for following these guidelines and can lose federal funding if the standards are not met. Despite the increased federal role, state and local governments are still the most important regulators of public education. Many states had already begun to introduce performance standards individually prior to passage of the Act, and the Act still allows states a considerable amount of discretion in how they implement many of its provisions.

In an effort to promote innovation in public education, many local and state governments have authorized the creation of public charter schools in the belief that, by presenting students and their parents with a greater range of instructional options, schools and students will be encouraged to strive for excellence. Charter schools, which usually are run by teachers and parents or, increasingly, by private firms, operate independently of the school system, set their own standards, and practice a variety of innovative teaching methods. Businesses strive to improve education by donating instructional equipment, lending personnel for teaching and mentoring, hosting visits to the workplace, and providing job-shadowing and internship opportunities. Businesses also collaborate with educators to develop curricula that will provide students with the skills they need to cope with new technology in the workplace.

Quality improvements also are being made to career and technical education at secondary and postsecondary

Education, Health Care, and Social Services

schools. Academics are playing a more important role in career and technical curricula, and programs are being made more relevant to the local job market. Often, students must meet rigorous standards, set in consultation with private employers, before receiving a certificate or degree. Career and technical students in secondary school programs must pass the same standardized tests in core subject areas as students who are enrolled in academic programs of study. A growing number of career and technical programs are emphasizing general workplace skills, such as problem solving, teamwork, and customer service. Many high schools now offer technical preparatory ("tech-prep") programs, which are developed jointly by high schools and community colleges to provide a continuous course of study leading to an associate's degree or other postsecondary credential.

Computer technology continues to affect the education field. Computers simplify administrative tasks and make it easier to track student performance. Teachers use the Internet in classrooms as well as to communicate with colleagues around the country; students use the Internet for research projects. Distance learning continues to expand as more postsecondary institutions use Internet-based technology to conduct lessons and coursework electronically, allowing students in distant locations access to educational opportunities formerly available only on campus.

Despite these improvements in quality, problems remain. Dropout rates have not declined significantly over the decade, and employers contend that numerous high school students still lack many of the math and communication skills needed in today's workplace. School budgets often are not sufficient to meet the institution's various goals, particularly in the inner cities, where aging facilities and chronic teacher shortages make educating children more difficult.

Working Conditions

School conditions often vary from town to town. Some schools in poorer neighborhoods may be run down, have few supplies and equipment, and lack air conditioning. Other schools may be new and well equipped and maintained. Conditions at postsecondary institutions are generally very good. Regardless of the type of conditions facing elementary and secondary schools, seeing students develop and enjoy learning can be rewarding for teachers and other education workers. However, dealing with

unmotivated students or those with social or behavioral problems can be stressful and require patience and understanding.

Most educational institutions operate 10 months a year, but summer sessions for special education or remedial students are not uncommon; institutions that cater to adult students and those that offer educational support services, such as tutoring, generally operate year-round as well. Education administrators, office and administrative support workers, and janitors and cleaners often work the entire year. Night and weekend work is common for teachers of adult literacy and remedial and self-enrichment education, for postsecondary teachers, and for library workers in postsecondary institutions. Part-time work is common for this same group of teachers, as well as for teacher assistants and school bus drivers. The latter often work a split shift, driving one or two routes in the morning and afternoon; drivers who are assigned to drive students on field trips, to athletic and other extracurricular activities, or to midday kindergarten programs work additional hours during or after school. Many teachers spend significant time outside of school preparing for class, doing administrative tasks, conducting research, writing articles and books, and pursuing advanced degrees.

Despite occurrences of violence in some schools, educational services is a relatively safe field. There were 2.7 cases of occupational injury and illness per 100 full-time workers in private educational establishments in 2003, compared with 5.0 in all fields combined.

Table 1. Employment in educational services by field segment, 2004 (Employment in thousands)

Field segment	Employment Public	Private
Educational services, total	10,010	2,766
Elementary and secondary schools	7,338	829
Junior colleges	664	84
Colleges, universities and professional schools	1,954	1,378
Other educational services	56	475

Important Characteristics of the Field

Skills: Instructing; Learning Strategies; Social Perceptiveness; Service Orientation; Persuasion; Time Management. **Abilities:** Speech Recognition; Speech Clarity; Written Expression; Oral Expression; Originality; Category Flexibility. **Work-Related Values:** Social Service; Authority; Working Conditions; Creativity; Activity; Co-workers.

Employment

The educational services field was the second largest field in the economy in 2004, providing jobs for about 13.0 million workers—about 12.8 million wage and salary workers and 199,000 self-employed and unpaid family workers. Most jobs are found in elementary and secondary schools, either public or private, as shown in table 1. Public schools also employ more workers than private schools at both levels because most students attend public educational institutions. According to the latest data from the Department of Education's National Center for Education Statistics, close to 90 percent of students attend public primary and secondary schools and about 75 percent attend public postsecondary institutions.

Table 2. Employment of wage and salary workers in educational services by occupation, 2004 and projected change, 2004–2014 (Employment in thousands)

Occupation	Employment, 2004		Percent change, 2004–2014
	Number	Percent	
Total, all occupations	12,778	100.0	16.6
Management, business, and financial occupations	823	6.4	21.8
Education administrators	363	2.8	15.6
Professional and related occupations	8,440	66.0	19.4
Computer specialists	180	1.4	29.1
Medical scientists	24	0.2	39.5
Clinical, counseling, and school psychologists	46	0.4	22.2
Educational, vocational, and school counselors	186	1.5	13.3

Occupation	Employment, 2004		Percent change, 2004–2014
	Number	Percent	
Child, family, and school social workers	40	0.3	11.3
Postsecondary teachers	1,553	12.2	32.7
Preschool teachers, except special education	68	0.5	22.2
Kindergarten teachers, except special education	156	1.2	21.7
Elementary school teachers, except special education	1,411	11.0	17.9
Middle school teachers, except special and vocational education	622	4.9	13.6
Secondary school teachers, except special and vocational education	1,017	8.0	14.3
Vocational education teachers, secondary school	99	0.8	8.9
Special education teachers, preschool, kindergarten, and elementary school	195	1.5	22.6
Special education teachers, middle school	96	0.7	19.7
Special education teachers, secondary school	135	1.1	17.7
Adult literacy, remedial education, and GED teachers and instructors	52	0.4	20.0
Self-enrichment education teachers	86	0.7	29.8
Librarians	96	0.8	4.8
Library technicians	52	0.4	15.6
Instructional coordinators	85	0.7	29.6
Teacher assistants	1,067	8.4	10.9
Coaches and scouts	95	0.7	24.6
Registered nurses	82	0.6	16.4
Speech-language pathologists	49	0.4	8.9
Service occupations	1,417	11.1	10.5
Cooks, institution and cafeteria	162	1.3	–10.4
Food preparation workers	83	0.6	3.3
Fast food and counter workers	140	1.1	10.1
Janitors and cleaners, except maids and housekeeping cleaners	483	3.8	14.5

Occupation	Employment, 2004		Percent change, 2004–2014
	Number	Percent	
Child care workers	119	0.9	21.1
Office and administrative support occupations	1,498	11.7	5.1
Bookkeeping, accounting, and auditing clerks	94	0.7	8.3
Secretaries and administrative assistants	595	4.7	1.5
Office clerks, general	367	2.9	8.1
Transportation and material moving occupations	311	2.4	9.4
Bus drivers, school	268	2.1	8.9

Note: May not add to totals due to omission of occupations with small employment

Occupations in the Field

Workers in the educational services field take part in all aspects of education, from teaching and counseling students to driving school buses and serving cafeteria lunches. Although 2 out of 3 workers in educational services are employed in professional and related occupations, the field employs many administrative support, managerial, service, and other workers. (See table 2.)

Teachers account for almost half of all workers in the field. Their duties depend on the age group and subject they teach as well as on the type of institution in which they work. Teachers should have a sincere interest in helping students and should also have the ability to inspire respect, trust, and confidence. Strong speaking and writing skills, inquiring and analytical minds, and a desire to pursue and disseminate knowledge are vital prerequisites for teachers.

Preschool, kindergarten, and elementary school teachers play a critical role in the early development of children. They usually instruct one class in a variety of subjects, introducing the children to mathematics, language, science, and social studies. Often, they use games, artwork, music, computers, and other tools to teach basic skills.

Middle and *secondary school teachers* help students delve more deeply into subjects introduced in elementary school. Middle and secondary school teachers specialize in a specific academic subject, such as English, mathematics, or history, or a career and technical area, such as automobile mechanics, business education, or computer repair. Some supervise after-school extracurricular activities, and some help students deal with academic problems, such as choosing courses, colleges, and careers.

Special education teachers work with students—from toddlers to those in their early twenties—who have a variety of learning and physical disabilities. While most work in traditional schools and assist those students who require extra support, some work in schools specifically designed to serve students with the most severe disabilities. With all but the most severe cases, special education teachers modify the instruction of the general education curriculum and, when necessary, develop alternative assessment methods to accommodate a student's special needs. They also help special education students develop emotionally, feel comfortable in social situations, and be aware of socially acceptable behavior.

Postsecondary teachers, or *faculty*, as they are usually called, generally are organized into departments or divisions based on their subject or field. They teach and advise college students and perform a significant part of our nation's research. They prepare lectures, exercises, and laboratory experiments; grade exams and papers; and advise and work with students individually. Postsecondary teachers keep abreast of developments in their field by reading current literature, talking with colleagues and businesses, and participating in professional conferences. They also consult with government, business, nonprofit, and community organizations. In addition, they do their own research to expand knowledge in their field, often publishing their findings in scholarly journals, books, and electronic media.

Adult literacy and remedial education teachers teach English to speakers of other languages (ESOL), prepare sessions for the General Educational Development (GED) exam, and give basic instruction to out-of-school youths and adults. *Self-enrichment teachers* teach classes that students take for personal enrichment, such as cooking or dancing.

Education administrators provide vision, direction, leadership, and day-to-day management of educational activities in schools, colleges and universities, businesses, correctional institutions, museums, and job training and community service organizations. They set educational standards and goals and aid in establishing the policies and procedures to carry them out. They develop academic programs; monitor students' educational progress; hire, train, motivate, and evaluate teachers and other staff; manage counseling and other student services; administer recordkeeping; prepare budgets; and handle relations with staff, parents, current and prospective students, employers, and the community.

Instructional coordinators evaluate school curricula and recommend changes to them. They research the latest teaching methods, textbooks, and other instructional materials and coordinate and provide training to teachers. They also coordinate equipment purchases and assist in the use of new technology in schools.

Educational, vocational, and school counselors work at the elementary, middle, secondary, and postsecondary school levels and help students evaluate their abilities, talents, and interests so that the students can develop realistic academic and career options. Using interviews, counseling sessions, tests, and other methods, secondary school counselors also help students understand and deal with their social, behavioral, and personal problems. They advise on college majors, admission requirements, and entrance exams and on trade, technical school, and apprenticeship programs. Elementary school counselors do more social and personal counseling and less career and academic counseling than do secondary school counselors. School counselors may work with students individually or in small groups, or they may work with entire classes.

Librarians help people find information and learn how to use it effectively in their scholastic, personal, and professional pursuits. Librarians manage library staff and develop and direct information programs and systems for the public as well as oversee the selection and organization of library materials. *Library technicians* help librarians acquire, prepare, and organize material; direct library users to standard references; and retrieve information from computer databases. *Clerical library assistants* check out and receive library materials, collect overdue fines, and shelve materials.

Teacher assistants, also called *teacher aides* or *instructional aides*, provide instructional and clerical support for classroom teachers, allowing the teachers more time to plan lessons and to teach. Using the teacher's lesson plans, they provide students with individualized attention, tutoring and assisting children—particularly special edu-

cation and non–English speaking students—in learning class material. Assistants also aid and supervise students in the cafeteria, in the schoolyard, in hallways, or on field trips. They record grades, set up equipment, and prepare materials for instruction.

School bus drivers transport students to and from schools and related activities.

Training, Other Qualifications, and Advancement

The educational services field employs some of the most highly educated workers in the labor force. Postsecondary teachers who teach at 4-year colleges and universities generally must have a doctoral or other terminal degree for full-time, tenure-track employment, and usually also for part-time teaching at these institutions as well, though a master's degree is sometimes sufficient. At 2-year colleges, however, most positions are held by teachers with a master's degree. Most faculty members are hired as instructors or assistant professors and may advance to associate professor and full professor. Some faculty advance to administrative and managerial positions, such as department chairperson, dean, or president.

Kindergarten, elementary, middle, and secondary school teachers in public schools must have a bachelor's degree and complete an approved teacher training program with a prescribed number of subject and education credits as well as supervised practice teaching. All states require public school teachers to be licensed; however, licensure requirements vary by state. Many states offer alternative licensure programs for people who have bachelor's degrees in the subject they will teach but lack the education courses required for a regular license. With additional education or certification, teachers may become school librarians, reading specialists, curriculum specialists, or guidance counselors. Some teachers advance to administrative or supervisory positions—such as department chairperson, assistant principal, or principal—but the number of these jobs is limited. In some school systems, highly qualified, experienced elementary and secondary school teachers can become senior or mentor teachers, with higher pay and additional responsibilities.

Special education teachers have many of the same requirements as kindergarten, elementary, middle, and secondary school teachers. In addition, most states require specialized training in special education. A

Education, Health Care, and Social Services

master's degree in special education, involving at least 1 year of additional course work, including a specialization, is also required by many states.

Teachers in private elementary, middle, and secondary schools do not have to meet state licensing standards; however, schools prefer candidates who have a bachelor's degree in the subject they intend to teach for secondary school teachers or in childhood education for elementary school teachers. They seek candidates among recent college graduates as well as from those who have established careers in other fields. Private schools affiliated with religious institutions also desire candidates who share the values that are important to the institution.

Vocational, or career and technical, education teachers typically need work or other experience in their field—and a license or certificate when required by the field—for full professional status. Most states require career and technical education teachers and adult literacy and remedial education teachers to have a bachelor's degree, and some states also require teacher certification. Self-enrichment teachers need only practical experience in the field in order to teach.

School counselors are required to hold state school counseling certification; however, certification procedures vary from state to state. A master's degree is generally required, and some states also require public school counselors to have teaching certificates and a number of years of teaching experience in addition to a counseling certificate. Experienced school counselors may advance to a larger school; become directors or supervisors of counseling, guidance, or student personnel services; or, with further graduate education, become counseling psychologists or school administrators.

Training requirements for education administrators depend on where they work. Principals, assistant principals, and other school administrators in school districts usually have held a teaching or related job before entering administration, and they generally need a master's or doctoral degree in education administration or educational supervision as well as state teacher certification. At postsecondary institutions, academic deans usually have a doctorate in their specialty. Other administrators can begin with a bachelor's degree, but generally will need a master's or doctorate to advance to top positions. In addition to climbing up the administrative ladder, advancement is also possible by transferring to larger schools or school systems.

Training requirements for teacher assistants range from a high school diploma to an associate's degree. The No Child Left Behind Act mandates that all teacher assistants working in schools that receive Title I funds either have a minimum of two years of postsecondary education or an associate's degree or pass a state-approved examination. Districts that assign teaching responsibilities to teacher assistants usually have higher training requirements than those that do not. Teacher assistants who obtain a bachelor's degree, usually in education, may become certified teachers.

Librarians normally need a master's degree in library science. Many states require school librarians to be licensed as teachers and to have taken courses in library science. Experienced librarians may advance to administrative positions, such as department head, library director, or chief information officer. Training requirements for library technicians range from a high school diploma to specialized postsecondary training; a high school diploma is sufficient for library assistants. Library workers can advance—from assistant to technician to librarian—with experience and the required formal education. School bus drivers need a commercial driver's license and have limited opportunities for advancement; some become supervisors or dispatchers.

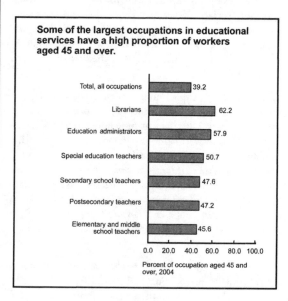

Some of the largest occupations in educational services have a high proportion of workers aged 45 and over.

Occupation	Percent aged 45 and over
Total, all occupations	39.2
Librarians	62.2
Education administrators	57.9
Special education teachers	50.7
Secondary school teachers	47.6
Postsecondary teachers	47.2
Elementary and middle school teachers	45.6

Percent of occupation aged 45 and over, 2004

Outlook

Wage and salary employment growth of 17 percent is expected in the educational services field over the 2004–2014 period, higher than the 14 percent increase projected for all fields combined. In addition, a greater-than-average number of workers are over the age of 45 in nearly all the major occupations that make up the field—from janitors to education administrators—so it is likely that retirements will create large numbers of job openings in addition to those due to employment growth. (See chart 1.)

School districts, particularly those in urban and rural areas, continue to report difficulties in recruiting qualified teachers, administrators, and support personnel. Fast-growing areas of the country—including several states and cities in the South and West—also report difficulty recruiting education workers, especially teachers. Retirements are expected to remain high over the 2004–2014 period, so the number of students graduating with education degrees may not be sufficient to meet this field's growing needs, making job opportunities for graduates in many education fields good to excellent. Currently, alternative licensing programs are helping to attract more people into teaching, especially those from other career paths, but opportunities should continue to be very good for highly qualified teachers, especially those in subject areas with the highest needs, such as math, science, and special education.

At the postsecondary level, increases in student enrollments and projected retirements of current faculty should contribute to a favorable job market for postsecondary teachers. As children of the baby boom generation continue to reach college age and as more adults pursue continuing education to enhance or update their skills, postsecondary student enrollments are expected to increase rapidly, spurring much faster-than-average employment growth for postsecondary teachers. However, candidates applying for tenured positions will continue to face keen competition as many colleges and universities rely on adjunct or part-time faculty and graduate students to make up a larger share of the total instructional staff than in the past.

Over the long term, the overall demand for workers in education services will increase as a result of a growing emphasis on improving education and making it available not only to more children and young adults, but also to those currently employed but in need of improv-ing their skills. Reforms, such as universal preschool and all-day kindergarten, will require more preschool and kindergarten teachers. However, low enrollment growth projections at the elementary, middle, and secondary school level are likely to slow growth somewhat, resulting in average growth for these teachers.

The number of special education teachers is projected to experience faster-than-average growth through 2014, stemming from an increasing enrollment of special education students, continued emphasis on the inclusion of disabled students in general education classrooms, and an effort to reach students with problems at younger ages. Employment of teacher assistants also will grow about as fast as the average; school reforms call for more individual attention to students, and additional teacher assistants will be needed in general education, special education, and English-as-a-second-language classrooms.

Despite expected increases in education expenditures over the next decade, budget constraints at all levels of government may place restrictions on educational services, particularly in light of the rapidly escalating costs associated with increased college enrollments, special education, construction for new schools, and other services. Funding constraints generally affect student services (such as school busing, library and educational materials, and extracurricular activities) before employment of administrative, instructional, and support staff, though supplementary programs, such as music and foreign language instruction, also often face cuts when budgets become tight. Even if no reductions are required, budget considerations also may affect attempts to expand school programs, such as increasing the number of counselors and teacher assistants in elementary schools.

Earnings

Earnings of occupations concentrated in the educational services field—education administrators, teachers, counselors, and librarians—are significantly higher than the average for all occupations because the workers tend to be older and have higher levels of educational attainment. Among teachers, earnings increase with higher educational attainment and more years of service. Full-time postsecondary teachers earn the most, followed by elementary, middle, and secondary school teachers. Most teachers are paid a salary, but part-time instructors in postsecondary institutions usually are paid a fixed amount per course.

Education, Health Care, and Social Services

Educational services employees who work the traditional school year can earn additional money during the summer in jobs related to, or outside of, education. Benefits generally are good, but, as in other fields, part-time workers often do not receive the same benefits that full-time workers do. Earnings for selected occupations within the education field appear in table 3.

About 38 percent of workers in the educational services field—the largest number being in elementary, middle, and secondary schools—are union members or are covered by union contracts, compared with only 14 percent of workers in all fields combined. The American Federation of Teachers and the National Education Association are the largest unions representing teachers and other school personnel.

Table 3. Median annual earnings of the largest occupations in educational services, May 2004

Occupation	Educational services	All fields
Education administrators, elementary and secondary school	$74,380	$74,190
Educational, vocational, and school counselors	50,420	45,570
Secondary school teachers, except special and vocational education	45,700	45,650
Middle school teachers, except special and vocational education	43,690	43,670
Elementary school teachers, except special education	43,220	43,160
Secretaries, except legal, medical, and executive	26,660	26,110
Office clerks, general	22,790	22,770
Janitors and cleaners, except maids and housekeeping cleaners	22,620	18,790
Bus drivers, school	22,340	23,250
Teacher assistants	19,670	19,410

Sources of Additional Information

Information on unions and education-related issues can be obtained from the following organizations:

- American Federation of Teachers, 555 New Jersey Ave. NW, Washington, DC 20001.
- National Education Association, 1201 16th St. NW, Washington, DC 20036.

Health Care

- Annual Earnings: $32,149
- Job Growth: 27.3%
- Size of Workforce: 13,062,102
- Self-Employed: 2.7%
- Part-Time: 20.0%

Significant Points

- As the largest field in 2004, health care provided 13.5 million jobs—13.1 million jobs for wage and salary workers and about 411,000 jobs for the self-employed.

- 8 out of 20 occupations projected to grow the fastest are in health care.

- More new wage and salary jobs—about 19 percent, or 3.6 million—created between 2004 and 2014 will be in health care than in any other field.

- Most workers have jobs that require less than 4 years of college education, but health diagnosing and treating practitioners are among the most educated workers.

Nature of the Field

Combining medical technology and the human touch, the health care field administers care around the clock, responding to the needs of millions of people—from newborns to the critically ill.

About 545,000 establishments make up the health care field; they vary greatly in terms of size, staffing patterns, and organizational structures. About 76 percent of health care establishments are offices of physicians, dentists, or other health practitioners. Although hospitals constitute only 2 percent of all health care establishments, they employ 40 percent of all workers (table 1).

Table 1. Percent distribution of wage and salary employment and establishments in health services, 2004

Establishment type	Establish-ments	Employ-ment
Health services, total	100.0	100.0
Hospitals, public and private	1.9	41.3
Nursing and residential care facilities.............	11.6	21.3
Offices of physicians.....................................	37.0	15.5
Offices of dentists...	21.0	5.7
Home healthcare services..............................	3.0	5.8
Offices of other health practitioners	18.7	4.0
Outpatient care centers..................................	3.2	3.4
Other ambulatory healthcare services	1.5	1.5
Medical and diagnostic laboratories................	2.1	1.4

The health care field includes establishments ranging from small-town private practices of physicians who employ only one medical assistant to busy inner-city hospitals that provide thousands of diverse jobs. In 2004, about half of nonhospital health care establishments employed fewer than 5 workers (chart 1). By contrast, 7 out of 10 hospital employees were in establishments with more than 1,000 workers (chart 2).

The health care field consists of the following nine segments:

Hospitals. Hospitals provide complete medical care, ranging from diagnostic services to surgery to continuous nursing care. Some hospitals specialize in treatment of the mentally ill, cancer patients, or children. Hospital-based care may be on an inpatient (overnight) or outpatient basis. The mix of workers needed varies, depending on the size, geographic location, goals, philosophy, funding, organization, and management style of the institution. As hospitals work to improve efficiency, care continues to shift from an inpatient to outpatient basis whenever possible. Many hospitals have expanded into long-term and home health care services, providing a wide range of care for the communities they serve.

Nursing and residential care facilities. Nursing care facilities provide inpatient nursing, rehabilitation, and health-related personal care to those who need continuous nursing care but do not require hospital services. Nursing

aides provide the vast majority of direct care. Other facilities, such as convalescent homes, help patients who need less assistance. Residential care facilities provide around-the-clock social and personal care to children, the elderly, and others who have limited ability to care for themselves. Workers care for residents of assisted-living facilities, alcohol and drug rehabilitation centers, group homes, and halfway houses. Nursing and medical care, however, are not the main functions of establishments providing residential care as they are in nursing care facilities.

Chart 1. Over 85 percent of nonhospital health services establishments employ fewer than 20 workers.

Percent

Legend: Establishments, Employment

- 1 to 4: Establishments 48.2, Employment 6.5
- 5 to 19: Establishments 38.4, Employment 24.0
- 20 to 99: Establishments 10.5, Employment 30.7
- 100 or more: Establishments 2.9, Employment 38.8

Number of workers employed by establishment, March 2004

Chart 2. More than 70 percent of jobs in hospitals are in establishments with 1,000 or more workers.

Percent

Legend: Establishments, Employment

- 1 to 19: Establishments 25.9, Employment 0.2
- 20 to 249: Establishments 31.1, Employment 6.1
- 250 to 999: Establishments 24.9, Employment 23.1
- 1,000 or more: Establishments 18.1, Employment 70.5

Number of workers employed by establishment, March 2004

Education, Health Care, and Social Services

Offices of physicians. About 37 percent of all health care establishments fall into this field segment. Physicians and surgeons practice privately or in groups of practitioners who have the same or different specialties. Many physicians and surgeons prefer to join group practices because they afford backup coverage, reduce overhead expenses, and facilitate consultation with peers. Physicians and surgeons are increasingly working as salaried employees of group medical practices, clinics, or integrated health systems.

Offices of dentists. About 1 out of every 5 health care establishments is a dentist's office. Most employ only a few workers, who provide general or specialized dental care, including dental surgery.

Home health care services. Skilled nursing or medical care is sometimes provided in the home under a physician's supervision. Home health care services are provided mainly to the elderly. The development of in-home medical technologies, substantial cost savings, and patients' preference for care in the home have helped change this once-small segment of the field into one of the fastest-growing parts of the economy.

Offices of other health practitioners. This segment of the field includes the offices of chiropractors, optometrists, podiatrists, occupational and physical therapists, psychologists, audiologists, speech-language pathologists, dietitians, and other health practitioners. Demand for the services of this segment is related to the ability of patients to pay, either directly or through health insurance. Hospitals and nursing facilities may contract out for these services. This segment also includes the offices of practitioners of alternative medicine, such as acupuncturists, homeopaths, hypnotherapists, and naturopaths.

Outpatient care centers. The diverse establishments in this group include kidney dialysis centers, outpatient mental health and substance abuse centers, health maintenance organization medical centers, and freestanding ambulatory surgical and emergency centers.

Other ambulatory health care services. This relatively small field segment includes ambulance and helicopter transport services, blood and organ banks, and other ambulatory health care services, such as pacemaker monitoring services and smoking cessation programs.

Medical and diagnostic laboratories. Medical and diagnostic laboratories provide analytic or diagnostic services to the medical profession or directly to patients following a physician's prescription. Workers may analyze blood, take X rays and computerized tomography scans, or perform other clinical tests. Medical and diagnostic laboratories provide the fewest number of jobs in the health care field.

In the rapidly changing health care field, technological advances have made many new procedures and methods of diagnosis and treatment possible. Clinical developments, such as organ transplants, less-invasive surgical techniques, skin grafts, and gene therapy for cancer treatment, continue to increase the longevity and improve the quality of life of many Americans. Advances in medical technology also have improved the survival rates of trauma victims and the severely ill, who need extensive care from therapists and social workers as well as other support personnel.

In addition, advances in information technology continue to improve patient care and worker efficiency with devices such as hand-held computers that record notes on each patient. Information on vital signs and orders for tests are transferred electronically to a main database; this process eliminates the need for paper and reduces record-keeping errors.

Cost containment also is shaping the health care field, as shown by the growing emphasis on providing services on an outpatient, ambulatory basis; limiting unnecessary or low-priority services; and stressing preventive care, which reduces the potential cost of undiagnosed, untreated medical conditions. Enrollment in managed care programs—predominantly preferred provider organizations, health maintenance organizations, and hybrid plans such as point-of-service programs—continues to grow. These prepaid plans provide comprehensive coverage to members and control health insurance costs by emphasizing preventive care. Cost-effectiveness also is improved with the increased use of integrated delivery systems, which combine two or more segments of the field to increase efficiency through the streamlining of functions, primarily financial and managerial. These changes will continue to reshape not only the nature of the health care workforce, but also the manner in which health care is provided.

Working Conditions

Average weekly hours of nonsupervisory workers in private health care varied among the different segments of the field. Workers in offices of dentists averaged only

26.9 hours per week in 2004, while those in psychiatric and substance abuse hospitals averaged 36.4 hours, compared with 33.7 hours for all nongovernment fields.

Many workers in the health care field are on part-time schedules. Part-time workers made up about 20 percent of the workforce as a whole in 2004, but accounted for 39 percent of workers in offices of dentists and 33 percent of those in offices of other health practitioners. Students, parents with young children, dual jobholders, and older workers make up much of the part-time workforce.

Many health care establishments operate around the clock and need staff at all hours. Shift work is common in some occupations, such as registered nurses. Numerous health care workers hold more than one job.

In 2004, the incidence of occupational injury and illness in hospitals was 8.7 cases per 100 full-time workers, compared with an average of 5.0 for nongovernment fields overall. Nursing care facilities had a much higher rate of 10.1. Health care workers involved in direct patient care must take precautions to prevent back strain from lifting patients and equipment; to minimize exposure to radiation and caustic chemicals; and to guard against infectious diseases, such as AIDS, tuberculosis, and hepatitis. Home care personnel who make house calls are exposed to the possibility of being injured in highway accidents, all types of overexertion when assisting patients, and falls inside and outside homes.

Important Characteristics of the Field

Skills: Social Perceptiveness; Service Orientation; Instructing; Time Management; Learning Strategies; Active Listening. **Abilities:** Speech Recognition; Problem Sensitivity; Arm-Hand Steadiness; Gross Body Coordination; Speech Clarity; Stamina. **Work-Related Values:** Social Service; Co-workers; Activity; Variety; Security; Achievement.

Employment

As the largest field in 2004, health care provided 13.5 million jobs—13.1 million jobs for wage and salary workers and about 411,000 jobs for self-employed and unpaid family workers. Of the 13.1 million wage and salary jobs, 41 percent were in hospitals; another 22 per-

cent were in nursing and residential care facilities; and 16 percent were in offices of physicians. About 92 percent of wage and salary jobs were in nongovernment fields; the rest were in state and local government hospitals. The majority of jobs for self-employed and unpaid family workers in health care were in offices of physicians, dentists, and other health practitioners—about 282,000 out of the 411,000 total self-employed.

Health care jobs are found throughout the country, but they are concentrated in the largest states—in particular, California, New York, Florida, Texas, and Pennsylvania.

Workers in health care tend to be older than workers in other fields. Health care workers also are more likely to remain employed in the same occupation, due in part to the high level of education and training required for many health occupations.

Occupations in the Field

Health care firms employ large numbers of workers in professional and service occupations. Together, these two occupational groups account for 3 out of 4 jobs in the field. The next largest share of jobs, 18 percent, is in office and administrative support. Management, business, and financial operations occupations account for only 4 percent of employment. Other occupations in health care made up only 3 percent of the total (table 2).

Professional occupations, such as *physicians and surgeons*, *dentists*, *registered nurses*, *social workers*, and *physical therapists*, usually require at least a bachelor's degree in a specialized field or higher education in a specific health field, although *registered nurses* also enter through associate degree or diploma programs. Professional workers often have high levels of responsibility and complex duties. In addition to providing services, these workers may supervise other workers or conduct research.

Other health professionals and technicians work in many fast-growing occupations, such as *medical records and health information technicians* and *dental hygienists*. These workers may operate technical equipment and assist health diagnosing and treating practitioners. Graduates of 1-year or 2-year training programs often fill such positions; the jobs usually require specific formal training beyond high school, but less than 4 years of college.

Service occupations attract many workers with little or no specialized education or training. For instance, some of these workers are *nursing aides, home health aides, building cleaning workers, dental assistants, medical assistants,* and *personal and home care aides. Nursing* or *home health aides* provide health-related services for ill, injured, disabled, elderly, or infirm individuals either in institutions or in their homes. By providing routine personal care services, *personal and home care aides* help elderly, disabled, and ill persons live in their own homes instead of in an institution. Although some of these workers are employed by public or private agencies, many are self-employed. With experience and, in some cases, further education and training, service workers may advance to higher-level positions or transfer to new occupations.

Most workers in health care jobs provide clinical services, but many also are employed in occupations with other functions. Numerous workers in management and administrative support jobs keep organizations running smoothly. Although many *medical and health services managers* have a background in a clinical specialty or training in health care administration, some enter these jobs with a general business education.

Each segment of the health care field provides a different mix of wage and salary health-related jobs.

Hospitals. Hospitals employ workers with all levels of education and training, thereby providing a wider variety of services than is offered by other segments of the health care field. About 3 in 10 hospital workers are *registered nurses.* Hospitals also employ many *physicians and surgeons, therapists,* and *social workers.* About 1 in 5 hospital jobs are in a service occupation, such as *nursing, psychiatric, and home health aides* or *building cleaning workers.* Hospitals also employ large numbers of office and administrative support workers.

Nursing and residential care facilities. About 2 out of 3 nursing and residential care facility jobs are in service occupations, primarily *nursing, psychiatric, and home health aides.* Professional and administrative support occupations make up a much smaller percentage of employment in this segment, compared to other parts of the health care field. Federal law requires nursing facilities to have licensed personnel on hand 24 hours a day and to maintain an appropriate level of care.

Table 2. Employment of wage and salary workers in health care by occupation, 2004 and projected change, 2004–2014 (Employment in thousands)

Occupation	Employment, 2004		Percent change, 2004–2014
	Number	Percent	
Total, all occupations	13,062	100.0	27.3
Management, business, and financial occupations	574	4.4	28.3
Top executives	101	0.8	33.3
Medical and health services managers	175	1.3	26.1
Professional and related occupations	5,657	43.3	27.8
Psychologists	33	0.3	28.1
Counselors	152	1.2	31.8
Social workers	169	1.3	29.3
Health educators	17	0.1	27.0
Social and human service assistants	99	0.8	38.6
Chiropractors	21	0.2	47.8
Dentists	95	0.7	18.5
Dietitians and nutritionists	32	0.2	20.1
Optometrists	18	0.1	29.6
Pharmacists	63	0.5	17.3
Physicians and surgeons	417	3.2	28.7
Physician assistants	53	0.4	54.8
Podiatrists	7	0.1	22.2
Registered nurses	1,988	15.2	30.5
Therapists	358	2.7	32.8
Clinical laboratory technologists and technicians	257	2.0	22.7
Dental hygienists	153	1.2	43.7
Diagnostic related technologists and technicians	269	2.1	26.4
Emergency medical technicians and paramedics	122	0.9	27.8
Health diagnosing and treating practitioner support technicians	226	1.7	18.0
Licensed practical and licensed vocational nurses	586	4.5	14.2
Medical records and health information technicians	134	1.0	30.0

Occupation	Employment, 2004		Percent change, 2004–2014
	Number	Percent	
Service occupations	4,152	31.8	33.2
Home health aides	458	3.5	66.4
Nursing aides, orderlies, and attendants........................	1,230	9.4	22.2
Physical therapist assistants and aides	95	0.7	41.0
Dental assistants	257	2.0	43.6
Medical assistants	361	2.8	53.7
Medical transcriptionists	81	0.6	22.1
Food preparation and serving related occupations	462	3.5	12.6
Building cleaning workers	365	2.8	20.6
Personal and home care aides..	312	2.4	60.5
Office and administrative support occupations	2,379	18.2	16.2
Billing and posting clerks and machine operators	179	1.4	10.9
Receptionists and information clerks	353	2.7	31.3
Medical secretaries	347	2.7	17.3

Note: May not add to totals due to omission of occupations with small employment

Offices of physicians. Many of the jobs in offices of physicians are in professional and related occupations, primarily *physicians*, *surgeons*, and *registered nurses*. About two-fifths of all jobs, however, are in office and administrative support occupations, such as *receptionists* and *information clerks*.

Offices of dentists. Roughly one-third of all jobs in this segment are in service occupations, mostly *dental assistants*. The typical staffing pattern in dentists' offices consists of one *dentist* with a support staff of *dental hygienists* and *dental assistants*. Larger practices are more likely to employ office managers and administrative support workers.

Home health care services. About 57 percent of all jobs in this segment are in service occupations, mostly *home health aides* and *personal and home care aides*. Nursing and therapist jobs also account for substantial shares of employment in this segment.

Offices of other health practitioners. Professional and related occupations, including *physical therapists*, *occupational therapists*, *dispensing opticians*, and *chiropractors*, accounted for about 2 in 5 jobs in this segment. Office and administrative support occupations and healthcare practitioners and technical occupations also accounted for a significant portion of all jobs—about 33 percent each.

Outpatient care centers. This segment of the health care field employs a high percentage of professional and related workers, including *counselors*, *social workers*, and *registered nurses*.

Other ambulatory health care services. Because this field segment includes ambulance services, it employs 2 out of every 5 *emergency medical technicians and paramedics* and *ambulance drivers and attendants*.

Medical and diagnostic laboratories. Professional and related workers, primarily *clinical laboratory* and *radiologic technologists and technicians*, make up about 43 percent of all jobs in this field segment. Service workers employed in this segment include *medical assistants*, *medical equipment preparers*, and *medical transcriptionists*.

Training and Advancement

A variety of programs after high school provide specialized training for jobs in health care. Students preparing for health careers can enter programs leading to a certificate or a degree at the associate, baccalaureate, or graduate level. Two-year programs resulting in certificates or associate degrees are the minimum standard credential for occupations such as dental hygienist or radiologic technologist. Most therapists and social workers have at least a bachelor's degree. Health diagnosing and treating practitioners—such as physicians and surgeons, optometrists, and podiatrists—are among the most educated workers, with many years of education and training beyond college.

The health care field also provides many job opportunities for people without specialized training beyond high school. In fact, more than half of workers in nursing and residential care facilities have a high school diploma or less, as do a quarter of workers in hospitals.

Some health care establishments provide on-the-job or classroom training as well as continuing education. For example, in all certified nursing facilities, nursing aides must complete a state-approved training and competency evaluation program and participate in at least 12 hours of in-service education annually. Hospitals are more likely than other facilities to have the resources and incentive to provide training programs and advancement opportunities to their employees. In other segments of health care, the variety of positions and advancement opportunities are more limited. Larger establishments usually offer a broader range of opportunities.

Some hospitals provide training or tuition assistance in return for a promise to work at their facility for a particular length of time after graduation. Many nursing facilities have similar programs. Some hospitals have cross-training programs that train their workers—through formal college programs, continuing education, or in-house training—to perform functions outside their specialties.

Persons considering careers in health care should have a strong desire to help others, genuine concern for the welfare of patients and clients, and an ability to deal with people of diverse backgrounds in stressful situations.

Health specialists with clinical expertise can advance to department head positions or even higher-level management jobs. Medical and health services managers can advance to more responsible positions all the way up to chief executive officer.

Outlook

Job opportunities should be excellent in all employment settings because of high job turnover, particularly from the large number of expected retirements and tougher immigration rules that are slowing the numbers of foreign health care workers entering the U.S. Wage and salary employment in the health care field is projected to increase 27 percent through 2014, compared with 14 percent for all fields combined (table 3). Employment growth is expected to account for about 3.6 million new wage and salary jobs—19 percent of all wage and salary jobs added to the economy over the 2004–2014 period. Projected rates of employment growth for the various segments of the field range from 13 percent in hospitals, the largest and slowest-growing field segment, to 69 percent in the much smaller home health care services.

Table 3. Employment in health care by field segment, 2004 and projected change, 2004–2014 (Employment in thousands)

Field segment	2004 Employment	Percent change, 2004–2014
All fields	145,612	14.0
Health services	13,062	27.3
Hospitals, public and private	5,301	13.1
Nursing and residential care facilities	2,815	27.8
Offices of physicians	2,054	37.0
Home health care services	773	69.5
Offices of dentists	760	31.7
Offices of other health practitioners	524	42.7
Outpatient care centers	446	44.2
Other ambulatory health care services	201	37.7
Medical and diagnostic laboratories	189	27.1

Many of the occupations projected to grow the fastest in the economy are concentrated in the health care field. For example, over the 2004–2014 period, total employment of home health aides—including the self-employed—is projected to increase by 56 percent, medical assistants by 52 percent, physician assistants by 50 percent, and physical therapist assistants by 44 percent.

Employment in health care will continue to grow for several reasons. The number of people in older age groups with much greater than average health care needs will grow faster than the total population between 2004 and 2014; as a result, the demand for health care will increase. Employment in home health care and nursing and residential care should increase rapidly as life expectancies rise and as aging children are less able to care for their parents and rely more on long-term care facilities. Advances in medical technology will continue to improve the survival rate of severely ill and injured patients, who will then need extensive therapy and care. New technologies will make it possible to identify and treat conditions that were previously not treatable. Medical group practices and integrated health systems will become larger and more complex, increasing the need for office and administrative support workers. Field growth also will occur as a result of the shift from inpatient to less-expensive outpatient and home health care because of improvements in diagnostic tests and surgical procedures along with patients' desires to be treated at home.

Many job openings will result from a need to replace workers due to retirements and high job turnover. Occupations with the most replacement openings are usually large, with high turnover stemming from low pay and status, poor benefits, low training requirements, and a high proportion of young and part-time workers. Nursing aides, orderlies and attendants, and home health aides are among the occupations adding the most new jobs between 2004 and 2014, about 675,000 combined. By contrast, occupations with relatively few replacement openings—such as physicians and surgeons—are characterized by high pay and status, lengthy training requirements, and a high proportion of full-time workers.

Another occupation that will add many new jobs is registered nurses. The median age of registered nurses is increasing, and not enough younger workers are replacing them. As a result, employers in some parts of the country are reporting difficulties in attracting and retaining nurses. Imbalances between the supply of and the demand for qualified workers should spur efforts to attract and retain qualified registered nurses. For example, employers may restructure workloads and job responsibilities, improve compensation and working conditions, and subsidize training or continuing education.

Fast growth is expected for workers in occupations concentrated outside the inpatient hospital sector, such as medical assistants and home health aides. Because of cost pressures, many health care facilities will adjust their staffing patterns to reduce labor costs. Where patient care demands and regulations allow, health care facilities will substitute lower-paid providers and will cross-train their workforces. Many facilities have cut the number of middle managers while simultaneously creating new managerial positions as the facilities diversify. Traditional inpatient hospital positions are no longer the only option for many future health care workers; persons seeking a career in the field must be willing to work in various employment settings. Employment growth in hospitals will be the slowest within the health care field because of efforts to control hospital costs and the increasing use of outpatient clinics and other alternative care sites.

Demand for dental care will rise due to population growth, greater retention of natural teeth by middle-aged and older persons, greater awareness of the importance of dental care, and an increased ability to pay for services.

Dentists will use support personnel such as dental hygienists and assistants to help meet their increased workloads.

In some management, business, and financial operations occupations, rapid growth will be tempered by restructuring to reduce administrative costs and streamline operations. Office automation and other technological changes will slow employment growth in office and administrative support occupations, but because the employment base is large, replacement needs will continue to create substantial numbers of job openings. Slower-growing service occupations also will provide job openings due to replacement needs.

Health care workers at all levels of education and training will continue to be in demand. In many cases, it may be easier for jobseekers with health-specific training to obtain jobs and advance in their careers. Specialized clinical training is a requirement for many jobs in health care and is an asset even for many administrative jobs that do not specifically require it.

Earnings

Average earnings of nonsupervisory workers in most health care segments are higher than the average for all nongovernment fields, with hospital workers earning considerably more than the average and those employed in nursing and residential care facilities and home health care services earning less (table 4). Average earnings often are higher in hospitals because the percentage of jobs requiring higher levels of education and training is greater than in other segments. Those segments of the field with lower earnings employ large numbers of part-time service workers.

Table 4. Average earnings and hours of nonsupervisory workers in health services by field segment, 2004

Field segment	Earnings Weekly	Hourly	Weekly hours
Total, nongovernment	$528.56	$15.67	33.7
Health care	572.83	17.32	33.1
Hospitals	715.12	20.31	35.2
Medical and diagnostic laboratories	634.79	18.15	35.0
Offices of physicians	613.82	18.41	33.4
Outpatient care centers	631.38	18.57	34.0

Education, Health Care, and Social Services

| Field segment | Earnings | | Weekly |
	Weekly	Hourly	hours
Other ambulatory healthcare services	498.65	14.32	34.8
Offices of dentists	510.81	18.96	26.9
Offices of other health practitioners	453.91	16.00	28.4
Home health care services	415.12	14.41	28.8
Nursing and residential care facilities	393.58	12.05	32.7

As in most fields, professionals and managers working in health care typically earn more than other workers in the field. Earnings in individual health care occupations vary as widely as the duties, level of education and training, and amount of responsibility required by the occupation (table 5). Some establishments offer tuition reimbursement, paid training, child day care services, and flexible work hours. Health care establishments that must be staffed around the clock to care for patients and handle emergencies often pay premiums for overtime and weekend work, holidays, late shifts, and time spent on call. Bonuses and profit-sharing payments also may add to earnings.

Earnings vary not only by type of establishment and occupation, but also by size; salaries tend to be higher in larger hospitals and group practices. Geographic location also can affect earnings.

Table 5. Median hourly earnings of the largest occupations in health services, May 2004

Occupation	Ambulatory health care services	Hospitals	Nursing and residential care	All fields
Registered nurses	$23.69	$25.66	$22.93	$25.16
Licensed practical and licensed vocational nurses	15.59	15.71	16.95	16.33
Dental assistants	13.60	14.02	–	13.62
Medical secretaries	12.88	12.60	12.00	12.76
Medical assistants	11.77	12.03	10.85	11.83
Office clerks, general	11.07	11.08	9.62	10.50
Receptionists and information clerks	10.76	11.79	10.40	10.95

Occupation	Ambulatory health care services	Hospitals	Nursing and residential care	All fields
Nursing aides, orderlies, and attendants	9.82	10.43	9.78	10.09
Home health aides	8.58	9.69	8.84	8.81
Personal and home care aides	7.05	8.54	8.85	8.12

Although some hospitals have unions, the health care field is not heavily unionized. In 2004, only 11 percent of workers in the field were members of unions or covered by union contracts, compared with about 14 percent for all fields.

Sources of Additional Information

For additional information on specific health-related occupations, contact

- American Medical Association/Health Professions Career and Education Directory, 515 N. State St., Chicago, IL 60610. Internet: http://www.ama-assn.org/go/alliedhealth

For information on physician careers and applying to medical school, contact

- Association of American Medical Colleges, 2450 N Street NW, Washington, DC 20037. Internet: http://www.aamc.org/students

General information on health careers is available from

- Bureau of Health Professions, Parklawn Rm. 8A-09, 5600 Fishers Lane, Rockville, MD 20857. Internet: http://bhpr.hrsa.gov/kidscareers

For a list of accredited programs in allied health fields, contact

- Commission on Accreditation of Allied Health Education Programs, 35 E. Wacker Dr., Suite 1970, Chicago, IL 60601. Internet: http://www.caahep.org

A wealth of information on health careers and job opportunities also is available through the Internet, schools, libraries, associations, and employers.

Social Assistance, Except Child Day Care

- Annual Earnings: $22,979
- Job Growth: 32.6%
- Size of Workforce: 1,305,420
- Self-Employed: 3.7%
- Part-Time: 24.6%

Significant Points

- About 1 out of 3 jobs are in professional and service occupations.

- Job opportunities in social assistance should be numerous through the year 2014 because of job turnover and rapid employment growth.

- Some of the fastest-growing occupations in the nation, such as home health aides and personal and home care aides, are concentrated in social assistance.

- Average earnings are low because of the large number of part-time and low-paying service jobs.

Nature of the Field

Careers in social assistance appeal to persons with a strong desire to make life better and easier for others. Workers in this field usually are good communicators and enjoy interacting with people. Social assistance establishments provide a wide array of services that include helping the homeless, counseling troubled and emotionally disturbed individuals, training the unemployed or underemployed, and helping the needy to obtain financial assistance. About 61,000 establishments in the private sector provided social assistance in 2004. Thousands of other establishments, mainly in state and local government, provided additional social assistance. (For information about government social assistance, see the descriptions of federal government and state and local government, excluding education and hospitals.)

Social assistance consists of four segments—individual and family services, community food and housing and emergency and other relief services, vocational rehabilitation services, and child day care services. The child day care services segment, including day care and preschool care centers, is covered in a description elsewhere in part II.

Individual and family services establishments are primarily engaged in providing nonresidential social assistance for children, the elderly, or persons with mental or physical disabilities. Services provided for children may include adoption and foster care, drug prevention, life skills training, and positive social development. Services also are provided to the elderly and persons with disabilities through adult day care, nonmedical home care or homemaker services, social activities, group support, and companionship.

Community food and housing and emergency and other relief services establishments provide various types of assistance to members of the community. Community food and housing and emergency and other relief services is further divided into three sectors: Community food services, community housing services, and emergency and other relief services.

Establishments in the *community food services* subsector collect, prepare, and deliver food for the needy. Establishments in this field may also distribute clothing and blankets to the poor. These establishments may prepare and deliver meals to persons who by reason of age, disability, or illness are unable to prepare meals for themselves; collect and distribute salvageable or donated food; or prepare and provide meals at fixed or mobile locations. Food banks, meal delivery programs, and soup kitchens are included in this field.

Establishments in the *community housing services* sector provide short-term emergency shelter for victims of domestic violence, sexual assault, or child abuse. Also included in this sector are establishments that provide transitional housing for low-income individuals and families as well as temporary residential shelter for the homeless, runaway youths, and patients and families caught in medical crises. Community housing establishments also perform volunteer construction or repair of low-cost housing in partnership with the homeowner, who may assist in construction or repair work and repair of homes for elderly or disabled homeowners. These establishments may operate their own shelter or may provide subsidized housing using existing homes.

Establishments in the *emergency and other relief services* sector provide food, shelter, clothing, medical relief,

Education, Health Care, and Social Services

resettlement, and counseling to victims of domestic or international disasters or conflicts.

Vocational rehabilitation services establishments provide vocational rehabilitation or life skills services, such as job counseling, job training, and work experience, to unemployed and underemployed persons; persons with disabilities; and persons who have a job market disadvantage because of lack of education, job skills, or experience. Vocational rehabilitation job training facilities and sheltered workshops, such as work experience centers, are included in this field.

Working Conditions

Some social assistance establishments operate around the clock. Thus, evening, weekend, and holiday work is common. Some establishments may be understaffed, resulting in large caseloads for each worker. Jobs in voluntary, nonprofit agencies often are part time.

Some workers spend a substantial amount of time traveling within the local area. For example, home health and personal care aides routinely visit clients in their homes; social workers and social and human service assistants also may make home visits.

Important Characteristics of the Field

Skills: Social Perceptiveness; Service Orientation; Persuasion; Learning Strategies; Active Listening; Writing. **Abilities:** Speech Recognition; Speech Clarity; Stamina; Problem Sensitivity; Dynamic Strength; Oral Comprehension. **Work-Related Values:** Social Service; Variety; Authority; Autonomy; Supervision, Technical; Security.

Employment

Social assistance provided 1.4 million nongovernment wage and salary jobs in 2004. About 63 percent were in individual and family services (table 1).

Table 1. Employment in of nongovernment wage and salary workers in social assistance, except childcare, by field segment, 2004 and projected change, 2004–2014 (Employment in thousands)

Field segment	Employment, 2004	2004–2014 Percent change Number	Percent
Total, social assistance, except childcare	1,365	100.0	32.6
Individual and family services	853	62.5	36.0
Vocational rehabilitation services	381	27.9	28.5
Community food and housing, and emergency and other relief services	131	9.6	22.1

In 2004, about 77 percent of social assistance establishments employed fewer than 20 workers; however, larger establishments accounted for most jobs (chart 1).

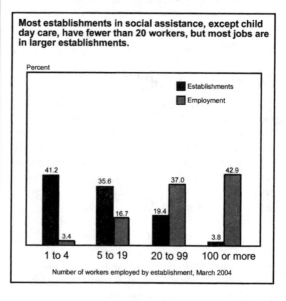

Most establishments in social assistance, except child day care, have fewer than 20 workers, but most jobs are in larger establishments.

Social assistance workers were somewhat older than workers in other fields (table 2). About 40 percent were 45 years old or older, compared with 39 percent of all workers. Jobs in social assistance are concentrated in large states with heavily populated urban areas, such as New York and California.

Table 2. Percent distribution of employment, by age group, 2004

Age group	Social assistance, except child day care	All fields
Total	100.0%	100.0%
16–19	3.8	4.2
20–24	10.2	9.9
25–34	23.0	21.8
35–44	23.6	24.8
45–54	22.7	23.3
55–64	12.6	12.4
65 and older	4.2	3.5

Occupations in the Field

More than one-third of nongovernment social assistance jobs are in professional and related occupations (table 3). *Social workers* counsel and assess the needs of clients, refer them to the appropriate sources of help, and monitor their progress. They may specialize in child welfare and family services, mental health, medical social work, school social work, community organization activities, or clinical social work. *Social and human service assistants* work in a variety of social and human service delivery settings. Job titles and duties of these workers vary, but they include human service worker, case management aide, social work assistant, mental health aide, child abuse worker, community outreach worker, and gerontology aide. *Counselors* help people evaluate their interests and abilities and advise and assist them with personal and social problems.

Almost one-third of employment in the social assistance field is in many of the service occupations. *Personal and home care aides* help elderly, disabled, and ill persons live in their own homes instead of in an institution by providing routine personal care services. Although some are employed by public or private agencies, many are self-employed. Persons in *food preparation and serving related occupations* serve residents at social assistance institutions. *Home health aides* provide health-related services for ill, injured, disabled, or elderly individuals in their homes.

As in most fields, office and administrative support workers—secretaries and bookkeepers, for example—as well as managers account for many jobs. However, social assistance employs a much smaller percentage of production; installation, maintenance, and repair; and sales jobs than does the economy as a whole.

Training, Other Qualifications, and Advancement

Some occupations in social assistance have very specific entrance requirements. These include most of the professional and related occupations. Those requiring specific clinical training, such as clinical social workers and clinical psychologists, also require appropriate state licensure or certification. Nevertheless, people with a limited background in social assistance or little education beyond high school can find a job in the field. Nursing aides, orderlies, and attendants; home health aides; and personal and home care aides are some of these occupations. Many establishments provide on-the-job or classroom training, especially for those with limited background or training.

Many employers prefer social and human service assistants with some related work experience or college courses in human services, social work, or one of the social or behavioral sciences. Other employers prefer an associate degree or a bachelor's degree in human services or social work. A number of employers provide in-service training, such as seminars and workshops.

Entry-level jobs for social workers require a bachelor's degree in social work or in an undergraduate major such as psychology or sociology. However, most agencies require a master's degree in social work or a closely related field. Public agencies and private practice clinics that offer clinical or consultative services require an advanced degree in clinical social work; supervisory, administrative, and staff training positions usually require at least a master's degree.

Education, Health Care, and Social Services

Table 3. Employment of wage and salary workers in social assistance, except child day care by occupation, 2004 and projected change, 2004–2014 (Employment in thousands)

Occupation	Employment, 2004		Percent change, 2004–2014
	Number	Percent	
Total, all occupations	1,365	100.0	32.6
Management, business, and financial occupations	138	10.1	33.3
Top executives	26	1.9	31.4
Social and community service managers	42	3.1	32.5
Human resources, training, and labor relations specialists	21	1.5	35.0
Accountants and auditors	9	0.7	32.5
Professional and related occupations	486	35.6	35.1
Clinical, counseling, and school psychologists	8	0.6	33.5
Substance abuse and behavioral disorder counselors	14	1.0	32.0
Educational, vocational, and school counselors	23	1.7	30.2
Marriage and family therapists	9	0.7	32.3
Mental health counselors	18	1.3	32.2
Rehabilitation counselors	52	3.8	23.6
Child, family, and school social workers	52	3.8	33.4
Medical and public health social workers	12	0.9	39.2
Mental health and substance abuse social workers	23	1.7	33.3
Health educators	7	0.5	32.4
Social and human service assistants	99	7.3	45.6
Preschool teachers, except special education	15	1.1	33.8
Adult literacy, remedial education, and GED teachers and instructors	8	0.6	33.1
Teacher assistants	22	1.6	33.7
Registered nurses	17	1.2	33.9
Service occupations	449	32.9	36.8
Home health aides	91	6.7	33.5
Cooks and food preparation workers	21	1.5	31.3
Building cleaning workers	36	2.7	32.6
Child care workers	26	1.9	27.8
Personal and home care aides	184	13.5	44.2
Recreation workers	20	1.5	32.2
Residential advisors	10	0.8	31.3
Office and administrative support occupations	170	12.4	17.9
Supervisors, office and administrative support workers	12	0.9	20.2
Bookkeeping, accounting, and auditing clerks	17	1.3	19.5
Receptionists and information clerks	17	1.3	26.5
Secretaries and administrative assistants	45	3.3	18.8
Office clerks, general	37	2.7	18.1
Transportation and material moving occupations	65	4.7	27.4
Bus drivers, school	13	1.0	33.4
Laborers and material movers, hand	29	2.1	21.8

Note: May not add to totals due to omission of occupations with small employment

Volunteering with a student, religious, or charitable organization is a good way for persons to test their interest in social assistance and may provide an advantage when applying for jobs in this field.

Advancement paths vary. For example, some personal and home care aides as well as some nursing aides, orderlies, and attendants and home health aides get additional training and become licensed practical nurses. Formal education—usually a bachelor's or master's degree in counseling, human services, rehabilitation, social work, or a related field—almost always is necessary in order for social and human service assistants to advance. Social workers with an advanced degree and the appropriate license can advance to supervisor, program manager, assistant director, or executive director of an agency or department. They also may enter private practice and provide psychotherapeutic counseling and other services on a contract basis.

Outlook

Job opportunities in social assistance should be numerous through the year 2014. The number of nongovernment wage and salary jobs is expected to increase 33 percent, compared with only 14 percent for all fields combined. Expected growth rates for the various segments of the field are 36 percent in individual and family services, 29 percent in vocational rehabilitation services, and 22 percent in community food and housing and emergency and other relief services over the 2004–2014 period. In addition to those arising from employment growth, many job openings will stem from the need to replace workers who transfer to other occupations or stop working.

Projected job growth is due mostly to the expansion of services for the elderly and the aging baby-boom generation. Similarly, services for the mentally ill, the physically disabled, and families in crisis will be expanded. Increasing emphasis on providing home care services rather than more costly nursing home or hospital care, and on earlier and better integration of the physically disabled and mentally ill into society, also will contribute to employment growth in the social assistance field, as will increased demand for drug and alcohol abuse prevention programs. Employment in private social service agencies may be spurred as state and local governments contract out their social services in an effort to cut costs. The expansion and creation of employment in the social assistance field may depend in large part on the amount of funding made available by the government and managed-care organizations.

Some of the fastest-growing occupations in the nation are concentrated in social assistance. Compared with field growth of 33 percent, the number of home health aides within social assistance is projected to grow 34 percent between 2004 and 2014. The number of social and human service assistants is expected to grow 46 percent; personal and home care aides, 44 percent. Overall employment of social workers will continue to grow, but not as rapidly as that of social and human service assistants.

Earnings

Earnings in selected occupations in the social assistance, except child day care field in May 2004 appear in table 4. As in most fields, professionals and managers—whose salaries reflect higher education levels, broader experience, and greater responsibility—commonly earn more than other workers.

Table 4. Median hourly earnings of the largest occupations in social assistance, except child day care, May 2004

Occupation	Individual and family services	Community food and housing and emergency and other releif services	Vocational rehabilitation services	All fields
Mental health and substance abuse social workers	$15.77	$13.41	$14.12	$16.31
Child, family, and school social workers	14.75	13.78	13.90	16.74
Rehabilitation counselors	12.64	12.68	12.80	13.40
Secretaries, except legal, medical, and executive	11.54	11.47	11.48	12.55
Social and human service assistants	11.25	10.70	10.47	11.67
Office clerks, general	9.87	9.83	9.67	10.95
Child care workers	9.17	9.01	8.42	8.06
Personal and home care aides	8.48	8.15	8.76	8.12
Home health aides	8.47	7.94	8.95	8.81
Janitors and cleaners, except maids and housekeeping cleaners	7.97	8.88	8.00	9.04

Education, Health Care, and Social Services

Average earnings in the social assistance field are lower than the average for all fields, as shown in table 5.

Table 5. Average earnings of nonsupervisory workers in social assistance, 2004

Field segment	Earnings Weekly	Hourly	Weekly hours
All nongovernment fields	$528.56	$15.67	33.7
Social assistance	337.76	11.06	30.5
Community housing, emergency, and relief services	400.00	13.19	30.3
Individual and family services	374.86	12.14	30.9
Vocational rehabilitation services	320.62	10.78	29.7
Community food services	324.60	11.35	28.6

Sources of Additional Information

For information about careers in social work and voluntary credentials for social workers, contact

- National Association of Social Workers, 750 First St. NE, Suite 700, Washington, DC 20002-4241. Internet: http://www.socialworkers.org

For information on programs and careers in human services, contact

- Council for Standards in Human Services Education, Harrisburg Area Community College, Human Services Program, One HACC Dr., Harrisburg, PA 17110-2999. Internet: http://www.cshse.org

State employment service offices also may be able to provide information on job opportunities in social assistance.

Leisure and Hospitality

Arts, Entertainment, and Recreation

- Annual Earnings: $20,190
- Job Growth: 25.1%
- Size of Workforce: 1,842,820
- Self-Employed: 14.6%
- Part-Time: 32.0%

Significant Points

- The field is characterized by a large number of seasonal and part-time jobs and relatively young workers.
- About 40 percent of all workers have no formal education beyond high school.
- Rising incomes, more leisure time, and growing awareness of the health benefits of physical fitness will increase the demand for arts, entertainment, and recreation services.
- Earnings are relatively low.

Nature of the Field

As leisure time and personal incomes have grown across the nation, so has the arts, entertainment, and recreation field. This field includes about 115,000 establishments, ranging from art museums to fitness centers. Practically any activity that occupies a person's leisure time, excluding the viewing of motion pictures and video rentals, is part of the arts, entertainment, and recreation field. The diverse range of activities offered by this field can be categorized into three broad groups—live performances or events; historical, cultural, or educational exhibits; and recreation or leisure-time activities.

Live performances or events. This segment of the field includes professional sports as well as establishments providing sports facilities and services to amateurs. Commercial sports clubs operate professional and amateur athletic clubs and promote athletic events. All kinds of popular sports can be found in these establishments, including baseball, basketball, boxing, football, ice hockey, soccer, wrestling, and even auto racing. Professional and amateur companies involved in sports promotion also are part of this field segment, as are sports establishments in which gambling is allowed, such as dog and horse racetracks and jai alai courts.

A variety of businesses and groups involved in live theatrical and musical performances are included in this segment. Theatrical production companies, for example, coordinate all aspects of producing a play or theater event, including employing actors and actresses and costume designers and contracting with lighting and stage crews who handle the technical aspects of productions. Agents and managers, who represent actors and entertainers and assist them in finding jobs or engagements, are also included. Booking agencies line up performance engagements for theatrical groups and entertainers.

Performers of live musical entertainment include popular music artists, dance bands, disc jockeys, orchestras, jazz musicians, and rock-and-roll bands. Orchestras range from major professional orchestras with million-dollar budgets to community orchestras, which often have part-time schedules. The performing arts segment also includes dance companies, which produce all types of live theatrical dances. The majority of these dance troupes perform ballet, folk dance, or modern dance.

Historical, cultural, or educational exhibits. Privately owned museums, zoos, botanical gardens, nature parks, and historical sites make up this segment of the field; publicly owned facilities are included in sections on federal, state, or local government elsewhere in Part II. Each institution in this segment preserves and exhibits objects, sites, and natural wonders with historical, cultural, or educational value.

Recreation or leisure activities. A variety of establishments provide amusement for a growing number of customers. Some of these businesses provide video game, pinball, and gaming machines for the public at amusement parks, arcades, and casinos. Casinos and other gaming establishments offering off-track betting are a rapidly growing part of this field segment. This segment also includes amusement and theme parks, which range in size from local carnivals to multiacre parks. These establishments may have mechanical rides, shows, and refreshment stands. Other recreation and leisure-time services include golf courses, skating rinks, ski lifts, marinas, day camps, go-cart tracks, riding stables, waterslides, and establishments offering rental sporting goods.

This segment of the field also includes physical fitness facilities that feature exercise and weight loss programs, gyms, health clubs, and day spas. These establishments also frequently offer aerobics, dance, yoga, and other exercise classes. Other recreation and leisure-time businesses include bowling centers that rent lanes and equipment for tenpin, duckpin, or candlepin bowling.

These facilities may be open to the public or available on a membership basis. Sports and recreation clubs that are open only to members and their guests include some golf courses; country clubs; and yacht, tennis, racquetball, hunting and fishing, and gun clubs. Public golf courses and marinas, unlike private clubs, offer facilities to the general public on a fee-per-use basis.

Technology is a major part of producing arts, entertainment, and recreation activities; for example, lighting and sound are vital for concerts and themed events and elaborate sets often are required for plays. However, most of this work is contracted to firms outside of the arts, entertainment, and recreation field. (For more information about entertainment technology jobs, see the sources of additional information at the end of this description.)

Working Conditions

Jobs in arts, entertainment, and recreation are more likely to be part time than those in other fields. In fact, the average nonsupervisory worker in the arts, entertainment, and recreation field worked 25.7 hours a week in 2004, as compared to an average of 33.7 hours for all nongovernment fields. Musical groups and artists were likely to work the fewest hours due to the large number of performers competing for a limited number of engagements, which may require a great amount of travel. The majority of performers are unable to support themselves in this profession alone and are forced to supplement their income through other jobs.

Many types of arts, entertainment, and recreation establishments dramatically increase employment during the summer and either scale back employment during the

Leisure and Hospitality

winter or close down completely. Workers may be required to work nights, weekends, and holidays because that is when most establishments are busiest. Some jobs require extensive travel. Music and dance troupes, for example, frequently tour or travel to major metropolitan areas across the country in hopes of attracting large audiences.

Many people in this field work outdoors, whereas others may work in hot, crowded, or noisy conditions. Some jobs, such as those at fitness facilities or in amusement parks, involve some manual labor and, thus, require physical strength and stamina. Also, athletes, dancers, and many other performers must be in particularly good physical condition. Many jobs include customer service responsibilities, so employees must be able to work well with the public.

In 2003, cases of work-related illness and injury averaged 5.9 for every 100 full-time workers, higher than the average of 5.0 for the entire private sector. Risks of injury are high in some jobs, especially those of athletes. Although most injuries are minor, including sprains and muscle pulls, they may prevent an employee from working for a period.

Important Characteristics of the Field

Skills: Service Orientation; Social Perceptiveness; Instructing; Learning Strategies; Persuasion. **Abilities:** Stamina; Gross Body Coordination; Dynamic Strength; Static Strength; Trunk Strength; Dynamic Flexibility. **Work-Related Values:** Social Service; Co-workers; Supervision, Technical.

Employment

The arts, entertainment, and recreation field provided about 1.8 million wage and salary jobs in 2004. About 58 percent of these jobs were in the field segment *other amusement and recreation fields*—which includes golf courses, membership sports and recreation clubs, and physical fitness facilities (table 1).

Table 1. Employment in arts, entertainment, and recreation by field segment, 2004 (Employment in thousands)

Field segment	Employment
Arts, entertainment, and recreation, total	1,833
Other amusement and recreation fields	1,060
Gambling fields	154
Amusement parks and arcades	137
Spectator sports	120
Museums, historical sites, and other institutions	117
Performing arts companies	115
Promoters of performing arts, sports, and similar events	73
Independent artists, writers, and performers	42
Agents and managers for artists, athletes, entertainers, and other public figures	15

Although most establishments in the arts, entertainment, and recreation field are small, 42 percent of all jobs were in establishments that employ more than 100 workers (chart 1).

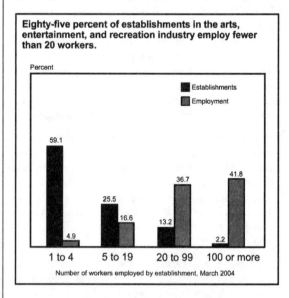

Eighty-five percent of establishments in the arts, entertainment, and recreation industry employ fewer than 20 workers.

The arts, entertainment, and recreation field is characterized by a large number of seasonal and part-time jobs and by workers who are younger than the average for all fields. About 46 percent of all workers are under 35.

Many businesses in the field increase hiring during the summer, often employing high school–age and college-age workers. Most establishments in the arts, entertainment, and recreation field contract out lighting, sound, set-building, and exhibit-building work to firms not included in this field.

Occupations in the Field

About 59 percent of wage and salary workers in the field are employed in service occupations (table 2). *Amusement and recreation attendants*—the largest occupation in the arts, entertainment, and recreation field—perform a variety of duties depending on where they are employed. Common duties include setting up games, handing out sports equipment, providing caddy services for golfers, collecting money, and operating amusement park rides.

Fitness trainers and aerobics instructors lead or coach groups or individuals in exercise activities and in the fundamentals of sports.

Recreation workers organize and promote activities, such as arts and crafts, sports, games, music, drama, social recreation, camping, and hobbies. They generally are employed by schools; theme parks and other tourist attractions; or health, sports, and other recreational clubs. Recreation workers schedule organized events to structure leisure time.

Gaming services workers assist in the operation of games, such as keno, bingo, and gaming table games. They may calculate and pay off the amount of winnings or collect players' money or chips.

Tour and travel guides escort individuals or groups on sightseeing tours or through places of interest, such as industrial establishments, public buildings, and art galleries. They may also plan, organize, and conduct long-distance cruises, tours, and expeditions for individuals or groups.

Animal care and service workers feed, water, bathe, exercise, or otherwise care for animals in zoos, circuses, aquariums, or other settings. They may train animals for riding or performance.

Other service workers include *waiters and waitresses*, who serve food in entertainment establishments; *fast food* and *counter workers* and *cooks and food preparation workers*, who may serve or prepare food for patrons; and *bar-*

tenders, who mix and serve drinks in arts, entertainment, and recreation establishments.

Building grounds, cleaning, and maintenance occupations include *building cleaning workers*, who clean up after shows or sporting events and are responsible for the daily cleaning and upkeep of facilities. *Landscaping and groundskeeping workers* care for athletic fields and golf courses. These workers maintain artificial and natural turf fields, mark boundaries, and paint team logos. They also mow, water, and fertilize natural athletic fields and vacuum and disinfect synthetic fields. Establishments in this field also employ workers in protective service occupations. *Security guards* patrol the property and guard against theft, vandalism, and illegal entry. At sporting events, guards maintain order and direct patrons to various facilities. *Gaming surveillance officers and gaming investigators* observe casino operations to detect cheating, theft, or other irregular activities by patrons or employees.

Professional and related occupations account for 11 percent of all jobs in this field. Some of the most well-known members of these occupations, *athletes and sports competitors*, perform in any of a variety of sports. Professional athletes compete in events for compensation, either through salaries or prize money. Organizations such as the Women's National Basketball Association (WNBA) and the National Football League (NFL) sanction events for professionals. Few athletes are able to make it to the professional level, where high salaries are common. In some professional sports, minor leagues offer lower salaries with a chance to develop skills through competition before advancing to major league play.

Coaches and scouts train athletes to perform at their highest level. Often, they are experienced athletes who have retired and are able to provide insight to players from their own experiences. Although some *umpires, referees, and other sports officials* work full time, the majority usually work part time and often have other full-time jobs. For example, many professional sport referees and umpires also officiate at amateur games.

Musicians and singers may play musical instruments, sing, compose, arrange music, or conduct groups in instrumental or vocal performances. The specific skills and responsibilities of musicians vary widely by type of instrument, size of ensemble, and style of music. For example, musicians can play jazz, classical, or popular

Leisure and Hospitality

music, either alone or in groups ranging from small rock bands to large symphony orchestras.

Actors entertain and communicate with people through their interpretation of dramatic and other roles. They can belong to a variety of performing groups, ranging from those appearing in community and local dinner theaters to those playing in full-scale Broadway productions. *Dancers* express ideas, stories, rhythm, and sound with their bodies through different types of dance, including ballet, modern dance, tap, folk, and jazz. Dancers usually perform in a troupe, although some perform solo. Many become teachers when their performing careers end. *Choreographers* create and teach dance, and they may be called upon to direct and stage presentations. *Producers and directors* select and interpret plays or scripts and give directions to actors and dancers. They conduct rehearsals, audition cast members, and approve choreography. They also arrange financing, hire production staff members, and negotiate contracts with personnel.

Archivists, curators, and museum technicians play an important role in preparing museums for display. Archivists appraise, edit, and direct safekeeping of permanent records and historically valuable documents. They may also participate in research activities based on archival materials. Curators administer a museum's affairs and conduct research programs. Museum technicians and conservators prepare specimens, such as fossils, skeletal parts, lace, and textiles, for museum collection and exhibits. They may also take part in restoring documents or installing and arranging materials for exhibit.

Audio and video equipment technicians set up and operate audio and video equipment, including microphones, sound speakers, video screens, projectors, video monitors, recording equipment, connecting wires and cables, sound and mixing boards, and related electronic equipment for theme parks, concerts, and sports events. They may also set up and operate associated spotlights and other custom lighting systems.

About 8 percent of all jobs in this field are in sales and related occupations. The largest of these, *cashiers*, often use a cash register to receive money and give change to customers. In casinos, *gaming change persons and booth cashiers* exchange coins and tokens for patrons' money. *Counter and rental clerks* check out rental equipment to customers, receive orders for service, and handle cash transactions.

Another 9 percent of jobs in this field are in office and administrative support occupations. *Receptionists and information clerks*, one of the larger occupations in this category, answer questions and provide general information to patrons. Other large occupations in this group include *general office clerks* and *secretaries and administrative assistants*. *Gaming cage workers* conduct financial transactions for patrons in gaming establishments. For example, they may accept a patron's credit application and verify credit references to provide check-cashing authorizations or to establish house credit accounts. Also, they may reconcile daily summaries of transactions to balance books or sell gambling chips, tokens, or tickets to patrons. At a patron's request, gaming cage workers may convert gaming chips, tokens, or tickets to currency.

Management, business, and financial occupations make up 6 percent of employment in this field. Managerial duties in the performing arts include marketing, business management, event booking, fundraising, and public outreach. *Agents and business managers of artists, performers, and athletes* represent their clients to prospective employers and may handle contract negotiations and other business matters. *Recreation supervisors* and *park superintendents* oversee personnel, budgets, grounds and facility maintenance, and land and wildlife resources. Some common administrative jobs in sports are *tournament director, health club manager,* and *sports program director.*

Installation, maintenance, and repair occupations make up 4 percent of this field's employment. *General maintenance and repair workers* are the largest occupation in this group.

Table 2. Employment of wage and salary workers in arts, entertainment, and recreation by occupation, 2004 and projected change, 2004–2014 (Employment in thousands)

Occupation	Employment, 2004		Percent change, 2004–2014
	Number	Percent	
Total, all occupations	1,833	100.0	25.1
Management, business, and financial occupations	101	5.5	28.1
Top executives	39	2.1	27.2

Occupation	Employment, 2004		Percent change, 2004–2014
	Number	Percent	
Agents and business managers of artists, performers, and athletes	7	0.4	20.0
Professional and related occupations	199	10.9	28.4
Archivists	2	0.1	16.3
Curators	5	0.2	18.7
Museum technicians and conservators	4	0.2	23.4
Artists and related workers	7	0.4	37.8
Set and exhibit designers	3	0.2	11.9
Actors	14	0.8	9.2
Producers and directors	7	0.4	24.4
Athletes, coaches, umpires, and related workers	39	2.2	29.8
Dancers and choreographers	9	0.5	24.7
Musicians, singers, and related workers	34	1.9	33.6
Service occupations	1,088	59.3	25.7
Security guards and gaming surveillance officers	42	2.3	6.7
Lifeguards, ski patrol, and other recreational protective service workers	33	1.8	30.1
Supervisors, food preparation and serving workers	24	1.3	24.8
Cooks and food preparation workers	68	3.7	26.2
Bartenders	40	2.2	19.0
Fast food and counter workers	57	3.1	30.9
Waiters and waitresses	93	5.1	16.4
Dining room and cafeteria attendants and bartender helpers	18	1.0	20.5
Dishwashers	19	1.0	19.4
Building cleaning workers	58	3.1	30.5
Landscaping and grounds-keeping workers	115	6.3	24.5
Gaming supervisors	6	0.4	42.8
Animal care and service workers	14	0.8	39.8
Gaming services workers	36	2.0	28.4

Occupation	Employment, 2004		Percent change, 2004–2014
	Number	Percent	
Ushers, lobby attendants, and ticket takers	37	2.0	18.1
Amusement and recreation attendants	155	8.5	30.0
Tour and travel guides	16	0.9	24.8
Child care workers	31	1.7	27.3
Recreation and fitness workers	137	7.5	28.5
Sales and related occupations	145	7.9	23.9
Cashiers	65	3.5	18.8
Counter and rental clerks	23	1.2	35.5
Office and administrative support occupations	172	9.4	16.8
Gaming cage workers	8	0.5	25.2
Receptionists and information clerks	39	2.1	22.6
Secretaries and administrative assistants	28	1.5	12.5

Note: May not add to totals due to omission of occupations with small employment

Training, Other Qualifications, and Advancement

About 40 percent of all workers in the arts, entertainment, and recreation field have no formal education beyond high school. In the case of performing artists or athletes, talent and years of training are more important than education. However, upper-level management jobs usually require a college degree.

Most service jobs require little or no previous training or education beyond high school. Many companies hire young, unskilled workers, such as students, to perform low-paying seasonal jobs. Employers look for people with the interpersonal skills necessary to work with the public.

In physical fitness facilities, fitness trainer and aerobic instructor positions usually are filled by persons who develop an avid interest in fitness and then become cer-

Leisure and Hospitality

tified to teach. Certification from a professional organization may require knowledge of cardiopulmonary resuscitation (CPR); an associate degree or experience as an instructor at a health club; and successful completion of written and oral exams covering a variety of areas, including anatomy, nutrition, and fitness testing. Sometimes, fitness workers become health club managers or owners. To advance to a management position, a degree in physical education, sports medicine, or exercise physiology is useful.

In the arts, employment in professional and related occupations usually requires a great deal of talent. There are many highly talented performers, creating intense competition for every opening. Performers such as musicians, dancers, and actors often study their professions most of their lives, taking private lessons and spending hours practicing. Usually, performers have completed some college or related study. Musicians, dancers, and actors often go on to become teachers after completing the necessary requirements for at least a bachelor's degree. Musicians who complete a graduate degree in music sometimes move on to a career as a conductor. Dancers sometimes become choreographers, and actors can advance into producer and director jobs.

Almost all arts administrators have completed 4 years of college, and the majority possess a master's or a doctoral degree. Experience in marketing and business is helpful because promoting events is a large part of the job.

Entry-level supervisory or professional jobs in recreation sometimes require completion of a 2-year associate degree in parks and recreation at a junior college. Completing a 4-year bachelor's degree in this field is necessary for high-level supervisory positions. Students can specialize in such areas as aquatics, therapeutic recreation, aging and leisure, and environmental studies. Those who obtain graduate degrees in the field and have years of experience may obtain administrative or university teaching positions. The National Recreation and Parks Association (NRPA) certifies individuals who meet eligibility requirements for professional and technical jobs. Certified park and recreation professionals must pass an exam; earn a bachelor's degree with a major in recreation, park resources, or leisure services from a program accredited by the NRPA or by the American Association for Leisure and Recreation; or earn a bachelor's degree and have at least 5 years of relevant full-time work experience, depending on the major field of study.

Outlook

Wage and salary jobs in arts, entertainment, and recreation are projected to grow about 25 percent over the 2004–2014 period, compared with 14 percent for all fields combined. Rising incomes, leisure time, and awareness of the health benefits of physical fitness will increase the demand for arts, entertainment, and recreation services.

Employment opportunities should be available in a wide range of settings, including golf courses, parks and outdoor recreational facilities, and amusement parks. Employment in fitness centers and similar establishments also will grow substantially, driven by several factors. Aging baby boomers are concerned with staying healthy, physically fit, and independent and have become the largest demographic group of health club members. The reduction of physical education programs in schools, combined with parents' growing concern about child obesity, has rapidly increased child health club membership. Membership among young adults has also grown steadily, driven by concern about physical fitness and funded by rising incomes. The proliferation of group exercise classes and the focus on overall wellness in health clubs should also increase the demand for workers in this field.

Strong employment growth is expected in the gaming field, spurred by the increase in casinos on American Indian reservations and the introduction of slot machines at racetracks. Many states are looking to relax gambling regulations so that they can increase state revenues from gaming establishment taxes.

In addition to these increases, employment in the performing arts will grow steadily, along with demand for entertainment from a growing population. However, the supply of workers in performing arts also will expand because of the appeal of these jobs, ensuring continued intense competition.

The arts, entertainment, and recreation field has relied heavily on workers under the age of 25 to fill seasonal and unskilled positions. About one-fourth of all jobs in this field are held by workers under age 25, compared to 14 percent in all fields combined. Opportunities should be available for young, seasonal, part-time, and unskilled workers. In addition, the field is expected to hire a growing number of workers in other age groups.

Earnings

Earnings in arts, entertainment, and recreation generally are low, reflecting the large number of part-time and seasonal jobs. Nonsupervisory workers in arts, entertainment, and recreation averaged $313 a week in 2004, compared with $529 throughout nongovernment fields.

Earnings vary according to occupation and segment of the field. For example, some professional athletes earn millions, but competition for these positions is intense, and most athletes are unable to reach even the minor leagues. Many service workers make the minimum wage or a little more. Actors often go long periods with little or no income from acting, so they are forced to work at second jobs. Earnings in selected occupations in arts, entertainment, and recreation appear in table 3.

Table 3. Median hourly earnings of the largest occupations in arts, entertainment, and recreation, May 2004

Occupation	Performing arts, spectator sports, and related	Museums, historical sites, and similar institutions	Amusement, gambling, and recreation fields	All fields
Fitness trainers and aerobics instructors	$9.89		$13.78	$12.25
Security guards	9.85	10.16	9.64	9.77
Receptionists and information clerks	9.80	8.93	8.26	10.50
Landscaping and groundskeeping workers	8.96	10.41	9.13	9.82
Janitors and cleaners, except maids and housekeeping cleaners	8.57	9.24	8.31	9.04
Cashiers	8.56	8.04	7.86	7.81
Amusement and recreation attendants	8.07	10.11	7.69	7.42
Ushers, lobby attendants, and ticket takers	7.61	7.72	7.67	7.30
Amusement and recreation attendants	7.20	7.78	7.20	7.47
Waiters and waitresses	6.90	8.24	7.69	6.75

Because many amusement and theme parks dramatically increase employment during vacation periods, employment for a number of jobs in the field is seasonal. Theme parks, for example, frequently hire young workers, often students, for summer employment. Also, many sports are not played all year, so athletes and people in the service jobs associated with those sports often are seasonally employed.

Employers in some segments of this field offer benefits that are not available in other fields. For example, benefits for workers in some theme parks include free passes to the park, transportation to and from work, housing, scholarships, and discounts on park merchandise.

Sources of Additional Information

For additional information about careers in the parks and recreation field and a listing of colleges and universities offering accredited programs in parks and recreation studies, contact

- National Recreation and Parks Association, 22377 Belmont Ridge Rd., Ashburn, VA 20148. Internet: http://www.nrpa.org

For more information about a career in the field of dance, contact

- Dance/USA, 1156 15th St. NW, Suite 820, Washington, DC 20005-1726. Internet: http://www.danceusa.org

For more information on employment with carnivals and other outdoor amusement businesses, contact

- Outdoor Amusement Business Association, 1035 S. Semoran Blvd., Suite 1045A, Winter Park, FL 32792. Internet: http://www.oaba.org

For information about careers in museums, contact

- American Association of Museums, 1575 Eye Street NW, Suite 400, Washington, DC 20005. Internet: http://www.aam-us.org

For more information about careers in entertainment services and technology, contact

- Entertainment Services and Technology Association, 875 Sixth Avenue, Suite 1005, New York, NY 10001. Internet: http://www.esta.org
- U.S. Institute for Theater Technology, 6433 Riddings Road, Syracuse, NY 13206-1111. Internet: http://www.usitt.org

Leisure and Hospitality

Food Services and Drinking Places

⊚ Annual Earnings: $15,720

⊚ Job Growth: 16.4%

⊚ Size of Workforce: 8,918,610

⊚ Self-Employed: 2.6%

⊚ Part-Time: 41.1%

Significant Points

- Food services and drinking places provided many young people with their first jobs—in 2004, more than 21 percent of workers in these establishments were aged 16 to 19, about 5 times the proportion for all fields.

- Cooks, waiters and waitresses, and combined food preparation and serving workers comprised more than half of field employment.

- About 2 out of 5 employees worked part time, more than twice the proportion for all fields.

- Job opportunities will be plentiful because large numbers of young and part-time workers will leave their jobs in the field, creating substantial replacement needs.

Nature of the Field

Food services and drinking places may be the world's most widespread and familiar field. These establishments include all types of restaurants, from casual fast-food eateries to formal, elegant dining establishments. The food services and drinking places field comprises about 500,000 places of employment in large cities, small towns, and rural areas across the United States.

As shown in table 1, about 45 percent of establishments in this field are *limited-service eating places,* such as fast-food restaurants, cafeterias, and snack and nonalcoholic beverage bars, that primarily serve patrons who order or select items and pay before eating. *Full-service restaurants* account for about 39 percent of establishments and cater to patrons who order, are served, and consume their food while seated and then pay after eating. *Drinking places (alcoholic beverages)*—bars, pubs, nightclubs, and tav-

erns—primarily prepare and serve alcoholic beverages for consumption on the premises. Drinking places comprise about 11 percent of all establishments in this field. *Special food services,* such as food service contractors, caterers, and mobile food service vendors, account for less than 6 percent of establishments in the field.

Table 1. Establishments and wage and salary employment in food services and drinking places, by detailed field, 2004

Field segment	Employment	Establishments
Total	100.0	100.0
Full-service restaurants	47.5	38.7
Limited-service eating places	42.1	45.2
Limited-service restaurants	36.6	37.0
Cafeterias	1.5	1.4
Snack and nonalcoholic beverage bars	4.0	6.9
Special food services	6.0	5.5
Food service contractors	4.3	3.0
Caterers	1.7	2.2
Mobile food services	0.1	0.3
Drinking places (alcoholic beverages)	4.4	10.6

The most common type of limited-service eating place is a franchised operation of a nationwide restaurant chain that sells fast food. Features that characterize these restaurants include a limited menu, the absence of waiters and waitresses, and emphasis on limited service. Menu selections usually offer limited variety and are prepared by workers with minimal cooking skills. Food typically is served in disposable, take-out containers that retain the food's warmth, allowing restaurants to prepare orders in advance of customers' requests. A growing number of fast-food restaurants provide drive-through and walk-up services.

Cafeterias are another type of limited-service eating place and usually offer a somewhat limited selection that varies daily. Cafeterias also may provide separate serving stations for salads or short-order grill items, such as grilled sandwiches or hamburgers. Patrons select from food and drink items on display in a continuous cafeteria line. Cafeteria selections may include foods that require more complicated preparations and greater culinary skills than are required in fast-food restaurants. Selections usually are prepared ahead in large quantities and seldom are cooked to the customer's order.

Limited-service snack and nonalcoholic beverage bars carry and sell a combination of snacks, nonalcoholic beverages, and other related products but generally promote and sell a unique snack or beverage for consumption on or near the premises. For example, some prepare and serve specialty snacks including ice cream, frozen yogurt, cookies, or popcorn. Others serve primarily coffee, juices, or soda.

Full-service restaurants offer more menu categories, including appetizers, entrées, salads, side dishes, desserts, and beverages, and varied choices within each category. Chefs and cooks prepare items to order which may run from grilling a simple hamburger to composing a more complex and sophisticated menu item. Waiters and waitresses offer table service in comfortable surroundings.

Cost-conscious and time-strapped patrons increasingly eat at midscale or family-type restaurants rather than at more elegant dining establishments. National chains are a growing segment of full-service restaurants. These restaurants usually offer efficient table service, well-priced familiar menu items prepared by moderately skilled kitchen workers, and a substantially nicer physical setting than limited service establishments. By contrast, customers at upscale dining places tend to seek a more relaxed and elegant atmosphere with skillfully prepared cuisine and leisurely but professional service.

Many popular full-service restaurants remain independently owned and locally operated. Independent full-service restaurants generally focus on providing a one-of-a-kind dining experience and distinctive design, décor, and atmosphere. Food and service remain the primary focus of the restaurant's offerings, but physical setting and ambience are important components of that experience. They help establish a restaurant's reputation and build a steady clientele.

Some drinking places also offer patrons limited dining services in addition to providing alcoholic beverages. In some states, they also sell packaged alcoholic beverages for consumption off the premises. Establishments selling alcoholic beverages are closely regulated by state and local alcoholic beverage control authorities.

Finally, the food services and drinking places field covers a variety of special food services establishments, including food service contractors, concession stands at sporting events, catering firms, and mobile food services such as ice cream trucks and other street vendors who sell food.

Technology influences the food services and drinking places field in many ways, enhancing efficiency and productivity. Many restaurants use computers to track orders, inventory, and patron seating. Point-of-service (POS) systems allow servers to key in a customer's order, either tableside using a hand-held device or from a computer terminal in the dining room, and send the order to the kitchen instantaneously so preparation can begin. The same system totals and prints checks, functions as a cash register, connects to credit card authorizers, and tracks sales. Many managers use inventory-tracking software to compare the record of sales from the POS with a record of present inventory to minimize food costs and spoilage. Some establishments enter an inventory of standard ingredients and suppliers into their POS system. When supplies of particular ingredients run low, additional inventory can be ordered directly from the supplier using this preprogrammed information. Computers also allow restaurant and food service managers to more efficiently keep track of employee schedules and pay.

Food service managers use the Internet to track field news, find recipes, conduct market research, purchase supplies or equipment, recruit employees, and train staff. Internet access also makes service to customers more efficient. Many restaurants maintain Web sites that include menus and online promotions, provide information about the restaurant's location, and offer the option to make a reservation. Wireless communication headsets are now being used by some managers, hosts and hostesses, and chefs. Headsets allow a means of hands-free communications with other staff so that they can prevent order backups in the kitchen; better serve patrons in the dining room; or more easily accommodate special requirements, such as large groups, diners with special dietary needs, or accessible seating requirements for people with disabilities. Other wireless technology systems allow managers to monitor orders placed through individual terminals or by particular employees, instantly

Leisure and Hospitality

check inventories, and ensure timely preparation of customers' orders.

Working Conditions

Many food services and drinking places establishments in this field are open long hours. Staff typically is needed to work during evening, weekend, and holiday hours. Full-time employees, often head or executive chefs and food service managers, typically work longer hours—12-hour days are common—and also may be on call to work at other times when needed. Part-time employees, usually waiters and waitresses, dining room attendants, hosts and hostesses, and fast-food employees, typically work shorter days (4–6 hours per day) or fewer days per week than most full-time employees.

Food services and drinking places employ more part-time workers than other fields. About 2 out of 5 workers in food services and drinking places worked part time in 2004, more than twice the proportion for all fields. This allows some employees flexibility in setting their work hours, affording them a greater opportunity to tailor work schedules to personal or family needs. Some employees may rotate work on some shifts to ensure proper coverage at unpopular work times or to fully staff restaurants during peak demand times.

Food services and drinking places must comply with local fire, safety, and sanitation regulations. They also must provide appropriate public accommodations and ensure that employees use safe food handling measures. These practices require establishments to maintain supplies of chemicals, detergents, and other materials that may be harmful if not used properly.

Typical establishments have well-designed kitchens with state-of-the-art cooking and refrigeration equipment and proper electrical, lighting, and ventilation systems to keep everything functioning. However, kitchens usually are noisy and may be very hot near stoves, grills, ovens, or steam tables. Chefs; cooks; food preparation workers; and other kitchen staff, such as dishwashers, may suffer minor cuts or burns, be subject to scalding or steaming liquids, and spend most of their time standing in a relatively confined area. Chefs and cooks are under extreme pressure to work quickly to stay on top of orders in a busy restaurant. The fast pace requires employees to be alert and quick-thinking, but also may result in muscle strains from trying to move heavy pots or force pressurized containers open without safely taking the proper precautions.

Dining areas also may be well-designed, but can become crowded and noisy when busy. Servers; attendants; and other dining-room staff, such as bartenders and hosts or hostesses, need to protect against falls, spills, or burns while serving diners and keeping service areas stocked. Also, dining-room staff must be aware of stairs, raised platforms, or other obstacles when directing patrons through narrow areas or to distant seating areas.

Most food services and drinking places workers spend most of their time on their feet—preparing meals, serving diners, or transporting dishes and supplies throughout the establishment. Upper body strength often is needed to lift heavy items, such as trays of dishes, platters of food, or cooking pots. Work during peak dining hours can be very hectic and stressful.

Employees who have direct contact with customers, such as waiters and waitresses or hosts and hostesses, should have a neat appearance and maintain a professional and pleasant manner. Professional hospitality is required from the moment guests enter the restaurant until the time they leave. Sustaining a proper demeanor during busy times or over the course of a long shift may be difficult.

Kitchen staff also need to be able to work as a team and to communicate with each other. Timing is critical to preparing more complex dishes. Coordinating orders to ensure that an entire table's meals are ready at the same time is essential, particularly in a large restaurant during busy dining periods.

In 2003, the rate of work-related injuries and illnesses was 4.6 per 100 full-time workers in eating and drinking places, slightly less than the average of 5.0 for the private sector. Work hazards include the possibility of burns from hot equipment, sprained muscles, and wrenched backs from heavy lifting and falls on slippery floors.

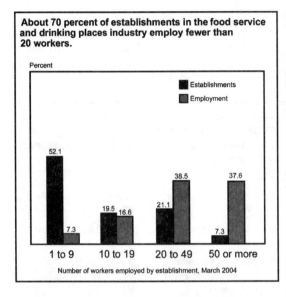

About 70 percent of establishments in the food service and drinking places industry employ fewer than 20 workers.

Percent

■ Establishments
■ Employment

| | 1 to 9 | 10 to 19 | 20 to 49 | 50 or more |
| | 52.1 / 7.3 | 19.5 / 16.6 | 21.1 / 38.5 | 7.3 / 37.6 |

Number of workers employed by establishment, March 2004

45 percent were under age 25, more than 3 times the proportion in all fields.

Table 2. Percent distribution of employment, by age group, 2004

Age group	Food services and drinking places	All fields
Total	100.0%	100.0%
16–19	21.2	4.2
20–24	23.3	9.9
25–34	23.1	21.8
35–44	15.7	24.8
45–54	10.5	23.3
55–64	4.4	12.4
65 and older	1.8	3.5

Important Characteristics of the Field

Skills: Service Orientation; Social Perceptiveness; Instructing. **Abilities:** Stamina; Gross Body Coordination; Trunk Strength; Speed of Limb Movement; Speech Recognition; Extent Flexibility. **Work-Related Values:** Co-workers; Social Service; Supervision, Technical; Moral Values.

Employment

The food services and drinking places field, with about 8.9 million wage and salary jobs in 2004, ranks among the nation's leading employers. Food services and drinking places tend to be small; about 72 percent of the establishments in the field employed fewer than 20 workers (see chart). As a result, this field often is considered attractive to individuals who want to own and run their own businesses. An estimated 248,000 self-employed and unpaid family workers were employed in the field, representing about 3 percent of total employment.

Establishments in this field, particularly fast-food establishments, are leading employers of teenagers—aged 16 through 19—providing first jobs for many new entrants to the labor force. In 2004, about 21 percent of all workers in food services and drinking places were teenagers, about 5 times the proportion in all fields (table 2). About

Occupations in the Field

Workers in this field perform a variety of tasks. They prepare food items from a menu or according to a customer's order; keep food preparation and service areas clean; accept payment from customers; and provide the establishment managerial or office services, such as bookkeeping, ordering, and advertising. Cooks, waiters and waitresses, and combined food preparation and serving workers accounted for more than half of food services jobs (table 3).

Employees in the various food services and related occupations deal with customers in a dining area or at a service counter. *Waiters and waitresses* take customers' orders, serve food and beverages, and prepare itemized checks. In fine-dining restaurants, they may describe chef's specials and take alcoholic beverage orders. In some establishments, they escort customers to their seats, accept payments, and set up and clear tables. In many larger restaurants, however, these tasks may be assigned to, or shared with, other workers.

Other food services occupations include *hosts and hostesses*, who welcome customers, show them to their tables, and offer them menus. *Bartenders* fill drink orders for waiters and waitresses and from customers seated at the bar. *Dining room attendants and bartender helpers* assist waiters, waitresses, and bartenders by clearing, cleaning, and setting up tables, as well as keeping service areas stocked with supplies. *Counter attendants* take orders and serve food at counters, cafeteria steam tables, and fast-food counters. Depending on the size and type of establishment, attendants also may operate cash registers.

Combined food preparation and serving workers, including fast food, prepare and serve items in fast-food restaurants. Most take orders from customers at counters or drive-through windows at fast-food restaurants. They assemble orders, hand them to customers, and accept payment. Many of these workers also cook and package food, make coffee, and fill beverage cups using drink-dispensing machines.

Workers in the various food preparation occupations prepare food in the kitchen. *Institution and cafeteria cooks* work in the kitchens of schools, hospitals, industrial cafeterias, and other institutions where they prepare large quantities of a small variety of menu items. *Restaurant cooks* usually prepare a wider selection of dishes for each meal, cooking individual servings to order. *Short-order cooks* prepare grilled items and sandwiches in establishments that emphasize fast service. *Fast-food cooks* prepare and package a limited selection of food that is either prepared to order or kept warm until sold in fast-food restaurants. *Food preparation workers* clean and prepare basic food ingredients such as meats, fish, and vegetables for use in making more complex meals; keep work areas clean; and perform simple cooking tasks under the direction of the chef or head cook. *Dishwashers* clean dishes, glasses, pots, and kitchen accessories by hand or by machine.

Food service managers hire, train, supervise, and discharge workers in food services and drinking places establishments. They also purchase supplies, deal with vendors, keep records, and help whenever an extra hand is needed. *Executive chefs* oversee the kitchen, select the menu, train cooks and food preparation workers, and direct the preparation of food. In fine-dining establishments, *maitre d's* may serve as hosts or hostesses while overseeing the dining room. Larger establishments may employ *general managers* as well as a number of assistant managers. Many managers and executive chefs are part owners of the establishments they manage.

Food services and drinking places may employ a wide range of other workers, including accountants, advertising and public relations workers, bookkeepers, dietitians, mechanics and other maintenance workers, musicians and other entertainers, human resources workers, and various clerks. However, many establishments may choose to contract this work to outside establishments who also perform these tasks for several food services and drinking places outlets.

Table 3. Employment of wage and salary workers in food services and drinking places by occupation, 2004 and projected change, 2004–2014 (Employment in thousands)

Occupation	Employment, 2004		Percent change, 2004–2014
	Number	Percent	
Total, all occupations	8,850	100.0	16.4
Management, business, and financial occupations	261	2.9	17.9
Top executives	76	0.9	16.8
Food service managers	160	1.8	18.2
Professional and related occupations	16	0.2	15.6
Dancers	5	0.1	12.9
Service occupations	7,910	89.4	16.8
Chefs and head cooks	87	1.0	16.9
First-line supervisors/ managers of food preparation and serving workers	548	6.2	17.9
Cooks, fast food	620	7.0	16.4
Cooks, institution and cafeteria	50	0.6	23.6
Cooks, restaurant	668	7.6	16.3
Cooks, short order	173	2.0	10.8
Food preparation workers	425	4.8	25.3
Bartenders	337	3.8	14.2
Fast food and counter workers	1,988	22.5	17.0
Waiters and waitresses	1,893	21.4	16.4
Food servers, nonrestaurant	52	0.6	6.3
Dining room and cafeteria attendants and bartender helpers	267	3.0	15.9
Dishwashers	390	4.4	15.5

Occupation	Employment, 2004		Percent change, 2004–2014
	Number	Percent	
Hosts and hostesses, restaurant, lounge, and coffee shop	282	3.2	16.5
Food preparation and serving related workers, all other	24	0.3	13.8
Janitors and cleaners, except maids and house-keeping cleaners	50	0.6	18.5
Sales and related occupations	324	3.7	7.6
Cashiers, except gaming	285	3.2	6.5
Office and administrative support occupations	82	0.9	6.0
Production occupations	46	0.5	18.2
Bakers	33	0.4	18.6
Transportation and material moving occupations	196	2.2	18.0
Driver/sales workers	153	1.7	18.2

Note: May not add to totals due to omission of occupations with small employment

Training, Other Qualifications, and Advancement

The skills and experience required by workers in food services and drinking places differ by occupation and type of establishment. Many entry-level positions, such as waiters and waitresses or food preparation workers, require little or no formal education or previous training. Similarly, work in limited-service eating places generally requires less experience than work in full-service restaurants.

Many fast-food worker or server jobs are held by young or part-time workers. For many youths, this is their first job; for others, part-time schedules allow more flexible working arrangements. On-the-job training, typically under the close supervision of an experienced employee or manager, often lasts a few weeks or less. Some large chain operations require formal training sessions, many using online or video training programs, for new employees.

Formal training and prior food-service experience for managers, however, is more common. Training may take the form of field-sponsored seminars; short-term, subject-specific certificate programs; or associate or bachelor's degree programs in culinary arts or hospitality, hotel, or restaurant management. Seminars often address a variety of complex issues faced by food service managers and suggest ways to resolve problems as they occur and to improve the firm's profitability, worker morale, and customer service. Some training topics cover proper food handling and safety issues or methods for recruiting and motivating quality employees. As more restaurants use computers to keep track of sales and inventory, computer training is becoming increasingly integrated into management training programs.

Larger establishments or regional offices of nationwide chain or franchise operations increasingly use video and satellite TV training programs or online employee-development software to educate newly hired staff. This type of corporate training generally covers the restaurant's history, menu, organizational philosophy, and daily operational standards. Nationwide chains often operate their own schools for prospective assistant managers so that they can attend training seminars before acquiring additional responsibilities. Eventually, successful assistant managers may advance to general manager of one of the chain's establishments, to a top management position in another large chain operation, or to a management position in an independent restaurant. Assistant managers in smaller independent restaurants may learn their duties on the job, while assistant mangers in most chain-affiliated establishments receive training through more formal programs.

Completion of postsecondary training is increasingly important for advancement in the food services and drinking places field. Whether it is in the form of a bachelor's degree or as specialized training in culinary arts or hospitality management, completion of such programs demonstrates both the maturity and motivation required for work in a hectic fast-paced field. Appropriate training often enables graduates to start as assistant managers. Management programs may last from 18 months, for tailored certificate or associate degree programs, to 4 years, for more comprehensive bachelor's degree programs. A

Leisure and Hospitality

growing number of master's degree programs in hospitality management provide training for corporate-level management involving site selection and feasibility assessments in addition to training for restaurant-level customer service responsibilities. Courses are available through community and junior colleges, trade and vocational schools, 4-year colleges and universities, hotel or restaurant associations, and trade unions. The Armed Forces are another source of training and experience in food service work.

Training options for chefs and other kitchen staff are more varied. Some start out in kitchens as food preparation workers and gradually work their way up to cook and chef positions with experience and improved skills. Or they may start in smaller restaurants or in less demanding work stations, such as the cold station, preparing comparatively simple salads or appetizers, and then move up to stations where more complicated dishes are made and more sophisticated cooking techniques are used. Working under an experienced chef and gaining progressively more responsible and difficult assignments is one way many cooks advance.

Formal culinary training for chefs and cooks is available through a wide variety of sources—independent cooking schools or academies, community and junior colleges, trade and vocational schools, and 4-year colleges and universities. Many trade associations and unions also certify cooking programs conducted at selected schools or sponsor federally approved apprenticeship programs that combine formal classroom instruction with on-the-job experience in a working kitchen. Many formal training programs offer job placement opportunities that help recent graduates find work in kitchens, generally at the sous-chef level or higher. Many cooks without the formal training gain experience through structured internships, working under the direction of experienced chefs. Some advance to more responsible cooking positions by moving up the line in the same restaurant or by moving from one kitchen to another.

Most culinary programs now offer more business courses and computer training to better prepare chefs to assume greater leadership and managerial roles in the field and to manage large, complex food service operations. Culinary training also has adapted to reflect changing food trends and eating habits. For example, chefs and cooks must know a wide variety of food preparation techniques and cooking styles. They also must know how to prepare foods to accommodate various dietary restrictions, to satisfy health-conscious eating styles, and to meet the needs of an increasingly international clientele. Chefs and cooks also need to be creative and know how to inspire other kitchen staff to develop new dishes and create inventive recipes.

Promotion opportunities in food services and drinking places vary by occupation and the size of individual establishments. As in other fields, larger establishments and organizations usually offer better advancement opportunities. As beginners gain experience and basic skills, those who choose to pursue careers in food services and drinking places can transfer to other jobs that require greater skill and offer higher earnings. Many workers earn progressively higher incomes as they gain experience or switch to jobs in establishments offering higher pay. For example, waiters and waitresses may transfer to jobs in more expensive or busier restaurants where larger tips are more likely.

Many food service workers start as untrained food preparation workers. As they pick up kitchen skills and demonstrate greater responsibility, they may advance to cook positions preparing routine or simple dishes. Advancement opportunities for food preparation workers, as well as for cafeteria and institution cooks and short-order cooks, generally require that they move into positions in full-service restaurants. In full-service restaurants, kitchen workers at all levels may acquire the appropriate experience and expand their skills, which may lead to work as a line cook. Line cooks also develop and acquire new skills, moving to more demanding stations and eventually to more challenging chef positions. As chefs improve their culinary skills, the opportunities for professional recognition and higher earnings increase. Chefs may advance to executive chef positions and oversee several kitchens within a food service operation, open their own restaurants as chef-proprietors, or move into training positions as teachers or culinary educators. Other chefs may go into sales or demonstrator careers, testing recipes, products, or equipment for sale to chefs and restaurateurs.

Many managers of food services and drinking places obtain their positions through hard work and years of restaurant experience. Dining room workers, such as hosts and hostesses or waiters and waitresses, often are promoted to *maitre d'* or into managerial jobs. Many managers of fast-food restaurants advanced from the ranks of hourly workers. Managers with access to the necessary capital may even open their own franchises or independent restaurants.

Outlook

Job opportunities in food services and drinking places should be plentiful because the large number of young and part-time workers in the field will generate substantial replacement needs. As experienced workers find jobs in other higher-paying establishments, seek full-time opportunities outside the field, or stop working, a large number of job openings will be created for new entrants. Field expansion also will create many new jobs as diners continue to seek the convenience of prepared meals. Wage and salary jobs in food services and drinking places are expected to increase by 16 percent over the 2004–2014 period, compared to 14-percent growth projected for wage and salary employment in all fields combined. Numerous job opportunities will be available for people with limited job skills, first-time job seekers, senior citizens, and those seeking part-time or alternative work schedules.

Increases in population, dual-income families, and dining sophistication will contribute to job growth. Consumer demand for convenience and ready-to-heat meal options also will offer cooks and other food preparation workers a wider variety of employment settings in which to work. Moderately-priced restaurants that offer table service will afford increasing job opportunities as these businesses expand to accommodate the growing demand of an older and more mobile population and cater to families with young children. Fine dining establishments, which appeal more to affluent, often older, customers, also should grow as the 45-and-older population increases rapidly. The numbers of limited-service and fast-food restaurants that appeal to younger diners should increase more slowly than in the past. As schools, hospitals, and company cafeterias contract out institutional food services, jobs should shift to firms specializing in these services. Some of the increased demand for food services will be met through more supermarket food service options—self-service facilities such as salad bars, untended meal stations, and automated beverage stations.

Occupational projections reflect different rates of growth among the various segments of the food services and drinking places field (table 3). Employment in occupations concentrated in full-service restaurants—including

skilled chefs and head cooks, waiters and waitresses, and hosts and hostesses—is expected to grow slightly faster than overall employment in the food services and drinking places field. On the other hand, employment in many occupations concentrated in limited-service and fast-food restaurants—including fast-food and short-order cooks—is expected to increase more slowly than overall employment in the food services and drinking places field. Duties of cooks in fast-food restaurants are limited; faster growth is expected for combined food preparation and serving workers who both prepare and serve items in fast-food restaurants.

Those who qualify—either through experience or formal culinary training—for skilled head cook and chef positions should be in demand because of the need for skilled cooks to work in the growing number of new outlets among the fast-casual chains and independent fine-dining restaurants. The greatest number of job openings will be in the largest occupations—waiters and waitresses and combined food preparation and serving workers—which also have high replacement needs.

Employment of salaried managers is projected to increase faster than the average for the field as a result of sustained growth in chain and franchised establishments. Graduates of college hospitality programs, particularly those with good computer skills, should have especially good opportunities. The growing dominance of chain-affiliated food services and drinking places also should enhance opportunities for advancement from food service manager positions into general manager and corporate administrative jobs. Employment of self-employed managers in independent food services and drinking places is expected to grow more slowly.

Table 4. Average earnings of production or nonsupervisory workers in food services and drinking places by field segment, 2004

Field segment	Weekly	Hourly
Total, nongovernment fields	$528.56	$15.67
Food services and drinking places	194.47	7.84
Full-service restaurants	200.70	7.95
Limited-service eating places	180.54	7.36
Special food services	255.51	10.42
Drinking places (alcoholic beverages)	175.36	7.77

Leisure and Hospitality

Earnings

Earnings in food services and drinking places usually are much lower than the average for all fields (table 4). In 2004, average weekly earnings were highest in special food services ($256) and lowest in drinking places, alcoholic beverages ($175). Average weekly hours in all food service fields were lower than the average for nongovernment fields. Low earnings are supplemented for many workers by tips from customers. Waiters, waitresses, and bartenders, for example, often derive the majority of their earnings from tips, which depend on menu prices and the volume of customers served. In some establishments, workers who receive tips share a portion of their gratuities with other workers in the dining room and kitchen.

Earnings vary by occupation, geographic area, and type and size of establishment. Usually skilled workers, such as chefs, have the highest wages, and workers who are dependent upon tips to supplement earnings have the lowest. Many workers in the field earn the federal minimum wage of $5.15 an hour, or less if tips are included as a substantial part of earnings. A number of employers provide free or discounted meals and uniforms to employees. Earnings in the largest occupations employed in food services and drinking places appear in table 5.

Unionization is not widespread in the food services and drinking places field. In 2004, less than 2 percent of all employees were union members or covered by union contracts, compared with about 14 percent for all fields.

Table 5. Median hourly earnings of the largest occupations in food services and drinking places, May 2004

Occupation	Food services and drinking places	All fields
First-line supervisors/managers of food preparation and serving workers	$11.84	$12.22
Cooks, restaurant	9.23	9.39
Food preparation workers	7.69	8.03
Hosts and hostesses, restaurant, lounge, and coffee shop	7.43	7.52
Bartenders	7.33	7.42
Dishwashers	7.22	7.35
Cashiers	7.20	7.81

Occupation	Food services and drinking places	All fields
Cooks, fast food	7.04	7.07
Combined food preparation and serving workers, including fast food	6.87	7.06
Waiters and waitresses	6.71	6.75

Sources of Additional Information

For additional information about careers and training in the food services and drinking places field, contact

- National Restaurant Association, 1200 17th St. NW, Washington, DC 20036. Internet: http://www.restaurant.org
- The American Culinary Federation, 180 Center Place Way, St. Augustine, FL 32095. Internet: http://www.acfchefs.org

For a list of educational programs in the food services and drinking field, contact

- The International Council on Hotel, Restaurant, and Institutional Education, 2613 North Parham Rd., 2nd Floor, Richmond, VA 23294. Internet: http://www.chrie.org

Information on vocational education courses for food preparation and service careers may be obtained from your state or local director of vocational education or superintendent of schools.

Hotels and Other Accommodations

- ◎ Annual Earnings: $18,840
- ◎ Job Growth: 16.9%
- ◎ Size of Workforce: 1,771,380
- ◎ Self-Employed: 2.7%
- ◎ Part-Time: 18.7%

Significant Points

- Service occupations, by far the largest occupational group, account for 65 percent of the field's employment.
- Hotels employ many young workers and others in part-time and seasonal jobs.
- Average earnings are lower than in most other fields.

Nature of the Field

Hotels and other accommodations are as diverse as the many family and business travelers they accommodate. The field includes all types of lodging, from upscale hotels to RV parks. Motels, resorts, casino hotels, bed-and-breakfast inns, and boarding houses also are included. In fact, in 2004 nearly 62,000 establishments provided overnight accommodations to suit many different needs and budgets.

Establishments vary greatly in size and in the services they provide. *Hotels* and *motels* comprise the majority of establishments and tend to provide more services than other lodging places. There are five basic types of hotels—*commercial, resort, residential, extended-stay,* and *casino.* Most hotels and motels are *commercial* properties that cater mainly to business people, tourists, and other travelers who need accommodations for a brief stay. Commercial hotels and motels usually are located in cities or suburban areas and operate year round. Larger properties offer a variety of services for their guests, including a range of restaurant and beverage service options—from coffee bars and lunch counters to cocktail lounges and formal fine-dining restaurants. Some properties provide a variety of retail shops on the premises, such as gift boutiques, newsstands, drug and cosmetics counters, and barber and beauty shops. An increasing number of full-service hotels now offer guests access to laundry and valet services, swimming pools, and fitness centers or health spas. A small, but growing, number of luxury hotel chains also manage condominium units in combination with their transient rooms, providing both hotel guests and condominium owners with access to the same services and amenities.

Larger hotels and motels often have banquet rooms, exhibit halls, and spacious ballrooms to accommodate conventions, business meetings, wedding receptions, and other social gatherings. Conventions and business meetings are major sources of revenue for these hotels and motels. Some commercial hotels are known as conference hotels—fully self-contained entities specifically designed for meetings. They provide physical fitness and recreational facilities for meeting attendees in addition to state-of-the-art audiovisual and technical equipment, a business center, and banquet services.

Resort hotels and *motels* offer luxurious surroundings with a variety of recreational facilities, such as swimming pools, golf courses, tennis courts, game rooms, and health spas, as well as planned social activities and entertainment. Resorts typically are located in vacation destinations or near natural settings, such as mountains, the seashore, theme parks, or other attractions. As a result, the business of many resorts fluctuates with the season. Some resort hotels and motels provide additional convention and conference facilities to encourage customers to combine business with pleasure. During the off season, many of these establishments solicit conventions, sales meetings, and incentive tours to fill their otherwise empty rooms; some resorts even close for the off-season.

Residential hotels provide living quarters for permanent and semi-permanent residents. They combine the comfort of apartment living with the convenience of hotel services. Many have dining rooms and restaurants that also are open to residents and to the general public.

Extended-stay hotels combine features of a resort and a residential hotel. Typically, guests use these hotels for a minimum of 5 consecutive nights. These facilities usually provide rooms with fully equipped kitchens, entertainment systems, ironing boards and irons, office space with computer and telephone lines, fitness centers, and other amenities.

Casino hotels provide lodging in hotel facilities with a casino on the premises. The casino provides table wagering games and may include other gambling activities, such as slot machines and sports betting. Casino hotels generally offer a full range of services and amenities and also may contain conference and convention facilities.

In addition to hotels and motels, *bed-and-breakfast inns, recreational vehicle (RV) parks, campgrounds,* and *rooming and boarding houses* provide lodging for overnight guests. *Bed-and-breakfast inns* provide short-term lodging in private homes or small buildings converted for this purpose and are characterized by highly personalized service and inclusion of breakfast in the room rate. Their appeal is quaintness, with unusual service and decor.

Leisure and Hospitality

RV parks and campgrounds cater to people who enjoy recreational camping at moderate prices. Some parks and campgrounds provide service stations, general stores, shower and toilet facilities, and coin-operated laundries. While some are designed for overnight travelers only, others are for vacationers who stay longer. Some camps provide accommodations such as cabins and fixed campsites and other amenities such as food services, recreational facilities and equipment, and organized recreational activities. Examples of these overnight camps include children's camps; family vacation camps; hunting and fishing camps; and outdoor adventure retreats that offer trail riding, white-water rafting, hiking, fishing, game hunting, and similar activities.

Other short-term lodging facilities in this field include *guesthouses*, or small cottages located on the same property as a main residence, and *youth hostels*—dormitory-style hotels with few frills, occupied mainly by students traveling on limited budgets. Also included are *rooming and boarding houses*, such as fraternity houses, sorority houses, off-campus dormitories, and workers' camps. These establishments provide temporary or longer-term accommodations that may serve as a principal residence for the period of occupancy. These establishments also may provide services such as housekeeping, meals, and laundry services.

In recent years, hotels, motels, camps, and recreational and RV parks affiliated with national chains have grown rapidly. To the traveler, familiar chain establishments represent dependability and quality at predictable rates. National corporations own many chains, although many properties are independently owned but affiliated with a chain through a franchise agreement. Many independently operated hotels and inns participate in national reservations services, thereby appearing to belong to a larger enterprise. Also, many hotels join local chambers of commerce, boards of trade, convention and tourism bureaus, or regional recreation associations in order to support and promote tourism in their area.

Increases in competition and in the sophistication of travelers have induced the chains to provide lodging to serve a variety of customer budgets and accommodation preferences. In general, these lodging places may be grouped into properties that offer luxury, all-suite, moderately priced, and economy accommodations. The numbers of limited-service or economy chain properties—economy lodging without extensive lobbies,

restaurants, or lounges—have been growing. These properties are not as costly to build and operate. They appeal to budget-conscious family vacationers and travelers who are willing to sacrifice amenities for lower room prices.

While economy chains have become more prevalent, the movement in the hotel and lodging field is towards more extended-stay properties. In addition to fully equipped kitchenettes and laundry services, the extended-stay market offers guest amenities such as in-room access to the Internet and grocery shopping. This segment of the hotels and other accommodations field has eliminated traditional hotel lobbies and 24-hour front desk staffing, and housekeeping is usually done only about once a week. This helps to keep costs to a minimum.

All-suite facilities, especially popular with business travelers, offer a living room or sitting room in addition to a bedroom. These accommodations are aimed at travelers who require lodging for extended stays, families traveling with children, and business people needing to conduct small meetings without the expense of renting an additional room.

Increased competition among establishments in this field has spurred many independently owned and operated hotels and other lodging places to join national or international reservation systems, which allow travelers to make multiple reservations for lodging, airlines, and car rentals with one telephone call. Nearly all hotel chains operate online reservation systems through the Internet.

Working Conditions

Work in hotels and other accommodations can be demanding and hectic. Hotel staffs provide a variety of services to guests and must do so efficiently, courteously, and accurately. They must maintain a pleasant demeanor even during times of stress or when dealing with an impatient or irate guest. Alternately, work at slower times, such as the off-season or overnight periods, can seem slow and tiresome without the constant presence of hotel guests. Still, hotel workers must be ready to provide guests and visitors with gracious customer service at any hour.

Because hotels are open around the clock, employees frequently work varying shifts or variable schedules. Employees who work the late shift generally receive additional compensation. Many employees enjoy the opportunity to work part-time, nights or evenings, or other schedules that fit their availability for work and the hotel's needs. Hotel managers and many department supervisors may work regularly assigned schedules, but they also routinely work longer hours than scheduled, especially during peak travel times or when multiple events are scheduled. Also, they may be called in to work on short notice in the event of an emergency or to cover a position. Those who are self-employed, often owner-operators, tend to work long hours and often live at the establishment.

Food preparation and food service workers in hotels must withstand the strain of working during busy periods and being on their feet for many hours. Kitchen workers lift heavy pots and kettles and work near hot ovens and grills. Job hazards include slips and falls, cuts, and burns, but injuries are seldom serious. Food service workers often carry heavy trays of food, dishes, and glassware. Many of these workers work part time, including evenings, weekends, and holidays.

Office and administrative support workers generally work scheduled hours in an office setting, meeting with guests, clients, and hotel staff. Their work can become hectic—processing orders and invoices, dealing with demanding guests, or servicing requests that require a quick turnaround—but job hazards typically are limited to muscle and eye strain common to working with computers and office equipment.

In 2003, work-related injuries and illnesses averaged 6.7 for every 100 full-time workers in hotels and other

accommodations, compared with 5.0 for workers throughout nongovernment fields. Work hazards include burns from hot equipment, sprained muscles and wrenched backs from heavy lifting, and falls on wet floors.

Important Characteristics of the Field

Skills: None met the criteria. **Abilities:** Stamina; Trunk Strength; Wrist-Finger Speed; Spatial Orientation; Speed of Limb Movement; Static Strength. **Work-Related Values:** Social Service; Co-workers; Moral Values; Supervision, Technical.

Employment

Hotels and other accommodations provided 1.8 million wage and salary jobs in 2004. In addition, there were about 33,000 self-employed and unpaid family workers in the field who worked in bed-and-breakfast inns, camps, and small motels.

Employment is concentrated in densely populated cities and resort areas. Compared with establishments in other fields, hotels, motels, and other lodging places tend to be small. About 91 percent employed fewer than 50 people; about 56 percent employ fewer than 10 workers (chart). As a result, lodging establishments offer opportunities for those who are interested in owning and running their own business. Although establishments tend to be small, the majority of jobs are in larger hotels and motels with more than 100 employees.

Hotels and other lodging places often provide first jobs to many new entrants to the labor force. As a result, many of the field's workers are young. In 2004, about 19 percent of the workers were younger than age 25, compared with about 14 percent across all fields (table 1).

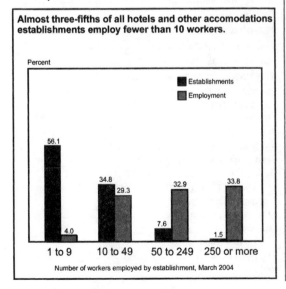

Almost three-fifths of all hotels and other accomodations establishments employ fewer than 10 workers.

Percent

Establishments
Employment

56.1
34.8
29.3
4.0
7.6
32.9
1.5
33.8

1 to 9   10 to 49   50 to 249   250 or more

Number of workers employed by establishment, March 2004

Table 1. Percent distribution of employment, by age group, 2004

Age group	Hotels and other accommodations	All fields
Total	100.0%	100.0%
16–19	5.3	4.2
20–24	13.7	9.9

Leisure and Hospitality

Age group	Hotels and other accommodations	All fields
25–34	22.4	21.8
35–44	23.7	24.8
45–54	20.2	23.3
55–64	11.4	12.4
65 and older	3.3	3.5

Occupations in the Field

The vast majority of workers in this field—more than 8 out of 10 in 2004—were employed in service and office and administrative support occupations (table 2). Workers in these occupations usually learn their skills on the job. Postsecondary education is not required for most entry-level positions; however, college training may be helpful for advancement in some of these occupations. For many administrative support and service occupations, personality traits and a customer-service orientation may be more important than formal schooling. Traits most important for success in the hotel and motel field are good communication skills; the ability to get along with people in stressful situations; a neat, clean appearance; and a pleasant manner.

Service occupations, by far the largest occupational group in the field, account for 65 percent of the field's employment. Most service jobs are in housekeeping occupations—including maids and housekeeping cleaners, janitors and cleaners, and laundry workers—and in food preparation and service jobs—including chefs and cooks, waiters and waitresses, bartenders, fast food and counter workers, and various other kitchen and dining room workers. The field also employs many baggage porters and bellhops, gaming services workers, and grounds maintenance workers.

Workers in *cleaning* and *housekeeping occupations* ensure that the lodging facility is clean and in good condition for the comfort and safety of guests. *Maids and housekeepers* clean lobbies, halls, guest rooms, and bathrooms. They make sure that guests not only have clean rooms, but have all the necessary furnishings and supplies. They change sheets and towels, vacuum carpets, dust furniture, empty wastebaskets, and mop bathroom floors. In larger hotels, the housekeeping staff may include assistant housekeepers, floor supervisors, housekeepers, and

executive housekeepers. *Janitors* help with the cleaning of the public areas of the facility, empty trash, and perform minor maintenance work.

Table 2. Employment of wage and salary workers in hotels and other accommodations by occupation, 2004 and projected change, 2004–2014 (Employment in thousands)

Occupation	Employment, 2004 Number	Percent	Percent change, 2004–2014
Total, all occupations	1,796	100.0	16.9
Management, business, and financial occupations	99	5.5	26.6
Top executives	16	0.9	25.8
Food service managers	10	0.6	16.2
Lodging managers	28	1.6	27.4
Meeting and convention planners	7	0.4	27.3
Service occupations	1,169	65.1	16.0
Security guards and gaming surveillance officers	34	1.9	–2.3
Chefs and head cooks	13	0.7	16.9
First-line supervisors/ managers of food preparation and serving workers	22	1.2	16.5
Cooks, restaurant	56	3.1	16.7
Food preparation workers	23	1.3	27.1
Bartenders	39	2.2	13.1
Fast food and counter workers	27	1.5	25.2
Waiters and waitresses	133	7.4	9.5
Food servers, nonrestaurant	39	2.2	11.9
Dining room and cafeteria attendants and bartender helpers	43	2.4	9.1
Dishwashers	38	2.1	8.3
Hosts and hostesses, restaurant, lounge, and coffee shop	21	1.2	9.1
Supervisors, building and grounds cleaning and maintenance workers	37	2.0	26.6
Janitors and cleaners, except maids and housekeeping cleaners	49	2.7	20.2

Occupation	Employment, 2004		Percent change, 2004–2014
	Number	Percent	
Maids and housekeeping cleaners	405	22.5	17.0
Landscaping and grounds-keeping workers	23	1.3	20.3
Gaming supervisors	11	0.6	10.3
Gaming dealers	35	2.0	25.0
Baggage porters and bellhops	25	1.4	21.5
Concierges	7	0.4	17.0
Recreation and fitness workers	13	0.7	22.1
Sales and related occupations	54	3.0	18.3
Cashiers, except gaming	16	0.9	14.3
Gaming change persons and booth cashiers	10	0.6	7.6
Office and administrative support occupations	320	17.8	15.0
Supervisors, office and administrative support workers	22	1.2	7.7
Bookkeeping, accounting, and auditing clerks	24	1.4	14.6
Gaming cage workers	5	0.3	5.7
Hotel, motel, and resort desk clerks	183	10.2	17.4
Reservation and transportation ticket agents and travel clerks	13	0.7	15.7
Installation, maintenance, and repair occupations	75	4.2	26.8
Maintenance and repair workers, general	64	3.6	27.2
Production occupations	39	2.2	19.0
Laundry and dry-cleaning workers	32	1.8	18.0
Transportation and material moving occupations	24	1.3	7.0

Note: May not add to totals due to omission of occupations with small employment

Workers in the various *food service* occupations deal with customers in the dining room or at a service counter. *Waiters and waitresses* take customers' orders, serve meals, and prepare checks. In restaurants, they may describe chef's specials and suggest appropriate wines. In smaller establishments, they often set tables, escort guests to their seats, accept payment, and clear tables. They also may deliver room service orders to guests. In larger restaurants, some of these tasks are assigned to other workers.

Hosts and hostesses welcome guests, show them to their tables, and give them menus. *Bartenders* fill beverage orders for customers seated at the bar or from waiters and waitresses who serve patrons at tables. *Dining room and cafeteria attendants* and *bartender helpers* assist waiters, waitresses, and bartenders by clearing, cleaning, and setting up tables; replenishing supplies at the bar; and keeping the serving areas stocked with linens, tableware, and other supplies. *Counter attendants* take orders and serve food at fast-food counters and in coffee shops; they also may operate the cash register.

Cooks and food preparation occupations prepare food in the kitchen. Beginners may advance to more skilled food preparation jobs with experience or specialized culinary training. *Chefs* and *cooks* generally prepare a wide selection of dishes, often cooking individual servings to order. Larger hotels employ cooks who specialize in the preparation of many different kinds of food. They may have titles such as salad chef, grill chef, or pastry chef. Individual chefs may oversee the day-to-day operations of different kitchens in a hotel, such as a fine-dining full-service restaurant, a casual or counter-service establishment, or banquet operations. Chef positions generally are attained after years of experience and, sometimes, formal training, including apprenticeships. Larger establishments also employ *executive chefs* and *food and beverage directors* who plan menus, purchase food, and supervise kitchen personnel for all of the kitchens in the property. *Food preparation workers* shred lettuce for salads, cut up food for cooking, and perform simple cooking steps under the direction of the chef or head cook.

Many full-service hotels employ a uniformed staff to assist arriving and departing guests. *Baggage porters and bellhops* carry bags and escort guests to their rooms. *Concierges* arrange special or personal services for guests. They may take messages, arrange for babysitting, make restaurant reservations, provide directions, arrange for or

Leisure and Hospitality

give advice on entertainment and local attractions, and monitor requests for housekeeping and maintenance. *Doorkeepers* help guests into and out of their cars, summon taxis, and carry baggage into the hotel lobby.

Hotels also employ the largest percentage of *gaming services workers* because much of gaming takes place in casino hotels. Some gaming services positions are associated with oversight and direction—supervision, surveillance, and investigation—while others involve working with the games or patrons themselves by tending the slot machines, handling money, writing and running tickets, dealing cards, and performing related duties.

Office and administrative support positions accounted for 18 percent of the jobs in hotels and other accommodations in 2004. Hotel desk clerks, secretaries, bookkeeping and accounting clerks, and telephone operators ensure that the front office operates smoothly. The majority of these workers are *hotel, motel, and resort desk clerks.* They process reservations and guests' registration and checkout, monitor arrivals and departures, handle complaints, and receive and forward mail. The duties of hotel desk clerks depend on the size of the facility. In smaller lodging places, one clerk or a manager may do everything. In larger hotels, a larger staff divides the duties among several types of clerks. Although hotel desk clerks sometimes are hired from the outside, openings usually are filled by promoting other hotel employees such as bellhops and porters, credit clerks, and other administrative support workers.

Hotels and other lodging places employ many different types of *managers* to direct and coordinate the activities of the front office; kitchen; dining room; and other departments, such as housekeeping, accounting, personnel, purchasing, publicity, sales, security, and maintenance. Managers make decisions on room rates, establish credit policy, and have ultimate responsibility for resolving problems. In smaller establishments, the manager also may perform many of the front-office clerical tasks. In the smallest establishments, the owners—sometimes a family team—do all the work necessary to operate the business.

Lodging managers or *general and operations managers* in large hotels often have several assistant managers, each responsible for a phase of operations. For example, *food and beverage managers* oversee restaurants, lounges, and catering or banquet operations. *Rooms managers* look after reservations and occupancy levels to ensure proper room assignments and authorize discounts, special rates, or promotions. Large hotels, especially those with conference centers, use an executive committee structure to improve departmental communications and coordinate activities. Other managers who may serve on a hotel's executive committee include *public relations* or *sales managers, human resources directors, executive housekeepers,* and *heads of hotel security.*

Workers at vacation and recreational camps may include camp counselors who lead and instruct children and teenagers in outdoor-oriented forms of recreation, such as swimming, hiking, horseback riding, and camping. In addition, counselors at vacation and resident camps also provide guidance and supervise daily living and general socialization. Other types of campgrounds may employ trail guides for activities such as hiking, hunting, and fishing.

Training, Other Qualifications, and Advancement

Although the skills and experience needed by workers in this field depend on the specific occupation, most entry-level jobs require little or no previous training. Basic tasks usually can be learned in a short time. Almost all workers in the hotel and other accommodations field undergo on-the-job training, which usually is provided under the supervision of an experienced employee or manager. Some large chain operations have formal training sessions for new employees; many also provide video or online training.

Hotel operations are becoming increasingly diverse and complex, but all positions require employees to maintain a customer-service orientation. Hoteliers recognize the importance of personal service and attention to guests, so they look for persons with positive personality traits and good communication skills when filling many guest services positions, such as desk clerk and host and hostess positions. Many hotel managers place a greater emphasis on customer service skills while providing specialized training in important skill areas, such as computer technology and software. Vocational courses and apprenticeship programs in food preparation, catering, and hotel and restaurant management, offered through restaurant associations and trade unions, provide training opportunities. Programs range in length from a few months to several years. About 800 community and junior colleges offer 2-year degree programs in hotel and restaurant management. The U.S. Armed Forces also offer experience and training in food service.

Traditionally, many hotels fill first-level manager positions by promoting administrative support and service workers—particularly those with good communication skills, a solid educational background, tact, loyalty, and a capacity to endure hard work and long hours. People with these qualities still advance to manager jobs but, more recently, lodging chains have primarily been hiring persons with four-year college degrees in the liberal arts or other fields and starting them in trainee or junior management positions. Bachelor's and master's degree programs in hotel, restaurant, and hospitality management provide the strongest background for a career as a hotel manager, with nearly 150 colleges and universities offering such programs. Graduates of these programs are highly sought by employers in this field. New graduates often go through on-the-job training programs before being given much responsibility. Eventually, they may advance to a top management position in a hotel, a corporate management opportunity in a large chain operation, or an investment or financial analysis position in the financial services sector.

Upper management positions, such as general manager, lodging manager, food service manager, or sales manager, generally require considerable formal training and job experience. Some department managers, such as comptrollers, purchasing managers, executive housekeepers, and executive chefs, generally require some specialized training and extensive on-the-job experience. To advance to positions with more responsibilities, managers frequently change employers or relocate within a chain to a property in another area.

For office and administrative support and service workers, advancement opportunities in the hotel field vary widely. Some workers, such as housekeepers and janitors, generally have few opportunities for advancement. In large properties, however, some janitors may advance to supervisory positions. Hotel desk clerks, hospitality workers, and chefs sometimes advance to managerial positions. Promotional opportunities from the front office often are greater than those from any other department because this vantage point provides an excellent opportunity to learn the establishment's overall operation. Front-office jobs are excellent entry-level jobs and can serve as a stepping-stone to jobs in hospitality, public relations, advertising, sales, and management.

Advancement opportunities for chefs and cooks are better than those for most other service occupations. Cooks often advance to chef or to supervisory and management positions, such as executive chef, restaurant manager, or food service manager. Some transfer to jobs in clubs, go into business for themselves, or become instructors of culinary arts.

Outlook

Wage and salary employment in hotels and other accommodations is expected to increase by 17 percent over the 2004–2014 period, compared with 14 percent growth projected for wage and salary employment in all fields combined. Recently, business and leisure travelers have resumed travel patterns of past years, rebounding from concerns over a weak economy and security matters. In addition, as more states legalize some form of gambling, the hotel field will increasingly invest in gaming, further fueling job growth.

Job opportunities should be concentrated in the largest hotel occupations, such as building cleaning workers and hotel, motel, and resort desk clerks, in part because they have the highest turnover. Many openings will arise in full-service hotels and resorts and spas because they employ the most workers. All-suite properties and extended-stay and budget hotels and motels usually do not operate restaurants, dining rooms, lounges, or kitchens; therefore, these limited-service establishments will offer a narrower range of employment and growth opportunities.

Employment outlook varies by occupation, geographic location, and service class of hotel. Employment of hotel, motel, and resort desk clerks is expected to grow faster than some other occupations in the field as responsibilities become more numerous and some of these workers take on tasks previously reserved for managers. However, the spread of computer technology will cause employment of other clerical workers—bookkeepers, accountants, and auditing clerks and secretaries, for example—to grow more slowly than employment in the field as a whole. Employment of waiters and waitresses will grow more slowly—reflecting the growing number of hotels and other accommodations that either do not offer full-service restaurants or contract them out to other food service establishments. Growth of full-service hotels and the small, but burgeoning, luxury hotel market which specializes in personal service will cause employment of

Leisure and
Hospitality

lodging managers to grow about as fast as other occupations. The growth of economy-class establishments—hotels with fewer frills and fewer departments to manage—will moderate some of this growth because these hotels have a flatter management structure. The accelerating trend toward chain-affiliated hotels and motels should provide managers with opportunities for advancement into general manager positions, manager jobs at larger and busier properties, and corporate administrative jobs. Opportunities should be more limited for self-employed managers or owners of small lodging places, such as bed-and-breakfast inns. Job opportunities at outdoor recreation and RV parks should grow as RVs and driving vacations gain popularity in the United States. Also, gaming services and gaming manager occupations should grow as more casino hotels are built.

Much new hotel construction is taking place in major urban and suburban areas, creating many new jobs. Also, hotels that emphasize personal service, such as luxury and boutique hotels, will have a greater need for front-of-the-house employees who provide guest services than for back office accounting and bookkeeping occupations.

Some occupations employed in this field have relatively high numbers of workers who leave their jobs and must be replaced. Many young people and others who are looking only for seasonal or part-time work, and not a career, take food service and clerical jobs that require little or no previous training. To attract and retain workers, the hotel and other accommodations field is placing more emphasis on hiring and training. Therefore, job opportunities in this field should be plentiful for first-time jobseekers and people with limited skills.

Earnings

Earnings in hotels and other accommodations generally are much lower than the average for all fields. In 2004, average earnings for all nonsupervisory workers in this field were $10.58 an hour, or $317 a week, compared with $15.67 an hour, or $529 a week, for workers throughout nongovernment fields. Many workers in this field earn the federal minimum wage of $5.15 an hour. Some states have laws that establish a higher minimum wage. Federal laws, however, allow employers to pay below the minimum wage when an employee is expected to receive a considerable portion of income from tips.

Food and beverage service workers, as well as hosts and hostesses, maids and housekeeping cleaners, concierges,

and baggage porters and bellhops, derive their earnings from a combination of hourly earnings and customer tips. Waiters and waitresses often derive the majority of their earnings from tips, which vary greatly depending on menu prices and the volume of customers served. Many employers also provide free meals and furnish uniforms. Food service personnel may receive extra pay for working at banquets and on other special occasions. In general, workers with the greatest skills, such as restaurant cooks, have the highest earnings, and workers who receive tips have the lowest. Earnings in the largest occupations in hotels and other lodging places appear in table 3.

Salaries of lodging managers are dependent upon the size and sales volume of the establishment and their specific duties and responsibilities. Managers may earn bonuses ranging up to 50 percent of their basic salary. In addition, they and their families may be furnished with lodging, meals, parking, laundry, and other services. Some hotels offer profit-sharing plans, tuition reimbursement, and other benefits to their employees.

About 9 percent of the workers in hotels and other accommodations are union members or are covered by union contracts, compared with 14 percent of workers in all fields combined.

Table 3. Median hourly earnings of the largest occupations in hotels and other accommodations, May 2004

Occupation	Accommodations	All fields
Maintenance and repair workers, general	$11.07	$14.77
Cooks, restaurant	10.68	9.39
Janitors and cleaners, except maids and housekeeping cleaners	9.12	9.04
Hotel, motel, and resort desk clerks	8.47	8.51
Bartenders	8.11	7.42
Dishwashers	8.07	7.35
Food servers, nonrestaurant	7.83	7.95
Maids and housekeeping cleaners	7.81	8.13
Dining room and cafeteria attendants and bartender helpers	7.70	7.10
Waiters and waitresses	7.06	6.75

Sources of Additional Information

For information on hospitality careers, write to

- International Council on Hotel, Restaurant, and Institutional Education, 2613 North Parham Rd., 2nd floor, Richmond, VA 23294. Internet: http://www.chrie.org

- American Hotel and Lodging Association, 1201 New York Ave. NW, Suite 600, Washington, DC 20005-3931.

General information on food and beverage service jobs is available from

- National Restaurant Association, 1200 17th St. NW, Washington, DC 20036-3097. Internet: http://www.restaurant.org

For information on the American Culinary Federation's apprenticeship and certification programs for cooks, write to

- American Culinary Federation, 180 Center Place Way, St. Augustine, FL 32095. Internet: http://www.acfchefs.org

Government and Advocacy, Grantmaking, and Civic Organizations

Advocacy, Grantmaking, and Civic Organizations

- Annual Earnings: $28,007
- Job Growth: 14.5%
- Size of Workforce: 1,121,940
- Self-Employed: 0.0%
- Part-Time: 24.6%

Significant Points

- Advocacy, grantmaking, and civic organizations had 1.2 million wage and salary jobs in 2004, with 75 percent in civic and social organizations or professional and similar organizations.

- Employers need individuals with strong communication and fundraising skills because organizations must constantly mobilize public support for their activities.

- Employment is expected to grow 15 percent as social and demographic shifts increase demand for services.

- Job opportunities should be excellent in most employment settings because of high job turnover, primarily because of the field's relatively low wages.

Nature of the Field

Advocacy, grantmaking, and civic organizations in the United states are distinct and, at some point, affect everyone's life. In every state, these types of organizations are working to better their communities by directly addressing issues of public concern through service, independent action, or civic engagement. These organizations span the political spectrum of ideas and encompass every aspect of human endeavor, from symphonies to little leagues and from homeless shelters and day care centers to natural resource conservation advocates. These organizations are collectively called "nonprofits," a name that is used to describe institutions and organizations that are neither government nor business. Other names often used include the not-for-profit sector, the third sector, the independent sector, the philanthropic sector, the voluntary sector, or the social sector. Outside the United States, these organizations often are called nongovernmental organizations (NGOs) or civil society organizations.

These other names emphasize the characteristics that distinguish advocacy, grantmaking, and civic organizations from businesses and government. Unlike businesses, these organizations do not exist to make money for owners or investors, but that doesn't mean that they cannot charge fees or sell products that generate revenue or that revenue must not exceed expenses. Instead, these groups are dedicated to a specific mission that enhances the social fabric of society. Unlike government, these organizations are not able to mandate changes through legisla-

Government and Advocacy, Grantmaking, and Civic Organizations

tion or regulations enforceable by law. Instead, they work toward the mission of their organization by relying on a small group of paid staff and voluntary service and financial support by large numbers of their members or the public. This field includes four main segments: business, professional, labor, political, and similar organizations; civic and social organizations; social advocacy organizations; and grantmaking and giving services. (Religious organizations, which also have legal status as nonprofits, are not included in this field.)

Business, professional, labor, political, and similar organizations comprised about half of the advocacy, grantmaking, and civic organizations field establishments in 2004 (table 1). Business associations are primarily engaged in promoting the business interests of their members. They include organizations such as chambers of commerce, real estate boards, and manufacturers' and trade associations. They may conduct research on new products and services; develop market statistics; sponsor quality and certification standards; lobby public officials; or publish newsletters, books, or periodicals for distribution to their members. Professional organizations seek to advance the interests of their members and their professional as a whole. Examples of professional associations are health professionals' and bar associations. Although contributions to these organizations are not tax-deductible, membership dues may be deductible as business expenses. Labor organizations promote the interests of the labor union members they represent by negotiating improvement in wages, benefits, and working conditions. They persuade workers to become members of a union and then seek to win the right to represent them in collective bargaining with their employer. Political organizations promote the interests of national, state, or local political parties and their candidates for elected public positions. Included are political groups organized to raise funds for a political party or individual candidates, such as political action committees (PACs). A variety of other similar organizations also are included in this segment of the advocacy, grantmaking, and civic organizations field. They include athletic associations that regulate or administer various sports leagues, conferences, or even entire sports at the amateur or professional level. Also included in this segment are condominium and homeowners' associations, property owners' associations, and tenant associations.

More than one-quarter of the establishments in the advocacy, grantmaking, and civic organizations field are associated with *civic and social organizations* engaged in promoting the civic and social interests of their members. These organizations include alumni associations, automobile clubs, booster clubs, youth scouting organizations, and parent-teacher associations. This segment also includes social clubs, fraternal lodges, ethnic associations, and veterans' membership organizations, some of which may operate bars and restaurants for their members.

Social advocacy organizations, which comprise 13 percent of advocacy, grantmaking, and civic organizations establishments, promote a particular cause or work for the realization of a specific social or political goal to benefit either a broad segment of the population or a specific constituency. They often solicit contributions and offer memberships to support their activities. There are three groups of social advocacy organizations: human rights organizations; environment, conservation, and wildlife organizations; and all other social advocacy organizations. Human rights organizations address issues such as protecting and promoting the broad constitutional rights and civil liberties of individuals and those suffering from neglect, abuse, or exploitation. They also may promote the interests of specific groups, such as children, women, senior citizens, or persons with disabilities; work to improve relations between racial, ethnic, and cultural groups; or promote voter education and registration. Environment, conservation, and wildlife organizations promote the preservation and protection of the environment and wildlife. They address issues such as clean air and water; global warming; conserving and developing natural resources, including land, plant, water, and energy resources; and protecting and preserving wildlife and endangered species. Other social advocacy organizations address issues such as peace and international understanding; organize and encourage community action; or advance social causes, such as firearms safety, drunk driving prevention, and drug abuse awareness.

Grantmaking and giving services comprised about 10 percent of advocacy, grantmaking, and civic organizations establishments and include grantmaking foundations; voluntary health organizations; and establishments primarily engaged in raising funds for a wide range of social welfare activities, such as health, educational, scientific, and cultural activities. Grantmaking foundations, also called charitable trusts, award grants from trust funds based on a competitive selection process or on the preferences of the foundation managers and grantors; some fund a single entity, such as a museum or university. There are two types of grantmaking foundations: private foundations and public foundations. Most of the funds of a private foundation come from one source—an individual, a family, or a corporation. Public foundations, in contrast, normally receive their funds from multiple sources, which may include private foundations, individuals, government agencies, and fees for services. Moreover, public foundations must continue to seek money from diverse sources in order to retain their public status. Voluntary health organizations are primarily engaged in raising funds for health-related research, such as the development of new treatments for diseases like cancer or heart disease, disease awareness and prevention, or health education.

Advocacy, grantmaking, and civic organizations receive the revenue that makes their operations possible from a variety of sources. Some organizations receive most of their funds from private contributions. Many organizations have experienced an increase in donors, stemming partially from more favorable treatment of donations by tax laws. Also, estates of many members of the Depression generation (those born during the 1920s and 1930s) have donated large sums to these organizations. However, many advocacy, grantmaking, and civic organizations—such as nonprofit hospitals and universities—generate revenue by charging fees for the services they provide, earning interest on investments, or producing and selling goods.

The formation of joint ventures or partnerships between advocacy, grantmaking, and civic organizations and corporations also has risen. The last few years also have seen a rise in three-sector partnerships formed between an advocacy, grantmaking, and civic organization; a corporation; and a government agency. These partnerships have ensured a steady flow of income to the advocacy, grantmaking, and civic organizations field and increased public awareness of these organizations and the importance of their missions. On the corporate side, partnerships help sell corporate products; enhance the civic image of the corporation; and allow corporations to provide additional revenue to advocacy, grantmaking, and civic organizations, which have traditionally relied on simple donations.

New information technology also is increasing the capacity of advocacy, grantmaking, and civic organizations to advocate their causes and to raise funds. Interactive Web sites, e-mail and electronic philanthropy, and electronically generated databases have transformed the way these organizations communicate with the public, grantmakers, and donors, reducing the costs of gathering constituents and connecting to policymakers and allies. The Internet has changed the way charitable organizations interact with government and its agencies as they continue to use "e-services" in order to remain efficient. For advocacy, grantmaking, and civic organizations, these advances provide an opportunity to reduce their paperwork, increase their efficiency in responding to regulatory demands, and improve their organizational capabilities. The Internet will continue to change the way these organizations collect and report data and will lead to greater consolidation of federal and state regulatory demands on the field.

Table 1. Percent distribution of establishments and wage and salary employment in advocacy, grantmaking, and civic organizations, by detailed field, 2004

Field segment	Establishments	Employment
Total	100.0	100.0
Business, professional, labor, political, and similar organizations	51.2	38.2
Civic and social organizations	25.6	36.7
Social advocacy organizations	13.2	14.6
Grantmaking and giving services	10.1	10.5

Working Conditions

In 2004, about three-fourths of the workers in advocacy, grantmaking, and civic organizations worked full time; the remainder worked part-time or variable schedules. Most workers spend the majority of their time in offices functioning in a team environment, often working with volunteers. The work environment may differ depending on the size of the organization. For those who work in small organizations, the equipment is sometimes outdated and their workspace cramped. But, in larger, well-funded organizations, conditions are very similar to those in large for-profit businesses. The work environment generally is positive—workers know that their work helps people and improves their communities. Top executives and workers responsible for fundraising may

Government and Advocacy, Grantmaking, and Civic Organizations

travel frequently to meet with supporters and potential donors, often in evenings and on weekends. Fundraising can be highly stressful because the financial health of the organization depends on being successful. Workers employed in the delivery of social services also work in very stressful environments because many of their clients are struggling with a wide range of problems related to child care, child welfare, juvenile justice, addiction, health, unemployment, and inadequate workforce skills.

Work in the advocacy, grantmaking, and civic organizations field is rarely hazardous. In 2003, the field had only 2.9 injuries and illnesses per 100 full-time workers, compared with an average of 5.0 throughout nongovernment fields.

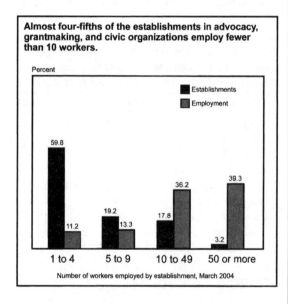

Almost four-fifths of the establishments in advocacy, grantmaking, and civic organizations employ fewer than 10 workers.

Percent

- Establishments
- Employment

59.8

19.2   17.8

11.2   13.3

36.2

39.3

3.2

1 to 4   5 to 9   10 to 49   50 or more

Number of workers employed by establishment, March 2004

Important Characteristics of the Field

Skills: Management of Financial Resources; Service Orientation; Social Perceptiveness; Persuasion; Time Management; Instructing. **Abilities:** Speech Recognition; Speech Clarity; Oral Expression; Time Sharing; Oral Comprehension; Problem Sensitivity. **Work-Related Values:** Social Service; Working Conditions; Co-workers; Activity; Company Policies and Practices; Supervision, Human Relations.

Employment

Advocacy, grantmaking, and civic organizations had 1.2 million wage and salary jobs in 2004. About 75 percent of them were in civic and social organizations or professional and similar organizations.

Advocacy, grantmaking, and civic organizations establishments are found throughout the nation, but the greatest numbers of jobs are found in California and New York, the states with the greatest population. Most establishments in this field are small (chart 1). The vast majority of jobs are in establishments that employ fewer than 5 people.

Table 2. Employment of wage and salary workers in advocacy, grantmaking, and civic organizations by occupation, 2004 and projected change, 2004–2014 (Employment in thousands)

Occupation	Employment, 2004 Number	Employment, 2004 Percent	Percent change, 2004–2014
Total, all occupations	1,231	100.0	14.5
Management, business, and financial occupations	285	23.1	17.6
Top executives	49	4.0	17.6
Public relations managers	10	0.8	21.5
Social and community service managers	19	1.5	19.1
Human resources, training, and labor relations specialists	71	5.8	11.1
Accountants and auditors	14	1.1	19.9
Professional and related occupations	224	18.2	21.8
Computer specialists	18	1.5	29.6
Social workers	21	1.7	18.4
Social and human service assistants	21	1.7	32.7
Community and social service specialists, all other	13	1.1	29.7
Preschool teachers, except special education	12	1.0	16.1
Self-enrichment education teachers	15	1.2	15.0
Teacher assistants	18	1.4	16.5

Occupation	Employment, 2004		Percent change, 2004–2014
	Number	Percent	
Athletes, coaches, umpires, and related workers	8	0.7	14.3
Public relations specialists	28	2.3	22.0
Service occupations	353	28.7	14.6
Security guards	18	1.5	–2.2
Lifeguards, ski patrol, and other recreational protective service workers	22	1.8	15.3
Cooks and food preparation workers	16	1.3	15.1
Bartenders	38	3.1	12.9
Waiters and waitresses	17	1.4	14.9
Janitors and cleaners, except maids and house-keeping cleaners	27	2.2	18.0
Maids and housekeeping cleaners	11	0.9	22.2
Landscaping and grounds-keeping workers	13	1.1	24.9
Nonfarm animal caretakers	9	0.7	18.0
Child care workers	32	2.6	12.4
Fitness trainers and aerobics instructors	37	3.0	13.2
Recreation workers	40	3.3	13.5
Sales and related occupations	36	2.9	13.3
Office and administrative support occupations	287	23.3	5.4
Supervisors, office and administrative support workers	23	1.9	8.0
Bookkeeping, accounting, and auditing clerks	31	2.5	4.9
Customer service representatives	19	1.6	22.7
Receptionists and information clerks	28	2.3	13.7
Secretaries and administrative assistants	97	7.9	2.2
Office clerks, general	52	4.2	5.6

Occupation	Employment, 2004		Percent change, 2004–2014
	Number	Percent	
Installation, maintenance, and repair occupations	23	1.9	22.6
Maintenance and repair workers, general	20	1.7	22.8

Note: May not add to totals due to omission of occupations with small employment

Occupations in the Field

Advocacy, grantmaking, and civic organizations employ many different types of workers, but 75 percent of the jobs are in management, business, and financial occupations; service occupations; or office and administrative support occupations (table 2).

Chief executives in advocacy, grantmaking, and civic organizations formulate policies and direct daily operations. In publicly held and nonprofit corporations, the board of directors ultimately is accountable for the success or failure of the enterprise, and the chief executive officer reports to the board. Chief executives perform a variety of duties depending on the size of their association and how it is organized. In a larger association, they may direct a number of operations specialty managers, each of whom is responsible for part of the organization's operations. In a small association, executives are likely to direct many or all of these functions themselves and be required to wear many hats at one time. The most common type of operations specialty managers in advocacy, grantmaking, and civic organizations is *social and community service managers,* who plan, organize, or coordinate the activities of a social service program or community outreach organization. They oversee the program or organization's budget and polices regarding participant involvement, program requirements, and benefits. Work may involve directing social workers, counselors, or probation officers. Larger organizations employ a variety of business and financial operations specialists. For example, *accountants and auditors* handle the financial affairs of an association. They also prepare financial statements, records, and reports. Accountants also contribute to fundraising efforts by figuring the costs of new programs and including those estimates in grant proposals. Larger organizations also may have

Government and Advocacy, Grantmaking, and Civic Organizations

human resources, training, and labor relations specialists.

Among professional specialty occupations that play an important role in advocacy, grantmaking, and civic organizations, *public relations specialists* handle functions such as media, community, consumer, and governmental relations; political campaigns; interest-group representation; conflict mediation; or employee and investor relations. They prepare press releases and contact people in the media who might print or broadcast their material. Many public relations specialists go on to specialize in fundraising, sometimes having the title director of development. Fundraisers find the money and other gifts needed to keep an organizations operations operating by asking for large gifts from individual donors, soliciting bequests, hosting special events, applying for grants, and launching phone and letter appeals. In small organizations, the director of development does all these things; in large ones, fundraisers specialize. *Social and human service assistants* provide direct and indirect client services to ensure that individuals in their care reach their maximum level of functioning. They assess clients' needs; establish their eligibility for benefits; and help them obtain services such as food stamps, Medicaid, or welfare.

Many advocacy, grantmaking, and civic organizations play an important role in education. *Self-enrichment education teachers* teach courses that students take for pleasure or personal enrichment; these classes usually are not intended to lead to a particular degree or vocation. Self-enrichment teachers may instruct children or adults in a wide variety of areas, such as cooking, dancing, creative writing, photography, or personal finance. If working for an association, for example, educators will be expected to possess strong management skills, exceptional people skills, event planning knowledge, extensive marketing talents, and an ability to work effectively with volunteers. *Teacher assistants* provide instructional and clerical support for classroom teachers, allowing teachers more time for lesson planning and teaching.

Among service occupations, *recreation workers* and *fitness trainers and aerobics instructors* plan, organize, and direct leisure and athletic activities, such as aerobics, arts and crafts, the performing arts, camping, and sports. Many work at playgrounds and recreation areas, community centers, health clubs, and fitness centers run by advocacy, grantmaking, and civic organizations. *Waiters and waitresses* take customers' orders, serve food and bever-

ages, prepare itemized checks, and sometimes accept payment at food service facilities. *Janitors and cleaners* clean floors, shampoo rugs, wash walls and glass, and remove rubbish. They may fix leaky faucets, empty trash cans, do painting and carpentry, replenish bathroom supplies, mow lawns, and see that heating and air-conditioning equipment works properly. While janitors typically perform a range of duties, cleaners tend to work for organizations that specialize in one type of cleaning activity, such as washing windows. *Security guards* patrol and inspect property to protect against fire, theft, vandalism, terrorism, and illegal activity. They protect their employer's investment, enforce laws on the property, and deter criminal activity or other problems. Security guards may be required to write comprehensive reports outlining their observations and activities during their assigned shift. They also may interview witnesses or victims, prepare case reports, and testify in court.

The larger the organization, the more administrative support occupations it needs. Advocacy, grantmaking, and civic organizations also employ *bookkeeping, accounting, and auditing clerks; receptionists and information clerks; executive secretaries and administrative assistants; office clerks;* and *first-line supervisors/managers of office and administrative support workers* commonly found in most business organizations.

Training, Other Qualifications, and Advancement

The types of jobs and skills required for advocacy, grantmaking, and civic organizations vary with the type and size of the organization. But all organizations need individuals with strong communication and fundraising skills because they must constantly mobilize public support for their activities. Creativity and initiative are important, as many workers are responsible for a wide range of activities, such as creating new events designed to communicate and sell an organization's goals and objectives. Basic knowledge about accounting, finance, management, information systems, advertising, and marketing provide an important advantage for those trying to enter the advocacy, grantmaking, and civic organizations field. In some cases, a second language may be needed for jobs that involve international activities. The highly competitive field also needs individuals who have adequate technical skills to efficiently operate and maintain their computer systems.

There are many ways that a person can enter the advocacy, grantmaking, and civic organizations field. One way to prepare for a job is to gain experience as a volunteer. Volunteering allows a person to try out an organization to see if he or she likes it, to make good contacts in the field, and to demonstrate a commitment to a cause. Volunteer work can be found through career and guidance counselors at high schools and colleges, as they often maintain a database of opportunities. County libraries and governments often have lists of opportunities as well. Many local schools and community groups also can identify organizations that need volunteers. The Internet is another good way to find volunteer openings. Paid work also can prepare job seekers for advocacy, grantmaking, and civic organizations. Many professionals in the field began their careers in for-profit business. Many organizations need marketing or technological expertise and often hire someone from the for-profit sector-especially if that person has volunteer experience.

As of 2004, more than 250 colleges and universities offered courses on the management of nonprofit organizations. In addition, about 72 programs offered noncredit courses in fundraising and nonprofit management. More than 50 programs offered continuing education courses. About 129 schools offered at least one course for undergraduate credit, and more than 70 were affiliated with American Humanics (an alliance of colleges, universities and nonprofit organizations preparing undergraduates for careers with youth and human service agencies).

In 2004, there were more than 90 master's degree programs, usually in business administration or in public administration with a focus on nonprofit or philanthropic studies. About 157 colleges and universities had at least one course related to management of nonprofits within a graduate department. Of these programs, about 114 offered a graduate degree with a concentration in the management of nonprofit organizations; about 41 universities offered one or two graduate courses, usually in financial management and generic nonprofit management.

The formal education and experience of chief executives or executive directors varies as widely as the nature of their responsibilities. There are many ways to prepare for the job of running an advocacy, grantmaking, and civic organization. Most paid executive directors in large organizations have graduate degrees, often in business or public administration, some specifically in nonprofit management. Some executive directors start their careers in other positions, such as fundraiser or communications director. Others start on the program side of an organization, offering services directly to the public. They might be teachers, health care workers, ecologists, or another type of professional. Accountants and auditors need a good understanding of business computer systems and some hands-on knowledge of accounting software. An accounting or finance degree with some management course work or a business administration degree with some accounting course work is a good background to have. A master of business administration or other advanced degree may be desirable for more senior positions. The certified nonprofit accounting professional (CNAP) accreditation also provides the additional credibility needed in some larger organizations. Social community service managers need a bachelor's degree. They must possess knowledge of principles and procedures for personnel recruitment, selection, training, compensation and benefits, labor relations and negotiation, and personnel information systems.

A bachelor's degree usually is not required in order to work as a social and human service assistant. However, employers increasingly seek individuals with relevant work experience or education beyond high school. Certificates or associate degrees in subjects such as social work, human services, gerontology, or one of the social or behavioral sciences meet most employers' requirements. Employers try to select applicants who have effective communication skills, a strong sense of responsibility, and the ability to manage time effectively. Formal education almost always is necessary for advancement. In general, advancement requires a bachelor's or master's degree in human services, counseling, rehabilitation, social work, or a related field. There are no defined standards for entry into a public relations career. A college degree combined with public relations experience, usually gained through an internship, is considered excellent preparation for public relations work. People who choose public relations as a career need an outgoing personality, self-confidence, an understanding of human psychology, and an enthusiasm for motivating people. Many public relations specialists advance to become directors of development or fundraisers. Directors of development find the money and other gifts needed to keep the organizations operations thriving. For self-enrichment teachers working in the advocacy, grantmaking, and civic organizations field, a college degree that encompasses education or human resources courses and

Government and Advocacy, Grantmaking, and Civic Organizations

general business courses is good preparation. Opportunities for advancement as a self-enrichment teacher vary from state to state and program to program. They may advance to administrative positions, or experienced self-enrichment teachers may mentor new instructors and volunteers. Educational requirements for teacher assistants vary by state or school district and range from a high school diploma to some college training, although employers increasingly prefer applicants with some college training. Teacher assistants must have good writing skills and be able to communicate effectively with students and teachers. Advancement for teacher assistants—usually in the form of higher earnings or increased responsibility—comes primarily with experience or additional education.

Office and administrative support occupations in the advocacy, grantmaking, and civic organizations field generally require a high school diploma or its equivalent. However, many employers prefer those who have familiarity or experience with computers. Good interpersonal skills are becoming equally important as the diploma to employers. In addition, employers may require previous office or business experience. Those who exhibit strong communication, interpersonal, and analytical skills may be promoted to supervisory positions. Advancement to professional occupations within an organization normally requires additional formal education, such as a college degree. While most workers receive on-the-job training, executive secretaries and administrative assistants acquire skills in various ways. Training ranges from high school vocational education programs that teach office skills and keyboarding to 1-year and 2-year programs in office administration offered by business schools, vocational-technical institutes, and community colleges.

Some service workers in the advocacy, grantmaking, and civic organizations field, such as waiters and waitresses and janitors, don't require any formal education and are trained on the job. Opportunities for advancement for waiters and waitresses are limited, but those workers who excel at their work can become food service managers. Food service managers supervise the work of cooks; they plan meals and oversee food safety. Educational requirements for recreation and fitness workers range from a high school diploma to a graduate degree for some administrative positions in large public recreation systems. Recreation and fitness workers need managerial skills in order to advance to supervisory or managerial positions. College courses in management, business

administration, accounting, and personnel management are helpful for advancement to supervisory or managerial jobs. Most states require that security guards be licensed. Some security guards may advance to supervisor or security manager positions. Guards with management skills may open their own contract security guard agencies.

Table 3. Employment in advocacy, grantmaking, and civic organizations by field segment, 2004 and projected change, 2004–2014 (Employment in thousands)

Field segment	2004 Employment	2004–2014 Percent change
Advocacy, grantmaking, and civic organizations, total	1,231	14.5
Grantmaking and giving services	126	18.5
Social advocacy organizations	178	18.1
Civic and social organizations	410	11.6
Business, professional, labor, political, and similar organizations	517	14.6

Outlook

Job opportunities should be excellent in most employment settings because of high job turnover, primarily because of the industry's relatively low wages, as workers retire or leave the industry for other reasons. Wage and salary jobs in advocacy, grantmaking, and civic organizations are projected to increase 15 percent over the 2004–2014 period, compared to 14 percent growth projected for all fields combined (table 3).

Social and demographic shifts will continue to increase the demand for services offered by advocacy, grantmaking, and civic organizations. For example, rapid growth of the elderly population will increase the demand for home health and nursing home care. Other demographic shifts include the increasing labor force participation of women; a high divorce rate creating more single-parent households; more out-of-wedlock births; growing numbers of immigrants and refugees; and greater ethnic and cultural diversity. These shifts will increase the demand for many services such as child day care, home health and nursing home care, family counseling, foster care, relocation assistance, and substance abuse treatment and prevention.

State and local governments usually are expected to fulfill new and growing social service roles, but increasingly many lack the resources to meet the rising demands. As a result, governments will increasingly turn to advocacy, grantmaking, and civic organizations, utilizing their experience at offering efficient and effective social services. In other cases, governments will form joint ventures or partnerships with these organizations to operate services more effectively. Governments also are expected to contract out some services, which will continue to be a major source of employment growth in the advocacy, grantmaking, and civic organizations industry.

Projected growth for some occupations in advocacy, grantmaking, and civic organizations differs from the 15 percent average growth projected for the industry as a whole (table 2). For example, employment of social and human service assistants is expected to grow faster than the industry because of the increased need for the services that these workers provide to the public. Employment of bookkeeping, accounting, and auditing clerks, on the other hand, is expected to grow more slowly than the industry because of the increasing use of office automation.

Table 4. Average earnings of production or nonsupervisory workers in advocacy, grantmaking, and civic organizations by industry segment, 2004

Industry segment	Weekly	Hourly
Total, private industry	$528.56	$15.67
Nonprofit organizations	441.00	14.78
Business, professional, labor, political, and similar organizations	568.17	17.78
Civic and social organizations	232.97	10.86
Social advocacy organizations	424.91	13.74
Grantmaking and giving services	555.56	18.33

Earnings

Earnings of wage and salary workers in advocacy, grantmaking, and civic organizations averaged $14.78 an hour, compared with $15.67 per hour for all workers in nongovernment fields in 2004 (table 4). The lower earnings reflect the large proportion of entry-level, part-time jobs. Weekly earnings among civic and social organizations were significantly lower than average, $233, compared with $529 for all workers in nongovernment fields in 2004.

Median hourly earnings of the occupations in advocacy, grantmaking, and civic organizations with the highest employment appear in table 5.

Directors and upper-level managers usually receive a salary. Entry-level salaries vary based on education; experience; and the size, budget, and geographic location of the association. The Nonprofit Times Annual Salary Survey reported the following average total compensation in 2004:

Director of International Activities $100,450
Director of Government Relations.....................................98,377
Chief Financial Officer 92,319
Director of Marketing 77,108
Director of Education/Certification 74,355
Director of Publishing 73,138
Director of Membership Development 72,953
Director of Administration...68,047
Director of Meetings/Conventions....................................67,997

About 9 percent of workers in the advocacy, grantmaking, and civic organizations field were union members or were covered by a union contract in 2004, less than the 14 percent rate throughout all fields.

Fringe benefits vary by region, sector, organization budget, geographic scope, number of employees, and type of organization. Most organizations appear to provide long-term disability, extended health care, dental, prescription drug, and life insurance coverage to all employees. Vision care has become a common benefit in the field. Most employers pay all of their employees' insurance benefit premiums, but none of the coverage for their dependents. Only some organizations allow their employees to purchase additional life insurance beyond the basic benefit amount provided, but most hold the line at somewhat less than one year's salary, with one and two years' salary being common as well.

Many advocacy, grantmaking, and civic organizations provide an automobile or car allowance to their senior managers, with most of them paying the entire cost for chief executive officers. Publication subscriptions and professional society and association memberships are generally provided for managers at all levels, and the overwhelming practice is to pay the entire registration fee to attend conferences, as well as associated travel, room, and meal expenses for the chief executive and other administrative and professional employees. Organizations rarely pay for club/social membership dues, first-class air travel, or travel expense for spouses. Most employers allow staff education leave without pay and contribute to tuition expenses for training considered relevant to the employee's job or the organization's current mission. Some workers have access to a sabbatical leave program.

Table 5. Median hourly earnings of the largest occupations in advocacy, grantmaking, and civic organizations, May 2004

Occupation	Grant-making and giving services	Social advocacy organizations	Civic and social organizations	Business, professional, labor, and similar organizations	All fields
General and operations managers	$38.09	$28.46	$28.46	$40.01	$37.22
Business operation specialists, all other	23.81	18.16	16.07	20.83	25.70
Human resources, training, and labor relations specialists, all other	22.57	19.20	15.02	19.50	22.85
Executive secretaries and administrative assistants	17.31	16.07	14.93	17.45	16.81
Fitness trainers and aerobics instructors	13.64	12.15	9.87	12.99	12.25
Secretaries, except legal, medical, and executive	13.30	11.81	10.48	13.19	12.55
Office clerks, general	10.58	10.14	8.73	11.24	10.95
Bartenders	9.87	7.22	7.24	7.10	7.42
Recreation workers	8.42	9.40	8.15	7.98	9.29
Child care workers	8.36	7.95	7.62	7.67	8.06

Sources of Additional Information

For more information about career opportunities in advocacy, grantmaking, and civic organizations, contact

- American Society of Associate Executives, 1575 I St. NW, Washington, DC 20005. Internet: http://www.asaenet.org

- Independent Sector, 1200 18th St. NW, Suite 200, Washington, DC 20036. Internet: http://www.independentsector.org
- The Foundation Center, 79 Fifth Ave., New York, NY 10003. Internet: http://fdncenter.org

Federal Government, Excluding the Postal Service

- Annual Earnings: $54,980
- Job Growth: 2.5%
- Size of Workforce: 1,768,370
- Self-Employed: 0.0%
- Part-Time: 5.5%

Significant Points

- With nearly 2 million civilian employees, the federal government, excluding the Postal Service, is the nation's largest employer.
- About 5 out of 6 federal employees work outside the Washington, DC metropolitan area.
- Job growth generated by increased homeland security needs may be largely offset by projected slow growth or declines in other federal sectors due to budgetary constraints, the growing use of private contractors, and the transfer of some functions to state and local governments.
- Competition is expected for some federal positions, especially during times of economic uncertainty, when workers seek the stability of federal employment.

Nature of the Field

The federal government's essential duties include defending the United States from foreign aggression and terrorism, representing U.S. interests abroad, enforcing laws and regulations, and administering domestic programs and agencies. U.S. citizens are particularly aware of the federal government when they pay their income taxes each year, but they usually do not consider the government's role when they watch a weather forecast, purchase fresh and uncontaminated groceries, travel by highway or air, or make a deposit at their bank. Workers employed by the federal government play a vital role in these and many other aspects of our daily lives.

Over 200 years ago, the founders of the United States gathered in Philadelphia, PA to create a constitution for a new national government and lay the foundation for self-governance. The Constitution of the United States, ratified by the last of the 13 original states in 1791, created the three branches of the federal government and granted certain powers and responsibilities to each. The legislative, judicial, and executive branches were created with equal powers but very different responsibilities that act to keep their powers in balance.

The legislative branch is responsible for forming and amending the legal structure of the nation. Its largest component is Congress, the primary U.S. legislative body, which is made up of the Senate and the House of Representatives. This body includes senators, representatives, their staffs, and various support workers. The legislative branch employs only about 2 percent of federal workers, nearly all of whom work in the Washington, DC area.

The judicial branch is responsible for interpreting the laws that the legislative branch enacts. The Supreme Court, the nation's definitive judicial body, makes the highest rulings. Its decisions usually follow the appeal of a decision made by the one of the regional Courts of Appeal, which hear cases appealed from U.S. District Courts, the Court of Appeals for the Federal Circuit, or State Supreme Courts. U.S. District Courts are located in each state and are the first to hear most cases under federal jurisdiction. The judicial branch employs about the same number of people as does the legislative branch, but its offices and employees are dispersed throughout the country.

Of the three branches, the executive branch—through the power vested by the Constitution in the office of the President—has the widest range of responsibilities. Consequently, it employed 96 percent of all federal civilian employees (excluding Postal Service workers) in 2004. The executive branch is composed of the Executive Office of the President; 15 executive Cabinet departments, including the newly created Department of Homeland Security; and nearly 90 independent agencies, each of which has clearly defined duties. The Executive Office of the President is composed of several offices and councils that aid the President in policy decisions. These include the Office of Management and Budget, which oversees the administration of the federal budget; the National Security Council, which advises the President on matters of national defense; and the Council of Economic Advisers, which makes economic policy recommendations.

Each of the 15 executive Cabinet departments administers programs that oversee an aspect of life in the United States. The highest departmental official of each Cabinet department, the Secretary, is a member of the President's Cabinet. Each, listed by employment size, is described here (table 1).

- *Defense:* Manages the military forces that protect our country and its interests, including the Departments of the Army, Navy, and Air Force and a number of smaller agencies. The civilian workforce employed by the Department of Defense performs various support activities, such as payroll and public relations.

- *Veterans Affairs:* Administers programs to aid U.S. veterans and their families, runs the veterans' hospital system, and operates our national cemeteries.

- *Homeland Security:* Works to prevent terrorist attacks within the United States, reduce vulnerability to terrorism, and minimize the damage from potential attacks and natural disasters. It also administers the country's immigration policies and oversees the Coast Guard.

- *Treasury:* Regulates banks and other financial institutions, administers the public debt, prints currency, and collects federal income taxes.

- *Justice:* Works with state and local governments and other agencies to prevent and control crime and ensure public safety against threats both domestic and foreign. It also enforces federal laws, prosecutes cases in federal courts, and runs federal prisons.

- *Agriculture:* Promotes U.S. agriculture domestically and internationally; researches new ways to grow crops and conserve natural resources; ensures safe meat and poultry products; and leads the federal anti-hunger programs, such as Food Stamps and School Lunch.

Government and Advocacy, Grantmaking, and Civic Organizations

- *Interior:* Manages federal lands, including the national parks and forests; runs hydroelectric power systems; and promotes conservation of natural resources.

- *Health and Human Services:* Performs health and social science research; assures the safety of drugs and foods other than meat and poultry; and administers Medicare, Medicaid, and numerous other social service programs.

- *Transportation:* Sets national transportation policy; plans and funds the construction of highways and mass transit systems; and regulates railroad, aviation, and maritime operations.

- *Commerce:* Forecasts the weather, charts the oceans, regulates patents and trademarks, conducts the census, compiles statistics, and promotes U.S. economic growth by encouraging international trade.

- *State:* Oversees the nation's embassies and consulates, issues passports, monitors U.S. interests abroad, and represents the United States before international organizations.

- *Labor:* Enforces laws guaranteeing fair pay, workplace safety, and equal job opportunity; administers unemployment insurance; regulates pension funds; and collects and analyzes economic data through its Bureau of Labor Statistics.

- *Energy:* Coordinates the national use and provision of energy, oversees the production and disposal of nuclear weapons, and plans for future energy needs.

- *Housing and Urban Development:* Funds public housing projects, enforces equal housing laws, and insures and finances mortgages.

- *Education:* Monitors and distributes financial aid to schools and students, collects and disseminates data on schools and other education matters, and prohibits discrimination in education.

Table 1. Federal government executive branch civilian employment, except U.S. Postal Service, November 2004 (Employment in thousands)

	United States	Washington, DC area
Total	1,767	279
Executive departments	1,582	227
Defense, total	616	64
Army	211	19
Navy	171	24
Air Force	150	6
Other	84	15
Veterans Affairs	234	7
Homeland Security	149	19
Justice	103	23
Agriculture	102	12
Treasury	95	9
Interior	71	8
Health and Human Services	61	28
Transportation	57	9
Commerce	36	20
Labor	16	5
Energy	15	5
State	13	11
Housing and Urban Development	10	3
Education	4	3
Independent agencies	183	50
Social Security Administration	65	2
National Aeronautics and Space Administration	20	4
Environmental Protection Agency	18	7
Tennessee Valley Authority	13	0
General Services Administration	13	5
Federal Deposit Insurance Corporation	5	2
Other	49	30

SOURCE: U.S. Office of Personnel Management

Numerous independent agencies perform tasks that fall between the jurisdictions of the executive departments or that are more efficiently executed by an autonomous agency. Some smaller, but well-known, independent agencies include the Peace Corps, the Securities and Exchange Commission, and the Federal Communications Commission. Although the majority of these agencies are fairly small, employing fewer than 1,000 workers (many employ fewer than 100 workers), some are quite large. The largest independent agencies are:

- *Social Security Administration:* Operates various old age, survivor, and disability insurance programs.

- *National Aeronautics and Space Administration:* Oversees aviation research and conducts exploration and research beyond the Earth's atmosphere.

- *Environmental Protection Agency:* Runs programs to control and reduce pollution of the nation's water, air, and lands.

- *Tennessee Valley Authority:* Operates the hydroelectric power system in the Tennessee River Valley.

- *General Services Administration:* Manages and protects federal government property and records.

- *Federal Deposit Insurance Corporation:* Maintains stability of and public confidence in the nation's financial system by insuring deposits and promoting sound banking practices.

Working Conditions

Due to the wide range of federal jobs, working conditions are equally variable. While most federal employees work in office buildings, hospitals, or laboratories, a large number also can be found at border crossings, airports, shipyards, military bases, construction sites, and national parks. Work environments vary from comfortable and relaxed to hazardous and stressful, such as those experienced by law enforcement officers, astronauts, and air traffic controllers.

The vast majority of federal employees work full time, often on flexible or "flexi-time" schedules that allow workers more control over their work schedules. Some agencies also offer telecommuting or "flexi-place" programs, which allow selected workers to perform some job duties at home or from regional centers.

Some federal workers spend much of their time away from the offices in which they are based. Inspectors or

compliance officers, for example, often visit businesses and worksites to ensure that laws and regulations are obeyed. Some federal workers frequently travel long distances, spending days or weeks away from home. Auditors, for example, may spend weeks at a time in distant locations.

Important Characteristics of the Field

Skills: Writing; Speaking; Science; Systems Evaluation; Systems Analysis; Judgment and Decision Making. **Abilities:** Written Expression; Problem Sensitivity; Inductive Reasoning; Oral Expression; Written Comprehension; Deductive Reasoning. **Work-Related Values:** Authority; Social Service; Co-workers; Responsibility; Social Status; Autonomy.

Employment

In 2004, the federal government, excluding the Postal Service, employed about 1.9 million civilian workers, or about 1.3 percent of the nation's workforce. The federal government is the nation's single largest employer. Because data on employment in certain agencies can not be released to the public for national security reasons, this total does not include employment for the Central Intelligence Agency, National Security Agency, Defense Intelligence Agency, and National Imagery and Mapping Agency.

The federal government makes an effort to have a workforce as diverse as the nation's civilian labor force. The federal government serves as a model for all employers in abiding by equal employment opportunity legislation, which protects current and potential employees from discrimination based on race, color, religion, sex, national origin, disability, or age. The federal government also makes an effort to recruit and accommodate persons with disabilities.

Even though the headquarters of most federal departments and agencies are based in the Washington, DC area, only 1 out of 6 federal employees worked in the vicinity of the nation's capital in 2004. In addition to federal employees working throughout the United States, another 93,000, which includes foreign nationals, are assigned overseas, mostly in embassies or defense installations.

Occupations in the Field

Although the federal government employs workers in every major occupational group, workers are not employed in the same proportions in which they are employed throughout the economy as a whole (table 2). The analytical and technical nature of many government duties translates into a much higher proportion of professional, management, business, and financial occupations in the federal government, compared with most fields. Conversely, the government sells very little, so it employs relatively few sales workers.

Table 2. Percent distribution of wage and salary employment in the federal government and for all fields by major occupational group, 2004

Occupational group	Federal government	All fields
Total	100.0	100.0
Professional and related	32.8	19.9
Management, business, and financial	27.4	9.0
Office and administrative support	16.7	17.6
Service	10.6	19.3
Installation, maintenance, and repair	4.8	4.0
Transportation and material moving	3.1	7.2
Production	2.1	7.6
Construction and extraction	1.9	4.7
Sales and related	0.4	10.1
Farming, fishing, and forestry	0.2	0.7

Professional and related occupations accounted for about one third of federal employment in 2004 (table 3). The largest group of professional workers worked in life, physical, and social science occupations, such as *biological scientists, conservation scientists and foresters, environmental scientists and geoscientists,* and *forest and conservation technicians.* They do work such as determining the effects of drugs on living organisms, preventing fires in the national forests, and predicting earthquakes and hurricanes.

Many health professionals, such as *licensed practical and licensed vocational nurses, registered nurses,* and *physicians and surgeons,* were employed by the Department of Veterans Affairs (VA) in VA hospitals.

Large numbers of federal workers also held jobs as *engineers,* including *aerospace, civil, computer hardware, electrical and electronics, environmental, industrial, mechanical,* and *nuclear engineers.* Engineers were found in many departments of the executive branch, but the vast majority worked in the Department of Defense. Some worked in the National Aeronautics and Space Administration as well as other agencies. In general, they solve problems and provide advice on technical programs such as building highway bridges or implementing agency-wide computer systems.

The federal government hires many *lawyers, judges,* and related workers, as well as *law clerks,* to write, administer, and enforce many of the country's laws and regulations.

Computer specialists—primarily *computer software engineers, computer systems analysts,* and *network and computer systems administrators*—are employed throughout the federal government. They write computer programs, analyze problems related to data processing, and keep computer systems running smoothly.

Management, business, and financial workers made up about 27 percent of federal employment and were primarily responsible for overseeing operations. Managerial workers include a broad range of officials who, at the highest levels, may head federal agencies or programs. Middle managers, on the other hand, usually oversee one activity or aspect of a program. One management occupation—*legislators*—is responsible for passing and amending laws and overseeing the executive branch of the government. Within the federal government, legislators are entirely found in Congress.

Other occupations in this category are *accountants and auditors,* who prepare and analyze financial reports, review and record revenues and expenditures, and investigate operations for fraud and inefficiency. *Management analysts* study government operations and systems and suggest improvements. *Purchasing agents* handle federal purchases of supplies, and *tax examiners, collectors, and revenue agents* determine and collect taxes.

About 17 percent of federal workers were in office and administrative support occupations. These employees aid management staff with administrative duties. Administrative support workers in the federal government include *information and record clerks, general office clerks,* and *secretaries and administrative assistants.*

Compared with the economy as a whole, workers in service occupations were relatively scarce in the federal government. About 7 out of 10 federal workers in service occupations were protective service workers, such as *correctional officers and jailers, detectives and criminal investigators,* and *police officers.* These workers protect the public from crime and oversee federal prisons.

Federally employed workers in installation, maintenance, and repair occupations include *aircraft mechanics and service technicians,* who fix and maintain all types of aircraft, and *electrical and electronic equipment mechanics, installers, and repairers,* who inspect, adjust, and repair electronic equipment such as industrial controls; transmitters; antennas; and radar, radio, and navigation systems.

The federal government employed a relatively small number of workers in transportation; production; construction; sales and related; and farming, fishing, and forestry occupations. However, they employ almost all the *air traffic controllers* in the country and a significant number of *agricultural inspectors* and *bridge and lock tenders.*

Table 3. Employment of wage and salary workers in the federal government, excluding the Postal Service, by occupation, 2004 and projected change, 2004–2014 (Employment in thousands)

Occupation	Employment, 2004		Percent change, 2004–2014
	Number	Percent	
Total, all occupations	1,943	100.0	2.5
Management, business, and financial occupations	533	27.4	5.5
Natural sciences managers	14	0.7	4.0
Purchasing agents, except wholesale, retail, and farm products	29	1.5	4.0
Compliance officers, except agriculture, construction, health and safety, and transportation	47	2.4	4.0
Management analysts	46	2.4	4.0
Accountants and auditors	33	1.7	–16.8
Tax examiners, collectors, and revenue agents	38	2.0	2.3

Occupation	Employment, 2004		Percent change, 2004–2014
	Number	Percent	
Professional and related occupations	636	32.7	6.8
Computer specialists	68	3.5	13.8
Engineers	90	4.6	8.4
Biological scientists	24	1.2	9.4
Physical scientists	31	1.6	3.5
Forest and conservation technicians	25	1.3	4.0
Lawyers	26	1.4	4.0
Physicians and surgeons	21	1.1	8.2
Registered nurses	52	2.7	14.4
Service occupations	207	10.6	8.8
Correctional officers and jailers	15	0.8	14.4
Detectives and criminal investigators	24	1.2	24.8
Police officers	21	1.1	24.6
Office and administrative support occupations	325	16.7	–14.2
Information and record clerks	163	8.4	–14.6
Secretaries and administrative assistants	38	2.0	–17.6
Construction and extraction occupations	36	1.8	3.9
Installation, maintenance, and repair occupations	94	4.8	1.0
Aircraft mechanics and service technicians	17	0.9	–7.3
Electrical and electronic equipment mechanics, installers, and repairers	16	0.8	–1.2
Production occupations	40	2.1	–2.2
Inspectors, testers, sorters, samplers, and weighers	13	0.7	–6.4
Transportation and material moving occupations	60	3.1	4.7
Air traffic controllers	22	1.1	14.4
Transportation inspectors	5	0.2	4.0

Government and Advocacy, Grantmaking, and Civic Organizations

Training, Other Qualifications, and Advancement

In all but a few cases, applicants for federal jobs must be U.S. citizens. Applicants that are veterans of military service may also be able to claim veteran's preference, which gives them preferred status over other candidates with equal qualifications. For an increasing number of jobs requiring access to sensitive or classified materials, applicants must undergo a background investigation in order to obtain a security clearance. This investigation covers an individual's criminal, credit, and employment history, as well as other records. The scope of the investigation will vary, depending on the nature of the position in the government and the degree of harm that an individual in that position could cause. Generally, the higher the level of clearance needed, the greater the scope of investigation.

The educational and training requirements for jobs in the federal government mirror those in the private sector for most major occupational groups. Many jobs in managerial or professional and related occupations, for example, require a 4-year college degree. Some, such as engineers, physicians and surgeons, and biological and physical scientists, require a bachelor's or higher degree in a specific field of study. However, registered nurse and many technician occupations may be entered with 2 years of training after high school. Office and administrative support workers in the government usually need only a high school diploma, although any further training or experience, such as a junior college degree or a couple of years of relevant work experience, is an asset. Most federal jobs in other occupations require no more than a high school degree, although most departments and agencies prefer workers with vocational training or previous experience.

Once employed, each federal department or agency determines its own training requirements and offers workers opportunities to improve job skills or become qualified to advance to other jobs. These may include technical or skills training; tuition assistance or reimbursement; fellowship programs; and executive leadership and management training programs, seminars, and workshops. This training may be offered on the job, by another agency, or at local colleges and universities.

Advancement for most workers in the federal government is currently based on a system of occupational pay levels, or "grades," although more departments and agen-

cies are being granted waivers to experiment with different pay and promotion strategies. Workers typically enter the federal civil service at the starting grade for an occupation and begin a "career ladder" of promotions until they reach the full-performance grade for that occupation. This system provides for a limited number of noncompetitive promotions, which usually are awarded at regular intervals, assuming job performance is satisfactory. The exact pay grades associated with a job's career track depend upon the occupation.

Typically, workers without a high school diploma who are hired as clerks start at grade 1, and high school graduates with no additional training hired at the same job start at grade 2 or 3. Entrants with some technical training or experience who are hired as technicians may start at grade 4. Those with a bachelor's degree generally are hired in professional occupations, such as economist, with a career ladder that starts at grade 5 or 7, depending on academic achievement. Entrants with a master's degree or Ph.D. may start at grade 9. Individuals with professional degrees may be hired at the grade 11 or 12 level. Those with a combination of education and substantive experience may be hired at higher grades than those with education alone.

Once nonsupervisory federal workers reach the full-performance level of the career track, they usually receive periodic step increases within their grade if they are performing their job satisfactorily. They must compete for subsequent promotions, and advancement becomes more difficult. At this point, promotions occur as vacancies arise, and they are based solely on merit and in competition with other qualified candidates. In addition to within-grade longevity increases, federal workers are awarded bonuses for excellent job performance.

Workers who advance to managerial or supervisory positions may receive within-grade longevity increases, bonuses, and promotions to higher grades. The top managers in the federal civil service belong to the Senior Executive Service (SES), the highest positions that federal workers can reach without being specifically nominated by the President and confirmed by the U.S. Senate. Relatively few workers attain SES positions, and competition is intense. Bonus provisions for SES positions are even more performance-based than are those for lower-level positions. Because it is the headquarters for most federal agencies, the Washington, DC metropolitan area offers the best opportunities to advance to upper-level managerial and supervisory jobs.

Outlook

Wage and salary employment in the federal government is projected to grow by 2.5 percent through the year 2014, compared to 14 percent growth projected for salaried employment in all fields combined. Job growth generated by increased homeland security needs may be largely offset by projected slow growth or declines in other federal sectors due to governmental cost-cutting, the growing use of private contractors, and continuing devolution—the practice of turning over the development, implementation, and management of some programs of the federal government to state and local governments.

Staffing levels in government, while relatively stable in the short run, can be subject to change in the long run due mainly to changes in public policies as legislated by Congress, which affect spending levels and hiring decisions for the various government departments and agencies. In general, over the coming decade, domestic programs are likely to see cuts in their budgets as Congress seeks to reduce the federal budget deficit, but the cuts will likely affect some agencies more than others. Any employment declines, however, generally will be carried out through attrition—simply not replacing workers who retire or leave the federal government for other reasons. Layoffs, called "reductions in force," have occurred in the past, but they are uncommon and usually affect relatively few workers. In spite of this, there still will be numerous employment opportunities in many agencies due to the need to replace workers who leave the workforce, retire, or accept employment elsewhere.

While there will be job openings in all types of jobs over the coming decade, demand will continue to grow for specialized workers in areas related to border and transportation security, emergency preparedness, public health, and information analysis.

A study by the Partnership for Public Service, which surveyed federal department and agency hiring needs for the 2005–2006 period, found that most of the new hires in the federal government will come in 5 major areas. They are security, enforcement, and compliance, which includes inspectors, investigators, police officers, airport screeners, and prison guards; medical and public health fields; engineering and the sciences, including microbiologists, botanists, physicists, chemists, and veterinarians; program management and administration; and accounting, budget, and business, which includes revenue agents and tax examiners needed mainly by the Internal Revenue Service. The Department of Health and Human Services will need health insurance specialists and claims and customer service representatives to implement the Medicare Prescription Drug benefit. Patent examiners, foreign service officers, and lawyers also are in high demand.

The distribution of federal employment will continue to shift toward a higher proportion of professional, business and financial operations, and protective service workers. Employment declines will be the greatest among office and administrative support occupations and production occupations due to increasing office automation and contracting out of these jobs.

Competition is expected for some federal positions, especially during times of economic uncertainty, when workers seek the stability of federal employment. In general, federal employment is considered to be relatively stable because it is not affected by cyclical fluctuations in the economy, as are employment levels in many private-sector fields.

Earnings

In an effort to give agencies more flexibility in how they pay their workers, there are now several different pay systems in effect or planning to be implemented over the next few years within the federal government. The two largest departments that are experimenting with new pay systems are the Departments of Defense and Homeland Security. The new systems incorporate fewer, but wider, pay "bands," instead of grade levels. Pay increases, under these new systems, are almost entirely based on performance, as opposed to length of service.

Table 4. Federal Government General Schedule pay rates, 2005

GS level	Entrance level	Step increase	Maximum level
1	$16,016	varies	$20,036
2	18,007	varies	22,660
3	19,647	$655	25,542
4	22,056	735	28,671
5	24,677	823	32,084
6	27,507	917	35,760
7	30,567	1,019	39,738

Government and Advocacy, Grantmaking, and Civic Organizations

GS level	Entrance level	Step increase	Maximum level
8	33,852	1,128	44,004
9	37,390	1,246	48,604
10	41,175	1,373	53,532
11	45,239	1,508	58,811
12	54,221	1,807	70,484
13	64,478	2,149	83,819
14	76,193	2,540	99,053
15	89,625	2,988	116,517

SOURCE: U.S. Office of Personnel Management

It is the case, however, that the majority of professional and administrative federal workers are still paid under the General Schedule (GS). The General Schedule, shown in table 4, has 15 grades of pay for civilian white-collar and service workers and smaller within-grade step increases that occur based on length of service and quality of performance. New employees usually start at the first step of a grade; however, if the position in question is difficult to fill, entrants may receive somewhat higher pay or special rates. Almost all physician and engineer positions, for example, fall into this category. In an effort to make federal pay more responsive to local labor market conditions, federal employees working in the continental U.S. receive locality pay. The specific amount of locality pay is determined by survey comparisons of private sector wage rates and federal wage rates in the relevant geographic area. At its highest level, locality pay can lead to an increase of as much as 26 percent above the base salary. Every January, a pay adjustment tied to changes in private-sector pay levels is divided between an across-the-board pay increase in the General Schedule and locality pay increases.

In March 2005, the average earnings for full-time workers paid under the General Schedule were $61,735. General attorneys, who earned $105,557 on average, was one of the higher paid occupations, while average earnings for nursing assistants was only about half the average for all occupations (table 5).

Table 5. Average annual salaries for full-time workers under the General Schedule in the federal government in selected occupations, 2005

Occupation	Salary
All occupations	$61,735
General attorney	105,577
General engineering	95,456
Financial management	95,257
Economist	89,441
Computer science	86,443
Chemistry	83,777
Statistician	81,262
Microbiology	80,798
Architecture	80,777
Criminal investigating	79,100
Information technology management	77,003
Accounting	74,907
Chaplain	74,730
Librarian	74,630
Mine safety and health	72,601
Ecology	72,021
Human resources management	71,232
Air traffic control	70,555
Budget analysis	67,767
Nurse	60,935
Engineering technician	60,543
Border patrol agent	56,297
Customs and border protection	53,533
Correctional officer	47,400
Legal assistance	42,279
Fire protection and prevention	41,061
Secretary	39,938
Police officer	39,579
Tax examining	36,963
Human resources assistance	36,576
Medical technician	35,526
Nursing assistant	31,460

SOURCE: U.S. Office of Personnel Management

The Federal Wage System (FWS) is used to pay workers in craft, repair, operator, and laborer jobs. This schedule sets federal wages so that they are comparable with prevailing regional wage rates for similar types of jobs. As a result, wage rates paid under the FWS can vary significantly from one locality to another.

In addition to base pay and bonuses, federal employees may receive incentive awards. These one-time awards, ranging from $25 to $10,000, are bestowed for a significant suggestion, a special act or service, or sustained high job performance. Some workers also may receive "premium" pay, which is granted when the employee must work overtime, on holidays, on weekends, at night, or under hazardous conditions.

Benefits are an important part of federal employee compensation. Federal employees may choose from a number of health plans and life insurance options; premium payments for these policies are partially offset by the government. In addition, workers hired after January 1, 1984, participate in the Federal Employees Retirement System (FERS), a three-tiered retirement plan including Social Security, a pension plan, and an optional Thrift Savings Plan. Worker participation in the Thrift Savings Plan is voluntary, but any contributions made are tax-deferred and, up to a point, matched by the federal government. In addition to other benefits, some federal agencies provide public transit subsidies in an effort to encourage employee use of public transportation.

Sources of Additional Information

Information on obtaining a position with the federal government is available from the Office of Personnel Management (OPM) through USAJOBS, the federal government's official employment information system. This resource for locating and applying for job opportunities can be accessed through the Internet at http://www.usajobs.opm.gov or through an interactive voice response telephone system at (703) 724-1850 or TDD (978) 461-8404. These numbers are not toll free, and charges may result.

For advice on finding a job with the federal government and more information on the federal hiring process and employment system, contact

- Partnership for Public Service, 1725 Eye St. NW, Suite 900, Washington, DC 20006. Internet: http://www.calltoserve.org

State and Local Government, Excluding Education and Hospitals

- Annual Earnings: $35,598
- Job Growth: 11.4%
- Size of Workforce: 7,619,390
- Self-Employed: 0.0%
- Part-Time: 5.5%

Significant Points

- Local government employs more than twice as many workers as state government; fire fighters and law enforcement workers, concentrated in local government, are the largest occupations.

- Employment growth will be dampened by budgetary constraints due to the rapidly increasing proportion of revenues devoted to the Medicaid program; reductions in federal aid, especially at the county level; public resistance to tax increases; and outsourcing of government jobs to the private sector.

- Employer-provided benefits are more common among state and local government employees than among workers in the private sector.

Nature of the Field

State and local governments provide their constituents with vital services, such as transportation, public safety, health care, education, utilities, and courts. Excluding education and hospitals, state and local governments employ about 7.9 million workers, placing them among the largest employers in the economy. Seven out of 10 of these employees work for local governments, such as counties, cities, special districts, and towns. In addition to these 7.9 million workers, large numbers of state and local workers work in public education. These workers form a large part of the Educational Services field, which is discussed elsewhere in Part II. Many state and local workers also work in public hospitals, which are included in the Health Care field elsewhere in Part II.

Government and Advocacy, Grantmaking, and Civic Organizations

In addition to the 50 state governments, there are about 87,500 local governments in 2002, according to the U.S. Census Bureau. These include about 3,000 county governments; 19,400 municipal governments; 16,500 townships; 13,500 school districts; and 35,100 special districts. Illinois had the most local government units, with more than 6,900; Hawaii had the fewest, with 20.

In many areas of the country, citizens are served by more than one local government unit. For example, most states have *counties*, which may contain various municipalities such as cites or towns, but which also often include unincorporated rural areas. *Townships*, which do not exist in some states, may or may not contain municipalities and often consist of suburban or rural areas. Supplementing these forms of local government, *special district* government bodies are independent, limited-purpose governmental units that usually perform a single function or activity. For example, a large percentage of special districts manage the use of natural resources. Some provide drainage and flood control, irrigation, and soil and water conservation services.

The Council of State Governments reports that state and local governments' responsibilities were augmented in the 1990s through "devolution," the practice through which the federal government turns over to state and local governments the development, implementation, and management of programs. Welfare reform typifies devolution in practice, with states receiving considerable leeway to devise programs that meet their needs as a result of the 1996 Congressional reform act that provided block grants to states. As the relationship between levels of government continues to change in the coming decade, so will the nature of services provided by state and local governments.

Working Conditions

Working conditions vary by occupation and, in some instances, by size and location of the state or local government. For example, chief executives in very small jurisdictions may work less than 20 hours a week; in larger jurisdictions, they often work more than 40 hours per week. Chief executives in large jurisdictions work full time year round, as do most county and city managers. Most state legislators work full time only when in session, usually for a few months a year, and work part time the rest of the year. Local elected officials in some small jurisdictions work part time.

Most professional, financial operations, and office and administrative support workers in state and local government work a standard 40-hour week in an office environment. However, workers in some of the most visible local government jobs have very different working conditions and schedules. Fire fighters' hours are longer and vary more widely than those of most workers. Many professional fire fighters are on duty for several days in a row, working over 50 hours a week, because some must be on duty at all times to respond to emergencies. They often eat and sleep at the fire station. Following this long shift, they are then off for several days in a row or for the entire next week. In addition to irregular hours, firefighting can involve the risk of death or injury. Some local fire districts also use the services of volunteer fire fighters, who tend to work shorter, regularly scheduled shifts.

Law enforcement work also is potentially dangerous. The injury and fatality rates among law officers are higher than in many occupations, reflecting risks taken in apprehending suspected criminals and responding to various emergency situations such as traffic accidents. Most police and detectives work 40 hours a week, with paid overtime when they testify in court or work on an investigation. Because police protection must be provided around the clock, some officers work weekends, holidays, and nights. Many officers are subject to call any time their services are needed and are expected to intervene whenever they observe a crime, even if they are off duty.

Most driver/operator jobs in public transit systems are stressful and fatiguing because they involve dealing with passengers, tight schedules, and heavy traffic. Bus drivers with regular routes and subway operators generally have consistent weekly work schedules. Those who do not have regular schedules may be on call and must be prepared to report for work on short notice. To accommodate commuters, many operators work split shifts, such as 6 a.m. to 10 a.m. and 3 p.m. to 7 p.m., with time off in between.

A number of other state and local government jobs also require weekend or night work. Because electricity, gas, and water are used continuously throughout each day, split, weekend, and night shifts are common for utility workers.

Important Characteristics of the Field

Skills: Social Perceptiveness; Service Orientation; Active Listening; Persuasion; Coordination; Judgment and Decision Making. **Abilities:** Night Vision; Glare Sensitivity; Response Orientation; Rate Control; Peripheral Vision; Spatial Orientation. **Work-Related Values:** Social Service; Co-workers; Security; Supervision, Human Relations; Social Status; Achievement.

Employment

State and local governments, excluding education and hospitals, employed about 7.9 million people in 2004. Seven out of 10 of these workers were employed in local government (table 1).

Table 1. Wage and salary employment in state and local government, except education and health, 2004 (Employment in thousands)

Jurisdiction	Employment	Percent
State and local	7,872	100.0
Local	5,486	69.7
State	2,386	30.3

Occupations in the Field

Service occupations made up the largest share of employment in state and local governments, accounting for 31 percent of all jobs (table 2). Of these, *police and sheriff's patrol officers, bailiffs, correctional officers and jailers*, and *fire fighters*, concentrated in local government, were the largest occupations (chart 1). Professional and related occupations accounted for 21 percent of employment; office and administrative support occupations accounted for 21 percent; and management, business, and financial occupations constituted 11 percent.

State and local governments employ people in occupations found in nearly every field in the economy, including chief executives, managers, engineers, computer specialists, secretaries, and health technicians. Certain occupations, however, are mainly or exclusively found in these governments, such as *legislators; tax examiners, collectors, and revenue agents; urban and regional planners;*

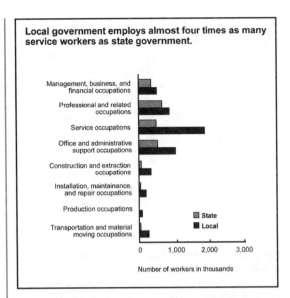

Local government employs almost four times as many service workers as state government.

judges, magistrates, and other judicial workers; police and sheriff's patrol officers; and *correctional officers and jailers.*

Chief executives, general and operations managers, and *legislators* establish government policy and develop laws, rules, and regulations. They are elected or appointed officials who either preside over units of government or make laws. Chief executives include governors, lieutenant governors, mayors, and city managers. General and operations managers include district managers and revenue directors. Legislators include state senators and representatives, county commissioners, and city council members.

Tax examiners, collectors, and revenue agents determine tax liability and collect past-due taxes from individuals or businesses. *Urban and regional planners* draft plans and recommend programs for the development and use of resources such as land and water. They also propose construction of physical facilities, such as schools and roads, under the authority of cities, counties, and metropolitan areas. Planners devise strategies outlining the best use of community land and identify the places in which residential, commercial, recreational, and other types of development should be located.

Judges arbitrate, advise, and administer justice in a court of law. They oversee legal processes in courts and apply the law to resolve civil disputes and determine guilt in criminal cases. *Magistrates* resolve criminal cases not involving penitentiary sentences, as well as civil cases involving damages below a sum specified by state law.

Government and Advocacy, Grantmaking, and Civic Organizations

Social workers counsel and assess the needs of clients, refer them to the appropriate sources of help, and monitor their progress. *Eligibility interviewers, government programs* interview and investigate applicants and recipients to determine eligibility to receive, or continue receiving, welfare and other types of social assistance. *Social and human service assistants'* duties vary with specific job titles. These workers include social service technicians, case management aides, social work assistants, residential counselors, alcoholism or drug abuse counseling aides, child abuse workers, community outreach workers, and gerontology aides. *Probation officers and correctional treatment specialists* assist in rehabilitation of law offenders in custody or on probation or parole.

Court, municipal, and license clerks perform a variety of state and local government administrative tasks. *Court clerks* prepare dockets of cases to be called; secure information for judges; and contact witnesses, lawyers, and attorneys to obtain information for the court. *Municipal clerks* draft agendas for town or city councils, record minutes of council meetings, answer official correspondence, keep fiscal records and accounts, and prepare reports on civic needs. *License clerks* keep records and help the public obtain motor vehicle ownership titles, operator permits, and a variety of other permits and licenses. State and local governments also employ many *secretaries and administrative assistants* and *general office clerks*.

Fire fighters control and extinguish fires, assist with emergency medical treatment, and help with the recovery from natural disasters such as earthquakes and tornadoes. *Fire inspectors* inspect public buildings for conditions that might present a fire hazard. *Emergency medical technicians and paramedics* assess injuries, administer emergency medical care, and extricate trapped individuals. They transport injured or sick persons to medical facilities.

Police and sheriff's patrol officers and *detectives and criminal investigators* have duties that range from controlling traffic to preventing and investigating crimes. They maintain order; enforce laws and ordinances; issue traffic summonses; investigate accidents; give evidence in court; serve legal documents for the court system; and apprehend, arrest, and process prisoners. *State and local correctional officers* guard inmates in jails, prisons, or juvenile detention institutions. *Bailiffs* keep order in courts.

Highway maintenance workers maintain highways, municipal and rural roads, airport runways, and rights-

of-way. They patch broken or eroded pavement, repair guardrails and highway markers, plow snow, and mow or clear brush from along roads. *Bus drivers* pick up and deliver passengers at prearranged stops throughout their assigned routes. Operators may collect fares, answer questions about schedules and transfer points, and announce stops.

Table 2. Employment of wage and salary workers in state and local government, excluding education and hospitals, by occupation, 2004 and projected change, 2004–2014 (Employment in thousands)

Occupation	Employment, 2004		Percent change, 2004–2014
	Number	Percent	
Total, all occupations	7,872	100.0	11.4
Management, business, and financial occupations	870	11.1	11.8
Top executives	162	2.1	8.1
Legislators	65	0.8	2.0
Accountants and auditors	75	1.0	–7.5
Tax examiners, collectors, and revenue agents	38	0.5	8.0
Professional and related occupations	1,625	20.6	15.1
Computer specialists	132	1.7	21.8
Engineers	90	1.1	16.4
Social workers	176	2.2	12.4
Probation officers and correctional treatment specialists	90	1.1	12.0
Social and human service assistants	98	1.3	6.0
Lawyers	84	1.1	35.1
Registered nurses	90	1.1	17.0
Emergency medical technicians and paramedics	61	0.8	25.5
Service occupations	2,466	31.3	14.3
Nursing, psychiatric, and home health aides	108	1.4	13.4
First-line supervisors/ managers of police and detectives	90	1.1	16.4
Fire fighters	265	3.4	25.4
Correctional officers and jailers	398	5.1	4.8

Occupation	Employment, 2004 Number	Percent	Percent change, 2004–2014
Police and sheriff's patrol officers	602	7.6	15.0
Janitors and cleaners, except maids and house-eeping cleaners	102	1.3	20.6
Landscaping and grounds-keeping workers	90	1.1	11.1
Recreation workers	106	1.4	12.7
Office and administrative support occupations	1,619	20.6	1.2
First-line supervisors/ managers of office and administrative support workers	116	1.5	5.3
Bookkeeping, accounting, and auditing clerks	103	1.3	1.8
Court, municipal, and license clerks	104	1.3	18.9
Eligibility interviewers, government programs	91	1.2	–10.3
Police, fire, and ambulance dispatchers	84	1.1	15.0
Secretaries and administrative assistants	322	4.1	0.6
Office clerks, general	338	4.3	0.3
Construction and extraction occupations	449	5.7	16.6
Construction equipment operators	89	1.1	15.1
Highway maintenance workers	134	1.7	23.2
Installation, maintenance, and repair occupations	281	3.6	13.5
Maintenance and repair workers, general	112	1.4	13.5
Production occupations	131	1.7	11.8
Water and liquid waste treatment plant and system operators	74	0.9	14.3
Transportation and material moving occupations	348	4.4	11.9
Bus drivers, transit and intercity	103	1.3	14.2

Note: May not add to totals due to omission of occupations with small employment

Training, Other Qualifications, and Advancement

The education level and experience needed by workers in state and local government varies by occupation. Voters elect most chief executives and legislators, so local support is very important. Taking part in volunteer work and helping to provide community services are valuable ways in which to establish vital community support. Those elected to chief executive and legislator positions come from a variety of backgrounds, but must conform to age, residency, and citizenship regulations regarding the positions that they seek. Advancement opportunities for most elected public officials are limited to other offices in the jurisdictions in which they live. For example, a local council member may run for mayor or for a position in state government, and state legislators may decide to run for state governor or for the U.S. Congress.

A master's degree in public administration is widely recommended, but not required, for city managers. They may gain experience as management analysts or assistants in government departments, working with councils and mayors. After several years, they may be hired to manage a town or a small city and eventually become manager of larger cities.

For most professional jobs, a college degree is required. To obtain an entry-level urban or regional planning position, most state and local government agencies require 2 years of graduate study in urban and regional planning or the equivalent in work experience. To become a judge, particularly a state trial or appellate court judge, one usually is required to be a lawyer. About half of all state judges are appointed, and the other half are elected in partisan or nonpartisan elections. Most state and local judges serve fixed terms, ranging from 4 or 6 years for limited jurisdiction judges to 14 years for some appellate court judges.

Most applicants for firefighting jobs must have a high school education or its equivalent and pass a civil service examination. In addition, they need to pass a medical examination and tests of strength, physical stamina, coordination, and agility. Experience as a volunteer fire fighter or as a fire fighter in the Armed Forces is helpful, as is completion of community college courses in fire science. Recruits study firefighting techniques, fire prevention, local building codes, emergency procedures, and the proper use of rescue equipment. Fire fighters may be

Government and Advocacy, Grantmaking, and Civic Organizations

promoted depending on written examination results and job performance.

Bus drivers must comply with federal regulations that require drivers who operate vehicles designed to transport 16 or more passengers to obtain a commercial driver's license from the state in which they live. To qualify for a commercial driver's license, applicants must pass a written test on rules and regulations and demonstrate that they can operate a commercial vehicle safely. For subway and streetcar operator jobs, applicants with at least a high school education have the best chance. In some cities, prospective subway operators are required to work as bus drivers for a specified period. Successful applicants generally are in good health; possess good communication skills; and are able to make quick, sound judgments. Because bus drivers and subway operators deal with passengers, they need an even temperament and emotional stability. Driving in heavy, fast-moving, or stop-and-go traffic and dealing with passengers can be stressful.

Police departments in most areas require applicants to be U.S. citizens of good character, at least 20 years old, and able to meet rigorous physical and mental standards. Police departments increasingly encourage applicants to take college courses, and some require a college degree. Many community and junior colleges, as well as colleges and universities, offer programs in law enforcement or criminal justice. Officers usually attend a local or regional police academy that includes classroom instruction in constitutional law, civil rights, and state and local law. They also receive training in patrol, accident investigation, traffic control, using firearms, self-defense, first aid, and emergency management. Promotions for police officers are highly influenced by scores on a written civil service examination and subsequent performance evaluations by their superiors.

Outlook

Wage and salary employment in state and local government is projected to increase 11 percent during the 2004–2014 period, slower than the 14-percent growth projected for all sectors of the economy combined. Job growth will stem from the rising demand for services at the state and local levels. An increasing population and state and local government assumption of responsibility for some services previously provided by the federal government are fueling the growth of these services. Despite the increased demand for the services of state and local governments, employment growth will be dampened by budgetary constraints due to the rapidly increasing proportion of revenues devoted to the Medicaid program; reductions in federal aid, especially at the county level; and public resistance to tax increases. Outsourcing of government jobs to the private sector will also limit employment in state and local government. When economic times are good, many state and local governments increase spending on programs and employment.

Professional and service occupations accounted for over half of all jobs in state and local government. Most new jobs will stem from steady demand for community and social services, health services, and protective services. For example, increased demand for services for the elderly, the mentally impaired, and children will result in steady growth in the numbers of social workers, registered nurses, and recreation workers. There will also be strong demand for information technology workers.

Employment of management, business, and financial occupations is projected to grow at about the same rate as overall employment in state and local government. Employment in office and administrative support occupations in state and local government is expected to remain close to current levels as these functions are increasingly outsourced to the private sector.

Earnings

Earnings vary by occupation, size of the state or locality, and region of the country. As in most fields, professionals and managers earn more than other workers. Earnings in the occupations having the largest employment in state and local government appear in table 3.

Table 3. Median hourly earnings of the largest occupations in state and local government, except education and health, May 2004

Occupation	State government	Local government	All fields
Police and sheriff's patrol officers	$23.55	$21.64	$21.74
First-line supervisors/ managers of office and administrative support workers	19.68	20.24	19.72

Occupation	State government	Local government	All fields
Child, family, and school social workers	16.86	19.53	16.74
Correctional officers and jailers	16.22	15.90	16.15
Fire fighters	14.94	18.78	18.43
Highway maintenance workers	14.81	14.10	14.21
Executive secretaries and administrative assistants	14.78	17.76	16.81
Secretaries, except legal, medical, and executive	14.17	13.78	12.55
Maintenance and repair workers, general	13.80	15.70	14.77
Office clerks, general	12.00	12.44	10.95

Occupation	Salary
Engineer	75,556
Chief financial officer	74,867
Economic development director	70,668
Public works director	70,135
Fire chief	70,000
Human resources director	70,000
Chief law enforcement official	69,837
Human services director	64,832
Parks and recreation director	62,988
Health officer	61,536
Purchasing director	59,013
Chief librarian	56,270
Treasurer	52,053
Clerk	46,779
Chief elected officials	7,740

The International City/County Management Association (ICMA) reported the 2004 median annual salaries of selected executive and managerial occupations in local government, shown in table 4.

Employer-provided benefits—including health and life insurance and retirement benefits—are more common among state and local government employees than among workers in the private sector.

Table 4. Median annual salary for selected executive and managerial occupations in local government, 2004

Occupation	Salary
City manager	$88,695
Assistant chief administrative officer	80,232
Information services director	75,582

Sources of Additional Information

Individuals interested in working for state or local government agencies should contact the appropriate agencies. City, county, and state personnel and human resources departments and local offices of state employment services have applications and additional information.

Information about careers related to human resources at the federal, state, and local levels of government is available from

- International Public Management Association for Human Resources, 1617 Duke St., Alexandria, VA 22314. Internet: http://www.ipma-hr.org

Government and Advocacy, Grantmaking, and Civic Organizations

APPENDIX A

Definitions of Skills and Crosswalks to Fields

B rowse this list to identify fields that can use your strongest skills, and use the definitions to understand the meaning of the skills listed in Part II under "Important Characteristics of the Field."

Skill	Field
Active Learning: Working with new material or information to grasp its implications.	Scientific Research and Development Services.
Active Listening: Listening to what other people are saying and asking questions as appropriate.	Banking; Health Care; Insurance; Management, Scientific, and Technical Consulting Services; Motion Picture and Video Industries; Securities, Commodities, and Other Investments; Social Assistance, Except Child Day Care; State and Local Government, Excluding Education and Hospitals.
Complex Problem Solving: Identifying complex problems and developing solutions.	Software Publishers.
Coordination: Adjusting actions in relation to others' actions.	State and Local Government, Excluding Education and Hospitals.
Critical Thinking: Using logic and reasoning to identify the strengths and weaknesses of different approaches.	Automobile Dealers.

Skill	Field
Equipment Maintenance: Performing routine maintenance and determining when and what kind of maintenance is needed.	Agriculture, Forestry, and Fishing; Automobile Dealers; Chemical Manufacturing, Except Drugs; Construction; Food Manufacturing; Machinery Manufacturing; Mining; Motor Vehicle and Parts Manufacturing; Oil and Gas Extraction; Pharmaceutical and Medicine Manufacturing; Printing; Steel Manufacturing; Textile, Textile Product, and Apparel Manufacturing; Truck Transportation and Warehousing; Utilities.
Equipment Selection: Determining the kind of tools and equipment needed to do a job.	Construction.
Installation: Installing equipment, machines, wiring, or programs to meet specifications.	Aerospace Product and Parts Manufacturing; Automobile Dealers; Computer and Electronic Product Manufacturing; Computer Systems Design and Related Services; Construction; Machinery Manufacturing; Mining; Motor Vehicle and Parts Manufacturing; Steel Manufacturing; Telecommunications; Textile, Textile Product, and Apparel Manufacturing; Utilities.
Instructing: Teaching others how to do something.	Advocacy, Grantmaking, and Civic Organizations; Arts, Entertainment, and Recreation; Automobile Dealers; Child Day Care Services; Educational Services; Food Services and Drinking Places; Health Care; Management, Scientific, and Technical Consulting Services; Scientific Research and Development Services.
Judgment and Decision Making: Weighing the relative costs and benefits of a potential action.	Federal Government, Excluding the Postal Service; State and Local Government, Excluding Education and Hospitals.
Learning Strategies: Selecting and using appropriate training/ instructional methods and procedures.	Arts, Entertainment, and Recreation; Child Day Care Services; Educational Services; Grocery Stores; Health Care; Social Assistance, Except Child Day Care.
Management of Financial Resources: Determining how money will be spent to get the work done and accounting for these expenditures.	Advertising and Public Relations Services; Advocacy, Grantmaking, and Civic Organizations; Agriculture, Forestry, and Fishing; Banking; Management, Scientific, and Technical Consulting Services; Oil and Gas Extraction; Scientific Research and Development Services; Securities, Commodities, and Other Investments; Wholesale Trade.
Management of Material Resources: Obtaining and seeing to the appropriate use of equipment, facilities, and materials needed to do certain work.	Agriculture, Forestry, and Fishing.
Management of Personnel Resources: Motivating, developing, and directing people as they work; identifying the best people for the job.	Agriculture, Forestry, and Fishing; Broadcasting; Grocery Stores; Motion Picture and Video Industries.
Mathematics: Using mathematics to solve problems.	Oil and Gas Extraction.

Skill	Field
Negotiation: Bringing others together and trying to reconcile differences.	Advertising and Public Relations Services; Broadcasting; Child Day Care Services; Insurance; Management, Scientific, and Technical Consulting Services; Motion Picture and Video Industries; Securities, Commodities, and Other Investments; Wholesale Trade.
Operation and Control: Controlling operations of equipment or systems.	Chemical Manufacturing, Except Drugs; Food Manufacturing; Machinery Manufacturing; Mining; Motor Vehicle and Parts Manufacturing; Oil and Gas Extraction; Pharmaceutical and Medicine Manufacturing; Printing; Publishing, Except Software; Steel Manufacturing; Textile, Textile Product, and Apparel Manufacturing; Truck Transportation and Warehousing; Utilities.
Operation Monitoring: Watching gauges, dials, or other indicators to make sure a machine is working properly.	Chemical Manufacturing, Except Drugs; Food Manufacturing; Machinery Manufacturing; Mining; Motor Vehicle and Parts Manufacturing; Oil and Gas Extraction; Pharmaceutical and Medicine Manufacturing; Printing; Steel Manufacturing; Textile, Textile Product, and Apparel Manufacturing; Truck Transportation and Warehousing; Utilities.
Operations Analysis: Analyzing needs and product requirements to create a design.	Computer Systems Design and Related Services; Internet Service Providers, Web Search Portals, and Data Processing Services; Software Publishers.
Persuasion: Persuading others to change their minds or behavior.	Advertising and Public Relations Services; Advocacy, Grantmaking, and Civic Organizations; Arts, Entertainment, and Recreation; Banking; Child Day Care Services; Educational Services; Insurance; Management, Scientific, and Technical Consulting Services; Motion Picture and Video Industries; Securities, Commodities, and Other Investments; Social Assistance, Except Child Day Care; State and Local Government, Excluding Education and Hospitals; Wholesale Trade.
Programming: Writing computer programs for various purposes.	Computer and Electronic Product Manufacturing; Computer Systems Design and Related Services; Food Manufacturing; Internet Service Providers, Web Search Portals, and Data Processing Services; Software Publishers.
Quality Control Analysis: Conducting tests and inspections of products, services, or processes to evaluate quality or performance.	Aerospace Product and Parts Manufacturing; Chemical Manufacturing, Except Drugs; Computer and Electronic Product Manufacturing; Machinery Manufacturing; Motor Vehicle and Parts Manufacturing; Pharmaceutical and Medicine Manufacturing; Printing; Steel Manufacturing; Textile, Textile Product, and Apparel Manufacturing.
Reading Comprehension: Understanding written sentences and paragraphs in work-related documents.	Scientific Research and Development Services.
Repairing: Repairing machines or systems using the needed tools.	Agriculture, Forestry, and Fishing; Automobile Dealers; Construction; Food Manufacturing; Machinery Manufacturing; Mining; Motor Vehicle and Parts Manufacturing; Steel Manufacturing; Telecommunications; Textile, Textile Product, and Apparel Manufacturing; Truck Transportation and Warehousing; Utilities.

Skill	Field
Science: Using scientific rules and methods to solve problems.	Aerospace Product and Parts Manufacturing; Agriculture, Forestry, and Fishing; Chemical Manufacturing, Except Drugs; Computer and Electronic Product Manufacturing; Federal Government, Excluding the Postal Service; Pharmaceutical and Medicine Manufacturing; Scientific Research and Development Services.
Service Orientation: Actively looking for ways to help people.	Advertising and Public Relations Services; Advocacy, Grantmaking, and Civic Organizations; Air Transportation; Arts, Entertainment, and Recreation; Banking; Child Day Care Services; Educational Services; Food Services and Drinking Places; Grocery Stores; Health Care; Insurance; Management, Scientific, and Technical Consulting Services; Securities, Commodities, and Other Investments; Social Assistance, Except Child Day Care; State and Local Government, Excluding Education and Hospitals; Wholesale Trade.
Social Perceptiveness: Being aware of others' reactions and understanding why they react the way they do.	Advertising and Public Relations Services; Advocacy, Grantmaking, and Civic Organizations; Arts, Entertainment, and Recreation; Banking; Broadcasting; Child Day Care Services; Clothing, Accessory, and General Merchandise Stores; Educational Services; Food Services and Drinking Places; Grocery Stores; Health Care; Motion Picture and Video Industries; Social Assistance, Except Child Day Care; State and Local Government, Excluding Education and Hospitals; Wholesale Trade.
Speaking: Talking to others to convey information effectively.	Advertising and Public Relations Services; Banking; Broadcasting; Federal Government, Excluding the Postal Service; Insurance; Motion Picture and Video Industries; Securities, Commodities, and Other Investments.
Systems Analysis: Determining how a system should work and how changes in conditions, operations, and the environment will affect outcomes.	Aerospace Product and Parts Manufacturing; Computer Systems Design and Related Services; Federal Government, Excluding the Postal Service; Internet Service Providers, Web Search Portals, and Data Processing Services; Software Publishers.
Systems Evaluation: Identifying measures or indicators of system performance and the actions needed to improve or correct performance.	Federal Government, Excluding the Postal Service; Internet Service Providers, Web Search Portals, and Data Processing Services.
Technology Design: Generating or adapting equipment and technology to serve user needs.	Aerospace Product and Parts Manufacturing; Computer and Electronic Product Manufacturing; Computer Systems Design and Related Services; Construction; Internet Service Providers, Web Search Portals, and Data Processing Services; Software Publishers; Telecommunications.
Time Management: Managing one's own time and the time of others.	Advocacy, Grantmaking, and Civic Organizations; Broadcasting; Educational Services; Health Care; Scientific Research and Development Services; Wholesale Trade.
Troubleshooting: Determining causes of operating errors and deciding what to do about them.	Aerospace Product and Parts Manufacturing; Automobile Dealers; Chemical Manufacturing, Except Drugs; Computer and Electronic Product Manufacturing; Computer Systems Design and Related Services; Construction; Internet Service Providers, Web Search Portals, and Data Processing Services; Mining; Oil and Gas Extraction; Pharmaceutical and Medicine Manufacturing; Software Publishers; Telecommunications; Utilities.
Writing: Communicating effectively in writing as appropriate for the needs of the audience.	Broadcasting; Federal Government, Excluding the Postal Service; Insurance; Social Assistance, Except Child Day Care.

APPENDIX B

Definitions of Abilities and Crosswalks to Fields

B rowse this list to identify fields that can use your strongest abilities, and use the definitions to understand the meaning of the abilities listed in Part II under "Important Characteristics of the Field."

Ability	Field
Arm-Hand Steadiness: Keeping your hand and arm steady while moving your arm or while holding your arm and hand in one position.	Health Care; Machinery Manufacturing; Motor Vehicle and Parts Manufacturing; Textile, Textile Product, and Apparel Manufacturing.
Auditory Attention: Focusing on a single source of sound in the presence of other distracting sounds.	Air Transportation.
Category Flexibility: Generating or using different sets of rules for combining or grouping things in different ways.	Educational Services; Oil and Gas Extraction; Scientific Research and Development Services.
Control Precision: Quickly and repeatedly adjusting the controls of a machine or a vehicle to exact positions.	Chemical Manufacturing, Except Drugs; Machinery Manufacturing; Motor Vehicle and Parts Manufacturing; Pharmaceutical and Medicine Manufacturing; Printing; Steel Manufacturing; Textile, Textile Product, and Apparel Manufacturing.

Ability	Field
Deductive Reasoning: Applying general rules to specific problems to produce answers that make sense.	Computer Systems Design and Related Services; Federal Government, Excluding the Postal Service; Internet Service Providers, Web Search Portals, and Data Processing Services; Software Publishers.
Dynamic Flexibility: Quickly and repeatedly bending, stretching, twisting, or reaching out with your body, arms, and/or legs.	Agriculture, Forestry, and Fishing; Arts, Entertainment, and Recreation; Printing; Publishing, Except Software; Textile, Textile Product, and Apparel Manufacturing.
Dynamic Strength: Exerting muscle force repeatedly or continuously over time.	Agriculture, Forestry, and Fishing; Arts, Entertainment, and Recreation; Construction; Employment Services; Food Manufacturing; Social Assistance, Except Child Day Care; Steel Manufacturing; Telecommunications.
Explosive Strength: Using short bursts of muscle force to propel yourself or to throw an object.	Aerospace Product and Parts Manufacturing; Agriculture, Forestry, and Fishing; Employment Services; Mining; Telecommunications; Truck Transportation and Warehousing.
Extent Flexibility: Bending, stretching, twisting, or reaching with your body, arms, and/or legs.	griculture, Forestry, and Fishing; Automobile Dealers; Clothing, Accessory, Aand General Merchandise Stores; Construction; Employment Services; Food Manufacturing; Food Services and Drinking Places; Grocery Stores; Steel Manufacturing; Utilities; Wholesale Trade.
Finger Dexterity: Making precisely coordinated movements of the fingers of one or both hands to grasp, manipulate, or assemble very small objects.	Computer and Electronic Product Manufacturing.
Fluency of Ideas: Coming up with a number of ideas about a topic.	Advertising and Public Relations Services; Broadcasting; Child Day Care Services.
Glare Sensitivity: Seeing objects in the presence of glare or bright lighting.	State and Local Government, Excluding Education and Hospitals; Utilities; Wholesale Trade.
Gross Body Coordination: Coordinating the movement of your arms, legs, and torso together when the whole body is in motion.	Arts, Entertainment, and Recreation; Automobile Dealers; Clothing, Accessory, and General Merchandise Stores; Food Services and Drinking Places; Grocery Stores; Health Care; Motion Picture and Video Industries.
Gross Body Equilibrium: Keeping or regaining your body balance or staying upright when in an unstable position.	Clothing, Accessory, and General Merchandise Stores; Construction; Telecommunications.
Hearing Sensitivity: Detecting or telling the differences between sounds that vary in pitch and loudness.	Child Day Care Services; Motion Picture and Video Industries.
Inductive Reasoning: Combining pieces of information to form general rules or conclusions.	Aerospace Product and Parts Manufacturing; Computer and Electronic Product Manufacturing; Computer Systems Design and Related Services; Federal Government, Excluding the Postal Service; Internet Service Providers, Web Search Portals, and Data Processing Services; Management, Scientific, and Technical Consulting Services; Scientific Research and Development Services; Software Publishers.

Ability	Field
Information Ordering: Arranging things or actions in a certain order or pattern according to a specific rule or set of rules.	Aerospace Product and Parts Manufacturing; Chemical Manufacturing, Except Drugs.
Manual Dexterity: Quickly moving your hand, your hand together with your arm, or your two hands to grasp, manipulate, or assemble objects.	Automobile Dealers; Construction; Employment Services; Food Manufacturing; Grocery Stores; Machinery Manufacturing; Motor Vehicle and Parts Manufacturing; Printing; Steel Manufacturing; Textile, Textile Product, and Apparel Manufacturing.
Mathematical Reasoning: Choosing the right mathematical methods or formulas to solve a problem.	Aerospace Product and Parts Manufacturing; Banking; Computer and Electronic Product Manufacturing; Computer Systems Design and Related Services; Insurance; Internet Service Providers, Web Search Portals, and Data Processing Services; Oil and Gas Extraction; Scientific Research and Development Services; Securities, Commodities, and Other Investments; Software Publishers.
Multilimb Coordination: Coordinating two or more limbs while sitting, standing, or lying down.	Automobile Dealers; Machinery Manufacturing; Mining; Motor Vehicle and Parts Manufacturing; Steel Manufacturing; Wholesale Trade.
Near Vision: Seeing details of objects at close range.	Publishing, Except Software.
Night Vision: Seeing under low light conditions.	Air Transportation; Publishing, Except Software; State and Local Government, Excluding Education and Hospitals.
Number Facility: Adding, subtracting, multiplying, or dividing quickly and correctly.	Banking; Insurance; Oil and Gas Extraction; Securities, Commodities, and Other Investments.
Oral Comprehension: Listening to and understanding information and ideas presented through spoken words and sentences.	Advocacy, Grantmaking, and Civic Organizations; Management, Scientific, and Technical Consulting Services; Scientific Research and Development Services; Social Assistance, Except Child Day Care; Software Publishers.
Oral Expression: Communicating information and ideas in speaking so others will understand.	Advertising and Public Relations Services; Advocacy, Grantmaking, and Civic Organizations; Banking; Broadcasting; Educational Services; Federal Government, Excluding the Postal Service; Insurance; Management, Scientific, and Technical Consulting Services; Motion Picture and Video Industries; Securities, Commodities, and Other Investments.
Originality: Coming up with unusual or clever ideas about a given topic or situation or developing creative ways to solve a problem.	Advertising and Public Relations Services; Broadcasting; Child Day Care Services; Computer Systems Design and Related Services; Educational Services; Software Publishers.
Perceptual Speed: Quickly and accurately comparing similarities and differences among sets of letters, numbers, objects, pictures, or patterns.	Computer and Electronic Product Manufacturing; Pharmaceutical and Medicine Manufacturing.
Peripheral Vision: Seeing objects or movement of objects to your side when your eyes are looking ahead.	Air Transportation; State and Local Government, Excluding Education and Hospitals; Wholesale Trade.

Ability	Field
Problem Sensitivity: Telling when something is wrong or is likely to go wrong.	Advocacy, Grantmaking, and Civic Organizations; Aerospace Product and Parts Manufacturing; Federal Government, Excluding the Postal Service; Health Care; Oil and Gas Extraction; Social Assistance, Except Child Day Care.
Rate Control: Timing your movements or the movement of a piece of equipment in anticipation of changes in the speed and/or direction of a moving scene.	Chemical Manufacturing, Except Drugs; Machinery Manufacturing; Mining; Motor Vehicle and Parts Manufacturing; Oil and Gas Extraction; Pharmaceutical and Medicine Manufacturing; Printing; Publishing, Except Software; State and Local Government, Excluding Education and Hospitals; object or Textile, Textile Product, and Apparel Manufacturing; Truck Transportation and Warehousing.
Reaction Time: Quickly responding with your hand, finger, or foot to a signal when it appears.	Chemical Manufacturing, Except Drugs; Machinery Manufacturing; Mining; Motor Vehicle and Parts Manufacturing; Pharmaceutical and Medicine Manufacturing; Truck Transportation and Warehousing; Utilities.
Response Orientation: Choosing quickly between two or more movements in response to two or more different signals.	Air Transportation; Chemical Manufacturing, Except Drugs; Mining; Pharmaceutical and Medicine Manufacturing; State and Local Government, Excluding Education and Hospitals; Truck Transportation and Warehousing.
Selective Attention: Concentrating on a task over a period of time without being distracted.	Chemical Manufacturing, Except Drugs; Oil and Gas Extraction; Pharmaceutical and Medicine Manufacturing.
Sound Localization: Telling the direction from which a sound originated.	Telecommunications; Utilities.
Spatial Orientation: Knowing your location in relation to the environment or knowing where other objects are in relation to you.	Agriculture, Forestry, and Fishing; Air Transportation; Hotels and Other Accommodations; State and Local Government, Excluding Education and Hospitals; Telecommunications; Truck Transportation and Warehousing; Utilities.
Speech Clarity: Speaking clearly so others can understand you.	Advertising and Public Relations Services; Advocacy, Grantmaking, and Civic Organizations; Banking; Broadcasting; Child Day Care Services; Educational Services; Health Care; Insurance; Management, Scientific, and Technical Consulting Services; Motion Picture and Video Industries; Securities, Commodities, and Other Investments; Social Assistance, Except Child Day Care.
Speech Recognition: Identifying and understanding the speech of another person.	Advertising and Public Relations Services; Advocacy, Grantmaking, and Civic Organizations; Automobile Dealers; Banking; Broadcasting; Child Day Care Services; Computer Systems Design and Related Services; Educational Services; Food Services and Drinking Places; Health Care; Insurance; Internet Service Providers, Web Search Portals, and Data Processing Services; Management, Scientific, and Technical Consulting Services; Motion Picture and Video Industries; Publishing, Except Software; Scientific Research and Development Services; Securities, Commodities, and Other Investments; Social Assistance, Except Child Day Care; Software Publishers; Wholesale Trade.

Ability	Field
Speed of Limb Movement: Quickly moving your arms and legs.	Food Services and Drinking Places; Hotels and Other Accommodations.
Stamina: Exerting yourself physically over long periods of time without getting winded or out of breath.	Arts, Entertainment, and Recreation; Child Day Care Services; Clothing, Accessory, and General Merchandise Stores; Construction; Food Manufacturing; Food Services and Drinking Places; Grocery Stores; Health Care; Hotels and Other Accommodations; Social Assistance, Except Child Day Care; Wholesale Trade.
Static Strength: Exerting maximum muscle force to lift, push, pull, or carry objects.	Agriculture, Forestry, and Fishing; Arts, Entertainment, and Recreation; Clothing, Accessory, and General Merchandise Stores; Construction; Employment Services; Food Manufacturing; Grocery Stores; Hotels and Other Accommodations; Mining; Steel Manufacturing; Truck Transportation and Warehousing.
Time Sharing: Shifting back and forth between two or more activities or sources of information.	Advocacy, Grantmaking, and Civic Organizations; Motion Picture and Video Industries.
Trunk Strength: Using your abdominal and lower back muscles to support part of the body repeatedly or continuously over time without tiring.	Arts, Entertainment, and Recreation; Automobile Dealers; Clothing, Accessory, and General Merchandise Stores; Employment Services; Food Manufacturing; Food Services and Drinking Places; Grocery Stores; Hotels and Other Accommodations.
Visual Color Discrimination: Matching or detecting differences between colors, including shades of color and brightness.	Computer and Electronic Product Manufacturing; Printing; Publishing, Except Software.
Visualization: Imagining how something will look after it is moved around or when its parts are moved or rearranged.	Aerospace Product and Parts Manufacturing; Computer and Electronic Product Manufacturing.
Wrist-Finger Speed: Making fast, simple, repeated movements of the fingers, hands, and wrists.	Air Transportation; Hotels and Other Accommodations; Printing; Telecommunications; Textile, Textile Product, and Apparel Manufacturing; Utilities.
Written Comprehension: Reading and understanding information and ideas presented in writing.	Computer Systems Design and Related Services; Federal Government, Excluding the Postal Service; Internet Service Providers, Web Search Portals, and Data Processing Services.
Written Expression: Communicating information and ideas in writing so others will understand.	Advertising and Public Relations Services; Banking; Broadcasting; Educational Services; Federal Government, Excluding the Postal Service; Insurance; Internet Service Providers, Web Search Portals, and Data Processing Services; Management, Scientific, and Technical Consulting Services; Scientific Research and Development Services; Securities, Commodities, and Other Investments.

The Bottom Line

Online merchants can be victims of all manner of fraud, including but not limited to fraudulent payments. PayPal offers a variety of tools and technologies to identify and help stop fraud before you're affected. Most important of these are a variety of Fraud Management Filters you can use to flag or deny questionable transactions. You can also deal with disputed transactions in PayPal's Resolution Center.

11

Dealing with Disputes and Chargebacks

Disputes and chargebacks can be difficult to handle. PayPal's systems can help—reducing the staff time and increasing customer's satisfaction. This is especially true if you have limited staff available to handle customer concerns.

The experience of resolving an issue strongly affects your customer's attitude and how they speak about you, for better or worse. Even if you've made a mistake, if you handle it well you often gain a customer for life!

If they don't choose to contact you directly, a dissatisfied customer has two avenues for complaint: filing a dispute with PayPal, or initiating a chargeback with their credit card company.

Understanding Disputes

To resolve an issue, the first thing a customer can do is file a *dispute* with PayPal. This is typically done as part of the PayPal Purchase Protection program.

When a customer has a complaint about an item purchased using PayPal (the item wasn't received or was significantly different than described), he files a dispute with PayPal. PayPal then freezes the associated funds in the merchant's PayPal account while it examines the transaction.

If PayPal rules in the customer's favor, the funds are withdrawn from the merchant's PayPal account and returned to the customer. If PayPal rules in the seller's favor, the funds are unfrozen and made available for use.

Understanding Chargebacks

A *chargeback* is similar to but different from a PayPal dispute in that it's not filed with PayPal. Instead, a chargeback occurs when a buyer requests his credit card issuer to reverse a transaction after it has been completed. Some chargebacks are legitimate, made after a customer has tried to work out a solution with a merchant, but without success; in this instance, a chargeback is the aggrieved customer's last means of recourse. Other chargebacks, however, are frivolous or even fraudulent, as customers try to avoid paying for legitimate purchases.

Most merchants hate credit card chargebacks even more than disputes; a chargeback is often a no-win situation, even for the most scrupulous sellers. Fortunately, PayPal can help you reduce chargebacks—and keep more money in your company's pockets.

CAUTION: As soon as PayPal is notified of the chargeback, PayPal puts a hold on your account for the amount in dispute. This hold is lifted if the dispute is settled in your favor, or if the transaction qualifies for Seller Protection.

Naturally, chargebacks are available only to users who make a payment funded by their credit or debit card. They are initiated and handled by the buyer's credit card issuer, not by PayPal. Therefore, the chargeback process follows the credit card issuer's regulations and timeframes.

Dealing with Unwarranted Chargebacks

If you find yourself the victim of what you feel is an unwarranted charge-back, follow these steps:

1. Log in to your PayPal account, select the My Account tab, and then select the Resolution Center subtab.

2. From the Resolution Center page, shown in **Figure 11.1**, navigate to the item in dispute and click Respond.

3. When the Chargeback Details page appears, you'll see the details about the nature of the chargeback. To respond to the case, click Resolve Chargeback Now at the bottom of the page.

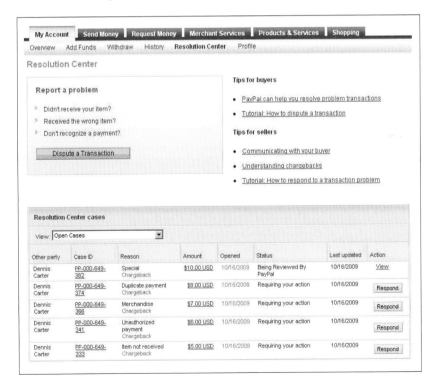

Figure 11.1

PayPal's Resolution Center.

Figure 11.2
Resolving a chargeback.

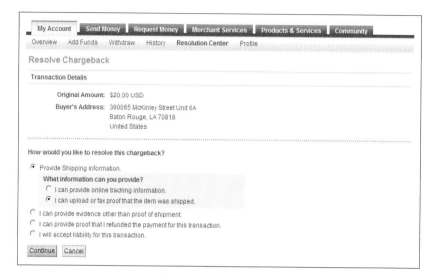

PayPal INSIDER

 ## Fighting Chargeback Fraud

Chargeback fraud is alarmingly widespread. This type of fraud occurs when a customer decides he wants his money back, without legitimate cause. Instead of trying to return the product and obtain a refund through your normal channels, the customer calls up his credit card company and says, in effect, "I'm not paying for this." The credit card company then attempts to file a chargeback, which would deduct the price of the original customer purchase from your account.

We don't think this is fair to merchants, which is why PayPal works to help protect you against fraudulent chargebacks. Credit card companies typically put buyers' needs before merchants'

needs, which makes it difficult to resolve chargeback disputes to a merchant's satisfaction. Not so with PayPal; we're equally concerned with buyers and sellers, and we're attuned to chargeback fraud.

When a buyer files a dispute over a transaction, we act as a mediator between the parties. Our goal is to resolve the situation before a chargeback is filed.

If mediation isn't successful and a chargeback is filed, we'll work on your behalf, using evidence you provide, to fight a fraudulent chargeback. Not only do we have a high success rate, you'll save time and frustration by letting us handle most of the work. Our goal is to protect you from chargeback fraud.

4. On the Resolve Chargeback page, shown in **Figure 11.2**, select the
    option that fits how you wish to remedy the chargeback. Each option
    has a few additional screens to complete in order to send the response
    to PayPal.

5. If you have any additional details to add to the case before it's closed
    by PayPal, you can always add files, notes, or a fax to the case by
    returning to the Chargeback Details page and clicking the Add link
    next to the medium you wish to add. Note that this option goes away
    once PayPal has reviewed your response.

It's then up to the credit card issuer to accept your version of the facts or to
side with the complaining customer. If you win the argument, the chargeback is withdrawn.

NOTE: You'll find helpful Tutorials in PayPal's Resolution Center which walk you
through some typical situations.

Minimizing Disputes with PayPal's Seller Protection

If you're the victim of an unwarranted dispute or chargeback, you may be
protected from any financial damages, thanks to PayPal's Seller Protection
program. As the name implies, this is a program designed to protect
PayPal sellers from fraudulent transactions—as well as items lost or
damaged in transit.

For those transactions eligible under the program,
PayPal covers you in the event of unauthorized
purchases, "item not received" claims, chargebacks,
and reversals. PayPal protects you for the full amount
of the eligible payment and waives any chargeback
fees, if applicable.

NOTE: A dispute is different
from a chargeback, in that it's a
complaint filed by the customer before
requesting a formal chargeback.

When You're Covered

To be covered under the Seller Protection program, the following criteria must be met:

- The transaction is marked either fully or partially eligible.

- The item in question is a physical, tangible item that can be shipped, i.e., no digital goods.

- Your primary business address or residence, as listed for your PayPal account, is in the United States.

- You ship the item to a PayPal confirmed address, and this is the same address listed on the PayPal Transaction Details page.

- You ship within seven calendar days of being paid by the buyer.

- You keep proof of shipment and delivery so that the item can be tracked online.

- For payments over $250 USD, including shipping and tax, you have a signature confirmation of delivery in addition to proof of shipment.

What's *Not* Covered

While most transactions are covered under Seller Protection, some are not. You're not covered under the following circumstances:

- The item is picked up locally or delivered in person, rather than by a traditional shipping service.

- The item is not shipped to the recipient's address. (This includes items originally sent to the recipient's address but later redirected to a different address.)

- The item in question is a service, digital good, or intangible item.

- You receive multiple payments for the same item.

- Claims or chargebacks alleging that the item is significantly not as described.

- Payments received via PayPal Direct Payments, Virtual Terminal, or PayPal Business Payments.

Using PayPal Seller Protection

How do you benefit from PayPal's Seller Protection Policy? It's easy—and PayPal does all of the work for you.

NOTE: You can tell whether a transaction qualifies for Seller Protection by examining the transaction details.

Seller Protection kicks in for eligible transactions when a buyer makes a claim against a seller for a transaction handled by PayPal. After the claim is filed, PayPal puts a temporary hold on the seller's PayPal account for the amount in dispute. This hold stays in place while PayPal reviews the case.

If the transaction fits the requirements for Seller Protection, PayPal then releases the hold on the merchant's funds. In this instance, you're not out a penny.

CAUTION: If the transaction in question does *not* fit the requirements for Seller Protection, PayPal will deduct the appropriate funds from the seller's account and transmit them to the buyer, as necessary.

The Bottom Line

Disputes and chargebacks are two ways for dissatisfied customers to gain refunds from a seller. PayPal's Seller Protection program helps protect your eligible transactions against most unwarranted chargebacks from disreputable buyers. The program also helps protect against items legitimately lost or damaged in transit. Seller Protection is automatically launched when a customer files a claim against any eligible transaction; there's nothing you have to do except let PayPal look into the matter.

MANAGING AND GROWING YOUR BUSINESS

12

Managing Business Info and Data

When you're running a business, you're constantly making decisions. To make good decisions, you need good information, information that's current, accurate, and relevant. In a retail or service business a key source of information is what people bought, how many they bought, what they paid—you get the idea.

PayPal helps you track and manage all of your customer transactions. PayPal keeps a record of every customer transaction for which it handles payment, and lets you view this data online and download it for further analysis.

Tracking Order Activity

You can view all of your PayPal transactions in several places on the PayPal site. How often you access this data—and what you use it for—is up to you.

Checking your Account Overview

When you want to view your most recent customer transactions, turn to your overview page. Depending on your preferences, it's probably the first thing you see after you've logged in. If not, just click the My Account tab, and then select the Overview subtab. Scroll to see your recent activity presented in a table near the bottom of the page.

As you can see in **Figure 12.1**, all of your recent customer transactions are listed here. You can filter transactions by payments sent or payments received, just by clicking the links above the data table.

Each item on this page lists different information about each transaction:

- **Date**, the date the transaction was completed.

- **Type**, the type of transaction recorded—payment, sale, debit, credit, refund, authorization, void, and the like.

- **Name/Email**, the name or email address of the customer.

- **Payment status**, the status of the current payment.

- **Details**, a link which, when clicked, displays the Transaction Details page for this item.

- **Order status/Actions**, which displays any pending actions you need to take regarding this transaction.

- **Gross**, the gross amount of funds generated (or debited) by this transaction.

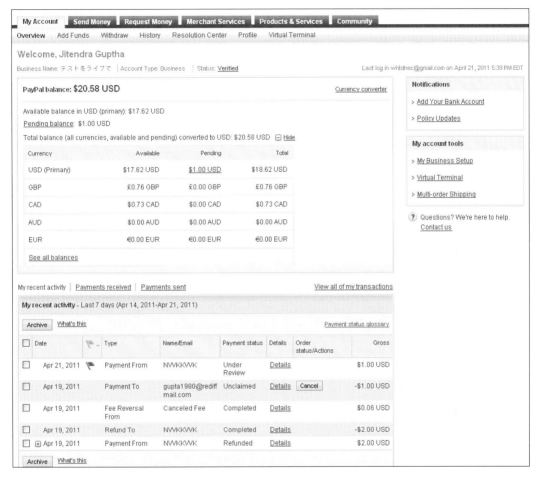

Figure 12.1 *Tracking recent order activity from your account overview page.*

Viewing Transaction History

A more complete transaction history is available from your History page. You get there by logging in to your account, clicking the My Account tab, and then selecting the History subtab. This is the place to go to view older transactions.

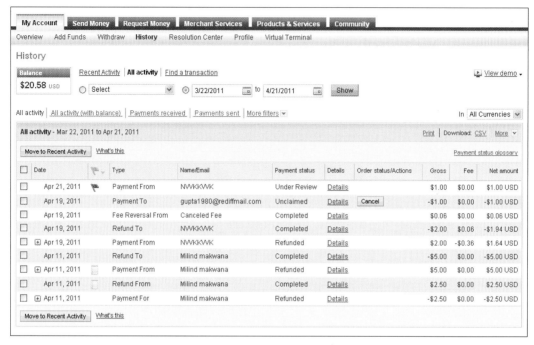

Figure 12.2 *Tracking all order activity from the History page.*

As you can see in **Figure 12.2**, the History page displays the same data for each transaction as was shown on the overview page, with two additions:

- **Fee**, the PayPal fees charged for this transaction.

- **Net amount**, the net value of the transaction transferred to your PayPal account—the gross amount paid less the PayPal fees.

By default, the History page displays all transactions for the past month or so. You can, however, display transactions for a selected data range (Today, This Week, Last Week, This Month, Last Month, or Last Three Months) by selecting a range from the first pull-down list (labeled Select) above the data table. Alternatively, you can display transactions from a custom date range by entering a start and end date in the boxes above the data table.

You can also filter the History page by a variety of criteria. Click the More Filters arrow above the data table and select one of the following filters:

- Payments received

- Payments sent

- Orders

- Credits

- Currency conversion

- eChecks

- Financial products and services (gift cards, PayPal credit, PayPal credit payment, or reward voucher)

- Money added and withdrawn (mass payments, money added, or money withdrawn)

- Payment received to a specific email address (if you hold multiple addresses)

- Payment received via PayPal Mobile

- Referrals

- Refunds

- Reversals

- Shipping (items to ship or items shipped)

- Subscriptions and agreements (billing agreements, pay list—payments received or payments sent, recurring payments, or subscriptions)

- Reserves (all, placed, or released)

- Payment holds (all, on hold, or released)

- Payment review transaction (all, under payment review, cleared by payment review, or canceled by payment review)

And, as with your account overview, click the Details link for any specific transaction to view the details for that transaction.

TIP: You can also use the History page to find a specific transaction. Click the Find a Transaction link at the top of the page; when the next page appears, enter one or more keywords and select where to search—in email, transaction ID, last name, last name/first name, receipt ID, invoice ID, auction item number, billing agreement, or profile ID. Select a date range for your search and then click the Search button.

Understanding Payment Status

What's the status of a given payment? The status is listed in the Status column of your account overview and History pages, but what types of status might you encounter? **Table 12.1** details the possible status types.

Table 12.1 PayPal Payment Status Types

Status	Description
Active	For subscriptions, automatic payments are scheduled.
Cancelled	The buyer has cancelled the payment, and that money has been refunded to her account.
Cleared	You received an eCheck payment, and the payment has cleared the buyer's account, with funds credited to your account.
Completed	A successful transaction, with funds credited to your PayPal account.
Denied	You decided not to accept this particular payment.
Expired	The transaction expired.
Failed	The customer's payment didn't go through.
Held	The customer's payment is being held, pending possible reversal, due either to a dispute or risk to seller (PayPal's assessment that the buyer's payment might not go through).
In progress	Payment has been sent but you haven't accepted it yet.
On hold	The payment is being held temporarily, typically because the buyer has filed a dispute or because PayPal is reviewing the transaction for some reason.
On hold–ship now	While you establish a successful sales history on eBay, in most cases, funds from eBay sales are available in 21 days—or sooner, based on how you ship the order. To help get your funds faster, print your shipping labels on eBay or PayPal, upload your tracking information, or mark the items as shipped on eBay. If your buyer reports a problem, it may take longer to get your funds.
Paid	For money requests, the recipient was paid the full amount.
Partially refunded by eBay	For eBay transactions, eBay ruled in favor of the buyer in a dispute filed with the eBay Resolution Center and issued a partial refund on your behalf. You need to reimburse eBay for this amount.

Table 12.1 **PayPal Payment Status Types** *(continued)*

Status	Description
Pending	For withdrawals from your PayPal account, the transfer to your bank or writing of a check is in progress.
Processed	For instances where you transfer funds from your bank account to your PayPal account, the transfer is in progress and funds should be available shortly.
Refunded	You have fully or partially refunded funds to the buyer.
Refunded by eBay	For eBay transactions, eBay ruled in favor of the buyer in a dispute filed with the eBay Resolution Center and issued a refund to the buyer on your behalf. If you have adequate funds in your PayPal account, PayPal will debit your account for the amount refunded; if you don't have the funds, you need to add them as soon as possible.
Refused	A bank transfer or check transfer was rejected.
Returned	For buyers, money was refunded because the recipient didn't claim the payment after 30 days.
Reversed	For withdrawals to your bank account, the transfer was denied and funds transferred back to your PayPal account. For check payments from PayPal, the check expired because it's been more than 180 days since the check was requested.
Temporary hold	PayPal sometimes places a short, temporary hold on funds during the authorization process. This process doesn't take long, and the status should quickly revert to Completed.
To be paid	For eBay transactions, eBay ruled in favor of the buyer in a dispute filed with the eBay Resolution Center. You didn't have enough money in your account to cover the refund, so eBay issued the refund on your behalf. You need to reimburse eBay as soon as possible for this refund.
Unclaimed	The recipient of a payment or funds transfer has not claimed the funds.
Uncleared	An eCheck payment is in progress, but has not yet cleared.
Under review	PayPal is reviewing this transaction. Do not ship the merchandise until the review is completed.

Downloading Transaction Data

You're not limited to viewing your transaction history online. You can also download your transaction history to your computer, to work with on your own time.

Downloading Data

To download PayPal transaction data, follow these instructions:

1. Log in to your PayPal account.

2. Go to the My Account tab, hover over the History subtab, then select Download History.

3. When the Download History page appears, as shown in **Figure 12.3**, select the date range to download (in the Custom Date Range section) or select the Last Download to Present option to download all transactions you haven't yet downloaded.

4. Pull down the File Types for Download list and select the type of file to download.

5. Click the Download History button (not shown).

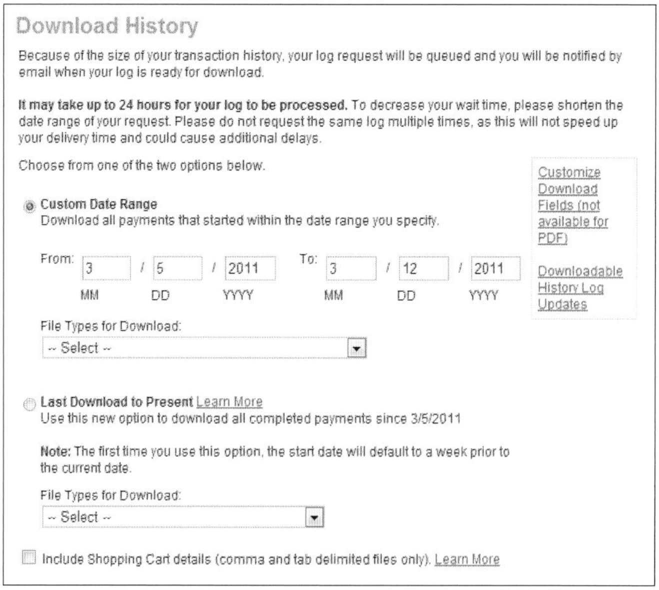

Figure 12.3

Downloading PayPal transaction history.

Download History

Because of the size of your transaction history, your log request will be queued and you will be notified by email when your log is ready for download.

It may take up to 24 hours for your log to be processed. To decrease your wait time, please shorten the date range of your request. Please do not request the same log multiple times, as this will not speed up your delivery time and could cause additional delays.

Choose from one of the two options below.

Customize Download Fields (not available for PDF)

○ **Custom Date Range**
Download all payments that started within the date range you specify.

From: 3 / 5 / 2011   To: 3 / 12 / 2011
MM   DD   YYYY   MM   DD   YYYY

Downloadable History Log Updates

File Types for Download:
-- Select --

○ **Last Download to Present** Learn More
Use this new option to download all completed payments since 3/5/2011

Note: The first time you use this option, the start date will default to a week prior to the current date.

File Types for Download:
-- Select --

☐ Include Shopping Cart details (comma and tab delimited files only). Learn More

Selecting a File Download Format

PayPal enables you to download your transaction history in a number of different file formats. Which file format you select depends on how you'll be using the downloaded information. **Table 12.2** details the available download formats.

Table 12.2 Transaction History Download Formats

File Format	Description
Comma Delimited – All Activity	Available for custom date ranges only. Downloads all activity for the selected date range in a comma-delimited text format. You can import this format into Excel and other spreadsheet programs, or into a custom database.
Comma Delimited – Completed Payments	Downloads completed payments only, in a comma-delimited text format. You can import this format into Excel and other spreadsheet programs, or into a custom database.
Comma Delimited – Balance Affecting Payments	Available for custom date ranges only. Downloads only those transactions that affect your account balance, in a comma-delimited text format. You can import this format into Excel and other spreadsheet programs, or into a custom database.
Tab Delimited – All Activity	Available for custom date ranges only. Downloads all activity for the selected date range in a tab-delimited text format. You can import this format into Excel and other spreadsheet programs, or into a custom database.
Tab Delimited – Completed Payments	Downloads completed payments only, in a tab-delimited text format. You can import this format into Excel and other spreadsheet programs, or into a custom database.
Tab Delimited – Balance Affecting Payments	Available for custom date ranges only. Downloads only those transactions that affect your account balance, in a tab-delimited text format. You can import this format into Excel and other spreadsheet programs, or into a custom database.
PDF – All Activity	Downloads all transactions into a PDF file for viewing with Adobe Acrobat Reader.

Of the major file formats available (comma delimited, tab delimited, Quicken, QuickBooks, or PDF), which should you use? Here are some tips:

- If you want to view and edit your data in Microsoft Excel, use either the comma- or tab-delimited formats; both of these formats import easily into an Excel spreadsheet.

- If you want to store your data in Microsoft Access or another database program, use either the comma- or tab-delimited formats; both of these formats import easily into most database programs.

- If you manage your business with Quicken, use a Quicken QIF.

- If you manage your business with QuickBooks, use a QuickBooks IIF.

- If you simply want to view your data onscreen or in printed format and not manipulate the data in any way, download to a PDF.

Customizing Download Fields

You can also customize the fields you download, for all download file formats except PDF. This lets you import only those fields you need for your own particular analysis or data storage. It's also a great way to import specific fields into Quicken or QuickBooks.

To select which fields to download, click the Customize Download Fields link on the right side of the History page. This displays the Customize My History Download page, shown in **Figure 12.4**.

By default, PayPal downloads the following fields:

- Date
- Time
- Time Zone
- Name
- Type

- Status
- Currency
- Gross
- Fee
- Net

- From Email Address
- To Email Address
- Transaction ID
- Reference Transaction ID
- Receipt ID

To select other fields, check those fields you wish to download and uncheck those you don't want to download. Click the Save button to save your preferences and return to the transaction download process.

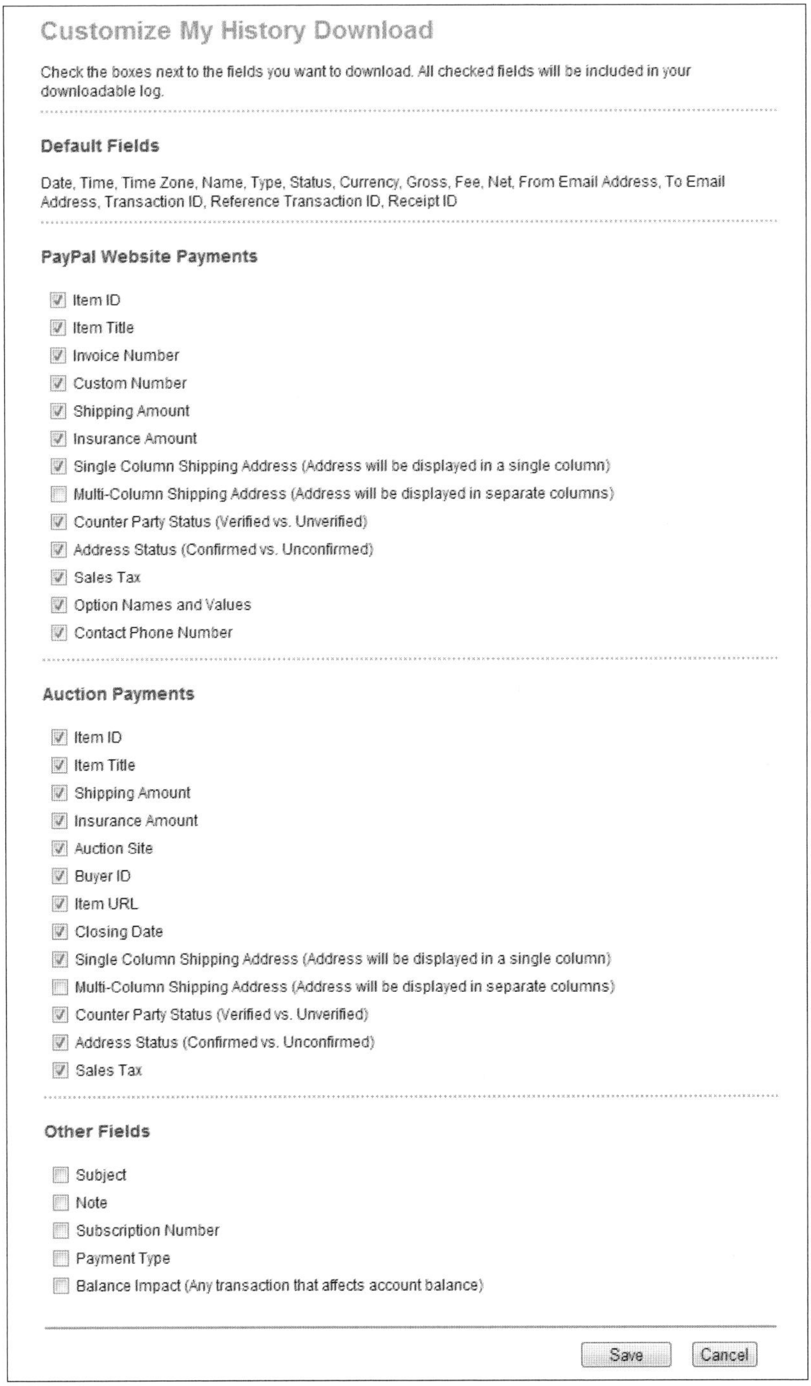

Customize My History Download

Check the boxes next to the fields you want to download. All checked fields will be included in your downloadable log.

Default Fields

Date, Time, Time Zone, Name, Type, Status, Currency, Gross, Fee, Net, From Email Address, To Email Address, Transaction ID, Reference Transaction ID, Receipt ID

PayPal Website Payments

- ☑ Item ID
- ☑ Item Title
- ☑ Invoice Number
- ☑ Custom Number
- ☑ Shipping Amount
- ☑ Insurance Amount
- ☑ Single Column Shipping Address (Address will be displayed in a single column)
- ☐ Multi-Column Shipping Address (Address will be displayed in separate columns)
- ☑ Counter Party Status (Verified vs. Unverified)
- ☑ Address Status (Confirmed vs. Unconfirmed)
- ☑ Sales Tax
- ☑ Option Names and Values
- ☑ Contact Phone Number

Auction Payments

- ☑ Item ID
- ☑ Item Title
- ☑ Shipping Amount
- ☑ Insurance Amount
- ☑ Auction Site
- ☑ Buyer ID
- ☑ Item URL
- ☑ Closing Date
- ☑ Single Column Shipping Address (Address will be displayed in a single column)
- ☐ Multi-Column Shipping Address (Address will be displayed in separate columns)
- ☑ Counter Party Status (Verified vs. Unverified)
- ☑ Address Status (Confirmed vs. Unconfirmed)
- ☑ Sales Tax

Other Fields

- ☐ Subject
- ☐ Note
- ☐ Subscription Number
- ☐ Payment Type
- ☐ Balance Impact (Any transaction that affects account balance)

Save   Cancel

Figure 12.4

Customizing the fields to download.

Downloading Shopping Cart Transactions

If you're downloading in comma- or tab-delimited formats (ideal for importing into Excel) and using the PayPal Shopping Cart in Website Payments Standard, PayPal lets you download details of each shopping cart transaction. With this option selected, each shopping cart line item appears on a new row under the transaction in the download file. The Type column indicates Shopping Cart Item for each of these rows.

What you get, then, are multiple rows in the download file for each shopping cart purchase. The first row (Type: Shopping Cart) holds transaction-level details; the second row (Type: Shopping Cart Item) displays item details. If there are multiple items in the shopping cart, there will be multiple Shopping Cart Item rows—one row for each item.

To include shopping cart details as part of your download, make sure you're downloading in either tab- or comma-delimited formats, and then check the Include Shopping Cart Details box on the Download History page.

PayPal INSIDER

When to Keep Hard Copies

While it's convenient to download PayPal data in electronic file formats, we recommend that as a safety measure you print and store hard copies of this data. If your electronic files are ever lost or damaged, you can reconstruct your data history from the printed copies.

When you plan to keep a hard copy of your transaction data, download it in PDF format. You can then print a copy of the PDF to file as appropriate.

Tracking Transactions via Multiple Email Addresses

If you maintain multiple websites, you can track sales by website by using a different email address for each site. You simply configure PayPal with up to eight separate email addresses corresponding to each of the sites you maintain. You can then track payments from different sites in your PayPal history.

Configuring PayPal for Multiple Email Addresses

Assuming that you have different email addresses (perhaps with different domains) for each of your websites, you then need to add each of these to your PayPal account. These site-specific addresses should be in addition to the main email address you used when you created your PayPal account.

Even if you maintain a single website, you can still add a separate PayPal email address for that site. This lets you route payment notices to one email address and PayPal news and information to a separate email address, as we'll discuss shortly.

Follow these steps to add multiple addresses to PayPal:

> **NOTE:** Your main PayPal address, dubbed your Primary PayPal address, is where PayPal sends general notices, news, and information. The site-specific addresses you add should be in addition to (and separate from) your Primary PayPal address.

1. Go to your profile, click My Business Info on the left, and click to update your email address(es).

2. When the Email page appears, click the Add button.

3. When the Add Email Address page appears, as shown in **Figure 12.5**, enter the new email address and click the Save button.

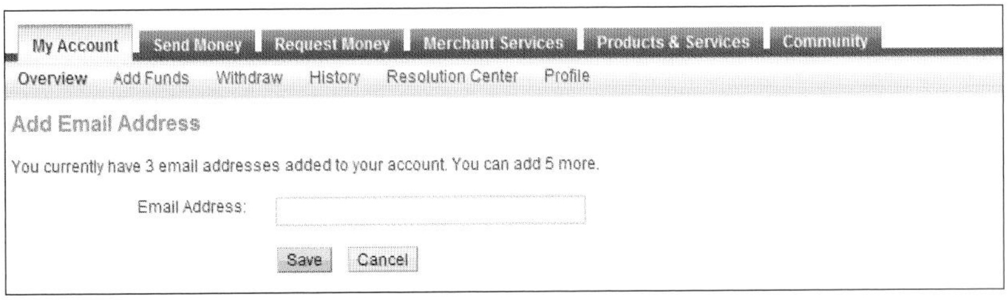

Figure 12.5
Adding a new email address to your PayPal account.

4. PayPal now sends a confirmation email to the new email address. Click the link in the email to confirm the address.

Configuring PayPal Payment Buttons for Multiple Email Addresses

After you've added site-specific email addresses to your PayPal account, you then need to configure your PayPal payment buttons with the email address associated with each website. You do this when you're creating your payment buttons.

From the Create Payment Button page, scroll to the Merchant account IDs section, shown in **Figure 12.6**. Select that site's email address from the email address list, and then proceed with the rest of the button-creation process.

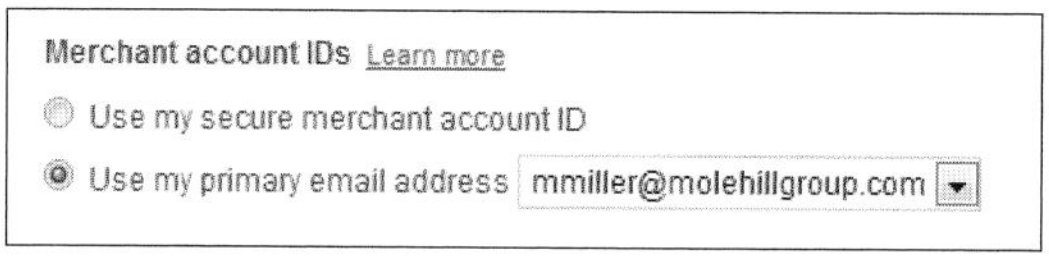

Figure 12.6

Selecting an email address for a PayPal payment button.

Tracking Transactions via Email Addresses

With your payment buttons configured properly, when a customer pays for a purchase at one of your websites, PayPal sends the transaction notification to the email address associated with that site. PayPal also tracks your transaction history via the site's email address, which makes it easy to sort or filter transactions for each site you maintain.

To display only transactions from a given website, go to your account History page and click the More Filters link. From the pull-down menu, select "Payment received to," and then select the email address associated with a particular website. PayPal then displays only those payments made on that site (i.e., sent to that email address).

Filtering Incoming PayPal Email

You can better manage all the emails sent to you by PayPal by creating some smart filters in your email program. For example, if you use Microsoft Outlook for email, you can filter your incoming messages so that emails associated with the different addresses you've registered with PayPal feed into different Outlook folders. How you do this, of course, varies from program to program; consult your email application's Help files for more detailed instructions.

If you maintain multiple websites, create a filter and a folder for transactions from each website. You should also create a filter and folder for email coming from your Primary PayPal email address; this is where all of PayPal's system notices, news, and information is sent to. Even if you maintain a single website, it's still good practice to have a separate email address (and filter and folder) for that address, and another filter and folder for the informational emails sent to your Primary PayPal address.

You can then check each of the PayPal-related folders separately for incoming messages. Put a priority on messages sent to your site-specific email addresses; this is where all of the payment and transaction notifications will come, and you should check them regularly. Less important are messages sent to the folder you created for your Primary PayPal address, so you don't need to check that folder as often.

The Bottom Line

PayPal tracks and keeps records of all the transactions for which it processes payments. You can access this data from your account overview (for most recent transactions) and your History page. You can view transaction data onscreen or download it in a variety of formats for import into Excel, Access, or other programs. If you run multiple websites, you can configure PayPal with different email addresses for each site, and then more easily track transactions (and transaction notification emails) for each site separately.

13

Reporting Tools

When it comes to managing your business, the more data you have, the better. PayPal offers a number of detailed business reports that track all aspects of the transactions for which PayPal handles payment processing. You can view this information in a variety of reports.

These reports let you analyze your business on a daily, monthly, or even yearly basis. Want to know how your sales are doing? Want to know how profitable your PayPal sales are, after all fees have been subtracted? PayPal has a report. You should be able to generate a PayPal report that presents only the data that matters to you.

Understanding PayPal's Reporting Tools

In addition to the detailed transaction history discussed in the previous chapter, PayPal offers a variety of reporting tools to help you better measure and manage your business. These tools—actually, a series of different reports—provide the information you need to identify and analyze important trends in your business.

PayPal's Reporting Tools let you better understand your customers' buying behavior by analyzing your revenue sources. They also automate time-consuming bookkeeping tasks and accurately settle and reconcile all PayPal-related transactions.

What Reporting Tools are available? In addition to the History log (discussed in Chapter 12, "Managing Business Info and Data"), PayPal offers the following:

- **Reporting Center**, which provides a quick summary of recent sales data.

- **Monthly Sales Report**, which details information for all payments and refunds on a day-to-day basis for a given month—and then lets you view all transactions for a given day.

- **Monthly Financial Summary**, which provides a snapshot of PayPal account activity for the selected month.

- **Yearly Financial Summary**, which creates a detailed financial statement for the given year.

- **Recurring Payments – User Profiles**, which displays details for all Recurring Payments profiles (with activity in the last 30 days).

- **Case Report**, which details all buyer complaint and chargeback cases.

- **Inventory and Profit & Loss Report**, which details current inventory levels and generates basic profit and loss data.

NOTE: Learn more about the Inventory and Profit & Loss Report in Chapter 8, "Managing Inventory."

In addition, PayPal lets you search your account history for specific transactions, via the Transaction Finder. Use this tool when you need more
details about a given transaction.

NOTE: PayPal also offers a Settlement and Reconciliation System, available to
high-volume Business accounts only. This system automatically settles your PayPal
payments and helps you avoid shipping items with incomplete or uncleared payments.

Your Business Overview

The Business Overview page is your home base for PayPal's Reporting Tools. Click the My Account tab, hover over the History subtab, and
select Reports. Or access this page—and all of the reporting tools—at
http://business.paypal.com.

As you can see in **Figure 13.1**, your Business Overview page provides a
quick overview of various key metrics as well as links to other reports and
useful information.

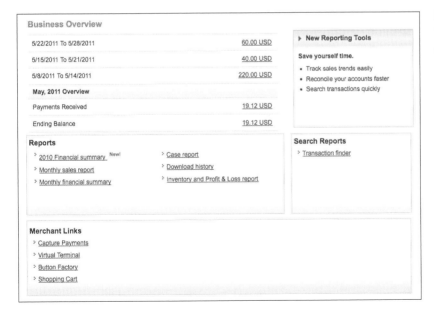

Figure 13.1

*Your Business
Overview page.*

TIP: Examine the Weekly Sales section for the past three weeks to determine sales trends—that is, whether your sales are increasing or decreasing over time.

At the top of your Business Overview page is a list of your weekly sales for the past three weeks. Click the amount to the right of any week to view the Sales Report for each day in that week.

Returning to your Business Overview, the next thing you see is information about the previous month's activities. This lists payments received and your ending PayPal account balance for the month. Click either the amount (Ending Balance or Payments Received) to view the Monthly Financial Summary page. This displays your Financial Statement for that month with controls to change the date range displayed.

Beneath this presentation of key metrics is the Reports section, which links to PayPal's various business reports. To the right of the Reports section is the Search Reports section; click the link here to search your payment history for specific transactions.

Viewing Sales Reports

PayPal's Sales reports provide detailed data about all payments and refunds processed on a given day. There are a number of ways to access the Sales reports; the easiest approach is to open your Business Overview page and then click Monthly Sales Report in the Reports section.

Viewing the Monthly Sales Report

After you select a date range (month-to-date by default) and currency, PayPal displays the Monthly Sales Report shown in **Figure 13.2**. This report displays a summary of activity for each day listed, including the following data:

- **Payments Received**, the number of individual payments registered.

- **Amount Received**, the total amount of money received in payment.

- **Payment Fees**, the amount of PayPal transaction fees charged.

- **Refunds Sent**, the number of individual refunds processed.

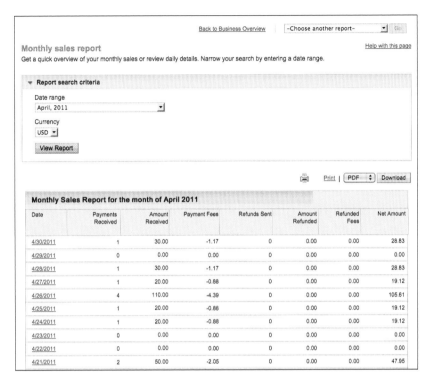

Figure 13.2
The Monthly Sales Report.

- **Amount Refunded**, the total amount of money refunded.

- **Refunded Fees**, the amount of PayPal fees refunded.

- **Net Amount**, the net amount of dollars transacted—amount received less payment fees less amount refunded plus refunded fees.

TIP: Peruse the Monthly Sales Report to quickly see your best-performing days and worst-performing days in terms of sales.

The Monthly Sales Report displays the default date range (month-to-date) and the default currency—until and unless you change either parameter. To display data from previous months, simply select a month from the Date Range list at the top of the report page. To change the currency displayed, select a new currency from the Currency list. Click the View Report button to redisplay the summary page after you make changes.

Downloading the Report

You can view the Monthly Sales Report onscreen, or download a copy in Microsoft Excel, tab-delimited, comma-delimited, or PDF format for further evaluation. To download this report, select a file format from the Download list at the top right corner of the page, and then click the Download button. If you select any of the non-PDF file formats, you can then import the downloaded file into Excel to manipulate as you please.

TIP: You can download most business reports the same way, using the Download button at the top of the individual report page.

Viewing Details for a Specific Day

To view a more detailed report for a specific day, click the link for that date in the Date column. The resulting report, like the one shown in **Figure 13.3,** provides more detailed views of the payments and refunds that were recorded on that particular day. There is an entry for each payment received and refund sent. For each entry you see the following data:

Figure 13.3
A report showing sales on a specific day.

- **Date**, when the transaction was concluded.
- **Type**, which describes the type of transaction.
- **Email**, of the customer for that transaction.
- **Gross Amount**, the total dollar amount of the transaction.
- **Fee Amount**, the amount of PayPal fees charged to this transaction.
- **Net Amount**, the Gross Amount less the Fee Amount.

Viewing Transaction Details

To view more details about a given transaction, click the amount in the Gross Amount column for that transaction. This displays a specific Transaction Details page, like the one in **Figure 13.4**, which shows just about everything PayPal knows about the transaction: amount received, customer email, total amount, fee amount, net amount, time and date transacted, the customer's shipping address, and so on.

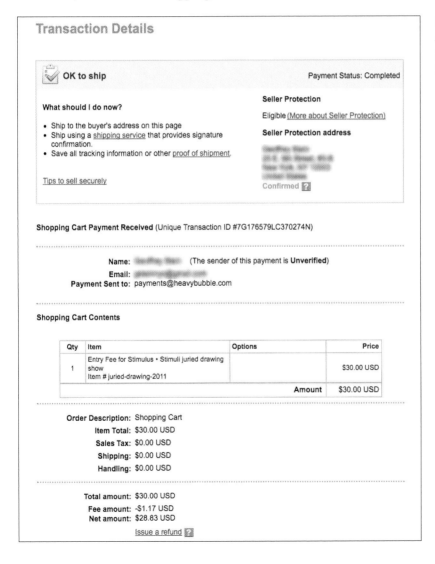

Figure 13.4
A typical Transaction Details page.

Viewing Financial Summary Reports

Next up are PayPal's financial summary reports. The Monthly Financial Summary report is a high-level overview of key transaction categories (sales activity, fees, disputes, and so on); it's a great report for viewing your various PayPal-related fees for the month. The corresponding Transaction Details report provides a line-by-line accounting of all transactions for the given time frame. Both are ideal reports to provide to your accountant—and to give you bird's-eye and detailed views of how your business is doing.

Viewing the Monthly Financial Summary

To access PayPal's financial summary reports, go to your Business Overview page and then click the Monthly Financial Summary link in the Reports section. This opens the Monthly Financial Summary report, like the one shown in **Figure 13.5**.

TIP: By default, the Monthly Financial Summary report summarizes all transactions so far in the current month. To view summary information from a different month, select that month from the Date Range list at the top of the report.

The major sections of this report include:

- **Balances**, including the Total Balance, Available Balance, and Payables Balance on both the beginning and ending dates of the report (by default, the start of the current month and today's date—although you can change the date range at the top of the summary page).

- **Sales Activity**, which summarizes all sales-related transactions, including Payments Received, Refunds Sent, and net sales (the Subtotal line).

- **Fees**, which summarizes all PayPal-related fees, including Payment Fees, Refunded Fees, Chargeback Fees, and Other Fees.

- **Dispute Activity**, which summarizes any transactions involved in customer disputes, including Chargebacks & Disputes and Dispute Reimbursements.

View details

Financial Statement for the month of April 2011		
		Amounts in USD
	Beginning	Ending
Total balance	63.24	112.81
Available balance	63.24	112.81
Payables balance	0.00	0.00
	Debit	Credit
Sales activity		**499.99**
Payments received		499.99
Refunds sent	0.00	
Fees	**-19.55**	
Payment fees	-19.55	
Refunded Fees	0.00	
Chargeback fees	0.00	
Account Fees Invoice	0.00	
Other fees	0.00	
Dispute activity	**0.00**	
Chargebacks & disputes	0.00	
Dispute reimbursements		0.00
Transfers & withdrawals	**-407.00**	
Currency transfers	0.00	
Transfers to PayPal account		0.00
Transfers from PayPal account	-407.00	
Purchase activity	**-23.87**	
Online payments sent	-23.87	

Figure 13.5
Your Financial Statement, displayed on the Monthly Financial Summary report (not shown in full).

- **Transfers & Withdrawals**, which summarizes all cash inflow and outflow to and from your PayPal account, including Currency Transfers, Transfers to PayPal Account, and Transfers from PayPal Account.
- **Purchase Activity**, which summarizes all payments you've made from your PayPal account to other sellers, including Online Payments Sent, Refunds Received, Debit Card Purchases, and Debit Card Returns.
- **Holds and Releases**, which summarizes transactions involved in holds, including Reserve Holds, Reserve Releases, Payment Review Holds, Payment Review Releases, Payment Holds, Payment Releases, Gift Certificate Purchases, and Gift Certificates Redeemed (not shown).
- **Other Activity**, including Money Market Dividends, Debit Card Cash Back, Credit Card Cash Back, and Other (not shown).

For all categories except account balances, you see two columns of numbers. The left column is for positive values (credits); the right column is for negative values (debits). The subtotal for each category (shown in the shaded row beside the category name) equals the difference between credits and debits.

As you can see, just about every category of transaction is summarized in this report. Want to know the value of gift certificates redeemed last month? Or how much you spent on purchases via debit card? Or how much you paid to PayPal in fees? Or the amount of money you refunded to customers? It's all here in the Monthly Financial Summary report.

Viewing Transaction Details

The Monthly Financial Summary report provides a bird's-eye view of all the income and outflow to and from your account in a given month. To view more details about each transaction processed, you need to view the Financial Summary: Transaction Details report. Display this report by clicking the View Details link at the top of the Monthly Financial Summary report.

TIP: Sometimes you don't want to view all transactions for a given month, but only certain types of transactions—sales activity, for example, or fees. To view a Transaction Details report for a specific category, open the Monthly Financial Summary report and click the dollar value for that category.

As you can see in **Figure 13.6**, the Transaction Details report lists all transactions processed in the selected month. The report is wider than a typical web page; you'll need to scroll to the right to view all data columns. These columns include the following data for each transaction:

- **Date**, of the transaction.

- **Type**, of transaction, including Payment Processed, Transfer Completed, and so forth.

Transaction Details for the month of April 2011

Amounts in USD

Date [M/D/YYYY]	Type	Transaction ID	Business/Recipient Name Address Line 1 Address Line 2/District	Email	Gross Amount	Net Amount	Fee Amount
4/1/2011	Subscription Payment Processed	292F809905Y069292F	Thomas C Fenner 2610 Fenner Road Cazenovia - 13035 NY	oldtom@wind.net	35.00	33.68	-1.32
4/4/2011	Transfer to Bank Initiated	1518186431N1441518	- -		-65.00	-65.00	0.00
4/4/2011	Payment Processed	110R6927AC561110P	Freshview Pty Ltd	payments@view.com	4.90	4.90	0.00
4/5/2011	Preapproved Payment Completed	633815756JB9016338	GoDaddy.com, Inc.	paypal@godaddy.com	-7.87	-7.87	0.00
4/6/2011	Subscription Payment Processed	83J52031TX924283J	Dan Summit 123 Summit Ave Lange - 19047 PA	dank@yahoo.com	20.00	19.12	-0.88
4/6/2011	Subscription Payment Processed	574054982KB1125740	Dan Summit 123 Summit Ave Lange - 19047 PA	dank@yahoo.com	20.00	19.12	-0.88
4/8/2011	Payment Processed	230R8013LW880230R	Margaret Church 10 Church Street Philadelphia - 19106 PA	ti@heavybubble.com	0.03	0.00	-0.03
4/11/2011	Payment Processed	372626930D93363726	Margaret Church 10 Church Street Philadelphia - 19106 PA	maggie@gmail.com	0.03	0.00	-0.03

Figure 13.6 *The Financial Summary: Transaction Details report.*

- **Transaction ID**, the unique identification number for this transaction.
- **Business/Recipient Name/Address**, the name and address of the customer (or other seller) involved in the transaction.
- **Email**, the customer's email address.
- **Gross Amount**, the total amount of the transaction.
- **Net Amount**, the net amount of the transaction (gross amount less fees).
- **Fee Amount**, the total amount of PayPal fees charged for this transaction.

TIP: As with the Monthly Sales Reports described previously, you can also view details for any given transaction from the Financial Summary: Transaction Details. To view individual transaction details, click the dollar amount in the Gross Amount column for that transaction.

Viewing the Yearly Financial Summary

While monthly reports are great for managing a business on a continuing basis, most businesspeople also like to view financial data for an entire year at a time. PayPal provides just such a report, in the form of the Yearly Financial Summary. This report, available in PDF format only, offers a similar format to the Monthly Financial Summary report, but for the entire previous year, as shown in **Figure 13.7**.

To download the Yearly Financial Summary report, go to your Business Overview page and click the *20XX* Financial Summary link in the Reports section. (To download the 2010 report, for example, click the 2010 Financial Summary link.) This downloads the report in PDF format to your computer; you can then use Adobe Acrobat Reader to view the report.

Figure 13.7
A portion of the Yearly Financial Summary report.

NVVKKVVK		
2136 Grow Drive #7,Pensacola-32591 FL		
Financial Statement from Jan 01, 2010 to Dec 31, 2010		
		Amounts in USD
Beginning Balance		24.58
Ending Balance		8.11
Beginning payables balance		0.00
Ending payables balance		0.00
	Debit	Credit
Sales Activity		284.38
Payments received		284.73
Refunds sent	-0.35	
Fees	-0.79	
Payment fees	-1.04	
Refunded fees*		0.25
Chargeback fees	0.00	
Account Fees Invoice	0.00	
Other fees	0.00	

Searching Payment History

If PayPal's various business reports don't quite meet your needs, you can use the Transaction Finder to search for and display information about any transaction recorded. To use the Transaction Finder, follow these steps:

1. Open your Business Overview page (business.paypal.com) and click the Transaction Finder link in the Search Reports section.

2. When the Transaction Finder page appears, as shown in **Figure 13.8**, enter your search criteria in the Search Keyword(s) box. You can search by customer name, business name, item name, or item number.

3. Enter starting and ending dates for your search in the Date Range boxes.

4. Pull down the Transaction Type list and select which types of transactions to search: Payments Received, Refunds Sent, Fees, and so forth. (The default is All.)

5. To further refine your search results (by currency, minimum or maximum amount, or card number), click the link to filter your results and fill in the desired information.

6. Click the Search button.

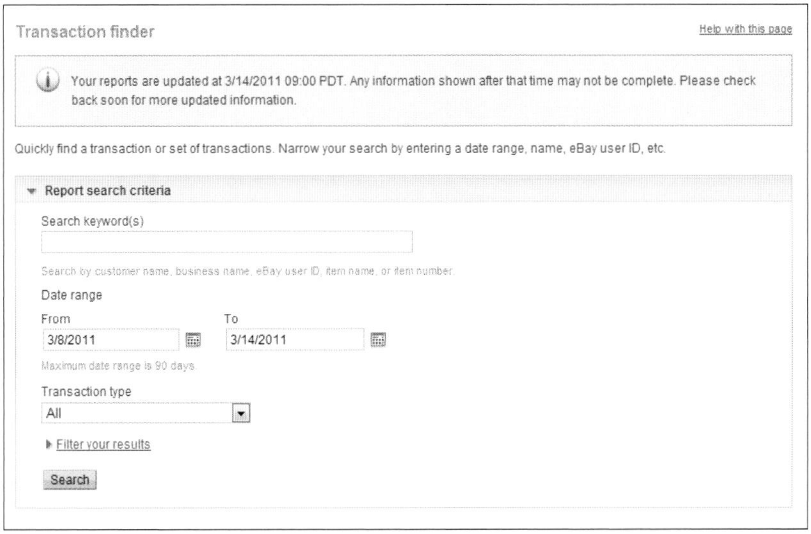

Figure 13.8
Using the Transaction Finder to search for a specific transaction.

PayPal now displays a list of transactions that match your search criteria. Click the dollar amount link in the Gross Amount column to view details for a given transaction.

 ## Analyzing Your Business

PayPal's various business reports let you view details about all of your PayPal-related transactions. More important, they help you track different categories of transactions—and analyze your business's performance.

For example, if you want to track overall sales on your website, look no further than the Monthly Sales Report. If you want to track sales by customer, use the Transaction Finder and search by that customer's name, ID, or email address. If you want to track how much money you owe to others, as well as all the fees you've amassed, turn to the Monthly Financial Summary report.

You can even use our reports to help you budget going forward. With several months' worth of data in hand, you should have a pretty good idea of how your sales are trending. (Importing into Excel and graphing the results really helps.) If things are on the upswing, you can start ordering more inventory. If things are looking down, it may be time to trim some expenses. You get the idea.

The point is to use all the tools at your disposal to track and analyze your business. Since we track all the transactions for which we process payments, PayPal's Reporting Tools are a good place to start. Just be sure you look at trends over time, in addition to daily or monthly snapshots. You want to see the big picture—and let that drive your business decisions.

The Bottom Line

PayPal's Reporting Tools are found at business.paypal.com. The most popular reports include your Business Overview page, the Monthly Sales Report, and the Monthly Financial Summary report. Using some combination of these reports—and their more detailed daily versions—you should be able to determine how well your business is doing, and observe ongoing trends.

14

Interacting with Your Customers

As you've learned throughout this book, PayPal offers many different products and services that help you manage and grow your business. But there's even more help available—in the form of tools that let you more effectively interact with your customers.

This chapter discusses two items you can add to your checkout process through PayPal. You can add a survey question to your checkout process to gather information about your customers, and you can invite customers to sign up for promotional emails from your company.

Surveying Your Customers

To grow your business, you need to know what your customers are thinking. One of the easiest ways to do this is to just ask them—via an online survey.

PayPal makes it easy to conduct this sort of online survey. You simply add a survey question to your checkout confirmation page, where it's integrated seamlessly into the PayPal checkout process. All the customer has to do is make a selection from a drop-down list—the process is not complicated or overly intrusive.

What Kind of Question Can You Ask?

PayPal lets you add a single survey question to the checkout confirmation page that all your customers see when purchasing from your site. Up to five possible answers appear in a drop-down menu, like the one shown in **Figure 14.1**. The customer answers the question by clicking an option from the list.

Figure 14.1

A typical survey question on a PayPal checkout confirmation page.

What kinds of questions, then, should you ask of your customers?

The most common survey question asked by PayPal merchants is how the customer heard about the merchant. This is a great way to find out which of your various promotional activities are working. Did the customer hear about you from an advertisement, another website, an email message, a Google search, a mention on Facebook or Twitter, or someplace else? It's important to know where your customers are coming from.

You can also ask customers what other items they might be interested in. They bought (at least) one thing from you; what else might they like to purchase in the future?

For that matter, you can ask them what other types of products they'd like to see on your site. Or, perhaps, you could ask them what type of item they might be interested in purchasing next.

You can also use your survey question to find out what customers think of you. You could ask how satisfied they were with the shopping experience: very, somewhat, or not at all. Or you could ask about any improvements they might like to see for your site, or your business in general.

Other retailers use their survey question to ask demographic questions about their customers. You can ask the customers' income level, level of schooling, profession, marital status, you name it. Just remember, you have only one question to ask, so make sure it counts!

Adding a Survey Question to Your Checkout Page

You can add a single survey question to the customer checkout page of any PayPal-hosted checkout solution. Your question can be up to 50 characters long, and have up to five possible answers, each up to 15 characters in length. The answers appear in a drop-down menu beside the question; the customer selects an option from the menu to answer the question.

To add a survey question to your checkout page, follow these steps:

1. Go to your profile and select My Selling Tools on the left.

2. Under the Selling Online heading, click to update your Custom Payment Pages.

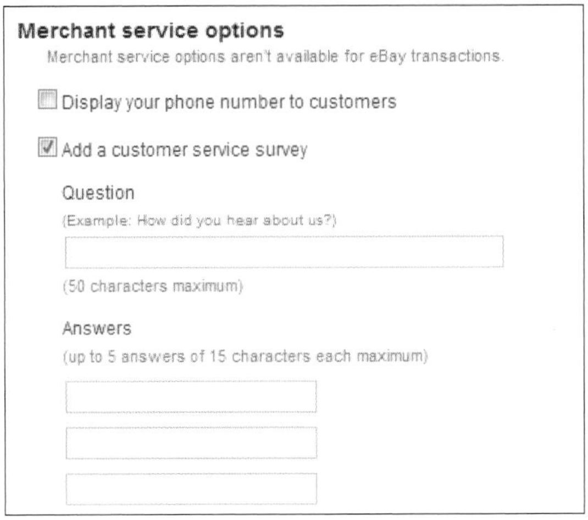

Figure 14.2

Creating a PayPal survey question.

Merchant service options
Merchant service options aren't available for eBay transactions.

☐ Display your phone number to customers

☑ Add a customer service survey

Question
(Example: How did you hear about us?)

(50 characters maximum)

Answers
(up to 5 answers of 15 characters each maximum)

3. When the Customize Your Payment page appears, click the Options tab.

4. Under the Merchant Service Options heading, check the "Add a customer service survey" box.

5. The page now expands, as shown in **Figure 14.2**. Enter your survey question (50 characters maximum) into the Question box.

6. Enter your first three answers (each up to 15 characters in length) in the first three Answers boxes.

7. To enter up to two more answers (for a total of five), click the Add More Answers link, and then enter the additional answers in the new boxes.

8. Click the Save button when done.

For example, you might enter the question "How did you hear about us?" Then you might provide the following answers:

- Online ad
- Search engine
- Website or blog
- Facebook
- Other

Once you've activated the survey, your buyers will see it when they reach the Review & Complete page in the checkout process—the page they're taken to after signing into PayPal. They have the option of answering or ignoring the question; it's not a requirement to proceed to the next page.

Viewing Survey Results

When a customer completes your survey, you can view the results for that individual transaction. Just go to your account overview or History page, identify a particular transaction, and then click the Details link. On the following Transaction Details page, the Survey Details section (shown in **Figure 14.3**) displays the customer's answer to your question.

NOTE: At present, there's no way to view a summary of survey results on the PayPal site. Instead, you can tabulate the results manually and then generate your own summary.

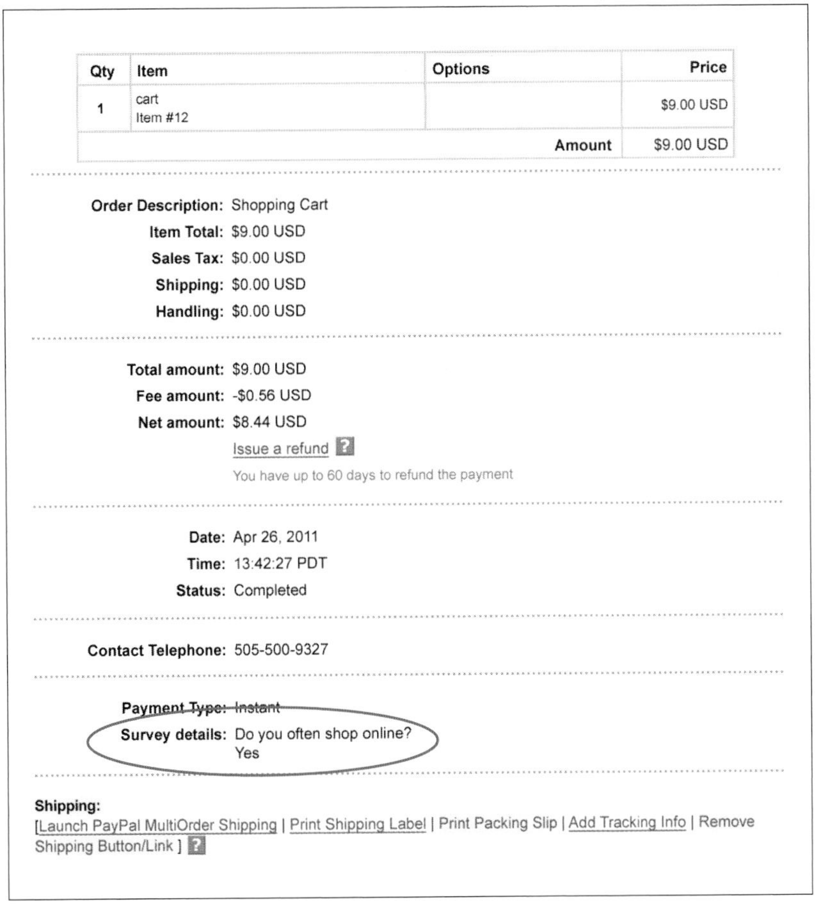

Figure 14.3

Viewing a customer survey response on the Transaction Details page.

Qty	Item	Options	Price
1	cart Item #12		$9.00 USD
		Amount	$9.00 USD

Order Description: Shopping Cart
Item Total: $9.00 USD
Sales Tax: $0.00 USD
Shipping: $0.00 USD
Handling: $0.00 USD

Total amount: $9.00 USD
Fee amount: -$0.56 USD
Net amount: $8.44 USD
Issue a refund [?]
You have up to 60 days to refund the payment

Date: Apr 26, 2011
Time: 13:42:27 PDT
Status: Completed

Contact Telephone: 505-500-9327

Payment Type: Instant
Survey details: Do you often shop online?
Yes

Shipping:
[Launch PayPal MultiOrder Shipping | Print Shipping Label | Print Packing Slip | Add Tracking Info | Remove Shipping Button/Link] [?]

What's a Good Response Rate?

It's great to be able to ask your customers a simple survey question when they complete the checkout process. But how many customers can you realistically expect to complete the survey?

In our experience, most retailers get between a 5 and 10 percent response rate to their survey questions. You'll probably get a higher response rate to general questions, and a lower response to questions that might be considered a bit more intrusive.

This response might not seem like a lot, but in the world of market research, that's a pretty good percentage. Some professional surveys have a response rate as low as 3 percent, so getting 5 to 10 percent of your customers to take the time to answer your question is a good deal.

Whether these responses are statistically representative of your total customer base is another question. Customers self-select to answer this type of survey, and you might wonder what types of people take the time to do so. Of course, it all depends on the question you ask. If you're asking about customer satisfaction, it's likely that only those customers with a strong response (positive or negative) will bother to answer—which means your survey answers might be skewed to the extremes. On the other hand, if you ask a relatively benign question about where customers heard about your website, the answers might better represent the whole.

Bottom line, while PayPal encourages you to use the survey feature on your checkout page, they caution you to take the results with a grain of salt. Remember, these are simple questions that you're asking your customers, not sophisticated queries devised by professional statisticians. Not everyone will answer, and not everyone who does answer will do so truthfully. Still, a survey can provide a good indication of what your customers are thinking or doing—just don't treat the results as a perfect reflection of what customers actually do.

Signing Up Customers for Email Promotions

As a retailer offering goods or services over the Internet, email marketing should be an essential part of promoting your business. That's because email marketing is a type of direct marketing; it's intended not simply to increase brand awareness or drive traffic to your website, but rather to solicit direct sales of a particular product or service.

An email marketing campaign involves sending targeted messages to your existing customer base; these emails can advertise upcoming promotions, new products, and the like. As such, you use email marketing to entice more sales from your current customers. And, as all marketers know, it costs a lot less to get more sales from a current customer than it does to create a new customer.

Smart merchants encourage their customers to sign up to receive their promotional emails. You can do this at any point in the purchase process, including on your checkout confirmation page. If you use PayPal for your checkout, you can let customers sign up for promotional emails on the checkout confirmation page itself.

CAUTION: To keep your promotional emails from being viewed as spam, ask your customers to opt in through an active sign-up process. Otherwise you'll be sending out unsolicited—and unwanted—emails. Even if customers opt in, you might be flagged as spam unless you use a sending email address known to your customers (and their email service).

To add this option to your PayPal checkout confirmation page, the process is similar to that for adding a survey question. Follow these steps:

1. Go to your profile and select My Selling Tools on the left.

2. Under the Selling Online heading, click to update your Custom Payment Pages.

Figure 14.4
Adding email signup to your checkout page.

Merchant service options
Merchant service options aren't available for eBay transactions.

☐ Display your phone number to customers

☐ Add a customer service survey

☑ Offer promotional emails
Offer promotional information like sale announcements or newsletters. If you choose this option, you also need to offer an unsubscribe service.

3. When the Customize Your Payment page appears, click the Options tab.

4. Under the Merchant Service Options heading, check the "Offer promotional emails" box, as shown in **Figure 14.4**.

5. Click the Save button.

Your customers can now sign up for your promotional emails during the checkout process. You can then use third-party software to send your customers a variety of emails to promote new products, upcoming sales, and the like. If you decide to pursue this, take the time to become familiar with email marketing regulations. And comply with them!

PayPal INSIDER

PayPal, a Powerful Promotional Tool

You might not think of PayPal in conjunction with marketing your business. We're a payment processing service, not an advertising network.

However, using PayPal for your payment processing actually serves as a form of promotion. When you put the PayPal logo on your website, it brands your site as a trustworthy and safer place to shop.

There's a reason that PayPal merchants are consistently more successful in attracting and retaining new customers than sites that don't have similar support; PayPal is a brand that consumers trust. When you associate with PayPal, that trust is shared with your site, giving you instant credibility.

Doing business with PayPal is a smart, cost-effective marketing strategy.

The Bottom Line

PayPal offers two features that help you more effectively interact with your customers. You can add a survey question to your PayPal checkout page, to better understand what your customers are thinking and experiencing. And you can offer customers the option of signing up for your email-based promotions and mailings. Both of these features are free, and available to any business using PayPal-hosted checkout services.

15

Mobile and PayPal

We're used to people accessing the Internet via personal computers, but more and more consumers are accessing the Web via smartphones and other mobile devices. This trend toward mobile access will affect the way you sell online—including the way you accept customer payments.

Suppose a potential customer sees a friend with your product and loves it, but is not near a computer? You don't want that moment to pass; in all sales, timing is critical. And when she gets to your site, can she find the product? Can she buy it easily? PayPal Mobile gives you access to those impulse buys, with a checkout process designed for mobile devices.

Why Mobile Matters

Why is mobile e-commerce important? It's a simple matter of numbers: mobile Web use is fast gaining on traditional computer-based Web use. You need to reach your customers no matter what type of device they use to access the Internet.

Look at the statistics. The International Telecommunication Union reports that there are more than 5 billion cellular telephone subscribers worldwide; CTIA—The Wireless Association reports that more than 300 million of these subscribers are in the U.S. CTIA also reports that 96 percent of all Americans had a mobile phone subscription at the end of 2010. IDC reports that there were close to 1.4 billion new mobile phones sold in 2010, making this the fastest-selling item in the entire consumer electronics industry.

These raw numbers dwarf those of the personal computer industry, but it gets even more interesting when you drill down to look at mobile Internet usage. In a 2009 report, the Pew Research Center found that 35 percent of all mobile phone users have used their phones to access the Internet; that's more than a billion people worldwide, and more than a hundred thousand in the U.S alone. This mobile access will only increase; Gartner estimates that mobile Web usage will surpass PC-based access by 2013.

And these mobile users are spending money. ABI Research reports that in 2009, $1.2 billion in purchases were made from mobile devices in the U.S.; ABI expects this number to increase to $119 billion by 2015. That's big money, and reason enough for savvy businesses to embrace the mobile Web. No business can dismiss hundreds of millions of potential customers; indeed, you want to reach Internet users no matter how they connect to the Web. A mobile phone is just another gateway to the products you sell online.

The importance of the mobile Internet is more than just numbers, of course. Customers don't need to be sitting in front of a computer, but instead can connect to the Web via mobile phone anytime and anywhere. People always have their phones with them; this gives you nonstop connectivity to your customers.

The mobile Web also promises increased access to location-based information about your customers. Being able to target buyers based on their location lets you provide them with information about shoes if they're in a shoe store, for example, or promotions for frozen food if they're in a grocery store. It's *narrowcasting*, as opposed to mass marketing, which should generate more effective results.

All this adds up to a channel that you can't ignore—and a real need for upgrading your e-commerce activities to embrace mobile users.

NOTE: PayPal's efforts in mobile extend beyond merchant services to services aimed squarely at mobile consumers. The very popular PayPal Mobile, for example, which lets consumers shop securely on eBay, speed through checkout on other mobile sites, send money to other users, and manage their PayPal accounts, all on their mobile phones. PayPal has apps for the iPhone, Android, and BlackBerry platforms, as well as a dedicated mobile version of our website (located at http://m.paypal.com).

Creating a Mobile-Friendly Website

The first step toward embracing mobile commerce is to design a version of your website specifically for mobile devices. The mobile screen is noticeably smaller (and of different dimensions) than a computer screen; what fits comfortably on a big monitor is overkill on a mobile phone.

It's not just about looks, either. Web functionality needs to be streamlined for mobile users. That's because it's more difficult to navigate a website on a phone than it is on a computer; you don't have a mouse to move around with. For that reason, a mobile website has to be navigable with many fewer clicks than a traditional site.

NOTE: When evaluating mobile website functionality, know that some mobile Web browsers do not display some technologies well or at all. As a prominent example, Apple's Safari browser, used on the popular iPhone, is not compatible with Flash media. If you have any Flash elements on your page, they simply won't display on an iPhone.

If you want to play on the mobile Web, then your website has to work with phones and other mobile devices. What do you need to do to create a great-looking and fully functional mobile website? Here are some things to keep in mind.

Reduce the Number of Elements

Designing a mobile e-commerce website is all about making things simple. The first thing to simplify is the number of elements on a page. The typical mobile phone screen isn't very large; only a few items can fit on the screen and still be legible.

To this end, you need to reduce the number of elements that appear on the screen at one time. Instead of displaying a dozen different elements, opt for a half dozen or less. Choosing those elements is most important.

TIP: When you're reducing the number of elements on your mobile site, make sure you prioritize the ones that remain. Browsing through pages on a mobile site can be quite time consuming; users should see the most important content at the top of the first page.

As an example, compare PayPal's regular website (**Figure 15.1**) with its website for mobile users (**Figure 15.2**). The regular site has lots and lots of options available, in a landscape (horizontal) orientation. The mobile site, on the other hand, presents only the most important options, in a portrait (vertical) orientation, with minimal graphics. It's a lot cleaner and to the point, and works much better on mobile devices.

Add a Search Box

When you limit the content you present on your mobile page, you reduce the number of navigational avenues into your site. Since there are fewer navigational options, it's important to provide a way for users to find specific content. That argues for a site search box, placed prominently on the homepage. You have to give customers a way to find what they're looking for, no matter what.

Design for Portrait Orientation

Pages on the traditional Web have a landscape orientation with horizontal menu bars, as users typically have widescreen computer monitors. Phone screens, however, are usually oriented vertically. This means you need to adjust your Web pages to be sure they display well in a vertical format.

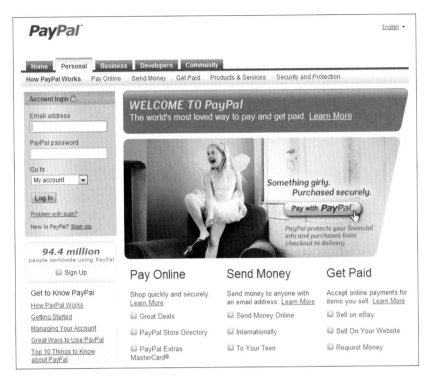

Figure 15.1
The traditional PayPal homepage, as viewed on a personal computer.

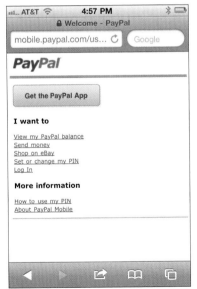

Figure 15.2
The PayPal Mobile homepage.

Limit the Use of Images

Here's something else about really good mobile websites: they don't use a lot of graphics. Space is at a premium, and you can't waste it with super-fluous images. In most instances, you can present content more efficiently in text than in pictures; let that drive your mobile page design.

Using text instead of images also affects the download time for your mobile pages. Mobile Web access is typically slower than a computer-based connection; everything takes longer on the mobile Web. Keep this in mind and limit the number of large elements that take a long time to download—don't make visitors suffer through an interminable download just to look at a pretty picture.

Reduce the File Size

With cellular data network speeds in mind (and knowing that even 3G networks aren't always speedy), you need to keep the file size for the entire web page as small as possible. You want to aim for a maximum page file size of 20KB. Smaller is better.

Don't Clutter the Screen

When designing for the mobile screen, it's tempting to try to cram as many elements as possible into the smaller space. Resist that temptation. White space is an important element of any page design, and even more so for small screens. Having too many elements in a small space is visually unappealing and difficult to navigate. The admonition to keep it simple applies to design as well as content.

Don't Do Tables

If you use tables on your main website, get rid of them for your mobile site. Tables simply don't display well on mobile devices; if a table is too wide (which it probably is), it throws off the entire page. Instead, pres-ent data in a bulleted list, or just in normal text format. Only use tables if you're sure they fit within the allotted screen width.

Use a High-Contrast Design

Getting into the design side of things, know that not all mobile devices have great screens. Some devices simply don't reproduce color well; some devices don't even have color screens. To that end, pay attention to the contrast on your page, and make sure the text color is in sharp contrast to the background color. When in doubt, remember that black text on a white background works best.

Minimize Text Entry

E-commerce websites require a fair amount of data entry on the part of your customers. That said, you need to rethink how you get that customer input. It's difficult to enter text on a mobile phone; you have to click here and press there and then tap an onscreen keyboard multiple times just to record a single letter. Consider accepting some input, such as demographic information, via simple radio buttons or lists that visitors can select from; also minimize the need to input non-alphanumeric characters and to capitalize input text. In other words, design your mobile site to require as few input keystrokes as possible.

Design for Multiple Phones

When designing a mobile website, it's tempting to focus your mobile efforts on Apple's iPhone, as it currently dominates the consumer smartphone market. But the iPhone isn't the only Web-enabled phone on the market; in fact, it only owns about a quarter of the smartphone market, let alone the market for all Web-enabled phones. If you focus on the iPhone exclusively, you'll be ignoring more than three-quarters of the potential mobile market.

This leads to the challenge of making sure your site can be displayed at a variety of screen sizes, shapes, and resolutions. Some mobile screens are tall and skinny, some are short and long, some are perfectly square. And resolution varies from 128 × 160 all the way to the iPhone 4's 960 × 640 pixels. It's tough to make a single site look good on all these different displays.

The best solution, then, is to keep your mobile site as clean and simple as possible, to maximize the viewing experience across multiple mobile platforms. Alternatively, you can design one site for web-kit mobile browsers (iOS, Android, etc.) and another for other feature phones. In any case, you have to take multiple phone models into account.

Adding PayPal Mobile Express Checkout to Your Mobile Website

Recognizing the growing importance of mobile e-commerce, PayPal has returned to its roots by offering a new way to accept payments. The new Mobile Express Checkout strikes a delicate balance between security and ease of use, both of which are crucial for acceptance by mobile customers.

Mobile Express Checkout provides a seamless, easy-to-use checkout experience for customers. It runs in most mobile Web browsers, using pages optimized for smaller mobile screens and mobile keyboards.

How Mobile Express Checkout Works

The mobile checkout experience begins on your mobile website when a buyer is ready to pay you. The process goes like this, as illustrated in **Figure 15.3**:

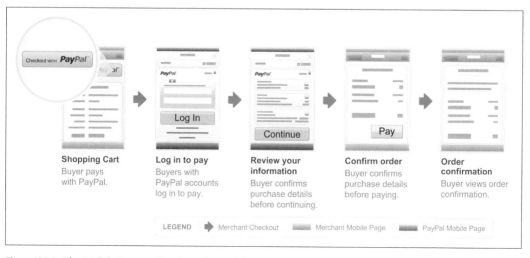

Figure 15.3 *The Mobile Express Checkout flow, with payment on the merchant's website.*

Figure 15.4 *The customer login page for Mobile Express Checkout.*

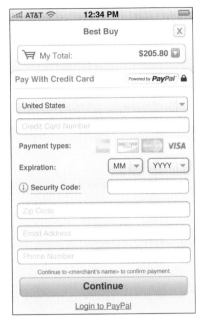

Figure 15.5 *How non-PayPal users enter payment information with Mobile Express Checkout.*

1. From your shopping cart page, the customer taps the Checkout With PayPal button.

2. This displays a login page, like the one shown in **Figure 15.4**. The customer logs in with his PayPal email address and password, or mobile phone ID and PIN, and then taps the Log In button.

3. An order review page now appears; the customer taps the Continue button if the information is correct.

4. When the page shown in **Figure 15.5** appears, the customer enters purchase details on your website, and then taps the Pay button. Payment information is transferred to PayPal, where the payment is confirmed.

5. Your site displays an order confirmation page. (Optional.)

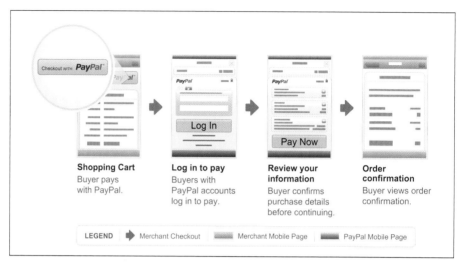

Figure 15.6 *The Mobile Express Checkout flow, with payment on PayPal's website.*

The process is even shorter if you let the customer pay on PayPal, as shown in **Figure 15.6**:

1. From your shopping cart page, the customer taps the Checkout with PayPal button.

2. This displays a login page on the PayPal site. The customer logs in with his PayPal email address and password, and then taps the Log In button.

PayPal INSIDER

 The Emerging Mobile Market

Navigating traditional checkout pages in a browser on a mobile device can be frustrating. At PayPal we are committed to providing a successful experience for your mobile customers.

We have found that by making the mobile checkout process easier for consumers, Mobile Express Checkout is very likely to increase sales for mobile merchants. A smoother checkout process generally results in fewer abandoned shopping carts. To that end, many of the merchants who did beta testing for us reported double-digit growth in their mobile stores since adding the feature. It's worth investigating as you develop your own mobile commerce website.

3. An order review page now appears; the customer reviews the order and then taps the Pay Now button. PayPal processes the payment.

4. The customer is returned to an order confirmation page on your website.

Implementing Mobile Express Checkout

Mobile Express Checkout currently supports Android-based mobile devices (software versions 2.0 and 2.1), the Apple iPhone (versions 3G, 3GS, and 4), and the iPod touch (2G and 3G). At present, Mobile Express Checkout is available to merchants and customers in the United States, Canada, and the United Kingdom. Expansion into additional markets is planned.

If you already use PayPal's Express Checkout, minimal programming changes are necessary to implement Mobile Express Checkout. All you need to do is add similar payment/shopping cart buttons to your mobile site to those you use on your regular site.

On the other hand, if you're developing a mobile app to enhance the shopping experience, you use the mobile APIs contained in the PayPal Mobile Express Checkout Library. This Library contains all the APIs and code you need to embed your mobile implementation of Express Checkout on select mobile devices. Everything you need is available (and explained) at www.x.com, PayPal's Developer Network website.

Using Mobile Marketing to Promote Your Website

When it comes to getting the word out about the mobile version of your website, you can turn to various mobile marketing activities that reach customers right on their mobile phones.

The most common of these marketing activities include mobile search engine optimization, mobile advertising, and marketing via mobile apps.

Mobile SEO

Now that you have a mobile website, you have to optimize it for mobile search—traditional Web searching conducted on mobile phones. And search engine optimization (SEO) is even more important in the mobile world than it is in computer-based search.

The big difference between mobile and traditional search is that while traditional Web-based search results pages show ten results or more per page, most mobile search results pages show only three or four results per screen. That makes it much more important to rank at the very top in terms of search results; lower rankings will get relegated to a subsidiary screen, with the resultant decrease in visibility and click-throughs.

The other big difference is the local nature of mobile searching. Much mobile searching is for local businesses and events: movie times, nearby restaurants, local retailers, and the like. You can take advantage of this by optimizing your mobile website for this mobile/local search.

The best way to optimize your mobile site for search is to identify keywords that help identify the location of your business. That can include any or all of the following:

- Your store address

- City name

- State name

- ZIP code, and nearby ZIP codes

- Neighborhood

- Region or regional nicknames (*tri-state region* or *Silicon Valley*, for example)

- Native nicknames (*Garden State*, *Hoosier State*, and so forth)

Add these local keywords to your regular list of keywords and mobile customers will be able to find you when they're searching locally. This should move your site nearer the top of mobile search results pages.

Mobile Advertising

When advertising on mobile devices, you have the typical choice of a Pay-per-click (PPC) text ad or clickable image ad. Both can be effective.

A mobile text ad looks much like a normal Web-based PPC text ad, but with less copy—typically just 24 to 36 characters, followed by your destination URL or phone number. A mobile image ad looks like a traditional Web-based banner ad, but with a very small banner that fits easily on the mobile screen.

Whichever type of ad you choose, you can decide what happens when a customer taps the ad. By default, tapping a mobile ad takes the consumer to a landing page on the advertiser's website—one designed for mobile viewing, ideally. But you can also opt to include a "call" link in your ad; tapping this link initiates a phone call to a number you specify. This is a great way to connect directly with customers on the go.

Mobile Apps

Finally, you can market your mobile website via a mobile app. The biggest market for mobile apps today is with Apple's iPhone and iPad; Android phones also represent a significant opportunity. Most apps are delivered via an app store, such as Apple's App Store or the Android Market, which is accessed directly from the mobile device.

Apps are extremely popular with mobile users. Nielsen Research reports that the average iPhone user has 37 apps installed on her phone; the average Android user, 22 apps; the average BlackBerry user, 10 apps.

A mobile app typically performs a single duty, or multiple duties within a defined area. Apps can display advertisements alongside more functional content, thus enabling a publisher to promote its website within the app. Publishers can also use in-app selling to market goods and services from within an application.

For marketing purposes, you need to develop an app that promotes your website and products. As such, the app needs to engage your current and future customers. The app needs to be useful, not just promotional; it can't just be an advertisement, it has to provide real value to users.

In addition to providing utility to users, your app also needs to promote the website behind the app. It should lead users directly back to your mobile website. This isn't just an image-building effort; you want to convert app users into customers. To that end, make it easy and worthwhile for app users to get to your website for more information or services or to make a purchase.

NOTE: To learn how to add PayPal to your mobile apps, visit www.x.com/mobile.

For that matter, you can design an app to facilitate purchases via a mobile device. If you own a restaurant that offers take-out or delivery services, you might want to design an app that lets customers order directly from their mobile phones. The key is to make your app useful and fun so it will lead directly to consumer purchases.

The Bottom Line

As more and more consumers access the Internet via their mobile phones, mobile e-commerce is becoming more important. To that end, you need to develop a mobile version of your website and employ various types of mobile marketing to promote it. You should also implement mobile checkout on your mobile site, such as that provided by PayPal's Mobile Express Checkout.

Index